Evaluating Pupil Growth

Principles of Tests and Measurement

Evaluating Pupil Growth

Principles of Tests and Measurement

THIRD EDITION

J. STANLEY AHMANN

Colorado State University

MARVIN D. GLOCK

Cornell University

ALLYN AND BACON, INC.

Boston

TO JUNE AND RUTH

Preface

A PERSON WHO WORKS HARD FOR A GOAL IS, understandably enough, very interested in the degree to which that goal has been realized. So it is with teachers, regardless of subject matter or grade level. Clearly, the evaluation of the degree to which educational goals have been achieved is a basic part of teaching and concerns everyone associated with the school.

It follows, therefore, that teachers, counselors, supervisors, administrators, and other educational specialists should have the following:

1. An appreciation of the usefulness of measuring instruments in education.
2. A knowledge of the characteristics of a satisfactory measuring instrument.
3. The ability to construct measuring instruments capable of showing the degree to which pupils have attained pertinent educational objectives.
4. A knowledge of common achievement and aptitude tests as well as personal-social adjustment inventories, which are often included in a schoolwide program of evaluation.
5. The ability to select appropriate measuring instruments for use in a continuous evaluation program.
6. The ability to interpret *properly* the data yielded by measuring instruments, to use them in diagnosing and remedying pupil deficiencies, and to report them efficiently and accurately to the pupils, their parents, and, possibly, the entire community.

This book was written for a one-term college course, whether at the undergraduate or "fifth-year" graduate level, which is designed on the basis of goals such as these. Each of its four parts contributes directly to one or more of the six goals and indirectly to several others. In many instances these relationships are self-evident. In Part I, "Evaluation in Education," the role of pupil evaluation in education is defined, the use of educational objectives as a basis of evaluating is established, and a number of measurement procedures are introduced. Part II, "Measuring Achievement in the Classroom," contains discussions of teacher-built objective and essay tests, methods by which such tests can be evaluated, and teacher-built instruments recording pupil performance. Part III, "Characteristics of a Good Measuring Instrument," is devoted to validity, reliability, and means of reporting the degree of pupil achievement. In Part IV, "Evaluating Pupil Behavior and Improving Learning," standardized achievement tests, aptitude tests, and personal-social adjustment inventories are described, the use of measurement data in diagnosis and remediation is explained, and methods of determining and reporting pupil growth are discussed.

Underlying this book are three significant and, indeed, axiomatic principles. In the first place, the measuring procedures of elementary and secondary school teachers are very similar. Moreover, in those instances in which the procedures differ, the secondary school teacher can profit from knowledge of the unique measuring problems and procedures of the elementary school teacher, and vice versa. Therefore, this book is designed to serve both groups in terms of general discussion as well as illustrations. Secondly, to be competent in educational measurement, a teacher must have a speaking knowledge of common statistical techniques such as the arithmetic mean, the standard deviation, and the correlation coefficient. This does not mean that he should be skilled in the theoretical aspects of statistics, helpful as that would be. It is assumed that students using this book have, for all practical purposes, no background in statistical methodology. To fill this need for a limited command of statistical procedures, descriptions of statistical techniques are included in the appendices. Each step to be followed when solving for one of these values is shown. The computations are so planned that no prior training in mathematics beyond fundamental arithmetic is needed in order to follow them with ease. Thirdly, before a teacher can successfully build his own measuring instruments or select appropriate commercial instruments for use in his classroom, he must be thoroughly familiar with the basic principles of measurement and evaluation. For this reason an entire chapter is devoted to the topic of validity and another to the topic of reliability. Understand, however, that these chapters as well as all of the others are not written for the theorist. The treatment is such that the teacher can make practical use of it in his classroom.

Most of the chapters in this book are inter-related. It is recommended that Part I and Part II be studied first and in that order. At this point the instructor may vary his choice as he wishes. If possible, Chapters 8, 9, and 10, dealing with norms, validity, and reliability, and Chapters 11, 12, 13, and 14, dealing with standardized instruments and the school-wide program of evaluation, should be kept together.

Scattered within each chapter are discussion questions, usually more than twenty in number. They are designed to challenge the student in that no readily determined answers are available. Often the question requires the student to apply what he is learning. Supporting references to educational and psychological literature are regularly given.

At the end of each chapter is a list of suggested readings that, in the opinion of the authors, provide suitable extensions of the material included in the chapter and are written at an appropriate level. These references will provide a more complete view of many of the more important topics. In addition, a list of free and inexpensive materials concerning educational measurement and evaluation is given in Appendix F.

Like all textbooks, this is the product of the efforts of many people. The authors are indebted to the many students at Colorado State University and at Cornell University and to the school personnel in Colorado and New York and other states who directly or indirectly provided ideas and illustrative material for this book. In addition, the authors are grateful to Professor Helen L. Wardeberg of Cornell University, who provided numerous suggestions for the improvement of the first edition of this book, and to the stenographers who typed various parts of the manuscript, particularly to Miss Grace Roetker of Colorado State University and to Mrs. Beverly Spencer Brown of Cornell University. Finally, many publishers have granted permission to reproduce parts of their publications in this volume. These are acknowledged as they occur.

J. Stanley Ahmann
Marvin D. Glock

Contents

Part Three: Characteristics of a Good Measuring Instrument

Part Four: Evaluating Pupil Behavior and Improving Learning

Evaluating Pupil Growth

Principles of Tests and Measurement

PART ONE

Evaluation

E<small>VALUATION IS</small> an integral part of our everyday activities. The merchant periodically inventories his stock to see whether he has realized a profit or a loss on his transactions and evaluate the merits of his present merchandising practices. The golfer carefully tabulates the strokes needed to play eighteen holes of golf, then checks the results against the listed par or perhaps his total of last Saturday, and on this basis he appraises the quality of his game. The surgeon examines his patient for postoperative developments so that he may better assess the success of the operation he performed and, hence, the well-being of his patient. The financier regularly reviews his portfolio of stocks and bonds, checks their values and earnings, and thus draws conclusions on the soundness of his present investment program.

Notice that in each of these illustrations a goal has been identified. For the merchant it is a successful merchandising policy; for the golfer it is an improved skill; for the surgeon it is a more healthy patient; for the financier it is a productive portfolio of stocks and bonds. Notice also that, to evaluate the effectiveness of the current procedure, style, or portfolio, it is necessary to gather information. On the basis of this information a value judgment is made. In the illustrations cited, a variety of information is needed. The merchant computes the amount of his sales and his expenses; the golfer counts strokes; the surgeon examines temperature charts, blood pressure readings, blood counts, and laboratory reports; the financier, like the merchant, is interested in dollars and cents as well as the trends of the stock market. After weighing the information with respect to a known goal, the individuals judge the current situation to be successful, with little or no changes necessary, or unsuccessful, with recommended changes to be made in the hope of improvement in the future.

A direct parallel can be found in education. Goals are established on the basis of pupils' needs. Educational programs are established so that pupils can reach these goals and do so in a reasonably efficient manner.

Finally, after the program has begun, information such as test scores and reports of observation of pupil behavior is periodically gathered. The success of the pupil in reaching the goal, and hence the success of the educational program, is evaluated in terms of the objectives. This is the core of educational evaluation.

This brief orientation to the nature of educational evaluation is also an overview of Part One. The purpose of Part One is to describe in limited detail the nature of the purposes and procedures of educational evaluation. Chapter 1, "The Role of Evaluation in Education," is devoted to discussions of the scope of pupil evaluation, its purposes, the major types of testing procedures, the heterogeneous nature of these procedures, and the problems resulting from the lack of accuracy of the information produced by these instruments. Chapter 2, "Educational Objectives in Pupil Evaluation," is concerned with the nature of pupil needs, the translation of these needs into educational objectives, and the role of educational objectives in evaluating pupil growth.

These two chapters will provide an overview of the entire field of pupil evaluation by identifying its perimeter and its principal parts, in addition to offering a basic vocabulary so necessary in a field of this complexity. In a sense, Part One can be compared to the large piece of heavy cardboard on which a child is to assemble the various pieces of an inlay jigsaw puzzle. On it is traced the outline of each piece of the puzzle and of the entire puzzle so that the child can speedily recognize the relationship of one piece to all the others. As a result, he can assemble the pieces much more rapidly than would otherwise be possible. These chapters provide similar outlines, so that in later chapters detailed descriptions of some of the topics mentioned can be more easily grasped and their position in the total outline of pupil evaluation more quickly recognized.

1 ✐

The Role of Evaluation in Education

A TRIP TO a crowded city beach in the summer is a revealing experience. Anyone but the most calloused and indifferent observer is impressed by this fascinating view of more or less undraped humanity. Some try to capture the sight on canvas or film; few forget it. Summer reminds us how unique each human body is.

With a moment's thought it is possible to identify readily the most obvious characteristics that contribute to individuality. Differences in height and weight, and the sometimes phenomenal distribution of that weight, are prominent. Hair or the lack of it, the size of feet and hands, and the posture are equally noticeable. So are the various parts of the head, the shape and position of the ears, the eyes, the chin, and the mouth. Other aspects of the physiological entity called man, which remain unseen but all none the less important, are visual and auditory acuity, breathing patterns, strength of grip, and sense of smell.

Most of the bathers are not acquainted with each other. If they were, an entirely new constellation of individual differences would reveal itself. These differences can be classified as psychological in nature. Variations in interests, attitudes, motives, and values certainly exist, as do aptitude differences, be they scholastic, mechanical, musical, artistic, or clerical. In terms of achievements there are literally thousands of additional dimensions that are sources of individuality. Achievement in the common subject-matter areas is just one part of the picture. To it must be added achievement in the multitude of additional activities necessary for everyday living, ranging from skill in driving an automobile to the art of making and keeping friends.

The picture is staggering. Small wonder that psychologists have spent lifetimes identifying sources of individuality and developing means of measuring the amount of a given characteristic a person might have at a given moment. The end results of these efforts have clearly established the principle that each person possesses a profile of traits, both physiological and psychological, that are the result of the unique heredity (except for identical twins) and environment of each individual.

Teachers are seldom surprised when the factors of individuality are listed. Some have observed individual differences among pupils for many years. Each succeeding class brings many new pupils before the teacher; no pupil is exactly like any other in this class or any pupil in one of the preceding classes. The appearance of new and refreshing changes in the educational "raw material" each year, is one of the joys of teaching. It is also the source of one of the most perplexing problems of teaching—learning to know your pupils so that educational experiences can be planned to capitalize on the individual differences in the class.

At this point it is appropriate to summarize the teacher's role in expediting the formal educational process for each of these pupils. This role can be conveniently reduced to four points (Tyler, 1951, p. 48).[1] In the first place, the teacher must identify the educational objectives sought. He must know the nature of the pupil behavior that will be displayed when the educational objectives have been achieved. Secondly, he must determine what educational experiences the pupils must have to achieve the objectives. Thirdly, he must know his pupils so well that he can design the educational experiences and arrange their order of presentation according to their varied interests, aptitudes and prior experiences. Lastly, he must evaluate the degree to which the desired changes in pupil behavior have taken place, the degree to which the educational objectives have been achieved. By means of the last step, the effectiveness of the various educational experiences can be inferred. Within the last two steps lie the purposes of pupil evaluation.

PURPOSES OF PUPIL EVALUATION

Evaluation in education has many aspects (Scriven, 1965; Stake, 1966). One of primary significance is pupil evaluation based on the rationale of individual differences mentioned in the foregoing paragraphs. Of course, there are many other types of differences of unusual importance in the educational process. For example, notable difference exists among teachers, curricula, books, and the physical plants of schools, and attempts are being made to measure these. Value judgments based on data reflecting these differences can be enormously important in the improvement of educational processes.

Furthermore, interactions among several of these evaluation attempts should not be ignored; for instance, the interaction between pupil and curriculum evaluation. The latter is typically defined as the process of

[1] The references are listed alphabetically at the end of each chapter.

gathering data about the goals, environments, personnel, methods, and content of an educational program on the basis of which decisions can be made about that program. In view of this, pupil evaluations are an integral part of curriculum revision (Cronbach, 1963).

Pupil evaluation has traditionally emphasized the pupil as an individual. Judgments about his educational growth are based on data concerning many aspects of it which may then be compared to similar data about him obtained at an earlier date or with similar data from his peer group obtained concurrently. On the other hand, more attention is being given to the assessment of educational progress on a national scale (Tyler, 1965). This is an attempt to determine what has been learned by various groups of individuals (for example, nine-year-olds, thirteen-year-olds, seventeen-year-olds, and adults) representing different geographic areas, socio-economic levels, and the like. Individual pupils will not receive test scores; each will contribute answers to only a few questions concerning his scholastic achievement. The sum of these for many individuals will permit evaluation of educational progress for groups.

The focus on educational evaluation here is restricted in general to pupil evaluation which concentrates on the pupil as an individual and as a member of a classroom unit. It has two purposes: (1) pupil evaluation helps the teacher determine the degree to which educational objectives have been achieved, and (2) pupil evaluation helps the teacher know his pupils as individuals. The first purpose is basic; changes in pupil behavior are always evaluated in terms of the goals of education. The second purpose is subsidiary to the first, since, naturally, if the teacher is intimately familiar with his pupils, he will be better able to plan educational experiences for them and determine the degree to which educational objectives have been achieved. It is important to realize this fundamental relation between the two purposes. In practice, information on the degree of achievement of educational objectives is always augmented by additional information on the pupil's earlier interests, values, aptitudes, and achievements. Thus, the second purpose supports the first.

Classroom teachers are quick to recognize these two purposes and their relationship to each other. On the other hand, they are sometimes slow to take planned and vigorous action to realize them. This reluctance seriously weakens the effectiveness of the teaching art.

Determining the Achievement of Educational Objectives

Briefly stated, the task of the classroom teacher is to assist his pupils in reaching the general and specific goals of education. These educational objectives guide every step of the teaching process. The professional activities of a teacher have meaning insofar as they are oriented toward the educational objectives of his class. In short, educational objectives serve the teacher as road maps serve the traveler; with these aids, the efforts of both are organized and the end of the journey draws steadily closer; without them, they walk in circles.

Some teachers appear to be quite indifferent to educational objectives. Others see an unnatural halo around them. The novice, for example, is occasionally inclined to view them as absolute and immutable criteria, thought up to serve as a perpetual "conscience" for classroom teachers. Actually, both points of view are badly distorted impressions. Educational objectives stem from the needs of youth as they are guided and molded by the democratic society in which they live. Suggestions for educational objectives commonly come from three sources: the study of the pupil, the study of the democratic society in which he lives, and the judgment of the informed educational specialist. Certainly the knowledges and skills a pupil already has, as well as his interests and goals, should influence the educational objectives of the class he is attending. Hence, objectives should be based in the last analysis upon pupil needs. By the same token, the democratic society in which the pupil lives has needs; it must be improved and perpetuated. Finally, the informed specialist in a subject-matter area can, after intensive study, identify important trends and interrelations that, when translated into new objectives or allowed to influence old ones, may ultimately improve the breadth and direction of the educational program as a whole.

STATING EDUCATIONAL OBJECTIVES. The modern way of expressing educational objectives is in terms of desired pupil behavior, that is, in terms of the behavior that the pupil should exhibit if he has achieved certain objectives. Often cited are behavioral patterns related to the pupil's knowledges, understandings, attitudes, appreciations, abilities, and skills in a specified subject-matter area. The following show the type of statement used in expressing objectives (Kearney, 1953, pp. 42–120):

Curriculum area: Physical development, health, and body care
Age-grade level: Primary (about the end of the third grade)

1. The pupil is growing in habitual attention to personal cleanliness; he covers nose and mouth with handkerchief when coughing, keeps hands and objects out of his mouth, uses his own towel, etc.
2. The pupil is becoming used to washing his hands before eating and after going to the toilet.

Curriculum area: Individual social and emotional development
Age-grade level: Intermediate (about the end of the sixth grade)

1. The pupil is interested in the point of view of other people and is respectful of their opinions, but is becoming more critical of adults.

   2. The pupil shows concern at unfinished work, and satisfaction at completed work.

Curriculum area: Communication
Age-grade level: Upper-grade (about the end of the ninth grade)

   1. The pupil can distinguish between literal and metaphorical language.
   2. The pupil can read all common punctuation marks.

From the point of view of pupil evaluation, objectives stated in terms of outwardly observable behavior are most suitable. Determining the degree to which objectives have been met is nothing more than finding out how the pupil is observably different after the educational experiences from what he was before them. Stating the objectives of education in these terms is deceptively difficult. The foregoing objectives indicate considerable success in this matter.

IDENTIFYING CHANGES IN BEHAVIOR.   There are many ways to discover what changes, if any, in pupil behavior have occurred as a result of educational experiences. By means of a few liberal interpretations, the multitude of methods can be classified into two groups: testing procedures and nontesting procedures. The testing procedures can be the common paper-and-pencil tests, oral tests, or performance tests. Nontesting procedures include teacher-pupil interviews, anecdotal records, sociometric techniques, general information questionnaires, and ranking and rating methods that summarize the results of observing samples of pupil behavior or products of that behavior. Properly or otherwise, the most commonly used is the paper-and-pencil achievement test.

No matter which of the suggested methods is used to identify changes in pupil behavior, the teacher needs considerable information in addition to knowledge of the technique. That information is a thorough grasp of the typical and atypical behavioral patterns of pupils he is teaching. Standardized testing devices attempt to provide these reference points by means of norms, that is, lists of typical scores made by a sample of pupils thought to be representative of a larger population of pupils for whom the test is designed. Nontesting procedures customarily require a full knowledge of what a given class or age group of pupils are like. The more complete this knowledge, the more adequate will be the evaluation of changes in pupil behavior.

Two notable obstacles prevent a comprehensive evaluation of the degree to which educational objectives have been achieved. First of all, certain educational goals, such as those pertaining to attitudes and interests, are difficult to translate into observable pupil behavior, and changes can be identified only crudely, if at all. Consequently it has not been possible to construct evaluation instruments which can adequately measure the degree to which the pupil has achieved all of the many and varied educational objectives. Secondly, in some instances the total desired change in pupil behavior may not be observable until months or years following the educational experience. Of course, the teacher most likely will not be on the scene at this auspicious moment. However, he may be able to observe changes in pupil behavior indicating partial achievement of an educational objective. For example, one of the broad educational objectives often mentioned is that the pupil will prepare himself adequately for a suitable vocation. The complete achievement of this objective may not be observable for some time. Yet the classroom teacher may observe partial achievement as the pupil masters, for example, verbal and mathematical skills.

Helping a Teacher to Know His Pupils

Every teacher subscribes to the obvious truth that, to be successful, he must know his pupils. He can begin by inquiring about their names, addresses, previous academic experiences, parents, and the occupations of their parents. By observation he may be able to appraise crudely the socio-economic level from which the pupil comes, his physical vigor, his social training, and even his enthusiasm concerning the anticipated educational experiences.

But what lies beneath the surface? A teacher is more than curious about the pupil's aptitudes, the complete story of his previous academic achievements, and the degree of his personal-social adjustment. These aspects of a pupil cannot be assessed without relying upon some of the many techniques here classified as a part of pupil evaluation. Considered guesses based upon informal observations are not sufficient. Appraisals need to be based upon objective data and to be organized in a systematic pattern.

Consider for a moment a given pupil about whom a teacher is questioned. Let's call him Mike. According to the teacher, Mike is a "fair" pupil who is "moderately bright" and who seems to be "rather well liked" by most of his classmates. In general, Mike is not very highly motivated, but appears to be content and causes little trouble. You may have often heard such a description. Undeniably it is a helpful thumb-nail sketch. Yet it could be infinitely more helpful if it were more specific and less subjective. One might ask how "fair" is "fair" and how "bright" is "moderately bright"? Test scores from achievement tests and a scholastic aptitude test could underpin this description to a sizable degree. Furthermore, according to the teacher's remarks, Mike seems to be an underachiever. Why? Test scores and teacher ratings of earlier academic achievements may shed light on this question, as may various aptitude test scores. Home conditions should not be ignored even though they can only be casually evaluated. Lastly, how "well liked" is "rather well liked"? What kind of trouble is "little trouble"? Sociometric devices and anecdotal records may jointly illuminate these questions.

The list of suggested evaluation techniques could be continued, but the point has been made. The picture of Mike can be brought into focus only by better evaluation techniques. These techniques will never paint a complete profile of a pupil, but they will reveal enough of that profile to justify the time and money their use demands.

Knowing a child is a prolonged, complex process. Ideally it combines the skill of the teacher as an impersonal, astute observer, the skill of the test technician who constructs and validates the standardized measuring instruments, and the skill of a clinician, who carefully amalgamates all the above information and ferrets out likely causes and effects. Although not confronted by the ideal situation, the average classroom teacher can, through extensive effort, attain useful though typically imperfect results.

The rewards for such effort are rich. The teacher can select and time educational experiences for his pupils much more effectively. He can also interpret more realistically the results of his attempts to find out how well his pupils achieved educational objectives.

PROBLEMS

1   Using a familiar class level and subject-matter for illustrative purposes, cite the major arguments supporting the contention that pupil evaluation is most successful when based on limited, well-defined educational objectives.

2   It is argued that an effective teacher is one who, in a minimum amount of instructional time, can help the pupil reach pertinent educational objectives commensurate with his abilities. In the light of this statement, to what degree should there be interaction between pupil evaluation and the evaluation of teacher effectiveness? Why?

3   Describe a real or ficticious instance in which a teacher's lack of insight into his own behavior reduced his ability to evaluate the degree to which one of his pupils had achieved an educational goal.

4   Does homogenous grouping of pupils on the basis of test scores yielded by a common group test of mental ability, significantly reduce the importance of the second purpose of pupil evaluation (a) insofar as a secondary school mathematics teachers is concerned, and (b) insofar as an elementary school teacher of the intermediate grade levels is concerned?

Differences Between Measurement and Evaluation

Differentiating between the terms "measurement" and "evaluation" is sometimes difficult. The two terms are related, yet decidedly different. Evaluation is a more inclusive term than measurement. In the last analysis, measurement is only a part, although a very substantial one, of evaluation. It provides information upon which an evaluation can be based.

Characteristics of Measurement

Educational measurement is the process that attempts to obtain a quantified representation of the degree to which a pupil reflects a trait. The use of a paper-and-pencil test to discover the scholastic aptitude or achievement of a pupil is an illustration of educational measurement. In the case of scholastic aptitude, for example, one can easily visualize it as a continuum, that is, as a trait that logically varies from much to some to none and that is theoretically capable of being divided into an infinite number of degrees. Each pupil has a specific position on the continuum. Educational measurement tries to represent that position by means of a numerical value, a scholastic aptitude test score, and to do so in as objective a manner as possible.

The measurement process is fundamentally descriptive. It strives persistently to describe the degree to which a trait is possessed by a pupil in terms of numbers rather than words. A teacher can characterize a fourth-grade pupil as "tall," "gifted," or "underweight." These are word descriptions of traits that are continuous. Measuring instruments can change "tall" to "61.5 inches," "gifted" to "*Stanford-Binet* IQ of 132," and "underweight" to "85 pounds." The advantage of reporting numbers rather than adjectives is obvious. The meaning of any adjective varies from teacher to teacher. The measurement data do not change if the measurement has been carefully executed with appropriate instruments. They are notably less ambiguous than verbal descriptions.

Educational measurement tends to concentrate on a narrow, specific, and well-defined trait or characteristic, and then strives to determine with precision the degree to which that trait is possessed by an individual pupil. This is in many ways comparable to the methods of a photographer who, in trying to capture the individuality of a physique, photographs each part separately, first the hand, then the foot, perhaps then the nose, and so forth. Such a photographer would hope that the result of his work would be a series of revealing photographs, each displaying clearly the status of the physique with regard to the particular part. If totally successful, he could assemble all photographs and recreate a picture of the total physique.

A teacher acts like a photographer when he examines specific pupil traits, such as reading comprehension, vocabulary, and scholastic aptitude, with a series of measuring instruments. Each test measures a certain pupil trait, just as each photograph pictures a part of the physique. Unfortunately, the teacher's task is not so simple as the photographer's. Whereas it is possible that some of the photographer's pictures might be blurred because his camera was out of focus or might have poor black and white contrast because they are underexposed, such lapses are unlikely, especially if he is a professional photographer. In contrast, the teacher using even the best measurement devices may have nothing but somewhat blurred and underexposed "photographs." Worse than that, some traits of the pupil can not be "photographed" at all since no measuring instruments are available. Hence the total picture of a pupil yielded by combining the results of many measurements of various pupil traits is often somewhat unclear, due to the failure of the instruments to yield precise, unequivocal results, and is invariably incomplete, due to the scarcity of suitable measuring instruments, particularly in the area of personal-social adjustment.

The statement that a measuring instrument fails to yield precise, unequivocal results means that the instrument does not adequately serve the purposes for which it is intended, and that it does not measure with perfect consistency. The failure of an instrument to serve the purposes for which it is intended is known as lack of validity; the failure of an instrument to measure consistently is known as lack of reliability. The concepts of validity and reliability are described and illustrated in Chapters 9 and 10 respectively.

Characteristics of Evaluation

Pupil evaluation is a process in which a teacher commonly uses information derived from many sources to arrive at a value judgment. The information might be obtained by using measuring instruments as well as other techniques that do not neecssarily yield quantitative results, such as general information questionnaires, direct observation, and teacher-pupil interviews. An evaluation may or may not be based upon measurement data, though appropriate measurements are customarily used if they are available. Thus, evaluation includes not only measuring or in some way identifying the degree to which a pupil possesses a trait or to which his behavior may have been modified as a result of an educational experience, but also judging the desirability and adequacy of these findings. Good measuring instruments can provide a sound basis for good evaluation.

The differences between measurement and evaluation can be easily illustrated. Suppose that you are about to buy a new four-door automobile and have decided to restrict your choice to three makes in the low-priced field. Now you face the happy dilemma of determining which of the three automobiles to buy. Your investigation of the three probably starts with measurement: the cost, the horsepower of the engine, the length of wheelbase, the gasoline consumption at various speeds, and the weight are useful measurement values. Perhaps then, you test-drive a demonstration car, forming judgments on riding ease, maneuverability, rapidity of acceleration, and interior and exterior beauty. Finally, you choose one of the three automobiles. The choice results from a careful consideration of quantitative evidence, qualitative evidence, and highly subjective impressions, and is the end result of an evaluation process.

Within the field of education an excellent example of the differences between measurement and evaluation can be found in the practice of assigning final marks to pupils at the end of a unit of work. Measurements of a pupil's prior achievement and aptitude may have been made before the unit began, and measurements of the changes in pupil behavior follow the termination of the unit. To these pieces of information the teacher frequently adds his reactions to the pupil's attitudes, cooperativeness, motivation, and possibly even his punctuality. The final result is generally a single letter or numerical mark that supposedly indicates the relative success of the pupil as he experienced the unit of work. As in the case of the choice of automobile, an evaluation process has taken place; a value judgment has been made.

PROBLEMS

5 According to Morgan (1959, p. 16), effective evaluation promotes the development of democracy. What does he mean by this statement? Do you agree or disagree with this statement? Why?
6 Identify the probable major aspects of measurement and evaluation in the case of a debutante attempting an intensive weight-reduction program with a controlled diet, or a candidate for the varsity football team attempting a strength-development program with isometric exercises.

EDUCATIONAL TESTING

Educational measurement is usually thought to include educational testing. Whether this is true or not depends, of course, on the manner in which educational testing is defined. "Test" is, paradoxically, a simple and widely used term and yet one of somewhat vague meaning. It can be defined in such a broad manner that some of the evaluation procedures known as tests yield only verbal descriptions of pupil traits (Cronbach, 1960, p. 21); these procedures cannot be included within the definition of educational measurement. On the other hand, educational testing can be defined in a more restricted manner so that, practically speaking, all tests can be called measuring instruments.

It is convenient for the purpose of this book to define the word "test" in the more restricted manner. In the first place, a test is nothing more than a group of questions or tasks to which a pupil is to respond. The questions might require the pupil to give the correct meaning of a word, solve an arithmetic problem, or identify missing parts in a picture of an animal. Tasks might require the pupil to thread beads on a string, assemble a small piece of apparatus, or arrange blocks in a prescribed design. These questions and tasks might be presented to the pupil orally or in writing; some are even presented by means of pantomime under certain circumstances. The questions and tasks are known as test items. They are intended to be a representative sample of all possible questions and tasks related to the trait measured by the test that are of suitable difficulty. A pupil's responses to the test items are scored in such a way that, ideally, the results indicate the degree to which he possesses the specified trait. The principal purpose of a test is to produce a quantitative representation of the pupil trait that it is designed to measure. Certainly educational testing is included within educational measurement when this restricted definition of a test is used.

Types of Tests

Tests can differ from each other in many ways. Some contain items of nearly constant difficulty, whereas others contain items of varying difficulty. Some require that rigid time limits be maintained; others do not. Some demand that the pupils to whom the test is to be administered have a complete command of the English language; others do not. Some can be administered to large groups of pupils simultaneously; others to only one pupil at a time. These and other variations have been used to subdivide tests into a relatively restricted list of fifteen types.

In the following discussion, two and sometimes three types of tests are grouped together, as in the case of oral, essay, and objective tests. This grouping is made because the types are more or less contrasting. Sometimes the relative merits of each are vigorously debated by both teachers and testing specialists. In any event, it is a useful way of remembering the types and their general characteristics.

Notice also that a given existing test can simultaneously be classified as more than one type. For example, one popular achievement test used in schools today is a group, verbal, objective, standardized, power test. Such a multiple classification of a test is actually a highly informative thumbnail description. Mastery of such terminology is a necessary prerequisite to an understanding of this part of educational evaluation.

INDIVIDUAL AND GROUP TESTS. Individual tests are tests that can be administered to only one pupil at a time. The examiner has an opportunity to establish rapport with the pupil and to gain insight into the pupil and his reaction to the testing situation. He can even ascertain possible reasons for many of the pupil's answers. Furthermore, the examiner practically always has the responsibility of making a written record of the pupil's answers. A common illustration of an individual test is the *Stanford-Binet Scale, Form L-M.*

Group tests can be administered to more than one pupil at a time. The number of pupils can range into the hundreds if sufficient test proctors are available. In elementary and secondary school situations, however, pupils are often tested as a class. Because of its simplicity and low cost, this type of test is far more popular than the individual test.

You have no doubt experienced the impersonal atmosphere in which group tests are typically given. As the group of pupils becomes larger, this problem increases. Certainly, a number of the desirable aspects of the individual test are found only to a reduced degree in group tests, since they have been sacrificed for economy of time and money.

INFORMAL AND STANDARDIZED TESTS. Informal tests are tests constructed by a classroom teacher for use in his particular classes under conditions of his choosing. In practically all instances these informal tests are group tests and measure pupil achievement. More of these tests are administered than any other kind. Unfortunately, they often are carelessly constructed.

The value of informal achievement tests stems from one major consideration—the individual nature of every class. This individuality can be traced primarily to the kind of educational objectives involved in the class as well as to the relative emphasis each received. It also can be traced to the quality of the pupils who compose the class. The teacher certainly knows better than anyone else the exact nature of these characteristics of his class. Since the appropriateness of any achievement test item is determined by the educational objectives of the class, the teacher is in an excellent position to build test items that measure suitable areas of the pupils' achievements and that are of suitable difficulty. Thus informal achievement tests, if properly prepared, are tailor-made for a certain class of pupils taught in a certain manner. On the other hand, standardized achievement tests are designed for many classes of a certain type; these tests attempt to cover those achievement areas though to be common to all classes for which they are designed.

Standardized tests are constructed almost invariably by teams of individuals rather than by a single person. In the case of standardized achievement tests, teachers qualified in the area tested work with measurement specialists by helping to identify the scope of an achievement test and its appropriateness. Often they contribute possible test items. In the case of standardized aptitude tests, the role of the teacher is considerably reduced, if not nonexistent.

Characteristically, standardized tests are carefully designed. They are pretested in order to determine the level of difficulty of the test items, the amount of testing time required, the sizes of typical scores made by various types of pupils, and so forth. The manuals accompanying the test contain information concerning the method of developing the test, its purposes, directions for its proper administration, directions for scoring, techniques for interpreting the scores, and reports of research in which the test was involved. In order that any standardized test be used properly, it must be administered only to those pupils for whom it is designed and strictly in accordance with the manual's directions. Furthermore, the scoring of the instrument and the interpretation of those scores must be performed in the manner prescribed for that test.

ORAL, ESSAY, AND OBJECTIVE TESTS. Although common in the early history of achievement testing, oral tests are not popular today. Their use as a means of testing the knowledges and understandings of a candidate for an advanced degree is no doubt their major single function now. Even in this situation they often are not used alone but in conjunction with paper-and-pencil tests.

The disadvantages of oral testing are not difficult to identify. First of all, it tends to be somewhat unplanned in total. The first questions asked by the teacher can be selected with care; after that, however, the nature of the responses of the pupils often influence the nature of later questions. Soon the sampling of the pupil's knowledges and understandings becomes quite narrow. Consciously or unconsciously, the teacher may be grossly unfair to the pupil. Secondly, pupils, like actors, are affected by their audience. The tension created by a face-to-face contact with an examiner has caused many a pupil, even though he actually knows the correct answer, to blurt out the most unusual conglomeration of words, complete with fractured syntax. Thirdly, oral tests generally require too much time of both teacher and pupil. Fourthly, there is no written record of the pupil's responses.

A major advantage of oral testing is that it can be diagnostic. Probing questions can reveal the causes of a pupil's error. Such information, needless to say, is extremely useful to a teacher. Oral testing has a further advantage in that it reveals how well a pupil can apply his knowledge to novel situations, though this can be tested by paper-and-pencil tests as well.

Since many of the difficulties associated with oral tests disappear when paper-and-pencil tests are used, essay testing has replaced oral testing in part. Instead of asking the pupil to answer a question orally, he is asked to write his answer. This simple change affects the testing situation drastically. Now many pupils can be tested simultaneously. Each can answer the same questions, except for an optional question or two which some teachers offer. Since only one set of questions is to be used for many pupils, extensive efforts to obtain a cross-sectional sampling of the subject matter in those questions are certainly justified. Moreover, each pupil has an opportunity to compose himself more leisurely as he attacks each question. The tension is noticeably reduced.

Objective tests are tests that can be scored in such a manner that subjective judgment is eliminated when determining the correctness of a pupil's answers. True-false tests, matching tests, and multiple-choice tests are objective tests in the true sense of the definition. Supply tests (for example, completion tests) are sometimes considered to be objective tests even though the subjective judgment is not entirely eliminated. Occasionally, they are called "semiobjective" test items.

Objective tests are very common. Informal as well as standardized achievement tests are so constructed. Paper-and-pencil aptitude tests are almost invariably of this type. Clearly, objective scoring is in keeping with the whole purpose of using a standardized test. After all, a standardized test tries to be a universal "yardstick" to measure a specified pupil trait. To prevent the "yardstick" from changing its units such precautions as uniform testing conditions are required. Uniform scoring procedures are equally vital. The test results obtained by a pupil should never be affected positively or negatively by the person who happens to score his paper.

SPEED, POWER, AND MASTERY TESTS. A speed test is one in which a pupil must, in a limited amount of time, answer a series of questions or perform a series of tasks of a uniformly low level of difficulty. The near constant level of difficulty of the questions or tasks is such that, if the pupil had unlimited time, he could easily answer each question or perform each task successfully. The average pupil finds that he does not have sufficient time to attempt all test items. It is the intent of a speed test to measure primarily the rapidity with which a pupil can do what is asked of him rather than whether he can do it at all.

Excellent illustrations of speed tests can be found in the case of some clerical aptitude tests. One such test requires the pupil to determine whether two numbers or two names are the same or different. In another the pupil must match combinations of two letters, a letter and a number, or two numbers. Rigid time limits which allow too little time for completion of the test are enforced. If this were not the case, any alert person would certainly have a perfect score.

Speed tests in the pure sense are not common in educational measurement. Not only are comfortable (though controlled) time limits usually allowed, but also the level of difficulty of the test items is not uniformly low. However, in achievement testing, some instruments tend to be speeded because of poorly chosen time limits. So little time is allowed the pupils that the number of unattempted test items becomes excessive. On the other hand, tests designed to measure speed of reading are closely timed and properly so. The very nature of the characteristic to be measured demands rigid time limits.

In aptitude testing, time limits of an instrument often are quite significant. For example, in group scholastic aptitude tests, time limits typically prevent most pupils from attempting every item. Yet, these instruments are not, strictly speaking, speed tests. The level of difficulty of test items changes; the test items become increasingly difficult as the test progresses.

In contrast to a pure speed test is a power test. The items of a power test have different levels of difficulty arranged in the order of increasing difficulty. Power tests are sometimes called scaled tests.

Technically, time limits for a power test do not exist. In reality, they frequently do exist. Little is to be gained by giving a pupil unrestricted time for writing a test. There seems to be a point in time after which further contemplation of the test items yields practically no profit for him. Builders of standardized instruments generally agree that a power test should be so timed that a very large percentage of the pupils for whom it is designed will have ample time to attempt all of the items. Although estimates vary as to the proper size of this percentage, 90 per cent seems to be an acceptable minimum.

Power tests are widely given, particularly when testing achievement. Teachers and pupils alike feel that minimizing the speed factors in a testing situation is desirable. This feeling no doubt stems from the conviction that knowing one's level of maximum achievement as indicated by a power test is more useful than knowing the rapidity with which one can perform simple tasks as indicated by a speed test.

A mastery test resembles both a speed and a power test. The level of difficulty of its items is uniformly low, and in this restricted sense it reminds us of a speed test. On the other hand, it typically has the liberal time limits of a power test. These are two principal characteristics of a mastery test.

A mastery test performs a limited function. It is designed to measure the knowledges and skills that every pupil of the class should have acquired. Hence it is expected that all or virtually all of the pupils will perform perfectly on the test. No attempt is made to discover how much a pupil may have acquired over and above the minimum everyone should have reached. Pupils completing a test are divided into two groups, those who answer all questions accurately and those who do not.

Mastery tests are customarily teacher-constructed. A spelling list, a vocabulary list, or a series of arithmetic computations may constitute such a test. Teachers have used them as quizzes with considerable effectiveness. However, as an end-of-unit or end-of-term achievement test, their usefulness is less than that of power tests, particularly at the secondary school level.

VERBAL, NONVERBAL, AND PERFORMANCE TESTS. A verbal test is a test in which the responding pupil utilizes written or spoken language. This use of language can occur in the directions needed by the pupil, or in his responses to the test items, or in both cases. The widespread use of paper-and-pencil achievement tests in the typical classroom situation clearly illustrates the popularity of verbal tests.

Not all persons can be given a verbal test, however. Illiterates, mentally deficient children, and very young children are incapable of understanding written directions and sometimes even oral directions. Some tests are so constructed that the instructions are orally given and the persons tested respond without use of language. These have been called nonverbal tests, although strictly speaking a nonverbal test does not require the use of language by either the examiner or the person taking the test. Pantomime is used as a means of giving directions. The person may only point to indicate his answer. Geometric drawings and three-dimensional materials have been used in this type of test.

When discussing performance tests, it is necessary to differentiate between aptitude performance tests and achievement performance tests. In aptitude testing, performance tests are often nothing more than nonverbal tests. They are designed to measure the aptitudes of those persons unfamiliar with the English language. For example, the manipulation of blocks and the tracing of a maze have been used to assess general mental ability. In achievement testing, performance tests are not devoted primarily to the illiterate. Performance tests attempt to appraise the degree to which a skill has been achieved. For example, a typing speed test is a performance test. The pupil's performance during a specific period of time is scored in terms of quantity and accuracy of the material typed. Athletic events, musical performances, food preparation, and machine operations can serve as performance tests.

READINESS AND DIAGNOSTIC TESTS.   Readiness tests are designed to determine the ability of a pupil to undertake a certain type of learning. Actually,
they resemble aptitude tests in that they try to forecast the achievement
that would occur if appropriate training were given. They differ from
aptitude tests in that they deal with a highly specific kind of achievement,
such as reading.

Readiness tests are designed to discover whether a pupil is sufficiently
advanced to profit from formal instruction in a subject area. To accomplish
this purpose, reading-readiness tests may use tests of visual discrimination,
auditory discrimination, vocabulary, and sometimes motor coordination.
Tests of pupil readiness in mathematics and language are also given in
secondary school; these are called aptitude or prognostic tests for a given
subject-matter area.

Whereas readiness tests are administered to pupils before formal
instruction is given, diagnostic tests are administered after formal instruction has taken place. The purpose of a diagnostic test is to reveal specific
deficiencies in a pupil's background. This information could also point to
specific deficiencies in the instruction given. The alert classroom teacher
tests in this manner continually, often with informal tests.

One outstanding characteristic of diagnostic tests is that any total test
scores they might give are of practically no value. The desired information
comes from part scores based upon a few related test items or from an item-
by-item analysis of the pupil's responses. Each individual item or small
group of items tests the pupils with regard to a particular part of the
materials taught. Thus a pupil's answers are studied on that basis.

PROBLEMS

7   According to the definition of a test used in this chapter, can the following
standardized instruments be called tests?
a.   *Mooney Problem Check List*
b.   *Kuder Preference Record*
c.   *Seashore Measures of Musical Talents, Revised Edition*
d.   *Vocational Interest Blank for Men*
For each of the foregoing considered to be a test, identify its classification
according to the fifteen types of tests described.

8   Occasionally, you hear the statement that "some test items are more objective than others." Is this a meaningful statement? Why?

9   The claim is made that no so-called standardized test is truly a standardized
test unless it is administered and its scores interpreted in the light of the
specifications included in its test manual. Give illustrations of testing situations which support this statement.

Indirect Nature of Measurement Procedures

When a carpenter builds a house, he engages in direct measurement. In other words, when he measures the length of a board or the size of the angles at which it is to be cut, the characteristic being measured certainly need not be inferred. It is clearly and obviously present and measurable. On the other hand, the teacher finds himself frequently engaged in indirect rather than direct measurement. For example, a pupil's general mental ability is inferred by measuring, by means of a test, what are considered to be the *effects* of general mental ability and not by measuring general mental ability as such. Let us examine this situation more closely.

The expression "general mental ability" (or its near synonym "general intelligence") is widely used today. But exactly what does it mean? Certainly this is a difficult question to answer. One writer claims that the general mental ability of a living organism is its "flexibility" or "versatility" of adjustment (Edwards, 1928). Another says that "an individual is intelligent in proportion as he is able to carry on abstract thinking" (Terman, 1921). Still another believes that, along with the strictly cognitive aspects of general mental ability, one must consider heavily "two additional factors; namely, (1) creativity and (2) resistance to emotional or other forces that distort the process of reasoning" (Stoddard, 1966).

These are but three of the multitude of definitions that have been proposed. The fact that they differ at least slightly among themselves and that other definitions differ to some degree from them is not of great concern to us for the moment. The important factor is their similarity. No matter which of the three one may choose as the most suitable definition, it is clear that general mental ability is definitely a less obvious human trait than others such as height and weight. In short, it is a trait that cannot be seen, touched, or handled in a direct manner.

To appreciate the relatively obscure nature of general mental ability, we need only recall how most individuals estimate informally, without the use of instruments, the general mental ability of their acquaintances. Rare is the person who has not identified a number of his acquaintances as having less mental ability than himself. Possibly (and with less certainty, perhaps) this same person also has classified a few of his acquaintances as having more mental ability than himself. How does he arrive at these decisions? Obviously he examines each acquaintance in terms of those aspects and products of his behavior that seemingly reflect the amount of general mental ability present. In other words, the behavior patterns and their products are assumed to be some of the effects of general mental ability.

Ordinarily informal estimates of general mental ability are based on such information as the academic or financial accomplishments of the person, his facility for quickly and correctly identifying the salient point of a humorous story, or perhaps his ability to carry on an interesting conversation. In addition, there may be numerous known instances in which he did or did not seem to "catch on" very rapidly. In spite of the fact that these pieces of information may not be a representative sample of a person's behavior, and that they may not necessarily be directly and completely related to variations in general mental ability, the judgment is nevertheless rendered.

Formal attempts to measure general mental ability resemble these informal attempts in one major respect. They too evaluate general mental ability in terms of its effects. Observable behavior thought to be directly related to general mental ability is identified, and the trait is measured indirectly by evaluating the observable behavior in some way.

A few of the common types of behavior sometimes used in this measurement are the ability to solve arithmetic problems, to identify the meanings of English words, spatial ability,[1] and the ability to solve number series problems.[2] If a pupil is "gifted," he should be able to answer correctly difficult questions concerning areas such as those mentioned. If he is "average," he should be able to answer correctly many of the pertinent questions in these areas but not the very difficult ones. If he is "dull," he should be able to answer correctly only the very easy questions and may find even these troublesome. Hence, by measuring a pupil's abilities to answer questions in suitable areas, the teacher can infer his general mental ability.

Observe that in this approach an important assumption is made. It is assumed that there is a direct and unchanging relationship between the general mental ability of a pupil and his ability to answer questions in the areas mentioned. If this assumption is not true, the indirect measurement procedure is worthless. Moreover, if the ability to answer these questions is an effect of only certain aspects of general mental ability whereas other aspects give rise to vastly different effects than the ability to answer ques-

---

[1] Spatial ability can be evaluated by determining whether a pupil can visualize how a geometric figure will look after it has been rotated or how it will look after it has been divided and the parts reassembled in different positions.

[2] A typical number series problem is the following:
The numbers in the following series proceed according to some rule. Select the next number from among the five possibilities listed.

Series	Next number
6 7 10 11 14 15 18	17 18 19 20 21

tions in the areas cited, then any measurement of general mental ability based only upon the type of questions mentioned is incomplete.

Indirect measurement procedures are common. Temperatures are ordinarily measured indirectly by means of a mercury thermometer. When temperatures rise, the column of mercury expands; when they fall, the column of mercury contracts. Traffic congestion and dangerous highway conditions are measured indirectly by means of automobile speed limits. When congestion is serious or when highway conditions are dangerous, speed limits are lowered; when the reverse is true, speed limits are raised. Aspects of a pupil's personal-social adjustment are inferred from his written answers to questions about himself. For example, he may be asked to respond with a "Yes," "Uncertain," or "No" to a question such as: "Are you frequently afraid of adults?" If he answers affirmatively it is assumed that his personal-social adjustment is probably less satisfactory than if he answered negatively. Attempts have even been made to determine how well a pupil can apply what he has learned by asking him to recite what he has learned. Presumably, the more information he can recall, the better he can apply it. Changes in a pupil's attitudes and appreciations have been estimated by rating changes in the pupil's overt behavior in the classroom or on the playground. Changes there have been interpreted to represent deep-seated, perhaps permanent changes, which will be manifested in the home or, in later years, in a vocation. These are but a few of many possible illustrations.

The commonness of indirect measurement procedures does not mean that they are necessarily desirable. Indirect procedures should be used only when direct procedures cannot be applied. Thus the repeated use of indirect measurement procedures in education stems from the fact that direct ones are often impossible or at least impractical. Psychological traits must be inferred on the basis of specified observable phenomena. This means that the measurement of such characteristics of a pupil as his general mental ability, interests, attitudes, and many aspects of his achievement is complicated.

PROBLEM

10 Which of the following can be best classified as direct measurement and which as indirect measurement?
    a. Determining the distance an automobile travels by means of an odometer.
    b. Determining the speed of a sprinter by using a stop watch to measure the time needed to run 100 yards.

    c.   Determining a pupil's ability to recall information about the American Revolution with the common paper-and-pencil testing method.
    d.   Determining the adequacy of a pupil's vision with a letter chart.
    e.   Determining the teaching effectiveness of an instructor with a paper-and-pencil opinionnaire administered to his pupils.

ACCURACY OF MEASUREMENT PROCEDURES

A carpenter building a new house continually varies the accuracy of his measurement according to the need, and chooses his measuring instruments on that basis. For instance, as he assembles rough scaffoldings to assist in the construction, he probably cuts the board needed at points found by estimating the desired lengths. The angles of the cuts are not drawn but are also estimated. When cutting the joists, however, a steel rule is used to measure lengths, and no greater than one-eighth of an inch error is allowed. Also, the right angles at the ends of the joists are not the result of estimation, but are drawn by a carpenter's square. Finally, when cutting the interior trim, he now uses the most precise of steel rules to measure length, allowing no more than one-sixteenth of an inch error.

Typically, the classroom teacher also varies the degree of accuracy of his measurement procedures as his purposes change. The measurement of general mental ability again offers a convenient illustration. In the first place, a teacher certainly wants to know whether each pupil in his class has a certain minimum amount of general mental ability without which that pupil cannot hope to profit from the learning experiences offered him. This need be only rough measurement for most pupils. Later the teacher may want to know whether each pupil is achieving in proportion to his capacity to learn. Such a classification of each pupil as an under-achiever, normal achiever, or over-achiever requires considerably greater accuracy of measurement of general mental ability as well as academic achievement. Should the teacher desire to determine the *amount* of over-achievement or under-achievement, the demand for accuracy of measurement is still greater.

Finally, certain pupils may be in competition for a highly specialized and technical training program to be started after completion of secondary school. Assume that the vast majority of pupils who are not qualified or interested are initially eliminated, and that only a few of the remaining pupils are to be chosen. Under these conditions, selecting those pupils who, because of their talents and earlier successes, have the greatest chance of success in such a program will demand even more sensitive measurements of general mental ability, prior achievement, and probably other factors.

The carpenter has an important advantage over the teacher in the matter of accuracy of measurement. The accuracy of his measurement when modern tools are used comfortably surpasses the minimal accuracy required. After all, he could determine the length of a joist to one-sixteenth or one-thirty-second of an inch if it were necessary. On the other hand, the teacher is confronted with a relatively low ceiling above which his accuracy of measurement has not, as yet, reached. For example, when measuring general mental ability, a teacher must be satisfied with identifying a pupil's mental ability test score, which *probably* does not differ from his true mental ability score by more than five or six points. We simply do not possess instruments that can measure psychological traits of a pupil with the accuracy that a carpenter can muster to determine the length of a board.

Level of Measurement Accuracy

What then, you may ask, is the level of accuracy teachers typically encounter in their measurement attempts? A detailed answer to this question is needed. As an introduction to the more elaborate discussion to follow, two facts can be mentioned. In the first place, the accuracy of measurement procedures varies with the pupil traits being investigated. Secondly, although the accuracy available to teachers is considerably less than what ideally should be present, it is often sufficient to cause the procedure in question to be highly useful.

ACCURACY VARIES WITH TRAITS.   That the level of accuracy should vary with the pupil trait being investigated is certainly understandable. Some traits are reasonably well-defined. Perhaps they have been studied more intensively than others, or perhaps they lend themselves to evaluation more readily than others. Accordingly, mental ability is repeatedly mentioned as an area in which the accuracy of evaluation procedures is relatively high, though far from perfect. Somewhat the same is said of the procedures used for evaluating academic achievement, especially when evaluating a pupil's ability to recall information. After all, it is not difficult to determine a pupil's ability to recall the year in which the Battle of Hastings was fought, or his ability to spell properly the word "parallel," or to find the product of 7 and 8.

The accuracy of the measurement procedures used in such relatively simple instances as those above is superior. We are able to determine a pupil's general mental ability, or the amount of knowledge that he can recall upon request. Furthermore, when well-developed standardized tests are administered, these amounts can be expressed in quantitative units that are of equal or near-equal size. In other words, a difference of one unit between two amounts is the same or essentially the same as a difference of one unit between any other two amounts, just as a difference of one pound between two weights is the same as a difference of one pound between any other two weights, and a difference of one inch between two distances is the same as a difference of one inch between any two distances. Measuring instruments yielding scores which have equal units are classified as "interval scales" (Selltiz and others, 1960, pp. 186–198).

In contrast, consider the efforts to measure aspects of a pupil's personal-social adjustment or the degree to which educational objectives pertaining to changes in attitudes and appreciations have been achieved. Now the pupil traits are subtle, almost nebulous. Such irrelevant factors as "lip service" and tendency to conform to majority opinion on the part of the pupil cloud the measurement attempts. Accuracy here is appreciably less than that found in the case of the measurement of general mental ability. To determine the amounts of some of these traits possessed by a pupil is often impossible. Our measuring procedures may yield information of such a crude nature that ranking the pupils within a group is the most accurate representation of the individual differences that is justified. For instance, Sammy's ability to cooperate willingly with his peers in completing various projects of mutual interest may be observably superior to Sandra's; her ability in this respect may be judged to surpass Jimmy's. Hence Sammy is ranked first, Sandra second, and Jimmy third. Unfortunately, we are not at all certain that Sammy surpasses Sandra to the same degree that she surpasses Jimmy. The intervals between successive ranks are not necessarily equal; thus ranking (that is, the "ordinal scale" of measurement) is clearly a less precise representation of individual differences than the determination of amounts.

All too frequently, the crudeness of the information produced by measuring procedures prevents us from even ranking pupils. Instead it is necessary to be content with a somewhat general verbal description. For example, instead of ranking Sammy first with respect to his ability to cooperate willingly with his peers our measuring procedures may be so imprecise that the teacher can say only that he "cooperates frequently," or "usually displays little reluctance when the opportunity to cooperate is presented." Verbal descriptions of this type obviously are less precise representations of individual differences than ranking members of a group. Classifying pupils in terms of categories which have no apparent sense of order is known as the "nominal scale" of measurement.

USEFULNESS OF AVAILABLE ACCURACY. So many negative statements can be written about the accuracy of educational measurements that you may well wonder whether the measurement movement has actually "moved" at all. Certainly the lack of accuracy in an absolute sense is disturbing. Yet sufficient accuracy does exist to justify the statement that measuring procedures are some of the most useful tools a teacher has. To obtain a realistic picture of the question of the accuracy of educational measuring instruments and the utility of these instruments for classroom teachers, it is convenient to examine a comparable situation in the field of meteorology.

In a number of respects, the teacher views his measurement results as the farmer views the weather forecasts he receives. The success of both parties is dependent in part upon accurate and timely evaluation results. Both recognize that information from their respective sources is not totally accurate, nor is it even timely in all instances. Both can, if they wish, supplement the reports with their own judgments and speculations, probably based upon appreciable experience.

The farmer generally follows the weather forecasts closely. They help him select dates for planting, cultivating, and harvesting his crop, as well as in other respects. He is quite aware of their inaccuracies, particularly in the case of the thirty-day forecasts, which predict the temperature and precipitation for the following month. They are couched in general terms, to say the least. The temperatures throughout the United States are often predicted in terms of five categories: much above normal, above normal, near normal, below normal, and much below normal. Precipitation is estimated as above normal, near normal, and below normal. No attempt is made to pinpoint the exact time or place for the periods of sunshine and rain; only the average temperature and rainfall for the thirty-day period are being predicted.

In spite of the generalities produced by the thirty-day forecasts, they represent a bold attempt. Short-term forecasts of one or two days are doubtful enough and, in the case of measurable precipitation, are often stated in terms of probabilities. On the other hand, the thirty-day forecasts are considerably less accurate despite the fact that they claim to predict only general trends. Even knowing this, the farmer rarely ignores either the long-range or the short-range weather forecasts. Inaccurate as they are, they represent a sizable improvement over his own forecasts made without the help of the meteorologist. Their utility is unquestioned.

Now it is clear that a classroom teacher is in much the same position as the farmer. The informed teacher recognizes the inaccuracies of the results produced by educational measurement procedures. But, before discarding them, he must ask himself the question: "Can the information yielded by these procedures, inaccurate though it be, tell me more about the pupil than I can discover by any other means?" Frequently the answer is in the affirmative. Many instruments can reveal consistently more accurate information than the most popular alternative method, namely, informal judgments by the teacher. Teacher judgments of pupils, as the farmer's own weather predictions, can be exceedingly accurate in a given instance and should be continually made, but they should be used in conjunction with, rather than independently of, evaluation procedures. As a teacher searches for information about his pupils he should use every means at his disposal, such as standardized tests, interviews, rating scales, and so on, and he should be keenly aware of the accuracy of the information that each will give him.

Problems

11 Classify each of the following in terms of the level of measurement (that is, nominal, ordinal, or interval) which they represent:
    a. Temperature in terms of degrees centigrade
    b. Scores from a well-developed achievement test
    c. Zip code numbers
    d. Dog show results
    e. High school grade-point averages

12 There is a fourth level of measurement known as the ratio level. In addition to having equal intervals as does the interval level, it also is characterized by an absolute zero (Selltiz and others, 1960, pp. 194–195). In other words, a zero reading means that zero amount exists of the characteristic being measured. Cite illustrations of this level of measurement within the realm of educational measurement.

13 According to Stanley (1964, p. 321), the application of the results is the crux of the whole testing program and, consequently, whatever value tests are to have depends in the last analysis on the use made of the results. Evaluate this statement in terms of the problems related to a lack of a high level of accuracy for many tests.

Pupil Evaluation Today

Pupil evaluation as we practice it today can be conveniently divided into two areas; namely, the evaluation of achievement and the evaluation of aptitudes. The former is the larger of the two and, in many ways, much more complex.

Evaluation of Achievement

Pupil achievement is subdivided into three categories or domains; namely, cognitive, affective, and psychomotor. The first is typically called academic achievement, the second the development of personal-social adjustment, and the third the development of motor skills.

Academic achievement means pupil achievement in all curriculum areas except physical development, emotional development, and ethical behavior. Hence, the evaluation of academic achievement includes all evaluation instruments designed to determine the degree to which education objectives in the remaining areas have been achieved. By definition, it includes all of the paper-and-pencil tests, performance tests, and non-testing procedures that measure changes in pertinent types of pupil behavior. The evaluation of academic achievement is as broad and varied as the educational objectives from which it springs, yet in practice it relies heavily on paper-and-pencil tests, most of which are informal rather than standardized tests. Improving these tests by significant degrees is one of the most serious tasks faced by the classroom teacher.

The importance of the evaluation of academic achievement cannot be overestimated. It dominates the entire fourth step of the teaching process mentioned at the beginning of this chapter. Considerable attention has been given to achievement evaluation problems by measurement specialists, and properly so. Tens of standardized achievement test batteries have been developed for all grade levels with the exception of the primary grades. Their popularity with teachers and counselors has steadily increased in recent years.

Evaluating a pupil's personal-social adjustment is not the same as evaluating his personality. Personality is, after all, an all-encompassing entity. It is the sum total of all the individual's psychological characteristics. Thus, it includes his abilities, emotions, motives, attitudes, interests, and whatever remains of all his past experiences. It follows, then, that evaluating a pupil's personality includes the evaluation of the other two categories of achievement and the evaluation of aptitudes. In contrast, the evaluation of personal-social adjustment is intended to represent a miscellaneous category containing those evaluation activities not included in the classifications mentioned.

Useful techniques in the evaluation of personal-social adjustment include attitude inventories, interest inventories, any teacher ratings of such pupil characteristics as "emotional maturity," and "cooperativeness," any paper-and-pencil personality inventories, sociometric devices, and self-rating scales. Projective techniques, such as Murray's *Thematic Apperception Test* (often called the *TAT*) and the *Rorschach Inkblot Test*, definitely belong in this category, but receive minor mention in this book because they are essentially clinical instruments. Home visitations, interviews, and analyses of autobiographies and anecdotal records are also a part of this area of evaluation.

Evaluation of Aptitudes

Simply stated, an aptitude is a person's capacity to learn. Hence, the instruments included in the evaluation of aptitude are designed to predict the achievement that would occur if a pupil were given proper training. Both general and specific aptitudes have been the focal points of testing attempts, many of which produced paper-and-pencil instruments. Tests of general mental ability are the most common of the general aptitude tests; a clerical aptitude test, a nursing aptitude test, or an art aptitude test typify testing for a much more specific aptitude.

Occasionally there is some confusion about the titles of aptitude tests. For instance, when considered in a broad sense, the expression "scholastic aptitude" cannot be considered as synonymous with the expressions "general mental ability" or "general intelligence." However, within the realm of paper-and-pencil aptitude testing, the expressions "scholastic aptitude test," "general mental ability test," and "general intelligence test" can be considered as essentially the same. They often have highly similar content and the same major purpose, namely, to predict future academic success in school work.

Also, there is some doubt about the difference between scholastic aptitude and academic achievement tests. In terms of the definitions, the evaluation of scholastic aptitude and the evaluation of academic achievement are distinctly different. Whereas the purpose of the latter is to reveal a pupil's accomplishments as of a particular moment, the purpose of the former is to predict those that the pupil can achieve with suitable training. From this point, the differentiation between academic achievement and scholastic aptitude evaluation becomes fuzzy. For instance, the difference between an achievement test and an aptitude test in terms of *test content* is virtually nonexistent. The best way to predict how well a pupil will perform in the future in a given area is to adopt the time-proven procedure of examining how well he performed in the past in that area or a similar area. Thus a scholastic aptitude test designed to predict future academic achievement might contain test items that could be found in an arithmetic achievement test or an English vocabulary test. Moreover, it is evident that a given test could serve both functions. For example, a reading test measuring speed comprehension may be used as an achievement test for sixth-grade pupils or as an aptitude test to predict their achievement in junior high school in such subjects as English and social studies. In short, aptitude tests differ from achievement tests in terms of purpose, but not necessarily in content.

Today we have tests designed to measure linguistic and quantitative aspects of scholastic aptitude, others designed to measure primary mental abilities, such as memory, reasoning, and word fluency, whereas still others are designed to measure differential aptitudes, such as verbal reasoning, numerical ability, mechanical reasoning, and clerical speed and accuracy. Add to these the many stenographic, artistic, musical, and mechanical aptitude tests, as well as aptitude tests for academic subject-matter areas, such as reading and mathematics, which often are identified as readiness tests or prognostic tests. Such is the list of tools available to help the teacher know his pupils better. It is indeed remarkable that such great strides have occurred in considerably less than one hundred years.

The Evaluation Movement Today

The principal developments that have contributed to pupil evaluation today have occurred since 1900. This fact more than any other clearly reveals the relative immaturity that characterizes the evaluation movement in psychology and education. Admittedly, modern efforts are less accurate and consistent than we might wish. The physical sciences far outstrip the behavioral sciences in ability to measure the phenomena being studied. Now the standard for measuring time is the rate of oscillation of cesium, whereas the standard for measuring distance is in terms of the wave lengths of light given off by electrically excited krypton 86. Such refinements as these vastly increase the accuracy of measurement possible and allow us to make even greater technological advances in the space age. Educational advances are less impressive by far. Yet, rather than being disappointed in the inability of behavioral sciences to match physical sciences in measuring, we should be impressed by the fact that evaluation in the behavioral sciences has progressed so far in so short a time.

Pupil evaluation is now a major activity of the school and of most teachers who compose its permanent staff. No one knows how many standardized tests are administered each year in the schools of the United States, but we are certain that the number exceeds 150,000,000 per year and is rapidly approaching 200,000,000. The number of teacher-constructed tests given annually cannot even be estimated, but must be many times the foregoing figure.

The merits of pupil evaluation are by no means universally acclaimed today. The history of the movement displays the familiar "pendulum" process. The popularity and general acceptance of the movement wax and wane, and the net result is a healthy skepticism on the part of well-read teachers, who have come to realize that these tools are but means to an end, and are an imperfect even though indispensable means. Thorough knowledge of the basic principles of evaluation is not only a necessary prerequisite to understanding and capitalizing upon today's tools but is a necessary preparation for tomorrow's progress.

PROBLEMS

14   Beginning with World War I, trace the role of the Armed Services in the development of standardized aptitude tests of all kinds.

15   The use of personality inventories is being criticized as unscientific, possibly immoral. Evaluate the response which Forehand (1964, pp. 853–860) has made to these claims.

SUMMARY

The nature and function of pupil evaluation stem from individual differences. The fact that pupils can and do differ from each other in terms of physiological and psychological traits automatically makes it necessary for a teacher to be familiar with the kinds and amounts of such differences to be able to teach successfully. Pupil evaluation deals primarily with psychological rather than with physiological differences.

The purposes of pupil evaluation are twofold: firstly, it helps the teacher evaluate the degree to which educational objectives have been achieved; secondly, it helps the teacher know his pupils to such a degree that educational experiences can be planned according to their varied interests, aptitudes, and prior experiences. Ideally, educational objectives should be stated in terms of the nature of the pupil behavior that will be displayed when they have been achieved.

The procedures used in pupil evaluation are varied. They include paper-and-pencil tests, ranking and rating scales, performance tests, anecdotal records, questionnaires, interviewing techniques, autobiographies, and sociometric procedures. The purpose of these and other evaluative methods is to provide information so that decisions can be made as to whether the changes in pupil behavior that occurred are compatible with pertinent educational objectives.

Educational measurement and educational evaluation are not synonymous expressions. Measurement is the process that attempts to obtain a quantitative representation of the degree to which a pupil reflects a trait. Educational evaluation is a process in which a teacher commonly uses information derived from many sources to arrive at a value judgment. The information may be obtained by using measuring instruments, as well as other techniques that do not necessarily yield quantitative results, such as questionnaires and interviews.

Fifteen different types of tests are briefly described. They are divided into six subdivisions, each of which contains two or three contrasting types. The subdivisions are: individual and group tests; informal and standardized tests; oral, essay, and objective tests; speed, power, and mastery tests; verbal, nonverbal, and performance tests; and readiness and diagnostic tests. A given test can be simultaneously classified in more than one of these subgroups. For example, an achievement test may be a group, standardized, objective, power, verbal test.

Educational measurement methods can be characterized by two features. First of all they are primarily indirect rather than direct. The pupil traits are appraised in terms of their effects, rather than in terms of the traits themselves. Thus, the traits are inferred. Secondly, measurement procedures are not remarkably accurate in terms of any absolute standards, but are dependable enough to be usable. The classroom teacher repeatedly discovers that his measuring instruments, inaccurate as they may be, reveal more information about pupils than do any other techniques at his disposal.

Pupil evaluation can be conveniently divided into two areas: the evaluation of achievement and the evaluation of aptitudes. The evaluation of achievement includes those techniques designed to measure the degree to which educational objectives have been achieved. Included are objectives pertaining to the cognitive, affective, and psychomotor domains. Aptitude evaluation is designed to predict the achievement that would occur if the pupil was given proper training.

Suggested Readings

Chauncey, Henry. Testing in perspective and context. In *Educational testing service annual report, 1960–61.* Princeton, N.J.: Educational Testing Service, 1961.
   The general status of educational testing today is described, and some of the more recent developments in testing are examined. Particular attention is given objective tests.

Chauncey, Henry, and J. E. Dobbin. *Testing: its place in education today.* New York: Harper and Row, 1963. Chapters 1, 2, 3.
   The purpose of this book is to provide a broad picture of what testing in schools is all about. The first three chapters deal with the history of the testing movement, the nature of mental ability tests, and the nature of achievement tests. These chapters are comparatively brief and well written.

Cook, Walter W. The functions of measurement in the facilitation of learning. In E. F. Lindquist (Ed.), *Educational measurement*. Washington: American Council on Education, 1951. Pp. 3–46.

> This is the first chapter of a book that can best be described as a comprehensive review of the theory and technique of educational measurement as of 1950. The chapter includes a general discussion of the functions of educational measurement in establishing individual learning situations, the diagnosis and treatment of learning difficulties, the motivation of learning, and the development and maintenance of skills and abilities.

Cronbach, Lee J. *Essentials of psychological testing*. (2nd ed.) New York: Harper & Row, 1960. Chapters 1 and 2.

> The first chapter is devoted to a brief discussion of the use of psychological tests. The second chapter includes a definition of a psychological test and a classification of tests into major types.

Ebel, Robert L. Inventories and tests. *Education*, 1960, 81, 67–99.

> Eight critical questions about the use of tests are posed. These deal with instruments for measuring achievement, aptitude, and personal-social adjustment. Answers to the questions have been prepared by six testing experts and are summarized in eight separate articles, each devoted to one of the eight questions.

Gerberich, J. R. The development of educational testing. *Theory into practice*, 1963, 2, 184–191.

> In a few pages, the author traces the history of the testing movement in education and identifies some of its major trends.

Lorge, Irving. The fundamental nature of measurement. In E. F. Lindquist (Ed.), *Educational measurement*. Washington: American Council on Education, 1951. Pp. 533–559.

> The pages cited contain a general definition of the term "measurement," following which classification and ranking are explained. Four scales of measurement are discussed. They are the nominal, the ordinal, the interval, and the ratio scales.

Thomas, R. M., and S. M. Thomas. *Individual differences in the classroom*. New York: David McKay, 1965. Chapters 1, 2, and 3.

> The general problem of individual differences in the classroom is treated in the first two chapters. The next seven chapters deal with intellectual differences among pupils. Chapter 3 is the first of this group and is a discussion of the recognition and measurement of these differences.

Tyler, L. E. *Tests and measurement*. Englewood Cliffs, N.J.: Prentice-Hall, 1963. Chapter 1.

> The first chapter of this paperback has two major topics; namely, the need for quantification in the study of human behavior and the four levels of measurement. The discussion of both is brief but effective.

Tyler, Ralph W. The functions of measurement in improving instruction. In E. F. Lindquist (Ed.), *Educational measurement*. Washington: American Council on Education, 1951. Pp. 47–67.

> Within this chapter are brief reviews concerning the manner in which educational measurement can assist in the selection of educational objectives, course content, learning experiences, and procedures of instruction, and the manner in which educational measurement can aid in organizing learning experiences.

References Cited

Cronbach, Lee J. *Essentials of psychological testing*. (2nd ed.) New York: Harper & Row, 1960.

Cronbach, Lee J. Evaluation for course improvement. *Tchers. Coll. Rec.*, 1963, **64**, 672–683.

Edwards, A. S. Intelligence as capacity for variability or versatility of response. *Psychol. Rev.*, 1928, **35**, 198–210.

Forehand, G. A. Comments on comments on testing. *Educ. psychol. Measmt*, 1964, **24**, 853–860.

Kearney, Nolan C. *Elementary school objectives*. New York: Russell Sage Foundation, 1953.

Morgan, H. Gerthon. What is effective evaluation? *NEA Journal*, 1959, **48**, 15–17.

Scriven, Michael. *The methodology of evaluation*. Unpublished manuscript. Bloomington: University of Indiana, 1965.

Selltiz, Claire; Marie Jahoda, Morton Deutsch, and Stuart Cook. *Research methods in social relations*. (Rev. ed.) New York: Holt, Rinehart and Winston, 1960.

Stake, R. E. *The countenance of educational evaluation*. Unpublished manuscript. Champaign, Ill.: University of Illinois, 1966.

Stanley, J. C. *Measurement in today's schools*. (4th ed.) New York: Prentice-Hall, 1964.

Stoddard, George D. On the meaning of intelligence. In *Proceedings of the 1965 Invitational Conference on Testing Problems*. Princeton, N.J.: Educational Testing Service, 1966. Pp. 3–11.

Terman, Lewis M. Intelligence and its measurement: a symposium. Part II. *J. educ. Psychol.*, 1921, **12**, 127–133.

Tyler, Ralph W. The functions of measurement in improving instruction. In E. F. Lindquist (Ed.), *Educational measurement*. Washington: American Council on Education, 1951. Pp. 47–67.

Tyler, Ralph W. Assessing the progress of education. *Phi Delta Kappan*, 1965, **47**, 13–16.

2 ✍

Educational Objectives in Pupil Evaluation

EACH PERSON organizes his life around a set of goals. Some of these are long-range, requiring almost a lifetime before they are realized. Others are more immediate; perhaps they can be attained in as little time as a month or so or in a matter of several years. Whatever they are, the attainment of them is important to us. The knowledge that our efforts directed toward a goal were sufficient to achieve that goal is a satisfying thing indeed.

The sources of these goals are difficult if not impossible to trace. It is clear, however, that they stem in one form or another from the needs that each of us experiences. The goals are direct outgrowths of social needs, such as the need for recognition, prestige, power, security, and companionship. The physiological needs such as hunger and thirst must also be included.

The nature of personal goals as well as their relative importance will vary from individual to individual. In spite of this variation, practically all of them can be classified into categories such as vocational, recreational, social, educational, and religious. This should not suggest that a goal in one category is independent of goals in any other. For example, an educational goal of acquiring a bachelor's degree from a first-class university may be closely related to a vocational goal of becoming a licensed physician. Again, a recreational goal of raising a bowling average to 175 pins per game may well be a part of a social goal of enlarging one's circle of friends.

At least for his more important goals each person organizes, formally or informally, programs that should lead him ever closer to them. Some may have tentative termination dates; others may not. Moreover, they may differ in terms of the degree to which they are structured. Those for educational and vocational goals are, for the most part, based upon formal schooling. Those for recreational and social goals may be designed by the individual and quite casual.

It is only reasonable that a person following a program would be concerned about his progress toward the intended goal. He may search for evidence that will identify his present position. For example, in the case of the educational goal mentioned, the evidence would include number of college credit hours accumulated and the grade-point average achieved; in the case of the bowling goal, it would be the bowling average for the past several games. With pieces of evidence such as these in mind, he can compare his present position with his initial position when the program began and with his goal. These two reference points allow him to evaluate the growth he has made.

Elementary and secondary schools contribute in a very substantial and basic way to the attainment of goals by the pupils enrolled in them. Educational objectives are extablished on the basis of the needs of the pupils that have been identified. School programs are designed to train pupils so that they may reach these goals and thereby learn how to satisfy their needs. Lastly, the teacher and the pupil evaluate the degree to which the pupil has achieved the educational objectives. Evaluation reveals the status of the pupil to him, his teacher, and his parents, and also contributes to any attempt to improve the school's program.

At this point we can easily see the role of pupil evaluation. Notice that it is necessary that we be extremely familiar with the capabilities and past experiences of each pupil before he is subjected to additional educational experiences, and that we determine how much he has changed or grown as a result of these new experiences. This is pupil evaluation.

To appreciate fully the importance of educational evaluation and the complexity of its mechanics, it is necessary to examine with some care the other aspects of the teaching process associated with it. Full treatment of these topics can be found in many textbooks devoted to curriculum development, methods of teaching, and educational psychology. It is appropriate here, however, to review briefly one of these topics—the identification of the needs of youth and the manner in which these needs are stated in terms of educational objectives. Only after this can a discussion of the degree to which pupils have achieved educational goals be meaningful.

IDENTIFYING THE NEEDS OF YOUTH

The needs of youth have been repeatedly investigated by psychologists and educators. Although the particular methods of inquiry used have varied appreciably, each can be classified under one of two general categories, the individual approach and the social approach (Low, 1953, pp. 30–38). The first category includes methods that concentrate upon a study of each youth as an individual, whereas the second category includes methods that try to identify the needs of youth by first analyzing the democratic society in which they live. The differences between the two categories are not as great as superficial inspection would lead one to believe.

Individual Approach

The methods in the individual approach attempt to identify the needs of youth by first studying the child as he is at a given moment and comparing his development with the behavior society expects him to display as an adult. The differences between his status of immaturity and society's standards for adulthood constitute his needs, whether or not he recognizes them at the moment. Studies of the status of youth at various ages have often been longitudinal in design and have characterized young people with regard to their physical, intellectual, and social development. From these findings has come a picture, inadequate as it may be, of the behavioral patterns and levels of maturation of typical children of a stated age with respect to these kinds of development.

To discover the kind of adult that society believes each child should become is no less difficult. Nevertheless, statements of authoritative tone have been formulated by a number of state, regional, and national organizations. The contents of the various statements resemble each other more than they differ, which may be due in part to the fact that some may have influenced others. A considerably more potent influence toward similarity is that all statements reflect to a substantial degree their authors' belief in a democratic society in which the individual is the dominant element.

Social Approach

The methods of inquiry included in the social approach attempt to discover the needs of youth by identifying first the present status of the democratic society in which the child lives, and then the goals that this society is to reach. The differences between the present position and the desired goals represent the needs of society and thus the needs of society's youth. This approach is based upon the assumption that each member of a democratic society must perpetuate and improve that society. His needs, then, can be traced to any deficiencies in his behavior patterns that in turn would prevent the democratic society from achieving its goals.

It is undoubtedly evident at this point that it is difficult to separate the personal needs of youth from the needs of a democratic society. The personal needs are, after all, guided and molded by the society in which the children live. Youth living in a democratic society will have needs different from those of youth living in some other type of society. Moreover, it can be argued that a democratic society achieves its goals only insofar as the needs of its members are appropriately satisfied. In other words, the members of a democratic society are obligated to serve it, and the society exists to serve them. The personal needs of youth and the broader needs of a democratic society are thus reciprocal in nature (Brink, 1953, p. 4).

Needs of Youth

Whether based upon the individual or upon democratic society as a frame of reference, the various statements of the needs of youth do not differ appreciably. Every child needs food, shelter, and rest. It is generally agreed that he also has needs related to preparation for his vocation, the utilization of his leisure time, his responsibilities as a citizen, and his future role as a homemaker and parent. Furthermore, each child has needs related to the acquisition of attitudes and values that will allow him to live in harmony with himself and other members of his society. Such needs are common to all youth.

Needs of the Individual

Identification of the major needs of youth such as those listed in the foregoing paragraph offers a basis for identification of the individual needs of each child. Although it is true that the needs of each child are similar in many respects, studies of the needs of youth would be badly oversimplified if allowances were not made for other pertinent factors. One of these factors is that all children do not recognize the relative importance of each need in the same way. An almost complete unawareness of some needs may exist, for a variety of reasons. For instance, needs related to vocational goals might easily be ignored insofar as children in the primary grade levels are concerned. A second factor is the degree to which the child has already learned to satisfy his own needs. Whereas one child may fail to realize that a need exists even though it actually does, another child of similar age may be equally indifferent about that area of need because he has already learned to meet them for the most part. A fortunate combination of environmental influences such as the home, the church, and the school, plus an unusual amount of innate talent possessed by the individual may have been sufficient to show him how to satisfy some of his needs at an abnormally early age.

Neither factor gives rise to situations that in any way refute the claim that certain general areas of need common to all children in a democratic society can be found. Their influence simply accounts for the fact that, at a given moment, one individual may recognize his needs and their relative importance differently than do his peers, even though all of them have common needs. Thus the needs of each child, although highly individualized, still fit into a pattern of needs common to all youth.

PROBLEMS

1   Select two school systems which you know well, preferably one in a metropolitan center and one not in such a center, and compare them in terms of the role which the schools must play in the process of helping pupils to learn how to satisfy their needs.

2   In view of the fact that children learn to satisfy some of their needs because of the experiences provided by agencies other than schools, and that the number, type, and effectiveness of these agencies vary from community to community and state to state, on what basis can one defend a relatively rigid "state curriculum" or a "national curriculum," perhaps developed along the lines of those in some foreign countries?

3   Murray (1938) says that, to understand the dynamics of human behavior, one must know both the psychological needs of the individual and the "press" of his environment as he perceives it. The behavior of the individual will be greatly influenced by his environment as he sees it. From Murray's point of view, what are the full implications of the statement that the central purpose of formal education is to educate pupils in such a way that they are better able to satisfy their needs?

TRANSLATING NEEDS INTO EDUCATIONAL OBJECTIVES

At one time the primary purpose of formal education was to teach each new generation all the knowledge that had been accumulated by all previous generations. This conception resulted in a highly rigid school curriculum that made the textbook the strongest single element in the classroom. At the present time this concept of the primary purpose of formal education has been largely superseded by another: to train pupils in such a way that they are better able to satisfy their needs (Tyler, 1953, p. 216). The kernel of this idea has been expressed by other writers in various ways. For instance, one writer said that "schools were created for the sole purpose of helping children to grow up properly" (Havighurst, 1953, p. 159). Another stated that the "major function of education is to foster, develop, and preserve democracy as a way of life" (Ahrens, 1953, p. 104). All three statements say in effect that the objectives of American schools must be derived from the needs of youth living in a democratic society.

The goals of formal education cannot be defined by simply restating each and every one of the known needs of youth. It is evident that children learn to meet some of their needs by experiences provided by agencies other than the school, such as the family, church organizations, private youth clubs, and tax-supported agencies designed to foster social, recreational, and athletic activities among youth. Since the school is not the only influential agency, the educational goals are not based upon all the needs of youth. Moreover, educational objectives may vary slightly from locality to locality.

The pertinent needs of youth are translated into educational objectives by identifying the new patterns of behavior that children must acquire to satisfy their needs. They involve the development of knowledges, understandings, attitudes and interests, skills, and abilities. Knowledge includes pupil behaviors which emphasize the remembering, either by recognition or recall, of ideas, material, or phenomena (Bloom, 1956, p. 62). If a pupil can comprehend the complete meaning of the pieces of information to the point that he can grasp the relationships among them, restate them in his own words, and take action intelligently on the basis of the information, then he has gained understanding. The patterns of behavior known as attitudes and interests pertain to a pupil's predisposition to react in a particular manner to certain ideas, objects, people, and events. He now has "points of view"; he has feelings of attraction or aversion toward aspects of his environment. Skills are often thought of as strictly motor in nature, but can be verbal and mathematical as well. Abilities are capacities to perform; for example, the pupil is able to demonstrate that he can read, write, listen, and speak effectively.

To classroom teachers and other education specialists falls the task of examining each area of need and deciding the nature of the new understandings, skills, abilities, and attitudes that each pupil must develop to be able to satisfy his needs. Then decisions must be made as to how and when each pupil will be trained. Such decisions must be based upon well-established principles gleaned from the study of the psychology of learning. These decisions should produce a curriculum in which attainable goals, carefully keyed to the maturity levels and various backgrounds of the pupils in question, have been selected for each area of instruction. Whether goals should be established for each grade level of each curriculum area is another question, since the grading system can be thought of as little more than a convenient administrative device for grouping pupils. In any event, within a framework of educational goals every teacher should still find sufficient flexibility so that he can exploit to the best of his abilities all the learning possibilities in his field, and can do so in terms of the individual needs of his pupils as he recognizes them.

The goals of education are pupil-oriented rather than teacher-oriented.

The manner in which they are stated should reflect this fact. In the not-too-distant past, educational objectives were stated in terms of the activities that the teacher was to perform. A certain topic was to be taught at a certain time in a certain manner. This was the objective, emphasizing subject-matter content and the sequence in which it was to be presented. The modern way of stating educational objectives reflects the fact that these objectives stem from pupil needs. The identification of educational objectives is nothing more than identifying the new patterns of behavior a pupil must acquire so that he will be able to satisfy his needs. To be consistent, therefore, educational objectives must be stated in terms of desired pupil behavior rather than in any other way. At the end of an educational experience the pupil should have knowledges, attitudes, interests, skills, or understandings that he did not possess before the experience. With these new behavioral patterns, he should be better able to satisfy his needs as he matures.

Problem

4   Low (1953, p. 25) believes that each need is dynamic; as an individual grows, his pattern of needs changes. Show how this fact is reflected in the educational objectives in the area of personal-social adjustment.

Taxonomy of Educational Objectives

Educational objectives can be classified into three domains, namely, the cognitive domain, the affective domain, and the psychomotor domain. The cognitive domain includes those educational objectives which are related to the recall of knowledge and the development of intellectual abilities and skills. The latter category involves pupil understandings. The effective domain includes those objectives concerning changes in pupil interests, attitudes, values, and appreciations. In other words, this is the domain of personal-social adjustment. The psychomotor domain includes objectives related to the motor skills which pupils are to develop.

Only the classifications of the objectives in the cognitive and affective domain are now developed. The taxonomy for the cognitive domain illustrates well the progress which has been made. Six major subdivisions of the cognitive domain are established and these in turn are subdivided as needed. The subdivisions are as follows (Bloom, 1956, pp. 201–207):

Knowledge

Knowledge involves the recall of specifics and universals, methods and processes, or a pattern, structure, or setting. The knowledge objectives emphasize most the psychological processes of remembering.

1.00 Knowledge
- 1.10 Knowledge of specifics
  - 1.11 Knowledge of terminology
  - 1.12 Knowledge of specific facts
- 1.20 Knowledge of ways and means of dealing with specifics
  - 1.21 Knowledge of conventions
  - 1.22 Knowledge of trends and sequences
  - 1.23 Knowledge of classifications and categories
  - 1.24 Knowledge of criteria
  - 1.25 Knowledge of methodology
- 1.30 Knowledge of the universals and abstractions in a field
  - 1.31 Knowledge of principles and generalizations
  - 1.32 Knowledge of theories and structures

Intellectual Abilities and Skills

Abilities and skills refer to organized modes of operation and generalized techniques for dealing with materials and problems. The abilities and skills objectives emphasize the mental processes of organizing and reorganizing material to achieve a particular purpose. The materials may be given or remembered.

2.00 Comprehension
- 2.10 Translation
- 2.20 Interpretation
- 2.30 Extrapolation

3.00 Application

4.00 Analysis
- 4.10 Analysis of elements
- 4.20 Analysis of relationships
- 4.30 Analysis of organizational principles

5.00 Synthesis
- 5.10 Production of a unique communication
- 5.20 Production of a plan or proposed set of operations
- 5.30 Derivation of a set of abstract relations

6.00 Evaluation
- 6.10 Judgment in terms of internal evidence
- 6.20 Judgment in terms of external criteria

An inspection of the foregoing outline reveals clearly the hierarchy of the types of educational objectives as they are known to exist. We move from knowledges, which can involve the simplest type of recall, to evaluation, which includes quantitative and qualitative judgments about the degree to which materials and methods approach criteria already established.

These are similar gradations for the affective domain. Five major categories have been identified, each of which has two or three subdivisions as follows (Krathwohl and others, 1964, pp 176–185):

1.0 Receiving (Attending)
At this level the learner is recognizing phenomena and stimuli presented by the teacher.
1.1 Awareness
1.2 Willingness to receive
1.3 Controlled or selected attention

2.0 Responding
At this level, the learner is actively attending. He is becoming involved in or committed to the phenomena or stimuli.
2.1 Acquiescence in responding
2.2 Willingness to respond
2.3 Satisfaction in response

3.0 Valuing
The learner recognizes a thing, behavior, or phenomenon as having worth. He displays this behavior consistently enough to be considered to be holding a value.
3.1 Acceptance of a value
3.2 Preference for a value
3.3 Commitment

4.0 Organization
The learner begins to organize his values into a system, determines their inter-relationships, and establishes the dominant and pervasive ones.
4.1 Conceptualization of a value
4.2 Organization of a value system

5.0 Characterization by a value or value complex
The learner is described and characterized as a person in terms of the controlling influence of his value hierarchy, and these beliefs and attitudes are integrated into a total philosophy or world view for him.
5.1 Generalized set
5.2 Characterization

It should be noted that the entire domain is organized with respect to one central factor called "internalization." This is a developmental sequence for an individual in which a characteristic or value becomes, in successive stages, a meaningful organizing principle for him. The internalization process is considered to be a hierarchical continuum and the five subcategories represent levels in the developmental sequence, starting with simple awareness of some characteristic or value and ending with its integration into a structure or "view of the world."

The cognitive, affective, and psychomotor domains represent the total framework of educational objectives for all types of educational institutions. They also represent, therefore, the total framework within which evaluation procedures are functioning. For every segment of the cognitive and the affective classification systems there is, or should be, a segment of evaluation. Hence, after careful study, a teacher can classify objectives pertinent to his teaching in appropriate categories, and devise a set of measurement procedures, some of which involve tests, to obtain appropriate data on the basis of which evaluations can be made. Use of the taxonomy in this way should add meaning to the educational objectives and define more sharply the limits of the scope of the evaluation attempted.

PROBLEMS

5   Classify each of the following objectives in terms of the six major levels of the taxonomy for the cognitive domain:
    a.   The pupil knows the physical and chemical properties of oxygen.
    b.   The pupil understands the scientific method as it is applied in the investigation of nutritional practices.
    c.   The pupil can interpret tables of data concerning the population, area, and economic wealth of various states of the United States.
    d.   The pupil can apply the Pythagorean principle to practical problems such as those in carpentry.
    e.   The pupil can recognize unstated assumptions in common advertising claims.
    f.   The pupil can write short creative stories for his own pleasure or the entertainment of others.
    g.   The pupil can analyze opposing arguments in a political debate and uncover any logical fallacies.

6   Classify each of the following objectives in terms of the five major levels of the taxonomy for the affective domain:
    a.   The pupil communicates directly with an individual in authority when he feels strongly about an issue within the jurisdiction of his office.
    b.   The pupil displays an interest in studying a foreign language.
    c.   The pupil evaluates people in terms of their behavior as individuals rather than in terms of factors such as race, religion, or national origin.
    d.   The pupil finds pleasure in the investigation of natural phenomena.
    e.   The pupil is developing a consistent philosophy of life.
    f.   The pupil recognizes that there may be more than one acceptable point of view about a given issue.
    g.   The pupil voluntarily reads articles in newspapers and magazines designed for his age group.

7   Stoker and Kropp (1964) discovered that, for an achievement test composed of carefully designed test items to represent each of the six major levels of the cognitive domain taxonomy, judges working independently had to classify most of the test items in the level intended by the test builder. List possible reasons why there was a lack of complete agreement among the judges with regard to the level in the taxonomy which a given test item was supposed to represent.

Formal Statements of Educational Objectives

Innumerable attempts have been made to formulate educational objectives. Many of these attempts have been quite narrow, often confined to a single subject-matter area such as reading or arithmetic; sometimes they have been restricted not only in terms of area but also in terms of class level. Some have been confined to a single subject-matter area and a single class level. On the other hand, a number of the most noteworthy attempts to devise educational objectives have been quite ambitious. Committees as well as individuals have prepared statements of the objectives of an elementary or secondary school program; these indeed have been prodigious tasks.

No attempt can be made here to list and describe all the results of these many efforts, or even to present a representative sample. Instead, several historically prominent reports are described as well as several that, because of their design and very precise statements, are making distinct contributions to pupil evaluation. Furthermore, the formal statements in this chapter in some instances emphasize the general objectives of formal education, whereas in others the specific objectives are emphasized. The general objectives spring from the major areas of the needs of youth. Specific objectives are simply subdivisions of the general objectives. A specific objective may be such a basic yet simple goal as the ability to add accurately any combination of two whole numbers, neither one of which is greater than 10. Or it might be the ability to use an apostrophe in simple words like "isn't" or "it's." Hosts of other specific objectives have been developed for each general objective and have been classified according to either age or grade level.

Cardinal Principles of Secondary Education

Of the many attempts to define the general objectives of secondary education, perhaps the most widely quoted is that formulated by the Commission on the Reorganization of Secondary Education, which was appointed by the National Education Association. These objectives are commonly called the "Seven Cardinal Principles of Secondary Education" (1918) and have unquestionably influenced the majority of all subsequent attempts of this kind. Briefly stated, they are as follows:

Good health
Command of fundamental processes
Worthy home membership

Vocational efficiency
Good citizenship
Worthy use of leisure time
Ethical character

According to these seven objectives, the functions of secondary schools extend considerably beyond simply "disseminating knowledge." Note also that they serve the elementary school teacher as well as the secondary school teacher. The objectives of education are additive. The secondary education objectives are the same as those of elementary education except that there is a different emphasis, and objectives peculiar to secondary education have been added.

Purposes of Education in American Democracy

The Educational Policies Commission of the National Education Association classified the objectives of secondary education in four categories (1938):

Self-realization
Human relationship
Economic efficiency
Civic responsibility

Within each of the four categories of objectives are listed many specific ones. The objectives of self-realization include skills in reading, writing, and arithmetic, intellectual and aesthetic interests, physical health, good character, and many others. Included in the category of human relationships are respect for humanity, appreciation of the home, and skills in homemaking. The objectives of economic efficiency are appreciation of good workmanship, consumer skills, and knowledge of occupations and their requirements. Within the category of objectives of civic responsibility are an understanding of democratic processes, respect for law, appreciation of social justice and tolerance, and many others.

A complete statement of all aspects of each category would constitute a sketch of an "educated person," the hope of a democratic society for each of its members. These statements represent an ideal person, and therefore are goals toward which each child strives. A school curriculum is designed to help him achieve these goals.

Developmental Tasks as Educational Objectives

Each child as he grows is subjected to three sets of pressures: those exerted by his maturing body, those exerted by the culture in which he lives, and those exerted by his personal values and aspirations. Because of these pressures, he is regularly confronted with lessons or tasks he must learn. If he learns them successfully at or about the age most children in his culture master them, his life will tend to be normal and happy. Should he fail to learn each lesson or task, or should he learn them at an atypical age, his life will seem less than normal and his membership in society less than satisfying.

The lessons or tasks that each individual must learn as he grows in his society are called *developmental tasks*. Havighurst defined a developmental task as "a task which arises at or about a certain period in the life of the individual, successful achievement of which leads to his happiness and to success with later tasks, while failure leads to unhappiness in the individual, disapproval by the society, and difficulty with later tasks" (Havighurst, 1953, p. 2). Some tasks may seem relatively easy to an individual; others extremely difficult. They are spread throughout the lifetime of each person.

Havighurst and others have attempted to list the developmental tasks common to all persons in the American society. Havighurst began by subdividing the life span into age periods, two of which are pertinent here: middle childhood and adolescence. Then on the basis of the evidence he had gathered he listed the developmental tasks for each period.

The middle childhood period begins at about six years of age and ends at about twelve or thirteen years of age. This period covers the elementary school years. The developmental tasks listed by Havighurst for this period are as follows:

1. Learning physical skills necessary for ordinary games.
2. Building wholesome attitudes toward oneself as a growing organism.
3. Learning to get along with age-mates.
4. Learning an appropriate masculine or feminine social role.
5. Developing fundamental skills in reading, writing, and calculating.
6. Developing concepts necessary for everyday living.
7. Developing conscience, morality, and a scale of values.
8. Achieving personal independence.
9. Developing attitudes toward groups and institutions (Havighurst, 1953, pp. 25–41).

The adolescent age period begins at about thirteen or fourteen years of age and ends at approximately eighteen years of age. These are the age levels of the secondary school. Havighurst's developmental tasks for this period are:

1. Achieving new and more mature relations with age-mates of both sexes.
2. Achieving a masculine or feminine social role.
3. Accepting one's physique and using the body effectively.

4. Achieving emotional independence of parents and other adults.
5. Achieving assurance of economic independence.
6. Selecting and preparing for an occupation.
7. Preparing for marriage and family life.
8. Developing intellectual skills and concepts necessary for civic competence.
9. Desiring and achieving socially responsible behavior.
10. Acquiring a set of values and an ethical system as a guide to behavior (Havighurst, 1953, pp. 111–158).

Developmental tasks that have been accurately determined for various age levels can be most useful in the determination of the objectives of education. They alert the teacher to the problems with which typical children of each age group are struggling, and in so doing, help the teacher improve the nature and the timing of the teaching process. Education should help each pupil achieve each of his developmental tasks when he is physiologically and psychologically ready and the pressures of his society are evident. Insofar as developmental tasks truly reflect the needs of youth, they can be considered general objectives of formal education or, at the very least, can appreciably influence the statement of such objectives.

Specific Objectives of Elementary Education

Of the hundreds of attempts to list part or all of the specific objectives of elementary education, only one is here reported. It is the statement of objectives prepared by the Mid-Century Committee on Outcomes in Elementary Education (Kearney, 1953). These objectives are particularly worthy of notice because an effort is made to state each in terms of observable pupil behavior. Each objective is also thought to be attainable by average children at some time prior to an age level of about fifteen or sixteen years. In other words, no matter how defensible a proposed objective might have been on a purely philosophical basis, it was not included unless it was also deemed attainable during the first fifteen years of the child's life, regardless of whether the school, the home, or some other community agency was instrumental in helping the child reach this goal. Moreover, in the case of those objectives in which the school is in some way involved, the manner in which they are stated makes the teacher aware of the ways in which a pupil is to behave after instruction. This greatly facilitates all evaluation attempts.

Nine curriculum areas are considered. They are:

Physical development, health, and body care
Individual social and emotional development
Ethical behavior, standards, and values

Social relations
The social world
The physical world
Esthetic development
Communication
Quantitative relationships

Physical development, health, and body care is a broad area, in that it includes individual health, physical education, safety, and personal grooming. Individual, social and emotional development pertains to mental health, emotional stability, and growth of personality. Ethical behavior, standards, and values are related to the observance of moral and civil laws. The area of social relations is devoted to the pupil's personal-social relations with others. Within the social world area is considered the behavior of the child in relation to a community, state, and nation; geography, civics, elementary economics, and government are studied. The physical world area encompasses the study of the natural environment. Esthetic development involves esthetic appreciation and expression in art, music, and the crafts. The communications area stresses reading, writing, composition, spelling, punctuation, speaking, and listening. Arithmetic and some parts of algebra and geometry constitute quantitative relationships.

Within each curriculum area, four types of behavioral patterns are cited:

Knowledges and understandings
Skills and competences
Attitudes and interests
Action patterns

Knowledges and understandings mean that the pupil will learn and retain certain things so well that they can be recalled easily. Skills are defined as those performances by the pupil that do not demand careful planning and preparation. The competences are intellectual in nature and pertain to decision making and related aspects. Interests and attitudes are centered around the emotions and motives of the pupil. Action patterns are broad, generalized ways of behaving in which the pupil uses the knowledges, understandings, skills, and competences, and is influenced in their use by his attitudes and interests.

The objectives of elementary education are not listed for each grade level. Instead, three points in time, called age-grade periods, are selected somewhat arbitrarily and the objectives are listed for each. The primary period corresponds to the end of the third grade, the pupils having attained an age of about nine years. The intermediate period corresponds to the end of the sixth grade, the pupils having attained an age of about twelve years. The upper-grade period corresponds to the end of the ninth grade, the pupils having attained an age of about fifteen years.

To illustrate the nature of the objectives reported by the Mid-Century Committee on Outcomes in Elementary Education (Kearney, 1953, pp. 68–73, 113–120), a few objectives of two curriculum areas are listed below. The two areas selected are dissimilar. One is ethical behavior, standards, and values, whereas the other is quantitative relationships. Note that only the intermediate period objectives have been cited.

Ethical behavior, standards, and values

A. Knowledges and understandings
  1. The pupil develops an awareness of property rights and of truth and falsehood.
  2. The pupil understands the basic principles of giving value in return for value received.

B. Skills and competences
  1. The pupil is able to like a person in spite of disliking his behavior in specific instances.
  2. The pupil's conception of "property" enable him to refrain from taking what does not belong to him.

C. Attitudes and interests
  1. The pupil is interested in altruistic club activities.
  2. The pupil protects other pupils, particularly the "underdog" or the handicapped.

D. Action patterns
  1. The pupil tends to be analytical in evaluating behavior.
  2. The pupil habitually acts in accord with a system of ethical values, although these are not always the same as adult values.

Quantitative relationships

A. Knowledges and understandings
  1. The pupil knows how numbers apply to time, weight, and dry and liquid measures.
  2. The pupil sees the relationship of division to fractions, and understands decimals as fractions or as small units or parts of larger units, with their places held by a decimal point and zeros or columns.

B. Skills and competences
  1. The pupil can add, subtract, and multiply decimals.
  2. The pupil performs the four fundamental processes, including long division, with whole numbers with a high degree of accuracy.

C. Attitudes and interests
  1. The pupil respects accuracy and arithmetical orderliness.
  2. The pupil enjoys estimating, playing with "short cuts," and number magic.

D. Action patterns
  1. The pupil is able to search for meaning behind the number or numerical relationships he uses.
  2. The pupil can interpret scale drawings, and can construct and read line and bar graphs.

These objectives are not designed to be minimal objectives for part or all of the pupils. The members of the committee expected that all pupils would not achieve all objectives to an equal degree or at the same rate. Furthermore, it is apparent that, for each curriculum area, the difficulty of the objectives varies within each of the three age-grade periods as well as among them. Within each period, there are objectives to be attained relatively early and hence they seem to be quite simple. With these are other objectives to be attained relatively late, because of this they seem more difficult.

Specific Objectives of Secondary Education

Following the publication of the statement of objectives prepared by the Mid-Century Committee on Outcomes in Elementary Education, it was proposed that a similar study be made of educational objectives at the secondary school level. As a result such a study was organized; the results were published (French and associates, 1957). As in the case of the elementary school objectives, the secondary school objectives are stated in terms of pupil behavior; in other words, they are descriptions of what pupils should be able to do or how they should act in certain situations.

Only the objectives for the general education program in the secondary school are included in this report. The basic purposes of this program are to help pupils realize their fullest potentialities and meet civic responsibility.

The lists of educational objectives are classified under three maturity goals and four areas of behavioral competence. The maturity goals are:

1. Growth toward self-realization. Self-realization is described as the development of "the common kinds of behaviors indicative of such personal growth and development as will enable them [the pupils] within the limits of their native environments, to live richer, more satisfying, more productive lives consonant with our ethical, aesthetic, and social standards and values."
2. Growth toward desirable interpersonal relations in small groups.
3. Growth toward effective membership or leadership in large organizations.

The four areas of behavioral competence are:

1. Attainment of maximum intellectual growth and development.
2. Cultural orientation and integration.
3. Physical and mental health.
4. Economic competence.

Combining the three maturity goals and the four areas of behavioral competence establishes twelve broad groups of behavior. In other words, a chart with twelve cells is formed. Each cell contains a group of related educational objectives. The cells are not considered mutually exclusive.

The educational objectives included in these cells are classified under the maturity goal of self-realization within the area of behavioral competence known as attaining maximum intellectual growth and development. The following five objectives are typical of those mentioned in the three major subgroups (1.11, 1.12, and 1.13) included in this cell.

1.111 (d) The pupil uses common sources of printed information efficiently; e.g., dictionary, encyclopedia, *Readers' Guide,* card catalog in a library.

1.121 (a) The pupil adjusts his reading rate and his method of reading to the material at hand.

1.123 (f) The pupil demonstrates that he can read and understand mathematical reports, charts and graphs, and simple statements of financial accounts.

1.131 (e) The pupil analyzes a problem and can follow the recognized steps involved in scientific thinking.

1.133 (c) The pupil recognizes the unsoundness of drawing generalizations from insufficient evidence (French and associates, 1957, pp. 92–102).

These educational objectives are designed to be reasonable goals for the most mature high school seniors. This means that, for each pupil, some of them will seem to be too high a standard. To assist the teacher in those instances in which they may seem to be too high, "developmental equivalents" are provided for each of the major subgroups of educational objectives. These are less mature behavioral patterns; they are indicative of the stages of development that we would expect to occur as the younger pupils progress toward the mature behavior of the older pupils.

PROBLEMS

8 In the statement of specific objectives of elementary education are cited "determining conditions," that is, the biological and sociological context in which children and the schools carry on together (Kearney, 1953, p. 36). In what way is this concept of "determining conditions," related to the basic thinking behind the developmental tasks as proposed by Havighurst?

9 Suggest reasons why the specific objectives in elementary and secondary education which are cited in this chapter are organized in noticeably dissimilar patterns.

10   What important differences in meaning, if any, exist between the term
     "self-realization" as used in the organization of the specific objectives of
     secondary education and "self-actualization" and "self-fulfillment" (Peck
     and Mitchell, 1962, pp. 12–14)?

Evaluating in Terms of Educational Objectives

The various published statements of the general and specific objectives
of education are most helpful to the classroom teacher. They point out the
ultimate goals that should be achieved by all American youth, regardless of
the family of which they are members, the schools in which they are
enrolled, or the communities in which the schools are located. In so doing,
these statements tend to keep the curriculum of all schools more or less
aligned without necessarily specifying the nature of all of its parts.

The formal statements of educational objectives cited in the preceding
sections have at least two common characteristics that have not been
previously mentioned. In the first place, none of the statements suggests
the relative importance of the objectives listed. The order in which they
are mentioned is not intended to reflect their order of importance. In the
second place, none of them suggests the particular objectives that are to
guide the instruction by a specific teacher on a stated day with a certain
group of pupils. These two omissions are deliberate—they should exist. It
is not the function of any group of consultants, no matter how gifted, to
dictate each movement of each teacher each day in his classroom. Instead,
they try only to state the common goals, and tacitly recognize that
individual differences among pupils, teachers, schools, and even among
communities will cause variations in the relative importance of the objectives and the timing of educational experiences designed to help the pupil
attain the goals.

For these reasons, the teacher is the most prominent single person
involved in the process of identifying educational objectives for the
classroom. It is he who must amalgamate the general and specific objectives of the kind mentioned with a variety of pertinent local factors to
arrive at the proper educational objectives for his class and to give each
objective its proper emphasis. Local factors usually considered are the
educational objectives of the courses previously completed by the pupils,
their success in achieving these objectives, the educational philosophy of
the school, the facilities of the community, the vocational goals of the
pupils, and the nature of their homes. In other words, difficult as it is, the
teacher must become acquainted with the individualized needs of the
pupils in his class. The influence of all local factors upon the formal
statements of educational objectives should yield a set of realistic and
pertinent objectives for classroom use.

Preparing Specific Educational Objectives

Teacher-derived educational objectives serve two functions: they are the basis on which the curriculum is developed; the teaching process organized, and data-gathering procedures planned. These functions are best served when the objectives are stated in specific terms of observable behavior. Knowing what changes his instruction should produce, the teacher is in a better position to plan it and evaluate the results.

Formal statements of elementary and secondary school objectives are nothing more than useful starting points for a teacher preparing the specific educational objectives needed for successful instruction and pupil evaluation. In spite of extensive efforts to formulate the so-called specific objectives of elementary and secondary education, each teacher normally will find these inadequate, since he needs a rather large series of concisely stated objectives.

What steps should the classroom teacher follow to prepare his own objectives? In recent years, considerable *attention* has been given to this question, particularly efforts to improve programmed instruction (Mager, 1962). Specific behavior-oriented objectives are needed to ensure the development of a successful programmed unit. This is also true of instruction and pupil evaluation not based on programmed learning.

Mager (1962, p. 12) believes that three basic steps must be taken to prepare the specific objectives. These are the following:

1. Identify specifically the kind of pupil behavior which is acceptable as evidence that he has achieved the objective in question. In other words, the objective must state explicitly what the pupil must be able to *do* in order to achieve it.
2. Describe the important conditions which influence pupil behavior. In other words, any support provided the pupil or any restrictions placed upon him when he must demonstrate his competence should be mentioned.
3. Specify the criteria of acceptable performance by describing at least the lower limit of such performance.

An illustration of the results of this procedure is the following taken from an elementary mathematics unit:

When provided with accurate drawings of a variety of triangles, each having all needed dimensions shown, the pupil can compute the area of each correctly to the nearest whole number, at least 75% of the time.

Note that an attempt has been made to follow each of the three steps. First of all, the pupil behavior is concisely described; that is, he must "compute the area of each correctly to the nearest whole number." Secondly, a condition is introduced; that is, the pupil is "provided with accurate drawings of a variety of triangles, each having all needed dimensions shown." Finally, the lower limit of performance is established; that is, answers must be correct to the nearest whole number "at least 75% of the time."

A properly designed educational objective should communicate the intent of the teacher quickly and completely to pupils and parents alike. An effective way of testing the wording of an educational objective is to present it to another teacher interested in the subject-matter and see if he can select successful pupils in terms of the objective. These should also be acceptable to you, the author of the statement.

The manner of preparation here described will produce specific educational objectives of considerable utility, especially in the cognitive domain. As one is forced to subdivide the general objectives and, perhaps, the so-called specific objectives to formulate those of direct concern to him, he gains an appreciably better insight into the problems of providing adequate instruction and designing appropriate measuring instruments.

Eliciting Pupil Behavioral Patterns

When objectives are stated in terms of pupil behavior, the basic intent of pupil evaluation can be described as the determination of the degree to which a pupil's behavior has changed so that it conforms more closely to that defined in the objectives. This sounds like a simple process; actually, it is tremendously complex. In the first place, the pupil must be given an opportunity to demonstrate that he has or has not reached the goal. Secondly, this demonstration must occur under circumstances that will allow critical evaluation in terms of the appropriate objectives. To accomplish this, a trained observer equipped with suitable measuring tools is needed. This is the only truly meaningful way of evaluating pupil growth. All other methods are indirect and, by this very fact, tend to be somewhat inadequate. The practical importance of these inadequacies varies considerably. In some cases they are so serious that the measurement results are practically worthless; in other cases their presence only modestly reduces the effectiveness of the measuring methods.

BEHAVIOR IN A NATURAL SITUATION. The first step requires that goal behavior by a pupil be elicited within a natural situation. The pupil involved feels no compulsion to say the "proper" thing or to behave in the "proper" manner. He is behaving as he truly has learned to, rather than in a feigned manner he might adopt if required to exhibit a pattern of behavior for teacher evaluation. In the natural situation, the true, unvarnished products of his educational experiences are voluntarily displayed.

This description of natural situations actually points out one of the major difficulties encountered in pupil evaluation. Since the very essence of natural situations prevents the teacher from controlling them, his efforts at evaluation are often hampered. Some natural situations will not occur in the classroom; in fact, some will not occur until after the formal education of the pupil has been completed. For example, it is reasonable to expect that pupil behavior related to aspects of educational objectives pertaining to citizenship, home membership, and vocational proficiency is best shown in natural situations, most of which occur outside the classroom. The natural situations that do occur during the pupil's elementary and secondary school career may take place at haphazard times and sundry places. Needless to say, the teacher should capitalize upon them when evaluating pupil behavior because they provide him with an opportunity to observe goal behavior freely. In view of this, it is clear that attempts to evaluate pupil behavior must occur at almost any time and in almost any place— which means, in effect, that evaluative efforts in natural situations are at times impractical, if not impossible.

To be sure, direct observation of pupil behavior in a natural situation can be made of the degree to which pupils have achieved some of the specific objectives of education. For example, a teacher can observe with relative ease and frequency whether a pupil consistently covers his nose and mouth with a handkerchief when sneezing or coughing, whether he can tell time and make change with accuracy, whether he enjoys active games, whether he uses conventional courtesies in his oral communications, whether he can read silently with little or no lip movement, or construct charts and graphs with only minor errors. These and other direct observations of pupil behavior can be made in lifelike situations outside the classroom or in connection with normal classroom routine. Class projects, teacher-pupil interviews, field trips, social functions, and other activities may be suitable opportunities for observation even though not necessarily designed for them.

SKILLFUL OBSERVATION. Although direct observations may be made in an informal atmosphere, the observation process that constitutes the second of the two steps of pupil evaluation cannot be as casual if it is to be successful. The skilled observer is one who is intimately familiar with the goals to be reached, the characteristics of pupil behavior that fall short of the goal to various degrees and in various ways, and the methods of reporting observations. This suggests that he have a full knowledge of human development, the psychology of learning, methods of educational evaluation, and the subject matter areas in which instruction takes place. The observer must know what he is looking for and must be able to search for it as systematically and objectively as possible. Vague "impressions" are not enough. Ranking and rating procedures, check lists, anecdotal records, and even sociometric devices are tools that can be used.

ARTIFICIAL SITUATIONS AND EVALUATION METHODS.   Evaluative attempts conducted in artificial situations are far more common than those conducted in natural situations. The pressures of time and convenience repeatedly cause the latter to be abandoned. Instead, the teacher establishes artificial situations as similar to natural situations as time and convenience will allow. It is hoped that the behavior exhibited by the pupil in the artificial situation is closely related to that he would have exhibited in a comparable natural situation if given the opportunity. The evaluation devices used in these situations are frequently paper-and-pencil achievement tests, but could be performance tests, written assignments, or work samples of a multitude of types.

The artificial situations and the evaluative devices used with them vary greatly in the degree to which they elicit pupil behavior closely related to that found in the corresponding natural situation (Lindquist, 1951, pp. 146–152). Some are quite successful in this respect. For example, paper-and-pencil tests, such as reading speed and comprehension tests, and performance tests, such as typing and shorthand tests, allow the pupil to demonstrate whether he has acquired the behavioral patterns described as objectives, and to do so in rather realistic settings. The same is true of performance tests given pupils in home economics classes, industrial art classes, and vocational agricultural classes. The products of the pupil's behavior as well as the behavior itself can be evaluated. A typed business letter, a meat roast, a wooden bookcase, or a welded wagon frame could serve this purpose. Note that in these instances the teacher does not wait until the pupil's behavioral patterns occur in the natural course of events, nor is he certain that the material involved in the evaluation is completely representative of that present in the natural situation.

On the other hand, there are countless other evaluation attempts involving artificial situations that do not elicit pupil behavior essentially the same as that the pupil would display in a natural situation. The teacher must assume that there is a sizable relationship between the pupil behavior elicited in the artificial situation and the behavior elicited in a natural situation. For example, attitude and interest inventories allow the pupil to indicate how he would (or should) behave in situations described to him, but do not actually place him in the situations so that he can overtly display his behavior. If there is a very strong relationship between what he says he would do and what he actually would do if given the opportunity, then these inventories are satisfactory. Such is not the case in actual practice.

Additional illustrations of the importance of the foregoing assumption are easily found. For instance, paper-and-pencil tests are sometimes used as a basis for evaluating the pupil's ability to perform laboratory and shop activities, which are a part of a number of secondary school classes. In a physics class, test items may describe the apparatus and materials necessary for laboratory experiments in electricity and magnetism. After the steps of the experiments have been recounted, the pupil is required to predict the outcome of each experiment and give reasons why this is the case. In an auto mechanics class, the test items may describe symptoms of an automobile engine that is not functioning properly. The pupil is required to diagnose the trouble by interpreting the symptoms, then select from a list of tools those necessary to repair the engine, and list the steps he would follow when making repairs. In an English class, artificial situations have been used to evaluate a pupil's writing ability. Rather than asking the pupil to write a composition, the teacher gives him a poorly written passage that he must improve by deleting or adding words, phrases, and punctuation marks.

In each of the three examples mentioned above, the response to the artificial situation is not the same as what would have been elicited in a natural situation. The test items in physics and in auto mechanics do not allow the pupil to display his skill in the actual manipulation of laboratory apparatus and tools. It is conceivable that he could answer the test items correctly and still not be able to perform the tasks. The same is true of the English composition test. Writing ability involves more than correcting the punctuation and rearranging the words of a passage written by someone else. It also includes selection and arrangement of ideas and style of expression. Elements of originality so important in superior writing ability are scarcely tapped by the test. Nevertheless, in the case of all three examples the teacher must make the assumption that the abilities of the pupil measured by the paper-and-pencil test items are related to his abilities to perform the tasks as they occur in natural situations.

Pupil evaluation should be planned as an integral part of the teaching process. As the teacher examines each of his objectives and designs experiences for his class, he should also design the method of evaluation to be used. It is not surprising to discover that methods of evaluation vary markedly from one kind of behavioral change to another. Recall of information is usually evaluated on the basis of test results yielded by paper-and-pencil tests, both teacher-constructed and standardized. The same is for the most part true of understandings, verbal skills, and mathematical skills. Motor skills are customarily evaluated on the basis of results, yielded by performance tests and the systematic use of ranking and rating devices. Attitudes and interests are sometimes evaluated in terms of paper-and-pencil inventory results, ranking and rating results, reports of teacher-pupil and teacher-parent interviews, anecdotal records summarizing direct observations, and, to a limited extent, sociometric results and other information from the pupil's peers.

Planning the Paper-and-Pencil Achievement Test

No doubt the most common measurement method used in schools today is the paper-and-pencil achievement test. In several respects its prominence is undeserved. Nevertheless, it shows the way in which measuring methods are designed in terms of a set of selected educational objectives.

The steps a teacher must take when constructing a paper-and-pencil achievement test are relatively few. First of all, he must separate from among his specific objectives those that have verbal and mathematical aspects. Many objectives of considerable merit will be excluded at this point. Secondly, he must determine the relative importance of the verbal and mathematical objectives. This is a purely subjective process. Teachers with the same specific objectives differ noticeably with respect to the relative importance they assign to each. As the relative importance of the specific objectives varies from teacher to teacher, so does the nature of the instruction. The relative emphasis that a specific objective receives in the process of instruction is a crude but effective indicator of the emphasis to be given that objective when an achievement test involving it is constructed. Finally, the teacher must build a group of test items, either of the essay or objective type, that constitute a representative sample of all materials included within the specific objectives. The importance of each objective is roughly equivalent to the number of test items related to it, the difficulty of these test items, the amount of credit allotted to right answers to the test items, or several or all of these simultaneously.

TABLES OF SPECIFICATIONS.   To illustrate the foregoing process, consider the case of the secondary school chemistry teacher who is conducting his educational program in terms of a number of general objectives, three of which are the following:

1. The pupil can remember and understand certain facts, definitions, laws, and theories of chemistry.
2. The pupil can understand the scientific method in its relations to the theories and principles of chemistry.
3. The pupil can apply the principles of chemistry in making predictions, explanations, and inferences.

When teaching a unit devoted to oxygen and some of its common compounds, he stresses the first and third objective insofar as this subject matter is concerned. From these are derived a large series of specific objectives, each of which establishes, for the most part, the criterion behavior which the pupil must display if he has achieved the objective, any restrictions placed upon him when he demonstrates his competence, and the lower limit of acceptable performance. The following three statements, based on the first general objective, show the kind of objectives used.

1. When given a list of twenty common compounds containing oxygen, the pupil can properly classify at least fifteen of them as to whether each is a gas, a liquid, or a solid when at normal temperature and pressure.

2. Of the ten oxides studied, the pupil can accurately identify each as an acidic oxide or a basic oxide at least 70% of the time.

3. When provided with an incomplete equation showing the ingredients and the conditions needed to synthesize each of twenty common compounds containing oxygen, the pupil can complete the equation and balance it properly at least 60% of the time.

The next step is to group the specific objectives as needed. Notice that the foregoing three deal with recall of chemical information, but each is concerned with a different subject-matter topic. Although each deals with common compounds of oxygen, the first speaks of their physical properties, the second of their chemical properties, and the third of their preparation.

A convenient way of gathering and organizing the specific objectives is a table of specifications. In its simplest form, the table of specifications is a two-way table, one dimension of which is a breakdown of behavioral changes, and the other of subject-matter topics. The behavioral changes can be classified into many categories; for example, the six major categories listed in the taxonomy of educational objectives for the cognitive domain. Less than six are commonly used in teacher-constructed tests. For the chemistry test, three categories were considered significant; the ability to recall chemical information, interpret chemical data, and apply chemical concepts and principles to new situations. These are the first three major categories of the cognitive domain taxonomy; that is, knowledge, comprehension, and application.

The subject-matter topics are subdivisions of the verbal and mathematical material included in the unit. Normally, many topics are listed. For example, the unit devoted to oxygen and some of its common compounds might be first subdivided into general topics—their physical properties, chemical properties, preparation, and uses. Each of these topics could be again subdivided into as many minor topics as the classroom teacher deems necessary.

To build a table of specifications the teacher must decide upon the relative importance of the behavioral changes and the topics. These judgments can be represented as percentages. In the oxygen unit, for example, the following decisions may be reached:

I. Behavioral changes
    1. Ability to recall information   35
    2. Ability to interpret data   35
    3. Ability to apply concepts and principles in new situations   30
      Total   100

II. Subject-matter topics
    1. Physical properties of oxygen and its common compounds   20
    2. Chemical properties of oxygen and its common compounds   30
    3. Preparation of oxygen and its common compounds   10
    4. Uses of oxygen and its common compounds   40
      Total   100

The two breakdowns and the assigned percentages are then combined into a simple table, as illustrated in Table 1. The entries in the twelve cells of the table are based upon the best judgment of the teacher, and are arranged so that the row and column totals are not changed. Should the four topics be expanded to many subtopics, additional table entries would be necessary. Thus, the various physical properties, chemical properties, methods of preparation, and uses can be listed and percentages assigned.

The number of behavioral changes in a table of specifications seldom varies appreciably. This is not true, however, of the number of topics. In a ninth-grade civics class, for instance, a unit concerning the structure and functions of the federal government might contribute only three topics to a table of specifications—the executive, judicial, and legislative branches. On the other hand, each branch might be given subtopics concerning its powers, duties, and relationships with the other two. The same is true of a plane geometry course. A unit concerning quadrilaterals may be subdivided

TABLE 1

TABLE OF SPECIFICATIONS FOR A CHEMISTRY UNIT DEVOTED TO OXYGEN
AND ITS COMMON COMPOUNDS

Subject-matter topic	Behavioral Changes			
	Recall of information	Inter-pretation of data	Application in new situations	Total
Physical properties	6%	10%	4%	20%
Chemical properties	10	10	10	30
Preparation	6	4	0	10
Uses	13	11	16	40
Total	35	35	30	100

into parallelograms, rectangles, squares, trapezoids, and rhombuses. Or, in addition, each kind of quadrilateral could be listed with subtopics concerning the determination of the size of its area, the length of its perimeter, and the relationships among its angles. Generally an attempt is made to subdivide the topics until the outline is quite detailed.

The percentages included in the table are rough approximations of the importance of each behavioral change in each topic. Therefore, if an objective test is to be constructed, the percentages could be used as rough approximations of the percentage of test items in the test devoted to the behavior changes of each topic. In actual practice, however, circumstances force the test builder to deviate somewhat from this point of view (Vaughn, 1951, pp. 168–170). For instance, a given test item may refer to more than one cell in the table. On the other hand, items for some cells might be extremely difficult to construct. Because of the short supply that results, the test may not reflect the designated importance of each cell as accurately as we might hope. Finally, it must be remembered the percentage weights in the table are, at best, very crude. As the test is being constructed, the builder will sometimes gain better insight into his table of specifications and change it accordingly.

In spite of the crudeness of a table of specifications and the difficulty of constructing a sufficient number of test items for all of its cells, the use of such a table for building paper-and-pencil achievement tests produces tests vastly superior to those yielded by a casual, unsystematic skimming of lesson plans and textbooks. Furthermore, the effort invested in the development of a table of specifications can pay dividends for a prolonged period of time. With revision as needed, the table may materially assist the construction of paper-and-pencil achievement tests for a number of years.

To use the percentage weights contained in the table of specifications, the teacher must first decide how many essay or objective items the test will contain. This in turn depends on the time available for testing, the type of test item to be used, and the anticipated difficulty of those items. The time factor is frequently determined by the administrative routine of the school. A class period may be the maximum amount of time available. The maturity level of the pupils and the possibility of the test causing excessive fatigue may be sufficient reasons for the teacher to reduce the time interval even more. In any event, knowing the testing time available, the teacher can estimate on the basis of past experience with his classes the number of test items of a given kind and difficulty that pupils can answer in the number of minutes allotted.

The techniques for constructing test items of various types are described in detail in the following chapters. However, it is important to recognize once again the position of item construction in the series of steps necessary to develop a paper-and-pencil achievement test. Rather than being the first, as commonly believed, it is the last of the three major steps. Test items are constructed only after the appropriate educational objectives have been selected, and their relative importance appraised. The results of these decisions are, in effect, summarized by means of one or more tables of specifications.

CONTENT VALIDITY.   Clearly, the central purpose of the procedure just described for building paper-and-pencil achievement tests is to develop a high quality test, that is, one which will satisfactorily serve the purpose or purposes for which it is intended. In the case of an achievement test such as the oxygen test, its purpose is to determine as of the moment it is administered, how well a pupil recalls, interprets, and applies the cross-section of the total amount of subject matter studied which it contains. The degree to which the achievement test serves this purpose is its content validity (French and Michael, 1966, pp. 12–16). This is one of three types of test validity (see pages 286–290).

The degree of content validity of a test rises and falls in accordance with (1) the extent to which its table of specifications accurately reflects the relative importance of the various subject-matter topics in relation to the various pupil behavioral changes stemming from verbal and mathematically oriented educational objectives, and (2) the degree to which the test items built on the basis of the table of specifications accurately mirror the balance of the cells. A high degree of content validity is customarily attained when carefully contrived tables of specification, or some similar device, are used, and when the many rules of test item construction described in Part Two are conscientiously followed.

General Considerations

Pupil evaluation is basically a function of the classroom teacher. It is he who must select the educational objectives for his class and establish their relative importance. After teaching his pupils in accordance with chosen objectives, it is he who must then evaluate the degree to which the desired modifications in pupil behavior have taken place. The teacher must design performance tests and paper-and-pencil achievement tests, and in doing so, call upon his vast fund of knowledge about the individual differences among his pupils and the intent of his educational objectives. It is difficult to conceive of a comprehensive program of pupil evaluation which does not utilize the classroom teacher and his resources more than any other single factor.

The conscientious teacher who fully accepts his responsibilities for pupil evaluation finds himself facing a difficult task. For every educational objective he should have a data-gathering method. Although the classroom teacher has at his disposal a large variety of these methods, they are still few in number and low in quality. Teacher-pupil and teacher-parent conferences, anecdotal records, pupil reports and records, ranking and rating devices, recitations, work samples, written assignments of many sorts, performance tests, and paper-and-pencil tests can be used. Nevertheless, even these are insufficient, and many of the results they yield are unreliable. New instruments are definitely needed. The supply of data-gathering devices is exceptionally inadequate for evaluating pupil behavior in curriculum areas such as esthetic development, social and emotional development, and moral values. Behavioral description as it is presently performed is at best incomplete and, even when its more highly developed methods inaccurate.

The true role played by paper-and-pencil tests in pupil evaluation is quite obvious at this point. The acknowledged purposes of elementary and secondary education have expanded greatly since the turn of the century. As they grew, the usefulness of the traditional paper-and-pencil test as a measuring instrument has steadily declined. For a curriculum based upon the idea that a school must, above all, serve as a vehicle for transmitting to the new generation all of the knowledge accumulated by previous generations, this kind of test would serve admirably. For a curriculum based upon the idea that a school must help á pupil learn how to meet his many needs as a member of a democratic society, this kind of test still is of major importance, but by no means should it dominate pupil evaluation to the degree that it now does.

The unjustified popularity of paper-and-pencil tests as measuring instruments can be most disconcerting to pupils, parents, and teachers alike. After everyone assures everyone else that the objectives of education should reflect the needs of the "whole" child, the teacher evaluates the behavioral patterns of his pupils on a highly restricted basis. The pupil and his parents are understandably confused; the teacher usually feels unduly frustrated. No doubt he recognizes the possibility of injustices when this method is followed, but he also knows that he does not have sufficient data-gathering tools and that many of those he has lack the respectability of paper-and-pencil tests.

This dilemma in which teachers repeatedly find themselves has no convenient solution. To use paper-and-pencil instruments to the point where most other techniques are ignored, however, is not the answer to the problem. Instead, consider the following:

> For many objectives of the type suggested, measuring or observational devices concerned with the student's overt behavior while he is yet in school, even though of a rough and opportunistic character, are perhaps much more worth while than any written type of tests. The actual behavior of the stu-

dent in school elections, for example, however fragmentary or limited in sampling, may provide a better clue to his future behavior than anything he professes that he will do in a written test; books actually read by the pupil in his free time may constitute a truer indication of his literary tastes than his score on a literary appreciation test; anecdotal records may be more meaningful than scores on personality tests; etc. The problem of deriving comparable measures from such opportunistic observational data now seems to present almost insuperable difficulties, but perhaps no worse than have been resolved before through determined and persistent effort (Lindquist, 1951, p. 157).

The foregoing remarks are, of course, intended to discourage the preference paper-and-pencil tests are so frequently given. These remarks should not be interpreted as a general denunciation of written tests, followed by a recommendation that they be abandoned completely. On the contrary, paper-and-pencil tests should be a sizable part of any pupil evaluation program. These tests should be used in conjunction with, rather than in the absence of, other methods. The very nature of many educational objectives requires that this be so. Paper-and-pencil tests can do a commendable job of determining the degree to which certain objectives have been achieved, but are totally inappropriate in the case of many others. Unfortunately, the results of such tests have also been used as estimates of the degree to which the pupil has achieved educational objectives far removed from the original ones. This has occurred in spite of the fact that the degree to which a pupil attains one educational objective is not necessarily the same as the degree to which he attains any other.

PROBLEMS

11   In educational evaluation, the teacher is to determine the degree to which pupils achieve pertinent objectives. On the other hand, Dressel (1960, pp. 4–5) wants educational objectives to be evaluated in terms of dimensions such as simple-complex, achievable-unachievable, explicit-implicit, and individual-social. In what ways will such study of educational objectives as proposed by Dressel improve the quality of educational evaluation?

12   When debating the suitability of using paper-and-pencil tests for measuring the degree to which a student attains important non-cognitive goals, Wrightstone expressed the opinion that the scope of written tests is broad enough to make important contributions in this realm, whereas Rummel believes the scope of paper-and-pencil tests in the non-cognitive domain is very limited at this time (Ebel, 1960, pp. 96–99). With whom do you agree? Why?

13   Prepare a statement of the verbal and mathematical objectives of a unit which you are teaching or soon will be teaching. On the basis of these objectives, build at least one table of specifications suitable for the construction of an informal achievement test.

14 Imagine that you are a member of a team of teachers who are to devise a social studies achievement test to be administered at the end of a unit which all are independently teaching to separate classes. How would you proceed to plan the test to guarantee a high degree of content validity for each class?

15 Show how the taxonomy of educational objectives in the cognitive domain can improve the chances of an informal achievement test having a high degree of content validity.

Summary

Each child has needs that he must be able to satisfy to live a happy and productive life in a democratic society. Common to all youth are organic needs, such as food, shelter, and rest. Each child also has needs related to preparation for his vocation, the utilization of leisure time, his responsibilities as a citizen, his role as a homemaker, and his personal-social adjustment. The areas of need have been identified by studying intensively both youth and the democratic society in which they live.

There are many agencies that can help youth learn how to satisfy their needs. Their families, churches, and clubs are important factors. However, the school is most important in practically all instances. The primary purpose of formal education is to train youth in such a way that they are better able to satisfy their needs. The objectives of education are developed on this premise.

The needs of youth are translated into educational objectives by identifying the new patterns of behavior the child must acquire in order to satisfy his needs. The educational objectives involve the development of new knowledges, understandings, attitudes, interests, skills, and abilities. Thus the objectives of education are pupil-oriented rather than teacher-oriented and are stated in terms of desired behavioral patterns in the pupil. Taxonomies for objectives in the cognitive and affective domains are now being used.

Many formal statements of educational objectives have been prepared by individuals and organizations. Prominent among them are the elementary and secondary school objectives prepared by committees sponsored by the Russell Sage Foundation. These and other statements have tended to keep the curriculum of all schools more or less aligned without necessarily specifying the nature of all its parts.

Having taught pupils with the guidance of educational objectives, the teacher must evaluate their achievement in terms of those objectives. The basic purpose of pupil evaluation is to determine the degree to which a pupil's behavior conforms to that defined in each of the educational objectives. Ideally this should be done by direct observation of the pupil's behavior in a natural situation. At times this is impractical, if not impossible. Instead, the teacher establishes artificial situations that are as similar to natural situations as time and convenience will allow and evaluates the pupil's achievement indirectly within these situations by means of a variety of data-gathering devices.

The artificial situations and the data-gathering devices used with them vary greatly in the degree to which they elicit pupil behavior closely related to that found in the corresponding natural situation. Performance tests are quire successful in this respect, as are some paper-and-pencil tests. However, many paper-and-pencil tests are considerably less successful, obvious illustrations being tests designed to measure attitudes or interests.

The construction of a paper-and-pencil achievement test involves three steps. Firstly, the educational objectives with verbal and mathematical aspects must be separated from all others. Secondly, the relative importance of these objectives and their subparts must be identified. Finally, a group of test items effectively sampling all materials within the educational objectives must be constructed. The second and third steps can be facilitated by using a table of specifications, and a high degree of content validity attained.

Evaluating pupil behavior in terms of educational objectives is a complex task. Many methods are used. Recall of information is usually evaluated on the basis of test results yielded by paper-and-pencil power tests, both informal and standardized. The same is for the most part true of understandings, verbal skills, and mathematical skills. Motor skills can be evaluated on the basis of results yielded by performance tests and the use of ranking and rating devices. Attitudes and interests are sometimes evaluated in terms of paper-and-pencil inventory results, ranking and rating results, reports of teacher-pupil interviews, and anecdotal records.

Paper-and-pencil tests, more refined than other techniques, can accurately reveal the pupil's verbal and mathematical achievement. However crude and opportunistic, observational devices such as anecdotal records and rating scales can provide better data on the degree to which other objectives have been achieved than written tests. Pupil evaluation is ordinarily centered around paper-and-pencil tests to an unrealistically high degree.

Suggested Readings

Bloom, Benjamin S. (Ed.) *Taxonomy of educational objectives: cognitive domain.* New York: David McKay, 1956.
This book provides an excellent basis for building evaluation instruments in

the cognitive domain. The cognitive domain includes those educational objectives dealing with the recall of knowledge and the development of intellectual abilities and skills. By classifying educational objectives, it offers a framework for improving the chances that achievement tests in this area will have acceptable content validity.

French, Will, and associates. *Behavioral goals of general education in high school*. New York: Russell Sage Foundation, 1957.

This is a report of the specific objectives of the general education program in the secondary school. Although organized in a different manner, it is, in a sense, a companion volume to *Elementary School Objectives* by Kearney. Part III is the most important part. It contains lists of behavioral outcomes classified according to three maturity goals and four areas of behavioral competence.

Havighurst, Robert J. *Human development and education*. New York: Longmans, Green, 1953. Parts 1, 2, and 3.

The developmental tasks for infancy and early childhood are described in Part 1, those for middle childhood in Part 2, and those for adolescence in Part 3. Of particular interest in Part 2 is Chapter 8 in which the developmental tasks of middle childhood are treated as objectives of elementary education, and in Part 3, Chapter 12, in which some of the relationships between developmental tasks and the school curriculum are explained.

Henry, Nelson B. (Ed.) *Adapting the secondary-school program to the needs of youth*. Fifty-Second Yearb. nat. Soc. Stud. Educ., 1953, Part I. Chicago: University of Chicago Press. Chapters 2, 12, and 14.

Chapter 2 is written by Camilla Low and contains discussions of the nature of the needs of youth and the methods of identifying these needs. In Chapter 12, Ralph Tyler discusses procedures for translating the needs of youth into teaching goals. Chapter 14, by Verner Sims, cites methods of evaluating pupil progress toward the satisfaction of needs. Although these chapters are keyed to the secondary school situation, they contain numerous ideas that are equally valuable in the elementary school.

Kearney, Nolan C. *Elementary school objectives*. New York: Russell Sage Foundation, 1953. Parts 2 and 3.

Part 2 lists the goals for the elementary school years as recommended by the Mid-Century Committee on Outcomes in Elementary Education. Their implications for educational practice, research, and measurement are treated in Part 3.

Krathwohl, D. R., B. S. Bloom, and B. B. Masia. *Taxonomy of educational objectives: affective domain*. New York: David McKay, 1964.

The first part of this book is an explanation of the rationale behind the taxonomy of educational objectives in the affective domain, including a discussion of internalization, the basic factor underlying the taxonomy. The second part contains a full description of the taxonomy and illustrative educational objectives and test items classified in the various levels.

Lindquist, E. F. Preliminary considerations in objective test construction. In E. F. Lindquist (Ed.), *Educational measurement*. Washington: American Council on Education, 1951. Pp. 119–158.

This chapter describes the role of general and specific objectives in achievement evaluation, direct and indirect methods of evaluating achievement, and the limitations of paper-and-pencil examinations.

Mager, R. F. *Preparing instructional objectives*. San, Francisco: Fearon Publishers, 1962.

    Techniques for stating objectives explicitly in behavioral terms are presented. Three considerations are: (1) identifying the terminal behavior which the pupil must demonstrate, (2) describing the conditions under which this behavior will be expected to occur, and (3) describing how well the pupil must perform in order to demonstrate mastery. Examples of well stated and poorly stated objectives are included.

Vaughn, K. W. Planning the objective test. In E. F. Lindquist (Ed.), *Educational measurement*. Washington: American Council on Education, 1951. Pp. 159–184.

    This chapter is essentially an overview of the various steps involved in building a standardized achievement test using objective test items. Tables of specifications are described and illustrations shown.

REFERENCES CITED

Ahrens, Maurice R. Developing a plan of action for improving programs for youth. *Adapting the secondary-school program to the needs of youth*. Fifty-Second Yearb. nat. Soc. Stud. Educ., 1953, Part I. Chicago: University of Chicago Press. Pp. 102–117.

Bloom, Benjamin S. (Ed.) *Taxonomy of educational objectives: cognitive domain*. New York: David McKay, 1956.

Brink, William C. The youth-needs motive in secondary education. *Adapting the secondary-school program to the needs of youth*. Fifty-Second Yearb. nat. Soc. Stud. Educ., 1953, Part I. Chicago: University of Chicago Press. Pp. 1–21.

Cardinal principles of secondary education. *U.S. Office of Education Bulletin*, No. 35, 1918.

Dressel, Paul L. Measurement and evaluation of instructional objectives. *The Seventeenth Yearb., Nat. Council Measmt in Ed.*, 1960. Ames, Iowa: National Council on Measurement in Education. Pp. 1–6.

Ebel, Robert L. Inventories and tests. *Education*, 1960, **81**, 67–99.

Educational Policies Commission. *The purposes of education in American democracy*. Washington: National Education Association and the American Association of School Administrators, 1938.

French, Will, and associates. *Behavioral goals of general education in high school*. New York: Russell Sage Foundation, 1957.

French, J. W., and W. B. Michael. *Standards for educational and psychological tests and manuals*. Washington: American Psychological Association, 1966.

Havighurst, Robert J. *Human development and education*. New York: Longmans, Green, 1953.

Kearney, Nolan C. *Elementary school objectives*. New York: Russell Sage Foundation, 1953.

Krathwohl, D. R., B. S. Bloom, and B. B. Masia. *Taxonomy of educational objectives: affective domain.* New York: David McKay, 1964.

Lindquist, E. F. Preliminary considerations in objective test construction. In E. F. Lindquist (Ed.), *Educational measurement.* Washington: American Council on Education, 1951. Pp. 119–158.

Low, Camilla M. Determining the nature of the needs of youth. *Adapting the secondary-school program to the needs of youth.* Fifty-Second Yearb. nat. Soc. Stud. Educ., 1953, Part I. Chicago: University of Chicago Press. Pp. 22–43.

Mager, R. F. *Preparing instructional objectives.* Palo Alto, Calif.: Fearon Publishers, 1962.

Murray, Henry A. *Explorations in personality.* New York: Oxford University Press, 1938.

Peck, Robert F., and James V. Mitchell. *Mental health.* What Research Says to the Teacher, No. 24. Washington: National Education Association, 1962.

Stoker, H. W., and R. P. Kropp. Measurement of cognitive processes. *J. educ. Measmt,* 1964, 1, 39–42.

Tyler, Ralph W. Translating youth needs into teaching goals. *Adapting the secondary-school program to the needs of youth.* Fifty-Second Yearb. nat. Soc. Stud. Educ., 1953, Part I. Chicago: University of Chicago Press. Pp. 215–229.

Vaughn, K. W. Planning the objective test. In E. F. Lindquist (Ed.), *Educational measurement.* Washington: American Council on Education, 1951. Pp. 159–184.

PART TWO

Measuring Achievemen

FOR THE HOMEOWNER, the do-it-yourself movement now dominates such areas as carpentry, painting, and landscaping. In some respects, the novelty of being your own designer, contractor, and artisan contributes to the popularity of this movement. Moreover, the self-satisfaction experienced at the completion of a project is virtually matchless.

The do-it-yourself idea is a familiar one to the teacher, both within the scope of his professional position and outside of it. Early in his training program he discovers that recipes for teaching are few, that prefabricated teaching techniques do not exist, and that hiring someone to perform part of his duties is seldom possible. In short, he learns that he must rely on his own skill and ingenuity practically all of the time. The unique characteristics of each teaching situation are too important to permit a standardization of the teaching art.

As one step in the teaching process, pupil evaluation offers an excellent opportunity for a teacher to display his skill and ingenuity. Although outside assistance is available in the form of standardized measuring instruments and measurement specialists who serve as consultants, the lion's share of the evaluation program must be shouldered by the classroom teacher. Frequently it is he who must design the instrument, administer it, score it, interpret the results, and, finally, appraise the worth of these activities. His responsibilities here are as clear as those related to the identification of his educational objectives and, on the basis of them, the determination of suitable learning experiences for his pupils.

The teacher's measuring efforts are often centered around the paper-and-pencil achievement test, either objective or essay type. Chapter 3, "Measuring Knowledges Objectively," is devoted to discussions of the construction and use of objective test items to be used as a classroom achievement test, emphasizing those test items that measure recall of information. Chapter 4, "Measuring Understandings Objectively," emphasizes those test items that measure pupil understandings. Chapter 5, "Preparing Essay Achievement Tests," identifies the role of essay test items in achievement testing and compares it with that of objective test items. Chapter 6, "Appraising Classroom Achievement Tests," contains descriptions of various methods of appraising paper-and-pencil tests, particularly those that are objective in nature.

Not all of the data-gathering instruments built by the classroom teacher are paper-and-pencil tests. Many are ranking and rating scales, check lists, product scales, and the like, that are used to evaluate pupil performance. Chapter 7, "Judging Procedures and Products," describes and illustrates these methods.

The classroom teacher generally cannot build measuring instruments as technically perfect as those produced by teams of testing specialists. On the other hand, he has a decided advantage over the specialists in that he is far better informed concerning the quality of the pupils whose achievements are to be measured and the nature of the learning experiences they have had. This in turn means that the classroom instruments that he builds with care will often compare favorably with standardized instruments designed to accomplish the same purpose.

Rather than being discouraged about the likelihood of building useful measuring instruments, teachers should be optimistic. The expenditure of reasonable amounts of effort coupled with careful observance of a group of simple rules are all that is really needed. If a teacher has a creative flair, the task is simpler and the product better.

3

Measuring Knowledges Objectively

As CONSUMERS, each of us repeatedly samples various products on the market and, on the basis of our reaction, we draw conclusions about the quality of the product. Consider for a moment any of the purchases of food we commonly make. Suppose that we enter a supermarket to buy three items—candy, bakery goods, and breakfast cereal. In the first instance we select a pound of gum drops. Within the pound are individual pieces of a variety of colors. A nibble of one of each color may quickly convince us to favor the green gum drops over those of all other colors and to avoid the black ones at all costs. For the second purchase we choose one dozen glazed doughnuts. These we find to be fresh and tasteful, and, as a result, our opinion of the bakery division is favorable. Finally, we select a well-publicized brand of breakfast cereal. If at breakfast on subsequent mornings we conclude that, as advertised, the cereal is indeed a "taste treat" and gives us that additional "go-power," we probably will continue to buy the product; if not, we will no doubt refuse to buy another box no matter how persuasive the exhortations of well-known motion picture personalities and baseball players.

How sound are these judgments? This question is difficult to answer. To the degree that our taste sensibilities are reasonably normal at the time we tested the product, and to the degree that the sample of the product we consumed is reasonably representative, the judgments are sound. If these two conditions are not met, the soundness of the decision is certainly in doubt. For example, had we been ill shortly before or during the trial, the first condition would very likely not be satisfied. Moreover, had the gum drops, doughnuts, or breakfast cereal been accidentally contaminated in some way, they would hardly be representative of these products when properly handled, and the second condition would not be satisfied.

When acting as a consumer of food products, the classroom teacher samples and judges them just like anyone else. When evaluating the achievement of his pupils, he follows essentially the same procedure. He is actually making the same two basic assumptions in both cases. In the first place, just as he assumes that his testing faculties are normal when he judges food products, he believes that the ability of his pupils to reveal the knowledges, understandings, skills, and attitudes they possess and their willingness to do so are not seriously impaired by any unusual factors. Such factors might be emotional disturbances, greatly reduced teacher-pupil rapport, physical fatigue, or any of a multitude of minor distractions.

Secondly, just as he assumes that the food products eaten are representative of similar ones in the supermarket on that day or, for that matter, on any future day, he concludes that the samples of pupil behavior that he observes and evaluates are typical of much unobserved pupil behavior both present and future. In the case of achievement testing, the samples of pupil behavior are elicited by the questions or tasks included in a test. Hence, to obtain a representative sample of all of the possible variations of the pupil behavior in question, the teacher tries to find a representative sample of all of the possible questions or tasks that might be presented to the pupil.

The justification for the use of samples for evaluating food products as well as achievement is essentially one of practicality. After all, you will no doubt agree that it is not feasible or necessary that a person eat all gum drops in sight before deciding that the green ones are the most pleasing. In the same manner, it is not feasible or necessary that a teacher ask a pupil all possible questions or provide opportunities for him to perform all possible tasks to determine the degree to which he has achieved certain educational objectives.

The teacher would of course like to be confident that these two assumptions are fulfilled in every instance in which he tries to evaluate pupil achievement. Complete certainty can never be attained. Steps can be taken, however, that improve the likelihood that both assumptions will be satisfied. As far as achievement tests are concerned, useful procedures for assuring that a pupil is responding willingly and to the best of his ability are discussed in Chapter 14. In addition, useful procedures for assuring that a representative sample of pupil behavior is being judged are mentioned in many parts of this book.

Preliminary Preparation for the Objective Test

Demanding that a paper-and-pencil achievement test contain a representative group of test items is equivalent to demanding that the test have a high degree of content validity. Notice again that content validity is inherently tied to educational objectives; in the case of paper-and-pencil achievement tests, it is tied to specific objectives with verbal and mathematical aspects. Thus, procedures such as the use of a table of specifications which are known to improve the degree of content validity of a paper-and-pencil test are important to us here.

A table of specifications is a miniature view of the test; it is actually a crude but helpful blueprint used by the teacher to devise a test, just as a contractor's blueprint is used by a carpenter. The relative weights the teacher attaches to each cell are his guides to building a test with representative items. As test items are written, they are identified with one or more of the cells, and this information recorded. The tendency to over-represent or to under-represent any cell or group of cells is greatly minimized by this procedure.

Tables of specifications in paper-and-pencil achievement tests guarantee that the subject matter will be properly sampled and all pertinent behavioral changes appropriately emphasized. In other words, they help the teacher determine the relative importance of each topic and behavioral change. For example, a sixth-grade teacher building a test for a health unit concerning teeth is first reminded by his table of specifications that 30 per cent of his test is to be devoted to the subject-matter topic entitled "the relationship between one's diet and the development and maintenance of good teeth." Moreover, he notes that, within this 30 per cent, 20 per cent is to concern recall of information, and 10 per cent is to concern the application of the information and principles in new situations. All other subject-matter topics are identified in a similar manner. In view of this, it is difficult to believe that representative paper-and-pencil test items can be constructed efficiently without tables of specifications or some comparable device.

Problems

1 Stodola (1961, pp. 3–13) describes the plans and procedures of four teachers, each teaching at a different grade level and in a different subject-matter area, for constructing an informal achievement test to meet a particular need. Several tables of specifications are shown. Evaluate the test construction efforts of the teachers in the light of their stated needs and the tables of specifications to be used.

2 Item-by-item analyses for the various achievement tests included in the *Sequential Tests of Educational Progress* have been published (1959). Select one of the tests of interest to you and evaluate it from the point of view of a classroom teacher in that area who teaches at a stated class level.

Types of Objective Test Items

An efficient and convenient way to measure the pupil's ability to recall the information identified by a table of specifications is to build and administer a series of pertinent objective test items. An objective test item is one that can be scored in such a way that judgment is for all practical purposes eliminated when determining the correctness of a pupil's answer. To be sure, this is a broad definition. It is not surprising, therefore, to find many different types of test items identified as objective test items yet seemingly quite dissimilar in form. A complete listing of all possible variations is not necessary in a book of this kind; instead, a broad classification of types followed by description of the most popular variations is sufficient.

One of the most useful ways of classifying objective test items is to designate them as the supply type of item or as the selection type of item (Ebel, 1951, p. 193). When responding to a supply type of item, the pupil has to provide the words, numbers, or symbols necessary. Possible answers are not listed as part of the item. An illustration of the supply type is the short-answer item, two varieties of which are shown below:

Short-answer question:

DIRECTIONS: Within the space provided, write the word or phrase that correctly answers the question.
What is the name of the author of the novel entitled *Pickwick Papers?*
(Charles Dickens)

Completion test item:

DIRECTIONS: Within the space provided, write the word or phrase that correctly completes the statement.
The name of the author of the novel entitled *Pickwick Papers* is (Charles Dickens).

The selection type of item allows the pupil to choose the correct response from the information provided. The well-known true-false test item, the multiple-choice test item, the matching test item, and countless variations of them typify this category.

True-false test item:

DIRECTIONS: Determine whether each of the following statements is true or false. If the statement is true, circle the "T" preceding the statement; if the statement is false, circle the "F."

(T) F 1. The novel entitled *Pickwick Papers* was written by Charles Dickens.

Multiple-choice test item:

DIRECTIONS: For each of the following questions choose the correct answer from among the four possible answers listed. Write the number of your choice in the blank to the left of the question.

(2) 1. Who wrote the novel entitled *Pickwick Papers?*
(1) William Thackeray
(2) Charles Dickens
(3) Anthony Trollope
(4) George Eliot

Matching test item:

DIRECTIONS: Match the title of each novel with its author by writing the letter identifying the author in the blank to the left of the title. It is possible that some authors have written more than one of the novels listed.

	Novels		Authors
(H)	1. *Barchester Towers*		A. Jane Austen
(B)	2. *David Copperfield*		B. Charles Dickens
(B)	3. *Great Expectations*		C. Alexandre Dumas
(B)	4. *Oliver Twist*		D. George Eliot
(B)	5. *Pickwick Papers*		E. Victor Hugo
(A)	6. *Pride and Prejudice*		F. William Thackeray
(D)	7. *Romola*		G. Leo Tolstoy
(B)	8. *Tale of Two Cities*		H. Anthony Trollope
(F)	9. *Vanity Fair*		
(H)	10. *The Warden*		

The similarities and differences in form among these major types of objective test items are obvious. There are, however, important similarities and differences, in ease of construction, applicability, and ease of scoring. These and related topics are discussed and illustrated in the following sections.

PROBLEMS

3 Some teachers argue that the differences among the various types of objective test items are seemingly large but actually small. In the case of the three major variations of the selection type of item, defend their point of view.

4 Many mathematics teachers build and use "computation" tests, that is, tests in which the pupil must arrive at numerical answers as the result of following certain computational procedures. Are these objective tests? Give reasons for your answer.

CONSTRUCTING OBJECTIVE TEST ITEMS

Building a paper-and-pencil test in terms of tables of specifications is, as we have seen, a major step toward assurance that the test will have high content validity. The value of this procedure, however, is noticeably lessened if the test items are carelessly devised. Even though the item may be carefully balanced in terms of the subject-matter topics and behavioral changes listed in the table of specifications, the test as a whole may lack some content validity if the teacher fails to apply properly a myriad of relatively simple, obvious, and seemingly unimportant rules when he builds the test items. Many "dos and don'ts" governing the construction of objective test items are listed and illustrated on the following pages.

You may quite naturally expect that if a teacher is intimately familiar with his educational objectives, his own tables of specifications, and the backgrounds of his pupils, then adhering faithfully to the spirit and letter of the suggestions for item construction would be a virtual guarantee that good test items would be produced. This expectation is not totally justified. The writing of test items has been properly called an art—an art demanding the utmost degree of creativity, ingenuity, and persistence on the part of anyone who practices it. Knowledge of specific educational objectives, pupils, and suggestions for construction of test items are not sufficient. The judgment of the teacher in the use of such knowledge is also a vital factor.

Supply Test Items

The supply test item can be crudely defined as an essay test item demanding a highly abbreviated answer. This answer is often only a single word or number, seldom more than several words or numbers. The pupil responds to a direct question or incomplete declarative statement by writing his answer in the space provided. Notice that there is little difference between these two. By means of a simple rearrangement of words a short-answer question becomes a completion test item, or a completion test item becomes a short-answer question. They are sometimes haphazardly intermixed in informal achievement tests; however, a better practice is to separate them, especially when young pupils are being tested.

SUGGESTIONS FOR CONSTRUCTING SUPPLY TEST ITEMS. *Design the supply test item so that it has only one correct answer, which is short and definite.* This is unquestionably the most difficult problem a teacher encounters when building supply test items. Although he has but one short and definite answer in mind for each item, he will be amazed at the pupils' facility for thinking of synonyms or near-synonyms of his answers, which in many instances must be considered as correct answers. For example, consider the following test item written in two different ways. It is intended for use in an achievement test in basic arithmetic for elementary school pupils.

Poor: In the mixed number 7⅔, the "2" is the (numerator).

Improved: In the mixed number 7⅔, which digit is the numerator? (2)

The first version of the item will elicit a variety of responses. Answers such as "top number," "even number," "smallest number," or "numerator" certainly will be given. In a sense, all of them are correct. Some are clearly better than others. Since the purpose of the test item is to see if the pupil can identify the numerator of a mixed number, the second version of the test item is an improvement. There is no doubt about the correctness of any answer given to this question.

The first version of the test item shown above can be quickly identified as a poor one. However, test items that, at a first glance, appear quite satisfactory can be equally inadequate. The following is such an item:

Poor: The novel entitled *Pickwick Papers* was written by (*Charles Dickens*).

Improved: The name of the author of the novel entitled *Pickwick Papers* is (*Charles Dickens*).

The first version of this completion test item could elicit such responses as "a man," "an Englishman," "an adult," a "novelist," or "a genius." All of these are technically correct, but none is the answer expected—"Charles Dickens." It is clear, therefore, that if a teacher wishes to avoid much needless quibbling over the correctness or incorrectness of answers, great care must be exercised in the development of the test items. Some proposed supply test items cannot be conveniently changed so that many correct or half-correct answers do not occur. To do so may cause the desired answer to be too obvious, and hence the item is practically worthless because its level of difficulty is too low. Changing the item form from a supply to a selection type sometimes helps in these cases.

Avoid removing statements verbatim from textbooks or other sources and trying to use them as short-answer test items. This practice will, of course, give an advantage to that pupil who can somehow detect a textbook expression and select his answers at least partially on the basis of whether they have a textbook flavor. Moreover, the use of verbatim statements may make the item ambiguous. For example, the first of the following statements is taken directly from a history textbook and one word is deleted to make it a completion item.

Poor: The power to declare war is vested in (*Congress*).

Improved: In the United States the power to declare war is vested in (*Congress*).

Since the test covered aspects of the governments of many other countries, the pupils are understandably confused by the first version of the test item. Obviously, the teacher will quickly recognize the trouble when it is called to his attention; however, he is less likely to anticipate this problem if he continually takes statements out of context and uses them as short-answer test items. In summary, each test item should be able to stand alone unless deliberately related to other items.

When building completion test items, avoid mutilating the statement until its meaning is all but lost. In an effort to increase the level of difficulty, or test for several pieces of information by means of one item, some teachers greatly increase the number of blanks in a completion item. The temptation to do so is rather strong at times, but seldom is the procedure successful. Using a relatively small number of well-chosen blanks is more satisfactory. For instance, notice how the following item is improved by reducing the number of omitted words:

Poor: The (process) by which (petroleum) is separated into various component (parts) having different (boiling points) is known as (fractional distillation).

Improved: The process by which petroleum is separated into various component parts having different boiling points is known as (fractional distillation).

To the pupil, the second version is a well-defined problem, whereas the first is not. In fact, the first statement would discourage anyone but the person who originally deleted the words.

When building completion test items, try to place the blank or blanks near the end of the statement rather than the beginning. Often it is a simple matter to place the blanks at either the beginning or end of the test item. Placing the blanks at the end prevents the test item from acquiring a noticeable awkwardness, as well as a degree of artificial difficulty. The following items illustrate the point:

Poor: (Ecology) is the name given to the study of the interrelationship of organisms among themselves and with their environment.

Improved: The study of the interrelationship of organisms among themselves and with their environment is known as (ecology).

Some pupils will need more time to arrive at the correct answer when confronted with the first version than with the second. This is particularly true of elementary school children.

Avoid the use of extraneous hints designed to help the pupil identify the correct answer. On occasion teachers try to help the pupil find the correct answer to a short-answer test item by inserting the first letter of each word of the answer, by drawing the length of the line indicating the omitted word so that it approximates the length of the answer, or by drawing several lines of appropriate length when the correct answer contains several words. The following short-answer test item in an elementary school geography test is typical of this procedure:

Poor: In which state is the most important seaport on the eastern seaboard located? N(ew) Y(ork).

Improved: In which state is the most important seaport on the eastern seaboard located? (New York)

The first version of the test item encourages guessing more than the improved version. In addition, offering such hints as these is not realistic; if a pupil were required to recall this information outside of the testing situation he undoubtedly would not be offered this assistance. The difference between the testing situation and the natural situation is increased, and therefore the form of the test item is open to criticism.

Also, the hints help him to use processes of elimination otherwise unavailable. In attempting to answer the test item, a pupil not knowing the correct answer could quickly eliminate possibilities by remembering that "N———" must mean "New" or "North." Therefore, the correct answer is New Jersey, New Mexico, New York, New Hampshire, North Dakota, or North Carolina. Of these states, only New York has the second word beginning with the letter "Y." This, then, is his answer.

Always indicate the units in which the answer is to be expressed for those supply test items that could have several correct answers depending upon the units chosen. For computational exercises this can be an annoying problem for both the pupils writing the test and the person who must later score it. For instance, the correct answer to the following exercise can be expressed in three different ways.

Poor: A four-foot piece of wire is to be cut into two pieces so that one piece will be six inches longer than twice the length of the second piece. What is the length of the longer piece? (2 ft., 10 in.)

Improved: A four-foot piece of wire is to be cut into two pieces so that one piece will be six inches longer than twice the length of the second piece. What is the length of the longer piece? Ans. (2) ft. (10) in.

The correct answer is 34 inches, $2\frac{5}{6}$ feet, or 2 feet and 10 inches. Demanding one type of unit rather than another can change the difficulty level of the exercise as well as the amount of time needed to solve it.

ADVANTAGES AND LIMITATIONS OF SUPPLY TEST ITEMS.   There are two advantages of using the supply test item rather than other kinds of objective test items. First of all, the supply form minimizes the likelihood that the pupil will guess the correct answer. Whereas in the case of the selection form, he need only recognize the correct response from among a relatively small number of given possibilities, in the case of the supply test item, he is confronted with a situation that is not as highly structured. The likelihood of guessing the correct response in the second instance is a less important consideration than in the first instance. As a result, some pupils argue that this type of item is more difficult for them.

A second advantage often attributed to supply test items is that they are relatively easy to construct. This is, in a sense, a deceptive statement. Although some teachers find them easier to build than the selection type of item, supply test items are by no means as simple to construct as a casual investigation might indicate. The foregoing suggestions for constructing supply test items offer ample supporting evidence.

Of all of the limitations of using supply test items usually cited, two are outstanding. In the first place, such items are more difficult to score than other kinds of objective test items. Despite the best efforts of the teacher building such a test item, often a variety of answers are totally or partially correct. Assigning total or partial credit can only be done by someone intimately familiar with the test items, the background of the pupils, and the teaching situation. In other words, it must be done by the teacher, and even he finds it to be a difficult and time-consuming task. The scoring of pupil responses is complicated by legibility of handwriting and faulty spelling. The latter may or may not be sufficient cause for reducing the amount of credit a pupil receives for an otherwise correct response. If one of the purposes of the test is to determine whether a pupil can spell the correct answer after he has recalled it, then loss of credit can be justified. If this is not the case, loss of credit for faulty spelling cannot be defended.

The second limitation is the kind of behavioral change involved in the item. Typically these items demand only recall of information rather than more complex aspects, such as the application of principles in new situations. This tendency is traceable in part to the fact that no matter what type of objective test item is to be used, test items requiring only recall of information are usually easier to construct. When building supply test items, the teacher strives to find items with correct answers that are short and clear, and in so doing, he often selects test items involving primarily factual details. Vocabulary is heavily emphasized.

PROBLEMS

5   In the light of the foregoing suggestions to be followed when constructing supply test items, improve each of the following:
   a.   A hogan is an almost round structure with walls made of   (logs)   and
        (mud plaster)

  b.   Selling price equals cost plus   <u>(profit)</u>

  c.   <u>(Sun)</u>   is the source of most of our heat.

  d.   A diameter which is   <u>(perpendicular)</u>   to a chord   <u>(bisects)</u>   the chord.

6 Engelhart (1964, p. 13) labels supply test items as "semiobjective." Defend his position.

True-False Test Items

The true-false test item is nothing more than a declarative statement to which the pupil responds in one of two ways—the statement is true or it is false. Occasionally, the statement is so worded that it is more convenient to ask the pupil to respond with "Right" or "Wrong" rather than "True" or "False." Moreover, changing the declarative statement to a question need not necessarily increase the number of possible responses. In these instances, the question can be phrased so that a "Yes" or "No" response is requested.

The most common type of true-false test items has already been illustrated. Less common variations are the following:

Correction variety:

DIRECTIONS: Determine whether each of the following statements is true or false. If the statement is true, circle the "T" following the statement. If it is false, circle the "F" and write in the blank provided the word or words that, when substituted for the word in italics, will make the statement true.

  1.   The earth is essentially *spherical in* shape.   Ⓣ F

  2.   The sun is a *planet.*   T Ⓕ (star)

  3.   The earth spins on its axis once each *month.*   T Ⓕ (day)

Cluster variety:

DIRECTIONS: The following statements pertain to the location of various European countries. Determine whether each statement about each country is true or false. If it is true, circle the "T" following the statement. If it is false, circle the "F."

  1.   Switzerland has a common border with

a. Italy on the south.	T	F
b. France on the west.	T	F
c. Austria on the east.	T	F
d. Czechoslovakia on the north.	T	F

T-F-CT-CF variety:

DIRECTIONS: Determine (1) whether each of the following statements is true or false, and (2) whether the converse of the statement is true or false. If it is true, circle the "T" preceding the statement; if it is false, circle the "F." If the converse of the statement is true, circle "CT"; if the converse is false, circle "CF." Two correct answers must be given for each statement.

Ⓣ F   CT (CF)   1. A square is always a quadrilateral.
Ⓣ F   (CT) CF   2. An equilateral triangle is also an equiangular triangle.
T (F) CT (CF)   3. A right triangle is necessarily an isosceles triangle.

T-F-TF variety:

DIRECTIONS: Determine whether each of the following statements is true, false, or true under some circumstances and false under other circumstances. If the statement is true under all circumstances, circle the "T" preceding the statement; if it is false under all circumstances, circle the "F"; if it is true under some circumstances and false under others, circle the "TF."

T F (TF)   1. The length on the earth surface of one degree of longitude is more than 69 but less than 70 statute miles.

T F (TF)   2. If a person is living at a latitude of 40° he is living north of the equator.

(T) F TF   3. The prime meridian is an imaginary line at 0° longitude.

SUGGESTIONS FOR CONSTRUCTING TRUE-FALSE TEST ITEMS. When constructing a test item requiring a response of either "True" or "False" and only that, search for statements that are true or false without additional qualifications. All too commonly a true-false test item is essentially true or false rather than absolutely true or false. This is perplexing to the pupil. Should he mark statements as true only if they are true under all possible cirumstances, and mark all others false even though some might be essentially true? On the other hand, should he mark those statements true that are in general true and those false that are in general false, thus ignoring specific and perhaps minor qualifications that might be pertinent? If his method of attack fails to be the one the teacher has in mind, his answer will be wrong even though his knowledge of the subject matter is superior.

The following test item illustrates the problem. The intended answer is "True."

Poor: The water vapor in the air will condense when the air is cooled.
Improved: If the temperature of the air in this room is progressively lowered, a temperature will ultimately be reached at which the water vapor in the air will start to condense.

The first version of the test item may trouble the pupil because the degree of cooling, the amount of water vapor in the air, and the temperature of the air are not stated. Slight cooling may or may not cause condensation; drastic cooling probably would. Hence, the statement is true under certain circumstances and false under others. A pupil who knows the information normally required to answer the test item correctly may fail to receive credit for his knowledge because he remembers too many facts. He judges the statement to be false. When confronted with the second version of the test item, he would mark it as "True." Incidentally, copying statements verbatim from textbooks or study guides customarily produces true-false test items that are not absolutely true or absolutely false.

Avoid the use of specific determiners. Specific determiners are words or expressions that frequently identify a statement containing them as true or false. Words often found in false statements are "only," "never," "all," "every," "always," "none," and "no." Those often found in true statements are "usually," "generally," "sometimes," "customarily," "often," may," "could," and "frequently." The test-wise pupil recognizes the situation. If he does not possess the knowledge necessary to answer correctly a true-false test item, he searches for a specific determiner. Should he find one and answer accordingly, his chances of having identified the correct answer are good. Consequently, the test item may discriminate among pupils on a basis other than their ability to recall information, and thus its usefulness is impaired.

In an effort to construct true-false test items that are absolutely true or absolutely false, teachers repeatedly resort to the use of specific determiners. The weakening of the test item that customarily occurs is illustrated in the case of the following:

Poor: None of the people of Switzerland is engaged in farming.
Improved: The mountains of Switzerland prevent the Swiss people from farming extensively.

A clever but ill-prepared pupil would quickly mark the first version of the test item as false. Even though he may know nothing of the farming problems of Switzerland, he is confident that at least one Swiss citizen is engaged in farming. The second version demands a knowledge of the geography of the country as well as the nature of its agriculture. It contains no specific determiners to provide hints as to its correct answer.

The teacher need not always avoid the use of such words as "all," "never," and "usually" because they can serve as specific determiners. On the contrary, they can be deliberately used, and with success, by including them in true-false test items that have correct answers the opposite of those suggested by the words in question. For example:

1. All planets revolve around the sun of our solar system.
2. The sum of the angles of a plane triangle is always 180°.
3. Each molecule of a given compound is chemically the same as every other molecule of that compound.
4. The galvanometer is the instrument usually used for the metering of electrical energy for determining the cost of electrical service in a home.

In these instances, the words "all," "always," "every" and "usually" are no longer specific determiners.

Try to keep the true-false test items reasonably short, and restrict each to one central idea. True-false test items that are extremely long require undue amounts of response time. The pupil must search out the truth or falsity of each phrase and dependent clause. Moreover, long true-false test items are more often true than false since the length is sometimes caused by the qualifying remarks needed to make the statement true. Strive to balance the true-false statements in terms of length. If lengthy statements are used, they should be false about as often as they are true.

A serious problem that is sometimes accentuated by lengthy true-false items is that several ideas become involved. The pupil has to answer the test item in terms of whether the statements made about all ideas are true or false. If one part of the test item is true, whereas another part is false, he customarily labels the test item as false. But this can be confusing to the pupil not only when he responds to the test item but also when he reviews his test at a later time. Misinformation may result.

An illustration of a true-false test item that is partially true and partially false is shown below:

Poor: Although today the members of the United States House of Repre-
           sentatives are elected by popular vote of the people of the districts
           they represent, the members of the United States Senate are se-
           lected by the state legislatures of the states they represent.

Improved: The members of the present Senate of the United States were
           selected by the state legislatures of the states they represent.

The length of the first version of this item makes it a forbidding thing indeed; it can be shortened easily. The clause at the beginning of the statement is unnecessary and should be eliminated, as illustrated by the second version of the test item. This deletion serves the additional purpose of reducing the scope of the item to one central idea, which can be judged as true or false.

If true-false tests are used regularly, be certain that the percentage of test items requiring a "True" answer, and hence the percentage of test items requiring a "False" answer, are not relatively constant from test to test. Some pupils quickly sense any tendency on the part of a teacher to maintain approximately the same per cent of true and false statements from test to test. This is true regardless of whether an even balance between the two statements is maintained or an overbalance of one type is used. If a noticeable consistency is detected, the pupil may use it as a basis for guessing the answers of some of the test items that baffle him. Moreover, some pupils quickly discover any pattern that the correct answers may take, such as, F-T-F-T-F-T or T-T-F-F-T-T. Occasionally a teacher arranges the test items so that the correct answers form a systematic pattern, thereby simplifying scoring. Such an arrangement also simplifies the task of the alert pupil when he responds to the test items. An otherwise good true-false test can be seriously damaged by this procedure.

ADVANTAGES AND LIMITATIONS OF TRUE-FALSE TEST ITEMS. The advantages accrued by using true-false test items are outweighed by the limitations also present. For the most part, the popularity of these test items is unjustified—a popularity which can be traced primarily to the fact that true-false test items allow the teacher to sample widely a large amount of subject matter without needing a great amount of testing time. Most pupils can respond quickly to well-constructed items of this type. Even pupils in the primary grades can respond to them without requiring prohibitive amounts of time. A second and less obvious advantage sometimes cited in the case of true-false test items is that they are essentially a realistic task for the pupil. Frequently, in everyday life, he is called upon to judge a statement as true or false in the manner required of him by the test items. A third advantage of even more doubtful merit is the claim that true-false test items are easy to build. As in the case of the supply test items, the true-false test item is by no means so easy to construct as you might suppose.

One of the most serious limitations of the true-false test item is that many are concerned only with small, relatively unimportant pieces of information. Like the supply test item, the true-false item serves best as a means of measuring the pupils' ability to recall information. Because of the teacher's efforts to find statements that are absolutely true or false, the information needed to answer the items correctly is frequently highly specific. It is difficult to build good true-false test items that involve generalizations, broad principles, and relationships, all of which may be notably more important than the pieces of information involved in the usual true-false test items.

A second serious disadvantage is that true-false test items encourage some pupils to try to guess the correct response. They argue that, after all, they have a fifty-fifty chance of identifying the right answer without even bothering to read the statement. The use of specific determiners, the tendency of long statements to be true statements, and the practice of arranging the correct responses in a systematic pattern encourage guessing and increase the likelihood of that guessing being successful. Means of correcting for guessing are discussed later in this chapter (see page 123).

Finally, true-false test items can be criticized on the basis that many of them are ambiguous. Although careful construction of a set of true-false test items reduces ambiguity, it is not eliminated. Words like "several," "many," "some," "frequently," "important," and "principal" can hardly be avoided. But what do they mean? Variations in the meanings of these and similar terms can mean variations in the pupils' responses to the statements containing them. Hairsplitting distinctions may be necessary, to the distress of teacher and pupil alike.

PROBLEMS

7   Evaluate the usefulness of true-false test items when used for the purpose of measuring pupil knowledge in the (a) elementary school and (b) the secondary school.

8   Suppose that the improved version of the true-false test item concerning Swiss agriculture on page 86 were changed to read:
    The terrain of Switzerland retards the development of a diversified agricultural program in that country.
    Criticize this version of the test item.

9   In the light of the foregoing suggestions to be followed when constructing true-false test items, improve each of the following:
    a.   If we feel heat traveling through a steel bar at a certain rate, we can assume that heat will travel through another kind of bar at that rate.
    b.   Heat can do work.
    c.   The Reader's Guide is the best source to use when looking for current material on a subject.
    d.   If (+) times (+) equals (+), then (−) times (−) equals (−).

Multiple-Choice Test Items

A multiple-choice test item is one in which a direct question or incomplete statement is presented and a number of possible responses or options are given. The pupil chooses the response that is the correct (or best) answer to the question or that is the correct (or best) expression for completing the statement. The question or incomplete statement introducing the test item is known as the *stem*. Any undesired answer is called a *distracter* or *foil*. Generally four or five responses are listed and all but one is a distracter.

Some multiple-choice test items require a correct answer, others a "best" answer. This difference can be traced to the subject matter. For instance, when selecting the name of the author of a book among four names listed, the pupil searches for the correct answer; all distracters are completely wrong. However, when selecting the principal reason from among four possible reasons that Ulysses S. Grant was elected to the presidency of the United States, the pupil searches for the "best" answer. It should be clearly the most outstanding of those listed. As you can easily see, in this illustration the distracters can be actual reasons, but relatively unimportant. Both of these kinds of multiple-choice test items are commonly used.

Introducing a multiple-choice test item by means of an incomplete statement seems to be equally as satisfactory as introducing it by means of a direct question. Often the factor governing the choice of stem is the length of the test item. If the direct question approach yields a short, easily understood test item, it is customarily used; should it not do so, the incomplete statement approach replaces it. For a person inexperienced in building multiple-choice test items, however, the direct question is recommended, since fewer technically weak items result (Ebel, 1951, p. 230). Both types of stems are popular and can be used regardless of whether a correct or "best" answer is desired.

There are numerous variations of the multiple-choice test item. The most familiar form is that illustrated earlier in this chapter. Three additional variations are shown below.

Negative variety:

DIRECTIONS: For each of the following questions, select from among the four responses listed that which is *not* the correct answer. Write the number of your choice in the blank to the left of the questions.

(1)   1.   Which of the following cities of the United States are located west of the Mississippi River?
        (1)   Chicago
        (2)   Denver
        (3)   Los Angeles
        (4)   Salt Lake City

Multiple-response variety:

DIRECTIONS: For each of the following questions, select the correct answer or answers from among the four listed. Note that for each question there may be as few as one and as many as four correct answers. Write the number(s) of your choice(s) in the blank to the left of the question.

(2, 3)   1.   Which of the following compounds are gases when at room temperature and under normal pressure?
        (1)   Benzene
        (2)   Ammonia
        (3)   Carbon dioxide
        (4)   Silicon dioxide

Incomplete-response variety:

DIRECTIONS: Solve each of the following mathematics exercises and express your answer in the units designated. Identify the digit of your answer that occupies the second place to the left of the decimal point. Find that digit in the list of five shown with each exercise. Write the letter identifying it in the blank to the left of the exercise.

(D)   1.   Four neighbors are to be assessed by their city for special repairs to the street in front of their houses. The amount to be paid is to be prorated among the neighbors according to the property frontage of each (i.e., the width of property along the street). The total assessment is $690, and the respective frontages are 50, 50, 60, and 70 feet. How much (to the nearest dollar) will the owner of the 60-foot frontage have to pay?

(A) 1
(B) 2
(C) 7
(D) 8
(E) 9

SUGGESTIONS FOR CONSTRUCTING MULTIPLE-CHOICE TEST ITEMS. *Select the distracters so that all of them are reasonably plausible and appealing to those pupils who do not possess the knowledge demanded by the item.* Your experiences as an examinee are no doubt sufficient to convince you of the importance of this suggestion. When you are confronted with a multiple-choice item to which you do not know the answer, you probably attack by a process of elimination. Any response that appears to be extremely unlikely you eliminate, even though you may have little or no knowledge of it. Often you are able to reduce the number of possibilities to two, sometimes to only one. If some of the distracters are implausible, the possibility of identifying the correct answer is greatly improved. Many a pupil arrives at the correct answer to a multiple-choice item by this means, yet he does not possess the knowledge or understanding which it contains.

The following test item shows the ease with which the correct answer to a multiple-choice test item can be found when the distracters are implausible or appealing.

Poor: Which of the following men was at one time the Chief Justice of the Supreme Court of the United States?
(1) Charles Evans Hughes
(2) Nikolai Lenin
(3) Chiang Kai-shek
(4) John Paul Jones

Improved: Which of the following men was at one time the Chief Justice of the Supreme Court of the United States?
(1) Charles Evans Hughes
(2) William E. Borah
(3) Oliver Wendell Holmes
(4) William Jennings Bryan

If a pupil does not know the answer to the test item as stated in the first instance, a few miscellaneous pieces of information can help him find it. After all, responses 2 and 3 are unlikely possibilities. Names such as these hardly sound "American," so they probably should be eliminated. Response 4 sounds "American" enough, but John Paul Jones will no doubt be remembered as a military hero, perhaps as a Revolutionary War naval hero. Since it seems improbable that a military hero would ever be elevated to the position of Chief Justice of the Supreme Court, this response is eliminated. Response 1 is therefore correctly selected despite the fact that the pupil knows nothing of Charles Evans Hughes, Nikolai Lenin, and Chiang Kai-shek, and very little about John Paul Jones and the Supreme Court.

The second statement of the test item is greatly improved. All of the persons listed were citizens of the United States and were prominent in public life. They were also contemporaries. All had sufficient qualifications to be considered for such a post as Chief Justice; one of them, Oliver Wendell Holmes, was a prominent associate justice of the Supreme Court but never the Chief Justice of that body. This should be a plausible and attractive distracter to the partially informed pupil. The distracters used in the second version of the test item are more homogeneous than those used in the first version.

It is possible to build a third version of the test item having even more homogeneous responses. For example, the distracters could be the names of prominent associate justices who served with Charles Evans Hughes. As you would expect, most pupils will find this version more difficult than the second version, just as they found the second more difficult than the first. Thus, increasing the homogeneity of the responses tends to increase the difficulty of the multiple-choice test item. This is a useful rule to remember, but it must be tempered with the reminder that, whether the responses are considered homogeneous or heterogeneous, each distracter must seem plausible to any inadequately prepared pupils.

Plausible distracters are often difficult to find. What is plausible to the teacher may not seem so to the pupils, yet the teacher must decide which distracters are used. With sufficient planning however, an alternate technique can be used. By tabulating wrong answers, the teacher can amass much helpful information for determining plausible distracters for future testing. Multiple-choice questions can be substituted for supply test items and wrong answers from earlier classes used as distracters.

Be certain that the length of the responses of a multiple-choice test item is not related to their tendency to be the correct (or best) answer. Because of the need to qualify to make one response the correct (or best) answer, the desired answer would regularly be the longest unless precautions are taken. Notice how obvious this is in the following illustration:

Poor: Sliced oranges are an excellent source of
        (1)   protein.
        (2)   starch.
        (3)   vitamin A.
        (4)   vitamin C, if the oranges are freshly sliced.

Improved: Freshly prepared orange juice is recommended for the diet because it is an excellent source of
  (1)　protein.
  (2)　starch.
  (3)　vitamin A.
  (4)　vitamin C.

If given the first version of the multiple-choice test item, the ill-prepared pupil will select response 4 more frequently than any other. Its length probably means that it is the correct answer. When confronted with the second version, he has no such irrelevant clue to help him.

If a multiple-choice test item requires a "best" answer, make certain that one and only one is clearly the best. "Hairsplitting" is a problem in practically all objective test items. This is especially true of "best" answer multiple-choice test items, for often a judgment is involved. It is a matter of opinion as to which of many reasons is the *most important* why a phenomenon occurred, or which of many is the *chief* result for a given cause. There are many counterparts to these possibilities, and they all too frequently appear in otherwise respectable multiple-choice tests.

Every multiple-choice test item should have a response that is clearly the best. For example:

Poor: The most serious health problem in the United States today is
  (1)　cancer.
  (2)　mental illness.
  (3)　heart disease.
  (4)　the common cold.
Improved: Of the following diseases, which hospitalizes the most people at the present time?
  (1)　pneumonia.
  (2)　mental illness.
  (3)　poliomyelitis.
  (4)　tuberculosis.

On the basis of the prevalence of the illness, the possibility of its being fatal, or the difficulty of relieving it, any one of the responses to the first version of the test item can be judged the "best." Unanimity or even near unanimity of opinion may be difficult to obtain. However, the test item as revised offers no such problem. Although all the diseases listed are health problems today, mental illness is the best answer here.

Whenever convenient, design the multiple-choice test item so that the stem includes as much of the item as is possible. Multiple-choice test items are usually improved if the stem is relatively long and the responses are relatively short. When this is done, the stem more clearly defines the problem on which the test item is based, and less response time is needed by most pupils. On the other hand, remember that it is sometimes awkward to build each multiple-choice test item with a long stem and short responses. The rule can be ignored to ensure clarity.

Examination of the following two versions of a multiple-choice item from a sixth-grade social studies test shows the advantages of relatively long stems coupled with short responses.

Poor: Yugoslavia
             (1)   is larger in area than France.
             (2)   borders on the Adriatic Sea.
             (3)   is located in western Asia.
             (4)   contains the Ural Mountains.

Improved: In which of the following continents is Yugoslavia located?
             (1)   Europe
             (2)   Asia
             (3)   Africa
             (4)   South America

The first version is more difficult to understand than the second. The pupil may read it several times before he recognizes that the item is designed to test his knowledge of the geography of Yugoslavia. On the other hand, the revised version is based on a single problem that is explicitly stated in the stem of the item. The pupil should have no trouble grasping the problem and, with this accomplished, he can devote his time to the selection of the correct answer.

Express the responses to a multiple-choice test item so that grammatical consistency is maintained. In other words, if the stem of the multiple-choice item is an incomplete sentence, each response must be worded so that it is a grammatically correct completion of the introductory statement. If the stem is a direct question, the responses should be suitable though brief statements of parallel construction. Failure to maintain grammatical consistency is often due to carelessness; happily, this defect can be easily corrected in most instances. The following test item illustrates this point:

Poor: If the north pole of one bar magnet is brought very near the south
             pole of another bar magnet, the two poles will
             (1)   repel each other.
             (2)   attract each other.
             (3)   no effect.
             (4)   an electric spark will be produced.

Improved: If the north pole of one bar magnet is brought very near the south
             pole of another bar magnet, the two poles will
             (1)   repel each other.
             (2)   attract each other.
             (3)   have no effect on each other.
             (4)   produce an electric spark.

The two versions of this test item make it clear that the teacher can avoid grammatical inconsistency by simply checking each response with the stem. If this is done and any appropriate changes in wording are made, the test item is not only more impressive from a grammarian's point of view but it is also less confusing from a pupil's.

ADVANTAGES AND LIMITATIONS OF MULTIPLE-CHOICE TEST ITEMS. The advantages of multiple-choice test items are much more impressive than the limitations. The outstanding feature of the multiple-choice item is its versatility. It can be used to determine how well a pupil can recall the most specific pieces of information as well as his ability to apply the most important principle in a novel situation.[1] Moreover, it can do so without introducing the problems of subjective scoring which weakens the short-answer test items or ambiguity, so noticeable when true-false test items are used. Successful guessing by the pupils is reduced but not eliminated. Any teacher with a reasonable amount of patience and ingenuity can build and use multiple-choice items with favorable results.

Multiple-choice test items are used at all grade levels with the possible exception of the primary. Even here they can be orally administered if practice test items correctly answered are shown. In addition, multiple-choice test items can be successfully used in all subject-matter areas when verbal and mathematical aspects are being tested. An objection is occasionally raised, however, to the use of these items in testing achievement in mathematics. A pupil may correctly answer the test item by using the four or five responses given as a basis for solving the problem backwards. This can be circumvented by using a variation of the standard multiple-choice form, such as the incomplete-response variety already illustrated.

Multiple-choice test items are not, of course, the panacea for the difficulties of achievement testing. They have distinct limitations, some of which have been mentioned in earlier discussions. They are difficult to build and suitable distracters are hard to find. Although a teacher's ingenuity can produce many, and others can be found among the wrong answers given to supply test items administered to preceding classes, surpluses are rare. More often than not the teacher lacks at least one distracter. He may try to fill the void by adding the response "none of the foregoing," "not given," or "can't tell." These cannot be used for "best" answer multiple-choice test items; also, they customarily weaken the correct answer variety if used consistently as a distracter, since they are recognized by the pupil as more often the wrong answer than the correct one. Such responses need not be avoided but they must be carefully presented.

Another limitation of multiple-choice test items is the response time they require. For a given amount of testing time, pupils can complete

[1] The usefulness of objective test items for measuring a pupil's ability to apply information and principles in a novel situation is discussed in Chapter 4.

fewer multiple-choice test items than true-false test items. This is particularly noticeable when the multiple-choice test items demand fine discriminations and fundamental understandings.

PROBLEMS

10 Attempts to improve the quality of "best" answer multiple-choice test items may actually change the test item to the "correct" answer variety. Examine the test item concerning diseases on page 93 and decide whether this has occurred.

11 Dunn and Goldstein (1959) discovered that the violation of certain rules for building multiple-choice test items reduced the level of difficulty but had no important effect on their general usefulness. Evaluate their position.

12 It has been suggested that instructions for multiple-choice tests be changed to enable pupils to identify whatever distractions they can and thereby reveal their partial knowledge (Coombs and others, 1956). Study this proposed scoring system and criticize it from the point of view of your educational experiences.

13 Hughes and Trimble (1965) studied the use of complex alternatives in multiple-choice test items such as "All of the above are correct," "Both 1 and 2 above are correct," or similar combinations. Do these complex alternatives increase or decrease the difficulty of the test item?

Matching Test Items

The matching test item in its simplest form consists of two lists of items and a set of instructions for matching each of the items in the first with one in the second. The first is known as a list of *premises*, the second as a list of *responses*. The instructions explain how the pupil is to match each premise with one or more of the responses. Premises and responses may be statements, names of people or places, titles of works of art, dates, formulas, symbols, or even parts of a picture or drawing. They may vary greatly but will tend to be homogeneous within a given list. Usually the length of each premise or response is (and should be) relatively short, perhaps no longer than a word or two.

In some matching exercises, the number of premises and responses is the same and each response can be used only once; this is a "perfect matching" exercise. In other instances, some of the responses do not match any of the premises; this is an "imperfect matching" exercise. An "imperfect matching" exercise can be constructed by making the list of responses longer than the list of premises or, if the lists are of equal length, by including some responses that must be used more than once. Earlier in this chapter an example is given of an "imperfect matching" test item having a shorter list of responses than premises; several responses are used more than once and some are not used at all.

In addition to the types of matching test items mentioned in the foregoing paragraph, there are a number of other variations. Two promising ones are illustrated here:

Compound matching variety:

DIRECTIONS: Below is a list of nineteenth century and early twentieth century novelists. For each novelist identify the title of one of his works that is listed in the second column by writing the letter opposite the title in the first of the two blanks to the left of the author's name. Identify his nationality from among those listed in the column below by writing the number opposite it in the second blank.

Authors				Novels	
(H)	(3)	1.	Alexandre Dumas	A.	*The Adventures of Tom Sawyer*
(G)	(2)	2.	George Eliot	B.	*Barchester Towers*
(F)	(3)	3.	Victor Hugo	C.	*Call of the Wild*
(C)	(1)	4.	Jack London	D.	*David Copperfield*
(E)	(1)	5.	Herman Melville	E.	*Moby Dick*
(J)	(2)	6.	William Thackeray	F.	*Notre Dame of Paris*
(B)	(2)	7.	Anthony Trollope	G.	*Romola*
(A)	(1)	8.	Mark Twain	H.	*The Three Musketeers*
				I.	*Uncle Tom's Cabin*
				J.	*Vanity Fair*
				K.	*War and Peace*

Nationalities

1. American
2. English
3. French

Classification variety:

DIRECTIONS: Each of the following statements is a complete sentence. Determine whether the sentence is a simple, complex, compound, or compound-complex sentence. Using the list below, find the letter corresponding to your choice and write it in the blank to the left of the sentence.

A. simple sentence
B. complex sentence
C. compound sentence
D. compound-complex sentence

(C) 1. During the winter the days are short and the nights are long.

(A) 2. Jane rode to school on her bicycle.

(B) 3. If Mary Lou had been home she could have visited with her grandparents and their friends.

(B) 4. Mother unpacked the picnic basket while I gathered wood.

SUGGESTIONS FOR CONSTRUCTING MATCHING TEST ITEMS. *Make lists of premises and responses as homogeneous as possible.* Each list should be confined to one type of subject. For example, it may be composed entirely of dates, names of people, or mathematical symbols. A title including every member can be placed above the list. In contrast, some poorly constructed matching test items are unnecessarily heterogeneous. Suppose that a certain list of premises contained names of inanimate objects, insects, animals, and people. For many pupils this simplifies the task of answering the test item correctly. They can eliminate many of the possible responses to a given premise not because they know much about the premise and response, but because there is no conceivable basis for matching some responses to a given premise.

Notice how this process of elimination is possible in the first version of a matching test item intended for use in a junior high school social studies achievement test.

Poor:

DIRECTIONS: Match each description in the first column with one of the names in the second column by writing the letter identifying the name in the blank to the left of the description.

		Descriptions		Names
(C)	1.	A river in southeastern Europe	A.	Bucharest
(F)	2.	One of the largest countries in the world	B.	Czechoslovakia
(G)	3.	Mountains in Russia	C.	Danube
(D)	4.	A level country	D.	Poland
(A)	5.	The capital of a country near Czecho-	E.	Romania
		slovakia	F.	Russia
			G.	Ural

Improved:

DIRECTIONS: Match each river with the body of water into which it flows by writing the letter identifying the body of water in the blank to the left of the name of the river. It is possible that several of the rivers flow into the same body of water.

		Rivers		Bodies of Water
(C)	1.	Danube	A.	Adriatic Sea
(G)	2.	Rhine	B.	Bay of Biscay
(F)	3.	Rhone	C.	Black Sea
(E)	4.	Seine	D.	Caspian Sea
(G)	5.	Thames	E.	English Channel
(F)	6.	Tiber	F.	Mediterranean Sea
			G.	North Sea

Both lists of the first test item are quite varied in content. The premises describe a river, two countries, a range of mountains, and a city.

The responses are name a city, four countries, a river, and a range of mountains. This lack of homogeneity certainly will help the relatively uninformed pupil find correct answers by a process of elimination. Moreover, the statement of some of the premises is poor. For example, premise 5 is "the capital of a country near Czechoslovakia." No matter how little a pupil might know about the geography of Europe, rarely would he choose the response "Czechoslovakia" as the answer.

The revised version of the matching test item is greatly improved. Notice that the titles "rivers" and "bodies of water" are much more accurate and definitive than those used in the first version. Any pupil, especially one with only sketchy knowledge of the topic, would find it difficult to use the process of elimination in this test item. Additional matching items dealing only with the location of various European cities, mountain ranges, and countries can also be constructed. In other words, several matching test items are needed to lessen the variation of the premises and responses in the first version without excluding any of that information from the test.

Always indicate as clearly as possible the basis on which the matching of premises and responses is to be made. In many instances the basis for matching is obvious. Sometimes it is doubtful at best. Every effort should be made to clarify the task the pupil is asked to perform. This can be done by improving the directions and the titles of the lists. After all, it is not the purpose of a matching test item to find out if a pupil understands the basis for matching, but rather to see if he can accurately match each premise with a response after he understands the basis of matching.

Below is a matching test item intended for an achievement test in elementary school science. Although it is not mentioned in the first version of the test item, the teacher wants the pupil to match each animal with the kind of food it ordinarily eats.

Poor:

DIRECTIONS: Match each animal with grass, insects, or other animals. Write the number in the box next to the name of the animal.

1	cow	1.	grass
1	sheep	2.	insects
3	fox	3.	other animals
3	lion		
2	robin		

Improved:

DIRECTIONS: Here is a list of animals. Each of these animals eats many different things each day. However, each animal will most often eat grass, or insects, or other animals. If an animal most often eats grass, write "1" in the box next to the animal's name. If it most often eats insects, write "2" in the box next to

the animal's name. If it most often eats other animals, write "3" in the box next
to the animal's name.

	Animals		Food
1	cow	1.	grass
1	sheep	2.	insects
3	fox	3.	other animals
3	lion		
2	robin		

When confronted with the faulty version of this test item, even the
most sophisticated elementary school pupil will at first be uncertain as to
how the matching should be done. Some of the less sophisticated may
never understand it and consequently skip the test item; or they may
unknowingly establish a false yet semi-plausible basis for matching. For
instance, several will choose the response "other animals" each time,
arguing that each animal is more like other animals in terms of its activities
and structures than it is like insects or grass.

The directions accompanying the improved version of the test item
are long and may need to be read to the pupils. Perhaps an illustration of
one animal correctly matched with the food it ordinarily eats should be
shown. Either or both of the steps should be taken if the teacher suspects
that the pupils are confused about the mechanics of the test item.

Arrange the premises and responses in a logical order. If the premises
or responses are names or titles, they should be arranged alphabetically. If
they are dates, they should be in chronological order; if numbers, they
should be arranged according to size. Unless there is an excellent reason for
doing otherwise, any logical order should be followed. This will noticeably
reduce the amount of response time needed for answering matching test
items.

In the following versions of a matching test item, the pupils are asked
to identify the 25-year period in which certain western states were admitted
to the Union.

Poor:

		States		Time periods
(E)	1.	Utah	A.	1900–1924
(A)	2.	New Mexico	B.	1825–1849
(D)	3.	Missouri	C.	1850–1874
(C)	4.	Kansas	D.	1800–1824
(A)	5.	Arizona	E.	1875–1899
(E)	6.	Colorado		
(C)	7.	Nevada		
(E)	8.	Washington		

Improved:

		States		Time periods
(E)	1.	Arizona	A.	1800–1824
(D)	2.	Colorado	B.	1825–1849
(C)	3.	Kansas	C.	1850–1874
(A)	4.	Missouri	D.	1875–1899
(C)	5.	Nevada	E.	1900–1924
(E)	6.	New Mexico		
(D)	7.	Utah		
(D)	8.	Washington		

Notice how much more rapidly a pupil can find the matching response in the second version than in the first. In addition, notice how the second version allows the pupil to check his answers with greater speed and certainty at a later time.

In every matching test item always include responses that do not match any of the premises, or responses that match more than one premise, or both. In other words, always construct "imperfect matching" test items rather than "perfect matching" ones. The latter have the serious disadvantage of increasing the likelihood of the uninformed pupil guessing one of the correct responses. Since in the "perfect matching" test item there are as many responses as premises, and each response can be used only once, the pupil answering it can determine the last response by a process of elimination.

The following is a "perfect matching" test item; the pupil is to match the description of a farming practice with its common title.

		Descriptions		Titles
(E)	1.	Planting a sloping field alternately with rows of corn, then rows of wheat, then rows of corn, etc.	A.	Clean farming
(D)	2.	Plowing a crop underground instead of harvesting it.	B.	Contour farming
(A)	3.	Removing brush and weeds along the fence between the fields.	C.	Crop rotation
(B)	4.	Planting around a hillside in level rows instead of planting up and down over the hill.	D.	Green manuring
(C)	5.	Planting a field one year with wheat, the second year with oats, the third year with alfalfa, the fourth year with corn.	E.	Strip cropping

Should a pupil have trouble matching a premise with such a response as "green manuring," he can pair all other premises and responses, thereby discovering that it matches the second premise. However, this is not possible if additional responses are added, such as "dry farming," "selective cutting," and "terracing." These three responses are attractive in their own right and, of course, prevent the pupil from arriving at a correct answer by a process of elimination.

Keep the list of responses relatively short. When attempting to answer matching test items, the pupil reads a premise and searches the list of responses. If this list is long, he may spend considerable time in spite of the fact that he may have a rather clear notion as to what the response should be. Thus, valuable test time is wasted. Incidentally, observe that a lengthy list of premises may likewise increase the amount of time needed by the pupil to respond to a matching test item. This cannot be called wasted time, however, unless some of the premises cannot be justified.

As you might expect, there is no well-established limit to the list of responses; however, the following is a good rule of the thumb: Allow the list to exceed twelve only when the maturity of the pupil and the nature of the subject matter in the test item permit; for immature pupils restrict the list to about half of this number. Should you find the list of responses becoming almost endless, consider the possibility of constructing more than one test item. This will allow you to sample a number of different subject-matter topics and simplify the job of finding lists of homogeneous premises and responses.

ADVANTAGES AND LIMITATIONS OF MATCHING TEST ITEMS. The major advantage gained by using matching items in an achievement test is that a lot of factual information can be included in the test without requiring much testing time. Such items are useful for seeing if a pupil can associate words with their definitions, events with their places and dates, results with their causes, concepts with their designated symbols, authors with their published works, statesmen with their countries and contemporaries, and so forth. Although it is not commonly done, matching test items can be used to measure a pupil's ability to apply the information he has learned. Notice the illustration given on page 97 in which the premises are a list of novel sentences that the pupil is to classify as simple, complex, compound, or compound-complex sentences. The classification variety can be successfully used to measure products of learning other than simple recall of information.

The major limitation encountered measuring achievement with matching test items is that good items are difficult to build. Sometimes the subject matter is insufficient in quantity or is not well suited for matching test items; in either case, homogeneous premises and responses are extremely hard to find. In others, the subject matter may seem to lend itself to this type of test item but the teacher has great difficulty in finding plausible but wrong responses as well as correct responses that are not completely obvious because of the terminology used.

PROBLEMS

14 Design a matching test item involving two lists in which several responses are, in at least one instance, matched with a single premise.
15 Design a compound matching test item involving three lists in which several responses in two of the lists are, in at least one instance, matched with a single premise.

OBJECTIVE TEST ITEMS BASED UPON PICTORIAL MATERIALS

It is said that a picture is worth ten thousand words. This is just as true in achievement testing as it is in any other aspect of everyday living. To demonstrate this, consider for a moment a teacher in the process of building objective items for an achievement test. Regularly he discovers that he needs a large number of words to develop sufficiently unambiguous test item. More words, he realizes, increase the pupil's reading load and the time required to answer the test item. Hence, he asks the logical question: Could a diagram, map, photograph, picture, or even a table of data be used to construct the test item? When this is done, the number of words needed to make the item specific and understandable is generally reduced, sometimes to less than half that required when no pictorial or tabular material is used. Furthermore, it is quite possible that the photograph or table does a much better job of explaining the intent of the test item than the words it replaces.

There is an even better argument for pictorial items. As discussed in detail in Chapter 1, paper-and-pencil tests are frequently used as indirect means of gathering information on which evaluations of achievement are based. How well they represent an artificial evaluation situation varies. Where pictorial test items are used, artificiality is reduced. We may very well be able to simulate the natural situation better by means of pictures than by means of words alone. Two vastly different illustrations make this clear. In a class in auto mechanics in a secondary school, paper-and-pencil test items may be used to determine in part the degree to which skills are acquired by the pupils. Although all such test items are admittedly indirect, one based upon an appropriate picture or diagram of a gasoline engine in disrepair is more realistic than one based upon only a verbal description. In a nature study unit in an elementary school, paper-and-pencil test items are used to discover how accurately the pupil can identify insects. Again, to identify pictures of insects is more realistic than to identify verbal descriptions.

Test items based upon well-designed pictorial materials can be interesting, succinct, understandable, and realistic; yet they are seldom used. There are two principal reasons. In the first place, many test items deal with subject matter of such a nature that pictorial representations are impossible to find. In other instances, they can be found but they fail to improve the test item significantly. Secondly, there are numerous practical difficulties encountered when designing and reproducing the map, diagram, or drawing for an achievement test. All teachers are not artists, yet the picture must be skillfully drawn. Fortunately, some pictures suitable for use can be copied from books and magazines, thereby insuring a better result. Even in these cases, however, reproducing copies of the picture by means of a mimeograph machine or a gelatin duplicating process can introduce another problem—the loss of fine details in the picture. To avoid this, some teachers make lantern slides for each test item.

Pictorial test items can be successfully used in both elementary and secondary school and in practically every subject-matter area. They are particularly useful in elementary school achievement testing because they reduce the reading comprehension difficulties. Also, they are quite useful in subject-matter areas such as science, mathematics, and some parts of social studies and industrial arts.

The illustrations shown below are confined to objective test items and sometimes reflect the pupil's ability to recall information as well as to apply one or more principles.

Supply Test Items

The following supply test items are intended for use in a ninth-grade class in general mathematics in which a unit in plane geometry is studied.

A real estate agent buys the city block shown in the diagram below and divides it into ten lots as indicated by the dotted lines. The lines CD, EF, GH, and IJ are parallel to the streets AB and KL. Street BL meets street AB at an angle of 72°.

1. What will the agent find to be the size of angle BDC? (108) degrees.
2. What will the agent find to be the size of angle IJL? (72) degrees.
3. Will the lots facing street AK have more, less or the same frontage as the corresponding lots facing street BL? (less)

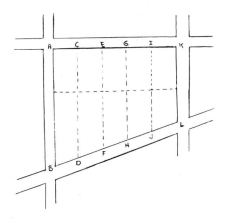

True-False Test Items

The following test items are designed for pupils in an upper elementary grade who have completed a unit in science devoted to weather.

DIRECTIONS: On the basis of the drawing shown below, decide whether each of the following statements is true or false. If it is true, circle the "T" to the left of the statement; if it is false, circle the "F."

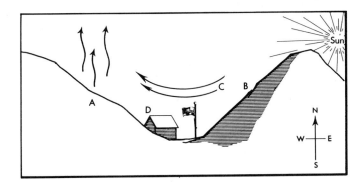

Ⓣ F 1. The air over point A is warmer than that over point B.
Ⓣ F 2. At point D you would feel a breeze from the east.
Ⓣ F 3. If the sun were behind the hill to the left rather than behind the hill to the right, the breeze should no longer blow from C to A.

Multiple-Choice Test Items

The following multiple-choice test items could be administered to pupils who have studied a sixth-grade social studies unit concerning measurement of the earth's surface and map reading.

DIRECTIONS: Carefully study the map below. Do not consider it to be any particular place. The dots represent cities. Each city is identified by a letter. For each of the questions following the map, choose the correct city from among the four listed. Write the letter of that city in the blank provided.

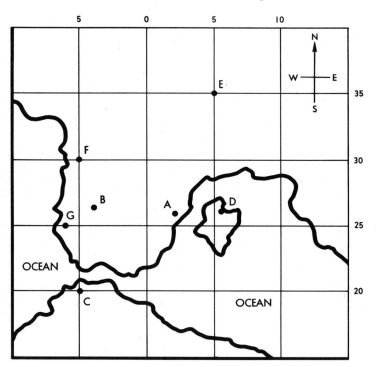

(C) 1. Which city is nearest the equator?
      City C
      City D
      City E
      City G
(A) 2. Which city is nearest the prime meridian?
      City A
      City B
      City D
      City F

(D)   3.   Which city has the greatest east longitude reading?
           City C
           City D
           City E
           City G

Problem

16   Suppose that, in the case of the second multiple-choice test item related to the map shown above, the distracter "City B" is changed to "City C." Would this improve the test item? Why?

Objective test items based upon pictures can be used with pupils as unfamiliar with test procedures as those in the first grade. The instructions to the pupil are given verbally as in the case of the multiple-choice test item shown in the example following. The pupils for whom the test item is designed are first graders who have completed a nature study unit concerning insects.

Teacher: *Draw a line through the number that tells you how many legs this insect has.*

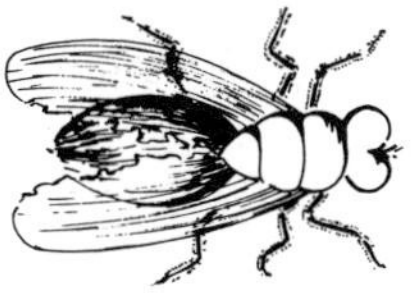

2
4
6
8
10

Teacher: *Draw a line through the number that tells you how many feelers this insect has.*

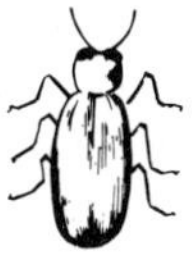

2
4
6
8

Teacher: *Draw a line through the number that tells you how many wings this insect has.*

0
2
4
6
8

Teacher: *Draw a line through the number that tells you how many eyes this insect has.*

2
4
6
8

Matching Test Items

Pictorial materials can be included in some matching test items with relative ease and notable success. For example, parts of a diagram or map are numbered and the pupil has to match each numbered part with a name selected from a list. The following illustration has a slightly different pattern. In it, not one but seven diagrams are shown and the pupil must select the one matching a description he has in mind. The test item deals with simple fractions as taught in elementary school arithmetic.

DIRECTIONS: Here are seven circles. Each circle has a letter written along side. Some are shaded a little, some almost completely. Match the description of the circle with the picture by writing the letter in the blank next to the description.

Description of circles			Circles
(D)	1.	¼ shaded	
(F)	2.	⅓ shaded	
(E)	3.	½ shaded	
(B)	4.	⅔ shaded	
(C)	5.	¾ shaded	

APPRAISING AND EDITING OBJECTIVE TEST ITEMS

Before any newly constructed objective test items can be incorporated into an achievement test, they should undergo a critical re-examination—essentially an appraising and editing procedure. It consists of verifying the relationship between each test item and the table of specifications, rechecking it for any ambiguity or irrelevant clues it might contain, and estimating its level of difficulty and reading load. The reexamination of test items in terms of these characteristics may simply reconfirm the worth of many well-constructed items; in some cases, it may reveal grammatical weaknesses that can be easily repaired; in others, it may uncover glaring faults in test items previously thought to be sound. Regardless of the outcome, it is a profitable procedure to follow. When building the test item, the teacher is often preoccupied with a myriad of details and, in the process, loses sight of one or more of its basic features. A later review of the test item customarily allows the teacher to see it in a new perspective, thereby giving him an opportunity to readjust any features that may be out of balance.

Appraising and editing objective test items can be done by the person who constructed the test items or by some other individual competent in the subject matter. The second possibility is recommended, but often not feasible. If it is impossible to find such a person, then the original item builder should make the review, but only some time after the building of the items.

No matter who is involved, a useful technique for appraising and editing is for that person to administer the test items to himself. He is now playing the role of the pupil. The answers he gives should then be compared to the answers as originally listed. Any lack of agreement between any two answers is a certain danger signal. It no doubt means that the test item is ambiguous. Perhaps a qualifying statement is missing, or some of the phraseology should be changed. It is possible, of course, that disagreement between two answers can be traced to the excessive difficulty of the test item. This flaw may be minor and easily corrected; it could be so serious that the item must be discarded.

The fact that the original answer to a test item and an independent answer later determined are the same, on the other hand, is no guarantee that the item is satisfactory. There may be other flaws in it that may not affect the answers arrived at by a reviewer, but that could seriously affect the role of the test item in a test and the pupil's response to it. In view of this, the teacher should review each test item by checking it in terms of five questions:

1. Is the test item properly identified with one or more cells of the table of specifications?
2. Is the test item ambiguous in any respect?
3. Does the test item contain any irrelevant clues?
4. Does the test item have an appropriate level of difficulty?
5. Does the test item have a suitable reading level?

After a test item has been examined in terms of each of the five questions and any differences corrected, a smooth copy of the test item is made. A highly useful and successful procedure is to type each test item on a 5 × 8 card. Generally there is ample room on the card to add additional pertinent information such as the correct answer to the test item, the name and page of the section of any book or outline on which it is based, and, at a later date, a summary of the responses pupils made when answering it. As a result, the teacher has all important information neatly summarized in a single place (see page 205).

Relationship Between Test Item and Table of Specifications

When building test items, the teacher uses his tables of specifications as blueprints to guide his selection of subject matter and behavioral changes to be included in each test item. The relationship between each test item and the part of the table of specifications from which it arose can be recorded by means of a simple coding technique. For example, the cells in the table are numbered, and the numbers of those related to the test item are listed on a card containing a statement of the test item. The numbers of the cells are listed in the order of their importance. In other words, the number of the cell to which the test item is primarily related is written first; the numbers of any cells to which it is secondarily related follow.

The first attempt to establish the relationship between a test item and the cells of a table of specifications is usually successful. Since the teacher began to build the test item with one or more cells in mind, he has little difficulty cross-referencing it and the cells. However, practically all test items undergo revisions. Perhaps the technical imperfections are corrected without regard to the manner in which these corrections might affect the relationship between the test items and the table of specifications. Sometimes they do not disturb this relationship. Many times they do. For instance, recall the differences between the two versions of many of the test items shown earlier in this chapter. Correcting a technical imperfection repeatedly may have necessitated a fundamental change in the test item. After revision, the test item may be primarily related to a different cell in the table of specifications.

Clearly, if these changes are numerous and go unnoticed, the test loses much content validity. To prevent this, the teacher must recheck the relationship between each test item and the cells in the table of specifications after all known technical imperfections have been removed.

Presence of Ambiguity

Many suggestions for constructing objective test items concentrate on one central weakness—ambiguity. The dangers of using verbatim quotes from text books and the difficulty pupils encounter when denied some relevant qualifications have already been stressed. Also, remember the importance of proper phraseology in the test item as well as in the directions to the pupil.

Individually, these suggestions for avoiding ambiguity can usually be followed with ease. Yet they must be applied in harmony with other suggestions not directly concerned with the problem, and this is not always easy to do. In some instances, a teacher building an objective test item will find two suggestions working more or less at cross-purposes. Following one by making a certain revision violates another. Escape from the dilemma may be difficult. No doubt a more common situation is the automatic adoption of the last suggestion. If the revision happens to violate another suggestion, this is not noticed.

Since ambiguity is one of the chief weaknesses of objective test items, a final check should be made. The teacher can reread each test item with one question in mind: Is it possible to word this test item more clearly and directly? In trying to answer his own question, the teacher may find himself improving test items he previously thought to be as polished as he could make them.

The importance of avoiding ambiguity in objective test items is primary. The pupil should never experience difficulty in trying to understand the question. After all, we are trying to find out if a pupil can answer a question he understands, not if he understands the question. (Ebel, 1951, p. 213).

Presence of Irrelevant Clues

Another weakness of objective test items is their tendency to include irrelevant clues. Such clues are those characteristics of the test items that allow some, perhaps most, of the unprepared pupils to answer correctly even though they do not possess the knowledge or understanding required. In other words, they reduce the value of the test item by changing the basis upon which it discriminates among the pupils to whom it is administered. Ideally, a test item should indicate whether they can do such things as recall one or more pieces of information or apply one or more principles to a new situation. Those who can do these things will answer a well-constructed test item correctly; those who cannot will respond incorrectly. If the test item contains irrelevant clues, the situation is changed. Some pupils who would normally respond incorrectly can give the right answer by properly interpreting the irrelevant clue.

There are many kinds of irrelevant clues. The suggestions for building objective test items reveal a number of them. Rechecking objective test items on the basis of these suggestions is generally not difficult work even though time-consuming. It is time well invested.

Proper Level of Difficulty

An important characteristic of objective test items, sometimes overlooked by the teacher as he strives to abide by all of the suggestions for constructing them, is the level of difficulty. Obviously this is not determined exclusively by the idea on which the test item is based, for the manner in which it is stated is also important. A single variation of a word or phrase can change it noticeably. Obtaining the proper level for each item and then the test as a whole is a perplexing problem.

The first question confronted by the teacher as he considers the level of difficulty of each item is whether he wishes to use it in a mastery test or a power test. As you will recall, in a mastery test the level of difficulty is uniformly low; in a power test, it varies somewhat, but concentrates in a zone around the 50% level of difficulty. This is the level at which half of the pupils have responded correctly to a test item.

A highly successful way of obtaining estimates of the level of difficulty of test items is to pretest them on a group of pupils similar to those for whom they are designed. Their answers to the test items can be tabulated and analyzed. On the basis of this analysis, the level of difficulty of each test item is determined. Unfortunately, this procedure is frequently impossible. Without pretesting data, the teacher must depend on his subjective judgements.

Subjective judgments are by no means precise. In reality they are rough approximations, even when the teacher is completely familiar with the situation, the maturity of the pupils, and many of their past experiences. At best, he can rate the test items on only a five-point scale: "very difficult," "moderately difficult," "average," "moderately easy," and "very easy." Sometimes a three-point scale of "difficult," "average," and "easy" is all that is appropriate. The principal reference point is the "average" category. Test items so rated are considered suitable for typical pupils in the class under consideration. When making these judgments, the teacher must weigh as best he can the nature of the test item, all pertinent factors related to the teaching situation, and whatever experience he has had in the past with similar test items and pupils.

Crude as these judgments are, they are useful. In devising power tests, for example, they are sufficiently accurate to prevent any test item from being so easy that all pupils respond correctly or so difficult that none do. Since the purpose of these tests is to differentiate among pupils in terms of their achievement, both extremes should be avoided.

Reading Level

Because test items are constructed by adults they regularly include words and expressions more typical of adults than children. This happens despite the most conscientious efforts of the teacher and can be a severe problem in the case of objective test items designed for elementary school pupils. After all, to the teacher these words and expressions seem to express the thought behind the test item very clearly. To the pupil, however, this probably is not true. If he were constructing the test item, he would no doubt choose different words. Often he would use more of them, thereby creating another difficulty. Since there is much to read, the pupil needs more response time for each test item. Consequently, fewer can be included, and the breadth of the sampling of the subject matter decreases.

A pupil with a slow reading rate or a modest vocabulary should not be appreciably penalized in a typical objective achievement test. To prevent any penalty, needlessly difficult terms appearing in the test items should be replaced with simpler synonyms. Complex arrangements of words should be simplified and unnecessary words or phrases removed. Also, ample testing time must be allowed.

Test items must be carefully reread to eliminate improper vocabulary and cut excessive length. It is not easy to play the role of the pupil in this case. Yet, if appropriate adjustments are not made, the pupil with superior reading ability and vocabulary may have an undue advantage over his less fortunate fellow pupil. Superior reading ability and vocabulary help him to understand more of the questions more quickly and, as a result, he has more time in which to concentrate upon obtaining the correct answers. When such items are included in a poorly timed test, they may actually measure the pupil's reading speed and comprehension more than his achievement in a chosen subject-matter area such as science or social studies. The basis on which the test items are differentiating among the pupils has changed.

PROBLEMS

17 Chauncey (1959, pp. 43–57) listed a number of criticisms of objective tests, four of which are the following:
   a. Objective tests measure only factual knowledge; hence students study accordingly.
   b. Objective tests are often ambiguous.
   c. When confronted with a predominance of objective tests, pupils do not learn to write.
   d. The scores from objective tests are overemphasized: evidence from nontest instruments receives little attention.
   Prepare your reaction to these criticisms and compare them with those of Chauncey.

ORGANIZING THE OBJECTIVE TEST

After each of a group of objective test items has been individually appraised and edited in the manner described, that part of the group which appropriately reflects the balance among the subject-matter topics and the behavioral changes established in the table of specifications is organized into an achievement test. To do so, we must decide the order in which the items are presented to the pupils and the number to be included. In addition, it is necessary to formulate directions for the pupils and to draw up a scoring key. Each of these steps must be taken carefully if the test items are to realize their maximum value.

Arranging Objective Test Items

Objective test items should not be arranged haphazardly in an achievement test. Instead, they should be organized on the basis of one or more of three characteristics: the type of item, the subject matter, and the level of difficulty.

When the items of an objective test are grouped according to type, all supply test items are placed together, as are all true-false, multiple-choice, and matching test items. This simplifies the directions given to the pupils. The number of times that new directions must be given is minimized. Furthermore, the pupil can no doubt complete a test so arranged more quickly. He acquires a mental set for each type of item and need not change it until all such items have been answered. This should speed his progress through the test. Incidentally, it is advisable to restrict the number of different types to as few as conveniently possible.

Arranging the test items according to the subject matter means that the test items are grouped according to a set of subject-matter topics. This appeals to the pupil because he sees the test as a miniature of the materials he learned. It is an integrated, orderly whole to him rather than a disorganized mosaic of unrelated questions. This arrangement may be attractive to the teacher, too, since it may help to reveal any stress or under-emphasis in the test.

Objective test items are grouped according to their difficulty; the easy ones first, the more difficult next, and the most difficult last. Such an arrangement has advantages for the average and below average pupil. With this kind of test he uses the time allowed more efficiently, and his morale is improved. If the difficult tests items appear first, many pupils of average or low achievement will waste a great deal of time trying to answer them. They may fail to answer easier items later in the test because so much time was spent on the first ones. Moreover, they may quickly become discouraged or even hostile. On the other hand, if the easier items are listed first, these same pupils will at first make smooth progress in the test, and consequently feel encouraged. When they later encounter the more difficult test items, they no doubt will have time to attack them. Even if they fail to answer some of them, as will very likely happen, the resulting disappointment will be moderated by the knowledge that they already have answered others correctly.

Certainly we can not expect to use all three ways of arranging test items simultaneously. In reality, all a teacher can hope to do is find the best possible compromise among the three. Sometimes he can escape partially or wholly from the dilemma by eliminating one of the possibilities. For example, suppose that only one type of test item is used. Now the test can be designed so that the items are grouped according to major subject-matter topic, and within each group they can be arranged in order of ascending difficulty. As a second example, suppose that the teacher is building a mastery test. This time the level of difficulty is unimportant as a basis for arranging the test items. As a result, the test can be designed so that the items are grouped according to type and, within each type, according to subject-matter.

In a power test the items can be grouped according to type or subject-matter, and, within each group, from easy to difficult. This means, in effect, that the achievement test is not one test but a group of subtests. The items in such subtests can be independently numbered and, to assure that each receives proper emphasis, separate time limits can be imposed.

Length of Objective Achievement Tests

Ideally, the length of an achievement test should be determined by two key factors; representative sampling and reliability. The test should contain as many items as are necessary to sample all the verbal and mathematical aspects of the educational objectives upon which the table of specifications is based. The smallest sample of test items (in other words, the shortest test) that can be used without jeopardizing fair representation varies with the nature of this table. If the subject-matter topics and behavioral changes in the table are too varied, then a larger sample is needed. If they are very much alike, a smaller sample can be used. Remember that too short a test may be unsatisfactory because it is impossible to include items based on some less important cells of the table of specifications. Consequently, the degree of content validity is lessened.

The second key factor is that the length of the test is also related to its reliability that is, the consistency of its results (see pages 311–313). In general, shortening the test decreases its reliability. If, therefore, the use of the test results demands a high degree of test reliability, the length of the test has to be increased. Test results used to diagnose an individual pupil's strengths and weaknesses in an area must be more reliable than those used only to determine differences between groups of pupils in terms of their achievement. In the first case, the test may be so long it is administered in parts and requires several hours. In the second, it may be so short that only one class period or less is needed.

In addition to these two factors governing the length of the informal achievement test, there is another and very practical one: the time available for the administration of the test. Although this factor lacks the theoretical justification of the first two, it is just as important. Indeed, it often influences the length of the test more than factors of content validity or reliability, because the teacher often has so little control over it. Ordinarily, he must administer the test during a regularly scheduled class period which usually lasts forty to sixty minutes. To change the length would, in the eyes of the school administrator at least, create havoc. Thus, time becomes the primary factor.

In this connection, it is appropriate to mention pupil fatigue. Writing achievement tests can be an exhausting task. For this reason, it is doubtful that time periods longer than one hour should be used for achievement testing even if they were available. Certainly time periods of more than two hours should be discouraged. The maximum length will of course vary with the maturity of the pupil and the environmental conditions at the time of the test administration. Any time pupil fatigue is suspected of being a noticeable influence on test performance, the test should be broken into parts with rest periods permitted between them.

The teacher customarily determines the length of his achievement test in a somewhat backward manner. First, he notes the maximum amount of time that administrative routine will allow for giving the test. Then he estimates the number of items to which the pupils should be able to respond in the time allotted. Finally, he selects this number from among those he has constructed. He selects these in such a way that, as a group, they reflect the established relative importance of the various cells of the table of specifications.

The first step is seldom a problem. The amount of time allotted is well known to the teacher. However, the second can be difficult. How many objective test items of a given type can the typical student answer in a given amount of time? The answers to this question vary. For example, some say that a mature pupil can answer about one hundred true-false test items or about sixty-five multiple-choice test items in a fifty-minute period. Such statements as these are not too helpful. After all, how mature is this pupil? Maturity here means test-wiseness, and this is hard to assess. Moreover, what is the nature of the test items being used? Items requiring only recall of information can generally be answered much more quickly than those measuring pupil understandings. Those that are short or that have a low vocabulary load require less reading time, hence less response time. In the last analysis, therefore, the teacher has to rely on his own judgment. On the basis of his experience with his pupils and various kinds of objective test items, he must decide how many to include in the test. Remember that if it is a power test, its length must be restricted so that at least 90 per cent of the pupils will have sufficient time to attempt all the items.

As the restrictions on testing time limit the number of items to be included in the test, so also do they weaken its content validity and reliability. All too frequently, there is no convenient way of overcoming this progression of troubles. Instead, the teacher must recognize the situation for what it is, build his achievement test accordingly, and temper his use and interpretation of the results to compensate for whatever content validity and reliability is lost.

Directions for Pupils

To perform to the best of his ability, the pupil must be completely oriented to the achievement test. Otherwise stated, he must know the purpose of the test and must be thoroughly familiar with its mechanics. To accomplish this, the teacher formulates directions that the pupil reads or that are read to him before he responds to any of the test items.

The purpose of most informal achievement tests, is quite clear to the pupils. No doubt the initial announcement of the test is supplemented with remarks concerning the reasons why it is being administered; or, perhaps it is one of a series and the pupils are well aware of its purposes. In both of these instances, the directions need not include statements concerning the purposes of the test. If, however, the teacher doubts for any reason the completeness of the pupil's understanding of the purposes of the test, the first part of the directions should be devoted to a brief statement about them. Failure to do so when the pupils are unacquainted when the purposes can cause an unnecessary loss of motivation.

The mechanics of the test typically command much more attention in the directions than the purposes. The pupil needs a complete knowledge of the "ground rules" under which he will operate. This means that he must be aware of the time allowed, the manner in which he is to select and record his answers, and in which the test is to be scored. He should even be instructed in test-room etiquette if circumstances dictate.

DIRECTIONS FOR SELECTING ANSWERS. Directions for selecting answers must be carefully written. Notice that the sample instructions of this kind given earlier assume that the pupil knows nothing about objective test items. This of course is an extreme assumption and, for the most part, an unnecessary one. Yet, stating the directions with too much detail is far less an evil than stating them with too little. The first procedure assures us that any pupil who has read the directions will not be penalized by lack of familiarity with the objective test items. This point is particularly important when novel or semi-novel items are being used.

To be certain that these directions are understood, practice test items may be included. These may consist of a typical item correctly answered in terms of the directions, as well as one or more to be answered by the pupil before beginning the test itself. He is told the correct answers to practice test items so that he can verify his understanding of the directions. Such items can be helpful when testing either elementary or secondary school pupils. The use of this procedure with the former group is quite common. Only after the pupils have independently solved the practice test items will many elementary school teachers begin the test.

DIRECTIONS FOR RECORDING ANSWERS. How the pupil is to record his answer is another small detail that cannot be overlooked. When the answer is to be written on the same sheet as the question, this is less of a problem. It is necessary to prepare directions such as those already illustrated, and to design a layout of the test items that allows generous space for circling letters, writing numbers, and filling blanks. When separate answer sheets are used, the directions are not so simple. The relationship between the test copy and the answer sheet must be explained as well as any features of the answer sheet that would speed or impair the marking of responses selected or that would increase or decrease the accuracy of scoring.

If separate answer sheets are used, teachers usually design their own. A typical one is shown in part in Figure 1. Notice that it can be used with a test having several types of objective items. These have been grouped according to type and each is numbered independently. The manner in which the pupil uses the answer sheet is described in the directions provided.

For many years, the most popular commercial answer sheets have been those distributed by the International Business Machines Corporation, usually IBM Form I. T. S. 1000 B 108. Space for responses to 150 true-false or multiple-choice test items is provided on each side of the answer sheet. With an electrographic pencil, the pupil carefully marks the space corresponding to his choice for each test item. The answer sheet is then scored electronically by a scoring machine (IBM Corporation, 1947) to which most schools have access.

Other methods of machine scoring are also being used; for instance, those employing the IBM Optical Mark Scoring Reader or the Optical Mark Page Reader and answer sheets designed for them. An answer sheet

Date _____   Name _____
                                        Last   First
Subject _____   Scores: Part A _____
                                      Part B _____
                                      Part C _____
                                      Part D _____
                                      Total _____

DIRECTIONS: Read with care the general directions at the beginning of the test and the directions preceding each subpart. Then read each test item and decide which answer is correct. Indicate your answer by filling the blank or circling the number or letter provided below. Be certain that the number of the test item corresponds exactly with the number on the answer sheet when you record each answer.

A: SUPPLY		B: TRUE-FALSE		C: MULTIPLE-CHOICE		D: MATCHING	
Item	Answer	Item	Answer	Item	Answer	Item	Answer
1	_____	1	T F	1	1 2 3 4 5	1	_____
2	_____	2	T F	2	1 2 3 4 5	2	_____
3	_____	3	T F	3	1 2 3 4 5	3	_____
4	_____	4	T F	4	1 2 3 4 5	4	_____
5	_____	5	T F	5	1 2 3 4 5	5	_____

FIGURE 1
SECTION OF A TEACHER-DESIGNED ANSWER SHEET

is shown in reduced size in Figure 2. It strongly resembles the original IBM answer sheets although the spaces for pupil responses are arranged horizontally instead of vertically. However, it is much more versatile. In addition to true-false and multiple-choice test items, it can be used for matching test items. The pupil marks his responses with an ordinary soft or medium lead pencil. The scoring machine optically reads the marks at an extremely high rate and prints part and/or total scores. Various scoring formulas (for example, formulas for correcting for guessing) can be applied by the scoring machine. Also, multiple-response test items can be scored. Finally, it is possible to transfer test score information directly into a computer which, in turn, can provide a wide variety of summary data about the test score distribution; for instance, the arithmetic mean of the scores.

Tests involving separate test copies and answer sheets can be success-

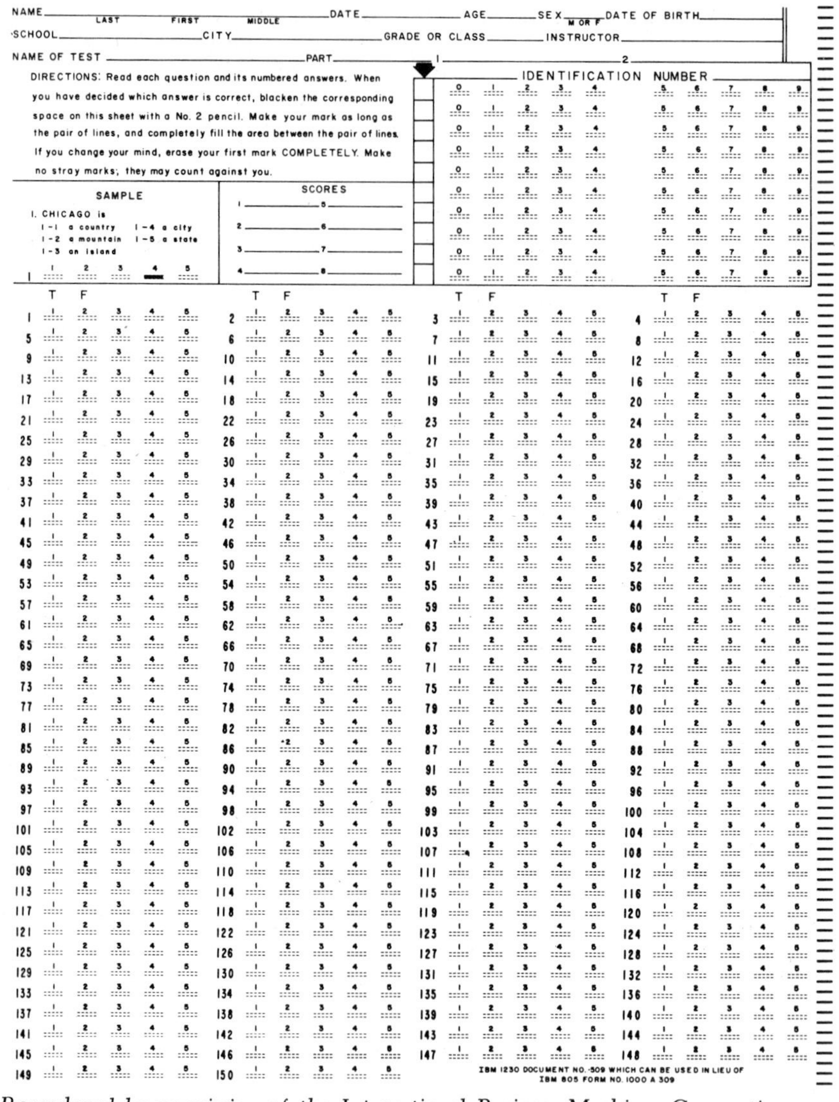

Reproduced by permission of the International Business Machines Corporation.

FIGURE 2

AN INTERNATIONAL BUSINESS MACHINE ANSWER SHEET, IBM 1230 DOCUMENT NO. 509

fully administered to pupils as inexperienced as those in the fourth grade. However, if they are used with elementary school pupils, a training period is necessary prior to testing. Even after this, they cannot handle the separate answer sheet efficiently. No doubt the time limits should be expanded for them. Secondary school pupils familiar with separate answer sheets lose very little time using them.

DIRECTIONS FOR SCORING ANSWERS.   The pupil should be informed of the scoring procedure when it is conveniently possible. He is entitled to ask how much credit he will get for each right answer. Usually this can be easily included in the directions because it is constant for each objective item within the subtests or possibly the total test.

Allowing the same number of points for each item is somewhat illogical. After all, they may vary in difficulty and importance, and thus more credit should be allowed for some correct answers than others. However, attempts to weigh the test items in terms of these characteristics tend to be highly subjective. Moreover, research has shown that scores made on an objective achievement test graded with a constant number of points for a right answer correlate very highly with scores obtained on the same test when the right answers are weighted in what is seemingly a more defensible manner. This means that, no matter which scoring procedure is used, the relative position of the pupils within the class remains unchanged in practically all cases. In view of this, most objective achievement tests are scored by means of the simpler method, which is to allow a constant amount of credit for each correct response to a given type of objective test item.

The directions should also include a statement about correction for guessing (see pages 123–125). Since the possibility of successfully guessing the correct answers appeals to some pupils, teachers may choose to discourage such attempts by penalizing the pupil for any wrong answers he makes. This is known as a correction for guessing. The pupil has the right to know whether one of these methods is to be used. This information could greatly affect his willingness to omit a test item or try to guess the correct answer with little or no information.

PRESENTING DIRECTIONS ORALLY.   Writing clear and explicit directions is of little help if the pupil refuses to read them or reads them carelessly. Therefore, a number of teachers read the directions aloud as the pupils read them silently. Any questions the pupils might have are answered, and then the test begins. This is wise procedure with elementary school pupils. With the primary grade levels it must be carried one step further. Copies of the directions for any objective test items are not given to the pupil. Instead, he is given an answer sheet that is meticulously tailored to the test. After the directions are read and explained, practice exercises are completed. Then the teacher reads the questions one by one, allowing time for a response to each. At the conclusion of the test, he might repeat some or all if time allows. Administering tests in this way removes a serious obstacle to the use of objective test items with elementary school pupils—the reading speed and comprehension problem.

Scoring the Objective Test

To many classroom teachers the least exciting task of informal achievement testing is the scoring of the pupil responses. To handle this task the pupils are sometimes asked to score their own papers or their neighbors'. Considering the importance of accurate scoring, the limitations of this procedure are obvious. Should the teacher score the papers himself, he commonly takes a blank copy of the test, fills in the correct responses, and compares this key with the responses on the test copy returned by each pupil. The number of correct responses by each pupil is determined and recorded. The total operation may not require much time, but being essentially clerical in nature, it is often viewed with distaste by those who must do it.

Various attempts have been made to reduce the time required for scoring objective tests. To do so means less boredom and fatigue for the scorer and, as a result, more accurate scores. These attempts have taken the form of scoring keys designed to assist in hand-scoring individual test copies or separate answer sheets containing the pupils' responses, and machine-scoring procedures using separate answer sheets.

SCORING KEYS FOR HAND-SCORING. A number of the more successful scoring keys for hand-scoring have been described and illustrated by Traxler (1951). Prominent among these are the fan key, the strip key, and the cut-out key.

The fan key is a sheet of paper on which the correct responses are written in a series of columns. The sheet of paper is the same size as the test copy or the separate answer sheet. Each column corresponds to a page of the test or a column on the answer sheet, and the correct responses are spaced in the column as the pupil responses are spaced on the page of the test or the column on the appropriate answer sheet. The key is folded along vertical lines separating its columns, thus taking the appearance of a fan. It is superimposed on the appropriate page of the test copy or placed next to the appropriate column on the answer sheet and matched with the corresponding responses.

The strip key is similar to a fan key except that the various columns are strips. Each strip is usually mounted on cardboard. It is used like a fan key.

The cut-out key is also a sheet of paper of the same size as the test copy or answer sheet. However, windows are cut in appropriate positions to reveal the correct responses if they are made. The key is superimposed on a page of the test copy or the separate answer sheet and the pupil's responses are scored. For a supply test item, the scorer sees only the pupil's written response and can quickly compare it with the correct response written on the key in a space immediately adjacent to the window. For a true-false or multiple-choice test item, the window corresponds to the letter or number of the response to be circled. If no circle appears in the window, the scorer marks the pupil's response as incorrect.

MACHINE-SCORING. The machine-scoring procedure now becoming popular for scoring informal objective tests utilizes the IBM Optical Mark Scoring Reader. If the separate answer sheets shown in Figure 2 are properly marked, the teacher can, if he chooses, turn over his task of scoring to a skilled clerk operating this machine. Under ideal conditions, the speed and accuracy of scoring can be superior.

The disadvantages of machine-scoring of this type are well known. First of all, it cannot be used with supply test items under any circumstances. Secondly, the pupils must be trained in the procedure of marking the answer sheets. The marks in the spaces must be reasonably heavy. Erasures must be complete and stray pencil marks avoided, because they might be recorded by the machine as wrong answers. A third disadvantage is the availability of the machine. Unless one is available on relatively short notice, machine-scoring may prove to be more trouble than it is worth as far as classroom achievement tests are concerned. Finally, there is no indication on the answer sheet as to whether an answer to a given test item is correct or incorrect. The pupil cannot identify his strong and weak areas by examining his answer sheet alone.

CORRECTING FOR GUESSING. A persistent problem encountered with objective achievement tests is the tendency of the pupil to guess when he does not know the correct answer. Sometimes this guess is based upon partial knowledge, other times on misinformation, and still other times on no information at all. In the last instance, he may not have even read the test item or, if he did, its answer is a total mystery to him. In either case, his chances of guessing the correct answer are greater in a true-false test than in a multiple-choice or matching test.

If the score is the number of correct responses, any success the pupil had when he guessed will raise it. Obviously, this is not a defensible situation. The test score should reflect his knowledge and understanding only, rather than these plus the pupil's willingness to guess and the amount of success he happened to have in this case. Therefore, some teachers argue that the pupil must be discouraged from wild guessing and be penalized if he does.

The formula for correcting for guessing in the case of the most common varieties of selection type objective test items is as follows:

$$S = R - \frac{W}{n-1}$$

where

    S = the test score

    R = the number of correct responses

    W = the number of incorrect responses

    n = the number of suggested responses from which one is chosen

R is often called the number of "rights," whereas W is thought of as the number of "wrongs."

For a true-false test, n is two and the formula reduces to

$$S = R - W$$

For a multiple-choice test having four suggested responses, the formula becomes

$$S = R - \frac{W}{3}$$

If the multiple-choice test items have five suggested responses, the formula becomes

$$S = R - \frac{W}{4}$$

Notice that to use the formula in any of these cases, you need only determine the number of correct and incorrect responses. The number of omitted test items is ignored.

These formulas assume that all incorrect responses and some of the correct ones are the result of wild guessing. This is, of course, not fully justified. The pupils are often taking "calculated risks" when selecting their responses. Rather than making wild guesses they are making more or less intelligent guesses based upon sound but incomplete knowledge and understanding. The pupil hopes, and legitimately so, that his chances of selecting the correct response are much better when he makes an intelligent guess than when he makes a wild guess.

Because the foregoing assumption is not completely satisfied, the formulas will overcorrect in some instances and undercorrect in others. Consequently, they are persistently criticized by teachers and pupils alike.

There is another disadvantage when a correction for guessing formula is applied. Informing the pupil that such a correction will be made customarily acts as a deterrent, but its effectiveness varies with the pupil.

Some are willing to gamble no matter what the penalty and guess wildly no matter what correction formulas are used. Others are cautious. A correction for guessing will cause them to answer only when they are certain of the correct response, and even intelligent guesses are not ventured. Hence, many more test items are omitted. More often than not, the first type of pupil gains higher test scores than the second. Thus, an extraneous personality factor unduly influences achievement tests designed to measure verbal or mathematical ability.

If sufficient time is allowed for the test so that every pupil can attempt every item, and if every pupil then answers every test item, no correction for guessing is needed. Determining the test score by counting the number of correct responses is perfectly acceptable. Despite the fact that the test scores are different in size when corrected than when not corrected for guessing, the relative position of each pupil in the class is the same in both cases. The relationship between the uncorrected and corrected test scores under these conditions is perfect. If the purpose of an achievement test is to determine the relative position of each pupil in the class, the simpler test score may as well be used.

To assure that all pupils will answer all test items, they must be instructed to guess when they do not know the answer, even if they must guess wildly. Needless to say, these instructions can hardly be considered good pedagogy. The pupil may lose respect for objective achievement testing, possibly even for the subject matter or the teacher. The full impact of these instructions is difficult to measure. Admittedly unsavory, they probably have no lasting effect upon most pupils.

PROBLEMS

18 What is your opinion of the practice of having pupils score their own test papers? Respond to this question both from the point of view of scoring accuracy and accepted principles of learning.
19 Demonstrate empirically that the relative position of each pupil in a class is the same whether or not the test scores are corrected for guessing by doing the following:
    a. Randomly list the words "True" and "False" ten times. Consider this to be the test key.
    b. Have a group of pupils do the same independently. Consider these to be pupil answer sheets.
    c. Score the answer sheets with and without a correction for guessing.
    d. Determine the relative rank of each pupil on the basis of both scores.
20 What are IBM mark-sense cards? Can they be used as answer forms for multiple-choice test items (Madril, 1959)?

Summary

An objective test item is one that can be scored so that subjective judgment is practically eliminated when determining the correctness of a pupil's answer. There are two types of objective test items, the supply type and the selection type. When responding to the supply type, the pupil has to provide the words, numbers, or symbols necessary. Possible answers are not listed as part of the item. In contrast, the selection type allows the pupil to choose the correct response from the information it provides.

Illustrations of the supply type are the short-answer question and the completion test item. Those teachers who use supply items in informal achievement tests do so because the likelihood of a pupil guessing the correct answer is minimized and they find them easier to construct than the selection type. However, they also find that pupil responses to supply test items are more difficult to score, and that often the items measure only the pupil's knowledge of factual details.

True-false, multiple-choice, and matching test items are all illustrations of the selection type. The true-false item in its simplest form is a declarative statement that the pupil must judge as true or false. A test containing this type can sample widely a large amount of subject matter without requiring much testing time. On the other hand, the true-false test item involves only trivial pieces of information and, because one of two responses must be correct, pupils not knowing the right one frequently guess.

A multiple-choice test item is one in which a direct question or incomplete statement is presented and a number of responses are given. The pupil is to choose the correct (or best) answer to the question or expression for completing the statement. This type of objective test is widely used in standardized as well as informal achievement tests because it is so adaptable. It can be used to measure recall of information or application of a principle in a novel situation in practically any subject-matter area with all but the most naive pupils. The principal disadvantage teachers experience when they attempt to use multiple-choice test items is that they are relatively difficult to build. A sufficient number of suitable distracters is sometimes hard to find.

The typical matching test item consists of two lists of items and a set of instructions for matching each in the first list with one in the second. Like the true-false test item, the matching item can include large quantities of factual information without requiring a proportionately large amount of testing time. However, some subject-matter material is not well-suited for matching test items. Homogeneous lists may be difficult if not impossible to develop.

After a group of objective test items have been constructed, they must be appraised and edited prior to being organized into an achievement test. This process involves rechecking the relationship between each item and the table of specifications, removing any ambiguity or any irrelevant clues that still remain, establishing its relative level of difficulty, and correcting any feature that seriously increases the amount of time needed by the pupil to read and understand it.

Organizing the objective items into an achievement test is a more complicated task than commonly supposed. For instance, the arrangement of the items within the test must be determined. This may be based upon the type of objective item, the level of difficulty, or a logical arrangement of the subject matter included. The length of the test must be established; generally the time available for testing is the key factor. Also, directions must be formulated and a scoring key prepared. In this connection, decisions must be made as to the use of a separate answer sheet and a correction-for-guessing formula for any selection type items the test contains.

Suggested Readings

Dressel, Paul L., and others. *Evaluation in higher education.* Boston: Houghton Mifflin, 1961. Chapters 4, 5, 6, and 7.

> These four chapters deal with evaluation in the social sciences, the natural sciences, the humanities, and communication skills. Each has been written by a different author. The role of objective test items is described in detail.

Dressel, Paul L., and Clarence H. Nelson. *Questions and problems in science, test item folio No. 1.* Princeton, N.J.: Educational Testing Service, 1956.

> This folio contains a large group of objective test items in biological and physical science. They are classified according to subject-matter topic and educational objective, and serve as a source of ideas for building informal achievement tests and as instructional materials.

Ebel, Robert L. *Measuring educational achievement.* Englewood Cliffs, N.J.: Prentice-Hall, 1965. Chapters 3, 5, 6, and 7.

> In four chapters, the planning of a classroom achievement test, the construction of true-false and multiple-choice test items, and the administration and scoring of achievement tests are discussed. Numerous faulty true-false and multiple-choice test items are shown and criticized.

Engelhart, Max D. *Improving classroom testing.* What Research Says to the Teacher, No. 31. Washington: National Education Association, 1964.

> All of the basic steps to be followed in the construction of classroom achievement tests are described, at least briefly, in this short pamphlet. Primary emphasis is given to the use of objective test items.

Furst, Edward J. *Constructing evaluation instruments.* New York: Longmans, Green, 1958. Chapters 8, 9, 10, and 11.

> Discussions of both objective and essay tests are included in these chapters. Chapter 9 is devoted to supply test items and Chapter 10 to selection test items.

Gerberich, J. Raymond. *Specimen objective test items.* New York: Longmans, Green, 1956. Parts 1, 2, and 3.

> The primary purpose of this book is to serve the classroom teacher as a guide in the construction of objective achievement tests. Part 1 describes the general procedures for building objective test items. Part 2 shows specimen objective test items of many varieties, which have been selected from many different standardized tests. Part 3 consists of several systems for classifying the specimen test items presented in Part 2.

Stodola, Quentin. *Making the classroom test, a guide for teachers.* (2nd ed.) Educational Testing Service Evaluation and Advisory Service Series, No. 4. Princeton, N.J.: Educational Testing Service, 1961.

> In relatively few pages the basic rules of test-making for both objective and essay tests are developed and illustrated. Elementary and secondary school examples are given.

Storey, Arthur G. A review of evidence or the case against the true-false item. *J. educ. Res.,* 1966, 282–285.

> The advantages and limitations of true-false test items are evaluated. Five major points are presented for restricting the use of this type of objective test item.

Traxler, Arthur E. Administering and scoring the objective test. In E. F. Lindquist (Ed.), *Educational measurement.* Washington: American Council on Education, 1951. Pp. 329–416.

> Although the pages cited are written with the standardized objective achievement test in mind, they are nevertheless a suitable reference for the teacher engaged in informal objective achievement testing. Particularly helpful are sections which describe techniques for administering tests, suggestions for writing directions to the pupils, and methods of scoring.

Wood, Dorothy A. *Test construction, development and interpretation of achievement tests.* Columbus, Ohio: Charles E. Merrill, 1960. Chapters 5, 6, and 7.

> This is a short book devoted to achievement testing by means of objective tests; only brief mention is made of essay tests. The three chapters cited concern the preparation of objective test items.

References Cited

Chauncey, Henry. Report of the president, 1958–1959. *Educational Testing Service Annual Report, 1958–1959.* Princeton, N.J.: Educational Testing Service, 1959.

Coombs, C. E., J. E. Milholland, and F. B. Womer. The assessment of partial knowledge. *Educ. psychol. Measmt,* 1956, **16,** 13–37.

Cooperative Test Division, *Sequential tests of educational progress teacher's guide.* Princeton, N.J.: Educational Testing Service, 1959.

Dunn, T. F., and L. G. Goldstein. Test difficulty, validity, and reliability as functions of selected multiple-choice item construction principles. *Educ. psychol. Measmt*, 1959, **19**, 171–179.

Ebel, Robert L. Writing the test item. In E. F. Lindquist (Ed.), *Educational measurement*. Washington: American Council on Education, 1951. Pp. 185–249.

Engelhart, Max D. *Improving classroom testing*. What Research Says to the Teacher, No. 31. Washington: National Education Association, 1964.

Hughes, H. H. and W. E. Trimble. The use of complex alternatives in multiple-choice items. *Educ. psychol. Measmt*, 1965, **25**, 117–126.

International Business Machines Corporation, Department of Education. *Methods of adapting tests for scoring by the IBM electric test scoring machine*. New York: The International Business Machines Corporation, 1947.

Madril, Ernest. The use of IBM mark-sense cards as multiple-choice paper-and-pencil test answer forms. *J. appl. Psychol.*, 1959, **43**, 296–301.

Stodola, Quentin. *Making the classroom test, a guide for teachers*. (2nd ed.) Educational Testing Service Evaluation and Advisory Service Series, No. 4. Princeton, N.J.: Educational Testing Service, 1961.

Traxler, Arthur E. Administering and scoring the objective test. In E. F. Lindquist (Ed.), *Educational measurement*. Washington: American Council on Education, 1951. Pp. 329–416.

4

Measuring Understandings Objectively

A FEW YEARS AGO a delightful book was published that contained countless "boners" made by pupils in the classroom (Abingdon, 1952). As nearly as can be determined, all that are listed are authentic errors made by pupils in examinations, themes, and occasionally in correspondence. The following are typical entries:

> In one instance, a pupil attempting to define the term "adolescence" asserted that it is "the stage between puberty and adultry." Another pupil claimed that Martin Luther died a horrible death because "he was excommunicated by a bull." In the realm of science, a pupil was asked to explain the effect of heat and cold and to give an illustration. His response is a classic: "Heat expands; in the summer the days are long. Cold contracts; in the winters the days are short." Finally, an English teacher was offered this unique differentiation between an active and a passive verb: "An active verb shows action, as, 'he kissed her'; and a passive verb shows passion, as, 'she kissed him.'"

Even parents occasionally experience difficulties in this respect. For instance, when explaining her son's absence from school, one mother said: "My boy can't come to school. He has indolent fever."

Aside from the humor present, these and other parts of the anthology make an important contribution. They reveal the pathetically inadequate grasp that some have of simple concepts, meanings, and relationships. Excessive verbalism is common. Words are only partially understood and, as a result, the pupil commits what might be called "logical errors." In other words, the boners repeatedly suggest that some parts of the pupil's verbal or mathematical achievements are at best superficial.

There are numerous less extreme illustrations of the same problem. In a science class it is generally possible to find a pupil who can quickly and properly define pH as the negative logarithm of the concentration of the hydrogen ion in gram atoms per liter, yet does not know what a logarithm or a hydrogen ion is or of what usefulness pH can be when his father tests the soil of his farm before deciding whether to spread lime on it. Another pupil can freely quote Newton's Laws of Motion but fail to see a connection between any of them and the fact that children of various weights travel varying distances when using the same sled on the same hill. A pupil in a modern language class can conjugate a French verb perfectly, but fail persistently to use the proper form of this verb when translating an English passage to French. In a social studies class we find a pupil who can recognize the relationship between latitude and climate north, but not south, of the equator. In a geometry class there are usually several pupils who have difficulty recognizing two parallel lines unless they are drawn vertically or horizontally, or have trouble solving problems with right triangles if the right angle is not the lower left-hand angle.

These are but a few of many frustrating situations confronting the classroom teacher almost daily. The achievement of the pupil is much more limited than is hoped. Within a restricted situation, he can recall partially or totally correct information, but it has little meaning for him. The pupil seems incapable of restating it in his own words or using it in a novel situation. When this occurs, his classroom success is meager.

These deficiencies have a far-reaching impact on achievement testing. If a test measures only the pupil's ability to recall information, it is possible that some of the pupils responding to the items may succeed admirably even though they possess only a superficial knowledge of the subject matter. Moreover, the teacher may erroneously assume that any pupil who can recall the information is also capable of using it properly. Although there is a consistent relationship between these two abilities, it is not large enough to justify this assumption. Therefore, the results of an achievement test measuring only recall of information provide limited information. To identify more closely the perimeters of the pupil's verbal and mathematical achievements, the tests must include items that measure understanding as well as knowledge. Both essay and objective test items can be used for this purpose.

Testing for Knowledges and Understandings

For the purposes of this book, a pupil's knowledges are those pieces of information that he commands. He can recall them when he wants to do so. According to this definition, the pupil may, but not necessarily, have some grasp of the meanings, implications, or significance of his knowledges. In other words, all the facts about people, places, events, and things that he acquired by rote and that he can still recall are a part of his knowledges, whether or not he grasps their meanings.

Understandings, on the other hand, are based upon the acquisition of meanings. The pupil gains understandings when he comprehends the meanings of the knowledges to the point that he can restate them in his own words, grasp the interrelationships among them, and take action intelligently on that basis. An understanding is knowledge with its meanings, implications, and significance attached. It represents utility, for it is by means of understandings that the pupil is able to meet the changing situations thrust upon him every day and to attack intelligently the problems they contain. In other words, it is essentially the same as a group of intellectual abilities and skills including comprehension, application, analysis, synthesis, and evaluation as reported by Bloom (1956).

Testing for Knowledges

Testing for verbal and mathematical knowledges with objective test items is illustrated in the preceding chapter. Most of them can be correctly answered by any pupil willing to memorize. If he fails to gain meaning as he memorizes, little is lost as far as these items are concerned.

Consider for a moment the matching test item in which a pupil must identify the twenty-five year period in which certain western states were admitted to the Union (see page 100). Certainly he can memorize the admission date of every state and thereby be able to answer the test item correctly. Any significance to the sequence in which the states were admitted or any factors determining the time at which a particular state was admitted are not needed to answer the test item. Quite possibly the pupil knows less about these than he does about the dates of admission.

Since testing for knowledge is comparatively easy, it receives considerable attention in the classroom. The teacher experiences little difficulty in constructing test items requiring the pupil to recall an isolated fact or a series of facts. Consequently, informal achievement tests and many standardized achievement tests are heavily overbalanced in this direction. This in turn has a profound influence on learning and teaching. Pupils quickly discover the advantages of concentrating on topics on which they are tested. They orient their learning procedures accordingly. Sometimes the teacher is no less susceptible to this pressure, particularly if his pupils are a part of a city-wide or state-wide testing program. When the tests stress recall of information, he generally teaches accordingly so that the class test results will compare favorably with those of the other classes. In brief, the educational objectives dealing with knowledges become the primary objectives.

The overemphasis on recall of information found in achievement tests today should not be replaced with a fault equally as serious: an underemphasis on testing for knowledge. Knowledges are, in a sense, the raw materials for understandings. Before a pupil can understand, he must have the pertinent knowledges at his disposal. A severe de-emphasis on testing for knowledges and their corresponding educational objectives could be as damaging as the present overemphasis.

Testing for Understandings

In knowledges testing, the material the pupil learns is essentially, if not exactly, the same as that included in the test items. Novel material is virtually nonexistent in the test. Appreciably novel test items require more of the pupil than simple recall of information. Understandings are also necessary if the correct answers are to be found.

When a pupil understands, he is able to use his knowledge effectively. Therefore, evidence of a pupil's understandings can be obtained by asking him questions about a carefully contrived situation that is new to him. Within this situation he is to apply the appropriate part of his total store of knowledge. To do so successfully, he must know the meanings of his knowledge and be able to reorganize them within a strange but plausible situation. The reason for using a novel situation for testing for understanding is quite clear. Only with this device can the teacher be confident that the pupil is doing more than merely parrotting memorized material.

An illustration of the use of novelty in testing for understanding can be found in the test item on tax assessment shown in the preceding chapter (see page 90). Assume that this situation is new to the pupil but the mathematical procedures involved have been studied. To answer it correctly he must recognize that the amount to be paid by each property owner is proportional to the frontage of his property. Therefore, he can proceed as follows:

$$\frac{230 \text{ feet}}{\$690} = \frac{60 \text{ feet}}{X}$$

Thus, the pupil selects from among his mathematical knowledges the part appropriate to this fictitious but realistic situation and applies it correctly.

What the Test Item Measures

There are instances when we are uncertain as to whether the test item is measuring the pupil's knowledges or his understandings. This is particularly true when the purpose of the test item is to measure knowledge. The teacher building the test item has no intention of measuring anything except recall of information and, as far as most members of the class are concerned, he succeeds. Consider, however, the pupil who for some reason did not acquire the knowledge in question, yet arrives at the correct answer by a process of deduction based upon related knowledge. For him the test item does not measure recall of information. Instead, more complex achievements are measured.

The problem can be illustrated easily. The multiple-choice test item shown below is a case in point:

In Shakespeare's *Hamlet* the following quotation appears:
  "This above all: to thine own self be true,
    And it must follow, as the night the day,
    Thou canst not then be false to any man."
Which of the following characters speaks these lines?
    (1) Claudius
    (2) Hamlet
    (3) Horatio
    (4) Laertes
    (5) Polonius

If the class studied the passage, the test item measures recall of information. No doubt most pupils memorized the fact that Polonius spoke these lines when giving advice to his son Laertes. To answer the question, they simply recall that fact. Yet a pupil who did not learn this as such but who is very familiar with the play may also arrive at the correct answer. He may do so on the basis of his knowledge of the play's plot and of the motives of the five characters listed. His response may be a reflection of his ability to interpret *Hamlet*, in which case the response represents a higher level of achievement than simply acquiring knowledge.

A similar line of reasoning may be used to answer the matching test item concerning the dates of admission of certain western states into the Union. The item is also intended to test recall of information. However, a pupil who cannot recall that Missouri was admitted in 1821 might be sufficiently familiar with the economic, political, and social aspects of this country in the nineteenth century to know that it was admitted some time after 1800 and before 1825. In other words, he may be able to arrive at the correct answer by analyzing the knowledge he has of the arguments concerning slavery, the balance of the free and slave states in the Senate, the Missouri Compromise, and the rate of growth in population and in wealth of the Mississippi valley. His answer may be a direct indication of his ability to interpret American history in the first half of the nineteenth century.

Test items designed to measure pupil understandings may measure only recall of information. If the situation on which the test item is based is familiar to a pupil, the teacher cannot be certain which aspect of the pupil's achievement is reflected in his answer. For example, it is possible in the case of the tax assessment item that the pupil memorized the steps needed to reach the correct answer and perhaps the answer itself. Certainly under these conditions he needs no understandings to handle the test item successfully.

Tests of Knowledges and Understandings Compared

The similarities and differences between tests measuring knowledges and those measuring understandings have been repeatedly investigated and reported. The studies were intended to answer two questions:

1. Are the gains made by pupils as measured in terms of tests of understandings more permanent than those measured in terms of tests of knowledges?
2. Is there a relationship between pupil achievement as measured by tests of understandings and pupil achievement as measured by tests of knowledges?

The answer to the first question is an affirmative one. Studies of secondary school and college academic achievement (Tyler, 1934; Wert, 1937; Weitman, 1965) have shown with remarkable consistency that, as the months pass following instruction, pupils retain more of the materials included in a test of understandings than those in a test of knowledges. In some studies, tests of both types were administered to classes as pretests at the beginning of the school year and as final tests at the end of the period of instruction. The difference between the score for each pupil was defined as his gain. Then, without an opportunity to review and relearn the subject matter, the pupils were retested one, two, and sometimes three years later. The gains in knowledge shrank alarmingly; however, the gains in understanding showed no such loss. On the contrary, in some instances they actually increased (Wert, 1937).

The relationship between pupil achievement as measured by tests of understandings and by tests of knowledges has been found to be positive and somewhat low (Tyler, 1936). Otherwise stated, the pupil who acquires knowledges in a subject-matter area ordinarily acquires understandings too, but this tendency is so imperfect that a pupil's understandings cannot be satisfactorily predicted on the basis of his knowledges. A pupil's understandings cannot be assessed indirectly by measuring his knowledges in that subject-matter area; instead, a test designed specifically for measuring understandings must be used.

Problems

1 Ebel and Damrin (1960, p. 1509) state that tests designed to measure abstract, general mental traits such as "critical judgment" and "logical reasoning" have been disappointing. Does this mean that the potential usefulness of tests of understandings is likely to be limited?
2 Give possible explanations why, as reported by Weitman (1965), tests composed of items which place little emphasis on rote learning will provide a good basis for predicting long-term learning by pupils.
3 Some say that achievement tests which measure pupil knowledges do not necessarily measure the degree to which the *ultimate* objectives of education are achieved (Lindquist, 1951, pp. 127–134). In what sense is this true?

Constructing Test Items for Measuring Understandings

Data concerning pupil understandings can be gathered in many different ways. The daily observation of pupil behavior by the teacher can provide a wealth of evidence concerning the scope of their understandings. Observation can take place in the classroom, on the playground, or in the pupil's home, and the information acquired can be organized by anecdotal records or rating scales. Pupil work products are also useful. An original theme for an English class, a collection or exhibit for a science class, a painting or clay model for a fine arts unit, an apron for a home economics class, or a book case for an industrial arts class will quickly reveal some of the pupil's understandings. Also helpful are teacher-pupil interviews, diaries of out-of-class activities, and, of course, paper-and-pencil tests.

The wide variety of possible ways of gathering evidence of pupil understandings is shown in the *Forty-Fifth Yearbook of the National Society for the Study of Education, Part I* (1946). This is one of the better discussions of the measurement of understandings. Illustrative procedures for evaluating understandings are shown for every major school subject. Considerable space is devoted to a measuring technique that is often overlooked: the objective test item. Although by no means a universal solution for the problems of measuring understandings, it can be extremely effective in science, social studies, mathematics, and the language arts. In such subjects as agriculture, home economics, and industrial arts, objective test items are used less frequently, but still provide much-needed information.

Procedure for Constructing Test Items

To construct test items that measure pupil understandings, two basic steps must be taken. First, the teacher must decide which pattern of pupil behavior related to understanding is to be measured. Behavioral patterns include the pupil's ability to apply facts and principles to new situations, his ability to interpret data, and recognize cause-and-effect relationships and assumptions underlying conclusions. Presumably, the pupil has learned these behavior patterns, and the teacher is understandably interested in the degree to which this is true. Secondly, the teacher must devise a novel but realistic situation with questions that, to be answered correctly, require the pupil to display the pattern of behavior being considered. The situations can be completely original or based upon some convenient source such as newspaper or magazine articles or even research reports unfamiliar to the pupils. If possible, they should resemble the everyday environment familiar to the pupil. He is generally impressed with the fairness of a testing approach that requires him to use what he has learned in school to answer questions about situations similar to his out-of-school experiences.

Combining an appropriate pattern of pupil behavior with a suitably novel situation is not simple. Initially, the teacher may be hard pressed to find the situation he wants and then experience difficulty in reducing it to an objective test item. Finding the situation is a matter of a teacher's sensitivity to the application of what he teaches in the world about him; reducing it to an objective test item is largely a matter of following many of the suggestions for constructing objective test items described in Chapter 3.

In his search for a novel situation, the teacher starts, of course, with a clear notion of the pattern of pupil behavior with which he is concerned. For example, in a mathematics class the pupils have mastered many theorems, one of which is the Pythagorean theorem. To see if they can use this information, the teacher may, in a test item, give them the outer dimensions of a baseball diamond and ask them to compute the distance that the ball must travel when the catcher throws it from home plate to second base. In an elementary school arithmetic unit, the pupils have studied simple areas. Therefore, the teacher might have them compute the number of square pieces of candy of 2×2 inch size that could be cut out of a 8×10 inch rectangular pan. In a science class the pupils learned of the law of refraction. Hence, the teacher builds a test item in which they must tell how they would judge the position of a rock at the bottom of a fish pond if they, standing on the bank, were to retrieve it. In a home economics class the pupils have completed a unit concerning nutrition. The teacher may wish to measure their ability to use this information for maintaining a balanced diet. The test item may list the foods eaten by an hypothetical pupil for breakfast and for lunch, and part of those selected at a cafeteria for dinner. The pupil must apply his knowledge by selecting one salad from among those on the menu which this person should eat, and giving reasons for this choice. Certainly these and many similar illustrations in other subject-matter areas are realistic, challenging problems to the pupils.

SINGLE-RESPONSE OBJECTIVE TEST ITEMS.   Some teachers prefer to ask only one question concerning the novel situation selected. It can be phrased to conform to any of the types of objective test items already described. Condensing the description of the novel situation and the question concerning it into a single test item can sometimes be accomplished without lengthening the test item excessively. For instance, in elementary school arithmetic the following short-answer and yes-no test items are typical.

Mrs. Johnson had 1½ pounds of butter in her refrigerator. She used ⅓ of it while baking this morning. How many pounds did she use?

Answer (½)

Yes (No) Joan had 25¢ with which to buy cookies. The cookies she wished to buy cost 36¢ per dozen. Did she have sufficient money to buy ¾ of a dozen?

In a secondary school English class the teacher may want to check on the pupil's skill in the proper use of the words *who, whose, whom, which,* and *that.* To do this he could give the pupil a series of sentences like those below and ask him to select the correct word from the two given, then write it in the space provided at the right.

1. The man (which, who) is speaking is our president.   1. (*who*)
2. Do you know the boy (who's, whose) model air-   2. (*whose*)
   plane is broken?

Sometimes not one but several questions can be asked about the novel situation. These questions can be more or less independent of each other— the response to one does not influence appreciably the response to any other. Each correct response may require the pupil to reveal a different aspect of his understandings.

The following novel situation is one on which a series of test items is constructed. These test items are intended to measure the ability of pupils in a home economics class to apply certain rules for meal planning. Typical menus are shown and proposed changes are to be accepted or rejected by the pupils. The pupils are also to identify the rule that supports the changes that are accepted. Since the rules are summarized for the pupil, these test items demand less recall of information than some of the others included in this chapter.

DIRECTIONS: Listed below are the menus of meals for two days and certain meal planning rules. Study them carefully.

Breakfast

A. Pear sauce
   Pouched egg on milk toast
   Coffee

D. Orange slices
   Soft cooked egg on toast
   Cocoa

Lunch

B. Tomato soup
   Bacon, lettuce, and tomato
   sandwich
   Peaches and cookie
   Milk

E. Chicken soup (broth)
   Cherry jello salad
   Orange
   Tea

Dinner

C. Fried pork chops
   French fried potatoes
   Spinach
   Mince pie
   Coffee

F. Pea soup
   Meat loaf
   Baked beans
   Rolls and butter
   Custard pie
   Coffee

Meal planning rules

1. Balance the different types of foodstuffs in each meal.
2. Do not serve the same food twice in the same meal, even in a different form.
3. Do not use many rich or hard-to-digest foods in one meal.
4. Combine bland or soft foods with those of more pronounced flavor or different texture.
5. Plan meals in which the colors harmonize and are appealing.
6. Plan at least one food in each meal that has high satiety value.

DIRECTIONS: Keeping in mind the above rules, consider the following changes. If the change would not improve the meal, place a zero in the blank. If the change would improve the meal, write the number of the rule supporting your decision in the blank opposite the change. Judge each change independently of all others.

(4) 1. Substitute scrambled egg and cinnamon toast for poached egg on milk toast in Menu A.

(2) 2. Substitute cream of mushroom soup for tomato soup in Menu B.

(3) 3. Substitute broiled steak for the fried pork chops in Menu C.

(0) 4. Substitute pecan pie for mince pie in Menu C.

(0) 5. Substitute half of grapefruit for orange slices in Menu D.

(6) 6. Substitute cream of chicken soup for chicken soup in Menu E.

(1) 7. Substitute baked potato for baked beans in Menu F.

Observe that the description of the novel situation is quite long. This is to be expected, since it provides ample material for a series of test items. Also observe that the objective test items following the description can be any one of several types. The true-false and multiple-choice types are commonly used.

Building test items such as the foregoing involves a series of revisions if a high quality product is obtained. The teacher begins by writing a description of the novel situation, then constructs test items on the basis of it. It is soon apparent that revision of the description will strengthen one or more of the proposed items. Minor deletions or additions of material may result in a wealth of new test item possibilities. Thus, the construction of test items suggests changes in the description, and changes in description suggest new or better test items. Persistent efforts along these lines by the teacher will produce a description of the novel situation that is virtually unambiguous and that contains no nonfunctional portions of any consequence; with this description will be a series of test items exploiting practically all the possibilities for measuring pupil understandings in terms of the situation used.

MULTIPLE-RESPONSE OBJECTIVE TEST ITEMS. Multiple-response objective test items are also used to measure pupil understandings. A common instance of this occurs when the teacher wishes to measure the pupil's ability to apply facts and principles to new situations. In this case the situation is described in some detail. A paragraph or more may be needed. The basic problem within the novel situation is defined and a question asked about it. The pupil answers the question by selecting the correct response from among several listed. Finally, he selects from among many reasons listed those that support his answer. In a sense he views each reason as he does a true-false test item. He must decide whether it is truly sound or faulty.

An illustration of the above is the following test item intended for use in a secondary school science class.[1] A knowledge of the principles of reproduction, how they operate in plants, and an ability to apply this information in a novel situation are measured by this test item.

> Since it takes several years for apple trees to mature, growing apples requires considerable patience and the ability to plan carefully for a profitable yield. In many sections of the country where apple growing is an important industry, bee hives are placed in orchards. What advantage is there in having bees in an orchard?

DIRECTIONS: Immediately following are given three possible answers to the questions asked above. Check the one that best answers the question.

_____ A. The bees will be able to get good nectar.
√ B. The number of apples formed on each tree will increase.
_____ C. The apple blossoms will be self-pollinated.

[1] This test item was adapted with modifications from materials prepared in the College of Sciences and Humanities of Iowa State University (1949).

DIRECTIONS: Following is a list of statements that are suggested as reasons for the above answer. Check the statements that are *good* reasons for the *answer* you selected above.

_____ 1. Yield of apples is increased if bees are present.

✓ 2. Fertilization makes possible the development of mature fruits.

_____ 3. Cross-pollination is necessary for the production of a good apple crop.

_____ 4. Cross-pollination frequently results in desirable variations.

_____ 5. Many fruit growers keep bees in their orchards.

_____ 6. The apple blossoms contain the most desirable type of nectar that can be used in commercial honey.

✓ 7. Flowers from which insects have collected nectar are usually pollinated.

_____ 8. The only completely satisfactory location for bee hives is in the orchard from which they can get nectar.

✓ 9. Even though self-pollination is possible in a flower, it frequently fails to occur.

_____ 10. Bees pollinate apple blossoms in order to aid in the production of a good crop.

_____ 11. All insect pollinated flowers are cross-pollinated.

_____ 12. Double fertilization increases the yield.

The construction of test items like the above is, unfortunately, not a simple task. Even after the difficulties of finding a suitable situation and identifying the central problem have been overcome, the teacher must still find two or more plausible answers, each of which is supported by a group of logical reasons. The latter are the most difficult to find. One way of simplifying the task is to submit the situation to groups of pupils as an essay test item, then screen their answers for attractive but wrong answers and logical reasons for them. These answers can be restated so that an objective test item results.

Two additional features of this kind of objective test item deserve mention. Observe that the pupils do not know how many of the suggested reasons are good reasons, and that some that are not relevant to the correct answer are nevertheless essentially true statements. An example of this is the fifth reason listed: "Many fruit growers keep bees in their orchards." To avoid confusion these two points are sometimes mentioned in the directions to the pupils.

USE OF PICTORIAL MATERIALS. We have already discussed the role of pictorial materials in measuring pupil achievement by means of objective test items (see page 103). They are particularly effective when the purpose of the test item is to measure pupil understandings. Occasionally the novel situation used is completely described by means of a picture, such as a graph or map, or perhaps a film strip or film. In other instances pictorial materials can serve as the principal means of description and need only supplementary remarks to augment them.

PROBLEMS

4   On the basis of each of the following principles in science, describe a novel situation and construct test items concerning it which will measure the pupil's ability to apply that principle.
   a.   Water tends to seek its own level.
   b.   An object floating in water will displace water equal to its weight.
   c.   The theoretical mechanical advantage of a lever used in conjunction with a fulcrum is related to the position of the fulcrum.
   d.   The earth rotates on its axis once a day and circles the sun once a year.
5   Using a table of specifications in a subject-matter area of interest to you, design one or more test items which measure pupil understandings. Then cross reference each test item with the table, that is, indicate the cells in the table with which it is primarily related and those with which it is secondarily related (for example, cells concerning knowledges).
6   Excellent illustrations of the use of pictorial and tabular materials as a part of test items to measure more than recall of information have been prepared and published by the Educational Testing Service (1963). Select one from this publication and analyze it with respect to the pupil knowledges and understandings involved.

ADMINISTERING AND SCORING TESTS OF UNDERSTANDING

The objective test items that measure pupil understandings are evaluated and edited in much the same way as those requiring only memory responses. Two variations of these procedures in Chapter 3, however, remain unmentioned. One concerns the merits of administering the test for understanding as an open-book test; the other concerns the method of scoring multiple-response test items.

Open-Book Testing

Teachers typically administer closed-book tests. The pupil has no source materials at his disposal that would provide him with the correct answers to any of the test items. He depends exclusively on his memory and his ability to manipulate successfully what he remembers. Occasionally the teacher modifies the rules slightly; although access to the textbook and many reference books is forbidden, a restricted number of source materials is allowed. For example, in some mathematics tests the pupils are permitted to use tables of logarithms, tables of trigonometric functions, or tables of squares, square roots, and reciprocals. During science tests the periodic table of elements is prominently displayed, and various chemical, zoological, and botanical handbooks are available to the pupils. In social studies tests, the pupils are sometimes allowed to refer to certain maps and charts. Furthermore, English teachers approve the use of a dictionary during some of their tests. Perhaps these should be called partially closed-book tests.

If the test being administered measures only pupil knowledges, the use of the traditional closed-book approach can be effectively defended. After all, an open-book administration with ample time limits may tell us little more about a pupil's achievement than whether he can use his textbook and other reference materials to find the correct answers to a list of questions. If the test being administered measures primarily pupil understandings, however, the use of the traditional closed-book procedure seems to be an unnecessary restriction. An open-book administration is much more realistic. Since a basic purpose of the test of understanding is to discover whether the pupil can use his knowledges in everyday living, the test situation should simulate the natural situation as much as possible and allow the pupil the use of the normal tools and aids he would have in the natural situation.

The debate on closed or open-book testing procedures gets complicated when we try to establish the degree to which the test or test item measures primarily pupil understandings. It is clear from inspection of the sample test items included in this chapter that both pupil knowledges and understandings are involved in each, that the relative amount of each varies from item to item, and that this balance can be controlled by the person building it. Furthermore, no matter what the test item may seem to measure on the surface, the learning experiences of the pupils answering the test item must also be known before the behavioral patterns it measures can be determined.

The final decision is, of course, in the hands of the classroom teacher. If he believes that tests for knowledges should be the traditional closed-book procedure and that tests for understandings should be open-book, then on the basis of his knowledge of the test items, the pupils, and their experiences, he may separate his test items and administer them accordingly. For those test items about which he is in doubt, he must decide which evidence of a pupil behavioral change is more important and classify the item accordingly.

Constructing test items for an open-book test is probably more difficult than constructing those for a closed-book test. Some of the suggestions for constructing objective test items already discussed must be followed with great care. For example, efforts to avoid textbook terminology should be redoubled. Copying verbatim from a textbook, even when designing test items for a closed-book test, is dangerous; for those items to be included in an open-book test it is very damaging.

Above all, the teacher must construct each test so that the textbook or reference materials will be used in much the same manner as they would be in a similar problem in a natural situation. Although this requirement cannot be fully satisfied, attempts to meet it typically yield good results. For instance, in a mathematics test the textbook may be of little direct help to a pupil as he decides which formula to use to solve the problem, but it does provide an accurate statement of any formula selected. In a social studies test an encyclopedia to which the pupil can refer may serve a similar function. The pupil need not trust his memory here any more than he would in a similar everyday situation in which he wanted to use a given formula or historical fact. In other words, the materials to which the pupil has access in a test should play a supporting role only. The test item should be designed so that this is essentially true.

If pupils are to be given an open-book test, they should be forewarned. The reference materials they can use should be carefully listed for them. Perhaps there will be no restrictions, or as some teachers prefer, the list may include only those materials that might be used in a typical out-of-class situation. In any event, the availability of the materials listed will greatly influence the manner in which the pupil prepares for the test. Quite possibly he will concentrate less on factual details and more on broad principles and relationships (Feldhusen, 1961). Moreover, he may try to become familiar with the reference materials, their content and organization.

Teachers sometimes argue that if an open-book test is to be used and no restrictions placed on the reference materials, class time need not be used for its administration. Instead, the pupil can write the test at home. Although the so-called take-home test has some merit, it suffers from two serious disadvantages. First, the teacher has no certainty that the pupil worked independently. Any assistance destroys the worth of the test results. Secondly, the pupil writing the test at home does not have an opportunity to ask legitimate questions about the items or procedure. Since tests are rarely so well-constructed that no questions are necessary, the pupil should not be denied the chance to ask pertinent questions.

Scoring the Multiple-Response Test Item

When a series of more or less independent questions is asked about the same novel situation, the pupil responses can be weighted and scored in essentially the same manner as any other objective test items of the same type; however, when pupil responses to one point of the test item are in some way dependent upon responses to another part, the weighting and scoring become more complicated. When scoring many of these test items, two questions can be asked:

1. How much credit should a pupil receive if he answers one part of the item incorrectly and, because of this, responds incorrectly to other parts dependent upon the first?
2. When the pupil is not told how many responses to make, how are his responses scored if he makes too few or too many, some of which are correct and some of which are wrong?

Both of these questions can be discussed in terms of the multiple-response objective test item concerning bee hives in an apple orchard. The pupil must select one of three alternatives as the principal advantage of placing bees in an apple orchard, and then indicate which of the twelve reasons listed support his answer. Suppose a pupil selects the wrong alternative and defends his choice well by checking appropriate reasons for it. How much credit should he receive? According to the scoring key, his responses are totally wrong. He argues, however, that only his first response is wrong. He did check the correct reasons for the wrong alternative. What should the teacher do? Although practices vary, one of the more popular is to allow no credit for any of the reasons checked if the correct alternative is not selected.

The second question deals with the case in which the pupil checks the correct alternative and receives whatever points are allowed for this answer, but does not check the proper reasons. Possibly he checks too many reasons, including the correct ones. Or possibly he checks too few reasons, yet those selected are correct. In either case, how should his choice of reasons be scored? Again, there is no single, widely accepted answer to this question. Sometimes teachers take the point of view that the pupil should be penalized if he checks any unacceptable reasons. Moreover, a pupil who indiscriminately checks all reasons should receive no credit.

According to this view, the penalty for any reason erroneously checked will be determined by the total number of reasons listed and the number correct. In the bee hives test item, four of twelve reasons are listed on the key as acceptable. Hence, if one point were allowed for each correct reason checked, then one-half of a point would be deducted for every incorrect reason. In this way a pupil who checks all reasons will receive four positive points and four negative points, a net of zero. If more than one point is allowed each correct reason checked, the penalty for each incorrect reason is proportionally increased.

PROBLEMS

7   Do open-book tests necessarily measure different pupil abilities from those measured by closed-book tests (Kalish, 1958)?

8   One study of college students showed that, in their opinion, they performed about as well on open-book achievement tests as on closed-book tests (Feldhusen, 1961). Is this finding surprising? Why?

9   Design an original method for scoring the multiple-response test item concerning bee hives shown on page 140.

ADVANTAGES OF MEASURING UNDERSTANDINGS WITH OBJECTIVE TESTS

The advantages gained by measuring pupil understandings with objective test items are somewhat the same as those obtained by any other means. In other words, their use enlarges the scope of the achievement evaluation program, which in turn increases the attention paid by both pupils and teachers to the role of understandings in educational objectives.

Moreover, pupils ordinarily find that objective test items designed to reveal understandings are challenging and practical. Pupil interest can reach the point where more than a few will voluntarily admit that the evaluation of understandings is enjoyable and meaningful. This reaction is considerably less common when instruments for measuring pupil knowledges are administered.

Measuring pupil understandings with objective test items has several additional advantages. For teachers skilled in objective testing who use it for measuring pupil knowledges, it serves as a convenient extension of familiar testing procedures to cover other parts of the table of specifications without sacrificing objectivity of scoring. Unlike the evaluation of pupil work products, for example, the objective test items provide highly structured problems to which the pupils are to react. Each pupil is confronted with the same novel situation and responds in terms of the same list of possible answers. This allows comparisons of pupil performances to be made more easily. Incidentally, the structuring of the problem may also limit the usefulness of objective test items. Understandings are reflected in the originality of pupil performance. Responses to objective test items do not reveal this originality, whereas a creative work product does.

Problems

10 Compare the value of information from objective test items with that gained by examining creative pupil products when the degree of pupil understandings is being evaluated in a subject-matter area of interest to you.

Limitations of Measuring Understandings with Objective Tests

There are three major limitations of measuring pupil understandings with objective test items. First, the methods tend to be more difficult to devise and execute than those for measuring pupil knowledges. They demand considerable ingenuity on the part of the teacher, especially if he attempts to determine the many kinds and levels of a pupil's understanding. Secondly, the time needed for pupil response may be excessive. Finally, the results yielded by this procedure cannot be attributed to one— and only one—pupil trait. Instead, they are the products of a combination of pupil traits, of which knowledges and mental ability are most prominent.

It is convenient to discuss the limitations of objective test items as a means of measuring pupil understandings in terms of these three points. The limitations of each type of objective test item mentioned in Chapter 3 are also important here.

Difficulty of Construction

The value of the objective test item measuring understandings depends directly upon the novel situation selected and the description provided. It is already apparent that the selection of the situation is a painstaking operation. After identifying the understanding to be incorporated in the test item, the teacher must find a reasonably simple, understandable, practical, and yet novel situation that illustrates it. Many possibilities are considered before one is selected.

The description of the situation must be prepared with equal care. Since the pupils answering the question cannot add or change any features of the description, it must be complete and, above all, unambiguous.

Several rewritings of the description are ordinarily necessary before this is accomplished. Needless to say, the teacher must also strive to maintain an appropriate vocabulary level and reasonable brevity.

Another factor that complicates the problem of construction is the relationship between the description of the novel situation and the basic question contained in the test item. These two parts must be clearly interdependent if the test item is to measure pupil understanding. In brief, it must be so designed that it can be answered correctly only if the pupil recalls appropriate facts and uses them in terms of the information contained in the description. Building this interdependence into the test item sounds like a relatively simple task, but it is not. The following is a case in point.

At the completion of a unit on the Constitution and its amendments, a teacher wishes to give his American history class a test measuring certain of their understandings. One group of test items is the following. The pupils must answer a series of true-false test items concerning the arrest and imprisonment of a high school pupil.

A janitor saw Jim walking near the high school on the same evening that many of its windows were broken. He reported this to the police who promptly arrested Jim on charges of having destroyed public property. Jim claimed that he was innocent. He was held incommunicado with his bail set at $500. Jim's father hired a lawyer, who immediately obtained a writ of habeas corpus.

(T) F   1. A writ of habeas corpus is a writ inquiring into the lawfulness of the restraint of a person who is imprisoned.

(T) F   2. When a person who is arrested is held incommunicado, he is not allowed to confer with his lawyer.

Observe that it is possible to answer both true-false test items correctly without reading the introductory material. They are measuring the pupil's ability to recall information rather than his ability to recall it and then use it effectively. As appropriate as the description of Jim's troubles seems to be, it is nothing but window dressing in the test.

Suppose that the last sentence of the introductory material were deleted and that the following two test items replaced the original pair:

(T) F   1. An effective way to help Jim would be to obtain a writ of habeas corpus.

T (F)   2. The manner in which Jim was held (i.e., incommunicado) is a violation of the Tenth Amendment of the Constitution.

It is clearly impossible for the pupil to answer the obove questions correctly without reading the description of the novel situation. Both test items require him to recall information and then apply it in the situation described. These changes make the introductory material functional and greatly improve the degree to which the responses reflect understandings rather than knowledges alone.

No doubt a number of teachers will find the second pair of test items more difficult to construct than the first. The reasons for this are not easy to trace. It may be that the item builder does not have a clear idea of the understandings he wishes to measure, or, possibly, he finds it difficult to break the habit of building completely self-contained test items. In any event, obtaining the proper relationship between the introductory material and the question is still another factor that lengthens the process of constructing appropriate items.

Response Time Needed

Class time is a precious commodity. The classroom teacher will be pleased with any measuring procedures that require less time and effort than the techniques already known to him, and concerned about any that seem less efficient. Objective test items for measuring understandings are usually placed in the latter category.

No doubt you are impressed with the length of many of the objective items in this chapter, especially the multiple-response type. The first reading consumes plenty of time, but the several which are usually required dangerously lengthen the response time. Unfortunately, attempts to shorten test items are only partially succesful. The description of the novel situation can be abbreviated only so much. Any inappropriate reading load will penalize the poor reader. This reduces the effectiveness of objective test items for measuring pupil understandings, particularly in the elementary school.

Another factor that increases a pupil's response time is lack of confidence in his answer. Unlike his responses to recall-of-information test items, his answers do not carry the conviction that he is correct. Hence, he rechecks. His relative lack of confidence carries over from item to item, which tends to slow his pace.

The limitation of extended pupil response time may have acquired exaggerated importance in some quarters. Although it is true that these objective test items often consume unduly large amounts of testing time and at best reflect a small sample of pupil understandings, the teacher can hardly justify not using them on this basis alone, unless he has better means of obtaining as much or more information about the pupil's understandings. An increase in testing time is, after all, a small price to pay when the reward is a measurement program broadened to obtain evidence of highly important educational outcomes.

Interpretation of Results

The interpretation of the results yielded by test items of understandings is clouded by the variety traits contributing to the pupil's response. Examination of the test items in this chapter shows us that, in keeping with their definitions, pupil knowledges and understandings are intermixed. For the most part the pupil cannot reveal his understandings unless he can recall appropriate information correctly. Therefore, his right answer indicates that several correct steps have been taken. Failure to answer a test item correctly means that the pupil failed to perform one or more steps correctly. Yet the teacher does not know which these are. In a simple case, the teacher might ask whether the pupil failed to give the right answer because he could not recall the necessary information correctly or could not use it in terms of the novel situation after he recalled it.

The manner in which the objective test items discussed here are constructed does not give the teacher any appreciable information with which to answer the question posed in the foregoing paragraph. Nor does it allow him to determine the full meaning of a correct response. If a pupil responds correctly, does this mean that he simply followed a correct procedure, or that he followed the *most efficient* correct procedure? A correct response does not mean that the pupil has full command of the understandings required any more than an incorrect response means that he has no command of them.

Testing techniques have been developed that reveal in greater detail the procedures that the examinee follows as he attempts to solve a problem. Prominent among these are the tab item technique reported by Glaser and his associates (1954), and a card technique reported by Rimoldi (1955). The tab item described is designed to measure a technician's proficiency in detecting the defective unit in a television set that is not operating properly. He is provided with a description of the malfunction, a diagram of the television set, a list of check procedures that might be employed to determine the cause, and a list of possibly defective units. Opposite each check procedure is a tab, under which is a verbal or diagrammatic description of the results the examinee would have obtained if he had actually performed the procedure. The examinee tries to locate the defective unit by making as few check procedures as possible. He begins by selecting one, tearing off the tab, and uncovering the information produced if the procedure is actually followed. He continues to do this until he has diagnosed the difficulty. The pattern of removed tabs reveals all of the steps he had to take; the sequence of the steps can also be recorded.

The card technique is similar to the tab item. The examinee is given a problem, such as the complaints made by a patient upon admission to a hospital. The examinee has to solve the problem by asking questions that he thinks necessary for its solution. The questions that he might be expected to ask are written on cards; the answers are written on the back of the card. The examinee selects a question and reads the answer. He continues to do this until he has solved the problem. The examiner records the order in which the questions are asked and thus knows the steps followed in the solution of the problem.

Certainly neither of these techniques has been developed to the point where the classroom teacher can conveniently use them in informal achievement testing, nor have attempts to establish their worth utilized elementary or secondary school pupils. Nevertheless, these techniques and their variations may appreciably influence future developments in informal testing for pupil understandings. It is from starting points such as these that many superior educational evaluation techniques have been developed.

A final question that is frequently asked is whether objective tests that measure understandings are appreciably different from tests of mental ability. In other words, are these tests achievement tests at all? Certainly the pupil's mental ability plays an important role in testing for understandings; there is evidence, however, that these are not the same as tests of mental ability (Furst, 1950; Glaser, 1941). The results yielded by the two tests are positively related, but not to a perfect degree. Therefore, tests of understanding can be called achievement tests; yet aptitude factors are thoroughly intermixed with them.

PROBLEMS

11   Study the scheme prepared by Ebel (1954) for classifying test items on the basis of the knowledge or ability which the test item requires of the pupil. Is it possible to accurately classify test items designed to measure understandings when the mental processes supposedly involved in solving them are not clearly known and may vary from pupil to pupil?

12   Using the card technique, build a test item for measuring pupil understandings in a subject-matter area of interest to you.

13   Different types of secondary school physics curricula produce different cognitive preferences by pupils (Heath, 1964). The cognitive preference test consists of four-option multiple-choice test items, frequently containing a diagram or graph in the stem. Since all options are correct answers, the pupil selects the one he prefers. Analyze this effort to evaluate curricula by means of an achievement test.

SUMMARY

A paper-and-pencil achievement testing program measuring only the pupil's knowledge is quite inadequate. Where possible, it should be extended to measure his understandings as well. In other words, it should determine whether the pupil knows the meaning of his knowledges, grasps the interrelationships among them, and can take action intelligently on the basis of them. With enough ingenuity and care, the classroom teacher can construct objective test items capable of eliciting these behavioral patterns from the pupil.

When a pupil understands, he can use his knowledge effectively. Therefore, suitable evidence of a pupil's understandings can be obtained by asking him questions about a carefully contrived situation that is new to him. To answer these questions correctly he must recall the appropriate part of his total store of knowledge and use it in terms of the novel situation described. If he can do so, he has achieved important, complex educational goals.

The novel situations are difficult to develop. First, they must reflect one or more understandings in which the teacher is interested. Secondly, they must be realistic, relatively commonplace, and plausible. Finally, they should require only a short description to be understood. Quite often, at least one of these requirements cannot be completely satisfied.

The question or questions concerning the novel situation can be presented as one or more objective test items. Any type of objective item can be used. To build them, the suggestions described in Chapter 3 can be followed, although minor variations are occasionally necessary.

The administration of the objective test for understandings is much like that of an objective test for knowledges. The possibility of using an open-book testing procedure, however, should be seriously explored when understandings are being measured, for such a procedure is a realistic method of administering this kind of test. Since a basic purpose of the test is to discover whether the pupil can use his knowledge in everyday living, the test situation should simulate the natural situation as much as possible. Hence, the pupil should be allowed to use the tools and aids normally available to him.

The principal advantage of using objective test items for measuring understandings is that they offer the teacher a convenient extension of familiar testing procedures to cover other parts of the table of specifications without sacrificing objectivity of scoring. The principal limitations are that the test items are difficult to build, the pupils need considerable time in which to respond, and the test results are hard to interpret.

Suggested Readings

Belt, Signey L. Teaching, testing, and conservation. *Science Teacher*, 1960, **27**, No. 3.

The "Test of Reasoning in Conservation" is described and sample test items are shown. These test items are useful illustrations of testing for more than recall of information and their use was considered successful.

Cieutat, Victor J. Reliability and validity of two types of objective test items. *Psychological Reports*, 1960, 7, 447–449.

A study was completed of the relative worth of test items measuring the pupil's ability to recall factual material and those measuring his ability to apply principles in general psychology. The former type was found to be better in some respects.

Dressel, Paul L., and Lewis B. Mayhew. *General education: explorations in evaluation*. Washington: American Council on Education, 1954. Chapters 3, 4, 5, and 6.

The materials in these chapters emphasize various evaluation problems in higher education, but are suitable in many respects for secondary school levels. Social science areas are discussed in Chapter 3, communication in Chapter 4, science in Chapter 5, and the humanities in Chapter 6. Companion handbooks concerning teaching or evaluating with respect to certain complex educational objectives are also available in the natural science and social science areas. They are *Science Reasoning and Understanding* and *Critical Thinking in Social Science, A Handbook for Evaluation and Teaching.*

Educational Testing Service, *Multiple-choice questions: a close look*. Princeton, N.J.: Author, 1963.

For the purpose of dispelling the myth that objective test items require no thought, insight, or understanding by the pupil who responds, twenty-two test items in a variety of subject-matter areas are reproduced in their entirety. Explanations of each and a description of the kinds of responses often given are provided.

Gerberich, J. Raymond. *Specimen objective test items*. New York: Longmans, Green, 1956. Chapters 5, 6, and 7.

These chapters do not contain descriptions of methods of constructing objective test items for measuring understandings but do include numerous illustrations of this kind of test item selected from standardized tests. These indirectly suggest variations of objective test items that can be used.

Henry, Nelson B. (Ed.) *The measurement of understanding*. Forty-Fifth Yearbook Nat. Soc. Stud. Educ., 1946, Part I. Chicago: University of Chicago Press.

This is an outstanding presentation of the methods of measuring understanding in the elementary and secondary schools. Of particular interest are Chapter 3, in which the nature of understanding is discussed, and Chapter 4, in which methods of obtaining evidence of understanding are described. In Section II are separate chapters devoted to the measurement of understanding in social studies, science, elementary school mathematics, secondary school mathematics, language arts, fine arts, health education, physical education, home economics, and agriculture. Methods other than the use of objective test items are also explained.

Monaghan, Floyd. Design of objective test items to evaluate thinking ability in science. *Science Education*, 1960, 44, 358–366.

Ways in which objective test items may be developed to measure pupil understandings in science are shown. These may be used as a means of gaining information about pupil achievement which has value in diagnosis.

Science in general education. Report of the Commission on the Secondary School Curriculum of the Progressive Education Association. New York: Appleton-Century-Crofts, 1938. Chapter 9.

This chapter is devoted to the evaluation of pupil achievement in science. It contains illustrations of objective test items designed to measure such pupil traits as the ability to observe phenomena accurately, the ability to interpret data, and the ability to apply facts and principles to new situations.

References Cited

Abingdon, Alexander (Pseud.). *Bigger and better boners.* New York: Viking Press, 1952.

Bloom, Benjamin S. (Ed.) *Taxonomy of educational objectives: cognitive domain.* New York: David McKay, 1956.

College of Science and Humanities. *Testing for more than memorization.* Unpublished manuscript. Ames, Iowa: Iowa State University, 1949.

Ebel, Robert L. Procedures for the analysis of classroom tests. *Educ. Psychol. Measmt,* 1954, **14**, 352–364.

Ebel, Robert L., and Dora E. Damrin. Tests and examinations. In Chester W. Harris (Ed.), *Encyclopedia of educational research.* (3rd ed.) New York: Macmillan, 1960. Pp. 1502–1517.

Educational Testing Service. *Multiple-choice questions: a close look.* Princeton, N.J.: Author, 1963.

Feldhusen, John F. An evaluation of college students' reactions to open book examinations. *Educ. Psychol. Measmt,* 1961, **21**, 637–646.

Furst, E. J. Relationship between tests of intelligence and tests of critical thinking and knowledge. *J. Educ. Res.,* 1950, **43**, 614–624.

Glaser, E. M. *An experiment in the development of critical thinking.* New York: Teachers College, Columbia University, 1941.

Glaser, Robert, Dora E. Damrin and Floyd M. Gardner. The tab item: a technique for the measurement of proficiency in diagnostic problem solving tasks. *Educ. Psychol. Measmt,* 1954, **14**, 283–293.

Heath, R. W. Curriculum, cognition, and educational measurement. *Educ. Psychol. Measmt,* 1964, **24**, 239–253.

Henry, Nelson B. (Ed.) *The measurement of understanding.* Forty-Fifth Yearb. Nat. Soc. Stud. Educ., 1946, Part I. Chicago: University of Chicago Press.

Kalish, R. A. An experimental evaluation of the open book examination. *J. Educ. Psychol.,* 1958, **49**, 200–204.

Lindquist, E. F. Preliminary considerations in objective test construction. In E. F. Lindquist (Ed.), *Educational measurement.* Washington: American Council on Education, 1951. Pp. 119–158.

Rimoldi, H. J. A. A technique for the study of problem solving. *Educ. Psychol. Measmt,* 1955, **15**, 450–461.

Tyler, Ralph W. The relation between recall and higher mental processes. In C. H. Judd and others, *Education as cultivation of the higher mental processes.* New York: Macmillan, 1936. Pp. 6–17.

Tyler, Ralph W. Some findings from studies in the field of college biology. *Science Education,* 1934, **18,** 133–142.

Weitman, Morris. Item characteristics and long-term retention. *J. Educ. Measmt,* 1965, **2,** 37–47.

Wert, James E. Twin examination assumptions. *J. Higher Educ.,* 1937, 8, 136–140.

5 ✍

Preparing Essay Achievement Tests

A SKILLED TRIAL LAWYER in action is a pleasure to watch. With great precision and organization, he carefully extracts information from witnesses—information that, of course, he hopes will be beneficial to his client. He may do this in such a way as to capitalize on any dramatic effects that are present, and he may later summarize the testimony presented to accentuate whatever casts a favorable light on his case and to deemphasize whatever does not.

For our purposes however, his most important task is the preparation of questions he will ask the witnesses.

It is difficult to imagine the amount of preliminary preparation that a lawyer must make before he ever appears in court. For instance, even the framing of the questions to be presented to the witnesses must be carefully planned. Obviously he does not want to use the questions to reveal all the information the witness can recall. Most of this information is irrelevant; some of it may even be damaging to his case. Framing and presenting helpful questions without resorting to leading questions, which the judge might disallow, is a genuine art.

The classroom teacher trying to measure academic achievement with essay tests might tear a page from the lawyer's book. He, too, is asking questions of reasonably cooperative subjects; he, too, is interested in soliciting certain kinds of information and no other. Therefore, it seems reasonable to expect that the task faced by the teacher as he frames questions for his pupils is essentially the same as that faced by the lawyer as he prepares to cross-examine a witness. Each has in mind distinct purposes that his questions are to serve. If the questions are to serve the respective purposes, they must be prepared deliberately.

Unfortunately, the teacher's questions designed to reveal pupil achievements are usually only partly successful. Consider for a moment oral questioning. Notice how frequently the pupil attempting to answer a question must ask his own questions to clarify his task. He may want to know the definition of some of the terms, or whether a certain basic assumption should be made when answering, or how much detail is desired. Only after this confusion has been dispelled can the original question be answered. The cost in time and frustration is sometimes considerable.

The essay test items included in a paper-and-pencil achievement test are generally a distinct improvement in this respect. Their preparation is much more systematic. Yet there is still unnecessary pupil confusion. In spite of the fact that few or no questions about the test are asked when it is administered, a review of the pupils' responses customarily reveals considerable uncertainty about one or more questions. Sometimes this review may even lead one to believe that the pupil would have written a correct answer if he had understood the question. In such cases, the questions are clearly not serving the purpose for which they were intended.

It has been said that to construct a good essay achievement test one need only be able to compose clear questions. This sounds simple. In reality, when compared to the procedures for constructing objective test items, those for constructing essay test items do seem simple. Nevertheless, as the skilled trial lawyer learns at an early stage, you cannot question anyone with consistent success unless the questions are planned. The fact that essay test items are deceptively simple in appearance and hence in construction is the reason why many of their potential values have not been entirely realized.

CHARACTERISTICS OF ESSAY TEST ITEMS

An essay test item is one for which the pupil selects, rather than supplies, the correct answer. More specifically, an essay test item demands a response composed by the pupil, usually in one or more sentences, of a nature that no single response or pattern of responses can be listed as correct, and the accuracy and quality of which can be judged subjectively only by one skilled and informed in the subject, customarily the classroom teacher (Stalnaker, 1951, p. 495). The important features of this description are the freedom of response allowed the pupil, and the difficulty of scoring the responses. The first is used as a basis for classifying essay test items; the second points up the most perplexing problem associated with essay test items, a problem treated in detail later in this chapter.

Freedom of Response

The freedom of response allowed the pupil may vary appreciably from one essay test item to another. Consider the following test items, both of which are designed for use in a secondary school, the first in an American history achievement test, and the second in an English and world literature achievement test.

> In your opinion is the federal government of the United States more or less democratic today than it was at the end of the eighteenth century? Give reasons for your answer.
>
> Explain how the study of English and world literature can help a person to understand better the political, economic, social, and religious aspects of past ages, and how it can influence his present understanding of and attitudes toward modern ways of life.

Both of these test items demand extended responses from the pupils. In fact the typical pupil reaction to each would be ". . . but I could write a book about it." This is justified in both instances. It is also apparent that both test items are tapping a higher order of learning than some objective test items; only those pupils who can recall what they have learned, evaluate it in terms of the question, and then organize it into a suitable answer will succeed.

In contrast, examine the following test items, one of which is taken from an elementary school test dealing with a health unit, the second from a junior high school general science test.

> Bill and Tom are pupils in the sixth grade. They try to take good care of their teeth. Both brush them immediately after their morning and evening meals, but do not brush them after their noon meal or after eating between meals. Both have the dentist inspect their teeth every six months. However, Bill's teeth decay more easily than Tom's. Give possible reasons why this is true.
>
> An athlete wishes to know the amount of time he needs to run 100 yards. He stations one man at the starting line with a revolver and a second at the finish line with a stop watch. In order to time the athlete accurately, should the man at the finish line start the watch at the moment he sees the flash of the revolver or the moment he hears the sound of the shot? Why?

In terms of freedom of response, these two essay test items represent the opposite extreme. The correct responses are now quite specific; notice also that, if the two situations described are novel, more than recall of information is required of the pupil.

The variations in freedom of response allowed the pupil offer a crude but useful means of classifying essay test items into types. At least two major types can be established, one being the *extended response* type, as illustrated by the first pair of test items, and the second being the *restricted response* type, as illustrated by the second pair of test items.

EXTENDED RESPONSE. The extended response has much to be said in its favor. It can be extremely challenging to pupils. To respond correctly, pupils must display such traits as their ability to organize, evaluate, write clearly, and be creative. Thus, the responses to these test items show how well the pupils have achieved important educational goals.

There is some evidence that this type of essay test item can serve as a projective technique (Sims, 1948); that is, as a relatively free expression by the pupil which can be analyzed to gain information about his motives, values, interests, modes of adjustment, and the like. If very few restrictions are placed on the pupil's response, additional evidence of his knowledge and understandings will be revealed. For instance, suppose that a general science teacher presented the following test item to his pupils:

Write a short composition on the topic "What Conservation Means to me."

The pupil responses to such a test item are more complex and varied than those to essay test items of the restricted response type. Presumably they contain helpful information about the pupil's difficulties and patterns of thought that can be used as a partial basis for remedial instruction. The latent content of the response is separated from the manifest content and interpreted; even the style of presentation and any omissions detected have possible significance.

The value of the extended response essay test item as a projective technique is not clearly established. Whether or not this type of item is considered a projective technique, the scoring of pupil responses is difficult, and the reliability low. This reason more than any other has restricted the use of extended response items. Although ample justification for the use of these test items can be found, especially in terms of the important educational objectives they reflect, their practical value is limited by the teacher's inability to score them reliably. To be sure, this in no way detracts from their use as a teaching device.

RESTRICTED RESPONSE. It follows, therefore, that the restricted response essay test item is of greater concern to us in the measurement of pupil achievement except in the case of his writing ability. This type of essay test item differs from the first in that the perimeter of pupil response is better defined. A specific problem is presented. It requires the pupil to recall the proper information, organize it in a suitable manner, arrive at a defensible conclusion, and express it in his own words. In several important respects, it requires the pupil to reveal abilities much like those required by a satisfactory answer to an extended response essay test item; however, this display must occur within well-defined restrictions. These restrictions simplify the scoring problem, thereby greatly improving the reliability of the scoring.

Observe that the restricted response essay test item is far removed from the supply type of test item described in Chapter 3. In the first place, it differs in the amount of freedom of response allowed the pupil. Although the restricted response essay sets limits in this respect, it does not confine the response to a word or two; on the contrary, a paragraph or more is usually needed if the question is to be answered properly. Secondly, it differs in terms of the behavioral changes reflected. The short-answer test is almost invariably used as a means of measuring pupil knowledges; the restricted response essay test item can be used for this purpose or designed to measure pupil understandings. The latter is a very important function of the essay test item.

Problems

1   Construct a supply item for an objective test and a restricted response item for an essay test. Design the latter so that it overlaps the scope of the objective test item. Compare the two in terms of the functions each might have in an achievement test.
2   Differentiate between essay test items which are designed to measure a pupil's achievement in a subject-matter area and those which are designed to measure his ability to write (Ebel and Damrin, 1960, pp. 1503–1504). Construct a test item of each type.

Constructing Essay Test Items

Essay test items are quite popular in the classroom as a method of measuring educational achievement. Objective items are almost exclusively used in standardized achievement tests. Although there are notable exceptions such as the essay writing test included in the *Sequential Tests of Educational Progress*, and the composition test from the *College Entrance Examination Board Tests*, even these constitute only a small part of the total battery, and their purpose is restricted to measuring pupil writing ability.

Preparing and scoring writing ability tests have received considerable attention from teachers and testing specialists (French, 1962; Diederich, 1965). To measure writing ability, objective and semi-objective items are being used alone and in conjunction with essay items which often require between 20 to 40 minutes of testing time. Combinations of these testing methods seem to be satisfactory means of measuring writing ability (Godshalk and others, 1966). Methods of evaluating essays are described in Chapter 7.

With the possible exception of those cases in which evidence of writing ability is desired, the extended response essay test item has limited value as a measuring tool. Therefore, the remainder of this chapter is devoted to the restricted response type.

Teachers usually consider essay items relatively easy to construct since they require less time and technical skill, than objective items. The task, however, is not a simple one. Four major considerations confront the teacher as he constructs essay test items:

1. Relating the essay test item to one or more cells of the table of specifications.
2. Adapting the essay test item to fit the academic background of the pupils to whom it is to be administered.
3. Determining the amount of freedom of response to be allowed the pupil.
4. Establishing a suitable time allotment for the pupil's response.

The four categories overlap each other to some degree and are not of equal importance; however, each is independent and important enough so that it cannot be ignored in the process of constructing essay test items. Failure to comply with the suggestions stemming from any one of the four categories will cause otherwise well-designed essay test items to fail.

Relating Essay Items to the Table of Specifications

As in the case of the objective test item, the essay test item is a direct outgrowth of one or more cells of the table of specifications. In other words, the fundamental relationship between the table and the test item is the same in both cases. Yet the objective and the essay test items do not merely duplicate each other. Like two competing makes of automobiles, they both perform all the functions demanded, but not with equal ease and efficiency.

As you know, the objective test item can be used to measure pupil knowledges with considerable success. Using them, the teacher can sample broadly with a minimum expenditure of time. Measuring pupil understandings with objective test items is an effective approach but not so effective as the measurement of knowledges. The difficulties of item construction and the lengthy response time pose problems. The essay test item, on the other hand, presents a different picture. It is not so efficient a means of measuring pupil knowledges as an objective test, one reason being that the scoring of the answers is a demanding task. As a means of measuring pupil understandings, however, it offers many encouraging possibilities. Test items measuring pupil understandings can be developed without spending the inordinate amounts of time often required when objective items are built for this purpose.

For these reasons, objective test items are often developed primarily in terms of the cells of the table involving knowledges, and the essay test items in terms of cells involving understandings. This means that the achievement test will frequently be composed of both types of items. Such tests offer the pupil some variety. They also distribute the teacher's work load. The construction of the objective item requires more of his time before the test, and the scoring of the essay item requires more of his time after the test.

In addition to differing in the kind of cells of the table of specifications with which they are associated, the objective and essay test items commonly differ in the number with which they are associated. Most often, the objective test item is primarily related to one cell and perhaps secondarily to several more. The essay test item quite frequently is related to several in both cases. It deals with a larger whole than the objective test item. The correct response to it has several subparts. These may easily involve one group of cells in the table of specifications in a primary manner and another in a secondary manner.

High content validity must be carefully maintained in an achievement test containing essay items. For instance, suppose that a teacher using an essay test item for measuring pupil understandings finds that it is primarily related to several cells pertaining to understandings as well as cells pertaining to knowledges. In addition, it may be secondarily related to a similar number of cells. If this is true, any objective test items included in the same test for measuring pupil knowledges must be readjusted accordingly. Only when the various subparts of the correct response to an essay test item are identified and analyzed can the relationship between that item and the table of specifications be determined. The contribution of the item to the content validity of the test obtaining it can then be established.

The true function of the essay test item in achievement measurement is to reveal the pupil's progress toward the more complex educational goals. Unfortunately, some of these goals are so ill-defined that no measurement method has been found useful. The essay test item should be designed with well-identified goals in mind. Pertinent behavioral changes are the abilities to apply principles, form generalizations, make inferences, interpret data, evaluate evidence critically, and recognize and use cause and effect relationships.

In summary, the teacher follows these steps as he builds essay test items according to the table of specifications. First, he must select the cell or group of cells dealing with understandings (and some dealing with knowledges) to which the item is to be related. With these in mind, he starts his search for suitable item content, most likely a novel situation. When the situation is identified, he frames one or more questions on its basis. Finally, he composes the correct response, separates it into its subparts, and cross-refers them with the cells in the table of specifications. He may discover that the cells he originally had in mind are not involved in the test item in exactly the manner initially intended. Therefore, he may alter the item to support his first plan, or he may expand or contract in an appropriate manner other essay and objective test items to be included.

Adapting Essay Items to the Pupils' Backgrounds

"How much detail should I give?" is a common question asked by a pupil confronted with an essay test item. The answer is particularly important to him if he is well aware of the fact that his response will be scored in terms of exactly what he writes; that is, no credit is allowed for what he seems to have written or for statements that are essentially correct but not pertinent. He recognizes that he will waste valuable testing time by making a very detailed response if detail is not required or that he will lose significant amounts of credit for his response if he erroneously assumes that the teacher allows no credit for minor but important detail.

The teacher also is penalized by any pupil uncertainty as to the amount of detailed information that the correct response should contain. If he expects a great deal but does not make this fact explicitly known, the pupils who did not include the details, but could have, will complain when penalized. If the teacher expects only the major elements but does not make this fact explicitly known, some pupils will include unnecessary information, thus lengthening their responses greatly, and complicating the scoring task.

The problem is illustrated by the following essay test item constructed by a physics teacher for use in a unit examination concerning electricity:

> A customer telephones your electrical shop concerning his doorbell, which will not ring when the door button is depressed. He wants to know what the trouble might be. Assuming that the electric current has not failed, describe to him two possible causes of this difficulty and how they could be corrected.

To answer this question the pupils will undoubtedly use such terms as "contact points," "armature," "magnetic field," "hammer," "gong," and so forth. Should they define these terms, or merely use them with the assumption that the teacher will consider proper use of the expressions to signify that the definitions are also known? With the test item stated in its original form the pupils will vary in their answers.

Suppose that the teacher wants somewhat limited detail; he is willing to assume that proper use of the expressions means comprehension of their meaning. In this event, he could improve the item by adding the following statement:

> Assume that the customer is familiar with the basic principles of electricity and magnetism as well as the names and functions of all parts of the common doorbell.

If he did not wish to make this assumption, he could add a statement such as the following:

> Assume that the customer has no knowledge either of the basic principles of electricity and magnetism or of the common doorbell. Be certain, therefore, that you define all technical expressions you use.

This illustration emphasizes a broader issue: adapting the essay test item to the academic background of the pupils. Pupils often have a large body of general knowledge. Asking them to reveal this knowledge in a response to an essay test item does nothing but demonstrate that they have it. No differentiation among the pupils has been accomplished. The teacher must decide on how much of this common knowledge is important in the correct response. For example, he must decide whether the correct use of the words "armature" and "gong" in a response to the foregoing test item are sufficient, or whether a description of what they mean must also be added.

If the purpose of a test item is to serve as a means of differentiating among pupils, it is difficult to defend any test item that requires the pupil to repeat great quantities of these so-called common knowledges. Instead, the test item should be built so that the pupils devote most of their response time to, and hence acquire most of their credit from, those aspects that will differentiate among them. This procedure shortens the response time needed and should result in a more efficient use of the testing time.

All these points have a direct bearing on the level of difficulty of the various parts of the essay test item and, therefore, of the item as a whole. Objective test items are quickly recognized as inadequate if their level of difficulty is very low or very high, a condition not so easily recognized in the case of essay test items. One or more subparts of the essay test item may have suitable levels of difficulty but the remainder may not. Adapting the essay test item to the academic background of the pupil is equivalent to minimizing those parts of the essay test item that are so easy or so difficult that they do not provide a basis for differentiating among the pupils responding.

Determining the Amount of Freedom of Response

How "restricted" is the response to a restricted response essay test item? No definite answer can be given. The illustrations given earlier suggest that the responses are fairly brief. However, they can exceed these limits and still be perfectly acceptable.

The suggestions for the adaptation of the essay test item to the background of the pupils indicate some ways in which the freedom of response is restricted. These suggestions help the pupil sort the important elements in the response from the unimportant; nevertheless, the pupil is still confronted with the question of which important elements are wanted. Perhaps the essay test item can be answered from more than one point of view. Although all types of response based on each of several points of view may be correct in a sense, only one is intended.

The essay test item must be so framed that each pupil will easily recognize exactly the task he is to perform. Even though he may not be able to give a perfect response, he should understand the question in the same way that all other pupils understand it. Any confusion or uncertainty that the pupil may experience should be attributed to his inability to answer correctly rather than his failure to understand the purpose of the test item.

To achieve this clarity in an essay test item is often difficult. On the other hand, violations of this principle can be easily identified and corrected, at least partially. For instance, consider the following essay test item, intended for use in a secondary school social studies test:

> Today both major political parties of the United States include members representing practically every shade of political conviction between arch conservatism and extreme liberalism. Suppose that a rearrangement of membership took place so that the Republican Party acquired a truly conservative philosophy, and the Democratic Party, a truly liberal philosophy. What would happen to the political situation in this country?

Imagine the great variety of responses that this test item would elicit. The impact of such a drastic rearrangement of the political parties could be discussed in terms of the changes in the sizes of the parties, their financial resources, leadership, appeal to the general public, platforms, and control of state legislatures, governorships, the presidency, and Congress. One pupil could have written successfully about several of these topics, another about several different topics, and yet both could have missed the point of the test item and consequently lost credit. In short, the task to be performed by the pupil is not clearly defined and, as a result, even the well-informed pupil will very likely be penalized.

Suppose the question at the end of the test item were replaced by the following:

> Compare the present platforms of the two parties with the platforms that you think the parties would adopt after the rearrangement of membership. Restrict your comparison to the areas of:
> 1. civil rights legislation
> 2. public works legislation
> 3. labor legislation

Now the task is better identified. It is only in terms of certain aspects of the platforms that comparisons are to be made between present and hypothetical party composition. A framework for the pupil's response is established. Incidentally, notice that the test item still requires the pupil to select information, organize it properly, and present it as an integrated whole. Although the framework restricts the pupil's freedom of response, it does not do so to the point where the test item elicits only an extremely specific response dealing with superficial knowledge.

Attempts to clearly define the pupil's task have contributed to the general decline in the use of expressions such as "discuss," "tell about," and "give your opinion of." In their place have come a series of different expressions that, when used individually or in combination, tend to clarify the intent of the test item. Typical of these expressions are the following (Stalnaker, 1951, p. 527): "explain," "relate," "interpret," "compare," "discriminate," "select significant ideas," "contrast," and "state the conclusion." The list is suggestive only.

Establishing Suitable Time Limits

Suitable time limits for essay tests are even more difficult to establish than those for objective tests. Several factors can account for this. First, some teachers find it more difficult to estimate the level of difficulty of essay test items and overestimate or underestimate the response time needed. Secondly, pupils vary in terms of the speed at which they can write or, as the test progresses, their susceptibility to fatigue. Third, a well-designed test item forces the pupil to marshall his facts and organize them in a suitable manner. To do so he may sketch out the preliminary notes or even a complete outline, then write his answer on the basis of such notes. The amount of time needed for this is another uncertain variable. Finally, if the pupil's response is to be scored partly in terms of organization, spelling, and grammatical accuracy, he will need more response time.

There is a tendency to allow too little response time for essay tests. The pupils must rush through at top speed if they hope to finish. The immediate results are, of course, a steady deterioration in the legibility of the handwriting and the organization of the answer. This complicates the task of scoring. Not only are the answers difficult to read and marred by unpardonable grammatical and spelling errors, but they are also replete with interlinear notations and endless footnotes representing afterthoughts.

Suitable time limits can be determined by pretesting the items on a similar group of pupils under normal conditions. Any needed adjustments can be made on the basis of this trial. Rarely can this be done, however. Therefore, in the absence of this information, the teacher must rely on his past experience with similar test items and pupils. Estimating time allotments for each item and listing them on the test copy helps him pinpoint his judgements. When in doubt, the teacher should allow too much rather than too little time. It is better to have fewer or shorter responses and not have to worry about a speed factor.

PROBLEMS

3 Redesign the essay test item concerning the two political parties (see page 167) so that the comparison between them is restricted to their positions on current domestic economic issues.

4 On the basis of a table of specifications in a subject-matter area of interest to you, build an essay test item which will measure pupil understandings. Identify the cells in the table to which it is primarily and may be secondarily related.

5 Criticize and strengthen as you see fit the following essay test items which were included in a ninth-grade social studies test administered at the completion of a unit devoted to government organization, functions, and services.

a. An amendment was proposed in the Congress to have the electoral college vote proportionately, according to actual vote of the people.
1. How would this change the present system?
2. Would this proposal strengthen the democratic control of the people and would it lead to a probable increased vote? Give reasons for your answers.

b. The Supreme Court has nine members. Do you feel this number is too large, too small, or just right to carry the responsibilities of the court? Give reasons.

c. In recent years the Federal government has increased its aid to the farmer. Again we are faced with the parity problem.
1. What is parity?
2. What is the soil bank program?
3. Do you favor either or both, and why?

ADMINISTERING THE ESSAY TEST

The administration of the essay test involves many of the same principles and procedures described in connection with the two preceding chapters dealing with objective tests. Hence, these need not be repeated here. Two features of test administration that deserve additional comment in connection with essay tests are the directions to the pupils and the use of open-book testing.

Unlike the directions given in objective tests, those for essay tests are quite simple. Most often the test items are sufficiently self-contained so that few pupils need any additional information to formulate satisfactory responses. In these cases, the directions are sometimes omitted, or, if given, are no more complicated than the following:

> DIRECTIONS: Answer the following questions in as brief a manner as possible. Only a few sentences will be necessary in order to cover the important points needed to answer each.

Special features of the test must be mentioned in the directions. For example, a brief description of the basis on which the responses are to be scored is sometimes included. If, as is occasionally the case, the classroom teacher plans to add or subtract credit for penmanship, style of writing, grammar, or spelling, this should be pointed out. Any restrictions on the time allowed or the type of paper to be used, the amount of space on the paper allowed for the response, or the use of pen or pencil should likewise be mentioned.

Using the essay test item primarily as a means of measuring understandings suggests an open-book test. If this point of view is accepted, then the question is raised as to whether the pupils could write the answers at home rather than in the classroom. The open-book, take-home administration of essay tests is somewhat common. The task may now fall under the classification of "homework" rather than a test, but, with the proper design of the questions and the cooperation of the pupils, it still can serve as a test with generous time limits.

SCORING THE ESSAY TEST

The scoring of the pupils' responses to an essay test item is unquestionably the most disagreeable task related to the use of these items. In the first place, the teacher is understandably reluctant to allot the great quantities of time that are needed if the job is to be done properly. Also, he is concerned about his ability to recognize the variation of quality in the responses. He suspects that his judgments are highly subjective. Perhaps his state of mind or the name of the pupil at the top of the page are more powerful factors in his determination of the quality of the response than the response itself. These and other doubts cause the scoring problem to be an important one.

The problem is also complicated by the "test-wiseness" of the pupil. This is the same element that reduces the effectiveness of objective achievement tests, but it manifests itself in a different manner here. An imaginative method of faking responses to the essay test item is to practice the art of "precise vagueness." The pupil takes great pains to write at length in a flowing, colorful style. He also takes great pains not to commit himself; he skirts the issue as closely as he can without actually facing it. In short, he wants to impress the scorer without revealing his ignorance. An illustration of this technique is the following response by a pupil to a test item requiring him to evaluate the causes of the fall from power of Napoleon Bonaparte.

> There was a day when Napoleon Bonaparte was at the pinnacle of success. People admired him and respected him. He was the outstanding leader in Europe. But this could not last forever. Difficulties arose. These difficulties were political, economical, social, and, of course, military. Moreover, they were not always obvious. Indeed, some were so subtle that even Napoleon himself was not aware of them. Nevertheless, obvious or subtle, these difficulties were sufficiently powerful that, in combination, they toppled him from power.
>
> The relative importance of these difficulties is hard to determine. It would seem that some were clearly more important than others. This is to say that some contributed more directly to Napoleon's fall than did others.

Paragraph after paragraph, perhaps page after page, the pupil continues to string one vague sentence to the end of another. Each rings of accuracy. Yet the true worth of such an answer is elusive; like a puff of smoke, it seems to disappear as you reach for it. The foregoing response is essentially empty. Yet, in the face of its impressive length and style, it would require a teacher well-schooled in the art of scoring responses to essay test items to recognize this and score accordingly.

Testing specialists have devoted considerable attention to simplifying the task of scoring responses to essay test items and to improving the reliability of the scoring process. Their efforts have been somewhat successful. Well-established general suggestions have been formulated and several methods of scoring have been devised and used.

Improving the Scoring of Essay Items

There are four general suggestions for improving the scoring of essay items.

Score the pupils' responses anonymously. It has been demonstrated that the "halo effect" can appreciably reduce the objectivity of the scoring. Because a certain pupil has written the response, the teacher expects a certain quality of response and has, in effect, prejudged it. The identical response written by a pupil with a decidedly different reputation will receive a different amount of credit.

The scoring of a response should be based exclusively on what is written and never should be influenced by knowledge of the identity of the pupil who wrote it. To conceal the identity of the examinee is not easy. If the teacher is familiar with the penmanship or style of writing of the pupils, it is virtually impossible. Should this not be the case, the use of numbers, rather than names, to identify the responses, or the practice of having the pupil's name written on the back of the paper, will provide a simple but effective means of maintaining anonymity.

Score all responses to each test item at one time. Only when this is done, and one item is completely finished, should the responses to any other item in the test be examined. This means that, instead of the responses to all test items by one pupil being scored at one time as is most often true of an objective test, the responses to one test item by all of the pupils are scored at one time.

Two advantages are gained by following this suggestion. First, it is easier to maintain a constant or near constant set of standards on the basis of which each response is to be judged. All details of the completely correct responses can be remembered, and comparisons between and among various pupil responses can be made. Secondly, any "halo effect" that might modify the scoring of all responses by one pupil in a test tends to be minimized. In other words, the way in which a pupil answers one test item will not influence the judgment of the teacher when he scores the pupil's response to a second test item that is more or less independent of the first. There is an unjustified feeling that, because the response to one test item by a pupil is poor or good, the responses to all other test items in the same test by that pupil must necessarily be of similar quality.

If the spelling, penmanship, grammar, and writing style of the responses are to be scored, it should be done independently of the subject-matter content. In other words, how a pupil writes should be judged apart from what he writes. You can easily imagine instances in which one might be of a very different quality from the other, and instances in which the quality of one affects the teacher's judgment of the quality of the other. An all too common occurrence is the case in which accurate spelling, legible handwriting, and pleasant style upgrade the rating of the quality of the content of the response, whereas substandard spelling, handwriting, and style function in the opposite direction.

The question is frequently asked whether the quality of grammar, spelling, handwriting, and style should be scored at all. The answer is simple. If any or all of these are a part of the educational objectives and hence the table of specifications on which the test is based, they should be scored. If they are not, any deficiencies in these respects can be noted and any superlative achievements can be acknowledged, but no loss or gain of credit can be given. In view of this it is easy to understand why, other than in tests in the language arts, such aspects as grammar, spelling, and writing style are seldom scored, or are scored on a restricted basis. An example of restricted scoring is the marking of spelling for technical words but not for nontechnical words.

If the results of the test are extremely important, have at least one other person score the responses independently. If this is not possible, score them a second time yourself, doing so without knowledge of your first judgments. The time-proven method of improving the scoring of responses to essay test items is to average independent judgments made by competent scorers guided by the same set of standards. The feasibility of this practice is questionable. The next best substitute is the procedure in which two independent judgments are made by the same teacher.

Any radical discrepancies between the scores yielded by independent judgments should be immediately investigated and resolved. Perhaps the services of a third scorer are needed. If the differences cannot be resolved, then the opinion of the person who knows the teaching situation best, the classroom teacher, should be followed.

Methods of Scoring Essay Items

A number of different methods of scoring the responses to essay test items have been developed; only two are discussed here. The first is called the *analytical method*; the second is known as the *rating method*.

ANALYTICAL METHOD. To use the analytical method of scoring, the teacher must first write out the perfect response to each test item, that is, the answer that would receive the highest possible score. Then it is analyzed and its component parts identified. The total number of raw-score points allowed for the correct response is distributed among the various subparts. The points may be distributed equally or unequally among the parts, depending upon the teacher's feelings about the matter and the importance of the cells in the table of specifications on which the subpart is based. Finally, each pupil's response to the test item is read, the various subparts of the correct response that it contains are noted, and the raw score determined accordingly. As far as the scoring is concerned, any extraneous material in the pupil's response is ignored, whether it is accurately stated or not. Note that this procedure does not prevent the teacher from marking any inaccuracies in the statements containing unnecessary information. Indeed, he should mark them. The steps of the foregoing procedure are then repeated for each of the other essay items.

The division of the correct response of an essay test item into its component parts and the assignment of raw-score points to each subpart are two key steps in the analytical method of scoring. A simple illustration of these procedures is the test item concerning possible reasons for the differences in incidence of tooth decay of two sixth-grade boys (see page 158). The teacher may decide that the correct response should contain three elements thought to be of approximately equal importance. Therefore, each is allotted one raw-score point.

1. Recognition that the nature of the boys' diets influences incidence of tooth decay.
2. Recognition that heredity factors can partly account for incidence of tooth decay.
3. Recognition that all factors causing tooth decay are not known; hence differences between the two boys in terms of these unknown factors could account partly for variations in the incidence of tooth decay.

A more complex illustration of the analysis of the correct response is the following. It is based on an essay test item designed for an informal achievement test to be administered to agriculture pupils completing a unit concerning dairy cattle. The item is in three parts.

A farmer is undecided whether two of the dairy cows in his herd should be fed the same or different amounts of a concentrate mixture he is using. The following information is available concerning the two cows:

COW	BREED	WEIGHT	AGE	MILK PRODUCTION	BUTTER-FAT CON-TENT	MONTHS IN CALF
A	Guernsey	1,000 lbs.	4 yrs.	37 lbs./day	5.1%	4
B	Holstein	1,200 lbs.	5 yrs.	49 lbs./day	3.5%	2

Both cows are fed adequate amounts of the same roughage.
1. Cite reasons why Cow A should be fed more concentrate mixture than Cow B.
2. Cite reasons why Cow B should be fed more concentrate mixture than Cow A.
3. Evaluate all the information and decide whether the farmer should feed more concentrate mixture to Cow A than to Cow B, or more to Cow B than to Cow A, or the same amount to both.

To answer the essay test item correctly, the pupil must recall that the amount of concentrate mixture fed a dairy cow is noticeably influenced by the cow's size, amount of butterfat produced per day, and stage of pregnancy, but is not appreciably influenced by differences in breed and age such as are shown in the chart. Then he must use this information accordingly.

If eight raw-score points were allowed for the correct response, one possible way of subdividing them among the subparts is as follows:

Subpart 1
  Total points: 3
  A.   (2 pts.) Amount of butterfat production is greater for Cow A (1.9 lbs./day) than Cow B (1.7 lbs/day).
  B.   (1 pt.) Cow A is in a more advanced stage of pregnancy than Cow B.

Subpart 2
  Total points: 1
  A.   (1 pt.) Cow B weighs more than Cow A.

Subpart 3
  Total points: 4
  A.   (1 pt.) If only the differences in breed and age are considered, both cows should be fed the same amount of concentrate mixture.
  B.   (3 pts.) The two reasons for feeding more concentrate mixture to Cow A than Cow B overbalance the reason for feeding more to Cow B than Cow A.

With this analysis of the correct response firmly in mind, the teacher should be able to score pupil responses more quickly and consistently. Moreover, later discussion of the test item, which would include a review of the pupils' responses and the scoring of items, is greatly facilitated when based on such an analysis as the foregoing. Both teacher and pupil are much more certain that the scoring is fair, and, in addition, they have isolated any gaps in each pupil's achievement revealed by the test item.

The analytical method offers several excellent advantages. In the first place, the analysis of the so-called perfect response will quite frequently cause the teacher to redesign the statement of the test item. He may realize that the item as originally stated will not necessarily elicit the response he desires, even when the pupil is very well informed. Any reframing of the test item or readjustment of the time limits that result from analyzing the correct response are generally distinct improvements. Secondly, the analytical method used by a conscientious grader can yield very reliable scores. This is true when the essay test item is of the restricted rather than extended response type.

RATING METHOD.   The rating method also requires that a so-called "perfect" response be written for each test item; however, this is not subdivided as such. The wholeness of the response is emphasized; the scorer attempts to grasp its complete scope. With this in mind, he reads the pupil's responses. On the basis of the wholeness of each response, he classifies it in one of three or one of five categories. The categories represent levels of quality such as, in the first case, good, average, or poor, and in the second case, very good, good, average, poor, or very poor. Seldom are more than five categories used.

Once the scorer has read and classified all responses, he rereads them a second time, possibly even a third. The answers in each category are compared with each other. Those that don't fit are shifted to a more suitable category. Homogeneity in each category is desirable, even though the scorer realizes that it depends on the number of categories used. The fewer categories used, the more variability exists within each.

When the scorer is completely satisfied that each response is in its proper category, it is marked accordingly. Total, partial, or no credit is allowed, depending on the category checked. The entire process is then repeated for all other essay items in the test.

By and large, the rating method of scoring essay test items has had only moderate success. To be sure, it is a distinct improvement over the single hasty reading in the absence of a clearly understood correct response that some teachers use as a means of scoring answers to their essay test items. On the other hand, it has not yielded the high scorer reliabilities of the analytical method. A scorer often has difficulty differentiating between the various categories and may even find that his basis for differentiating is likely to change.

Problems

6　Even though a teacher decides to score responses to essay test items on the basis of content without consideration of writing style, it is possible that he will be influenced, consciously or subconsciously, by the quality of writing. Scannell and Marshall (1966) found evidence of this. Do you agree?

7　Compare the difficulty of scoring the responses to an essay test measuring pupil writing ability with the difficulty of scoring responses to an "interlinear" test (Findley, 1954, p. 259); that is, a test requiring the pupil to make corrections and deletions for a badly garbled piece of prose.

8　Summarize the recent evidence of consistent scoring of responses to essay test items (Ebel and Damrin, 1960, pp. 1504–1505).

Advantages of Measuring with Essay Items

The use of essay test items for measuring pupil achievement offers a number of advantages. They can be conveniently classified under three headings:

1.　Relative ease of construction.
2.　Emphasis on integrated wholes of the subject matter.
3.　Usefulness for measuring achievement of important educational objectives.

These are important advantages. For instance, pupils regularly report that they prepare in a different way for an essay test than for an objective test, although one cannot be certain that great differences in study habits actually exist. They expect—unfortunately, with some justification—that the objective test will emphasize small details; a broad command of factual materials will be needed. On the other hand, many feel that the essay test is usually based on broad principles and relationships; in short, on integrated wholes.

If the essay test item is used for measuring pupil understandings as recommended, it will favorably influence study habits and teaching procedures. Both pupil and teacher will find themselves concentrating on the basic aspects of a field of study, the relationship between these and other fields, and their applications in everyday living. Thus, the proper use of essay test items can have a profound effect on the learning procedure. Teachers would do well to exploit this advantage.

To be able to respond successfully to an essay test item, a pupil must be able to select the information he needs, organize it into a cohesive whole, and express it in his own words. These steps represent vital educational objectives, such as the abilities to select, organize, relate, synthesize, and apply information. The well-designed essay test item can show how well a pupil can do these things but, as a measuring instrument, it is far from perfect.

Serious questions have been raised about the stability of such traits as the ability to organize and use knowledge creatively, and hence the success with which responses to essay test items reflect them (Stalnaker, 1951, pp. 509–510). In this respect, the value of the essay test-item is still in doubt.

LIMITATIONS OF MEASURING WITH ESSAY ITEMS

Essay test items suffer from two major limitations: the unreliability (that is, lack of consistency) of the scoring of the pupil's response and the inadequacy of the sampling of the subject matter. Both are important factors that differentiate between the usefulness of essay test items and objective test items for measuring pupil achievement.

Unreliability of Scoring

Research has shown that seemingly competent scorers frequently cannot agree with themselves, much less with each other, concerning the amount of credit to be allowed a pupil's response to an essay test item. The subjectivity in the scoring process varies according to the nature of the essay test item but is typically large. When the test item approaches the extended response type, subjectivity increases and reliable scoring becomes an extremely difficult problem. Unfortunately, the pupil does not always graciously accept any inconsistencies in the teacher's scoring efforts.

The suggestions for improving the two methods of grading essay responses can increase scorer reliability. To do so, three conditions must be met. First, the responses must have been elicited by carefully framed test items, which present the pupil with a well-defined task. Secondly, the teacher using the analytical or rating method should master and apply it carefully. Among other things, this may mean practicing the method by scoring pupil responses several times independently, then analyzing whatever differences occurred. Thirdly, ample time must be allowed. Essay test items, unlike objective ones, cannot be clerically graded. The teacher must be an alert, discerning judge at all times, which is a role he cannot play properly if pressed for time.

Inadequacy of the Sampling

The problems of sampling subject matter for an achievement test are essentially the same as those of a public opinion pollster or a reader picking a novel to borrow from the library. A basic problem in all cases is the size of the sample. How large must it be to guarantee that generalizations based upon it will truly represent the population from which it came? All three situations have practical restrictions on the size of the sample. The test cannot have more than a certain number of test items because of limited time. The pollster does not have the financial resources to draw huge samples. The reader thumbing pages at random will not scan endlessly because it requires too much time and may spoil the novel when he reads it in entirety.

The variety of the population sampled also affects the size of sample needed. For example, sampling a homogeneous mixture, such as a bottle of milk or a bag of well-mixed inorganic fertilizer, is comparatively simple; a relatively small sample will no doubt be sufficiently representative. On the other hand, sampling a heterogeneous mixture, such as subject matter, public opinion, or a lengthy novel is difficult. Inevitably, large samples are needed if one is to have confidence in the breadth of the sample.

In the light of this discussion, the inadequate subject matter sampling of the essay test comes into focus. Simply stated, the typical essay achievement test contains only a handful of test items; therefore, despite the fact that each item may have a number of subparts, the test is a distressingly small sample when the variety of most subject matter is considered. The possibility that the sample is unrepresentative is increased. Otherwise stated, its content validity is quite possibly less than satisfactory. As a result, there is greater likelihood that a rather well-prepared pupil might have the misfortune to find that one or more test items touch upon his weak areas; hence he responds poorly, and the total test results underestimate his true achievement.

USE OF OPTIONAL TEST ITEMS. Some teachers try to reduce the sampling limitation of the essay test item with optional items. For instance, twelve test items might be listed, and the pupil allowed to answer any eight of them. Rather than improving the sampling, this procedure weakens it. Since many pupils will make partially different selections, they are, in effect, confronted with partially different samples. The content validity depends upon the particular combination the pupil chooses, since test content and the meaning of the score varies from pupil to pupil. A direct comparison of the various test scores cannot be defended.

A different use of optional test items is that in which a series to be answered by all pupils is first presented, and a series of paired items follows. The pupil is to choose one of each pair. The members of each pair are considered to be equivalent test items; they are of the same level of difficulty, require approximately the same response time, are based on the same combination of cells in the table of specifications, and so forth. Thus, ideally, the content validity would be the same for all practical purposes no matter what choices the pupil made; yet the test is somewhat more flexible.

The foregoing use of optional test items is much more defensible than the first described. Nevertheless, it cannot be recommended. It doesn't relieve the basic difficulty, which is that certain cells of the table of specifications are not represented in the test. The pairs are merely independent test items representing the same combinations of cells. Building equivalent test items is, of course, no simple task. Moreover, they increase the scoring labor because the scorer has a greater variety of items to score.

PROBLEMS

9   After an essay test, some teachers asked the pupils to record the reasons for their answers on a 3″ x 5″ card. This information was then used for diagnosing pupil difficulties and strengthening similar future test items. Identify the advantages and limitations of this procedure.

10   It is recommended that the scoring key to an essay test be prepared before the test. In what respects would this policy be likely to strengthen essay test items?

Comparison of Essay and Objective Tests

At this point, we can identify a number of sizable differences between the essay test item and the objective test item as a means of gathering information on which pupil achievement can be evaluated. Seven general characteristics used as a basis for differentiating between the two types of items are as follows:

Difficulty of preparing the test item
Adequacy of the sampling of the subject matter
Relative ease with which knowledges and understandings are measured
Study procedures followed by the pupil as he prepares for the test
Originality of the response the pupil must make to the test item
Relative success of guessing correct responses
Difficulty of scoring the pupil responses

The differences between essay and objective test items in terms of these seven characteristics are summarized in Table 2. This table reveals the fallacy of the argument that one type of test item is unquestionably superior or inferior to the other. Each has unique advantages and limitations; there are testing needs for which each is particularly well suited. No teacher should needlessly restrict his measurement program by adhering to one type or the other. Recognizing this situation, many classroom teachers build and administer achievement tests containing both types of items. In these cases, pupils generally prefer to answer the objective test items first and the essay items later, thereby making better use of their testing time.

Problems

11   On the basis of your experience, compare the additional time required to build an objective test rather than essay test with that required to score the essay rather than the objective test.

12   Stodola (1961, p. 17) says that essay tests encourage the pupil to learn how to organize his own ideas and express them effectively, whereas objective tests encourage him to build a broad background of knowledges and abilities. Evaluate this comparison.

Summary

An essay test item demands a response composed by the pupil, usually in the form of one or more sentences. The quality of the pupil's response

TABLE 2
COMPARISON OF ESSAY AND OBJECTIVE TESTS

Characteristic	Essay test	Objective test
Preparation of the test item.	Items are relatively easy to construct.	Items are relatively difficult to construct.
Sampling of the subject matter.	Sampling is often limited.	Sampling is usually extensive.
Measurement of knowledges and understandings.	Items can measure both; measurement of understanding is recommended.	Items can measure both; measurement of knowledge is more common.
Preparation by pupil.	Emphasis is primarily on larger units of material.	Emphasis is often on factual details.
Nature of response by pupil.	Pupil organizes original response.	Except for supply test items, pupil selects response.
Guessing of correct response by pupil.	Successful guessing is minor problem.	Successful guessing is major problem.
Scoring of pupil responses.	Scoring is difficult, time-consuming, and somewhat unreliable.	Scoring is simple, rapid, and highly reliable.

can be judged subjectively by an informed scorer. This person is customarily one who instructed the pupil and built the test item, that is, the classroom teacher.

The freedom of response allowed on an essay test item can vary appreciable. In one case, few restrictions are placed on the nature of the pupil's response; such a test item is an extended response essay test item. Other test items define quite specifically the task to be performed by the pupil; these are restricted response essay test items. Because of the extremely difficult task of scoring answers to extended response essay test items, their value as a method of evaluating achievement is curtailed. On the other hand, since answers to the restricted response type can be scored reliably, it plays an important role in informal achievement testing.

There are four major considerations facing the teacher when he builds essay test items. First, he must relate the item to one or more cells in the table of specifications; those to be emphasized involve pupil understandings. Secondly, he must adapt it to the academic background of the pupils. Thirdly, he must determine the freedom of response to be allowed the pupil. Finally, he must establish suitable time limits.

Scoring responses to an essay test item is usually difficult. To help simplify this task and, at the same time, improve the reliability of the scoring process, four general rules should be followed. First, score the pupils' responses anonymously. Secondly, score all responses to each test item at one time. Thirdly, if spelling, penmanship, grammar, and so forth are to be graded, score them independently of the subject-matter content. Fourthly, if possible, have another person go over them; if this is not possible, score them a second time yourself.

Two prominent methods of scoring essay test items are the analytical method and the rating method. In the analytical method, the teacher breaks the correct response into subparts, assigns raw-score points to each, and awards points for a pupil's answer insofar as each subpart of the correct response is or is not included. In the rating method, the teacher tries to grasp the complete scope of the right answer, then, on the basis of the wholeness of a pupil's response, to classify it into one of three or five categories representing various levels of quality. The analytical method is often considered more satisfactory than the rating method for scoring responses to restricted response essay test items.

The use of essay test items for measuring pupil achievement offers three major advantages: they are relatively easy to construct, they emphasize integrated wholes of the subject matter, and they can facilitate the measurement of pupil achievement of some important educational objectives. The limitations commonly encountered are the unreliability of the scoring of pupil responses and the inadequacy of the sampling of the subject matter.

Suggested Readings

Anderson, C. C. The new STEP Essay Test as a measure of composition ability. *Educ. psychol. Measmt*, 1960, **20**, 95–102.
    A report is made of a study of the effectiveness of the *Essay Test* of the *Sequential Tests of Educational Progress*. Some variability in the scoring of the pupil responses was found.
Ebel, Robert L. *Measuring educational achievement*. Englewood Cliffs, N.J.: Prentice-Hall, 1965. Chapter. 4.
    The differences and similarities between objective and essay test items are recounted, and suggestions are given for the preparation, use, and scoring of essay tests.

Ebel, Robert L., and Dora E. Damrin. Tests and examinations. In Chester W. Harris (Ed.), *Encyclopedia of educational research*. (3rd ed.) New York: Macmillan, 1960. Pp. 1502–1517.

A large section of this article (pp. 1503–1506) is a review of recent research on the purposes, reliability, and validity of essay tests.

Page, E. B. Imminence of grading essays by computers. *Phi Delta Kappan*, 1966, 47, 238–243.

Initial efforts show that a computer can grade pupil compositions about as well as classroom English teachers. These promising results are leading to the study of the use of the computer to score limited response essay test items dealing with subject matter. These and other considerations are reviewed in a non-technical way in this article.

Palmer, Orville. Sense or nonsense? The objective testing of English composition. *The English Journal*, 1961, 50, 314–320.

An interesting argument is presented in favor of measuring a pupil's ability in written composition with objective test items. Pertinent activities of the staff of the College Entrance Examination Board testing program are mentioned.

Sims. V. M. The essay examination is a projective technique. *Educ. psychol. Measmt*, 1948, 8, 15–31.

This is a challenging article in that it views essay test items in a manner seldom used by classroom teachers. Sims argues that both the actual response to the essay question and the latent content, which unintentionally reveals aspects of the pupil's mental life, are important to the examiner. With this in mind, he offers suggestions for writing good essay test items and suggestions for evaluating the pupil's response. Since the essay test item is being viewed in a broad manner, a number of these suggestions differ from those given in Chapter 5.

Stalnaker, John M. The essay type of examination. In E. F. Lindquist (Ed.), *Educational measurement*. Washington: American Council on Education, 1951. Pp. 495–530.

This is a superior discussion of the value of essay test items as a means of measuring pupil achievement. In it are described the limitations of this type of test item, its potential value, suggestions for improving it, and reliable methods of scoring pupil responses.

Wood, Dorothy A. *Test construction, development and interpretation of achievement tests*. Columbus, Ohio: Charles E. Merrill, 1960. Chapter 10.

The advantages and limitations of essay tests are described, and suggestions for improving them listed. Using the essay test as a means of measuring pupil originality or creativity is considered.

References Cited

Diederich, Paul B. Reading and grading. In A. Jewett and C. E. Bish (Eds.), *Improving English composition*. Washington: National Education Association, 1965. Chapter 11.

Ebel, Robert L., and Dora E. Damrin. Tests and examinations. In Chester W. Harris (Ed.), *Encyclopedia of educational research*. (3rd ed.) New York: Macmillan, 1960. Pp. 1502–1517.

Findley, Warren G. Progress in the measurement of achievement. *Educ. Psychol. Measmt*, 1954, 14, 255–260.

French, John W. School of thought in judging excellence of English themes. In *Proceedings, 1961 Invitational Conference on Testing Problems*. Princeton, N.J.: Educational Testing Service, 1962.

Godshalk, Fred I., and others. *The measurement of writing ability*. New York: College Entrance Examination Board, 1966.

Scannell, D. P., and J. C. Marshall. Effect of selected composition errors on grades assigned to essay examinations. *Am. Educ. Pres. J.*, 1966, 3, 125–130.

Sims, Verner M. The essay examination is a projective technique. *Educ. Psychol. Measmt*, 1948, 8, 15–31.

Stalnaker, John M. The essay type of examination. In E. F. Lindquist (Ed.), *Educational measurement*. Washington: American Council on Education, 1951. Pp. 495–530.

Stodola, Quentin. *Making the classroom test, a guide for teachers*. (2nd ed.) Educational Testing Service Evaluation and Advisory Service Series, No. 4. Princeton, N.J.: Educational Testing Service, 1961.

6

Appraising Classroom Achievement Tests

THE USE OF MEASURING INSTRUMENTS in our commercial, scientific, and even recreational pursuits is commonplace. This would be a strange world indeed if the desk rulers, bathroom scales, milk cartons, clocks, thermometers, speedometers, and electrical meters were suddenly removed. These and countless other measuring instruments are constantly feeding information to us that we use to make decisions. Without such information, a significant part of our modern civilization would cease to function.

An interesting result of the dominance of measuring instruments is the great confidence we have in their accuracy. True, we may doubt the readings of an ancient wrist watch or an inexpensive outdoor thermometer, but only infrequently do we entertain doubts as to whether the desk ruler is twelve inches long and divided into twelve equal parts, or whether the water and gas meters are measuring volume properly, or whether the speedometer in our automobile is registering as it should. We assume that, for our purposes, their accuracy is sufficient.

Fortunately our confidence in such instruments is well-founded. Extensive efforts are made by the federal and sometimes the state governments as well as by industrial and scientific organizations to maintain accurate measuring instruments. For example, the United States Bureau of Standards works actively in this field. Among other functions, it maintains fireproof vaults in which platinum-iridium meter bars and kilogram weights are carefully stored; they are the standards against which some of the instruments for measuring distance and weight can be checked. Moreover, other governmental units appoint officials known as sealers who conduct systematic checks of devices such as the scales used in grocery stores and meat markets and the meters used in gasoline stations, thereby protecting the consumer. Also, scientists are constantly recalibrating the thermometers, burets, and weights used in their work to be certain that the accuracy of their measurements is maintained.

The perpetual vigilance in commercial, industrial, and scientific fields should be copied by the classroom teacher. He makes numerous measurements and, in so doing, uses instruments in which he has notably less confidence than the scales and meters mentioned. This is particularly true when classroom achievement tests are used. Although the product of much time and effort, they no doubt contain numerous unsuspected flaws. After all, many tentative decisions are made as they are constructed. Decisions concerning item difficulty, the attractiveness of distracters, or the length of the test, to name just a few, are made on the basis of inadequate evidence and could be at least partially wrong. The teacher will not know the success or failure of these decisions unless the test is carefully re-examined after its administration. Then and only then will he know how worthwhile it was and how meaningful the scores.

In addition to determining the worth of a classroom achievement test after it has been given, re-examining test results has other values. For instance, any errors or inadequacies discovered can serve as warnings to the teacher when he constructs other achievement tests. Although the methods and material used in a class may change from year to year, the major educational objectives are generally stable. Therefore, the classroom achievement testing program changes from year to year but seldom drastically. In view of this, any past failures and successes can assist the teacher immeasurably in future achievement test construction. Furthermore, a careful inspection of pupil responses to individual test items or groups of items has diagnostic value. The areas of strength and weakness for each pupil—or the class as a whole—can be identified.

Item Analysis Methods

Re-examining each test item to discover its strengths and flaws is known as *item analysis*. Item analysis usually concentrates on two vital features: level of difficulty and discriminating power. The former means the percentage of pupils who answer correctly each test item; the latter the ability of the test item to differentiate between pupils who have done well and those who have done poorly.

Essay or objective items from open- or closed-book tests can be subjected to item analysis. However, it is most useful to us when the items are a part of a power test. In other words, the purpose of the test is to measure the level of performance of each pupil; the scores are to be used as a basis for ranking pupil achievement. The purpose of a mastery test, on the other hand, is to separate the pupils into two groups, those who have achieved at least as high as a certain level and those who have not. Consequently, the level of difficulty and discriminating power of the items are much less important in a mastery test than in a power test. The remainder of this chapter is devoted to the analysis of power test items.

Methods of item analysis are essentially mathematical and can take many forms. Various statistical techniques are used, many of them requiring a considerable amount of computing. In addition, the relative merits of these methods are not clearly established. Testing specialists do not always agree as to which method should be used even though they produce results that seem to be more similar than dissimilar.

The methods described in the following sections are, in contrast to many, relatively simple. They are quite satisfactory for classroom teachers. Since teachers do not have the time, facilities, or number of cases often demanded by the more elaborate methods, such methods are of little practical value although widely used in the construction of standardized achievement tests.

Item Difficulty

It is easy to determine a test item's level of difficulty. First a tabulation is made of the number of pupils who successfully answer the item. This figure is then divided by the total number of pupils attempting the item, and the quotient is multiplied by 100. These steps are summarized in the following formula:

$$P = \frac{N_R}{N_T} (100)$$

where

P = percentage of pupils who answer the test item correctly
N_R = number of pupils who answer the test item correctly
N_T = total number of pupils who attempt to answer the test item

Suppose that an item in an informal achievement test is answered correctly by eighteen of the twenty-eight pupils who attempt to answer it. Then the level of difficulty of this test is found as follows:

$$P = \frac{18}{28} (100) = 64$$

In other words, 64 per cent of the pupils who attempted the test item answered it correctly.

The formula shown does not alert the teacher to two questions that are often raised about the determination of item difficulty. In the first place, is the number of pupils who attempt to answer the item the same as the total number who are administered the test? If the time limits are too restrictive, it is conceivable that some pupils did not have an opportunity to answer test items appearing near the end. Hence, the number of pupils who attempt to answer the test item is not the same as the number to whom the test was administered. Secondly, is the number of pupils who know the correct answer the same as the number who answer it correctly? In the case of objective test items, successful guessing may cause the two numbers to be different and thus, to some degree, destroy the value of the computation of item difficulty.

The first question is seldom a problem to the classroom teacher. Sufficient time is allowed for the administration of the test so that each pupil attempts each item. Therefore the denominator of the formula is the same for each test item. However, if it happens that some pupils do not attempt a test item, then the denominator is correspondingly reduced in size. Of course it is sometimes difficult to determine whether a pupil has attempted to answer an item. Failure to record an answer does not necessarily mean that the pupil did not try to answer. The rule usually followed is that the pupil is considered to have attempted to answer a test item if he records an answer either to this or any subsequent item. As you can see, the assumption underlying this rule is that the pupil works systematically through the test, mentally trying to answer all items up to and including the last one for which an answer is recorded (Conrad, 1948).

The second question is the source of widespread debate among measurement specialists. Simply stated, it is: Should a correction for guessing be made when the levels of difficulty of test items are being computed? Obviously the question concerns itself with objective test items of the selection type. Successful guessing of the answer to one of these test items will cause the number of pupils who answer it correctly to exceed the number who actually know the correct answer. Adjusting the former number with correction-for-guessing formulas appreciably improves the situation in the opinion of some measurement specialists. Others are disturbed by the fact that the conventional formulas may either overcorrect or undercorrect for successful guessing, and believe that such an adjustment creates about as many problems as it solves.

The arguments for and against correcting for guessing are concisely summarized by Davis (1951, pp. 268–281). He concludes that correcting for guessing is desirable in the case of intensive efforts to build objective achievement tests, and he shows formulas for computing item difficulty that incorporate this correction. On the other hand, it is more difficult to justify the use of these formulas when a classroom test is being analyzed. In the first place, the added computational burden, though not serious, can be troublesome. Also, the assumptions underlying the formula are not fully satisfied, and the pupils' reaction to the warning that a correction for guessing is to be made are so varied that extraneous personality factors influence the achievement test scores. Finally, the teacher ordinarily does not need a very accurate measure of item difficulty. Rough approximations are usually sufficient.

For these reasons, the formula for determining item difficulty contains no provision for correcting for successful guessing. The factor N_R is labeled as the number of pupils who answer the test item correctly. To the degree that successful guessing has occurred, the value of P yielded by the formula will be wrong.

Item Discriminating Power

The discriminating power of a test item is its ability to differentiate between pupils who have achieved well (the upper group) and those who have achieved poorly (the lower group). To determine the discriminating power of a test item we must first specify the characteristics of the upper and lower groups. Here we have considerable latitude. We may wish to use an independent criterion to classify the pupils. Such a criterion might be the score from a standardized test thought to measure the same aspects of achievement as the classroom test containing the item in question. Or we may wish to use final marks in the same or similar achievement areas, these having been determined without knowledge of the scores yielded by the classroom test. Ont the other hand, an internal criterion may be used, such as the total scores from the classroom achievement test, the items of which are being studied.

In most cases, the internal criterion is used. This is done not only because independent criteria are customarily unavailable, but also because they are not totally appropriate measures of the aspects of achievement involved in the classroom test. These achievement tests are, in a sense, "self-defining," that is, the test itself defines what it is to measure. Therefore, the independent criteria such as the two mentioned are automatically inappropriate to some, perhaps to a large degree. Incidentally, the use of the total test scores as the criterion for classifying pupils into upper and lower groups, followed by the use of these groups to determine an index reflecting the discriminating power of individual test items, is known as the *internal-consistency* method of computing indices of item discriminating power.

Selection of a criterion for determining the upper and lower groups must be followed by an arbitrary definition of their limits. For instance, if the total test score is used, a decision must be made as to which part of the distribution of scores is the upper group and which part is the lower group. Some choose the upper and lower halves, others the upper and lower thirds with the middle third discarded, and still others the upper and lower 27 per cent with the middle 46 per cent discarded. The last has received a great deal of support by testing specialists, and a number of tables designed to assist item analysis are based upon this division. However, for the classroom teacher analyzing his informal test, the upper and lower thirds is probably a suitable compromise. Fewer cases are lost than when the upper-lower 27 per cent method is used, and a more distinctive separation between the groups is provided than in the case of the upper-lower halves method.

The rationale behind the scheme for computing an index of item discriminating power is quite simple. A test item with maximum discriminating power would be one which every pupil in the upper group would answer correctly and every pupil in the lower would answer incorrectly; in short, it can discriminate between every pupil in the upper group and every pupil in the lower group. Thus, this test item produces a maximum number of correct discriminations. Of course, we cannot expect items to discriminate perfectly. The typical test item will yield some correct discriminations—part of the upper group will respond correctly and part of the lower group incorrectly—and will yield some incorrect discriminations in that the remainder of the upper group will respond incorrectly and the remainder of the lower group correctly.

The discriminating power of a test item is the difference between the number of correct and incorrect discriminations expressed as a percentage of the maximum possible correct discriminations. Several reports based on this idea have appeared (Johnson, 1951; Ebel, 1954; Findley, 1956). In simplified form, the formula to compute an index of discriminating power based on this idea is the following:

$$D = \frac{U - L}{N}$$

where

D = index of item discriminating power
U = number of pupils in upper group who answer the test item *correctly*
L = number of pupils in the lower group who answer the test item *correctly*
N = number of pupils in each of the two groups

To use this formula conventionally, it is first necessary to find the total raw scores on the test for all pupils. Then the test papers are ranked according to the raw scores, and the top and bottom thirds of the raw-score distribution are found; the middle third is ignored. For each test item, the number of pupils in the upper and lower groups who respond correctly are tabulated. Appropriate substitutions are then made in the formula. For instance, suppose that ten of twelve pupils in the upper third of the raw-score distribution answer an item correctly, and five of twelve in the lower third answer it correctly. The index of discriminating power for this test item is

$$D = \frac{10 - 5}{12} = +0.42$$

It is evident that the maximum size of the index is +1.00 and the minimum size is −1.00. In the first case, maximum discrimination occurs in the desired direction; in the second, in the opposite direction. Any negative value means that the test item discriminates—to some degree—in the wrong direction. Hence, the discriminating power of the test item is unsatisfactory. Positive values show that the test item discriminates in the desired direction, even though it may not be completely satisfactory. The larger the positive value the better. Although it is difficult to establish a suitable minimum positive value below which the discriminating power of a test item is considered faulty, certainly values less than +0.20 indicate that the discriminating power of the test item is questionable.

Difficulty Levels Near Fifty Percent

It has long been known that the discriminating power of an item is influenced by its difficulty. The manner in which it influences discriminating power depends upon the relative intercorrelation of the items, that is, the degree to which each test item is correlated with every other. In the case of tests containing items that have low intercorrelations, those composed of items with levels of difficulty near 50 per cent will display more discriminating power than those composed of items with widely varying levels of difficulty. In the case of tests containing items with high intercorrelations, the reverse is true. The reasons are beyond the scope of this book but can be found in any of several standard references pertaining to psychometrics (Guilford, 1954).

Since achievement tests rarely are composed of highly intercorrelated items, the recommendation is frequently made that they include only those test items with mid-range levels of difficulty, between 40 and 70 per cent (Ebel, 1954). This recommendation often disturbs teachers who feel that a wide distribution of levels of item difficulty is necessary to test very good and very poor pupils properly. In reality, the use of test items with mid-range levels does not mean that the very good pupil will automatically receive a raw score of maximum size or that the very poor pupil will receive a zero. To separate the very good, the good, the average, the poor, and the very poor pupils from each other, an achievement test with superior discriminating power is needed. To obtain this, it is necessary, strange as it may seem, to avoid the use of test items with widely varying levels of difficulty.

PROBLEMS

1 Using data obtained from an objective test which you have either administered or taken yourself, determine *P*-values and *D*-values for all test items. Interpret the results of your computations.
2 The statement has been made that homogeneous grouping of pupils often reduces the likelihood of sharp discriminations by test items, and also the need for such discriminations (Katz, 1961, p. 269). Describe situations for which this statement is true.
3 Study the nontechnical discussion by Wood (1960, pp. 82–83) of the principle that, for a single test item, the maximum number of discriminations that the item can provide is related to the 50 per cent level of difficulty. Restate her remarks in your own words.
4 Compare the discussion of the 50 per cent level of difficulty by Wood (1960, pp. 82–83) with that by Katz (1961, pp. 268–269) in which the latter supports, under certain conditions, a less demanding level of difficulty for multiple-choice test items as the number of options in the test item decreases.

USING ITEM ANALYSIS RESULTS

The results of item analysis can serve two major purposes. The first and more obvious one is that they provide important information concerning the problems encountered when classroom achievement tests are built. On the basis of such information the teacher can gain a much better view of the worth of the test he built and used; he can also profit by his mistakes in that he should be able to construct noticeably better tests in the future. The second use can be summarized in a single word: diagnosis. By examining the data from item analysis, the teacher can detect learning difficulties of individual pupils or the class as a whole, and, in consequence, can plan more suitable remedial programs. Studying the strengths and weaknesses of pupil achievement will also help him to evaluate more accurately the effectiveness of various parts of the learning situation (see Chapter 15).

Improving Classroom Achievement Tests

As he administers each achievement test, the classroom teacher is usually plagued by countless questions. Will the distracters of one item be attractive? Is another item so worded that the superior achievers may misunderstand its intent and respond incorrectly, yet, paradoxically, the poor achievers will not be misled and will tend to respond correctly? Is another item too difficult? Does the order of the test items reflect an increasing level of difficulty? The answers to questions such as these can cause a teacher to view the test results with confidence or doubt.

LEVELS OF ITEM DIFFICULTY. As a first step in the process of answering questions such as the foregoing, item difficulties can be computed. A quick scanning of these data reveals all items to which 100 and 0 per cent respond correctly. Since the purpose of a power test is to yield scores that will differentiate among the pupils, neither type of item is suitable. They contribute nothing in terms of differentiation and can be considered unnecessary "padding." On the other hand, a possible use of one or two test items to which 100 per cent responded correctly would be to place them at the beginning, thereby letting them serve as a gentle introduction to the remainder of the test.

Items of extremely high or low levels of difficulty can also be identified. Since any test items with levels of difficulty that are not in the general vicinity of 50 per cent (that is, between 40 and 70 per cent) tend to reduce the discriminating power of the test, these can be viewed with suspicion. Their indices of discriminating power should be checked. In all likelihood, the test items are also weak in this respect.

Further inspection of the item difficulties will reveal how closely the arrangement of the test items corresponds to an order of ascending level of difficulty. Also, the failure of certain test items to approximate the anticipated level of difficulty may be information of great value to the teacher. Is the item poorly designed? Is the effectiveness of the learning experiences far different than expected? If so, why? Is the level of difficulty of this test item affected by the presence of other items in the test? If so, which items? These and other avenues of explanation can be explored.

INDICES OF DISCRIMINATING POWER. The second step that can partly answer some of the questions posed by the teacher is to compute and interpret indices of discriminating power. Any D-values above +0.40 can be considered very good, any between +0.40 and +0.20 satisfactory, and any between +0.20 and zero poor. It is clear that negative values identify items that differentiate among pupils in the wrong way. Ebel (1954) suggests that, in a well-built, classroom achievement test composed of objective test items, more than 50 per cent of the test items should have D-values exceeding +0.40, less than 40 per cent should have values between +0.40 and +0.20, less than 10 per cent should have values between +0.20 and zero, and none should have negative values. Obviously, these are only guides and can be changed at the discretion of the teacher.

Examining All Responses to an Item.   An even closer inspection of the effectiveness of test items can be obtained by tabulating and comparing all of the responses of the pupils in the upper and lower groups. For example, in the case of a multiple-choice test item, the responses to each of the distracters—as well as the correct response—are counted. Incidentally, this tabulation can be made quickly and accurately by a test scoring machine or a computer if the proper answer sheets have been used (Michael, 1965).

To demonstrate the kinds of information that can be obtained by scrutinizing all responses, several multiple-choice items can be used. For instance, the following item was included in an achievement test administered to thirty-six pupils completing a percentage unit in arithmetic.

> Mr. Miller purchased a dress shirt from a department store. The retail cost was $4.40, and the sales tax 5%. What was the total cost of the shirt which Mr. Miller must pay?
> (1) $0.22
> (2) $4.18
> (3) $4.40
> (4) $4.62

The responses to all options by the pupils in the upper and lower thirds are shown below. Option 4 is the correct response.

Option	Upper third	Lower third
1	0	0
2	3	6
3	0	1
4	9	5
(Omits)	0	0
Total	12	12

Although the item is discriminating fairly well ($D = +0.33$) the attractiveness of the distracters is extremely unbalanced. The first option is chosen by no one, whereas the third is selected by only one pupil. Clearly these distracters are not sufficiently attractive. If this or a similar item were to be used again, perhaps changing the first to $4.45, that is, $4.40 + 0.05, and the third to $4.42, that is, $4.40 + 0.02, would improve the situation. No doubt these changes would make the item more difficult; they would also provide a better basis for determining whether the pupils are committing some of the more common mistakes in percentage computations.

Some teachers will estimate the level of difficulty of the test item by using the data from the upper and lower groups. Since fourteen pupils out of twenty-four marked the item correctly, P is estimated to be 58 per cent. Such estimates are usually fairly accurate for our purposes. The middle third often divides itself between correct and incorrect answers much as the other two-thirds combined.

Although the first and third options of the arithmetic test item are criticized because they attracted practically no response, it cannot be said that the ability of a distracter to attract responses is necessarily a sign that a distracter is performing effectively. It must do more than this. A good distracter should have a differential attractiveness, that is, it should be more attractive to the lower group than the upper group. In this way it contributes to the discriminating power of the test item.

This point is illustrated by the following item from a general science test. The correct response is the first option.

Which of the following diseases may be readily contracted from water that is polluted with sewage?
  (1)   typhoid fever
  (2)   rickets
  (3)   rheumatism
  (4)   heart disease

The responses of the upper and lower groups are:

Option	Upper third	Lower third	Difference $(U - L)$
1	9	4	+5
2	3	2	+1
3	1	4	−3
4	1	4	−3
(Omits)	0	0	
Total	14	14	

Observe that the discriminating power of the test item (+0.36) and its level of difficulty (46 per cent estimated) are satisfactory.

The relative power of each distracter is shown in the far right-hand column. Notice that the second option is as attractive as the other two distracters but is not distractive. Any properly functioning distracter will yield a relatively large negative value in this column. Therefore, if changes are to be made and the item re-used in a modified form, the second option should be replaced.

A third illustration of some of the kinds of information produced by a close scrutiny of pupil responses to test items is one administered to an English class concerning library skills.

If you wish to find quickly the page on which a particular topic or subject appears in a reference book, to which of the following would you refer?
(1) the appendix
(2) the subject index
(3) the table of contents
(4) the bibliography

The responses of the pupils in the upper and lower groups are as follows:

Option	Upper third	Lower third
1	0	1
2	13	11
3	1	2
4	0	0
(Omits)	0	0
Total	14	14

This test item is too easy, the estimate of P being 86 per cent. Moreover, its discriminating power is poor, D being $+0.14$.

Quite possibly, the weakness in the test item is due to the inclusion of the word "subject" in the second option. This may be a clue to the correct response so obvious that the pupils quickly notice it and choose their answer accordingly. The uninformed pupil will profit more by such a clue than the informed pupil who didn't need one in the first place. If this word were deleted, it is conceivable that the differential attractiveness of the distracters would increase, thereby improving the level of difficulty of the item and its discriminating power.

A final illustration is a test item with a satisfactory level of difficulty but negative discriminating power. It appeared in an elementary school social studies test. The first option is the correct response.

The capital of Switzerland is
(1) Bern
(2) Zurich
(3) Lucerne
(4) Geneva

The responses of the pupils in the upper and lower groups are as follows:

Option	Upper third	Lower third
1	5	6
2	2	3
3	1	1
4	5	3
(Omits)	0	0
Total	13	13

The estimated level of difficulty is 42 per cent and the index of discriminating power is −0.08.

We can only speculate as to why more pupils in the lower group than in the upper responded correctly and so many of the pupils in the upper group selected the fourth option. Possibly their familiarity with the League of Nations and the many important international conferences that were held in Geneva caused the pupils in the upper group to think of Geneva as the most important city in Switzerland and thus the capital of the country. The pupils in the lower group, on the other hand, may not have known this about Geneva and therefore were not misled by it. Having no preconceived ideas about the importance of these four cities, almost half of them learned that Bern is the capital and responded accordingly. Perhaps the relative importance of the cities of Switzerland and their relationship to each other and the world are not well taught. Certainly these data indicate that further clarification of the status of Bern is needed.

The four previous illustrations make it clear that a rich fund of information concerning his test is available to the teacher who takes the trouble to examine all responses to the test items. Although only multiple-choice items are shown, similar information can be obtained from other types of objective test items and even essay test items of the restricted response type. At the very least, this information should give the teacher a much more realistic view of the value of his test. Ideally, it should also warn him of some of the pitfalls encountered in achievement test construction and suggest means of overcoming or circumventing these. With item analysis information, the teacher should be able either to improve older test items if he wishes or build better new ones. Without it we can fully expect that, with rare exceptions, the flaws present in a classroom test will be found in succeeding tests constructed by the same teacher.

Diagnosing Inadequacies in Achievement

As informative as a pupil's total raw score can be in many respects, it does not provide very much information about the sources of his successes and failures. In other words, the raw score of a pupil or the arithmetic mean of the raw scores of a class may be interpreted to mean that one or more pupils are having trouble, but such scores will not tell what the trouble is or where it is located. To locate the nature of the trouble, an item-by-item inspection of the test is necessary.

The first step in diagnosing inadequacies in achievement is to build a chart showing the item-by-item performance by each pupil. A section of such a chart based upon an objective achievement test is shown in Table 3. The plus signs indicate correct responses, the negative signs incorrect responses, and the zeros omitted responses. Incidentally, some teachers have their pupils participate in the construction of such a chart as this.

The totals listed at the bottom of the table reveal the number of pupils who responded correctly and incorrectly to each test item. The totals pinpoint the areas of difficulty for the pupils as a class. Notice that, of the first ten test items, seven pupils found items 2, 3, 4, 6, and 8 to be relatively easy, whereas they found 1, 5, and 10 to be moderately difficult, and 7 and 9 quite difficult. Now the strengths and weaknesses in the achievement of the pupils can be quickly found by examining the areas of achievement involved in the test items identified and noting the cells of the table of specifications on which they are based. Discussing this information with members of the class immediately following the administration of the test can be most enlightening to them.

Very likely the teacher will wish to study the test items that cause difficulty before those that do not. After satisfying himself that there is nothing technically wrong with such a test item and its scoring, he can pose questions as to the reasons why it is difficult: Is little emphasis placed on the point of the test item during the period of instruction? If so, is this lack of emphasis deliberate or accidental? Is there widespread misunderstanding among the pupils in spite of the fact that careful instruction is given? If so, what is the nature of the misunderstanding? Should the learning experiences related to the areas of difficulty be changed in any way? Do the pupils omit the test item frequently? If so, is this because the test might be too long?

There is profit as well in examining test items that the class found to be easy. Again, after a search for technical imperfections fails to reveal any defects, the teacher can raise questions about why the test items are relatively easy: Are the items found to be easy those that primarily measure recall of information rather than understandings? If so, does this indicate that undue emphasis is being placed on the objectives related to knowledges with a corresponding de-emphasis on those involving understandings? Can the idea behind one or more of the relatively easy test items be traced to a particular learning experience? If so, is there some feature of that learning experience such as a visual aid or supplementary instructional

TABLE 3

SAMPLE CHART FOR ANALYZING PUPIL RESPONSES
TO EACH ITEM IN AN ACHIEVEMENT TEST

Name of Pupil	Test Item Number										Total score
	1	2	3	4	5	6	7	8	9	10...60	
1. Steve	$+^a$	$-^b$	+	+	+	−	−	+	−	+	+	39
2. Mary	−	+	+	−	+	−	+	−	−	+	0^c	21
3. Dick	−	+	+	+	−	+	−	−	+	−	−	18
4. Carol	+	−	−	+	+	+	+	+	−	−	−	37
5. Becky	+	+	+	−	−	+	−	+	−	+	+	41
6. June	+	+	+	+	−	+	+	+	+	−	+	55
7. Sheri	−	+	−	+	+	+	−	+	0	+	−	44
Total No. correct	4	5	5	5	4	5	3	5	2	4... 3	
Total No. wrong	3	2	2	2	3	2	4	2	4	3... 3	
Omissions	0	0	0	0	0	0	0	·0	1	0... 1	

a Correct response
b Incorrect response
c Omitted response

material that is responsible for the pupils' successes and should be re-used with subsequent classes? Is extreme success with a test item caused by unwarranted hints given before or during the administration of the test? If so, should the test be rescored with this item omitted?

After these questions have been answered to his satisfaction, the teacher can turn to the responses of each individual pupil. Just as he attempted to analyze the areas of strength and weakness for the class as a whole, he can now do the same for each pupil. Following a thorough examination of the item-by-item performance of the pupil, other records of his achievement can be consulted, observations of his study habits made, and, in many instances, a teacher-pupil conference held. In this manner, many additional pieces of information come to light as to why the pupil is successful or unsuccessful, details which can be used along with the initial information concerning what the areas are, as a basis for building a remedial program. Such a program is individually tailored to the needs of the pupil. If it succeeds, it will not only correct his past inadequacies but also provide him with the means of preventing a number of future difficulties.

SAMPLING PROBLEM. Analyzing the item-by-item performance of each pupil has one serious weakness that must be recognized. This is the problem of adequate sampling—the same problem we encounter with other aspects of educational measurement. According to the procedures outlined in the foregoing paragraphs, the teacher may regularly make decisions concerning the pupil's achievement on the basis of his response to one or perhaps several test items. Frequently these are very small samples of the achievement areas in question; and, consequently, the probability that they do not present an accurate picture of the pupil's accomplishments is uncomfortably large. This means that the information gleaned from the item-by-item analysis must be considered suggestive rather than definitive.

The sampling problem can be corrected in part without destroying all of the diagnostic features of the analysis by modifying Table 3 slightly. Instead of listing the test items individually across the top of the table, we can organize them into meaningful groups and list them in place of the individual items. For instance, in an arithmetic test the test items may be grouped in four categories: those requiring addition, subtraction, multiplication, and division. The number of correct and incorrect responses to each group of items by each pupil can be tabulated.

A recommended scheme for organizing the test items into groups is to use the table of specifications. Items representing the same or similar cells may be combined into one group. The number of groups used, as well as their size, are determined by the teacher and, of course, can vary widely. However, to make the grouping process effective, the two extremes should be avoided. If only two groups are used, little information is gained that cannot be obtained from inspection of the total test scores. If the number of groups is only slightly less than the number of test items, the process will not sufficiently relieve the sampling problem to justify the work it entails.

PROBLEMS

5 Study the steps described by Katz (1961, pp. 266–268) with which the teacher prepares a homemade answer sheet for objective achievement tests having selection test items, which will reduce the effort required to complete an item analysis of the test. Demonstrate this procedure with an achievement test to be used in a class which you are now teaching or attending. Evaluate the demonstration.

6 Study the steps described by Diederich (1964, pp. 2–8) with which the pupils to whom an achievement test was administered, perform most of the

work involved in the item analysis by raising their hands in response to instructions from the teacher. Demonstrate this procedure with a class which you are now teaching or attending. Evaluate the demonstration.

7 Compare the Katz item analysis procedure and that proposed by Diederich in terms of their feasibility and accuracy.

8 When large groups of pupils are available, Wood proposes that the discriminating power of a test item be determined by finding a tetrachoric correlation coefficient (1960, pp. 84–86). Using the chart she provides, find and interpret the tetrachoric correlation coefficient for each of the following three test items.

Test item	Percentage of upper half passing the item	Percentage of lower half passing the item
a.	60	30
b.	55	40
c.	47	55

Limitations of Item Analysis

As useful as item analysis data are for evaluating an achievement test and diagnosing weaknesses, there are several serious limitations when the techniques described are applied. In the first place, the internal-consistency method so commonly used when computing indices of discriminating power presents some problems. This method is suitable for tests containing items that measure somewhat the same mental functions; achievement tests generally contain test items that are relatively heterogeneous in this respect. Second, the classroom teacher frequently must base his item analysis on a small number of pupils. This means that judgments are made on limited evidence. Third, analysis of responses to essay test items is less informative than that of responses to objective test items such as multiple-choice items. This lessens the utility of the techniques for the teacher using essay test items. Finally, item analysis results are more relative than some teachers realize. The level of difficulty and discriminating power of a test item are influenced by the test in which the item appears, the conditions in which the test is administered, and the quality of the pupils.

Use of Internal-Consistency Methods

The internal-consistency method for computing indices of item discriminating power is appropriate when the pupil traits measured by the total test scores are homogeneous for all practical purposes. Successful items in a test of this kind are those that are closely related to each other and, of course, that tend to measure whatever the total test scores measure. These items will display satisfactory discriminating power in terms of indices based on the internal-consistency method. As any test items with low discriminating power are eliminated or changed so that their discriminating power increases, the resulting test will become more and more homogeneous. In other words, it is becoming more and more internally consistent; all test items are reflecting the same unitary pupil trait.

The total scores of achievement tests typically represent hctcrogeneous rather than homogeneous aspects of the pupils. They contain test items that measure several different kinds of behavior (knowledges and understandings) in unequal amounts. The total score is actually a composite representation of these behaviors. The biggest part contributes greatly to the size of the total test score and will, in a sense, dominate the results of the discriminating power determinations. In other words, if one pupil trait stands out in the total test scores, well constructed items which reflect it will have satisfactory indices of discriminating power. On the other hand, test items reflecting less important and somewhat unrelated traits, even though they are well constructed in many technical respects, will tend to have low indices of discriminating power.

This problem can be easily illustrated. Suppose that an achievement test contains forty-five recall-of-information items that are fairly homogeneous and five application-of-principles items that are noticeably unlike the first group. The total score is found by counting the number of correct responses, regardless of which type of test item is being scored. All other factors being equal, we would expect that the items in the larger group would have markedly higher indices of discriminating power than those in the smaller group, if the internal-consistency method of computation is used. The pupil's ability to recall certain kinds of information is the dominant trait reflected in the total test scores. Items such as those in the smaller group that do not contribute appreciably to the measurement of this trait likewise do not improve the internal consistency of the test. Therefore, they typically have low indices of discriminating power.

EFFECT ON CONTENT VALIDITY. The true significance of the foregoing statements comes into focus when the problem of content validity is considered. Certainly maintaining high content validity in each achievement test is the primary goal of each teacher who designs and builds it. Yet indices of discriminating power may actually encourage the teacher to reduce the degree of content validity of future tests. This would occur if, in the illustration of the 50-item achievement test, the teacher wishes someday to use it again and either eliminates the items with low indices of discriminating power or modifies them in the hope that the indices will improve. In both cases, large or potentially large changes in content validity could take place. Obviously more is lost than gained.

Indices of discriminating power based on the internal-consistency method must be interpreted with some caution. We are continually faced with the prospect that a test item may have a low index of discriminating power not because it is faulty but because it measures a trait making a secondary contribution to the total test score. Of course the problem is largely corrected if it is possible to break down an achievement test in homogeneous subtests with reliable scores and use each as the internal criterion for computing indices of discriminating power for items within that subtest. Although this is regularly done with standardized achievement tests, such is not the case with classroom achievement tests because it is often impracticable.

Inadequate Numbers of Pupils

One measurement specialist believes that the minimum number of cases to be used in item analysis is 500 (Conrad, 1948, p. 38). This is more than ten times the number of pupils usually available to classroom teachers who are analyzing classroom achievement test results. This difference shows how extremely small are the samples with which teachers are working in their item analysis determinations.

Re-examine for a moment the distributions of the responses made by pupils in the upper and lower groups to the four test items shown earlier in this chapter. Note how a shift of one response from one option to another can change your opinion of the power of a distracter, or how it might even change the P- or D-value noticeably. Remembering that some of the reasons why a pupil selects one option rather than any of the other three can be vague and obscure, you can imagine how easily a shift in choice could have taken place. All of this means that the profile of pupil responses to an item must be considered tentative as long as the number of pupils is so small.

The teacher's alternatives are simple. Either he bases his item analysis on an inadequate number of pupils or he must continue to build and interpret his achievement tests without item analysis data. His choice is obvious. Tentative item analysis information followed by tentative judgments based upon it is clearly better than no information at all. Although the fact that only a few cases are available weakens the value of item analysis data, it does not totally destroy it.

Analyzing Responses to Essay Test Items

Item analysis techniques can be applied to the responses to essay test items as well as to objective test items; however, it is definitely more difficult, and the results are sometimes considered less meaningful. The difficulty is traced to the problems of reliable scoring of essay responses and tabulating the incorrect responses. Both of these activities are time consuming. The relative lack of meaning of the data is attributed to the fact that the various subparts of the correct response to an essay test item are frequently related to each other. The level of difficulty of one subpart may affect the level of difficulty of another; the correctness or incorrectness of a pupil's response to one part of an essay test item may affect the correctness or incorrectness of his response to a subsequent part. These are the principal reasons why responses to essay test items are analyzed much less frequently than objective test items.

The analysis of responses to essay test items is most successful if they are of the restricted response type and are scored by the analytical method. If at all possible, each subpart should be separately considered. In effect, this is equivalent to considering each an independent test item with its own level of difficulty and discriminating power. When some or all subparts cannot be logically separated, they should be combined as necessary and the composites treated as separate test items. An analysis based on the internal-consistency method can be used here as it is with responses to objective test items.

Relative Nature of Item Analysis Data

We would like to believe that data from item analysis are completely accurate and meaningful. Clearly this is not justified, both because of the limitations introduced by the use of an internal criterion and a small sample of pupils, but also because of the special circumstances surrounding every test item as it is administered.

Some of those special circumstances relate to the pupils as they respond to the item—their alertness, motivation, and emotional tone. Some relate to the environment in which the test is given—the time of day, the amount of extraneous noise, the temperature of the room, and the ventilation. Some relate to the test containing the item in question—its length, the levels of difficulty of the other items, and the order in which they are arranged.

It is hard to determine how much these factors influence item analysis data. Generally, the influence is slight. But in a given instance it could be prominent. Regardless of which it is, a qualification must be added to every interpretation of item analysis data. It must be understood that the P-value and D-value are merely representations of the level of difficulty and discriminating power of an item as it appeared in a certain test administered under specified circumstances to one group of pupils. It is clear that if the test or environment is changed, the values can certainly change.

General Considerations

The foregoing sections point out many of the functions of item analysis and the limitations commonly incurred. However, at no point is notice taken of a somewhat strange misconception that is occasionally found concerning the relationship between item construction and analysis. Some teachers believe that a careful analysis of test results somehow makes careful construction of items less important. This is not true. The many suggestions given in Chapters 3, 4, and 5 for improving test items should be followed, regardless of whether techniques for the analysis of items are later used. Item analysis results can be successfully used to improve subsequent measurements of pupil achievement but do not improve the test being analyzed. Even here it operates imperfectly since all flaws in a test item are not necessarily revealed by analysis. Bear in mind, therefore, that item analysis in no way relieves the teacher of the responsibility of building the best achievement test possible.

Persistent attempts to follow the suggestions for improving test items should directly and indirectly help produce test items with encouraging item analysis data. There is no guarantee, however, that this will happen. Very careful construction and even very ingenious revision based on item analysis data may fail to improve the P-value and D-value of a test item satisfactorily. This creates a dilemma: considerations of content validity make it necessary to include the material in the test, yet item analysis suggests that the related items are inferior in some respects. Preference must be given to the content validity. Items based on the material must be included and repeated efforts made to improve their quality. If this fails, then the table of specifications can be changed so that the material can be properly excluded from the test. As a result, the meaning of the total score is changed and evaluation of the pupil achievement in the area omitted must be made by other methods. The areas of achievement omitted can usually be evaluated in terms of the pupils' procedures and products. The techniques used are non-testing procedures such as rating methods, product scales, and check lists. These are discussed and illustrated in the following chapter.

Problems

9 Select a suitable criterion other than the total score on an achievement test and describe how you would use it as a basis for computing an item analysis for that test. To what degree, if any, would this procedure increase the likelihood that a satisfactory level of content validity would be present in the test if it were to be used again after modification on the basis of the item analysis data obtained?

10 It is widely recognized that, for classes of about 30 pupils or less, item analysis data are undependable. Demonstrate the degree to which P-values and D-values will change by systematically altering the response of one pupil in the upper third and one in the lower third of the test item concerning Switzerland (see page 194), and recomputing the two values each time.

Test Item File

The teaching notes maintained by many classroom teachers are voluminous. A syllabus, a variety of outlines, numerous references, several study guides, and a quantity of newspaper clippings and miscellaneous pamphlets are usually a part of this collection. In one way or another, each assists the teacher as he pursues his instructional duties. Some of these are highly prized; they are considered to be proven teaching aids. Although other notes may be of more doubtful value, the practicing teacher would rarely be willing to part with them.

The portion of this mass of teaching notes that often receives the least attention is the evaluation section. Usually it consists of a copy or two of each of the classroom achievement tests administered during the past year or so, and possibly the tables of specifications on which they were based. Nevertheless, more complete materials concerning these techniques could easily simplify the teacher's measurement functions as much as teaching notes simplify his instructional functions. As far as classroom achievement tests are concerned, a highly successful means of organizing much of the pertinent information is a test item file.

Item Data Card

A test item file is nothing more than a series of cards which record a great deal of the information obtained by item analysis procedures. Usually the file contains as many cards as there are test items, although sometimes the length of the item or the nature of the information about it requires several cards. The cards are customarily 5 × 8 in size and are arranged in any order the teacher desires.

The front of a sample item data card is shown in Figure 3. Notice that the multiple-choice test item shown is typed so that ample space is allowed for revision. Interlinear notations can be made if the stem is to be changed; new options can be written to the right of the original ones if desired. Notice also that the item is cross-referenced with the cells of the table of specifications on which it is based. Each cell is identified by the row (the Arabic number) and the column (the English letter) of the table that intersect to form it. Additional useful information is the page or chapter number of a book or other reference directly related to the subject matter of the item. This allows the teacher to check quickly any detail that might be questioned.

The reverse side of the item data card is shown in Figure 4. Space is allowed for summarizing the item analysis data for as many as three

---

No. 143

If both the President and the Vice President of the United States are unable to serve, which of the following officials will act as President?

(1) Secretary of State
(2) Speaker of the House of Representatives
(3) Secretary of Defense
(4) President pro tempore of the Senate

Cells in table of specifications:			Reference(s):
Table No.	Primary	Secondary	Doe and Colofort
2	4B	—	American Government Today, Revised Ed.
			1967, pp. 273–274.

FIGURE 3
FRONT SIDE OF ITEM DATA CARD

Test	Unit 2						Comments:
Class	11th grade						4-22-67—Pupils are confused about the meaning of the expression "unable to serve." Possible this should be changed to "die while in office."
Date	4-22-67						
Item No.	18						
N_T	33						
Type of Adm.	Closed book						
Options	Upper	Lower	Upper	Lower	Upper	Lower	
1	2	4					
2	⑦	②					
3	0	2					
4	2	3					
5	—	—					
Omits	0	0					
P (Est.)	41%						
D	+0.45						

FIGURE 4
REVERSE SIDE OF ITEM DATA CARD

separate administrations of the test item or a revision of it and for any appropriate comments made by teacher or pupils. For each administration the name of the test, the class to which it was administered, its size, the date of administration, the test item number, and the type of administration are noted. Below these, the responses to all options by the upper and lower third of the class, and the *P*- and *D*-value of the test item are recorded.

Clearly, maintaining item data cards is a serious clerical problem. Fortunately it is not insurmountable. Item data cards such as the one shown can be easily prepared with a mimeograph machine or a gelatin duplicating process. Once an ample supply is available and the necessary item analysis tabulation is completed, the item data card can be filled out rather rapidly. Regular attention will prevent a backlog of unrecorded data from accumulating and provide a smooth, permanent, and up-to-date record for every test item used.

Some teachers reduce the clerical load by using less elaborate cards. For instance, the data concerning the name of the test, the class to which it was administered, its size, and the type of administration are omitted. By filing the cards for each test in a separate group, this information need be recorded only once. Others do not fill out cards for all the test items they use. Instead, only very promising test items are filed.

Advantages of a Test Item File

The advantages of maintaining a test item file are obvious if the teacher intends to use his test items again. On the basis of the item analysis information and the comments made, he can revise the item. A quick check of the table of specification will reveal whether the relationship between the item and the table of specifications has changed. Moreover, the fact that the items are on cards facilitates separating and counting them in terms of the cells in the table of specifications. In this way, the content validity of the total test can be measured. Having the items on cards also simplifies the reproduction of the test. Since the test is built by accumulating a pack of cards, the arrangement of the items in the test can be changed by simply rearranging the cards, and the final copy of the test can be typed directly from them.

Much can be said in favor of using test items again. By constantly reworking his test items and adding new ones as needed, the conscientious classroom teacher can develop some excellent achievement tests. In this way, the teacher's investment of time and effort in maintaining a test item file becomes reasonable and profitable. However, he cannot use test items again if there is any chance that pupils in succeeding classes will be familiar with them before the test is given. To prevent this, some teachers withhold the test copies and answer sheets after the test.

Withholding test materials, however, is neither fair to the pupils nor good teaching procedure. The pupil who is aware of his successes and failures can take action to improve his deficiencies and gain a much more realistic view of his achievements. His attitudes toward school work are also affected. It is difficult, to say the least, to provide the pupil with a true and complete record of his achievements if he is not allowed to keep his test materials. Therefore, the teacher must, if at all possible, return them and discuss the results with him.

Re-using test items, therefore, becomes considerably more difficult. Only after a teacher has developed a large pool of test items over a period of years should he use any of them again. Under these conditions it is unlikely that any pupils will have any unfair advantage worth mentioning. After all, the vast majority of the previous test copies have been discarded or lost. On the other hand, even if a pupil had access to all of them, the task of studying them would be more forbidding than preparing for a test in the normal manner. Finally, the test items that are used again are usually revisions of the original items. Even when the revision is minor, it helps prevent a pupil who may have studied the original item and memorized the answer from gaining a tremendous advantage over others.

Maintaining a test item file also offers advantages to teachers who do not intend to use any of them again. Restudying test items used in the past can provide helpful hints for constructing new ones. Old items can serve as valuable guides in the development of new ones. The new item may be totally original yet based on the same idea as one in the file, or it might be such a drastic revision of an older test item that its relationship to it is not easily recognized by the pupils.

In addition, restudying the results of earlier tests can alert the teacher to those cells in the table of specifications that very often are the basis of successful test items and those, if any, that are the basis of unsuccesful test items. If cells of the latter type are found, efforts at item construction can be focused on them. Likely weaknesses of a new test can be detected before it is given.

Limitations of a Test Item File

One of the major limitations of maintaining a test item file has already been mentioned, and that is the great clerical task it creates. Another limitation is that the method of recording the data is not equally applicable to all types of test items. Although the form shown in Figure 3 can be used for many different items, that shown in Figure 4 cannot. It is suitable for the common multiple-choice and true-false test items but must be modified if short-answer or some of the longer matching items are used. The essay test item presents even more problems, since the scoring and analyzing of the responses are so difficult.

Still another possible limitation is that maintaining a test item file will actually have an adverse effect on the teacher's instructional and measurement efforts. The first part of the argument goes this way: if teachers are very familiar with past test items, and if the same or similar test items are used in the future, they may teach toward the test without knowing it. In reality, they may be coaching the pupils; the instruction may slavishly follow the achievement tests instead of the reverse. The second part is that intimate knowledge of the old test items will tend to dull the teacher's creativity when building new test items. In other words, the teacher falls into a testing rut. The new test items strongly resemble old ones, novel types are typically ignored, and, as a result, the classroom achievement tests become stereotyped.

Certainly these adverse effects are possible. It is difficult to believe, however, that the discerning teacher would tolerate any of them for any length of time. The advantages gained by maintaining a test item file far outweigh these limitations.

Problems

11   Design a data card for a restricted response essay test item.

12   Can the data card be used successfully with multiple-response objective test items designed to measure pupil understandings; for example, the item concerning beehives in an apple orchard shown on page 140? Give reasons for your answer.

Summary

Since many tentative decisions are made in the construction of class-room achievement tests, teachers are understandably concerned about the worth of the test. They want to know its strengths and weaknesses so that they can interpret the results more properly. To do so, each test item must be re-examined to discover its strengths and weaknesses. This is known as item analysis.

Item analysis concentrates on two vital features: level of difficulty and discriminating power. The former means the percentage of pupils who answer each test item correctly; this is expressed in terms of P-values. The latter means the ability of the test item to differentiate between pupils who achieve well and those who achieve poorly; this is expressed in terms of D-values. The pupils who achieve well and those who achieve poorly are usually identified by the internal-consistency method. The total scores on the test containing the items to be analyzed serve as the criterion. Those pupils in the upper one-third of the raw-score distribution are said to achieve well; those in the lower one-third are said to achieve poorly.

Results of item analysis can serve two major purposes. In the first place, they provide important information concerning the problem encountered in the construction of achievement tests. On the basis of this information, the teacher can gain a much better idea of the value of the test he has built, and he should also be able to construct noticeably better tests in the future. The second use is diagnosis. By examining the data from item analysis, the teacher can detect learning difficulties of individual pupils or the class as a whole. He can plan more suitable remedial programs. Studying the strengths and weaknesses of his pupils' achievement will also help him evaluate more accurately the effectiveness of various parts of the learning situation.

There are four prominent limitations in the application of item analysis. Firstly, the internal-consistency method is suitable for tests containing items that measure somewhat the same mental functions. Achievements typically are not of this type. Secondly, only a very small sample of pupils is available for the analysis. Thirdly, it is difficult to analyze pupil responses to essay test items. Lastly, item analysis data are relative in that they are influenced by the remainder of the test in which the item appears and the particular conditions in which it is administered.

A convenient means of organizing much of the pertinent information yielded by item analysis is a test item file. This file is a series of 5×8 cards on which are typed the item, information about the test administration, and the item analysis data. Although maintaining a file creates a difficult clerical problem, it can greatly assist the teacher who wishes to use some or all of his original test items in later tests, as well as the teacher who plans to build new test items and, in so doing, wants to capitalize on past experiences.

SUGGESTED READINGS

Anderson, Scarvia B. Can tests teach? *California J. second. Educ.*, 1960, **35**, 50–55.

A strong argument is presented in favor of building tests designed specifically to teach rather than for any other purpose. Time limits, security precautions, item analysis techniques, and other procedures usually followed would be changed. As in the case of the use of teaching machines, pupil responses to the tests would be reinforced.

Cox, R. C. Item selection techniques and evaluation of instructional objectives. *J. educ. Measmt*, 1965, **2**, 181–185.

Empirical evidence is presented indicating that item analysis data may inadvertently cause objective test items related to some educational objectives to be disproportionately eliminated from an achievement test. The first four categories of the cognitive domain taxonomy were used to classify the educational objectives.

Davis, Frederick B. Item selection techniques. In E. F. Lindquist (Ed.), *Educational measurement*. Washington: American Council on Education, 1951. Pp. 266–328.

In this chapter, Davis discusses methods for determining measures of level of difficulty and discriminating power. He also reviews the problem of correcting for guessing and describes procedures for organizing a test item file.

Diederich, Paul B. *Short-cut statistics for teacher-made tests.* (2nd ed.) Educational Testing Service Evaluation and Advisory Service Series, No. 5. Princeton, N.J.: Educational Testing Service, 1964. Pp. 2–8.

All needed instructions are given for completing an item analysis of an achievement test by pupils' "show of hands" in the classroom. It is possible to complete an item analysis of a one-period test in ten to twenty minutes of class time, thereby conserving much teacher time and effort.

Ebel, Robert L. Procedures for the analysis of classroom tests. *Educ. psychol. Measmt*, 1954, **14**, 352–364.

The procedures for analyzing teacher-constructed objective achievement tests at the State University of Iowa are explained in this article. The tests are analyzed for relevance and discriminating power. The work sheets used are shown.

Findley, Warren G. A rationale for evaluation of item discrimination statistics. *Educ. psychol. Measmt*, 1956, **16**, 175–180.

In this article the derivation of the D-formula for measuring discriminating power and the rationale behind it are explained. The effectiveness of D-values as representations of item discriminating power is illustrated by several sets of item analysis data.

Katz, Martin. Improving classroom tests by means of item analysis. *Clearing house*, 1961, **35**, 265–269.

Detailed instructions are given for the teacher who wishes to prepare an item analysis for his achievement tests. The method described is very useful and is based in part on the rationale for the D-formula presented by Findley.

Wood, Dorothy A. *Test construction, development and interpretation of achievement tests*. Columbus, Ohio: Charles E. Merrill, 1960. Chapter 9.

Both the question of item difficulty and discriminating power are discussed. In the former case, attention is given to the issue of a 50% level of difficulty; in the latter the determination of tetrachoric correlation coefficients with a chart is shown. These coefficients serve as measures of discriminating power.

REFERENCES CITED

Conrad, Herbert S. Characteristics and uses of item analysis data. *Psychol. Monogr.*, 1948, **62**, 8.

Davis, Frederick B. Item selection techniques. In E. F. Lindquist (Ed.), *Educational measurement*. Washington: American Council on Education, 1951. Pp. 266–328.

Diederich, Paul B. *Short-cut statistics for teacher-made tests*. (2nd ed.) Educational Testing Service Evaluation and Advisory Service Series, No. 5. Princeton, N.J.: Educational Testing Service, 1964.

Ebel, Robert L. Procedures for the analysis of classroom tests. *Educ. psychol. Measmt*, 1954, **14**, 352–364.

Findley, Warren G. A rationale for evaluation of item discrimination statistics. *Educ. psychol. Measmt*, 1956, **16**, 175–180.

Guilford, J. P. *Psychometric methods*. (2nd ed.) New York: McGraw-Hill, 1954.

Johnson, A. Pemberton. Notes on a suggested index of item validity: the U-L index. *J. educ. Psychol.*, 1951, **42**, 499–504.

Katz, Martin. Improving classroom tests by means of item analysis. *Clearing house*, 1961, **35**, 265–269.

Michael, William B. (Ed.) Electronic computer programs and accounting machine procedures. *Educ. psychol. Measmt*, 1965, **25**, 199–243.

Wood, Dorothy A. *Test construction, development and interpretation of achievement tests*. Columbus, Ohio: Charles E. Merrill, 1960.

7 ✐

Judging Procedures and Products

THE FULL EXTENT OF OUR ACHIEVEMENTS cannot always be predicted on the basis of information about part of them. For instance, an investor may reveal widespread knowledge about the economic laws of supply and demand, the histories of prominent industrial companies, and the characteristics of economic cycles in the United States and the world, but still fail to realize anything more than an occasional modest profit when playing the stock market. An avid football fan can no doubt quote at length the rules of the game, recall accurately outstanding contests of past seasons, and even diagnose a quarterback's offensive strategy and plan effective defenses to contain it, yet be unable to play the game himself on a par with his twelve-year-old son. The music critic may command extensive knowledge of the musical score, the instruments played, and perhaps the life of the composer, but not be able to play a single note. Likewise, the mechanical engineer may be completely familiar with the principles of an internal combustion engine, the transmission and the suspension system of a modern automobile, yet not be able to drive or repair it with ease.

There are obvious parallels in formal education. A pupil studying general science may be able to cite accurately the laws upon which an experiment is based and even draw schematically the apparatus needed to conduct the experiment, yet experience great difficulty when trying to set up the apparatus and reproduce the results of the original experiment. In the language arts, a pupil may quote the rules of English grammar without hesitation, spell a great variety of words, and command a large vocabulary, but be unable to write an acceptable original theme. Pupils in vocational education courses may know many facts and principles of woodworking, cooking, or animal nutrition, yet fail in their attempts to build a set of wooden shelves, prepare baked custard, or conduct a profitable hog-feeding enterprise.

It is clear that attempts to predict the quality of a performance involving physical activity on the basis of verbal and mathematical knowledge are often unsuccessful, not only in everyday experiences but also in the classroom. If we wish to gain information concerning the pupil's ability to perform, we must do so by direct inspection of the quality of that performance. This means that the pupil must be given an opportunity to perform under suitable conditions.

The evaluation of pupil performance has all too often been accorded a secondary place in the pupil evaluation program. A quick study of educational objectives reveals, however, that such an attitude is unjustified. Sprinkled liberally throughout the listings of educational objectives for both elementary and secondary school, are objectives directed toward the development of motor skills, the ability to create products of approved quality, perform services efficiently, and so forth. These are a part of the psychomotor domain.

Note that some of the objectives of physical and biological science require that the pupil be able to manipulate apparatus and create products such as drawings of specimens, logs and diaries, precipitates, and operational mock-ups. In physical education, driver education, art, and music, many of the most important objectives are not verbal or mathematical in nature. The vocational programs, such as business, agriculture, industrial arts, and home economics, also are dominated by educational objectives that stress pupil performance. Finally, in the language arts, handwriting skill and speaking ability are integral parts of the program.

The importance of these objectives cannot be overestimated. Quite regularly, pupil success or lack of success in reaching such goals as these shows how much understanding he has acquired. As pointed out in several of the preceding chapters, paper-and-pencil achievement tests, whether informal or standardized, are a useful but somewhat limited means of measuring pupil understandings. They need to be supplemented. Systematic examination of pupil performance is often an excellent means of doing this. Moreover, the behavior to be studied is usually much more complex than that elicited by paper-and-pencil tests. Instead of being restricted to primarily verbal and mathematical aspects, it can involve these in addition to nonlanguage aspects such as motor skills. Such behavior can incorporate originality, creativity, and the ability to organize and coordinate many parts of pupils' past achievements.

No doubt the principal reasons that a relatively small part of the teacher's evaluative effort is directed toward the study of pupil performance are that (1) the techniques tend to be more subjective and less dependable than paper-and-pencil achievement testing, and (2) they are, as suggested in the foregoing paragraph, aimed at more complex aspects of pupil behavior, and hence are difficult to administer, score, and interpret. In spite of these two problems, a number of highly useful instruments have been developed in this area. Some are directed primarily toward the procedure displayed by the pupil, whereas others are directed toward a product yielded by that procedure. Therefore, as a first step in examining these measurement efforts, it is convenient to divide pupil performance into two parts—procedures and products.

Procedures and Products

Procedure and product are clearly interdependent. Yet in terms of their descriptions, are easily distinguished. Procedures are the sequences of movements executed by the pupil; products are the results of these procedures. A good illustration can be found in typing. The procedure learned by the pupil involves assuming a proper posture, placing the fingers on certain keys before beginning, watching the material to be typed rather than the keyboard, and striking only designated keys with each finger, doing so with the proper stroke. The product can be a typed business letter or several paragraphs or pages of prose. Similar illustrations can be found in art, mechanical drawing, handwriting, home economics, agriculture, and industrial arts.

In some educational areas, however, it is difficult to separate the two. Some of the objectives in music, physical education, and speaking are so stated that procedure and product are inextricably intermixed. The procedures could be singing a song, dribbling a basketball, or reciting a poem. The corresponding products are identified in the same manner.

Measurable Characteristics of Procedures

The complex nature of many procedures prevents a teacher from measuring all their subtle aspects. Indeed, he often feels fortunate if he can record sufficient data on just their major features. Since the time available is generally short, and a number of the characteristics of many procedures defy measurement for all practical purposes, the teacher is generally faced with a difficult task.

The characteristics that virtually defy measurement may be extremely important. For example, speaking ability should be evaluated in terms of such attributes as rhythm of talking, variety of word usage, and appropriateness of pitch and tone of voice. Shop procedures should display, among other things, an adaptability by the pupil when unforeseen difficulties arise. Performance in a physical education class should often be characterized by grace, ability, and coordination. Since these are essential features of a pupil's performance, they must be judged. But how? Clearly, the teacher must, on the basis of training and experience, establish standards for such features as these and then, in a subjective manner, classify the performance by comparing it with the standards.

The characteristics of measurable procedures can usually be classified in one of two categories—those related to the efficiency of the procedure and those related to its accuracy. Efficiency suggests a smoothness of action coupled with rapidity and a general economy of effort. Very often key data in this category are the speed of performance, as in a typing exercise, or the identification of the sequence of steps followed, as in the use of a microscope. Accuracy means that few errors are committed; moreover, those committed are relatively unimportant. For example, tabulations can be made of the number of words mispronounced and grammatical errors made during a speech. In a singing or instrumental exercise, a similar count could be made of the instances in which the pupil misjudges the pitch of a note or its duration, or the length of a rest. Clearly it is possible for a given pupil performance to have some of the characteristics in the efficiency category, but none in the accuracy category, and vice versa.

Measurable Characteristics of Products

Since the quality of a product is basically a reflection of the quality of the procedure that yielded it, the tendency of products to be complex is as great as it is for procedures. Again, this factor increases the difficulty of the measurement. On the other hand, the time available is an important difference. Seldom does the teacher feel the extreme pressure of time limitation when examining products, as is often the case with procedures. Moreover, some products can, if necessary, be broken down into their component parts and each part analyzed; many can be subjected to rigorous measurement of various types without such a breakdown—all at a relatively leisurely pace, which simplifies the process.

The study of pupil products is highly subjective. For instance, the teacher must answer questions such as the following: Is the drawing of the biological specimen sufficiently accurate? How "light" must a cake be before it is a good product? Is the wood-working project in question esthetically attractive? What must a typing exercise look like before one can say that it is "professional" work? These and a myriad of similar questions can only be answered by the teacher applying his standards in the same subjective manner as in the case of procedure evaluation.

Measurable characteristics of products are typically numerous. For example, laboratory products from a chemistry course can be measured in terms of their volume or weight; a cake can be measured in terms of its height or volume; a wood-working project can be measured in terms of its length and weight; a typing exercise can be measured in terms of its length and the number of errors. Notice that these characteristics of the products tend to be specific rather than general, and that the measurement of them is often reliable.

Importance of a Natural Situation

Procedures and products are usually studied in a natural situation or one very much like it. This is one of the great strengths of these methods. The elaborate equipment found in the gymnasium, the science laboratories, the industrial and agricultural shops, the art and music studios, the business education rooms, and the home economics kitchens and sewing quarters of the modern school offer not only realistic settings in which to teach but also to evaluate pupil growth. Certainly samples of pupil behavior concerning procedures and products are being observed in a much more natural situation and much more directly when these facilities are used than when paper-and-pencil tests based upon the same specific educational objectives are administered.

The realism of these observation settings is a function of several factors, one of which is the nature and amount of equipment available. For instance, in vocational education or science courses, the equipment may differ greatly from that later used by the pupil when he leaves secondary school for a job or college. Close liaison with business, industry, and colleges plus a flexible budget for purchasing can prevent any serious gap.

Observation Techniques

The instruments used in the observation of procedure and product are primarily of the nontesting type. In other words, they can but do not necessarily yield quantitative information. Instead, they commonly include qualitative information coupled with personal impressions or opinions. Many times they function as recording devices. They provide a convenient means of organizing and summarizing the teacher's observations of pupil performances and his reaction to them.

The most widely used techniques for procedure and product observation are ranking and rating methods, check lists, product scales, and anecdotal records. Of these, teachers often rely on ranking and rating methods more than any of the others.

RANKING. Ranking is one of the lower levels of measurement. All that is attempted is an ordering of the pupils according to the merits of the procedures they displayed or of the products according to their excellence. Under certain circumstances, it can be fairly reliable, that is, consistent. This is usually true when a competent judge is ranking a procedure or product on the basis of only one of its characteristics. Thus, members of a driver training class may be reliably ranked according to their ability to brake properly, or the drawings of a mechanical drawing class in terms of the uniformity of thickness of the straight lines. The more clearly defined the characteristic, the more likely that the ranking will be reliable.

As the basis for the ranking broadens, its reliability tends to drop. Rankings of general merit of a procedure or product in which not one but several characteristics are simultaneously considered, are notoriously unreliable. Certainly the ranking of pupils' general driving ability (including posture, starting, steering, and stopping) and the general quality of their drawings (including lettering, dimensions, accuracy, and neatness) are no doubt less reliable than the rankings of single characteristics described. This drop in reliability can be traced to two causes. First, it is difficult to define clearly the meanings of these many characteristics. Second, the relative importance of each characteristic in terms of its contribution to the composite rank is rarely, if ever, completely established. Thus, it is clear that successful ranking normally must be based on a single well-defined characteristic. Moreover, if possible, the ranking should be repeated by the same (but without knowledge of the results of the first attempt) or other competent observers.

RATING. Rating scales, which take many forms, are popular devices for summarizing procedure and product information. One of the most common is the continuum form. The basic steps followed in its construction and use are as follows. Characteristics of the performance or product are identified, and a continuum representing degrees of merit is established for each characteristic. The continuum may be divided into as few as two positions or as many as ten or more, each position representing a different degree of merit or quality. The various positions along the continuum are often identified by number and a brief description of the corresponding degree of merit. The observer then rates each characteristic of the procedure or product in question by checking the number or description that corresponds most closely to the degree of merit observed. Illustrations of this type of rating scale are included in the following sections.

Rating based upon over-all general merit is as difficult a process as ranking on that basis. The failure to define clearly the characteristics to be included and to establish definitely the relative importance of each destroy much of the worth of this type of rating. Again, successful rating, like successful ranking, usually should be based on a single well-defined characteristic and should be repeated.

CHECK LISTS. Check lists are highly serviceable instruments for recording pupil procedures. Usually they list a series of actions, whether desirable or not, that are a part of a typical pupil's performance. These are arranged in a convenient manner, usually in the order in which you would expect them to occur. For instance, in the case of the check list for softball batting form shown in a following section, the sequence is: (1) grip of the bat, (2) preliminary stance, (3) stride, (4) pivot, and (5) swing.

The type of response for each entry in the check list can vary. Very often, it is simply a check mark indicating that the action listed had occurred. In other cases, a "yes-no" response is required, the "yes" response meaning that the action had been performed in a satisfactory manner, the "no" response meaning the opposite. A third type of response is one in which numbers are placed after the actions. The numbers, starting with "1," indicate the sequence in which the actions occurred. In other words, the completed check list is a step-by-step summary of the procedure followed by a particular pupil.

The development and use of check lists sensitizes the teacher to the subparts of each procedure. In this way, he gains a better view of the totality of the procedure and a more reliable technique for reporting information about it.

PRODUCT SCALES. A product scale is a carefully selected series of products representing various levels of quality. Each product in the scale is usually identified by a number or letter. Generally each scale is composed of five or more products, and an attempt is made to select these so that they are evenly spaced along an "inferior-superior" continuum of quality.

The application of a product scale is quite simple. Each pupil prepares a product of the kind included in the product scale. This is then compared with those of the scale and as close a match as possible is made. The pupil's product is then assigned the letter or number of the one in the scale it most closely resembles. An excellent example of this procedure is found in the case of handwriting, which is described in a following section.

Teachers can build product scales without great difficulty. For instance, pupil products such as drawings involving orthographic projection, sewing samples of hemming, basting, and backstitching, woodworking samples of sawing and nailing, and typing products such as a business letter, can be accumulated over a period of a few years. No doubt their quality will vary widely. Repeated independent attempts to arrange them by quality in equal-appearing intervals will eliminate many products that are near duplicates or about which there is disagreement. The remainder can serve as a product scale.

ANECDOTAL RECORDS.   Anecdotal records are the most informal of the five techniques mentioned here. The teacher does little more than summarize in writing the major actions of a procedure performed by a pupil. A definite attempt is made to produce a factual report. A single such record may mean little; however, a series of related anecdotal records can contribute appreciably to the study of pupil procedures.

Anecdotal records are used most frequently when so little is known about the procedures in question that its characteristics cannot be well defined. Thus, suitable check lists and rating scales cannot be constructed. It is not surprising, therefore, to find anecdotal records used in those cases in the fine arts, physical education, social studies, and home economics in which the teacher is interested in educational objectives concerning esthetic development, health attitudes, interpersonal relationships, and worthy home membership respectively.

PROBLEMS

1   Identify the measurable aspects of each of the following procedures:
    a.   Shooting free throws in basketball.
    b.   Bending a piece of glass tubing to form a right angle.
    c.   Parking an automobile parallel to the curb.
    d.   Hemming a dress.
2   Identify the measurable aspects of each of the following products:
    a.   A map which is an enlargement of a professionally-drawn map.
    b.   A short poem.
    c.   An apron.
    d.   A set of wooden whatnot shelves.
3   Illustrate how observation of performance could be useful when determining an elementary school pupil's skill in mathematical computation and the ease with which he finds social applications of mathematics.
4   Five major types of rating scales cited by Wrightstone (1960, pp. 929–931) are descriptive rating scales, graphic rating scales, product scales, man-to-man rating scales, and numerical rating scales. Study each type and determine its merits as a means of gathering data about pupil achievement.
5   Time samples are defined as the observation of a pupil's behavior for definite, short periods of time and the recording of the occurrence or non-occurrence of specific types of pupil behavior during each. (Wrightstone, 1960, p. 928). How might this technique be used to determine the degree to which pupils have achieved specific social studies objectives in the affective domain?

Observing Procedures

Techniques most often used in observing procedures are ranking procedures, rating scales, check lists, and anecdotal records. Among the many variations of these techniques that have been developed are the following: (1) rating scales for evaluating speaking, (2) a check list for evaluating softball batting form, (3) a check list for recording skill in the use of a microscope, (4) a check list for reporting pupil behavior when engaged in group work, and (5) a sample anecdotal record concerning achievement in elementary school mathematics.

Rating Scales for Speaking

The characteristics of speaking have been defined quite clearly. Among those usually listed are enunciation, pronunciation, loudness, word usage, rhythm, pitch, rate, and posture and movements. The skilled observer can separate one from another without much difficulty and, with appropriate rating scales, can record his judgments of the quality of a pupil's performance.

Typical of the rating scales constructed and used by teachers are the pair shown in Figure 5, the first pertaining to enunciation and the second to pronunciation. Here only a three-point scale is used. If desired, they could be expanded to five points and appropriate descriptions added as required.

The descriptions beneath each number, though brief, are helpful. They add meaning to the numbers; as a result, the rating scales are improved. The space for comments is often an invaluable addition to the scale. Much useful specific information for evaluation as well as in remediation can be added. If desired, a tally of the frequency of a flaw in procedure can be added as in the case of the "agin" for "again" error in Scale B.

When a pupil is to deliver a prepared speech, some teachers prefer rating scales tailored more closely to this activity than a series such as that in Figure 5. For example, scales can be constructed for judging the effectiveness of such elements of the speech as the introduction used by the pupil, the body of the speech, the transition from topic to topic, and the conclusion. Added to these might be scales for judging gestures and movements, eye contact, voice, and so forth.

DIRECTIONS: Below are scales for various characteristics of speaking. Check the position on each scale that represents to the greatest degree the speaking ability of the pupil. Add comments concerning his performance in the space provided.

A.   *Enunciation*

√

1	2	3
Poor	Average	Good
Many words indistinct. Few can be understood without effort.	Some words are indistinct. Mumbles occasionally.	Most words can be clearly understood. Rarely is a word not clear.

Comments: The suffixes "-ing" and "-ness" are indistinct.

B.   *Pronunciation*

√

1	2	3
Poor	Average	Good
Many words are mispronounced. Some words are mispronounced in several different ways.	Some words are mispronounced. Mispronunciations greatly resemble correct pronunciation.	Most words are pronounced correctly. Rarely is a word mispronounced.

Comments: "pitcher" for "picture," "yeller" for "yellow," "agin" for "again" (3)

FIGURE 5
SAMPLE RATING SCALES FOR JUDGING SPEAKING ABILITY

Check List for Batting Form

Check lists and rating scales may not differ as much as descriptions of them would suggest. The "comments" sections frequently included in rating scales allow space in which the observer can note specific features of the pupil's behavior; in a check list the most common of these features would be listed and, hence, checked only when appropriate. On the other hand, some check lists have crude representations of continua much like those found in rating scales.

Date   Rater's initials   Player's name _____

                                   Captain's name   _____

INSTRUCTIONS: Rate the player each time he bats. Place a tally mark in the space which precedes the best description of player's form in each of six categories. Indicate your observation of errors in the right-hand half of the page, again with a tally mark. Write in any additional errors and add comments below.

1. *Grip*   *Errors*
   - _____ good   _____ Hands too far apart
   - _____ fair   _____ Wrong hand on top
   - _____ poor   _____ Hands too far from end of bat

2. *Preliminary stance*
   - _____ good   _____ Stands too near plate
   - _____ fair   _____ Stands too far away
   - _____ poor   _____ Rear foot closer to plate than
   -                                _____   forward foot
   -                                _____ Stands too far forward
   -                                _____ Stands too far backward
   -                                _____ Bat not in readiness position

3. *Stride or footwork*
   - _____ good   _____ Fails to step forward
   - _____ fair   _____ Fails to transfer weight
   - _____ poor   _____ Lifts back foot from ground

4. *Pivot or body twist*
   - _____ good   _____ Fails to twist body
   - _____ fair   _____ Fails to wind up
   - _____ poor   _____ Has less than 90° of pivot

5. *Arm movement or swing*
   - _____ good   _____ Arms held too close to body
   - _____ fair   _____ Rear elbow held too far up
   - _____ poor   _____ Bat not held parallel to ground

6. *General* (Eyes on ball, judgment of pitcher, etc.)
   - _____ good   _____ Jerky action
   - _____ fair   _____ Tries too hard
   - _____ poor   _____ Poor selection of bat
   -                                _____ Lacks confidence

From Scott and French, 1945; reproduced by permission of A. S. Barnes and Company.

FIGURE 6

SAMPLE CHECK LIST FOR SOFTBALL BATTING FORM

An illustration of a check list that resembles in part a series of rating scales is that shown in Figure 6. This is designed to record observations of batting form (Scott and French, 1945, p. 168). Each time a pupil bats, an observer checks "good," "fair," or "poor" with respect to his grip, stance, stride, pivot, and swing. Then the observer checks in the right-hand column the errors that are committed. The list of errors is expanded if necessary. An experienced observer can complete such a check list as this very quickly and with acceptable accuracy.

Check List for Operation of a Microscope

One of the most widely known check lists is that devised by Tyler (1930) for use in reporting a pupil's ability to use a microscope. It is shown in Figure 7. Although the check list as such may have only limited application in a secondary school science program, it is interesting because it represents a high degree of development in the use of check lists and can serve as a pattern for the construction of additional lists.

The teacher observes a pupil who is operating a microscope in an attempt to find a specified substance present in a culture. All needed materials, such as slides, cheese cloth, lens paper, are provided. As the pupil attacks the problem, the teacher records the sequence of actions by numbering them as they occur. He also checks the most obvious characteristics of the pupil's behavior and his mount and the skills in which he needs further training.

The numbers and checks in Figure 7 represent the kind of description of the pupil's procedure available at the completion of the exercise. All important desirable and undesirable actions that he made and the order in which he made them are a matter of record. Also shown are some of the intervening directions that he might have been given, such as "Find the object under low power" (see aaa).

Check List for Behavior in Group Work

Teachers frequently want to determine whether their pupils are acquiring and practicing desirable social habits and attitudes. Some of these are revealed when the pupils are engaged in committee and group work. Of interest in these instances are such pupil behaviors as willingness to cooperate, volunteer for duties, make worthwhile suggestions, and display democratic leadership. To provide a situation in which these behaviors can be displayed, a committee of pupils is formed to perform some task, such as drawing a map of the playground or planning a class

	Student's actions	Sequence of actions
a.	Takes slide	1
b.	Wipes slide with lens paper	2
c.	Wipes slide with cloth	
d.	Wipes slide with finger	
e.	Moves bottle of culture along the table	
f.	Places drop or two of culture on slide	3
g.	Adds more culture	
h.	Adds few drops of water	
i.	Hunts for cover glasses	4
j.	Wipes cover glass with lens paper	5
k.	Wipes cover with cloth	
l.	Wipes cover with finger	
m.	Adjusts cover with finger	
n.	Wipes off surplus fluid	
o.	Places slide on stage	6
p.	Looks through eyepiece with right eye	
q.	Looks through eyepiece with left eye	7
r.	Turns to objective of lowest power	9
s.	Turns to low-power objective	21
t.	Turns to high-power objective	
u.	Holds one eye closed	8
v.	Looks for light	
w.	Adjusts concave mirror	
x.	Adjusts plane mirror	
y.	Adjusts diaphragm	
z.	Does not touch diaphragm	10
aa.	With eye at eyepiece turns down coarse adjustment	11
ab.	Breaks cover glass	12
ac.	Breaks slide	
ad.	With eye away from eyepiece turns down coarse adjustment	
ae.	Turns up coarse adjustment a great distance	13, 22
af.	With eye at eyepiece turns down fine adjustment a great distance	14, 23
ag.	With eye away from eyepiece turns down fine adjustment a great distance	15
ah.	Turns up fine adjustment screw a great distance	
ai.	Turns fine adjustment screw a few turns	
aj.	Removes slide from stage	16
ak.	Wipes objective with lens paper	
al.	Wipes objective with cloth	
am.	Wipes objective with finger	17
an.	Wipes eyepiece with lens paper	
ao.	Wipes eyepiece with cloth	
ap.	Wipes eyepiece with finger	18
aq.	Makes another mount	
ar.	Takes another microscope	
as.	Finds object	
at.	Pauses for an interval	

Student's actions	Sequence of actions
au. Asks, "What do you want me to do?"	
av. Asks whether to use high power	
aw. Says, "I'm satisfied"	
ax. Says that the mount is all right for his eye	
ay. Says he cannot do it	19, 24
az. Told to start new mount	
aaa. Directed to find object under low power	20
aab. Directed to find object under high power	

Skills in which student needs further training

a.	In cleaning objective	√
b.	In cleaning eyepiece	√
c.	In focusing low power	√
d.	In focusing high power	√
e.	In adjusting mirror	√
f.	In using diaphragm	√
g.	In keeping both eyes open	√
h.	In protecting slide and objective from breaking by careless focusing	√

Noticeable characteristics of student's behavior

a.	Awkward in movements	
b.	Obviously dexterous in movements	
c.	Slow and deliberate	√
d.	Very rapid	
e.	Fingers tremble	
f.	Obviously perturbed	
g.	Obviously angry	
h.	Does not take work seriously	
i.	Unable to work without specific directions	√
j.	Obviously satisfied with his unsuccessful efforts	√

Characterization of the student's mount

a.	Poor light	√
b.	Poor focus	
c.	Excellent mount	
d.	Good mount	
e.	Fair mount	
f.	Poor mount	
g.	Very poor mount	
h.	Nothing in view but a thread in his eyepiece	
i.	Something on objective	
j.	Smeared lens	√
k.	Unable to find object	√

FIGURE 7

CHECK LIST FOR REPORTING SKILL IN USING A MICROSCOPE

DIRECTIONS: Below are eight kinds of behavior that a pupil might display when participating in committee or group work. Check "Yes" if it occurred; check "No" if it did not. If the evidence available is insufficient or conflicting, check "Uncertain."

BEHAVIOR	YES	NO	UNCERTAIN
1. Starts working promptly			
2. Volunteers for assignments			
3. Displays interest			
4. Cooperates with other pupils			
5. Displays cheerfulness			
6. Makes worthwhile suggestions			
7. Is a follower occasionally			
8. Is a leader occasionally			

FIGURE 8

SAMPLE CHECK LIST FOR REPORTING PUPIL BEHAVIOR IN GROUP WORK

observance of a national holiday. The behaviors displayed can be recorded on a check list.

A sample check list of the kind that might be used in these situations is shown in Figure 8. Eight kinds of behaviors are listed. The teacher is to check whether each occurred. Should the evidence be insufficient or conflicting, he checks the category labeled "Uncertain." Observe that this category is not a middle position between "Yes" and "No." Instead it is a position that indicates that the teacher is unable to make a judgment for any number of reasons. Perhaps the pupil has no opportunity to display the behavior in question throughout the period that the committee is at work. Perhaps the teacher is unable to observe the pupil as long as he desires. Perhaps the pupil behaved inconsistently. The last might be the subject of anecdotal records that would then supplement the check list.

Anecdotal Record in Mathematics

Recording observations of spontaneous procedures is seldom an easy task. Yet much of this behavior is very indicative of learning already acquired, and hence it cannot be ignored. The anecdotal record reports the principal details of the procedures observed and, when a series of them is available concerning related procedures, interesting insights into learning can be gained.

The sample anecdotal record shown in Figure 9 concerns behavior reflecting an elementary level of achievement in arithmetic. Without prompting or coaching of any kind, a pupil is satisfying himself in his own way that $8 \times 6 = 6 \times 8$, thereby convincing himself that the multiplicand and the multiplier are arbitrarily designated. The pupil procedure, that of counting the windows and stories in a picture of a six-story building, differs in type from those previously considered. In speaking, batting, and using a microscope, the observer is interested in the efficiency and accuracy with which the procedure is executed. These, too, might be the subjects of anecdotal records. Here, however, the observer is concerned with the fact that the procedure is executed at all. In other words, a helpful insight into a pupil's achievement in multiplication is obtained by observing his several attempts to count windows and stories and multiply his results. Whether he counts them slowly or rapidly, one or two at a time, is not so important.

ANECDOTAL RECORD FORM

Date: November 16   *Pupil's name:* James Rainer
Observer: M. B. Grant
Description of incident:

James was examining with great interest the windows in a picture of a six-story building. There were forty-eight windows in all, eight in each story. All were the same size and were arranged in vertical columns.

First he counted the number of windows in each story, then the number of stories. He multiplied the two numbers and obtained an answer of 48. Secondly, he counted the number of windows in each column, then the number of columns. Again he multiplied and obtained an answer of 48. He repeated this several times.

Comment:

James demonstrated to his own satisfaction that $8 \times 6 = 6 \times 8$, and seemed extremely pleased with himself.

FIGURE 9
SAMPLE ANECDOTAL RECORD PERTAINING TO ACHIEVEMENT IN ARITHMETIC

PROBLEMS

6   Construct a graphic rating scale to use as a basis for reporting a pupil procedure in a subject-matter area of interest to you.

7 Would the check list for reporting pupil behavior in group work shown in Figure 8 be improved if a column entitled "Sometimes" were inserted between the "Yes" and "No" columns and the directions changed appropriately? Why?

8 Using the anecdotal record shown in Figure 9 as an example, list the inherent limitations present in this reporting technique.

JUDGING PRODUCTS

Ranking procedures, rating scales (including score cards), and product scales are popular means by which pupil products are studied. To illustrate some of the many possibilities offered by these techniques, four instruments are shown here: (1) rating scales for theme analysis, (2) rating scales for judging pupil success in fastening pieces of wood with nails, (3) score cards for food products, and (4) product scales used for judging handwriting specimens.

Rating Scales for Themes

Many subjects occasionally require a largely original written product of the pupil. English courses are—and should be—especially demanding in this respect. The well-known English theme calls upon the pupil to select a topic, arrange its subparts in a suitable manner, and develop them in appropriate written form. From a measurement point of view, a theme is both an important and a complex product.

The complex nature of a theme makes its evaluation difficult. To overcome this problem, some teachers divide the characteristics of a theme into two categories, content and matters of form and style. The content categories include the selection of the topic (if topics are not assigned), organization, and the quantity and quality of investigation. The form and style category includes the elements of grammar, punctuation, vocabulary, spelling, capitalization, division of words, documentation, and so forth.

The relative importance of the two categories and their respective subparts no doubt varies radically from teacher to teacher, depending upon the purpose of the theme and the maturity of the pupil. For example, themes in a social studies class should be scrutinized more carefully in terms of content than form and style. The reverse may be true for most themes in an English class. In addition, the subparts of a category, such as the quantity and quality of investigation of the topic and the documentation of the theme, will probably lose importance when one is judging themes from lower grade levels.

Sample rating scales for themes are shown in Figure 10. Only two are

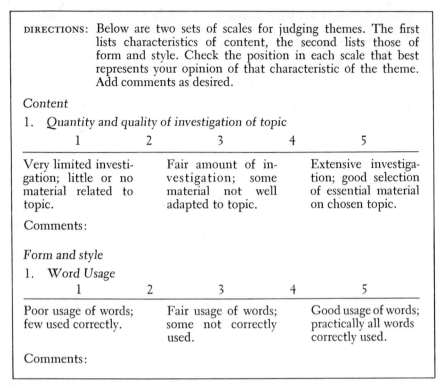

DIRECTIONS: Below are two sets of scales for judging themes. The first lists characteristics of content, the second lists those of form and style. Check the position in each scale that best represents your opinion of that characteristic of the theme. Add comments as desired.

Content

1. Quantity and quality of investigation of topic

1	2	3	4	5

| Very limited investigation; little or no material related to topic. | | Fair amount of investigation; some material not well adapted to topic. | | Extensive investigation; good selection of essential material on chosen topic. |

Comments:

Form and style

1. Word Usage

1	2	3	4	5

| Poor usage of words; few used correctly. | | Fair usage of words; some not correctly used. | | Good usage of words; practically all words correctly used. |

Comments:

FIGURE 10

SAMPLE RATING SCALES FOR JUDGING THEMES

shown, one from each category. Notice that these are five-point scales although only three descriptions are included. An observer vacillating between two of the positions for which descriptions are available may want to select the intermediate position. Obviously a series of similar scales for other characteristics in each category can be developed.

Further suggestions for analyzing themes have been prepared by Dressel and Mayhew (1954), whose handbook contains themes of varying quality together with analyses of them. In addition, principles for analyzing themes are discussed. These include: (1) judging a theme according to the nature of the assignment, (2) judging it in terms of the pupil's purposes, and (3) judging it according to neglected opportunities for more effective writing. Although this handbook is oriented toward higher education, it can be helpful to secondary school teachers.

Diederich (1964) suggests two sets of five-point rating scales which could be used for judging English compositions. One category deals with general merit and has four scales; namely, (1) quality and development of ideas, (2) organization, relevance, and movement, (3) style, flavor, and individuality, and (4) wording and phrasing. The other deals with mechanics, and its four scales are (1) grammar and sentence structure, (2) punctuation and capitalization, (3) spelling, and (4) handwriting and neatness.

Some doubt exists as to the need for sets of criteria such as those mentioned in this section. There is little evidence that they are consistently used (Fostvedt, 1965). Moreover, other investigations have established that a fast impressionistic reading of essays by several qualified readers is a reliable method of measuring pupil writing ability (Godshalk, 1966). This method requires the readers of themes and essays to make "global or holistic" judgments of each paper rather than analytical judgments. The theme is read quickly for total impressions and given one of three ratings: a score of "3" for a superior paper, "2" for an average paper, and "1" for an inferior paper.

Rating Scales for Shop Products

Many shop products must conform to prescribed dimensions and, as a result, mechanical devices can be used as one means of determining their quality. For instance, rulers, combination squares, calipers, and gauges of various kinds are employed in this process. In a very direct manner, one or more measurements are obtained that reveal the success or failure of the pupil to develop a product of a certain size, with certain proportions, or within certain tolerance limits.

Helpful as mechanical devices are, they are not capable of measuring all of the important characteristics of a shop product. Anyone who has carefully examined wood, metal, or plastic shop products realizes that two such products may have nearly identical dimensions, but still differ noticeably in workmanship. Characteristics such as esthetic attractiveness, strength, finish, design, and neatness, must be judged by other techniques.

A set of rating scales reported by Adkins (1947, p. 231) for fastening edges of pieces of wood with nails is shown in Figure 11. Many of these rating scales are related to the characteristics of strength, attractiveness, and neatness mentioned in the foregoing paragraph. For example, the splitting, spacing, and utility scales are a part of the strength characteristic; the hammer marks and depth scales are a part of the attractiveness and neatness characteristics.

Notice that a ten-point scale is given for each factor. It is quite possible that a teacher will find that he is unable to identify this many degrees of quality. If he finds that fewer than ten points will suffice, the scale should be so revised. Also notice that, unlike the other rating scales

| (1) | Straightness | 1 | 2 | 3 | 4 | 5 | 6 . | 7 | 8 | 9 · | 10 |

Are nails driven straight, heads square with wood, no evidence of bending?

| (2) | Hammer marks | 1 | 2 | 3 | 4 | 5 | 6 | 7 | 8 | 9 | 10 |

Is wood free of hammer marks around nails?

| (3) | Splitting | 1 | 2 | 3 | 4 | 5 | 6 | 7 | 8 | 9 | 10 |

Is wood free of splits radiating from nail holes?

| (4) | Depth | 1 | 2 | 3 | 4 | 5 | 6 | 7 | 8 | 9 | 10 |

Are depths of nails uniform and of pleasing appearance?

| (5) | Spacing | 1 | 2 | 3 | 4 | 5 | 6 | 7 | 8 | 9 | 10 |

Are nails spaced too close or too far apart?

| (6) | Utility | 1 | 2 | 3 | 4 | 5 | 6 | 7 | 8 | 9 | 10 |

Will the nails hold?

From Adkins, 1947; reproduced by permission of D. C. Adkins.

FIGURE 11
SAMPLE RATING SCALES FOR FASTENING

included in this chapter, a question is posed as a part of each scale and the brief descriptions of the positions are omitted. Whether this device is a gain or not is for you to decide. Perhaps both techniques could be used to advantage.

Score Cards for Food Products

An extensive study of pupil achievement in home economics programs has been done by Arny (1953). Since food preparation is an important part of these programs, and since food products are excellent representations of a pupil's achievement, she and others developed a set of food score cards (1946), a revised edition of which was later published.

There are 57 different cards in each set. Practically every food product that a pupil might prepare in the foods laboratory is included. Typical of the score cards is that for plain muffins shown in Figure 12.

The muffins are judged on the basis of seven major characteristics, one of which has three subparts, another two. Each characteristic or subpart is

		1	2	3		Score
			MUFFINS (Plain)			35
Appearance	1.	Not symmetrical	Symmetrical		1.	_____
	2.	Peaked or knobbed top	Definitely rounded top		2.	_____
	3.	Smooth surface	Pebbled surface		3.	_____
Color: Exterior	4.	Dark brown, pale, or uneven	Golden brown		4.	_____
Interior	5.	Yellow spots or evidence of unmixed flour	Creamy white		5.	_____
Moisture Content	6.	Dry or soggy	Slightly moist		6.	
Texture	7.	Large holes or tunnels or very compact	Medium size, fairly uniform holes		7.	
Lightness	8.	Heavy	Light		8.	
Tenderness of Crust	9.	Hard or tough	Tender		9.	
Taste and Flavor	10.	Flat or unpleasant flavor of certain ingredients	Pleasing flavor		10.	_____
					SCORE	_____

From Brown, 1946; reproduced by permission of the University of Minnesota and the Educational Testing Service.

FIGURE 12

SCORE CARD FOR PLAIN MUFFINS

rated in terms of a three-point scale; thus ten scores are obtained. The two extremes of each scale are described, one based on an improperly prepared product, the second on a standard product. After the ten scores have been determined, they are added to obtain a total score. The score cards increase the objectivity of the study. In addition, they require very little scoring time. Finally, they can be used as a teaching device in that the pupils can, by studying the cards, learn the important characteristics of a standard product.

Product Scales for Handwriting

Two styles of writing are generally taught in the elementary school. One is the manuscript style, in which the letters are disconnected and made in a form similar to printed letters. The other is the cursive style, in which the letters of each word are connected. The general practice is to teach manuscript writing first, and then change to cursive writing at about the third grade.

The easiest way to gather information about pupil achievement in handwriting, whether manuscript or cursive style, is to examine specimens that have been obtained under controlled conditions. Both speed and quality can be determined. The speed or rate at which pupils write is the easier of the two characteristics to measure. Quality can be defined in many ways. Thorndike, who built the first scale for measuring quality of handwriting, interpreted quality to mean beauty, legibility, and character. Ayres, whose scale is shown in part in Figure 13, considered quality to mean legibility only.

Speed of handwriting can be measured by a teacher-made test if it is carefully administered. First the teacher selects a simple statement such as "Mary had a little lamb" or "The quick brown fox jumps over the lazy dog." The statement should be so simple that it can be easily memorized; it should have no unusual words or expressions that will in any way hinder the pupil in his speed test. After the statement has been memorized by the pupils, they are told that, when given a signal, they should start to write the statement as well and as rapidly as they can, and continue to do so until told to stop. Either two or three minutes are allowed. The number of letters written by each pupil is counted and divided by the number of minutes allowed.

One of the most widely used scales for measuring the quality of handwriting is the *Ayres Measuring Scale for Handwriting, Gettysburg Edition* (1915). Before the scale can be used, the pupils must be thoroughly familiar with the first three sentences of Lincoln's Gettysburg Address. Then they are given exactly two minutes in which to copy them. To determine quality, each pupil's handwriting specimen is then compared with a scaled series of printed samples. There are eight samples in all, four of which are included in Figure 13. The comparison is made by sliding each specimen along the scale until a printed sample of the same or very similar quality is found. The number above this sample is the value assigned to the pupil's specimen. The numbers increase as the quality of the specimen improves. This scale is designed for elementary school pupils and contains only cursive writing samples. Rate scores can be obtained in the same manner as described earlier.

Teachers have not been able to get consistent results when using product scales to study handwriting samples (Feldt, 1962). To improve this situation, at least three handwriting samples should be obtained independently from each pupil and the ratings averaged. This can be repeated each time pupil growth is to be checked in this area of achievement.

PROBLEMS

9 Seventh-grade pupils in social studies were required to draw a map showing the major rivers and lakes in their home state. They were allowed to refer

MEASURING SCALE FOR HANDWRITING

20	40	70	90
(handwriting specimen)	*(handwriting specimen)*	*(handwriting specimen)*	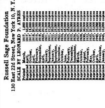

This scale for measuring the quality of handwriting is a revised edition of a scale first published in 1912 and subsequently reprinted 12 times with a total of 62,000 copies. The purpose of the present edition is to increase the reliability of measurements of handwriting through standardizing methods of securing and scoring samples, and through making numerous improvements in the scale itself designed to reduce variability in the results secured through its use.

The present scale is usually referred to as the "Gettysburg Edition" because the opening sentences of Lincoln's Gettysburg Address are used. It is priced at ten cents for single copies, and in quantity at the rate of $9.00 per hundred and $75.00 per thousand copies.

To secure samples of handwriting the teacher should write on the board the first three sentences of Lincoln's Gettysburg Address and have the pupils read and copy until familiar with it. They should then copy it, beginning at a given signal and writing for precisely two minutes. They should write in ink on ruled paper. The copy with the count of the letters is as follows:

Four 4 score 9 and 12 seven 17 years 22 ago 25 our 28 fathers 35 brought 42 forth 47 upon 51 this 55 continent 64 a 65 new 68 nation 74 conceived 83 in 85 liberty 92 and 95 dedicated 104 to 106 the 109 proposition 120 that 124 all 127 men 130 are 133 created 140 equal 145. Now 148 we 150 are 153 engaged 160 in 162 a 163 great 168 civil 173 war 176 testing 183 whether 190 that 194 nation 200 or 202 any 205 nation 211 so 213 conceived 222 and 225 so 227 dedicated 236 can 239 long 243 endure 249. We 251 are 254 met 257 on 259 a 260 great 265 battlefield 270 of 272 that 282 war 285.

To score samples slide each specimen along the scale until a writing of the same quality is found. The number at the top of the scale above this shows the value of the writing being measured. Disregard differences in style, but try to find on the scale the quality corresponding with that of the sample being scored. With practice the scorer will develop the ability to recognize qualities more rapidly and with increasing accuracy. If the scoring is done twice, the results will be considerably more accurate than if done only once. The procedure may be as follows: Score samples and distribute them in piles with all the 20's in one pile, all the 30's in another, and so on. Mark these values on the backs of the papers, then shuffle the samples and score them a second time. Finally make careful decisions to overcome any disagreements in the two scorings.

Russell Sage Foundation
130 East 22d Street, New York 10, N. Y.
SCALE BY LEONARD P. AYRES

(Bar charts by grade: Fifth grade, Sixth grade, Seventh grade, Eighth grade — Quality of writing. Columns represent per cent of pupils in each of four upper grades commonly found to have handwriting of qualities shown below each column.)

(Bar charts by grade: Fifth grade, Sixth grade, Seventh grade, Eighth grade — Rate of writing. Columns represent per cent of pupils in each of four upper grades commonly found to write the number of letters per minute shown below each column.)

Printed in U.S.A.

From Ayres, 1915; reproduced by permission of the Educational Testing Service.

FIGURE 13

SAMPLE SCALES FROM AYRES MEASURING SCALE FOR HANDWRITING, GETTYSBURG EDITION

to, but not to copy directly, printed maps. The following rating scales were to be used first by each pupil and then by the teacher to judge the product of his efforts. Revise these scales in any manner which, in your opinion, will strengthen them.

RATING SCALE

5	4	3	2	1
Very neat	neat	fairly neat	somewhat messy	messy
Words are printed not written	printed	some words might not be printed	written	written
Has title and key	Both title and key	Might lack correct title or key	Might lack title or key	Lacks both
Has shown rivers and lakes most clearly	Has shown all rivers and lakes	Lacks one or two required items	Lacks several items	Lacks a lot of items
Turned in at required time	Turned in at required time	One day late	More than one day late	More than one day late

RELIABILITY OF JUDGING PERFORMANCE

It is clear that judging pupil performance is an integral part of the total pupil evaluation program conducted by a teacher; it is also one of the most difficult. It is typically less objective and organized than paper-and-pencil testing, and sometimes less satisfying to both teacher and pupil. Many of these problems contribute directly to a serious weakness of judging performance; that is, to its relatively high degree of unreliability. A high degree of unreliability means that the procedures frequently yield inconsistent results.

This can be traced both to the performance evaluated and the observer. In other words, the reliability of the process is directly related to the degree of successful sampling of pupil performance and the consistency of the observer when judging that performance.

Sampling Pupil Performances

Sampling pupil performances is necessarily limited in scope. How many times is it possible for a pupil to deliver a prepared speech, build a pair of book ends, or cut out and sew an apron? The teacher may have only one or two opportunities to observe these performances, and they may not take place under conditions that he can control as much as he would like. Yet he must assume that they are typical representations of pupil achievement.

Some pupil products require considerable quantities both of class and out-of-class time in which to be completed. As a result, unauthorized assistance by a second party is likely. The product then becomes much less useful in terms of judging pupil achievement in that it is a poor sample of his work.

Ideally, then, the teacher should have at least several opportunities to observe an important pupil performance. Such samples should truly reflect the pupil's achievement and his alone, and should take place under suitable conditions.

Observer Reliability

Fatigue, boredom, and indifference can destroy the worth of the observer's attempts to examine pupil performance. To eliminate these factors, the teacher can preplan his observations as much as possible, being certain that he spreads them out over a reasonable period of time. On the other hand, since these and other factors can never be eliminated, multiple observation is desirable. This means that, in the case of judging procedures, several competent teachers observe independently, then reconcile any differences that exist. In the case of judging products, several persons can participate, or one can judge the product more than once without knowledge of earlier decisions.

Unfortunately, consistent results yielded by efforts to judge a pupil's performance do not necessarily mean that a proper analysis has been made. After all, the observer or even a team of observers could be consistently wrong. This, of course, is unlikely if the observers are reasonably competent. On the other hand, such factors as the well-known "halo effect," so often present in efforts of this kind, can make the analyses more consistent but less accurate. To improve observer reliability, well-defined reference points are needed. In the case of procedures, these may be careful descriptions of the important aspects of various degrees of quality; in the case of products they may be a variety of specimen products of known quality.

Problems

10 It has been recommended that, to judge pupil compositions properly, files of various sorts of pupils' writings should be kept from year to year (Burrows, 1959, pp. 27–28). Speculate as to how this system might be organized. How much would the foregoing procedure reduce the limitations of judging performance?

11 Tripp and others (1957) discuss problems of measuring handwriting variables such as pressure and speed. Also, they describe new devices for measuring variables such as these. Study this report and appraise the measuring techniques mentioned from the point of view of the reliability of the data produced.

Judging by Pupils

Pupils as well as teachers can judge performances—their own and also those of their classmates. For example, in speaking, the audience of pupils can rate the speaker, and he can rate himself. In a foods laboratory, all pupils including the cook can examine the roast that is prepared. In the case of a handwriting exercise, the pupil who submits the specimen can arrive at his own judgment of its merits by following the same procedures the teacher follows.

As a learning experience there is much to be said for this type of multiple evaluation. When both pupils and teacher use the same instruments to judge the same performance simultaneously, and the results are examined, the pupils gain a much better perspective of the important features of the performance and the teacher's standards concerning them. Particularly informative is the comparison of the self-evaluation by the pupil with that made independently by his teacher. Certainly the diagnosis of defects and their causes as well as remediation can be based on such a conference. Most important to the pupil is the realistic view of his achievement or lack of it that he gains.

From the point of view of sound principles of evaluation, there are serious objections to using the pupils' judgments or a composite of them in reporting pupil achievement. Certainly we cannot assume that the average pupil is as competent a judge of the quality of another's performance or of his own as the teacher. This automatically reduces the value of pupil observations to a point where they are often of minor importance. The successful observer has a maturity of judgment and sense of impartiality rarely found in pupils. Pupils should be regularly allowed to gain experience in observing, but they should not be expected to make sound judgments with great consistency.

Problem

12 Some teachers believe that, as pupils become skilled in self-evaluation, they actually raise the standards by which evaluations are made. Do you agree? Why?

Summary

Some of the educational objectives for elementary and secondary school are such that paper-and-pencil measuring instruments cannot reveal the degree to which pupils have achieved them. These goals pertain to pupil performances such as the ability to deliver a speech, write a paragraph, conduct an experiment, or hem a garment. Generally they are quite complex, involving both language and nonlanguage aspects.

Judgments of pupil performance can be based on the procedure displayed by the pupil or the products yielded by the procedure. Both have some characteristics that lend themselves readily to measurement and some that do not. Efficiency and accuracy are the easiest procedure characteristics to measure. Product characteristics can often be measured more easily; in fact, mechanical devices are available for this purpose for such articles as shop products.

The instruments used in judging procedures and products are primarily of the nontesting type. For procedures, ranking and rating methods, check lists, and anecdotal records are frequently applied. Illustrations of these are rating scales for speaking, a check list for softball batting form, a check list for the operation of a microscope, a check list for pupil behavior when engaged in group work, and an anecdotal record reflecting achievement in arithmetic. For products, ranking and rating methods and product scales are used. Illustrations of these are rating scales for theme analysis, rating scales for determining pupil success in fastening pieces of wood with nails, score cards for food products, and product scales for handwriting specimens. In all cases a competent observer is needed.

Performance evaluation is not always reliable because pupil performance is not always successfully sampled and the observer not always consistent. Repeated sampling of pupil performances and independent observations by one or more qualified teachers increase the reliability of the process. When pupils judge their own performances or those of their classmates, they gain excellent experience in this process, although their attempts seldom produce superior evaluative data.

Suggested Readings

Adkins, Dorothy C. *Construction and analysis of achievement tests.* Washington: U.S. Civil Service Commission, 1947. Chapter 5.
> In this chapter, Adkins describes the nature of performance tests and their administration. Many illustrations of evaluation instruments and procedures are included.

Ahmann, J. Stanley, Marvin D. Glock, and Helen L. Wardeberg. *Evaluating elementary school pupils.* Boston: Allyn and Bacon, 1960. Chapters 11, 12, and 13.
> The three chapters cited deal with appraisal in the language arts, mathematics, and the content areas, respectively. A number of rating scales and check lists to be used with elementary school pupils are shown.

Arny, Clara M. *Evaluation in home economics.* New York: Appleton-Century-Crofts, 1953. Chapter 7.
> Techniques suitable for judging pupil performance in home economics are discussed in this chapter. They include rating scales, check lists, and anecdotal records. Illustrations are given of one or more of these techniques in the areas of foods and nutrition, textiles and clothing, and family relationships.

Bradfield, James M., and H. Stewart Moredock. *Measurement and evaluation in education.* New York: Macmillan, 1957. Chapter 13.
> Measurable dimensions of pupil procedures and products of various kinds are identified. Examples are provided of rating scales to be used in art, driving, music, industrial arts, typing, home economics, physical education, and speech.

Dressel, Paul L., and Lewis B. Mayhew. *Handbook for theme analysis.* Dubuque, Iowa: Wm. C. Brown, 1954.
> The Communications Committee of the Cooperative Study of Evaluation in General Education collected a number of themes and analyzed them according to a group of formulated principles. The principles as well as the themes and a lengthy commentary about each are arranged in handbook form. This handbook is designed for either teachers or pupils.

Dressel, Paul L., and others. *Evaluation in higher education.* Boston: Houghton Mifflin, 1961. Chapter 7.
> Rating scales for judging pupil writing and speaking ability are shown. Ranking techniques are mentioned briefly.

Godshalk, Fred I., and others. *The measurement of writing ability.* New York: College Entrance Examination Board, 1966. Chapters 1 and 2.
> The first two chapters of this research report describe the problem of measuring writing ability and the measuring devices to be tested. Of particular

interest are the illustrations of the objective test items and interlinear exercises used to measure writing ability indirectly. A short description of the "global or holistic" method of scoring essays is included.

Ryans, David G., and Norman Frederiksen. Performance tests of educational achievement. In E. F. Lindquist (Ed.), *Educational measurement*. Washington: American Council on Education, 1951. Chapter 12.

This chapter contains discussions of the types of performance tests, the use of them as measures of achievement, and their reliability. Seven steps to be followed in building a performance test are described in detail.

Wrightstone, J. Wayne. Observational techniques. In Chester W. Harris (Ed.), *Encyclopedia of educational research*. (3rd ed.) New York: Macmillan, 1960. Pp. 927–933.

Recent research on observational techniques of all kinds is reviewed. Separate sections are devoted to time samples, rating methods, and anecdotal records.

REFERENCES CITED

Adkins, Dorothy C. *Construction and analysis of achievement tests*. Washington: U.S. Civil Service Commission, 1947.

Arny, Clara M. *Evaluation in home economics*. New York: Appleton-Century-Crofts, 1953.

Ayres, Leonard P. *Ayres Measuring Scale for Handwriting, Gettysburg Edition*. Distributed by the Cooperative Test Division of the Educational Testing Service, 1915.

Brown, Clara M., and others. *Minnesota Food Score Cards*. (Rev. ed.) Distributed by the Cooperative Test Division of the Educational Testing Service, 1946.

Burrows, Alvina T. *Teaching composition*. What Research Says to the Teacher, No. 18. Washington: National Education Association, 1959.

Diederich, Paul B. Problems and possibilities of research in the teaching of English. In *Research design and the teaching of English*, Proceedings of Conference of National Council of Teachers of English. Champaign, Ill.: National Council of Teachers of English, 1964.

Dressel, Paul L., and Lewis B. Mayhew. *Handbook for theme analysis*. Dubuque, Iowa: Wm. C. Brown, 1954.

Feldt, L. S. The reliability of measures of handwriting quality. *J. educ. Psychol.*, 1962, **53**, 288–292.

Fostvedt, D. R. Criteria for the evaluation of high school English composition. *J. educ. Res.*, 1965, **59**, 108–112.

Godshalk, Fred I., and others. *The measurement of writing ability*. New York: College Entrance Examination Board, 1966.

Scott, M. G., and French, E. *Better teaching through testing*. New York: A. S. Barnes, 1945.

Tripp, Clarence A., and others. Measurement of handwriting variables. *Perceptual and Motor Skills*, 1957, **7**, 279–294.

Tyler, Ralph W. A test of skill in using a microscope. *Educ. Res. Bull.*, 1930, 9, 493–496.

Wrightstone, J. Wayne. Observational techniques. In Chester W. Harris (Ed.), *Encyclopedia of educational research.* (3rd ed.) New York: Macmillan, 1960. Pp. 927–933.

PART THREE

Characteristics of a

An unknown wit of several generations ago remarked that the only good thing about error was that it created jobs. The truth of this can be demonstrated in many areas including pupil evaluation. All of our measuring instruments are somewhat inadequate, a number of them to an appreciable degree. To reduce error, the builders of these instruments are striving constantly to refine their products; this is, in a sense, an endless job. These efforts in turn complicate the problems of those who must choose from among many available measuring instruments the ones that are best suited for a particular need. Each new instrument means a repetition of the job of selection by anyone needing an instrument of that type.

The classroom teacher may find himself cast in either or both of the following roles: in one case, he may be constructing a paper-and-pencil achievement test to measure the academic achievement of his pupils; in a second, he may be a member of a teacher committee organized to select a scholastic aptitude or standardized achievement test to be used as a part of the school testing program. In either case the teacher needs standards. To construct his own test to appraise its value, he must be familiar with the characteristics of a good measuring instrument and the methods of determining the degree to which a given instrument may possess them.

The characteristics of a good measuring instrument can be classified in many different ways. Here they are grouped under three headings: norms, validity, and reliability. These three headings identify the three chapters that compose Part Three. In Chapter 8, "The Use of Test Scores and Norms," the need for an instrument to yield information that is easily understood and utilized is discussed. This is ordinarily satisfied by computing norms, that is, by identifying the relative performance of a pupil in terms of a group of pupils much like him. Chapter 9, "The Validity of Measurement Methods," is devoted to the most important of the three characteristics. A measuring instrument is valid to the degree that it serves the purpose or purposes for which its use is intended. In Chapter 10, "The Reliability of Measurement Methods," the need for an instrument to yield consistent or dependable information is discussed. An instrument that strongly reflects this characteristic will yield virtually the same information each time it is used in an unchanging situation.

Some statistical methodology must be introduced to describe these characteristics and how they are measured. The arithmetic mean, the median, the standard deviation, and the product-moment coefficient of correlation are discussed at appropriate points in Part Three. In Appendix A is an additional explanation of these statistical measures, as well as a step-by-step description of the easiest means of computing each. Although classroom teachers are seldom required to compute such values, they are often required to interpret them in connection with the validity, reliability, and norm determinations found in test manuals and educational literature.

The purpose of Part Three is to identify the characteristics of a good measuring instrument, to illustrate the most common methods of determining how strongly a specific instrument reflects them and to provide an adequate background for those statistical techniques commonly used in such determinations. The importance of Part Three can hardly be over-emphasized.

8 ✐

The Use of Test Scores and Norms

EVERY MORNING AT SOME SPECIFIED TIME PRIOR TO 9:00 A.M., practically every radio station in the United States broadcasts a summary of the weather conditions in the locality at that moment and as they probably will be for the remainder of the day. Typical of the kind of announcement that might be heard on a morning in mid-April is the following:

> The temperature at 7:00 A.M. this morning was 50° F., the barometric pressure was 29.8, the wind velocity was 10 to 20 miles per hour from the northwest, and the relative humidity was 70 per cent. Today will be cloudy and mild, with a high temperature of about 60° F. The probability of measurable precipitation today is 5%.

To most listeners, this report, brief as it is, is useful. As he prepares for the day's activities the informed citizen can readily decide such questions as to whether he should wear a spring topcoat rather than a winter overcoat, make his son of preschool age button his woolen sweater before leaving the house, or plan an early season golf or tennis match.

The teacher, of course, is no different from his neighbors in his reliance on a daily weather report. In addition, he may well ponder two prominent aspects of the problem confronting the meteorologist in his attempts to describe the weather to the public; and he may note the importance of these same two aspects when he, as a teacher, attempts to describe a pupil to a parent.

In the first place, the complexity of the entity being described is almost overwhelming. A description of one word or one number in the case of the weather or a pupil would be unhappily inadequate. Multiple measurements must be made to sketch even a crude profile of the weather or a pupil. The weather report attempts this, and so do well-designed school testing programs.

The second aspect is the meaning of the measurements when they are reported to a relatively uninformed audience. In this respect, the meteorologist has a vast advantage over the educator. Each of us learns at a tender age that temperatures in the vicinity of 70° F. are comfortable, whereas those in excess of 90° F. and less than 60° F. tend to be uncomfortable unless appropriate adjustments in dress or physical activity are made. A barometric pressure is almost automatically compared to 30 inches of mercury, the ordinary barometric pressure at sea level. Wind velocities of less than 10 miles per hour are conceded to be practically unnoticeable; velocities between 30 and 75 miles per hour are called gales. Little more need be said to prepare most individuals for this aspect of the weather. Much the same is true of relative humidity. When thinking only of our comfort, we usually believe that the lower the relative humidity the better. Furthermore we have learned to associate temperature, wind velocity, and relative humidity when we consider the probability of a comfortable day.

Teachers may envy the meteorologist's ability to present succinct, understandable descriptions of something as intricate as the weather. To be sure, the meteorologist has not achieved perfection in his efforts. Yet he can point to notable success. A teacher may well question whether those same individuals who seem to comprehend so much of a ninety-second report on the day's weather would understand comparable amounts if given a ninety-second report on the academic achievement of their child that day in school.

Although the comparison of the teacher's position with that of the meteorologist may not be totally justified, it is interesting nevertheless. Certainly one of the reasons the teacher's position is less satisfactory than the meteorologist's is that the units of measurement reported by the former are not as meaningful as degrees Fahrenheit or miles per hour. It is understandable, therefore, why many people involved in pupil evaluation pay considerable attention to the nature of test scores and their interpretation.

RAW SCORES

The difficulty of meaningfully presenting the results yielded by educational measurement can be illustrated in many ways. Assume, for example, that a battery of achievement tests is administered to the pupils in all of the seventh grades of a city school system. One is a vocabulary test composed of 110 words, the meanings of which have to be identified by each pupil. The success of each pupil is then expressed in terms of the number of words correctly identified. Therefore, for each of the 360 pupils who wrote the vocabulary test, a numerical representation of his effort is available, and it can be no smaller than zero nor larger than 110.

Let us consider for a moment the position of a teacher whose pupils are involved in the testing program. One of his pupils correctly identified the meaning of 58 of the 110 words. Hence in his record book opposite this pupil's name the teacher wrote a "58." This he properly calls a *raw score*, that is, the quantitative report that is the immediate end product of scoring the test. In the case of this test and many others like it, each pupil is credited with one point for every correct answer and zero points for every wrong or omitted answer. To be sure, the amount of credit could have varied for each right answer, increasing to two points or more as the words became more difficult. Furthermore, correction for guessing on the part of the pupil could have been made by subtracting points for wrong answers. Had either or both of these procedures been used, the result of the scoring process would still be called a raw score.

Simply labeling the "58" as one of many raw scores is useful but does not answer other questions concerning this representation of success. For example, the teacher may wonder whether 58 indicates that this pupil's vocabulary of words is twice as great as another pupil's, since this second pupil's vocabulary test score is only 29. Certainly it is tempting to assume that this is true. Yet the whole idea, in reality, is absurd. Unfortunately, a meaningful comparison of the raw scores of 58 and 29 cannot be made unless the units of measurement possess certain characteristics. For instance, the fact that a raw score of zero does not represent zero knowledge of words is sufficient to render useless any such comparison.

Absolute Zero

The failure of the raw score of size zero to indicate zero knowledge of vocabulary is equivalent to saying that the raw score of zero is not an absolute zero. In other words, unlike the customary measurement of height and weight, the units of measurement of the vocabulary test are relative. This is a common characteristic of test scores.

Like many achievement tests, the vocabulary test is deliberately constructed in such a way that a score of zero does not indicate zero knowledge. If for no reason other than economy of time and energy, such simple words as "dog," "house," and "bicycle" are not included in the test, since they do not differentiate among pupils of a typical seventh-grade class. On the other hand, words like "immaculate," "formula," and "conscientious" may very likely be of acceptable difficulty for the class and hence are included in the test. Instruments such as the vocabulary test are generally designed to have a relatively small difficulty spread so that all pupils to be measured will fall on the scale rather than somewhere below or above it. Hence raw scores of zero and 110 will be virtually nonexistent. The test then differentiates among the pupils measured even though absolute zero has not been identified.

This information can be translated into a diagram such as Figure 14. Although this figure is but an approximate representation of the relation-

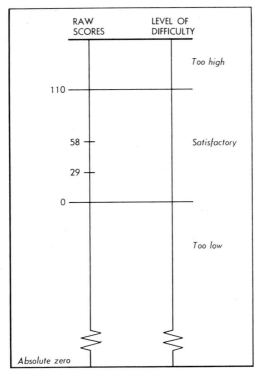

FIGURE 14

RAW SCORES AND LEVEL OF DIFFICULTY OF AN ENGLISH VOCABULARY TEST
FOR SEVENTH-GRADE PUPILS

ship between the raw scores of the vocabulary achievement test and its level of difficulty, it nevertheless illustrates two noteworthy points. First of all, it is evident that a raw score of zero differs from absolute zero by some large and unknown distance. Obviously, the distance between a raw score of 58 and absolute zero is not twice the distance between a raw score of 29 and absolute zero. The second point concerns the level of difficulty of the instrument. Of course, the satisfactory level of difficulty for this achievement test varies with the group of pupils for whom it is designed. It would move up the scale for eighth-grade pupils and down for sixth-grade pupils. If the test is carefully constructed, its raw-score spread will fall directly opposite the satisfactory level of difficulty as illustrated. Previous test results are invaluable aids in identifying the test items that, being too easy or too difficult, are therefore useless for a specific achievement test. Note again that the position of absolute zero is of no direct concern to the test builder as he identifies the proper level of difficulty.

Figure 14 resembles the situation that might exist if a school nurse wished to obtain the relative rather than the absolute heights of a group of secondary school girls. To do so she could nail a yardstick vertically to the wall at a position such that every girl would be found to be at least as tall as the distance between the floor and the lower edge and no taller than the distance between the floor and the upper edge of the yardstick. Her knowledge of typical heights of girls of this age group would help her to make a satisfactory approximation of the position. After the yardstick is in place, each girl stands barefooted at a point beneath the yardstick and a reading can be made.

There are two similarities between this determination of relative height and the vocabulary test. In the first place, the relative heights would be very acceptable information for differentiating among the girls in terms of height, just as the vocabulary test scores can differentiate among the seventh-grade pupils. Ratios between these heights, however, like ratios between the test scores, defy interpretation. Certainly a girl with a relative height of 22 inches is not twice as tall as a girl with a relative height of 11 inches. Thus, as in the case of the test scores, the zero point of the yardstick differs from an absolute zero by some unknown distance. Secondly, determining a suitable position on the wall at which to nail the yardstick is essentially the same as selecting the vocabulary test items of satisfactory difficulty. In both cases, changes would be made if different groups of subjects were measured. For example, if elementary school girls were used in the determination of relative height, the yardstick would be lowered; if sixth-grade pupils were tested, less difficult vocabulary test items would be used.

The failure of educational measuring instruments to have an absolute zero is not as serious as it may first seem. The continued successful use of the Fahrenheit and centigrade scales to measure temperature is ample evidence that scales without absolute units still have superior utility. The absence of absolute units simply means that ratios between raw scores lack meaning when generalizations about the attribute measured are being made. To question whether one pupil's vocabulary is twice that of another pupil's is no different than to question whether a room at 100° F. is twice as warm as a room at 50° F.

Differences Between Raw Scores

As the teacher examines the raw scores reported for his class, he may find himself grappling with other uncertainties. He notices, for example, that another pupil received a raw score of 59 in contrast to the first pupil's 58. Does this pupil in fact surpass the first in terms of the vocabulary test? When answering this question remember that this test, like all tests, is somewhat unreliable. In other words, it does not yield completely consistent results. Test unreliability forces us to interpret each score as an interval rather than a point. These intervals, sometimes called "confidence intervals" or "bands" (Educational Testing Service, 1955), are found by using the standard error of measurement (see pages 324–325).

UNEQUAL UNITS. Further examination of the vocabulary raw scores may reveal a situation such as the following:

Pupil	Raw score
Sheri	88
Carol	68
Arthur	37
Donald	17

Since the raw-score difference between the two members of each pair is 20 in both instances, can it be said that Sheri surpasses Carol in terms of the vocabulary test by the same amount that Arthur surpasses Donald? If the raw-score units are equal, the question can be answered affirmatively. In all likelihood, however, the difference of 20 raw-score units between the two girls is not exactly the same as the difference of 20 raw-score units between the two boys. It is all too true that educational measurement habitually yields unequal units. A specified difference, such as 20 raw-score units, cannot be identified at any position along the range, as 5 inches can be isolated in any position on an accurate yardstick.

In all probability, increasing a raw score in a vocabulary test from 68 to 88 represents greater accomplishment than increasing a raw score from 17 to 37. Hence, Sheri surpasses Carol to a greater degree than Arthur surpasses Donald. It is typical of achievement tests to find the "rubber units" contracted at the lower end of the raw-score distribution and expanded at the upper end.

Interpreting Raw Scores

The individual most vitally concerned about the 58 his teacher wrote in the record book is the pupil himself. When informed of his achievement, he is understandably puzzled. Unlike the previously described weather data, which he interprets without effort, the results of the vocabulary test as reported to him defy interpretation. Obviously he lacks reference points against which to compare his information. He needs a raw-score counterpart of "70° F." to help him interpret "58" as "70° F." helps him interpret temperature reports.

His first reaction might be to convert the number of correct responses, 58, to a per cent. However, to know that he correctly identified 53 per cent of the words is not particularly helpful. If the test were composed of simple words, 53 per cent might indicate inferior achievement. Had the test been composed of difficult words, on the other hand, 53 per cent might indicate superior achievement for a seventh-grade pupil.

No doubt the pupil requests information concerning the number of words correctly identified by the other class members. Should all other class members have correctly identified fewer than 58 words, he would certainly be elated about his achievement; however, if all other class members correctly identified more than 58 words, he may very well be downcast. If the average number of words correctly identified by his classmates is reported, then he can describe his position as "above average" or as "below average" in terms of the vocabulary test.

Three helpful reference points are now available to the pupil. They are the maximum number of words correctly identified by any classmate, the minimum number of words correctly identified by any classmate, and the average number of words correctly identified by the entire class. Meager as this information is, it nevertheless provides the pupil with the opportunity to interpret his "58" in much the same manner as he would a reported temperature. Both numerical reports have some meaning in terms of certain relative criteria.

FREQUENCY DISTRIBUTION. To provide the pupil with information that will help him interpret his raw score, the teacher must follow several steps. Initially he explains that, in view of the similarity of curriculum and educational environment in general, it is reasonable to compare the raw score of 58 not only with those of other members of his class at his school, but also with those of all 360 pupils of the seventh-grade classes in all schools in the city. Then he decides to show his pupil the scores of all other pupils tested. Needless to say the columns upon columns of unarranged raw scores (often called the ungrouped data) are hardly informative. On the other hand, the raw scores can be grouped into intervals and a *frequency distribution* constructed. The procedure is illustrated in Table 4. The total spread of the scores from 15 (the lowest raw score) to 94 (the highest raw score) is arbitrarily subdivided into 16 intervals of a constant size of five raw-score units. This procedure forms the first column of Table 4, which is called the raw-score intervals columns. Then each raw score is tallied in the proper interval, as indicated by the vertical marks adjacent to the intervals. Counting the tallies yields the frequencies listed in the last column.

The interpretation of the values of the frequency column is by no means difficult. It is clear that three of the pupils have raw scores somewhere between 15 and 19 inclusive, whereas five have raw scores between 20 and 24 inclusive. Forty-six have raw scores between 55 and 59 inclusive, one of these being the pupil in question.

TABLE 4

WORK TABLE FOR DETERMINING A FREQUENCY
DISTRIBUTION OF 360 VOCABULARY RAW SCORES

Raw-score intervals	Tallies	Frequency
90–94	IIII	4
85–89	ꟷHꟷ I	6
80–84	ꟷHꟷ ꟷHꟷ II	12
75–79	ꟷHꟷ ꟷHꟷ ꟷHꟷ ꟷHꟷ	20
70–74	ꟷHꟷ ꟷHꟷ ꟷHꟷ ꟷHꟷ ꟷHꟷ III	28
65–69	ꟷHꟷ ꟷHꟷ ꟷHꟷ ꟷHꟷ ꟷHꟷ ꟷHꟷ ꟷHꟷ I	36
60–64	ꟷHꟷ ꟷHꟷ ꟷHꟷ ꟷHꟷ ꟷHꟷ ꟷHꟷ ꟷHꟷ ꟷHꟷ	40
55–59	ꟷHꟷ ꟷHꟷ ꟷHꟷ ꟷHꟷ ꟷHꟷ ꟷHꟷ ꟷHꟷ ꟷHꟷ ꟷHꟷ I	46
50–54	ꟷHꟷ ꟷHꟷ ꟷHꟷ ꟷHꟷ ꟷHꟷ ꟷHꟷ ꟷHꟷ ꟷHꟷ III	43
45–49	ꟷHꟷ ꟷHꟷ ꟷHꟷ ꟷHꟷ ꟷHꟷ ꟷHꟷ ꟷHꟷ IIII	39
40–44	ꟷHꟷ ꟷHꟷ ꟷHꟷ ꟷHꟷ ꟷHꟷ ꟷHꟷ II	32
35–39	ꟷHꟷ ꟷHꟷ ꟷHꟷ ꟷHꟷ IIII	24
30–34	ꟷHꟷ ꟷHꟷ III	13
25–29	ꟷHꟷ IIII	9
20–24	ꟷHꟷ	5
15–19	III	3
Total		360

To help the pupil understand even more clearly his relative position in the group of 360 pupils, Table 4 is changed to Table 5. Now two columns of percentages are available, one based upon cumulative frequencies. Approximately 13 per cent of the seventh graders fall within the same interval as the pupil we are considering, and 47 per cent fall within the intervals below his. Thus about 40 per cent of the pupils fall within intervals above the one containing his raw score.

CONSTRUCTING A GRAPH. A further step the teacher may take in his attempts to improve the meaningfulness of the pupil's raw score would be to convert the frequency distribution to graphic form. It is common practice to plot the data included in Table 4 by spacing the raw-score intervals along a horizontal axis and the frequencies along a vertical axis. In this manner, Figure 15 is constructed. The frequency of each interval is plotted directly above its midpoint.

The curve in Figure 15 is characteristic of those resulting from similar plotting of the scores yielded by many different kinds of measuring instruments used in education and elsewhere. Had the pupils involved

TABLE 5
FREQUENCY DISTRIBUTION OF 360 RAW SCORES

Raw-score intervals	Frequency	Per cent	Cumulative frequency	Cumulative per cent
90–94	4	1.1	360	100.0
85–89	6	1.7	356	98.9
80–84	12	3.3	350	97.2
75–79	20	5.6	338	93.9
70–74	28	7.8	318	88.3
65–69	36	10.0	290	80.6
60–64	40	11.1	254	70.6
55–59	46	12.8	214	59.4
50–54	43	11.9	168	46.7
45–49	39	10.8	125	34.7
40–44	32	8.9	86	23.9
35–39	24	6.7	54	15.0
30–34	13	3.6	30	8.3
25–29	9	2.5	17	4.7
20–24	5	1.4	8	2.2
15–19	3	0.8	3	0.8
Total	360	100.0		

been infinite in number and unselected with respect to vocabulary, it is expected that the curve would be smooth and symmetrical rather than erratic. The group of 360 pupils somewhat approximates these conditions, and thus the line resulting approximates a smooth symmetrical curve.

NORMAL CURVE. The curve in Figure 15 is shaped, for all practical purposes, like a normal curve. The normal curve is distinctively bell-shaped, with the peak of the curve above a point on the horizontal axis corresponding to the average score of the distribution. From the peak, the curve drops rapidly on either side, yielding a symmetrical tapering as it approaches either end of the raw-score distribution.

The fact that the raw scores from the vocabulary test tend to be normally distributed assists considerably in their description. It is immediately possible to say that few pupils have high raw scores, few pupils have low scores, whereas many have scores clustering around the average raw score. The statement can be appreciably strengthened by wording it in terms of the standard deviation and the arithmetic mean of raw scores. If the standard deviation is added to and subtracted from the arithmetic mean, points along the horizontal axis are found between which fall a fixed percentage of the scores.

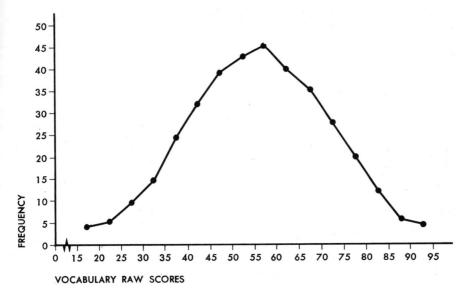

FREQUENCY

VOCABULARY RAW SCORES

FIGURE 15

DISTRIBUTION OF 360 VOCABULARY RAW SCORES
AS PRESENTED IN GRAPHIC FORM

The arithmetic mean is often called the "average." It is a measure of central tendency, that is, a point at or near which the test scores are clustering. With ungrouped data, it is computed by adding all the scores and dividing by the number of scores. However, this procedure cannot be followed when they are arranged in a frequency distribution since, in these instances, the exact test score for a particular pupil is unknown. A modified formula for computing the arithmetic mean of scores in a frequency distribution is shown in Appendix A (see pages 000–000). When applied to the 360 vocabulary raw scores, an arithmetic mean of 55.7 is found.

Like the range, the standard deviation is a measure of the variability or dispersion present in a distribution of test scores. It is a distance expressed in test-score units rather than a point such as the arithmetic mean. Relatively small standard deviations are obtained when the test scores of a distribution are clustered in the vicinity of the arithmetic mean. As the test scores of a distribution spread widely above and below the arithmetic mean, the size of the standard deviation increases.

As in the case of the arithmetic mean, the standard deviation can be computed for test scores which are ungrouped or for test scores arranged in a frequency distribution. Appropriate formulas are shown in Appendix A (see pages 000–000). For the 360 vocabulary test scores shown in Table 4, a standard deviation of 15.3 was computed.

We can add and subtract the standard deviation (σ) from the arithmetic mean (M) in the following manner:

$$M + \sigma = 55.7 + 15.3 = 71.0$$
$$M - \sigma = 55.7 - 15.3 = 40.4$$

and

$$M + 2\sigma = 55.7 + (2)(15.3) = 86.3$$
$$M - 2\sigma = 55.7 - (2)(15.3) = 25.1$$

Because the distribution is approximately normal, about 68 per cent of raw scores are higher than 40.4 but no larger than 71.0. Of the 360 pupils, about 245 have attained such scores. On the other hand, about 95 per cent of the raw scores are larger than 25.1 and smaller than 86.3. Of the 360 pupils, about 342 have attained such scores. Only when a normal distribution is being examined can the foregoing values of 68 and 95 per cent be used in this manner.

Because finite groups of raw scores never conform to a perfect normal distribution, it is common to speak of the 68 per cent of the scores falling between $M + \sigma$ and $M - \sigma$ as the "middle two-thirds" of the distribution. Thus the two remaining tails of the distribution are identified as the "upper one-sixth" and the "lower one-sixth," respectively. Rough as this subdivision is, is quite useful. For example, the teacher confronted with 360 normally distributed vocabulary raw scores can quickly add the standard deviation to the arithmetic mean, then subtract the standard deviation from the arithmetic mean, and visualize a diagram such as the one in Figure 16. He can accordingly classify any raw score above 71 as in the

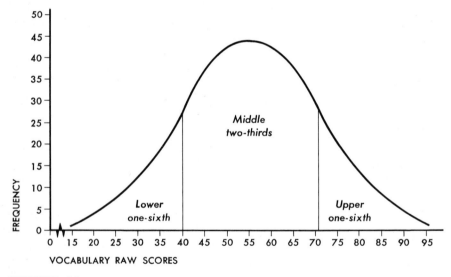

FIGURE 16

NORMAL DISTRIBUTION OF VOCABULARY RAW SCORES

upper one-sixth of the distribution, any raw score larger than 40 but no larger than 71 as in the middle two-thirds of the distribution, and, finally, any raw score below 40 as in the lower one-sixth of the distribution. Although the teacher may be wrong in his classification of raw scores in the immediate vicinity of 71 and 40, he will very likely classify all other raw scores correctly. For example, 58 is clearly within the middle two-thirds of the distribution.

PROBLEMS

1 Assume that the following data are a part of the distribution of vocabulary raw scores:

Pupil	Raw score	Pupil	Raw score
A	40	C	52
B	60	D	57

Is it appropriate to say that the difference in achievement between the first two pupils is four times as great as that between the second two? Why?

2 On the basis of data shown on page 251 the statement is made that Sheri surpasses Carol in terms of the vocabulary test to a greater degree than Arthur surpasses Donald. Is this consistent with your experiences? Explain.

3 In addition to the arithmetic mean, what other measures of central tendency are commonly computed for raw-score distributions?

4 For the distribution of 360 vocabulary raw scores, find the range, that is, the difference between the highest and lowest raw scores. How many times larger is the range than the standard deviation? Do you expect that this relationship between the sizes of the two measures of variability would change appreciably when determined for other groups of normally distributed raw scores? Why?

IDENTIFYING RELATIVE PERFORMANCE

Attempts to identify the relative performance of a pupil in terms of a test have been numerous. Furthermore, these attempts have yielded procedures that are vastly less cumbersome and casual than the manipulations of the raw-score distribution described above. The gist of the problem of simplifying the identification of relative performance is to convert the raw scores yielded by a test to some kind of derived scores that have, by their very nature, considerably greater interpretability. The many variations of derived scores are classified under the heading of *test norms*.

Test norms are representations of average or common performance, based upon the results of testing a normal group of pupils. This group is usually large and supposedly representative of those pupils for whom the test is designed. The test is of course administered under the conditions specified by its author.

Test norms are sometimes confused with test standards. The two expressions are not synonymous. Test norms represent *actual* performance of certain groups of pupils. In contrast, test standards represent *desired* performance in terms of a specific test. In the case of the vocabulary test, for example, the average number of words correctly identified is 55.7, or about one-half of the total number of items. This value is an indication of average or common performance on the part of the seventh-grade pupils and hence falls within the notion of test norms. However, it is possible that the teachers feel that any raw score below 60 is unsatisfactory. If this position is taken, the teachers have obviously established a standard. Such a standard may coincide with a value such as the mean raw score, and then again it may not. Presumably, standards are based upon the considered judgment of teachers and supervisors who are intimately familiar with the teaching environment related to the characteristic·measured by the test and with the talent of the group of pupils tested.

The most common types of norms can be classified into four groups:

Quartiles, deciles, and percentiles
Standard scores
Grade equivalents
Age equivalents

The very length of this list suggests that none seems to be completely satisfactory. It is common to find test authors and consumers reporting several kinds of norms for the same test. Thus, each type of norm deserves a separate, though brief, description.

Quartiles, Deciles, and Percentiles

Quartiles, deciles, and percentiles are points in a distribution of test scores below which fall specified percentages of the scores. The quartiles are three points dividing the distribution into four equal parts in terms of the number of test scores; deciles are nine points dividing the distribution into ten equal parts; percentiles are ninety-nine points dividing the distribution into one hundred equal parts.

The interpretation of a quartile, decile, or percentile is quite uniform. The first quartile, often identified as Q_1, is the point below which 25 per cent of the scores fall. The first decile, D_1, is the point below which 10 per cent of the scores fall. The first percentile, P_1, is the point below which 1 per cent of the scores fall. In a similar manner, the remaining quartiles, deciles, and percentiles are identified symbolically and interpreted. In other words, in the case of the quartile, 25 per cent of the scores fall below Q_1, 25 per cent between Q_1 and Q_2, 25 per cent between Q_2 and Q_3, and 25 per cent above Q_3.

By definition, equalities have been established between certain quartiles, deciles and percentiles. For example,

$$Q_1 = P_{25}$$
$$Q_3 = P_{75}$$
$$D_1 = P_{10}, \text{ etc.}$$

The most notable equality is

$$Q_2 = D_5 = P_{50}$$

Interestingly enough, the point in question, namely, the point below which 50 per cent of the scores fall, is not known as Q_2, D_5, or P_{50}, but as the median. The median also plays a role in other types of norms described in this chapter.

The computation of any quartile, decile, or percentile can be based upon a frequency distribution of raw scores such as the distribution of vocabulary scores shown in Table 5. The formula necessary for the determination of any of these values is shown in Appendix A (see pages 577–580). Repeated application of this formula yields the raw-score equivalents of all of the quartiles, deciles, and percentiles; these are listed in the fourth column of Table 6.

The fact that quartiles, deciles, and percentiles are points and nothing more is re-emphasized by examination of the raw-score equivalents. Consider D_1 for a moment. Its raw-score equivalent is 35.8. This value, as are the others, is arbitrarily rounded back to one decimal since additional decimal places are of little value. Furthermore, like a great majority of its fellow values, it is not an integer. Hence we can say that a raw score of 35 is slightly below D_1, whereas a raw score of 36 is slightly above. No raw score exactly corresponds to D_1. Note that it is not correct to say that any raw score of less than 36 is in the first decile. Quartiles, deciles, and percentiles are points, not parts. Raw scores can be above a given one of them, below it, occasionally at it (for example, $P_{65} = 62.0$) but never in it. To refer carelessly to Q_1 as the lowest quarter, or to D_1 as the lowest tenth of the distribution is naive, inaccurate, and unnecessarily confusing.

The raw-score equivalents of the quartiles, deciles, and percentiles as presented in Table 6 lack utility to some degree. We might now ask, for example, what statement can be made about the raw score of 58. Can it be

TABLE 6
QUARTILES DECILES, PERCENTILES, AND PERCENTILE RANKS
BASED UPON A DISTRIBUTION OF 360 RAW SCORES

Percentile	Decile	Quartile	Raw-score equivalent	Percentile rank	Raw scores
				100	91 and above
99			90.0	99	87, 88, 89, 90
98			86.8	98	85, 86
97			84.2	97	83, 84
96			82.7	96	82
95			81.2	95	80, 81
94			79.7	94	79
93			78.7	93	78
92			77.8	92	77
91			76.9	91	
90	9		76.0	90	76
89			75.1	89	75
88			74.3	88	74
87			73.6	87	
86			73.0	86	73
85			72.4	85	72
84			71.7	84	
83			71.1	83	71
82			70.4	82	70
81			69.8	81	
80	8		69.2	80	69
79			68.7	79	
78			68.2	78	68
77			67.7	77	
76			67.2	76	67
75		3	66.7	75	
74			66.2	74	66
73			65.7	73	
72			65.2	72	65
71			64.7	71	
70	7		64.3	70	64
69			63.8	69	
68			63.4	68	63
67			62.9	67	
66			62.5	66	
65			62.0	65	62
64			61.6	64	

TABLE 6 (Continued)

Percentile	Decile	Quartile	Raw-score equivalent	Percentile rank	Raw scores
63			61.1	63	61
62			60.7	62	
61			60.2	61	60
60	6		59.8	60	
59			59.3	59	59
58			58.9	58	
57			58.5	57	
56			58.2	56	58
55			57.8	55	
54			57.4	54	
53			57.0	53	57
52			56.6	52	
51			56.2	51	56
50	5	Median	55.8	50	
49			55.4	49	
48			55.0	48	55
47			54.6	47	
46			54.2	46	54
45			53.8	45	
44			53.4	44	
43			53.0	43	53
42			52.5	42	
41			52.1	41	52
40	4		51.7	40	
39			51.3	39	51
38			50.9	38	
37			50.5	37	
36			50.0	36	50
35			49.6	35	
34			49.2	34	49
33			48.7	33	
32			48.2	32	48
31			47.8	31	
30	3		47.3	30	47
29			46.9	29	
28			46.4	28	46
27			45.9	27	
26			45.5	26	
25		1	45.0	25	45

TABLE 6 (Continued)

Percentile	Decile	Quartile	Raw-score equivalent	Percentile rank	Raw scores
24			44.6	24	
23			44.0	23	44
22			43.4	22	43
21			42.9	21	
20	2		42.3	20	42
19			41.8	19	
18			41.2	18	41
17			40.6	17	
16			40.1	16	40
15			39.5	15	39
14			38.8	14	
13			38.0	13	38
12			37.3	12	37
11			36.5	11	36
10	1		35.8	10	
9			35.0	9	35
8			34.0	8	33, 34
7			32.7	7	32
6			31.3	6	30, 31
5			29.9	5	29
4			28.1	4	27, 28
3			26.1	3	24, 25, 26
2			23.7	2	21, 22, 23
1			20.1	1	20 and below

reported that it fell somewhere between P_{55} and P_{56}? Certainly this is true, but it is an awkward way to identify relative performance. Simplification of the wording is not possible if it is necessary to speak of percentiles. However, if *percentile ranks* are to be used, the statement reduces itself appreciably.

PERCENTILE RANKS. Quartile ranks, decile ranks, and percentile ranks are not points, but ranges of raw scores. In the case of percentile ranks, these ranges are customarily quite small. By definition, any raw score of the same size as P_1 or less is given a percentile rank of one. Symbolically, this is PR_1. Any raw score larger than P_1 but no larger than P_2 is given a percentile rank of two, that is, PR_2. The process continues until PR_{100} is reached. Any raw score larger than P_{99} is so identified. Thus the distribution is divided into one hundred percentile ranks.

The last two columns of Table 6 list the percentile ranks and the corresponding raw scores. The latter are found by simply inspecting the size of the raw-score equivalents of the percentiles and applying the definition of percentile ranks. A less laborious means of determining percentile ranks is to read them from an accurately plotted ogive curve; that is, the curve resulting when cumulative percentages are plotted against the raw scores (Downie and Heath, 1965).

It follows then that a raw score of 58 is equivalent to a percentile rank of 56. This can be interpreted to mean that a pupil with a score of 58 in a vocabulary test ranks fifty-sixth from the bottom in a standard group of one hundred seventh-grade pupils.

The relationships among raw scores, percentiles, and percentile ranks are worth examining in some detail. Figure 17 facilitates the discussion; the lower part of the raw-score distribution from the vocabulary test is reproduced on the left-hand vertical line, the corresponding percentiles on the center vertical line, and the percentile ranks on the right-hand vertical

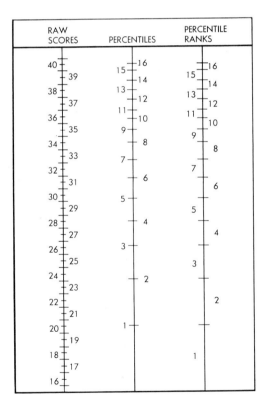

FIGURE 17

RELATIONSHIPS AMONG RAW SCORES, PERCENTILES AND PERCENTILE RANKS line. The raw scores are represented as the mid-points of tiny theoretical ranges, the size of the range being a function of the sensitivity of the measurement. Since, in the case of the vocabulary test, the characteristic is measured to the nearest whole number, a raw score such as 16 is considered to be the mid-point of a tiny theoretical range between 15.5 and 16.5. The size of the range is unity throughout these raw scores. Because percentiles are defined as points, the identifying numbers in the center vertical line are placed opposite the appropriate mark. In contrast, the percentile ranks are ranges, and are numbered on the right-hand vertical line by centering the numbers midway in the proper interval.

Clearly, Figure 17 is nothing more than a graphic presentation of part of the data included in Table 6. Even though incomplete, the figure is a suitable adjunct to the table in that it shows strikingly that raw scores are equivalent to theoretical ranges, percentiles are points, and percentile ranks are ranges of raw scores isolated by consecutive percentile points. Notice that the size of the ranges of the percentile ranks does not remain constant.

Percentile ranks are more commonly reported and used than percentiles. Tables converting raw scores to percentile ranks are standard equipment in many test manuals. Although the last two columns of Table 6 perform the conversion function, they are probably not shown in that fashion. Rather, the two columns are rearranged so that the raw-score column is first and the percentile-rank column is second.

UTILITY OF PERCENTILE NORMS. The use of percentiles and percentile ranks to represent relative performance is extremely popular. This fact is perhaps the most powerful reason why test authors seldom fail to include these norms in their test manuals. Nor that teachers, pupils, and even parents have been educated to a point that the term " percentile" has become almost a household word, test authors capitalize on the situation and view percentile norms as a convenient way of communicating with a large, heterogeneous audience.

There is a second reason for the continued use of percentile norms: the tables of norms can always be interpreted exactly no matter what the nature of the distribution of raw scores from which they are derived. Because the percentiles and percentile ranks discussed in this chapter are based upon a normal distribution of raw scores, the casual generalization may have been made that only when raw scores are normally distributed can the percentiles and percentile ranks be computed and interpreted as described. This is not true. The distribution of raw scores can vary immensely from a normal distribution without changing the interpretation of percentile norms.

The disadvantages of using percentile norms for representing relative performance of pupils are, however, somewhat damaging. Firstly, and most important of all, the size of units of percentiles and percentile ranks is not constant. Differences between percentiles are not equivalent to differences between raw scores. The failure of the percentile norm to reflect the characteristic measured in the same manner as the original raw score is serious indeed.

Inspection of Table 6 and Figure 17 reveals this situation in a typical case. Certainly the percentiles and percentile ranks are hiding large differences between raw scores when they occur at either the high or low extremity of the raw-score distribution, and also are enlarging small differences between raw scores when they occur near the center of the distribution. A pupil with a raw score of 15 is no different in terms of percentile rank from a pupil with one of 20. Both are at the first percentile rank. Similarly, a pupil with a raw score of 94 is no different in terms of percentile rank from a pupil with a raw score of 91. Both have a percentile rank of 100. On the other hand the raw score of 58 yields a percentile rank of 56. With the present system of scoring the vocabulary test, it is not possible for a pupil to have a percentile rank of 54 or 55.

Percentile norms have "rubber units." The extent to which the units have been "rubberized" depends upon the nature of the distribution of the raw scores. If that distribution is normal or nearly normal, the amount of distortion is large, as in the illustration. In Table 6 notice that a pupil at PR_{96} is much farther away from a pupil at PR_{86} in terms of raw-score units than is a pupil at PR_{56} from a pupil at PR_{46}. The difference in raw-score units is nine in the first instance and four in the second.

The second objection is less serious than the first and sometimes of little concern to teachers. Simply phrased, it states that percentiles and percentile ranks as such cannot be treated arithmetically and a meaningful end product obtained. One cannot legitimately compute an arithmetic mean of these values or correlate them with other measurements by means of a product-moment coefficient of correlation. Percentiles and percentile ranks are, in effect, terminal values. Once computed they can be interpreted; then their utility is exhausted. Test norms such as standard scores do not suffer from this limitation.

Standard Scores

Another popular system for representing relative performance on a test is the standard score. The intent of the standard score is to transform the raw-score distribution to a derived-score distribution having a desired arithmetic mean and standard deviation. If the arithmetic mean and standard deviation are known, and if the derived-score distribution is normal, identification of the relative performance of individual pupils is a simple matter. The same approach is used here as is described in connection with Figure 16 when normally distributed raw scores were involved.

Z-SCORES. There are many types of standard scores, each with its own arithmetic mean and standard deviation. The "parent" of the group is the well-known z-score. From this base have sprung the others, three of which are commonly encountered and are described below.

The z-scores are computed from the formula

$$z = \frac{X - M}{\sigma}$$

where

$z =$ standard score
$X =$ any raw score of a given distribution
$M =$ arithmetic mean of the raw-score distribution
$\sigma =$ standard derivation of the raw-score distribution

Examination of the formula reveals that any raw score smaller than the arithmetic mean of the raw scores yields a z-score with a negative sign, whereas any larger than the arithmetic mean yields a z-score that is positive. When a raw-score distribution is transformed into z-scores, the arithmetic mean of the resulting z-scores is zero, and the standard deviation to the z-scores is unity.

To change a raw score to a z-score, a table of norms similar to that used for percentile ranks is consulted. Such a table is Table 7, the second column of which is constructed by successively solving the z-score equation for all obtained raw scores ($M = 55.7, \sigma = 15.3$) resulting from the administration of the vocabulary test. Any raw score can be readily converted to a z-score by merely glancing at the table. For example, a z-score of $+0.15$ corresponds to the raw score of 58. Note that the practical limits of the z-score distribution do not exceed $+3.00$ and -3.00.

OTHER MULTIPLE-DIGIT STANDARD SCORES. Because z-scores have negative signs and decimal points, their usefulness decreases. Clerical errors too easily and too often create havoc when test results are reported. To avoid these difficulties, linear transformations of the original z-scores are made and an entire family of standard scores is automatically born. One such transformation is

$$\text{Standard score} = 10\,(z) + 50$$

This equation produces a distribution of standard scores with an arithmetic mean of 50 and a standard deviation of 10. In Table 7 these standard scores are listed opposite the corresponding z-score and vocabulary

TABLE 7
STANDARD SCORES OF RAW SCORES BASED UPON 360 SEVENTH-GRADE PUPILS

Raw score	z	Standard score (M = 50, σ = 10)	Raw score	z	Standard score (M = 50, σ = 10)
94	2.50	75	54	−0.11	49
93	2.44	74	53	−0.18	48
92	2.37	74	52	−0.24	48
91	2.31	73	51	−0.31	47
90	2.24	72	50	−0.37	46
89	2.18	72	49	−0.44	46
88	2.11	71	48	−0.50	45
87	2.05	71	47	−0.57	44
86	1.98	70	46	−0.63	44
85	1.92	69	45	−0.70	43
84	1.85	69	44	−0.76	42
83	1.78	68	43	−0.83	42
82	1.72	67	42	−0.90	41
81	1.65	67	41	−0.96	40
80	1.59	66	40	−1.03	40
79	1.52	65	39	−1.09	39
78	1.46	65	38	−1.16	38
77	1.39	64	37	−1.22	38
76	1.33	63	36	−1.29	37
75	1.26	63	35	−1.35	36
74	1.20	62	34	−1.42	36
73	1.13	61	33	−1.48	35
72	1.07	61	32	−1.55	34
71	1.00	60	31	−1.61	34
70	0.93	59	30	−1.68	33
69	0.87	59	29	−1.75	32
68	0.80	58	28	−1.81	32
67	0.74	57	27	−1.88	31
66	0.67	57	26	−1.94	31
65	0.61	56	25	−2.01	30
64	0.54	55	24	−2.07	29
63	0.48	55	23	−2.14	29
62	0.41	54	22	−2.20	28
61	0.35	54	21	−2.27	27
60	0.28	53	20	−2.33	27
59	0.22	52	19	−2.40	26
58	0.15	52	18	−2.46	25
57	0.08	51	17	−2.53	25
56	0.02	50	16	−2.60	24
55	−0.05	49	15	−2.66	23

test raw score. It should be noted that this type of standard score is often called a T-score, although the original T-score as proposed by McCall (1939) is somewhat different.

Another transformation is

$$\text{Standard score} = 20\,(z) + 100$$

Now the arithmetic mean of the standard scores is 100 and the standard deviation is 20. This type of standard score is used with the Army General Classification Test administered during and after World War II.

Also, the equation can read

$$\text{Standard score} = 100\,(z) + 500$$

The arithmetic mean of these standard scores is 500, whereas the standard deviation is 100. Standard scores of this type are used in connection with the College Entrance Examination Board Tests.

The above information is summarized in the following table. In addition to the arithmetic means and standard deviations, the practical limits of the standard score distribution are given. The practical limits are the points that are three standard deviation units above the arithmetic mean and three below the arithmetic mean.

The interpretation of any standard score of any type depends directly upon the knowledge of the arithmetic mean of the standard-score distribution and its standard deviation. If the distribution of standard scores is normal, the interpretation is not difficult; if it is not normal, the interpretation is quite uncertain.

| | Arithmetic | Standard | Practical imits | |
Type	mean	deviation	High	Low
z	0	1	+3.00	−3.00
10 (z) + 50	50	10	80	20
20 (z) + 100	100	20	160	40
100 (z) + 500	500	100	800	200

To assume that standard scores are always normally distributed simply because they are standard scores is a common mistake. If the raw scores are normally distributed, then the standard scores computed from them are automatically normally distributed. In view of the fact that many raw-score distributions, as in the vocabulary test, are for all practical purposes normally distributed, the interpretation of most standard scores is based upon the normal curve.

To interpret standard scores based upon normally distributed raw scores, it is helpful to think of a diagram such as Figure 16. For z-scores, the middle two-thirds of the distribution falls between $+1.00$ and -1.00, whereas the upper one-sixth is composed of z-scores that exceed $+1.00$ and the lower one-sixth contains z-scores that fail to reach -1.00. For the other three types of standard scores, the following reference points are available:

Standard score characteristics		Middle two-thirds	Upper one-sixth	Lower one-sixth
M	σ	Between	Greater than	Less than
50	10	40 and 60	60	40
100	20	80 and 120	120	80
500	100	400 and 600	600	400

Unlike the percentile rank procedure, no attempt is made here to interpret more exactly the relative performance of each pupil. Occasionally, percentile ranks are criticized for leaving a largely artificial impression of exactness. In any event, the normal curve can be broken into more segments than the three mentioned. Should this be desirable for whatever reason, a table of areas under the normal curve can be consulted. Such a table, along with a description of its functions, can be found in most of the available textbooks devoted to statistical methodology (Downie and Heath, 1965).

STANINES. The outstanding single-digit standard score used today is the stanine (pronounced *stay-nine*). This word was originally derived from the expression "standard *nine*-point scale," which is a system of standard scores developed during World War II. At that time, a simple and workable type of norm was sought. The stanine scale was found to be satisfactory since it employs a single digit to represent relative performance and yet is precise enough for most practical testing problems. It is being used more and more now for standardized and teacher-constructed tests.

When stanine norms are used, raw scores are converted to one of nine stanine scores which vary from a low of 1 to a high of 9. The mean of the stanine distribution is 5 and its standard deviation 2. On the other hand, when large numbers of pupils are involved, some measurement specialists will subdivide the two extreme positions on the scale, thereby creating an eleven-point scale with a low of zero and a high of ten.

The determination of stanine scores is simple (Durost, 1961). For example, when working with raw scores from smaller groups of pupils, a teacher can arrange the raw scores from high to low, then determine the median of the distribution, and, with this as a starting point, apply the theoretical percentages of the stanine subgroups. These percentages are as follows:

Stanine	1	2	3	4	5	6	7	8	9
Percentage of Pupils	4	7	12	17	20	17	12	7	4

The median is theoretically in the center of the middle 20% of the distribution. This subgroup is given a stanine of 5. By working upward and downward from this subgroup the remaining subgroups are found and the stanines assigned. Certain minor adjustments of the subgroups are usually necessary to bring the actual percentages into the closest possible agreement with the theoretical percentages. This is necessitated by the principle that every pupil having the same raw score will, of course, have the same stanine score.

UTILITY OF STANDARD SCORE NORMS. After comparing the interpretation of the vocabulary raw scores and the interpretation of the standard scores based upon those raw scores, you may wonder what advantages standard scores have over raw scores. One of these is the fact that standard scores have a specified arithmetic mean and standard deviation. Raw-score distributions have a habit of producing arithmetic means and standard deviations that have somewhat quaint sizes and are seldom integers. On the other hand standard-score distributions have arithmetic means which are easily remembered—0, 5, 50, 100, or 500—and a standard deviation that can be speedily added to or subtracted from that mean. In the case of the vocabulary test, it would be faster to manipulate the standard-score distribution with its arithmetic mean of 50 and standard deviation of 10 than the raw-score distribution with its arithmetic mean of 55.7 and standard deviation of 15.3. Also, fewer arithmetical errors would occur.

The two disadvantages of percentile norms cannot be attributed to standard-score norms. When computed for normally distributed raw scores, the standard-score unit is constant throughout the range and not a changing unit, as is that of percentile norms. Furthermore, standard scores can be treated arithmetically. To find the arithmetic mean or standard deviation of standard scores is just as legitimate as finding those values for raw scores.

Another important advantage of standard scores is the ease of comparison of scores for a pupil who has been given several tests, and the ease of determining a composite score if desired. For instance, reporting each of a series of achievement test scores in a subject-matter area in terms of stanines permits the teacher to compare levels of achievement from one test to another for a specific pupil; for example, when a graphic profile of stanines is prepared. He can also combine these stanines to obtain a composite score representing the over-all achievement of the pupil. Such a composite score is often the arithmetic mean of the stanines in question. Finding the arithmetic mean weights each test score equally. If desired, various weights can be assigned the stanines before the arithmetic mean is computed.

Percentiles and all types of standard scores are interrelated if the raw-score distribution from which they are computed is normal. The normal distribution restriction is highly important. In Figure 18 these relationships are shown in part (Seashore, 1955). Before the relationships shown in this figure can be considered useful, there must be statistical evidence that the distribution of raw scores is essentially a normal one.

The major disadvantage of standard scores is that they are difficult to

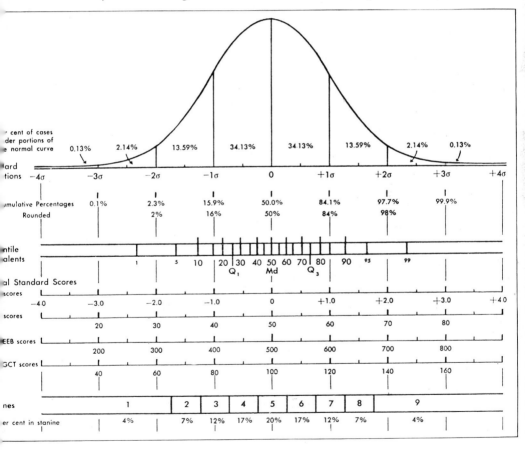

FIGURE 18

RELATIONSHIPS AMONG NORMALLY DISTRIBUTED RAW SCORES, PERCENTILES, AND CERTAIN STANDARD SCORES

interpret when they are not normally distributed. This fact, plus the general public's lack of familiarity with them, somewhat restricts their use.

Grade Equivalents

Representing the relative performance of pupils with grade equivalents is still another popular method. A grade equivalent of a particular raw score is the grade level of those pupils whose median is the same as the raw score in question. In other words, if the median raw score happened to be 63 for a test administered to sixth-grade pupils just beginning that grade level, all raw scores of 63 have a grade equivalent of 6.0.

The generally accepted way of reporting grade equivalents is in terms of two numbers. The first of the two numbers is designated as the year and second as the month. For example, a grade equivalent of 5.4 is the median raw score of pupils tested at the fourth month of the fifth grade. Note that the calendar year is divided into ten parts, nine representing the academic year and one representing summer vacation months.

The process of computing grade equivalents is systematic but not unusually impressive. In the first place, the test is administered to large groups of pupils in consecutive grade levels. This takes place at the same time of year for all pupils. The median raw score of each grade level is found and plotted against the grade level. Then the "best fitting" curve is passed through the points, and sometimes extended (extrapolated) dangerously far beyond the upper and lower grade levels involved in the initial testing. The grade equivalents of raw scores are read directly from the curve.

Figure 19 is the type of curve that could have resulted from the above procedure when an achievement test is administered to elementary school pupils. Raw-score units have been laid off on the vertical axis and grade equivalents on the horizontal axis. The smooth curve yielded by the plotted points (not shown) is identified by a solid line. The extrapolated sections representing grade levels not tested are drawn as dotted lines and supposedly follow the general curvature of the solid line. To find that as much as one-half of the diagram is obtained by extrapolation as illustrated in Figure 19 is relatively common.

The weaknesses of the method of determination are apparent. The "best fitting" curve is a matter of judgment. So is the extension of the curve to grade levels not included in the testing. Furthermore, the smoothness of the curve suggests regular and gradual pupil growth throughout the academic year, and summer vacation growth comparable to one month of growth during the academic year. These assumptions are more easily attacked than defended.

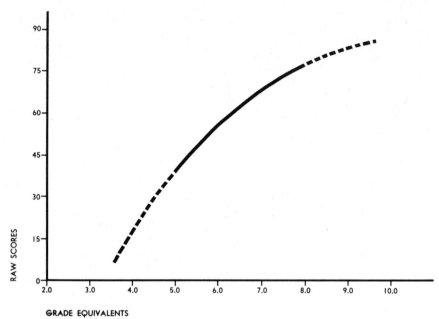

FIGURE 19

A TYPICAL CURVE FOR DETERMINING GRADE EQUIVALENTS OF ACHIEVEMENT
TEST RAW SCORES OF ELEMENTARY SCHOOL PUPILS

UTILITY OF GRADE EQUIVALENTS. Despite the limitations in the plotting
procedure for computing grade equivalents, these scores are amazingly well-
received, especially in the elementary grade levels. The reason for this is
that grade equivalents are easily understood. Contrast these derived scores
with standard scores or even percentile ranks. Comparing a pupil's actual
grade level with his grade equivalents yielded by tests in various subject-
matter areas is definitely more comprehensible to many teachers, administrators, and parents than standard scores and percentile ranks. Moreover,
grade equivalents offer convenient units for plotting profiles of pupil
achievement. Such profiles are graphic representations of a pupil's test
scores and typically emphasize the areas of over- and under-achievement.
Again, the reference point most useful for interpreting the profile is the
present grade level of the pupil.

Several basic restrictions of grade equivalents must be remembered if
they are to be properly used and interpreted. The most important of these
is that a grade equivalent cannot always be taken at face value. When the
"best fitting" curve used to determine the grade equivalents of raw scores
has been extended to grade levels higher and lower than those used in the
initial testing, this trouble becomes pronounced. Suppose, for example,
that a pupil beginning the fifth grade is given a fifth-grade arithmetic test

and receives a grade equivalent of 8.0. This does not necessarily indicate that he has mastered all of the arithmetic subject matter in the fifth, sixth, and seventh grades. Although he is displaying superior arithmetic achievement when compared to the typical fifth-grade pupil, in all probability he is not sufficiently well trained at that moment to compete successfully in arithmetic with pupils beginning the eighth grade. In other words, had he been tested by an *eighth-grade* arithmetic test, he very likely would fall below the grade equivalent of 8.0.

A second restriction limits the highest grade level to which equivalents may extend. Grade equivalents should not extend beyond the ninth grade since, with the exception of English, there is no continuous and systematic instruction beyond the ninth grade for those subject-matter areas taught in elementary school. Remember that the plotting method of determining grade equivalents assumes regular and gradual pupil growth over the period of time selected. Since this does not occur in secondary school in such areas as reading, arithmetic, and spelling, grade equivalents like 10.3 and 11.0 are meaningless. Standard or scaled scores should be used to represent relative performance of secondary school pupils when tested in pertinent subject-matter areas.

Finally, grade equivalents suffer from that ancient malady we call "rubber units." There is no assurance that a given difference between two grade equivalents is comparable to the same difference between two other grade equivalents, even though the same test is involved. However, the seriousness of this difficulty varies with the subject-matter area being tested. Within the elementary school levels, grade equivalents yielded by tests in areas such as reading, arithmetic, and spelling tend to have equal units. This is true because the subject-matter areas are given a consistent emphasis throughout a relatively long period of time. For subject-matter areas that are not given consistent emphasis over a prolonged period of time, the units of grade equivalents are customarily unequal.

Age Equivalents

Age equivalents are very similar to grade equivalents. Years of age have simply replaced grade levels in the method of computation and interpretation. It follows then that an age equivalent of a particular raw score is the chronological age of those pupils whose median (or arithmetic mean) raw score is the same as the raw score in question. For example, a pupil who received a raw score of 48 on a certain test finds, upon consulting a table converting raw scores to age equivalents, that it corresponds to an age equivalent of 10-4. The median (or arithmetic mean in some cases) raw score of pupils ten years and four months of age is therefore 48.

The above illustration lists the age equivalent by means of two numbers separated by a dash, a typical way of reporting these values. The first number represents the number of years, whereas the second represents the number of months. Unlike grade equivalents, the calendar year is divided into twelve parts, so that the second number varies from a minimum of zero to a maximum of eleven.

Computing age equivalents strongly resembles the computation of grade equivalents. Both processes utilize plotted points to determine a "best fitting" smooth curve as in Figure 19, from which derived scores are read off for any raw score. Both processes commonly extend the curve rather liberally beyond the limits of the data and thereby automatically inject serious possibility of error for derived scores in the regions of the extended curve.

UTILITY OF AGE EQUIVALENTS. Many of the remarks concerning the utility of grade equivalents can be attributed to age equivalents. For instance, age equivalents are most suitable for the chronological years covered by the elementary grade levels. Also, they are based upon the assumption that the characteristic represented changes continually and smoothly during the years spanned by the norms. They are simple to grasp and convenient to talk about, just as are grade equivalents.

On a number of occasions, the authors of tests list both age and grade equivalents as suitable derived scores for their achievement tests. The choice of the score the teacher is to use may or may not be difficult. If the pupils in question are members of an elementary school that practices automatic promotion based on chronological age, and the teachers recognize this in their teaching, the two types of norms will differ little from each other. If this is not the case, then the nature of the characteristic measured by the test plays a more important role.

Age equivalents are suitable for representing characteristics that change as a part of the pupil's general development. In other words, age equivalents have, in the last analysis, a biological base. For this reason physiological traits like height and weight can be appropriately represented by age equivalents. Of the psychological traits, general intelligence can be suitably expressed in terms of age equivalents.

In contrast, it is logical to represent relative performance of pupils in terms of grade equivalents when the characteristic measured is influenced primarily by the formal educative processes of school systems. Subject-matter areas such as arithmetic, spelling, nature study, and reading fall in these categories, even though certain gains take place outside the classroom. As far as summer vacation is concerned, the grade equivalent tries to compensate for the change by allowing one month for the period. This probably undercompensates for the amount of change, especially in such an area as reading. Age equivalents consider every month to be the same as all other months and thus undoubtedly overcompensate for the amount of change occurring during summer vacation in the subject-matter areas mentioned.

The age equivalents obtained by measuring a pupil are most readily interpreted by comparing them with his present chronological age. If the age equivalent noticeably surpasses his chronological age, he is above average; if the two are approximately the same, he is average; if the age equivalent is definitely lower than his chronological age, he is below average. In an attempt to refine this method, some age equivalents are divided by the chronological age and the quotient multiplied by 100. The final result is called an educational quotient if the age equivalent represents general achievement, or a subject-matter quotient (such as a reading quotient) if the age equivalent indicates progress in a subject-matter area.

Symbolically the formula for general achievement is

$$EQ = \frac{EA}{CA} (100)$$

where

EQ = educational quotient
EA = educational age (i.e., age equivalent)
CA = chronological age

According to the formula, an EQ of about 100 is average. Any value well above 100 is above average, whereas any value well below 100 is below average. Notice that this is the same approach as was used for representing degrees of general mental ability with the ratio type intelligence quotient. The popularity of this type of intelligence quotient has declined rapidly in recent years.

PROBLEMS

5   Teachers are often interested in pupil growth or improvement in achievement in a given subject-matter area and will administer the same test before and after a period of instruction hoping that the difference between the two scores will measure pupil growth. Identify the principal measurement problems present in this process. How successfully can the various types of norms reflect pupil growth (Tiedeman, 1951)?

6   Construct an ogive curve based on Table 5 and determine several percentile ranks by means of it (Downie and Heath, 1965, Chapter 3). Check your results against those shown in Table 6.

7 A differentiation is made between "normative" standard scores and "content" standard test scores (Wesman and others, 1962). On what basis is this differentiation made and of what significance is it to classroom teachers?

STANDARDIZATION GROUPS

When the pupil's raw score of 58 was compared to those of all the other members of his class, undoubtedly no one seriously complained about the fairness of the procedure. After all, in terms of vocabulary formal training, he and his classmates probably had had almost identical opportunities. In addition, his class represented a small geographic area within a city, and thus a smaller socio-economic range than in the city at large, certainly a smaller range than in the state or nation. If these conditions existed, it is likely that the range of scholastic aptitude among the pupils of his class was somewhat restricted in comparison to the range in the entire city or state. Very possibly the class was relatively homogeneous in many other respects. If so, one might ask whether there is a group of pupils to whom he might more suitably be compared than these seventh-grade classmates, many of whom were his neighbors and had attended the same classes with him since kindergarten.

Throughout the discussion of derived scores, repeated mention is made of the standardization or norm group, that is, the group of pupils whose raw scores are used to identify the raw-score equivalents of the derived scores. The standardization group consists of pupils for whom the test is designed and who are given the test under conditions recommended by its author. For our illustration, this group is more than the seventh-grade class; it is the 360 seventh-grade pupils within the city school system. The appropriateness of interpreting achievement in the light of the results of this larger group must be established before taking the trouble to compute any of the derived scores.

A regularly observed principle is that the expression of a pupil's relative performance in derived scores is meaningful when the standardization group used to determine them resembles that pupil in terms of any of a variety of salient characteristics. It follows, therefore, that comparison of a pupil's vocabulary with that of the 360 pupils is suitable since, within a single city school system, there is appreciable similarity in amount and quality of instruction in any subject-matter area among the various component schools, and similarity in the pupils' ability to profit from that instruction.

It is only rarely appropriate to compare a pupil's vocabulary achievement to that of a seemingly very different group. Hence to support the use of the 360 pupils as a standardization group, they should be described in terms of the amount of their previous formal schooling in the area tested, their age distribution, scholastic aptitude distribution, socio-economic ratings, and so forth. Since the averages of these measures do not differ greatly from the pupil's position, the comparison of his achievement with theirs would seem to make sense. Should the 360 pupils as a group be vastly unlike him, the interpretation of his relative performance based upon this group is less useful, barring unusual reasons.

Sampling Problem

The problem so often faced by teachers who wish to use test norms is that their pupils are not a part of the standardization group. Hence, the teacher must know whether his pupils can be considered a part of the population of which the standardization group is a cross-sectional sample. Unless they can be considered a part of such a population, the tables of norms cannot be used.

The sampling problem with test norms has been vastly underestimated. Tables of norms that are labeled "national" or "regional" without bothering to specify the manner in which the nation or region is sampled, are contributing by omission to the fuzzy notion that the worth of a sample is determined only incidentally by the method of obtaining it. More often than not, the size of the sample is impressive and is noted with pride, notwithstanding the fact that it is incidental to the method of selecting its members.

The whimsical nature of some methods of sampling pupils to be used as standardization groups can be neatly illuminated by changing the scene slightly. Suppose you want to find the average body temperature of human adult males. This is a norm, of course, and you already recognize that, if you use the thermometer-under-the-tongue technique, the answer is 98.6°F. In any event, assume that this information is unknown, even though the measurement technique has been perfected. Had you attacked the problem as some test authors attack the problem of norms, you would immediately search for a group (preferably large) of readily available and unusually co-operative subjects. What better place is there to find them than in the local hospitals? Hospital authorities will probably co-operate because it means an inexpensive way of acquiring more information about their patients; the patients can't complain, nurses can be quickly trained to measure temperature reliably. You proceed happily with your research and discover the average body temperature of human adult males to be 100.2°F.

There is a remarkable parallel between the foregoing illustration and the all-to-common procedure for establishing norms of some educational tests. However, results of the temperature measurements are summarily rejected by the medical profession and for good reason. The method of measurement is not questioned, but the accurate representation of the sample certainly is. On the other hand, in educational measurement, tables of norms yielded by equally faulty sampling procedures are sometimes accepted uncritically. Those pupils that serve as standardization groups because they are conveniently available are more likely atypical than typical of the regional and national population that they are supposed to represent.

The task of satisfactorily sampling a group of pupils is admittedly difficult and highly expensive. If there is no evidence to the contrary, national norms should include, in proportion to their numbers, boys and girls, some white and some colored, native born and foreign born, intelligent and not intelligent, some who live in cities, some in suburban areas and some in rural areas, those who are wealthy and those who are poor, who attend large schools and small schools, public schools and private schools, and who have received superior and inferior instruction. Even this list is not complete. Any factor that could conceivably affect the test results should be considered in the selection of the sample.

A number of test authors strengthen the utility of their tables of norms by publishing not one but several such tables, each designed for a relatively homogeneous population. If the sexes are found to differ in terms of a test, such as a paper-and-pencil personality inventory, separate tables of norms for boys and girls are listed. In some instances, separate tables are shown for rural schools and urban schools, for schools in southern states and in northern states, for various levels of scholastic aptitude within a grade level, and for pupils specializing in various types of secondary school curricula. For each group of pupils so used, the author then reports data concerning the group's age, educational status, and the like. Every additional piece of information characterizing the standardization group helps a teacher decide whether his pupils logically belong in the population sampled by the standardization group.

LOCAL NORMS. Even though a variety of tables of norms is available, consideration should be given to the possibility of constructing local norms. These are usually expressed in terms of percentile ranks or standard scores. If several hundred or more test scores from a certain test are available, and if future use is to be made of that test, local norms should be found, and should be revised from time to time as additional raw scores become available. After all, a particular raw score on a test may be equivalent to a standard score of 60 in terms of national norms, 57 in terms of regional norms, 58 in terms of local norms based upon one city, or 52 in terms of local norms based upon one school. All these indications of relative performance may be helpful, but, generally speaking, those derived from local norms tend to be the most realistic appraisals of the pupil's position. Variations in school admission and promotion policies, in curriculum and teaching methods, and in pupil ability cause norms based upon a scattered, poorly defined group of schools and pupils to be reference points of somewhat vague stability and meaning.

Problems

8   A senior whose percentile rank on a scholastic aptitude test was 85, had a percentile rank of 60 on an achievement test in advanced mathematics. His mathematics teacher concluded that he was under-achieving. What information must you know about the standardization groups used before you can evaluate the teacher's conclusion on that basis?

9   Study the description of procedures used to select a standardization group and the description of the standardization group finally used for the *Iowa Tests of Basic Skills* (Lindquist and Hieronymous, 1956, pp. 76–82). Compare this with similar information provided by any other achievement test battery for the elementary school.

10   In addition to norms for pupil scores, manuals of the *Iowa Tests of Educational Development* provide information concerning norms for school averages. Evaluate the worth of the school norms.

11   An attempt has been made to develop norms for a long test by administering only a few of its items to each pupil in the standardization group (Lord, 1962). What practical gains are realized by this technique?

Summary

The results yielded by evaluation instruments frequently lack meaning. For instance, raw scores, which are the immediate quantitative end product of scoring the test, defy interpretation until suitable reference points are known. Three such reference points are the arithmetic mean of a group of raw scores and the values of the largest and smallest raw scores. Other reference points can be readily located if the distribution of raw scores is normal or practically normal. When this is true, the standard deviation of the raw scores can be successively added to and subtracted from the arithmetic mean to identify distribution points, including fixed percentages of raw scores.

Raw-score distributions are habitually characterized by two inadequacies. In the first place, a raw score of zero does not correspond to absolute zero. This is not a serious deficiency in terms of lessening raw score interpretability. Secondly, raw-score distributions tend to have "rubber units," that is, unequal units. This deficiency is considerably more serious but hardly disastrous in well-constructed instruments.

There have been many efforts to improve the meaningfulness of raw scores. Raw scores are changed to derived scores, which more readily show the relative performance of a pupil in terms of the test. Derived scores (better known as norms) are obtained by giving a test to a group of pupils for whom it is designed and under conditions recommended by the author, and, now having a distribution of raw scores, applying the necessary formulas or plotting the necessary graphs. The group of pupils so used is called a standardization group.

The most common norms in educational measurement are quartiles, deciles, and percentiles; standard scores; grade equivalents; and age equivalents. Quartiles, deciles, and percentiles are points in a distribution below which specified percentages of raw scores will fall. Standard scores are derived scores with known arithmetic means and standard deviations. Grade equivalents represent average test performance of pupils of various grade levels, whereas age equivalents represent average test performance of pupils of various chronological ages.

The standardization group used to compute tables of norms must be carefully chosen. It is a sample of a population of pupils and, ideally, should be selected in accordance with the sampling procedures designed by a competent statistician. Before tables of norms can be used, a teacher must be convinced that his pupils can legitimately be considered a part of the population represented by a standardization group. Many test manuals contain several tables of norms representing various populations, since, for most purposes, norms become more meaningful as the standardization group used to determine them more closely resembles the pupils involved in the comparison. This resemblance should occur for any and every characteristic known to influence test performance. The need for similarity between a pupil and the standardization group with which he is being compared contributes heavily to the importance of local norms.

Suggested Readings

Anastasi, Anne. *Psychological testing.* (2nd ed.) New York: Macmillan, 1961. Chapter 4.
   This chapter includes sections dealing with age scores, percentiles, and standard scores. It concludes with a discussion of standardization groups.
Downie, N. M., and R. W. Heath. *Basic statistical methods.* (2nd ed.) New York: Harper & Row, 1965. Chapters 3, 4, 5, and 6.
   Methods of computing quartiles, deciles, and percentiles are shown in Chapter 3. Standard scores and the normal curve are treated in Chapter 6. Chapters 4 and 5 deal with the computation of measures of central tendency and measures of variability respectively.

Durost, W. N. *The characteristics, use, and computation of stanines.* Test Service Notebook, No. 23. Tarrytown, N.Y.: Harcourt, Brace and World, 1961.
  All aspects of stanines which are important to classroom teachers are covered in this bulletin. Illustrations are given of their computation and uses.

Flanagan, John C. Units, scores, and norms. In E. F. Lindquist (Ed.), *Educational measurement.* Washington: American Council on Education, 1951. Pp. 695–763.
  The pages cited include discussions of the problem of interpreting test scores, the principal types of norms, and the difficulty of finding suitable standardization groups. Parts of the material presented are somewhat technical.

Lennon, R. T. Norms: 1963. In *Proceedings of the 1963 Invitational Conference on Testing Problems.* Princeton, N.J.: Educational Testing Service, 1964. Pp. 13–22.
  The author gives particular emphasis to the determination of standardization groups for standardized achievement test batteries. Illustrations are provided and discussed.

Lyman, H. B. *Test scores and what they mean.* Englewood Cliffs, N.J.: Prentice-Hall, 1963. Chapters 5 and 6.
  Written for individuals such as classroom teachers who must interpret test scores, this book covers its topics well. Chapter 5 concerns norm tables and standardization groups, and Chapter 6 types of derived scores. A thirteen-page glossary to testing terms ends the book.

McLaughlin, K. F. *Interpretation of test results.* Washington: U.S. Government Printing Office, 1964. Chapters 8 and 9.
  Classroom interpretation of test scores is the topic for Chapter 8, whereas Chapter 9 is devoted to the interpretation of test results to parents. Both chapters are short and clearly stated.

Ricks, James H., Jr. *On telling parents about test results.* Test Service Bulletin, No. 54. New York: Psychological Corporation, 1959.
  The principle of informing parents about the test scores of their children is warmly supported. Suggestions for explaining intelligence quotients, grade equivalents, standard scores, and percentile ranks are given.

Wesman, Alexander G., and others. Symposium: standard scores for aptitude and achievement tests. *Educ. psychol. Measmt,* 1962, **22,** 5–39.
  The virtues and limitations of various kinds of standard scores are compared and evaluated. Five testing specialists contributed to the symposium.

REFERENCES CITED

Downie, N. M., and R. W. Heath. *Basic statistical methods.* (2nd ed.) New York: Harper & Row, 1965.

Durost, Walter N. *The characteristics, use, and computation of stanines.* Test Service Notebook, No. 23. Tarrytown, N.Y.: Harcourt, Brace and World, 1961.

Educational Testing Service. *Examiner's manual, Co-operative School and College Ability Tests.* Princeton, N.J.: Author, 1955.

Lindquist, E. F., and A. N. Hieronymous. *Manual for administrators, super-visors, and counselors, Iowa Tests of Basic Skills.* Boston: Houghton Mifflin, 1956.

Lord, Frederic M. Estimating norms by item-sampling. *Educ. psychol. Measmt,* 1962, **22,** 259–267.

McCall, William A. *Measurement.* New York: Macmillan, 1939.

Seashore, Harold G. *Methods of expressing test scores.* Test Service Bulletin, No. 48. New York: Psychological Corporation, 1955.

Tiedeman, David V. Has he grown? *Occupations,* 1951, **30,** 106–111.

Wesman, Alexander G., and others. Symposium: standard scores for aptitude and achievement tests. *Educ. psychol. Measmt,* 1962, **22,** 5–39.

9 ✍

The Validity of Measurement Methods

SOME YEARS AGO, so it is reported, an anthropologist studying the culture of a primitive community wanted to determine the number of children of each age living there. Since birth records were available for only a few children and parental reports were quite undependable, the anthropologist decided to measure the heights of the children to obtain an estimate of their ages. He did this by first measuring the heights of those few children whose ages were known. Then, by comparing the heights of children of unknown age with the heights of children whose ages were available, he estimated the ages of children on the basis of their heights. This desperate resort on the part of the anthropologist was probably received sympathetically by his colleagues. It is possible that, had he not estimated ages from heights, he would have departed with no information about ages.

The anthropologist's action is not unlike that of a high school senior in his search for a university; he may assess the quality of a university's academic offerings on the basis of the size of its undergraduate student body, or perhaps the number of games won by its football team, or both. In somewhat the same category is the political pundit who evaluates the popularity of his party's agricultural program in terms of the number of unsolicited favorable letters received from the public at large, and also the economic soothsayer who describes the economic health of the nation solely in terms of the rise and fall of the stock market.

Each of the foregoing illustrations may be cynically interpreted by discerning observers. The causes for such cynicism can be traced to such questions as the following: Do differences in heights of children always indicate differences in age? Is the quality of a university's academic program necessarily a function of its size? Do unsolicited letters received at a political party's headquarters represent a cross section of voter opinion? Is the stock market completely sensitive to all of the subtle changes in the economic structure? These and similar questions would undoubtedly tend to yield nothing more than hesitant answers surrounded by embarrassment.

The individuals using the foregoing measurement methods in such potentially dangerous fashions are possibly somewhat innocent. The very accessibility of such data as height, enrollment, number of letters, and stock market reports tempts most investigators. Furthermore, the accuracy of these data is generally considered good. Height can readily be measured to the nearest one-fourth of an inch. College enrollment reports are seldom in error. Favorable and unfavorable letters as well as stock market fluctuations can be easily tabulated. The difficulty then is not centered in the accuracy of the data involved, but rather in the interpretation of them. To argue that unwarranted interpretations have been made is to argue that validity, to some degree, is absent.

DEFINITION OF VALIDITY

In educational measurement, validity is often defined as the degree to which a measuring instrument actually serves the purposes for which it is intended. A scholastic aptitude test is a valid measurement of scholastic aptitude if it truly measures scholastic aptitude. An achievement test in spelling is valid to the extent that it assuredly measures achievement in spelling. In the illustrations just cited, it is obvious that the data concerning height, enrollment, favorable letters, and stock market fluctuations are valid insofar as they are used in measuring height, enrollment, favorable letters and stock market fluctuations, respectively. This statement sounds needlessly repetitious. Nevertheless it re-emphasizes the idea that a measurement of height by means of an accurate tape measure applied under controlled conditions is unquestionably a valid measurement of height, but a doubtful measure of age. Likewise, counting the number of undergraduates engaged in full-time academic programs is a valid measure of size of an undergraduate student body, but a decidedly uncertain basis on which to evaluate the quality of the academic program of that institution. By the same token, scores yielded by a scholastic aptitude test may very well be valid indicators of degrees of scholastic aptitude but inadequate representations of emotional stability. An excellent test measuring achievement in spelling most certainly will yield scores that do not reflect individual differences in finger dexterity.

Validity is clearly the most important characteristic of a measuring instrument. No matter what other characteristics an instrument may possess, if it is not adequately valid it is of no value whatsoever.

PROBLEMS

1 Perhaps you have heard someone make statements such as the following:
"The test that I am using measures general mental ability. General mental ability means that pupil trait which this test measures."

Are these statements meaningful in terms of a discussion of test validity? Why?

2 The claim is made that some definitions of validity are virtually synonymous with that for test value (Ebel, 1961). If this is true, then ease of administration, adequacy of norms, reliability, etc., become aspects of validity. Should the definition of validity be this encompassing? Give reasons for your answer.

TYPES OF VALIDITY

The definition of validity already stated is useful, but still inadequate. To say that a measuring instrument is "valid" in the sense that validity has been defined is not enough. The statement is too vague. An instrument is valid in terms of its purpose or purposes. Examples already have been presented which vividly illustrate the fact that results yielded by a measuring instrument may be highly valid for one purpose and not at all for another. Since the relative validity of an instrument indicates the degree to which its purposes or aims are being achieved, and since the aims of tests vary, somewhat different types of validity are under consideration in various measuring instruments. As the aims differ, so do the types of validity involved.

The aims of measurement methods are divided into three categories (French and Michael, 1966, p. 12):

1. To determine how well a pupil performs today in a certain type of situation or subject matter, a cross-sectional sample of which is present in the measuring instrument. For example, a teacher might administer a spelling test to his class to determine how much they know at that moment about spelling. In all likelihood, the test would include only a sample of all the words for which the pupils are responsible.

2. To predict a pupil's future behavior or to estimate his present standing with respect to some characteristic not directly measured by the instrument. For example, in the case of future behavior, a scholastic aptitude test could be given to pupils completing junior high school to predict their academic success in senior high school. In the case of a pupil's present standing, a teacher can administer a paper-and-pencil arithmetic test composed of addition and subtraction problems involving representations of pennies, nickels, dimes, quarters, half dollars, and dollar bills. The size of the test score is intended to show the accuracy with which each pupil can make change when purchasing articles from retail stores.

3. To infer the strength of a pupil trait or quality as reflected in the results yielded by the measuring instrument. For example, a teacher might give a memory test to a class to make inferences about each pupil's scholastic aptitude.

There are certain similarities and dissimilarities among the three aims of measuring instruments. These may be conveniently examined after each of the aims has been translated into its corresponding type of validity. The three types of validity are commonly identified as content validity, criterion-related validity, and construct validity.

Each can be defined as the degree to which a measuring instrument accomplishes the aim associated with that type. Of course, an instrument may be designed to meet more than one of the three aims, and hence the person who developed it must investigate more than one type of validity. Also, some types of validity tend to be more vital in certain kinds of tests. For example, content validity plays a key role in achievement testing and criterion-related validity in aptitude testing. To examine these and other ramifications resulting from the classification of validity types, separate consideration of each type is necessary.

Content Validity

Finding the content validity of a measuring instrument is equivalent to showing how well it samples certain types of situations or subject matter. The instrument claiming high content validity clearly attempts to include a cross-sectional sample of a great variety of items representing the area in which the pupil's performance is being measured.

You recall that the primary purpose of achievement measurement is to discover how well pupils have achieved educational objectives. Prominent educational objectives are those concerning mastery of specific facts and general principles related to the subject matter already covered. These are the objectives toward which many measurement efforts are directed. For example, a teacher may wish to know how well his pupils can add whole numbers, or how rapidly they can read. Another may want to determine how much information his class retains from prolonged discussions and readings about the political, economic, and social causes of World War II. Still another teacher may want to know how well his pupils understand and apply the Pythagorean theorem. These and countless similar illustrations typify the rather well-defined areas of subject matter in terms of which achievement tests are constructed. The validity of such a test is determined by the representativeness of its contents. Since all possible questions cannot be included, the test is necessarily a sample. To the degree that the sample is not representative, the test lacks content validity.

In addition to achievement tests, content validity is a useful characteristic of other types of measuring instruments, such as scholastic aptitude tests and personal-social adjustment inventories. In each of these types of instrument it is generally true that content validity is secondary to another kind. In scholastic aptitude tests criterion-relayed validity is paramount, yet content validity is involved in the identification of the great variety of items from which the test items and the description of the methods used to select them are selected.

Criterion-Related Validity

Criterion-related validity can be divided into two parts; namely, the validity of instruments designed to predict future performance, and of those designed to estimate present status with respect to a characteristic different from the test. In the past, the former was known as predictive validity and the latter as concurrent validity. The principal difference between these two classifications is the time at which the pupil displays the behavior in question.

INSTRUMENTS PREDICTING FUTURE PERFORMANCE

The foregoing discussion of content validity has already indicated the importance of criterion-related validity in aptitude measurement. The fact that aptitude tests are designed to predict what a pupil can accomplish with training is another way of saying that aptitude tests, by definition, are fundamentally dependent upon the establishment of a high degree of criterion-related validity. The uses of scholastic aptitude scores for sectioning classes, anticipating success in reading, estimating the likelihood of graduating from secondary school, or guiding a pupil toward a career in law, amply illustrate the use of a test score or scores to infer tomorrow's successes and failures. The criterion-related validity of a measuring instrument depends on the accuracy of its predictions of future pupil behaviour.

In spite of the fact that achievement tests are constructed for the primary purpose of determining how much a pupil knows or how well he can perform as of that moment, another and less common use is forecasting subsequent achievement. For instance, reading tests are used to section classes in various subject-matter areas and predict academic success in secondary school and college. In these cases, high criterion-related validity is unquestionably necessary (Hansmeier, 1960).

INSTRUMENTS ESTIMATING PRESENT STANDING

Some measuring instruments try to determine a pupil's present standing indirectly. The pupil behavior elicited by this type of instrument is thought to correspond closely to a certain external behavior criterion. If it does, the instrument has acceptable criterion-related validity.

Like content validity, this type is usually a necessary attribute of achievement-measuring instruments. Consider, for example, the measurement of the quality of a pupil's handwriting. General quality may be broken down into elements such as correctness of letter formation, spacing, and uniformity of size and slant. A specimen of the pupil's handwriting might then be compared with a series of specimens of increasing merit with respect to the foregoing elements, and an estimate of the quality of his handwriting obtained. It seems reasonable to argue that this is useful only if it shows the quality of the pupil's handwriting when he writes a letter to his grandmother to thank her for a birthday present or copies the grocery order as dictated by his mother. If, therefore, the data resulting from the measurement of the quality of handwriting are closely related to the quality of handwriting in somewhat less formal simultaneous attempts, then there is sufficient criterion-related validity.

Since paper-and-pencil achievement tests tend to measure a characteristic indirectly rather than directly, additional illustrations of criterion-related validity in achievement testing are readily found. A reading comprehension score from a test might be interpreted as the pupil's reading comprehension when he reads for pleasure. The results of an arithmetic test may be interpreted as related to the accuracy with which a pupil can compute his hourly wages when he shovels snow after school. A teacher may wish to interpret scores on a language usage test as closely correlated with a tabulation of the pupil's actual verbal usage at the time.

Criterion-related validity is also important when considering the validity of instruments in personal-social adjustment. These instruments must have a great deal when they are used to classify pupils in groups. For example, an interest inventory may reflect one or more differences between pupils who have hobbies involving manual skills and those who do not. Also, pupils in need of immediate counseling may be detected by personal-social adjustment inventory scores and other evidence.

Construct Validity

To describe construct validity, it is first necessary to establish the meaning of the term "construct." A construct is a characteristic assumed to exist to account for some aspect of human behavior. In psychology many constructs are used, such as cautiousness, tendency to conform, rigidity, insecurity, dominance, and ability to apply principles. These terms serve the useful purpose of providing a convenient means of identifying the psychological concepts they represent. By themselves, however, they do not explain the concept or any theory underlying it.

Whenever a measuring instrument is believed to reflect a particular construct, its construct validity must be investigated. This amounts to determining how well certain constructs account for pupil performance as measured by the instrument. To make a suitable investigation possible, the construct should be sufficiently well defined so that verifiable inferences can be drawn from it. Testing the accuracy of the inferences with a measuring instrument is a way of confirming or denying the claim that a certain construct accounts for variations in the performance elicited by the instrument. If the instrument has construct validity, its findings will vary from one kind of individual to another, or from one situation to another, as the theory underlying the construct would predict. In many ways, establishing construct validity is the same as validating the theory that defines the construct (Cronbach and Meehl, 1955).

Examples of the importance of construct validity can be found in the measurement of achievement, aptitude, and personal-social adjustment. In the case of achievement measurement, construct validity is a pertinent characteristic of those tests claiming to measure study skills and ability to reason. Is there any proof that the tests actually measure study skills or reasoning ability as defined by the authors of the tests? Aptitude tests can be challenged by questioning whether evidence is available that can describe the complete meaning of the aptitude measured. A teacher using a general mental ability test may demand of its author an explanation of his concept of general mental ability and how the pupil's activities as he writes the test correspond to that concept. Finally, when a personal-social adjustment inventory is thought to reveal the composition of the pupil's personality, the inventory must have a high construct validity.

PROBLEMS

3 Give illustrations of cases in which a teacher might be concerned about the content validity of (a) a paper-and-pencil personality inventory and (b) a paper-and-pencil test of clerical aptitude.

4 Cite arguments for and against the statement that content and construct validity have little in common with criterion-related validity, as well as little in common with each other (Ebel, 1961, p. 640).

5 Cronbach (1960, p. 106) believes that the central question asked when the construct validity of a test is being determined, is the following:
  "How can scores on this test be explained psychologically?" What is the full meaning of this question? Illustrate.

6 Does construct validity encourage the reification of human traits (Campbell, 1960, pp. 551–552; Bechtoldt, 1959)? Give reasons for your answer.

Determination of Degrees of Validity

Since validity is classified into three types for descriptive purposes, it is appropriate to discuss the determination of the validity of measuring instruments in terms of the same classification. It has already been shown that, as the purposes of instruments vary, so do the types of validity. Furthermore, a given instrument may have more than one purpose, and thus should be characterized by more than one type of validity. The demonstration of high validity, then, is commonly a multiple approach rather than a single attempt.

These facts are of vital concern to the builders of measuring instruments. After all, acceptable validity is the most critical quality an instrument can have. Thus the author is obliged to carefully examine the aims of his instrument and, for each aim, present evidence that the instrument can validly perform that function. The burden of proof is in the hands of the author. If he fails for some reason to prove that his instrument has sufficient appropriate validity, then his test's value is doubtful.

Content Validity

Because content validity is oriented toward achievement testing, which is such a formidable part of pupil evaluation, this section is restricted to achievement testing. Achievement tests are developed on the basis of educational objectives with verbal or mathematical aspects and are designed to show how well pupils have achieved those objectives. Therefore, to construct a test with high content-validity, the teacher must begin with the same educational objectives that guided his classroom instruction. On the basis of the objectives chosen, tables of specifications are built, which in turn guide the selection of test items.

To ensure acceptable content validity, the teacher should devise achievement tests for his class. Who knows better than the teacher which of many proposed test items are probably "trick" or "unfair" items? Such test item labels, when attached after considered thought by either teacher or pupil, can be regarded as vernacular expressions, equivalent to saying that the test items, and hence the test as a whole, lack content validity to some degree. The teacher's knowledge of the class and its educational objectives are the most important factors in the superior content validity of classroom achievement tests.

STANDARDIZED ACHIEVEMENT TESTS. To some teachers standardized achievement tests are unknown quantities. The impressive titles of the tests, coupled with sometimes equally impressive authorship and precisely stated directions for administration, tend to add to, rather than subtract from, their doubts. Yet these instruments are nothing more than classroom achievement tests that have been refined, perhaps several times, and probably will have additional refinements in the future. They usually represent the thinking of teachers, supervisors, school administrators, and others, and have withstood a rigorous statistical assault by professional testing specialists.

The educational objectives of a course of study and their tables of specifications, which are so important in the identification of the content validity of teacher-built achievement tests, are equally important in the identification of the content validity of standardized achievement tests. Hence, for a standardized achievement test to have high content validity for a subject-matter area, it must be constructed in terms of the same educational objectives as subscribed to by the teacher of that subject matter and must reflect the relative weight of each educational objective as the teacher judges them. Beyond question, these are impossible conditions for the test author to satisfy. Since his test is to be used by not one teacher but hundreds, and since each teacher has his own peculiar set of educational objectives and tables of specifications, despite much common ground in many subject-matter areas, the author can hope only to orient his instrument toward those educational objectives that appear to be most prevalent. Each teacher who proposes to use a standardized achievement test is automatically obliged to find convincing evidence that the educational objectives involved and their weighting closely correspond to his own.

To aim a standardized achievement test at popularly held educational objectives, the test builders do considerable investigation. A year or more may be spent in the laborious process of scanning lesson plans, state study guides, and widely used textbooks covering the subject matter in question as well as in interviewing teachers and supervisors directly involved in the selected field. The process finally yields a core of reference materials thought to be most representative, and possibly a panel of subject-matter specialists thought to be well-informed. On the basis of these sources of information, test items are constructed.

Since the reference materials are identical with or closely related to those used by a teacher, the possibility of the standardized achievement test having high content validity for that teacher's use is considerably improved. Obviously, the textbooks and courses of study composing the reference materials should be identified for the potential test user. Some, but by no means all, manuals accompanying standardized achievement tests include complete titles and dates of publication of each of the reference materials. If a panel of subject-matter specialists in the field is used, either independently of or in conjunction with the reference materials, they should be identified by name and pertinent facts about their professional qualifications listed.

Unfortunately, detailed information about the reference materials and any panel of specialists is not given in some test manuals. The inquiring teacher finds only glib statements about the "careful selection" of the test items and the "popular modern textbooks" that were consulted. This is meager fare indeed for any astute reviewer.

Regardless of the limited data of this kind that might be offered in the test manual, at least two other avenues relative to content validity should be explored. In the first place, manuals usually supply ample statements about the purposes of the test and its limitations in terms of subject matter covered. These statements bear careful perusal for evident reasons. Secondly, the test items themselves should be carefully scrutinized. It is highly recommended that a teacher play the role of pupil and write the answers under similar conditions. Then there should be an additional item-by-item examination. For each item the question must be asked: In view of my educational objectives, the tables of specifications derived from them, and the method of teaching I followed, is this test item appropriate for my pupils this term? Answers will be regularly affirmative if there is acceptable content validity.

The item-by-item examination should not be a casual operation. On the contrary, it should be tied directly to the teacher's educational objectives and his tables of specifications. A tabulation should be made by copying each item number opposite the cell of the table of specifications with which it is associated. If a test item is related to more than one cell, it should be tabulated accordingly. If it is primarily related to one cell of the table and secondarily related to another, a simple coding scheme can identify these differences. Although this process is lengthy, it is necessary if the content validity of a standardized achievement test is to be assessed.

Some standardized achievement tests simplify the tabulation process by including with the test materials a printed outline summarizing the various subject-matter areas covered and listing opposite each the numbers of the test items related to that area (Cooperative Test Division, 1959, pp. 21–85).

Problems

7 The classifications of test items published for standardized achievement tests are usually based on subject-matter categories only. The type of pupil

behavioral change is not included. Is the determination of the content validity of the achievement test in question seriously hampered by this omission? Why?

8   Compare the categories used to classify the test items from (a) the mathematics test and (b) the science test of the *Sequential Tests of Educational Progress* (Cooperative Test Division, 1959, pp. 72–85) with the categories for the corresponding tests included in the *High School Basic Battery* of the *Stanford Achievement Test* (Gardner and others, 1965, pp. 25–26). Identify the similarities and dissimilarities and suggest reasons for them.

9   Dizney (1965) has found evidence that pupil comments on the fairness of the items do little to improve achievement tests. Do you agree?

Criterion-Related Validity

The degree of criterion-related validity for various types of tests can be determined by using aptitude tests as illustrations. The practical value of tests designed to measure mechanical aptitude, clerical aptitude, scholastic aptitude, art aptitude, and similar areas is centered in the accuracy with which a teacher can make predictions on the basis of their scores. It is logical, then, to take a longitudinal approach to the problem of determining criterion-related validity. A scholastic aptitude test can be administered to a group of pupils today and predictions of academic achievement can be made in one or more future subjects. At that time, actual academic success can be measured by achievement tests or, possibly, final marks. Finally, predicted achievement can be compared with actual achievement, and the criterion-related validity of the scholastic aptitude test as applied in these prediction situations can be evaluated.

Predictions of future academic achievement can also be made in terms of the same units as those of the achievement measurement criterion, but are not always made in this manner. With statistical techniques beyond the scope of this book, a teacher or administrator may be able to say, for example, that a pupil whose scholastic aptitude test score is 117 should be expected to score in the vicinity of 82 on a particular English test. However, the predictions usually made are informal, thus making it awkward to compare predicted and actual achievement. They are often equivalent to saying that pupils who do well on the scholastic aptitude test will probably achieve well in school, whereas those who do badly will probably achieve poorly. In view of this, comparison of the scholastic aptitude scores and the measures of academic success would yield information concerning criterion-related validity.

Some of the basic steps in establishing the validity of an aptitude test can be examined most directly with an illustration. Suppose that an eighth-grade teacher of social studies wishes to know how satisfactorily achievement in that class can be predicted from scholastic aptitude test scores from a test given one year earlier. For the sake of simplicity, he is willing to define achievement in the social studies in terms of the scores of a comprehensive achievement test given at the end of the term. The result is a double measurement of each pupil, the data from which may be compiled in a fashion similar to Table 8.

The twenty pupils are arranged according to their scores on the scholastic aptitude test. Their achievement scores are listed opposite the scholastic aptitude scores. To facilitate interpretation, both sets of scores are ranked from 1 to 20 according to the position of the pupil in the class with respect to each test. If the scholastic aptitude test possesses high validity, the rank of any pupil in the scholastic aptitude test should be approximately the same as his rank in the achievement test. Table 8 shows that the aptitude and achievement scores of some pupils differ by a single point. These cases support the contention that the scholastic aptitude test

TABLE 8

SCHOLASTIC APTITUDE TEST SCORES AND ACHIEVEMENT TEST SCORES
OF EIGHTH-GRADE SOCIAL STUDIES PUPILS

Name	Scholastic Aptitude Test Fall Term, Seventh Grade		Social Studies Test Fall Term, Eighth Grade		Difference in rank
	Score	Rank	Score	Rank	
Jim	135	1	66	9	8
Sam	130	2	90	1	1
Ruth	120	3	68	8	5
Mary	117	4	85	3	1
John	116	5	81	4	1
Louise	114	6	47	17	11
Ralph	113	7	69	7	0
Mae	112	8	77	5	3
Quinton	111	9	65	10	1
Sandra	109	10	56	15	5
Larry	107	11	89	2	9
Norma	106	12	49	16	4
Frank	101	13	57	14	1
Milton	100	14	58	13	1
Dave	97	15	71	6	9
Joe	95	16	60	11	5
Bill	94	17	38	19	2
Sally	90	18	31	20	2
Margaret	88	19	40	18	1
Sue	87	20	59	12	8

can predict achievement in eighth-grade social studies. Since other pupils, however, have differences of eight or more, these cases tend to refute the contention concerning the validity of this test.

The foregoing analysis is casual, if not crude. A precise statement of the validity of the test is still lacking. Figure 20 was prepared to give a more comprehensive picture of the entire class of twenty pupils. In this figure are plotted twenty points, one for each pupil. The position of a point is found by locating on the vertical axis the scholastic aptitude test score of that pupil, and moving to the right, parallel to the horizontal axis, until his achievement in social studies is located. The points are numbered in terms of the ranks of the pupils on the scholastic aptitude test.

A moment of thought will indicate that, if the scholastic aptitude test has high criterion-related validity in this example, the points should arrange themselves in a straight line. Thus, the greater the tendency of the points to approximate a straight line, then the greater the validity. All points in Figure 20 obviously do not fall in a straight line, yet the eye can detect a definite elongated pattern that certainly suggests linearity. It is interesting now to observe the positions of points representing the five pupils whose ranks differ so greatly. The points are numbered 1, 6, 11, 15, and 20, and are represented by squares rather than circles. It is not surprising that they are all found along the perimeter of the pattern, and that their deletion would strengthen the impression that the points tend to form a straight line.

Figure 20 strongly suggests, as did Table 8, that the scholastic aptitude test has at least some validity in this situation. To identify the degree even more precisely, another step is necessary. This is the computation of the *Pearson product-moment coefficient of correlation*, often known as simply the correlation coefficient, and represented by the letter r.

THE CORRELATION COEFFICIENT.   The correlation coefficient is a number representing the straight-line relationship between the values of two variables, such as the values of the two variables resulting from double measurement of the pupils listed in Table 8. If points are plotted, as in Figure 20, and all of them fall in a straight line, the value of r will be 1.00. As the points deviate from a straight line, the value of r decreases to zero. In addition, when high values of one variable are associated with high values of the second variable, and low values of one variable are associated with low values of the other, as in the data in Table 8, the relationship is called positive and the r-value carries a positive sign. If high values of one variable are associated with low values of the other, and low values of the first are associated with high values of the second, the relationship is called negative and the r-value carries a negative sign. Thus, r-values vary from -1.00 to $+1.00$. The number is indicative of the degree to which the

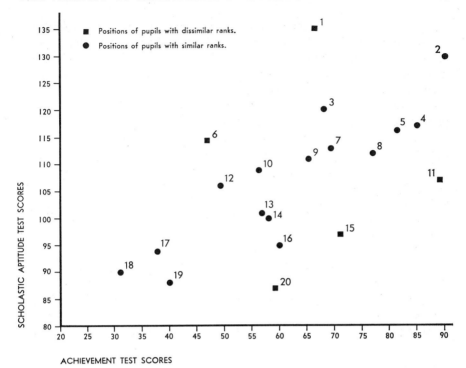

FIGURE 20

SCATTER DIAGRAM OF SCHOLASTIC APTITUDE TEST SCORES
AND ACHIEVEMENT TEST SCORES

points form a straight line, and the sign reveals the direction of the relationship. It should be noted that positive r-values are much more common than negative values in educational evaluation.

The computation of an r-value provides a succinct representation of the validity of the scholastic aptitude test in achievement in social studies. The extent to which the points plotted in Figure 20 tend to form a straight line determines the r-value computed from the data, and also shows how efficiently the scholastic aptitude test predicts the eighth-grade achievement in social studies.

Computation of the correlation coefficient is somewhat lengthy, but simple. One formula of r that can be applied to the data in Table 8 is shown in Appendix A (see pages 574–577). With the formula is a complete description of the manner in which the values in Table 8 are summarized and substituted into the formula. An r-value of 0.61 is found.

The interpretation of this value has, in reality, already been given. It represents the degree to which the points fall into a straight line or, stated differently, the rate of change in social studies achievement test scores compared to a given change in scholastic aptitude test scores. Unfortunately, some uninitiated observers try to improve upon the interpretation by considering the r-value as a percent. The fact that r-values, with the sign ignored, vary from 0.00 to 1.00 undoubtedly encourages this error. In any event, the reasoning follows essentially this path: An r-value of 1.00 results from data that, when plotted, yield a perfectly straight line. Hence, prediction of achievement on Test Y from scores from Text X will be 100 per cent accurate. On the basis of this evidence, the accuracy of the prediction decreases as the r-value decreases, in such a fashion that an r-value of 0.61 would mean that estimates of social studies achievement test scores based upon scholastic aptitude test scores will be 61 per cent accurate. This latter argument is not true.

Although it is correct to say that an r-value of 1.00 indicates a prediction of 100 per cent accuracy, the decrease in prediction accuracy is not proportional to the decrease in the r-value. Table 9 shows the percentage reductions in the margins of prediction error of scores on Test Y from scores derived from Test X as the correlation between the two sets of scores changes. This percentage reduction is known as the index of forecasting efficiency. Rather than being 61 per cent, the forecasting efficiency of an r-value of 0.61 is slightly greater than 20 per cent. In other words,

TABLE 9

FORECASTING EFFICIENCY OF PRODUCT-MOMENT
COEFFICIENTS OF CORRELATIONS OF VARIOUS SIZES

Coefficient of correlation	Index of forecasting efficiency (per cent)
1.00	100.0
0.99	85.9
0.97	75.7
0.95	68.8
0.90	56.4
0.80	40.0
0.70	28.6
0.60	20.0
0.50	13.4
0.40	8.4
0.30	4.6
0.20	2.0
0.10	0.5
0.00	0.0

predicting social studies achievement test scores on the basis of scholastic aptitude test scores will have a margin of error about 80 per cent of error that would occur if we predict social studies achievement test scores *without* knowledge of the scholastic aptitude test scores. The reduction in the margin of error is about 20 per cent, which can be considered the percentage of improvement over chance. As the correlation increases, so does the reduction in the margin of error of prediction (Guilford, 1965, pp. 376–379).

Although they represent by no means the only method, product-moment coefficients of correlation are popular representations of the criterion-related predictive validity claimed for a test. Other types of coefficients of correlation, discussions of which can be found in many textbooks of statistical methodology, are also used, but in a minority of instances. It is clear, certainly, that an adequate grasp of the demonstration of criterion-related validity is highly dependent upon an adequate grasp of the meaning of the correlation coefficient. Although teachers generally do not find themselves confronted with computations of an r-value, they are regularly obliged to interpret them.

EXPECTANCY TABLES. Computing product-moment coefficients of correlation and interpreting them in terms of the information on forecasting efficiency in Table 9 is an investigation of the relative validity of an instrument when its data are used for making very fine "pinpoint" predictions. Note that the scholastic aptitude scores in Table 8 are to be used to predict the *exact* social studies achievement test scores. Often such close prediction is unnecessary. Rather than trying to predict the exact achievement test score, many teachers wish to predict only in terms of broad categories: they may wish to predict whether a pupil will achieve "above average," "average," or "below average" in his class. If this is the intended use of the scholastic aptitude test, the predictive validity of the instrument can be much more realistically appraised by *expectancy tables* (Wesman, 1949, 1966).

An expectancy table is merely a condensed version of plotted data similar to that in Figure 20. In the figure, each gradation of the scores of each test is shown; in an expectancy table, the scores are grouped into a convenient number of intervals. Table 10 is an expectancy table based on the data in Table 8 in which each set of test scores is grouped into three intervals. The number within each cell of the table represents the number of pupils who have scholastic aptitude and social studies achievement scores within the limits indicated. Percentages may also be used if preferred.

The interpretation of the table is simple. For instance, we can say that

TABLE 10
EXPECTANCY TABLE FOR SCHOLASTIC APTITUDE AND
SOCIAL STUDIES ACHIEVEMENT TEST SCORES

Scholastic aptitude test scores	*Social Studies Achievement Test Scores*			
	Below average (Below 55)	*Average (55–75)*	*Above average Total*	*(Over 75)*
Above average (Over 115)	0	2	3	5
Average (95–115)	2	7	2	11
Below average (Below 95)	3	1	0	4
Total	5	10	5	20

none of the pupils whose aptitude score is "below average" (less than 95) has an achievement score that is "above average" (greater than 75). Moreover, none of the pupils with "above average" aptitude scores (greater than 115) receives a "below average" achievement score (less than 55). More inclusive statements could be made in a slightly different manner. Pupils with aptitude scores of 95 or more rarely (2 out of 16) receive achievement scores of less than 55. Or, pupils with aptitude scores of 115 or less rarely (2 out of 15) receive achievement scores of more than 75.

If a teacher wishes to predict in terms of relatively crude approximations, his probable accuracy is well illustrated by an expectancy table such as that shown in Table 10. It is advisable, of course, to include more than twenty pupils in an expectancy table before it can be used as a basis for a conclusive statement on the criterion-related validity of the instrument.

DEGREES OF CRITERION-RELATED VALIDITY. It is certainly clear at this point that the scholastic aptitude test in question does not have the greatest possible predictive validity. On the other hand, although the r-value is no larger than 0.61 and the expectancy table shows some pupils classified in cells other than the ones desired, we cannot automatically say that the validity of the instrument is unsatisfactory. On the contrary, the instrument may be judged as useful for prediction purposes if, in spite of its inaccuracies, it can predict future achievement of these pupils better than any other means.

Predictions of future achievement based upon aptitude test data must be viewed in much the same manner as the predictions of life expectancy made by insurance companies and of deaths due to automobile accidents made by national safety organizations. Life insurance companies can predict with striking accuracy the percentage of thirty-year-old men who will be living twenty-five or fifty years from now; yet they cannot predict with similar accuracy which *members* of the group will be alive or dead at these future dates. The number of deaths in automobile accidents during a fourth of July weekend can be predicted with small error, but the identity of the victims cannot be predicted with the same minimum of error. This is true of achievement predicted from aptitude test data. If predictions are made for a group, the accuracy is customarily quite good; a prediction made for an individual member of that group may be distressingly inaccurate.

TEST MANUAL AS A SOURCE OF INFORMATION. The primary source of information for most teachers as they investigate the validity of standardized aptitude tests and personal-social adjustment inventories is the test manual. Although this compilation is usually highly abbreviated, it regularly provides sizable amounts of data about the author's attempts to establish acceptable validity and perhaps references to research conducted by other investigators interested in the problem. Examination of the test manual by the potential test purchaser is always sound practice.

The test author who wishes to present the most comprehensible discussion of his test's validity is certain to find it an exacting task. Among other things, he must carefully describe the criterion with which his test is correlated and the nature of the pupils who cooperated in the validation attempt. Both of these descriptions emphasize the fact that the determination of validity as it is outlined is relative to the criterion used and the pupils measured. To the degree that the criterion is weak or the standardization group inadequate in any way, the determination of validity becomes less meaningful.

In the illustration summarized in Table 8, the scholastic aptitude test has some validity in terms of the social studies test as administered to eighth-grade pupils. If this illustration were a formal attempt to determine the relative validity of the scholastic aptitude test, the author of that test should report in the test manual such characteristics of the social studies achievement test as its length, level of difficulty, the nature of its items, and its content validity. Furthermore, the test author would identify the pupils tested as to their sex, age, level of education, socio-economic status, and, for that matter, any pertinent factor that would help the teacher decide whether this group of pupils was similar to those for whom the author's test is designed and in turn similar to the pupils which he, the teacher, plans to test.

PROBLEMS

10   What is cross-validation (Langmuir, 1954)? Of what significance is it in the determination of the relative validity of a scholastic aptitude test? Give an illustration to support your answer.

11   When test performance is reported in terms of pupil ranks such as in Table 8, the criterion-related validity can be easily estimated by computing a Spearman rank-order coefficient of correlation (Guilford, 1965, pp. 305–308). Compute this value for the data in question and compare its size with the r-value reported.

12   What is a standard error of estimate (Guilford, 1965, pp. 360–361)? Of what use is this value when a validity determination is being made for a scholastic aptitude test and its results interpreted?

13   What major types of expectancy tables are being used? Study the illustrations shown by Schrader (1965) and compare them with Table 10.

Construct Validity

Many of the methods used to determine the relative validity of the first two types are also suitable when construct validity is being investigated. In fact, an analysis of construct validity is supported by total available knowledge of the validity of the instrument in question. In other words, demonstrating what constructs account for variations in the performance elicited by a measuring instrument is a difficult task. It involves many methods, some of which can also be properly used in connection with other types of validity.

The basis on which the investigation of construct validity proceeds is provided by the theory underlying the construct supposedly involved in the measuring instrument. On the basis of the theory, predictions are made: one group of individuals will differ from another in terms of the data yielded by an instrument involving the construct, or individuals will or will not change in terms of an instrument involving the construct after they have experienced certain environmental conditions. The evaluation instrument is then used to test the predictions. If the predictions and the data produced by the instrument concur, evidence in support of the construct validity has been found. If they do not, a state of uncertainty exists. Either the instrument does not involve the construct, or the theory is not sound. In any event, the degree of construct validity is in doubt (Cronbach and Meehl, 1955).

COMPARISONS WITH OTHER INSTRUMENTS.   One method of determining construct validity is to correlate the data from the instrument under study with a second instrument thought to measure the same construct. This is sometimes done with group tests of general mental ability of the type regularly used in elementary and secondary schools. For example, an experimental group test of general mental ability and the *Stanford-Binet Scale, Form L-M,* are administered to a sample of pupils. The scores from the experimental test and the *Stanford-Binet* test are then correlated. If the *Stanford-Binet* test is an acceptable measure of general mental ability, and its scores are closely correlated with those of the experimental test, the experimental test is said to have high construct validity.

Since complete agreement is seldom obtained as to the quality of the test serving as a standard, the correlation process is often repeated with several tests. When a group test of general mental ability is being studied, the standards are usually individual general mental ability tests or well-known group general mental ability tests. In areas other than general mental ability testing there is a similar tendency, rightly or wrongly, to use popular tests reputed to measure the same construct as a test under investigation.

COMPARISONS WITH JUDGES' RATINGS.   The use of judges is another means of assessing construct validity and has been used in connection with a variety of tests. For example, suppose that a paper-and-pencil test has been constructed to measure the social adaptability of junior high school pupils. Each of the 100 items included in the test requires the pupil to select one of the five alternatives that best approximates his behavior should he be confronted with the social situation described. The test author defines social adaptability as the ability of a person, when participating in a social situation, to adjust his behavior in accordance with the nature of the situation and to do so easily.

To discover whether this test actually measures social adaptability, the author may employ a group of judges who are to observe independently— and somewhat surreptitiously—the social behavior of a group of pupils. The judges are, of course, ignorant of the pupils' test scores determined by the paper-and-pencil test. They may use rating scales and check lists to record each pupil's behavior at such events as a school dance, a class picnic, a basketball game, and a concert. If the test scores correlate well with the ratings, then the paper-and-pencil test has acceptable construct validity.

Serious doubts have been raised about the use of ratings of individuals as criteria against which to validate test scores (Guilford and others, 1962). These ratings are thought to be valid in that it is assumed that the raters know what they are measuring. Unfortunately, ratings regularly measure different traits than those intended.

PROBLEMS

14 When two testing instruments are compared to estimate the construct validity of one of them, while the second is considered a standard, is the investigator engaging in a "circular" argument?

15 Select a paper-and-pencil personality inventory such as the *Edwards Personal Preference Schedule* and suggest procedures which might be useful for establishing its construct validity.

General Considerations

Determining the relative strength of any one of the three types of validity in a measuring instrument is sometimes frustrating. If the instrument is commercially distributed, the teacher may faithfully scan the test manual and doggedly sift the references to articles in professional journals in which the instrument is mentioned. Yet it often happens that even this effort leaves the investigator unsatisfied. The information gleaned from the process is often too vague and too limited.

VAGUE TERMS

The complaint of vagueness is traceable in part to the widespread use of a handful of terms that are not as meaningful as often supposed. Expressions such as "face" validity, "statistical" validity, and "curricular" validity fall into this category. Even the expression "validity coefficient" is applied too generally to contribute much to a discussion of validity.

A paper-and-pencil test has "face" validity when it seems to be valid to someone reading it. In other words, if a person unsophisticated in achievement measurement is handed an English vocabulary test for high school seniors and, after reading it, agrees that it appears to be a "valid" vocabulary test for that group, "face" validity is claimed. Admittedly, this is important to the pupils writing a test. Certainly they will tend to cooperate more readily if they sense that the nature of the items logically corresponds to the over-all purpose of the test. Nevertheless, a flat claim for "face" validity of an instrument does not release its author from the responsibility of establishing the relative strength of one or more of the three types of validity. Also, "face" validity does not guarantee that the test has enough validity of any type.

"Statistical" validity is not a meaningful expression. As the title suggests, validity determinations in which correlation coefficients of some kind are computed are labeled determinations of "statistical" validity. Within this loose framework are some of the determinations of all three types of validity, particularly criterion-related validity and construct validity. The expression is, therefore, unnecessary.

The coefficients of correlation resulting from computations of "statistical" validity are known as "validity coefficients." This is a more helpful expression than "statistical" validity, but still cannot be applied in isolation. The "validity coefficient" indicates how much criterion-related or construct validity an instrument possesses. Thus, unless a "validity coefficient" is described in terms of one of these types, it is not definitive.

The expression "curricular" validity suggests the same type of validity as content validity. In achievement measurement both are acceptable. In aptitude and personal-social adjustment measurement, however, "curricular" validity becomes an awkward identification because the term "curricular" suggests only that an academic curriculum is implicated in some fashion. To speak of content validity does not inject any such restrictions. Therefore, the expression "curricular" validity is not as flexible and thus less satisfactory than "content" validity.

LIMITATION OF EVIDENCE. When appraising the validity of an instrument we sometimes grumble about the limited evidence offered. There are several reasons for this. In the first place, determining the strength of any one of the three types of validity is noticeably time-consuming and expensive in all but a minority of cases. Even the most conscientious author cannot exhaust all the possible avenues of approach or use many varieties of groups of pupils for his validation attempts. In the second place, evidence that a certain type of validity is *not* present in an instrument is rarely listed in a test manual. In many cases, however, it is reported in educational or psychological journals or test reviews in other publications.

THE MENTAL MEASUREMENTS YEARBOOKS. Fortunately, there is a yet unmentioned source of information about standardized instruments of all kinds. This helps fill the voids mentioned in the preceding paragraphs, and is known as *The Mental Measurements Yearbooks*, the first volume of which was published in 1938. Additional volumes are published at fairly regular intervals. The largest section of each of the *Yearbooks* is entitled *Tests and Reviews* and contains—among other items—materials related to validity. The many purposes of this section bear repeating. In part, it is to assist those who use measuring instruments to appraise the instruments by providing comprehensive and up-to-date bibliographies of recent instruments, frank and critical reviews of them, and comprehensive bibliographies of references concerning each. For a given instrument, it is common to find such information as its complete title, the age or grade levels of the individuals for whom it is designed, the date of publication, cost, time limits, and the name of the author and the publishing company. In addition, one or more reviews are usually included, and the author identified. Pertinent references are listed without comment and may be numerous, in a few instances as many as one hundred. These contain information on the construction, validity, use, and limitations of the instrument.

The magnitude of the yearbooks is somewhat startling. For instance, *The Sixth Mental Measurements Yearbook* (Buros, 1965) alone contains 1,219 test and inventory titles, 795 critical reviews of them, and 8,001 references. When it is remembered that this yearbook supplements rather than supplants the preceding five volumes, it is eminently clear that the volumes form a colossal body of material.

Counselors, supervisors, and research workers, as well as classroom teachers, find the *Yearbooks* of inestimable value · in their instrument appraisals. As a readily accessible compilation of facts about and considered criticisms of measuring instruments, they are unmatched. Certainly no validity appraisal other than a teacher-constructed instrument is complete without including whatever information about its validity the *Yearbooks* can provide.

Problems

16   Study the reviews in *The Mental Measurements Yearbooks* of two tests or test batteries of interest to you in the area of (a) academic achievement, (b) scholastic aptitude, and (c) interest patterns. On the basis of the evidence presented, compare each pair of tests or test batteries in terms of their various kinds of validity.

17   What is differential content validity (Hopkins and Wilkerson, 1962)? How is this concept related to the methods used to establish high content validity for achievement tests?

Summary

Validity, the most vital attribute of any measuring instrument, is commonly defined as the degree to which that instrument actually serves the purposes for which it is intended. Since the purposes of measurement are divided into three categories, validity is classified into three types: (1) content validity, (2) criterion-related validity, and (3) construct validity.

Content validity is defined as the degree to which an instrument can be used to measure the performance of a pupil today in a certain type of situation or subject matter of which its items are a cross-sectional sample. Criterion-related validity exists to the extent that (1) it can be used to predict a pupil's future performance, and (2) to the degree that the behavior elicited by a measuring instrument corresponds to external but concurrent pupil behavior. An instrument has construct validity if a specified construct accounts for the variations in pupil performance it elicits.

The demonstration of a measuring instrument's validity is almost invariably a lengthy and laborious task. It may be necessary, for example, to ascertain whether a given instrument is characterized by more than one of the three types of validity, perhaps all three. Furthermore, suitable criteria and samples of pupils must be found before the validity determination can be completed. This is particularly true of criterion-related validity investigations. Lastly, the end product of a validity determination may or may not be quantitative in nature. Studies of content validity often do not yield quantitative evidence, whereas studies of criterion-related and sometimes construct validity do yield quantitative evidence, such as a product-moment coefficient of correlation.

Before a teacher uses any measuring instrument, he is obliged to conduct a thorough investigation of its validity. Not only must he decide that his purposes are the same as those for which the instrument is designed, but also he must convince himself that its author has acceptable evidence that the instrument can accomplish the purposes claimed. A teacher's appraisal of the validity of a standardized instrument commonly utilizes the material presented in the instrument's manual, the information provided by *The Mental Measurements Yearbooks*, and the considered judgment of the teacher.

SUGGESTED READINGS

Anastasi, Anne. *Psychological testing.* (2nd ed.) New York: Macmillan, 1961. Chapter 6.
    This chapter includes descriptions of the various types of validity, including "face" validity.
Anastasi, Anne. Some current developments in the measurement and interpretation of test validity. In *Proceedings of the 1963 Invitational Conference*

on *Testing Problems*. Princeton, N.J.: Educational Testing Service, 1964, pp. 33–45.

> Five comparatively recent developments in test validation are reviewed briefly. One topic is "synthetic" validity, an approach sometimes used to predict job performance in business and industry. A lengthy bibliography is included.

Campbell, Donald T. Recommendations for APA test standards regarding construct, trait, or discriminant validity. *Amer. Psychologist*, 1960, 15, 546–553.

> The background of the debate concerning construct validity is reviewed. Objections raised by various testing specialists are listed, each of which is followed by a brief evaluation by the author.

Cronbach, Lee J. *Essentials of psychological testing*. (2nd ed.) New York: Harper & Row, 1960. Chapter 5.

> Within this chapter are discussions of the three types of validity. Steps for computing a product-moment and a rank order coefficient of correlation are given.

Cureton, Edward E. Validity. In E. F. Lindquist (Ed.), *Educational measurement*. Washington: American Council on Education, 1951. Pp. 621–694.

> This chapter is somewhat more technical than any of the other references mentioned here. The nature of validity, some of the problems of validity determination, and statistical aspects of validity estimation are explained.

Ebel, Robert L. Must all tests be valid? *Amer. Psychologist*, 1961, 16, 640–647.

> This is a provocative article. The author argues that all tests need not be "valid" if the term "valid" is not to be made synonymous with the term "good," and if validity is a clearly defined concept which can be quantified by correlating test scores and data from an independent criterion.

French, J. W., and W. B. Michael. *Standards for educational and psychological tests*. Washington: American Psychological Association, 1966. Pp. 12–24.

> This bulletin is the result of the second major attempt by the American Psychological Association and other organizations to develop an authoritative statement concerning test standards. Content, criterion-related, and construct validity are defined carefully and illustrations are provided.

Helmstadter, G. C. *Principles of psychological measurement*. New York: Appleton-Century-Crofts, 1964. Chapters 4, 5, and 6.

> These three short chapters are devoted to content, empirical, and construct validity respectively. Empirical validity is analogous to criterion-related validity.

Wesman, Alexander G. Expectancy tables—a way of interpreting test validity. Test Service Bulletin, No. 38. New York: Psychological Corporation, 1949.

> This bulletin is devoted to expectancy tables and their usefulness in the demonstration of criterion-related validity. Illustrations involving the *Differential Aptitude Tests* are shown, and the advantages and limitations of expectancy tables are listed.

Wesman, Alexander G. *Better than chance*. Test Service Bulletin, No. 45. New York: Psychological Corporation, 1953.

> In this publication, the value of the product-moment coefficient of correlation and expectancy tables as representations of criterion-related validity are compared. The practical utility of expectancy tables is explained and illustrated.

Wesman, Alexander G. *Double-entry expectancy tables*. Test Service Bulletin, No. 56. New York: Psychological Corporation, 1966.

Since predictions of future achievement are often made on the basis of two predictors rather than one, a double-entry expectancy table is needed. In this bulletin, such tables are described and one is developed for the relationship between college grade-point average and a combination of scholastic aptitude scores and rank in high school graduating class.

REFERENCES CITED

Bechtoldt, H. P. Construct validity: a critique. Amer. Psychologist, 1959, 14, 619–629.

Buros, Oscar K. (Ed.) The sixth mental measurements yearbook. Highland Park, N.J.: Gryphon Press, 1965.

Campbell, Donald T. Recommendations for APA test standards regarding construct, trait, or discriminant validity. Amer. Psychologist, 1960, 15, 546–553.

Cooperative Test Division. Sequential Tests of Educational Progress teacher's guide. Princeton, N.J.: Educational Testing Service, 1959.

Cronbach, Lee J. Essentials of psychological testing. (2nd ed.) New York: Harper & Row, 1960.

Cronbach, Lee J., and Paul E. Meehl. Construct validity in psychological tests. Psychol. Bull., 1955, 52, 281–302.

Dizney, Henry. Characteristics of classroom test items identified by students as "unfair." J. educ. Measmt, 1965, 2, 119–121.

Ebel, Robert L. Must all tests be valid? Amer. Psychologist, 1961, 16, 640–647.

French, J. W., and W. B. Michael. Standards for educational and psychological tests. Washington: American Psychological Association, 1966.

Gardner, Eric F., and others. Stanford Achievement Test, High School Battery manual. New York: Harcourt, Brace and World, 1965.

Guilford, J. P. Fundamental statistics in psychology and education. (4th ed.) New York: McGraw-Hill, 1965.

Guilford, J. P., and others. Ratings should be scrutinized. Educ. psychol. Measmt, 1962, 22, 439–447.

Hansmeier, Thomas W. The Iowa Tests of Educational Development as predictors of college achievement. Educ. psychol. Measmt, 1960, 20, 843–845.

Hopkins, K. D., and C. J. Wilkerson. Differential content validity: the California Spelling Test, an illustrative example. Educ. psychol. Measmt, 1962, 2, 413–419.

Langmuir, Charles R. Cross-validation. Test Service Bulletin, No. 47. New York: Psychological Corporation, 1954.

Schrader, W. B. A taxonomy of expectancy tables. J. educ. Measmt, 1965, 2, 29–35.

Wesman, Alexander G. Expectancy tables—a way of interpreting test validity. Test Service Bulletin, No. 38. New York: Psychological Corporation, 1949.

Wesman, Alexander G. Double-entry expectancy tables. Test Service Bulletin, No. 56. New York: Psychological Corporation, 1966.

10

The Reliability of Measurement Methods

PRODDED BY HIS TEENAGE SON, the proud owner of a near-new automobile decided to determine the number of miles that it traveled for each gallon of gasoline consumed. During a week in early May he carefully tabulated the gasoline consumption and the miles traveled, and computed the gasoline mileage to be 17.3 miles per gallon. Later that same month the owner selected another week, measured the gasoline consumed and miles traveled, and found that the gasoline consumption was 17.0 miles per gallon. The procedure was repeated during the first week of June, and a gasoline mileage of 17.4 miles per gallon resulted.

It did not surprise the owner that the gasoline mileages varied by only small amounts. Because the three one-week periods were separated by relatively short periods of time, and because such factors as weather and traffic conditions were, for all practical purposes, uniform during all three trials, it seemed reasonable that the results should be consistent if these measurements of gasoline mileage were at all accurate. No doubt the owner ignored the minor differences among the three values and concluded that the gasoline milage produced by his automobile under the existing traffic and weather conditions was fairly well identified. He might have even averaged the three measurements, and then used this value as the final product of his investigation.

Had he known that the true gasoline mileage had remained unchanged during the three trial periods and was really 17.3 miles per gallon, he would not have been dismayed. On the contrary, he might have been quite pleased with the accuracy of his estimates. Furthermore, if he had been pressed for an explanation as to why his three estimates varied although the true value did not vary, he might have shrugged his shoulders and attributed the small fluctuations to "chance" errors.

The chance errors that he had in mind are many. First of all, the measurement of the gasoline delivered by the pump might have been in error. Thus, exactly five gallons of gasoline drawn from the pump might not necessarily have been registered on the meter as exactly five gallons. It is possible that exactly five gallons in one case might be measured as slightly more than five gallons and in another as slightly less. Secondly, the reading of the meter introduced a possibility of error. The gasoline was measured to the nearest one-tenth of a gallon, and since the amount necessary to fill the tank probably fell somewhere between two such points, it had to be estimated to the nearest one-tenth of a gallon. Overestimates and underestimates are distinct possibilities. Thirdly, the attendant might have filled the gasoline tank to varying degrees of "fullness" each time the owner began and completed the measurement of the gasoline mileage. Haste and carelessness might have caused slightly different amounts of gasoline to be contained within the tank when it was classified as "full." Lastly, the odometer might not have registered the miles traveled with perfect accuracy, and the reading of it also might have involved certain amounts of estimation.

Despite these possibilities of error, the gasoline mileages were fairly consistent. Such consistency of measurement is equally desirable in education. A good measuring instrument must yield dependable information; in other words, if it is possible to use it repeatedly in the same unchanging situation, the information yielded by each administration of the instrument should be similar to that yielded by any other administration. For instance, the typing teacher who gives a speed test to his pupils on Friday would hope that the typing rates determined would be the same, for all practical purposes, as those obtained from such an exercise administered on Monday, if the pupils did not study or practice during the weekend. Likewise, the scholastic aptitude scores yielded by a test given to pupils at 10:30 A.M. on September 18th are assumed to be essentially the same as those that would be obtained were the test administered at 9:30 A.M. on September 19th.

Should there be no assurance that tests such as these do yield reasonably consistent results, their value would be severely limited. Before any measuring instrument should be used, therefore, the question might be asked: If repeated attempts are made to obtain information about an unchanging pupil attribute with this instrument, will the results tend to duplicate each other? The question can be stated much more simply: Is the measuring instrument reliable?

Definition of Reliability

Reliability means consistency of results. This is equivalent to saying that a highly reliable instrument can be used repeatedly in an unchanging situation and produce constant or near constant results. When, on the contrary, a measuring instrument is applied again and again and yields results that vary greatly, even though the situation has not changed, the instrument is labeled as highly unreliable. Unfortunately, all instruments are somewhat unreliable.

Chance Errors

To say all measuring instruments are somewhat unreliable is the same thing as saying that all measurements are subject to some *chance error*. Chance errors, or compensating errors as they are sometimes called, have one vital characteristic; they have a tendency to cancel each other when the instrument is used many times. There are a number of possibilities of chance error in the gasoline mileage determinations, one of which can be traced to the meter on the gasoline pump. Although a given withdrawal of precisely five gallons from the pump may be recorded on the meter as slightly more than five gallons, a second attempt might be recorded as slightly less. Were the process to be repeated an infinite number of times and the tendency to overestimate and underestimate found to be equal, then the error is a chance error and affects the reliability of the measurement.

There still remains, of course, the possibility that the meter habitually overestimates or underestimates; and that no canceling takes place no matter how many measurements are made. This is obviously an error of measurement, but not a chance error. It does not lessen the reliability of the measurement, but does lessen the validity. Thus, validity of the gasoline mileage measurement is affected if the readings on the gasoline meter were always one-tenth of a gallon less than the actual amount of gasoline delivered by the pump. In the case of the typing speed test and the scholastic aptitude test, similar errors are possible. Either one could have yielded erroneous measurements to the extent that every typing rate is seven words per minute too low, or every scholastic aptitude score is four points too large. In contrast to compensating errors, which are important in the reliability of measuring instruments, these errors are classified in the second group of errors called *biased errors*, or *constant errors*, and affect only the relative validity of these instruments. These errors do not tend to cancel each other when an instrument is used many times.

PUPIL-CENTERED AND INSTRUMENT-CENTERED FACTORS. Many factors affect the reliability of measuring instruments. Some are associated with the pupils themselves, whereas other factors arise from the instrument itself. Pupil factors ordinarily mentioned are state of health, fatigue, motivation, emotional strain, and the like.Two factors associated with the instrument itself are prominent in the paper-and-pencil test. First of all, the test is only a sample of an immense number of possible test items; secondly, the scoring of the test, particularly those with essay test items, may not be consistent, a factor known as lack of scorer reliability. Many additional factors related both to the pupils and to the instrument and its administration have been listed by Thorndike (1951).

Certainly the importance of these factors as they affect the information yielded by a measuring instrument is not uniform from pupil to pupil or instrument to instrument. The pupil-centered factors may easily fluctuate from day to day, perhaps from forenoon to afternoon, and, for many pupils, play only a small role in terms of influencing an instrument's results. Instrument-centered factors tend to be less damaging as, for example, a paper-and-pencil test is lengthened by adding suitable items and as the scoring becomes more objective. Trivial as some of the sources may seem to be, they can drastically reduce the value of a measuring instrument.

Perhaps it is disconcerting to find such factors as those listed classified as the originators of chance errors. Admittedly they may not fit as neatly into the scheme as does the gasoline meter and its errors. Yet we can argue that the errors from the sources listed would cancel out if it were possible to measure an unchanging pupil attribute many times with each of its many tests, which in turn were scored independently by many judges.

Problems

1 Define and illustrate scorer reliability.
2 Define and illustrate sampling error as it is a factor in reliability determinations (Hoyt, 1960, p. 1145).

Differentiating Between Validity and Reliability

The terms "validity" and "reliability" have too often been used as though they are synonymous or nearly so. Though the concepts are somewhat related, they are by no means identical. The validity of a measuring instrument is the degree to which it actually serves the purposes for which its use is intended; the reliability of an instrument is its capacity to yield consistent information regardless of whether it serves the purposes in question. Thus a highly reliable instrument is not necessarily an equally valid instrument. For example, the heights of male college seniors majoring in education can be measured with considerable reliability. Yet this fact would in no way support the statement that the tall male college senior will be a better classroom teacher in future years than a short one. Educational tests may likewise have superior reliability and still be woefully lacking in validity. An arithmetic achievement test used to measure qualities of leadership is one of many possible examples.

It is timely to re-emphasize that high validity is the most important characteristic of an instrument. The role of reliability is a vital but secondary one when a measuring instrument is being appraised. The importance of both characteristics can be summarized in the statement that the perfect instrument must serve the purpose or purposes for which it is intended and, in doing so, must produce consistent information.

Problem

3   One definition of validity (Wert and others, 1954, p. 328) proposes that an evaluation instrument is highly valid if neither chance nor biased errors appreciably affect the information it yields. Then reliability is a necessary condition for validity. Evaluate this definition in the light of the foregoing discussion and the position taken by Ebel (1961).

Determination of Coefficients of Reliability

Testing specialists concerned with methods for estimating the validity of a measuring instrument sometimes search for external evidence and try to appraise its validity in terms of such evidence. Reliability determination on the other hand, is not based on evidence of this kind. Instead, the instrument is compared with itself or some equivalent form. These procedures can be illustrated readily in the case of paper-and-pencil tests.

The determination of test reliability is based upon one central method. The instrument to be investigated is used (perhaps in conjunction with an equivalent form) to obtain one or more attribute measurements of each member of a group of pupils. Each measurement identifies the position of each pupil in terms of the attribute measured. The consistency with which he maintains his position within the group from measurement to measurement is a reflection of the reliability of the test. This consistency can be translated into a product-moment coefficient of correlation, called a coefficient of reliability. Moreover, a coefficient of reliability can often be interpreted more easily by converting it to a standard error of measurement. This is an attempt to estimate the size of the errors of measurement caused by the unreliability of the test.

Determination of Coefficients of Reliability

Coefficients of reliability can result from four separate processes known as the stability method, the equivalence method, the stability and equivalence method, and the internal consistency method. According to the stability method, a test is administered once, then a short period of time is allowed to pass and it is administered a second time to the same pupils. A coefficient of reliability is computed from the two sets of test scores. The equivalence method requires two equivalent forms of the test. They are given consecutively to a group of pupils, and a coefficient of reliability is computed. If a time interval of some size (for example, one week) occurs between the administration of the two equivalent forms, then the reliability determination follows the stability and equivalence method. Lastly, it is possible to analyze the data obtained from a single administration of a test and a reliability coefficient. This is the internal consistency method.

In the past, the coefficients of reliability resulting from the application of the four methods have been identified as the coefficient of stability, coefficient of equivalence, coefficient of stability and equivalence, and coefficient of internal consistency respectively. Although these are useful labels, they do not adequately describe the kind of reliability determination which yielded the coefficient of correlation (French and Michael, 1966, pp. 26–27). It is recommended that in their place more complete statements be used to describe the coefficient of correlation such as "coefficient of reliability representing stability of measurements obtained by administering two different forms of the test one week apart."

STABILITY METHOD. We can easily determine the reliability with which we can assess such dimensions as the length or weight of a block of wood. Repeated measurements of the object are made and compared. A similar procedure is sometimes applied when the reliability of educational measuring instruments is under study. Suppose that a test author constructs a 150-item test designed to measure eleventh-grade pupils' knowledge of American history, and that this test has satisfactory content validity. To determine the reliability of his instrument, the author may give the test to a sample of eleventh-grade pupils, tabulate the results, allow an interval of time to pass, and finally readminister the instrument to the same pupils under the same conditions as before. Unless there is evidence to the contrary, it is assumed that the group has not changed with respect to their knowledge of American history during the time interval. Ideally then, each pupil would receive the same test score the second time as the first. In reality, the most the author can hope for is that pupils who received high scores on the first test administration will receive high scores on the second test administration and that those who received low scores the first time will receive low scores the second time.

Plotting the results of the two test administrations is most profitable. Figure 21 is a partial reproduction of the kind of configuration that might occur if the test were highly reliable. Many more cases (perhaps 200 or more) would be used than are shown in Figure 21. Observe that in this figure, as in the case of Figure 20 shown in Chapter 9, the points arrange themselves in an elongated manner so as to approximate a straight line. If the test were very unreliable, the points would scatter considerably, even to the extent that no straight line could satisfactorily represent the total number of points.

Once again the product-moment coefficient of correlation is the most convenient and suitable means of representing the degree to which the points conform to a straight line. The scores of the two test administrations are substituted in the appropriate formula (see page 575) for the coefficient of correlation and a coefficient of reliability is computed. For a test such as described in this illustration, the r-value might be 0.90 or more. A value of 1.00 would represent perfect test reliability in terms of this method, whereas a value of 0.00 would represent no test reliability.

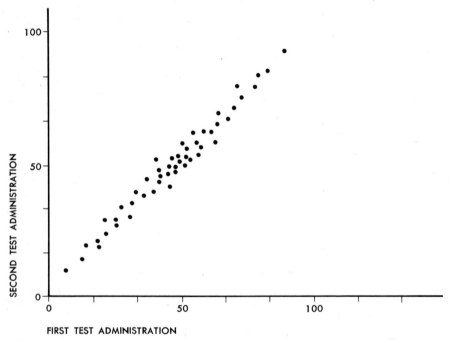

FIGURE 21

SCATTER DIAGRAM OF ACHIEVEMENT TEST SCORES
RESULTING FROM TWO TEST ADMINISTRATIONS

Further examination of Figure 21 reveals another noteworthy feature of the data. Observe that the straight line that seems to fit the points as plotted will not, if extended, touch the point at which the score resulting from each administration is zero. Instead it will intersect the vertical axis slightly above the zero-point. This commonly occurs when the reliability of achievement tests is determined by test-retest procedures. The scores from the second test administration are generally slightly higher than those from the first test administration, because of the practice effect that results from the first test administration. Unlike a block of wood, which can be measured endlessly without any noticeable effect on the block, a pupil will probably change as a result of the measurement. In the case of achievement tests, the change is customarily slight but discernible when a group of pupils is considered.

The length of time allowed between test administrations is critical and must be selected with care. If it is too short, pupils will remember the answers given at the first test when they answer the questions the second time; if it is too long, the pupils may change with respect to the characteristic measured. In many cases, a week or two is judged to be an appropriate compromise. Obviously there is no single, widely accepted time interval suitable for all types of test with all varieties of pupils.

The stability method is not considered the most defensible for establishing test reliability. Some of its weaknesses have been mentioned. Three apparent defects are the practice effect that may result from the first test administration, the difficulty of establishing a suitable interval of time between test administrations, and the failure to have identical testing conditions both times. More serious in the eyes of some, however, is the fact that the coefficient of reliability reflects pupil-centered chance errors but not one of the most vital instrument-centered chance errors, namely, the fact that tests are samples of an immense number of possible items. Repetition of a test at different times will reveal inconsistent pupil behavior, but, since the same test is used twice, the sampling of the items is held constant. Consequently, an important instrument-centered chance error is ignored and the coefficients of reliability tend to be unduly high. Some writers recommend that these coefficients not be computed for achievement tests.

RELIABILITY DETERMINATIONS BASED ON EQUIVALENT FORMS

Rather than administering the same test twice to a group of pupils, as in the case of the stability method, the equivalence method utilizes the scores from each of a pair of equivalent tests. The two equivalent tests are given to a suitable group of pupils with little or no time allowed between the two administrations. For each pupil two scores are available, one from each form of the test. When the scores are correlated, a coefficient of reliability results. If the two forms of the test were administered with an intervening time interval as in the test-retest method, then the stability and equivalence method is being followed. In many such cases, the time interval is at least a day and no longer than a week.

The requirement that a measuring instrument be available in two equivalent forms is, of course, a severe limitation. Equivalent forms of informal tests are seldom found. Teachers usually do not construct them except in the case of "make-up" tests, which are supposed to be equivalent to the tests they replace. Standardized tests, on the other hand, are often published with two equivalent forms, sometimes more. Suppose that the test author who developed the 150-item achievement test in American history wants to construct an equivalent form. The problem he faces is not incidental. One danger to be avoided is to design the equivalent form to be so "equivalent" to the original that it is essentially identical. Then he still has but one test in spite of his efforts. The second danger is to design the equivalent form to be so "unequivalent" that it is measuring something at least slightly different from the original. A satisfactory equivalent form is somewhere in between.

The problem of building an equivalent form of the American history achievement test can be attacked systematically. First of all, as is emphasized in the discussion of content validity of achievement tests, the test author must have identified certain specific educational objectives and developed one or more tables of specifications on the basis of them. To measure the degree to which these selected objectives have been achieved, he had to compose a vast number of test items. Pretesting the items at various times with appropriate pupils has helped screen them. In all likelihood, only part of the surviving items are included in the original form of the test. The balance are available for an equivalent form. Then the test author might dip into this supply in search of a second cross-sectional sample of test items that represent the same level of difficulty and the same relative importance of the pertinent educational objectives as the set of test items composing the original form. Evidence concerning the equivalence of the two forms can be obtained by methods beyond the scope of this book (Wilks, 1946).

Assume that the test author completes an equivalent form of the American history test and labels it Form B. The original test, now called Form A, and Form B can be administered consecutively to a group of 200 eleventh-grade pupils for whom the test is designed. The result is a pair of scores for each pupil, which in turn can be plotted and will yield a scatter of points very much like that in Figure 21. A coefficient of correlation computed from the data is a coefficient of reliability and will of course fall somewhere between 1.00 and 0.00. An r-value of 0.91 is found in the case of the history test.

This coefficient of reliability is clearly not the same representation of test reliability as the coefficient yielded by the stability method. The chance errors involved in the two methods are different. In the equivalence method, the pupil-centered chance errors are not reflected in the coefficient of reliability. This is because the time interval between the two tests administrations is virtually nonexistent. On the other hand, the instrument-centered chance error, associated with the fact that the test is necessarily a sample, is manifest in this method. Each form of the test is assumed to be a cross-sectional sample of the same group of items. The opposite is true in the case of the stability method: the pupil-centered chance errors are operative, whereas the instrument-centered chance error is not.

The use of two equivalent forms of a test is a recommended way of computing an estimate of test reliability. The test author may choose to give the two forms consecutively to an appropriate group of pupils, or he may choose to allow a time interval between the two tests. By the latter process, many pupil-centered as well as instrument-centered chance errors will influence the reliability estimate. Therefore, since reliability is defined as the relative absence of chance errors in the measurement results, the most logical procedure for estimating test reliability is to give equivalent forms with a time interval between the test administrations, and then compute a coefficient of reliability. Remember that this type of coefficient of reliability represents stability of performance by the pupil over a short period of time. This is essential information, since we often want assurance that the pupil would have obtained a similar test score had he been tested on a different day or with an equivalent instrument.

INTERNAL CONSISTENCY METHOD. The practical difficulties in the test re-test and equivalent forms methods of determining reliability emphasize the desirability of estimating test reliability with a single administration of a single form of the test in question. The savings in time and labor are obvious. To perform this feat, however, new formulas are necessary and new assumptions must be made.

There are two basic procedures for analyzing the results of a single administration of a test to assess the reliability of the instrument. The first, sometimes known as the split-half procedure, arbitrarily divides the total test into two halves, scores them separately, thereby yielding two scores per pupil, and correlates the pairs of scores. The resulting coefficient of correlation is a coefficient of reliability of one-half of the test rather than the total test, and is adjusted to be applicable to the total test. The second procedure, sometimes known as an analysis of variance procedure, involves examination of the responses to each test item in terms of the number of pupils who successfully answered the item and the number who failed it.

Usually the first controversy concerning the application of the split-half procedure is centered around the selection of the two halves. Imagine the number of possible halves that could be obtained by splitting the 150-item achievement test in American history previously mentioned. The most satisfactory set of all possible halves would be that pair composed of the two most equivalent members. In other words, the level of difficulty of the test items and the manner in which the items reflect the relative importance of the cells of the table or tables of specifications involved should be the same in both halves. Dividing a test haphazardly into halves without thought of equivalence reduces the split-half process of reliability determination to busy work of dubious value.

If two equivalent halves of a test are to be found in the same way as two equivalent forms of a test are constructed, little has been gained in terms of conserving time and labor when the split-half method is used. Therefore, some compromises generally are made. Again the achievement test in American history can illustrate a typical situation. Let us assume that this achievement test, as most achievement tests, follows two general principles of construction. In the first place the level of difficulty of the test items for the most part increases slightly from the beginning to the end of the test so that the least difficult items are found at the beginning of the test and the most difficult are found at the end. Secondly, the test items are crudely grouped according to content; items relating to each cell in the table of specifications are clustered in a systematic fashion. Under these conditions, a convenient way of selecting two halves that would tend to be equivalent is to separate the odd-numbered items from the even-numbered items. The level of difficulty of the items in the odd half will approximate the level of difficulty of those in the even half. So also will the content of the test items in the odd half approximate that of the items in the even half. Note that had the author decided to divide his test so that the items numbered from 1 to 75 composed one half, whereas the items numbered from 76 to 150 composed the second half, the second would be more difficult than the first and would sample different material. The lack of equivalence would be striking.

The odd-even division is a popular method of separating a test into two halves of approximate equivalence. Had the test author chosen to use this method, the remainder of the reliability determination is simple. First he gives the complete test (with odd and even test items in their proper order) to a representative group of eleventh-grade pupils for whom the test is designed. Then he separately scores the odd- and even-numbered items. Plotting the two scores for each pupil produces a diagram much like Figure 21, if the performance of the pupil tends to be consistent. The degree to which the points fit a straight line can again be represented by a correlation coefficient, which can be computed by substituting the odd-half and even-half scores into the appropriate formula. The correlation coefficient between their scores is 0.80. This is the coefficient of reliability for one-half of the test rather than for the total test. To estimate the expected coefficient of reliability of the total test, an adjustment formula known as the Spearman-Brown "Prophecy Formula" (Spearman, 1910) is used.

In modified form the formula is

$$r_{xx} = \frac{2\, r_{oe}}{1 + r_{oe}}$$

where

r_{xx} = coefficient of reliability of the total test

r_{oe} = coefficient of correlation between the odd-half scores and the even-half scores

In the case of the American history achievement test the coefficient of reliability is

$$r_{xx} = \frac{(2)\ (0.80)}{1 + 0.80} = 0.89$$

Observe in this case the noticeable increase in the size of the coefficient of reliability as the length of the test is doubled.

The major assumption underlying the applicability of the Spearman-Brown formulas is that the two halves are indeed equivalent. As the two halves fail to be ideally equivalent, so then is the coefficient of reliability of the total test as yielded by the Spearman-Brown formula an underestimate. Since the equivalence of the two halves is probably somewhat inadequate, the coefficients of the Spearman-Brown formula are conservative estimates test reliability.

Computation of a coefficient of reliability by an analysis of variance method most often utilizes one of the Kuder-Richardson formulas (Kuder and Richardson, 1937). This formula, identified as K-R #20, is relatively easy to apply, although its derivation is intricate and beyond the scope of this book. Important pieces of information necessary for solution of the formula are the proportions of pupils passing and failing each test item. This procedure estimates test reliability on the basis of consistency of pupil performance from item to item within the test. In the case of achievement tests, the r-values computed are usually smaller than expected because the item content of this type of test is not homogeneous.

The Kuder-Richardson and Spearman-Brown formulas are appropriate only for power tests, which are so administered that practically all pupils have an opportunity to attempt every test item. The r-values that will result from use of these formulas with a single administration of a pure speed test will be inflated, perhaps substantially. The amount of over-estimation is difficult to establish, but tends to decrease as the number of unattempted test items becomes smaller. The preferred procedure for determining the reliability of a speeded test is the stability and equivalence method.

You can readily see that, no matter which of the two methods of computation is used, the coefficients of reliability do not reflect chance errors associated with day-to-day variations of the pupils tested. Stated otherwise, pupil-centered chance errors are ignored in this type of relia-bility coefficient; however, the instrument-centered chance errors, arising from the fact that the test is but a sample of many possible test items, are reflected.

COMPARISON OF COEFFICIENTS OF RELIABILITY.   The various coefficients of reliability can be compared in two different ways. First of all, the similari-ties and dissimilarities in their methods of determination can be tabulated. In the second place, they can be compared on the basis of the chance errors they reflect. Both comparisons can be summarized by tables such as Table 11 and Table 12.

In Table 11 the methods of determination are considered. For each coefficient of reliability, the need for one or more forms of the test and the number of test administrations required are listed. It is apparent again that the coefficient or reliability most easily found is that yielded by the internal consistency method, whereas the one found with greatest difficulty is that yielded by the stability and equivalence method.

Two major types of chance errors and their relationship to each coefficient of reliability are shown in Table 12. Pupil- and instrument-

TABLE 11

TEST FORMS AND NUMBER OF ADMINISTRATIONS REQUIRED BY VARIOUS METHODS OF DETERMINING COEFFICIENTS OF RELIABILITY

| | Number of Test Administrations | | |
| | | Two test administrations | |
Test forms needed	One test administration	Same day	Different days
One form	Internal Consistency		Stability
Equivalent forms		Equivalence	Stability and Equivalence

TABLE 12

CHANCE ERRORS REFLECTED IN VARIOUS COEFFICIENTS OF RELIABILITY

		Chance Errors	
Method of determination	*Procedure*	*Pupil-centered*	*Instrument-centered*
Stability	Same test form given on different days	X	
Stability and Equivalence	Equivalent test forms given on different days	X	X
Equivalence	Equivalent test forms given on same day		X
Internal Consistency	Split-half procedure		X
Internal Consistency	Kuder-Richardson procedure		X

centered chance errors are reflected only in the stability and equivalence method.

PROBLEMS

4   To what degree would one expect the problem of the "practice effect" to reduce the value of a coefficient of reliability from the stability method as a representation of the reliability of a test? Is "practice effect" also a problem when the equivalence method is used? Explain your answer.

5   Compare the equivalence method with the internal consistency method in terms of chance errors which are reflected and the practical problems of completing the determination.

6   It is argued that, in spite of evidence presented by the test author, so-called equivalent forms of an achievement test may be far from equivalent for a particular pupil population, and therefore comparisons based on these forms of the test may be distorted (Howell and Weiner, 1961). Study this argument and the supporting data. Of what significance is it in terms of the equivalence method?

7   Differentiate between K-R #20 formula and K-8 #21 formula for determining a coefficient of reliability (Cronbach, 1960, pp. 141–142; Cureton, 1966).

Determination of the Standard Error of Measurement

Since every test is somewhat unreliable, each score obtained for a pupil must be considered as an estimate of his "true score," which would have been found had the test been totally reliable. Useful as the coefficients of reliability are when test reliability is being appraised, they do not directly offer an estimate of the actual magnitude of the error in a test score for a given pupil, that error having been caused by test unreliability. The standard error of measurement, on the other hand, attempts to do precisely this. In other words, the standard error of measurement affords the test consumer some indication of the size of the difference (resulting from the fact that the test is unreliable to some degree) between an obtained score for a pupil and his "true score" on the test. This difference is expressed in the same units as are the test scores. Observe that, when using the expressions "obtained score" and "true score" in the description of the standard error of measurement, considerations of validity are temporarily ignored.

COMPUTING STANDARD ERRORS OF MEASUREMENT. The computation of the standard error of measurement is not difficult. Its formula is

$$\text{S.E.}_{\text{m}} = \sigma\sqrt{1 - r}$$

where

$$
\begin{aligned}
\text{S.E.}_{\text{m}} &= \text{standard error of measurement} \\
\sigma &= \text{standard deviation of total test scores} \\
r &= \text{coefficient of reliability}
\end{aligned}
$$

The standard error of measurement of the achievement test in American history is 4.5. To obtain this value, the coefficient of equivalence of 0.91 is used along with the standard deviation, which is computed in accordance with a formula shown in Appendix A (see pages 571–574). The standard deviation value of 15.1 and the coefficient of equivalence are substituted in the standard error of measurement formula as follows:

$$\text{S.E.}_{\text{m}} = \sigma\sqrt{1 - r} = (15.1)\sqrt{1 - 0.91} = 4.5$$

INTERPRETING STANDARD ERRORS OF MEASUREMENT. It is *not* appropriate to say that, in the case of the American history achievement test, a pupil's "true score" differs from his obtained score by no more than 4.5 raw-score points. Rather, it can be said that the "true scores" will not differ from their respective obtained scores by more than 4.5 raw-score points in approximately two-thirds of the measurements we might make with this test. Or, the standard error of measurement can be doubled and the statement made that the "true scores" will not differ from their respective obtained scores by more than 9.0 raw-score points in approximately 95 per cent of the measurements we might make. Finally, we could triple the standard error of measurement and say that the "true scores" will not differ from their respective obtained scores by more than 13.5 raw-score points in approximately 99 per cent of the measurements.

Although the foregoing interpretations still do not offer a direct, unequivocal statement of the error caused by test unreliability in a given pupil's obtained score, teachers still consider the standard error of measurement to be a highly meaningful measure of test reliability. The fact that it is expressed in the same units as the test scores contributes greatly to its popularity. Teachers repeatedly argue that it offers a good basis for judging how satisfactory the reported test reliability is for a given testing function. In general, of course, it is pleasing to find low standard errors of measurement and most distressing to be confronted with large values. As the standard error of measurement increases, the confidence in obtained scores as estimates of "true scores" correspondingly decreases.

Because test unreliability, scores must be interpreted as regions rather than as points. Such regions, often known as "bands," are determined by the standard error of measurement of the test. Since a pupil's "true score" does not differ from his obtained score by more than the standard error in approximately two-thirds of the measurements we make, it is customary to find the limits of the "band" by adding the standard error of measurement to and subtracting it from the obtained score. Suppose that a pupil obtained a test score of 70 on a test with a standard error of measurement of 3. The "band" often used would have a lower limit of 67 and an upper limit of 73. A pupil with a score of 75 would have a 72-78 "band." By the way, because the two "bands" overlap, we can say that there is probably no difference between the two pupils in terms of this test. Should the two "bands" fail to overlap, there probably is a genuine difference between the pupils in question. This use of the standard error of measurement, crude as it is, serves to inject caution into the interpretation of small differences between raw scores.

Problems

8   Study the procedure for scoring and interpreting the *School and College Ability Tests*. Why does the width of the percentile bands vary?

9   The standard error of measurement is a standard deviation. Identify the theoretical distribution of which it is the standard deviation (Cronbach, 1960, pp. 126–127).

10   Differentiate between a standard error of measurement and the standard deviation of the test scores (Cronbach, 1960, pp. 126–127).

11   Describe a practical situation of interest to you in which the standard error of measurement of a test is used. Describe a second such situation in which a standard error of estimate is used (Anastasi, 1961, pp. 159–160). Compare the functions of these two statistical values.

Appraising Estimates of Reliability

Coefficients of Reliability

As is often true with statistical results, a simple judgment based upon the statistical value alone is probably foolhardy. Careful scrutiny of the source of the value generally produces an enlarged view of it. In the case of coefficients of reliability, careful scrutiny most often includes a prolonged look at (1) the test itself, (2) the characteristics of the group of pupils involved in the reliability determination, and (3) the testing conditions. The enlarged view embodies shrewd guesses as to why the reliability coefficient is the size it is and whether the test scores are sufficiently free of chance errors to permit the test to be satisfactorily applied in a specific situation.

CHARACTERISTICS OF THE TEST.   When examining the test itself in search of evidence to assist in appraising a coefficient of reliability, at least three characteristics deserve attention. These are the tendency of the test to be speeded, the homogeneity or heterogeneity of its content, and the length. The role of test speed as it affects the size of coefficients yielded by the internal consistency method and the role of homogeneity of test content when applying the Kuder-Richardson formula are mentioned earlier. The importance of test length in determining the size of coefficients of reliability is dramatically illustrated by the Spearman-Brown formula. If the number of items in a test is increased by adding items equal in quality to the original ones, the reliability of the test will improve noticeably. To apply the Spearman-Brown formula, it is necessary to assume the items added are indeed equal in quality to the originals. Unfortunately this assumption is not always remembered, and an overgeneralized statement results, namely, the longer the test, the more reliable it is. Although it is true that longer tests tend to be more reliable in repeated instances, lengthening a test does not automatically assure us of greatly improved reliability.

CHARACTERISTICS OF THE PUPIL GROUP.   The group of pupils cooperating in the reliability determination is a second source of information. As in the case of the determination of criterion-related validity, this group should be thoroughly characterized by the test author as to any attribute that can conceivably be related to the dimension being measured by the test. For example, the 200 eleventh-grade pupils involved in the experimental use of the American history achievement test should be identified as to grade level, age, average scholastic aptitude score on some well-known instrument, previous training in history, socio-economic level, and geographic location. These and other pieces of information will help the teacher immeasurably in reaching his decision as to whether the 200 eleventh-grade pupils are, for all practical purposes, comparable to his class for whom the test is being selected. If his class and the 200 eleventh-grade pupils seem to be the same, he can assume that the reliability estimates listed accurately reflect the reliability of the measurements he will make. If his class is vastly dissimilar when compared to the 200 pupils, the reliability estimates based upon the test scores of the latter group may well be meaningless for him.

The variability of the 200 eleventh-grade pupils with regard to the attribute being measured by the achievement test must never be ignored. A key value in describing the variability of the group in terms of this test is the standard deviation, in this instance 15.1. As the variability in American history achievement increases, so will the standard deviation. Moreover, as the variability increases, so will the coefficient of reliability. An extreme illustration involving the achievement test under consideration can readily illuminate the problem. Suppose that the 200 pupils had been drawn in about equal numbers from tenth, eleventh, and twelfth grades, in spite of the fact that the test is designed for eleventh-grade pupils who are completing a course in American history. The tenth-grade pupils know relatively little about the material covered in the test; the eleventh-grade pupils know more; the twelfth-grade pupils, now having completed both American history and (probably) world history courses, supposedly command even more knowledge. If this is true, the new group of 200 pupils is extremely variable in terms of American history achievement, and the standard deviation will exceed 15.1, which is really based upon 200 eleventh-grade pupils. Hence the coefficient of reliability will be larger. Obviously the robust size of a coefficient of reliability based upon a highly variable group of pupils does not indicate the reliability of measurements made on a more uniform group. Therefore, to interpret a coefficient of reliability, the standard deviation of the test scores should be studied. Coefficients of reliability become more and more interpretable as the standard deviation of the standardization group, the 200 eleventh-grade pupils, approaches that of the teacher's class.

STANDARDIZATION OF TESTING CONDITIONS. The uniformity or lack of uniformity of the testing conditions is another point of concern when reports of reliability determination are appraised. Certainly the testing conditions at the time the standardization group is measured must be essentially the same as those recommended by the test author. This prerequisite is generally attained without difficulty. A persistent problem, however, is pupil motivation. An appropriately-oriented pupil who is to be given the test only once, may be highly motivated throughout the measurement process. In contrast, a pupil who is the unwilling victim of double measurement, be it by test-retest or equivalent forms, and who is measured at some inopportune time for no reason known to him, is undoubtedly less motivated. These differences introduce error. They will, for example, tend to lower the coefficients of stability that might be computed.

MINIMUM COEFFICIENTS OF RELIABILITY. Thoughtful consideration of the test itself, the characteristics of the standardization group used, and the testing conditions, inevitably leads to a more intimate grasp of the meaning of the coefficient of reliability. The question is often posed, however, as to what minimum a coefficient of reliability must attain before the test can be used under any condition. The answer is not straightforward. For instance, tests whose reliability coefficients are in the vicinity of 0.50 are used. Either the teacher applied an instrument of limited reliability or he did not measure at all, since, as happens periodically in the measurement of personality traits, no other more satisfactory instruments exist. Needless to say, interpretation of scores from instruments with such low reliability coefficients must be made with extreme caution.

There is no single minimum size a coefficient of reliability must reach, since the minimum changes with the purpose for which the test scores are to be used. Sometimes listed as appropriate minimums for various purposes are those reported by Kelley (1927). On the basis of a selected difference in test scores that is assumed to be a desirable minimum, he establishes, among other values, 0.50 as the lowest correlation necessary if the level of group accomplishment is to be evaluated, and 0.94 as the minimum if the level of individual accomplishment is to be evaluated. By the latter he means that a test with a reliability coefficient of at least 0.94 is sufficiently reliable for discriminating between individual pupils with respect to the characteristic measured. These are considered by some to be quite stringent requirements. In any event, coefficients of reliability in the vicinity of 0.85 and higher are regularly found for many standardized achievement and aptitude tests distributed by well-known publishing companies. Values for personality inventories vary considerably but frequently are lower.

RELIABILITY OF THE DIFFERENCE BETWEEN TWO MEASUREMENTS. An important sidelight of the problem of appraising coefficients of reliability occurs when the purpose of the measurement is to identify differences between two measurements rather than to interpret each measurement as such. Determining the difference between two measurements is relatively common. A teacher may wish to know how much progress his pupils made as a result of a particular learning experience. He could measure the class before the learning experience, then again after it, and interpret the difference between the two scores. In another case, a test battery composed of three, four, or more achievement and aptitude tests may have been given to a class. Then a test profile for each pupil is found. Among others, the question might be raised as to whether a pupil or a class is more competent in English than in general science. Differences between the scores of the two appropriate tests would be most helpful.

Although the coefficient of reliability indicates the reliability of individual measurements, it does not directly show the reliability of the difference between two measurements. This, however, can be computed when we know the coefficients of reliability of the two tests involved in the determination of the differences in question, and the intercorrelation between these tests (Cronbach, 1960, pp. 287–288).

It is unfortunately true that, if there is any important correlation between the two tests yielding scores from which difference scores are obtained, the reliability of these difference scores is substantially lower than average reliability of the two tests in question. All users of tests should be keenly aware of this fact. In Table 13 notice the striking drop in

TABLE 13
RELIABILITY OF DIFFERENCE SCORES FOR TESTS HAVING
VARIOUS DEGREES OF RELIABILITY

Coefficient of reliability		Correlation between Test A and Test B	Reliability of difference scores
Test A	Test B		
0.90	0.90	0.60	0.75
		0.40	0.83
		0.00	0.90
0.80	0.80	0.60	0.50
		0.40	0.67
		0.00	0.80
0.70	0.70	0.60	0.25
		0.40	0.50
		0.00	0.70

the reliability of the difference scores as the correlation increases between the two tests used.

If the correlation between the two tests is zero, the reliability of the difference scores is the same as the average of the coefficients of reliability of the two tests. In other words, relatively uncorrelated tests are needed if suitable difference scores are to be obtained.

Standard Errors of Measurement

The foregoing discussion of the coefficients of reliability is appropriate in part to the standard error of measurement. Appraising the significance of standard errors of measurement embodies a searching examination of the test itself, the characteristics of the standardization group of pupils, and the testing conditions. However, fluctuations in the variability of the group with respect to the characteristic being measured are considerably less important when standard errors of measurement are being considered instead of coefficients of reliability. Whereas differences in variability of the characteristic measured cause considerable fluctuations in the coefficients of reliability, the standard errors of measurement are, for all practical purposes, independent of fluctuations in the variability of the test scores. Hence, the standard error of measurement is a desirable way of comparing the reliability of a particular test when administered to two different groups of pupils. This is precisely what happens when a teacher compares the reliability of a test when it is given to a standardization group with its reliability when it is given to his class.

There are no readily applied suggestions as to how big a standard error should or should not be to ensure that the test is useful for a given purpose. Since it is expressed in the same units as the test scores, and since these units typically vary from test to test, a standard error of measurement of a specific size may be considered small in the case of one test and large in the case of another. Consider for a moment the standard error of measurement of the American history achievement test, a value of 4.5. This can be interpreted to mean that the pupils' "true scores" will not differ from their respective obtained scores by more than 9.0 raw-score points in approximately 95 per cent of the measurements made. Should the teacher feel that a difference of 9.0 raw-score points does not represent a serious amount of variation in terms of the characteristic measured, then the test is judged to have satisfactory reliability. Evaluation of standard errors of measurement is centralized, for the most part, in the teacher's concept of the importance of score difference in terms of the purposes far which the test has been administered. In the event that a test author should report more than one standard error of measurement, as is sometimes the case, and identify them as being applicable to certain different score levels, the foregoing principle still holds.

Just as in his appraisal of the determination of validity of standardized tests, a teacher estimating reliability determinations finds himself extremely dependent upon two principal sources of information—the test manual, if one is available, and the reports included in *The Mental Measurements Yearbooks*. One or both often provide sufficient information to allow the teacher to make at least a tentative judgment.

PROBLEMS

12 Study the procedure for scoring and interpreting the *Differential Aptitude Tests*. Relate the discussion of the question of a vertical distance of one inch on the individual report form (see page 410) to the foregoing discussion of the unreliability of difference scores.

13 Identify the similarities and differences between a standard error of measurement and a standard error of the difference between two test scores (Anastasi, 1961, pp. 131–133). Explain why the standard error of the difference between two scores is larger than the standard error of measurement of either of the two scores.

SUMMARY

Reliability is defined as the tendency of a measuring instrument to yield consistent information. It is secondary to validity as a desirable characteristic and highly reliable instruments may be virtually invalid. A test is reliable if chance errors do not influence the information produced when it is given. Common chance errors in educational measuring methods are pupil-centered errors, such as fluctuations in level of health, emotional strain, and motivation, and instrument-centered errors, which arise from the fact that, for example, a paper-and-pencil test is actually a sample of an immense number of possible items, and that it may not be scored consistently. Unfortunately, all measuring instruments are somewhat unreliable.

Reliability is practically always expressed in quantitative terms, either as a coefficient of reliability or as a standard error of measurement. The coefficient of reliability, as discussed in this chapter, is a product-moment coefficient of correlation that can be determined in one of several ways. These are the stability method, the equivalence method, the stability and equivalence method, and the internal consistency method. According to the stability method, the coefficient of reliability is computed when a test is administered twice (with an intervening period of time) to a group of pupils, and the pair of scores correlated. For the equivalence method, the coefficient of reliability is found by administering (with no intervening period of time) two equivalent forms of a test to a group of pupils, then correlating the pairs of scores. When a time interval is allowed, the stability and equivalence method is being applied. For the internal consistency method, several procedures may be followed, the split-half method or an analysis of variance method. The split-half method may utilize the Spearman-Brown "Prophecy Formula." An analysis of variance method is described in terms of the Kuder-Richardson Formula #20.

The standard error of measurement affords some indication of the size of the error caused by test unreliability. To compute it, the size of the coefficient of reliability and the standard deviation of the test scores must be known. It is considered a useful indicator of test reliability because it is expressed in the same units as the test score and it is relatively independent of fluctuations in group variability in terms of the characteristic measured.

SUGGESTED READINGS

Anastasi, Anne. *Psychological testing.* (2nd ed.) New York: Macmillan, 1961. Chapter 5.
> The chapter cited contains sections dealing with the types of test reliability, the techniques for measuring test reliability, the reliability of speed tests, and the dependence of test reliability upon the sample used.

Cronbach, L. J., and G. C. Gleser. Interpretation of reliability and validity coefficients—remarks on a paper by Lord. *J. educ. Psychol.*, 1959, 50, 230–237.
> An explanation is put forward of the usefulness of tests of low reliability and validity when crude decisions about test score differences are made. In this connection, test score "bands" are used.

Diederich, Paul B. *Short-cut statistics for teacher-made tests.* (2nd ed.) Educational Testing Service Evaluation and Advisory Service Series, No. 5. Princeton, N.J.: Educational Testing Service, 1964. Pp. 9–33.
> The three major topics considered are the standard error of a test score, reliability, and correlation. Simple methods of computing needed statistical values are demonstrated.

Ebel, Robert L. *Measuring educational achievement.* Englewood Cliffs, N.J.: Prentice-Hall, 1965. Chapter 10.
> The purpose of this chapter is to clarify some of the more important aspects of estimating, interpreting, and improving the reliability of achievement tests. Attention is given to both the Kuder-Richardson Formula #20 and #21.

French, J. W., and W. B. Michael. *Standards for educational and psychological tests.* Washington: American Psychological Association, 1966. Pp. 25–32.
> In this section, a brief general discussion of reliability is given, and essential

information needed for evaluating any reported coefficients of reliability is cited.

Helmstadter, G. C. *Principles of psychological measurement.* New York: Appleton-Century-Crofts, 1964. Chapter 3.

Reliability is defined and procedures for estimating its relative presence in a test are given. The influence of factors such as test length, heterogeneity of the standardization group, and speed of reliability estimations is evaluated.

Hoyt, Cyril J. Reliability. In Chester W. Harris (Ed.), *Encyclopedia of educational research.* (3rd ed.) New York: Macmillan, 1960. Pp. 1144–1147.

Reliability is defined, and various means of obtaining evidence concerning its relative presence in a test are discussed. The author points out the major assumptions underlying these computations.

Thorndike, Robert L. Reliability. In E. F. Lindquist (Ed.), *Educational measurement.* Washington: American Council on Education, 1951. Pp. 560–620.

The author describes the sources of variance in test scores, the procedures for estimating the reliability of an instrument, the factors affecting the reliability of an instrument, and the interpretation of estimates of instrument reliability. Parts of the discussion are somewhat technical. A detailed list of possible sources of differences in test performance is given on page 568.

Thorndike, Robert L. Reliability. In *Proceedings of the 1963 Invitational Conference on Testing Problems.* Princeton, N.J.: Educational Testing Service, 1964. Pp. 23–32.

Some of the major issues concerning test reliability are listed. Particular attention is given to problems related to samples and populations in reliability determinations.

Wesman, Alexander G. *Reliability and confidence.* Test Service Bulletin, No. 44. New York: Psychological Corporation, 1952.

The purpose of this bulletin is to clarify some of the more important aspects of the reliability of measuring instruments. It includes discussions of reliability as an important characteristic of an instrument, factors affecting the interpretation of reliability coefficients, and some common misconceptions about the meaning of certain reliability determination.

REFERENCES CITED

Anastasi, Anne. *Psychological testing.* (2nd ed.) New York: Macmillan, 1961.

Cronbach, L. J. *Essentials of psychological testing.* (2nd ed.) New York: Harper & Row, 1960.

Cureton, E. E. Kuder-Richardson reliabilities of classroom tests. *Educ. psychol. Measmt,* 1966, **26**, 13–14.

Ebel, Robert L. Must all tests be valid? *Amer. Psychologist,* 1961, **16**, 640–647.

French, J. W., and W. B. Michael. *Standards for educational and psychological tests.* Washington: American Psychological Association, 1966.

Howell, John J., and Max Weiner. Note on the equivalence of alternate forms of an achievement test. *Educ. psychol. Measmt,* 1961, **21**, 309–313.

Hoyt, Cyril J. Reliability. In Chester W. Harris (Ed.), *Encyclopedia of educational research*. (3rd ed.) New York: Macmillan, 1960. Pp. 1144–1147.

Kelley, Truman L. *Interpretation of educational measurements*. Tarrytown, N.Y.: Harcourt, Brace and World, 1927.

Kuder, G. Frederic, and M. W. Richardson. The theory of estimation of test reliability. *Psychometrika*, 1937, 2, 151–160.

Spearman, Charles. Coefficient of correlation calculated from faulty data. *British J. of Psychol.*, 1910, 3, 271–295.

Thorndike, Robert L. Reliability. In E. F. Lindquist (Ed.), *Educational measurement*. Washington: American Council on Education, 1951. Pp. 560–620.

Wert, James E., Charles O. Neidt, and J. Stanley Ahmann. *Statistical methods in educational and psychological research*. New York: Appleton-Century-Crofts, 1954.

Wilks, S. S. Sample criteria for testing equality of means, variances, and covariances in a normal multi-variate distribution. *Ann. math. Statist.*, 1946, 27, 257–281.

PART FOUR

Evaluating Pupil Behavio

PART FOUR HAS TWO general purposes. One is to acquaint the reader with the nature and availability of standardized tests designed to measure achievement, aptitude, and aspects of personal-social adjustment. The second is to outline procedures for using the various measuring instruments to improve evaluation and instruction.

In the first three chapters of Part Four, considerable attention is given to standardized measuring instruments. Chapter 11, "Standardized Achievement Tests," discusses the construction of such tests, attempts to give the reader an understanding of their general nature, and emphasizes the differences in construction and use between these and teacher-constructed tests. Selected achievement tests and batteries are used to illustrate their contribution to the evaluation program. These include both survey and diagnostic tests, and their roles in the evaluation program are explained. Chapter 12, "Measuring Pupil Aptitudes," is devoted to an explanation of the various kinds of aptitude instruments. It discusses selected tests to clarify the different purposes for which each should be used, and outlines procedures for their effective use in the classroom and with individual pupils. A large part of the chapter is concerned with a discussion of scholastic aptitude and its testing both by individual and group instruments. The concepts of mental age and intelligence quotient, including the DIQ, are developed, and precautionary measures for their use discussed. Differential testing is also explored and its advantages delineated. In considering the "culture fair" scholastic aptitude test, certain questions are raised regarding its value. Those concerned with college admission will find a brief description of national aptitude tests. Chapter 13, "Evaluating Personal-Social Adjustment," is devoted to the third general area of evaluation. Emphasis is laid upon the strengths and weaknesses of the personal-social adjustment inventories, and suggestions are given for their use in conjunction with less formal methods of evaluation, including observation with use of anecdotal records, rating scales, check lists, and interviews. There is some consideration of sociometric techniques which provide helpful information about pupils' interaction with the group. Measurement of attitudes and interests is dealt with as an important aspect of understanding pupil growth.

The last three chapters in Part Four attempt to help the reader apply his understandings of measurement and evaluation to classroom use. Chapter 14, "A School-Wide Program of Evaluation," stresses the importance of organizing a program of evaluation rather than one of testing alone. It is suggested that the program be developed democratically rather than imposed on the teachers by the administration. Emphasis is given to the cumulative record and the part it plays in providing for continuous evaluation. The uses of standardized tests are discussed and suggestions given for proper administration and scoring. Chapter 15, "Diagnosis and Remediation of Problems," is devoted to outlining procedures and suggesting materials and tests to aid in diagnosing and prescribing remediation in severe learning difficulties. Practical examples are included to provide the teacher with information for the selection of tests and interpretation of test data. Specific difficulties in such subjects as reading, arithmetic, and writing are treated. The philosophy of diagnostic teaching as effective teaching directs the discussion throughout. Chapter 16, "Determining and Reporting Growth," focuses attention on the pupil's development and how we can best use the results of measurement to aid the school and the home in helping him achieve his potential. In this context, the purposes of marking by informing pupils, parents, and school personnel are discussed. It is suggested that specific evidences of pupil progress be based on the school's educational objectives, among these being data on test performance, procedure and product evaluation, class participation, and projects and reports. Various methods of marking and reporting these data are given, such as the letter-number systems, check lists, written correspondence, and teacher-parent conferences. Finally, suggestions for improving marking and reporting are outlined. The chapter concludes with a discussion of promotion as it relates to final marks.

11 ✐

Standardized Achievement Tests

WHEN A GOLFER "breaks seventy-five" for eighteen holes, he is considered an outstanding performer. The athlete who runs a mile in four minutes has finished a superlative race. The major league baseball player with a batting average over 0.300 will be surpassed by relatively few. On the other hand, the golfer who requires more than 100 strokes to complete eighteen holes is considered a duffer and the miler who is clocked over 4' 30" would not be likely to make a good college track team. Certainly a baseball player whose batting average is below 0.225 isn't considered a good hitter.

These performances are evaluated in terms of norms generally accepted as representing various degrees of competence. It makes no difference whether the game is played or the mile run in Kansas City or Seattle. The performances are regulated by specific rules so that the degree of excellence is affected by the ability of the performer. Even though an athlete may be considered outstanding when compared to limited competition, his performance may be mediocre on a national scale.

A similar situation exists when standardized tests are administered. There are prescribed conditions for testing. Norms are established. It follows that the examinee's performance can be evaluated by comparing it with that of a large number of his peers from many schools.

If you have studied the foregoing chapters carefully, you already know a great deal about standardized achievement tests. To understand the concepts of validity, reliability, item analysis, test scores and norms, the place of educational objectives in testing, and the building and appraisal of classroom tests means that you already know about the framework on which standardized achievement tests are constructed.

STANDARDIZED VS. TEACHER-CONSTRUCTED TESTS

The term *standardized* actually refers to specific instructions for administration and scoring. Norms can then be prepared that are representative of performance for similar groups. These give the teacher an independent yardstick for checking the achievement of his pupils. While his own tests can measure only the relative performance of the pupils in his class, norms provide the opportunity to compare their achievement with that of pupils in other schools. It is of particular importance for the college-bound pupil to know how well he does in comparison with those with whom he will be competing. The teacher, too, can use norms to judge in part the effectiveness of his teaching.

Of the factors that distinguish standardized and informal achievement tests, most relate to better test making. The planning and construction of a standardized test is customarily in the hands of specialists and so is more careful and thorough than for teacher-constructed tests; there is also a much more critical analysis of the objectives on which the measurement is based. Exacting procedures are followed in the construction and appraisal of individual test items, and extensive statistical analyses are applied to determine their level of difficulty and discriminating power. Often there are comparable forms of the instrument so the test can be administered periodically to measure growth.

In building a classroom test, teachers can take advantage of the individuality of the local community and the pupils in the classes, having pupils study that which best relates to their experiences. Appreciation of literature can be taught with different literary selections, and scientific method through different subjects. Obviously, individual variations in study materials cannot be considered on a test designed for wide use among many schools, and it becomes necessary to include the materials on which questions are based. This results in many short selections with a definite limitation on achievement measurement; it is impossible to ask an examinee to criticize complete literary works or determine his recall on wide reading. At the classroom level, however, teachers must be better trained in test construction to avoid using assigned materials to measure memorization of content for its own sake rather than as a vehicle for evaluating the lasting results of instruction (Lindquist, 1951).

PROBLEMS

1 What arguments might you, as a teacher, offer your school principal to justify using a standardized achievement test as a final examination in your course?
2 It is recognized that standardized tests are generally superior in planning and construction to tests prepared by classroom teachers. What techniques used by standardized test builders could be easily and profitably used by the classroom teacher?

3 A high school senior who hopes to enter a highly competitive university was given a standardized achievement test in mathematics designed for high school seniors. He and his parents were greatly encouraged because he received a percentile rank of 80 on this test. His counselor was less enthusiastic. Suggest reasons related to the test for his counselor's reaction.

USES OF STANDARDIZED TESTS

Standardized tests play an important role in strengthening the instructional program. One function is to provide the teacher with a criterion for checking his own emphasis in teaching. Of course, the use of norms implies that comparisons made between and among pupils or classes are restricted by the content of the test. If a class has a high mean score on an American history test, it has not necessarily achieved more in this subject-matter area than another class with a lower score. Emphasis in one class may have been on facts and details, while the other stressed critical thinking and broad relationships. Test content must be analyzed before making a final judgment. However, when a test proves to include important and generally accepted areas of knowledge and skills, a teacher had best make a critical evaluation of his own educational objectives and instruction if a class does poorly in relation to the pupils' ability.

A second use of standardized tests is for determining pupil progress. Generally there are comparable forms of the test, which makes it possible to administer one at the beginning and another at the end of the year. Although cautious interpretation should be made on the basis of individual test scores, group scores representing progress or the lack of it may emphasize particular strengths or weaknesses.

It must also be remembered that pupils' mental ability is positively correlated with achievement. Effective teaching cannot always be inferred just because the class average is at the median. On the other hand, a class average below the median may actually represent excellent progress in one case, while in another achievement above the median may still be far below the potential of the group.

A third function of standardized tests is to provide a comparison of achievement between various subject-matter areas and specific phases of a particular area. It is often desirable to determine how a pupil's arithmetic skill compares with his reading ability or to compare achievement in vocabulary, comprehension, and rate of reading. Obviously these comparisons can be made on an individual or group basis. If the group has a particular weakness, then an evaluation of class learning experiences is in order. When problems seem to relate to individual pupils, then the teacher must provide individual attention.

A fourth use of standardized tests is for diagnosis of difficulties in achievement. Often the source of pupils' difficulties may be determined through one or a number of very effective standardized instruments. Because test items have been constructed on the basis of studies that have determined frequent sources of difficulty, it is possible to analyze the adequacy of performance in these crucial areas. In diagnosing a reading disability, for example, one can discover whether the pupil knows the initial consonant sounds, whether he can break words into syllables, and whether he makes use of punctuation for improved comprehension. Naturally, the teacher will also use his own tests in diagnosis, but standardized tests are helpful in providing a systematic approach to diagnosis.

Finally, a fifth use is for purposes of selection and classification. Achievement tests can serve as aptitude tests predicting performance in a given subject area. Not only are achievement test results helpful in grouping for instruction, but scores are useful in determining whether pupils can be expected to do well or poorly in given courses.

Problems

4 During a weekly faculty meeting, a member of the mathematics department was critical of the time spent in the administration and scoring of standardized tests and the recording of the scores. He argued that, if each teacher could spend this time on curriculum development and class preparation, the pupils would be much better off. Moreover, report cards represent more meaningful measures of pupil achievement. A lively discussion ensued. What were some of the probable arguments? How do you feel about this question?

5 Before becoming elated or depressed over your pupils' scores on standardized achievement tests, what major factors related to the tests and the pupils would you consider carefully?

6 Mary James received a total percentile rank of 45 on a standardized arithmetic test. Part scores were as follows: Concepts: 65 PR, Computations: 35 PR, Problem Solving: 40 PR. What conclusion might you reach from these data? What further information would be valuable?

7 A major use of standardized tests is that of grouping pupils for instruction. Would you consider achievement or scholastic aptitude test results more appropriate for this purpose? Explain your choice.

Standardized Test Construction

One may gain better understanding of standardized tests through a discussion of some of the important steps in their construction. The expense and effort involved in constructing these tests demands a very careful appraisal of the need for a particular kind of instrument. First, it may be determined whether there is a group of individuals that provides a potential test market. Ideally, there should be a need for an instrument with no satisfactory test available to meet it. Unfortunately, the criterion for the construction of a new test sometimes becomes the soundness of the business venture, even though several good instruments that can serve the same purpose may be available.

Be that as it may, once it has been decided that a new instrument will be constructed, representatives from the population of test consumers are consulted to formulate specifications for the instrument. The purpose of the test must be spelled out clearly. Is it to be a survey or a diagnostic test? Is it to be primarily for individual or group guidance? Will there be subscores or just a total score? For what population of pupils is the test to be designed? Is it for a group of homogeneous ages or for grades three through twelve? Does it require reading ability? What will be its general contents? All of this must be answered before actual test construction begins.

Pretest Construction and Administration

In discussing paper-and-pencil achievement tests in Chapter 2, three steps are outlined for construction: (1) identifying educational objectives with verbal and mathematical aspects, (2) developing tables of specifications reflecting the relative importance of the objectives, and (3) building the test items on the basis of the tables of specifications. A similar approach is used in developing standardized achievement tests, though test items are generally constructed by several subject-matter specialists and examined by test specialists for technical considerations. Practical considerations, such as typical length of school class periods help determine test length. Although at times it would be desirable to improve the reliability and validity of a test by increasing its length, it is not always possible because test administration must be fitted into existing school schedules.

In the development of the better tests, more items are initially constructed than will be used in the final form of the test. These items are assembled into a form called a *pretest*. Before the pretest is administered, the individual items are carefully scrutinized by other subject-matter specialists and test experts for inaccuracies and technical flaws.

Directions and accessory materials must be prepared and provision made for recording answers either on separate sheets or the test booklet itself. When the test has been cast into its final form, these accessory materials, including scoring stencils, must be revised to fit it.

Analysis of Pretest Data

When the pretest form is ready, it is administered to a group of pupils comparable to those for whom the test is being designed. The results of the pretest administration are studied to determine which items should be kept. If the test is to discriminate among pupils, the items should neither be so difficult that some will answer them all incorrectly, nor so easy that some can make a perfect score. In neither case is it possible to obtain a true measure of the individual's achievement. It is absurd to conclude that he has achieved nothing; it is equally erroneous to assume that an individual has achieved the ultimate or that two individuals with a perfect score have equal achievement. Therefore, the levels of difficulty of the test items retained should be such that both zero and perfect scores will rarely, if ever, occur.

Items should also be chosen on the basis of their power to discriminate between good and poor pupils. Therefore, those items are retained which are answered correctly by more good pupils than poor. By the same token, the distracters or foils should be chosen more often by the poor than the good pupils.

The total number of items selected for the final form of the test depends on how many can be answered by the pupils in a given amount of time. One general rule of thumb is that about 90 per cent of an average class should have an opportunity to attempt all the items in the time allowed. If careful attention has been given to the level of difficulty of these items, an average pupil should answer somewhat more than fifty per cent of them correctly (Educational Testing Service, 1959).

Developing Norms

On the basis of the criteria discussed above and through use of the tables of specifications, items are selected for the final form of the test. It is then given to groups of pupils typical of those for whom the test is designed but who have not taken the pretest. Their scores provide the basis for setting up the norms of the test by which a teacher or school administrator can compare pupils' performance. These norms usually are standard scores, percentile ranks, age equivalents, or grade equivalents. Often several different kinds of norms are reported.

EQUIVALENT, PARALLEL, AND COMPARABLE TEST FORMS. It is often helpful to have two or more forms of a test so that a pupil may be tested more than once—perhaps at the beginning and end of a term of instruction. A second test may be helpful at times when there is reason to doubt the validity of a pupil's first test score—because of illness, for example.

Parallel forms of a test may be developed simultaneously. This is sometimes done by constructing pairs of items that measure the outcome of specific objectives and are of approximately the same level of difficulty. Obviously, the administration procedures and format of both tests should be alike. If when parallel forms are administered to a large population of pupils and they yield scores with identical distributions, we have *equivalent* forms. *Comparable* forms of a test are illustrated by the various sub-tests of the *Differential Aptitude Tests* (see p. 407). Unlike the approach in equivalent forms, various mental traits are measured. In the *DAT* all comparisons are based on the same norm group. The raw scores of each test can be converted into the same type of derived scores.

Accessory Materials

In addition to the test booklet, there may be special scoring stencils and, with all of the better tests, a manual. A set of test standards (French and Michael, 1966) recommends that certain kinds of information be placed in the manual. Procedures in administration and scoring should be stated so that it is possible to duplicate the conditions under which the test was standardized. The directions should be clearly phrased so the examinee will understand how the author intended him to perform. Although most standardized tests can be scored objectively, whenever there is an element of subjectivity, scoring variations leading to error should be discussed.

Because the name of a test does not always clarify its purpose and sometimes may even misrepresent what the test actually measures, the manual should state the objectives to be measured and assist in the correct interpretation of test results. Competencies required in administration, scoring, or interpretations beyond the typical classroom teacher should be indicated.

Detailed information on reliability and validity should include evidence that can be used in judging whether it is pertinent to the teacher's and the examinee's problems. The method of determining the reliability coefficient should also be reported. Discussion of validity should be specific in terms of whether it is content, criterion-related, or construct validity (see Chapter 9). The nature of any validating criteria and their desirability for a specific test purpose whould be reported fully. Statistical data for determining any validity coefficients should be so adequate that the test user may judge their worth.

The manual should contain a discussion of the development of the test norms. Norm groups must be defined, method of population sampling reported, and the time and conditions under which norm data were secured should be included. It is imperative that measures of central tendency and variability be reported.

Problems

8 Assume that you are the chairman of the social studies department of a public school system. Your project for the school year is to construct an achievement test to be used as a final examination in social studies for ninth-grade pupils graduating from junior high school. The test is to sample seventh-, eighth-, and ninth-grade subject-matter content and should reflect the philosophy of your department. Prepare a detailed, step-by-step outline of how you will proceed in this task and how you will evaluate the final product.

9 You have an appointment with your principal to present a request to purchase and use a certain standardized achievement test. What specific information about this test should you have prior to the conference? What will be your major selling point?

Selected Standardized Tests

There are many standardized achievement and diagnostic tests available to the classroom teacher. They attempt to measure a wide variety of areas, including such skills as critical thinking, reading, and listening. There are also tests in subject areas, such as arithmetic, physics, and history. A number of selected and illustrative tests are listed in Appendix C (see Appendix C). Rather than giving a brief description of sampling the many tests available, an extended discussion of a few selected tests and batteries is included here. The survey test, test battery, and diagnostic test are illustrated. Through this approach, the reader can become more familiar with standardized test construction and the general problems and approaches that apply to this type of instrument.

Survey Tests

Whether a test can be labeled as a survey test depends partly on the purpose for which it is used and also on the number of its subscores. Although generally a test yielding only one score is not thought of as being inherently diagnostic, it could well be used for diagnostic purposes if one were to analyze the performance of the examinee on individual questions.

As the number of subtests is increased, the instrument begins to assume a diagnostic flavor.

Tests generally thought of as survey instruments are often used along with scholastic aptitude tests to determine whether pupils are retarded. For example, the retarded reader is one who does not read as well as he should for his ability. He may be reading above his grade level, but if he is a bright child, he still may be an underachiever. Likewise, a child who reads below his grade level is not necessarily retarded; his performance may be adequate for his mental capacity. The reading survey test actually provides a measure of the level of difficulty at which the pupil can read. In general it contains at least two measures, one of vocabulary and the other of comprehension. A measure of reading rate is often included.

GATES-MACGINTIE READING TESTS.   The *Gates-MacGintie Reading Tests* is a series of tests replacing the well-known *Gates Primary Reading Test*, *Gates Advanced Primary Reading Tests*, and the *Gates Reading Survey*. The plan of the tests is as follows:

Primary A—Vocabulary and comprehension for grade 1 (Forms 1, 2)
Primary B—Vocabulary and comprehension for grade 2 (Forms 1, 2)
Primary C—Vocabulary and comprehension for grade 3 (Forms 1, 2)
Primary CS—Speed and accuracy for grades 2 and 3 (Forms 1, 2, and 3)
Survey D—Speed, vocabulary, and comprehension for grades 4 through 6 (Forms 1, 2, and 3)
Survey E—Speed, vocabulary, and comprehension for grades 7 through 9 (Forms 1, 2, and 3)
Survey F—Speed, vocabulary, and comprehension for grades 10 through 12 (Forms 1, 2, and 3)

Both *Survey D* and *E* contain thirty-six short paragraphs of approximately the same level of difficulty in the *Speed and Accuracy Test*. These paragraphs end in a question or incomplete statement. The pupil chooses a correct word from among four which best answers the question or completes the statement. Vocabulary tests contain fifty items. Each has a word to be defined from a choice of five other words. Items become progressively more difficult. The comprehension test contains twenty-one passages with fifty-two blank spaces. From five choices, the pupil picks the completion which best fits the passage meaning. In this test, too, passages increase in difficulty.

The vocabulary tests in *Primary A, B,* and *C* consist of items including four printed words and a picture which illustrates one of these words. In addition to this type of item, *Primary C* also has items containing a test word followed by four others, one of which means the same as the test words.

Comprehension tests are designed to measure a pupil's ability to read and grasp the meaning of whole sentences and paragraphs. In *Primary A* and *B*, passages are matched with a four-picture panel, one of which best conveys the meaning of the paragraph. In *Primary C*, there are two multiple-choice test items for each paragraph.

Primary CS, Speed and Accuracy Test, is similar in construction to this kind of test in *Survey D* and *E*. Short paragraphs of uniform difficulty end in a question or an incomplete statement followed by four words from which the pupil chooses one.

It appears that this series of tests has corrected a serious criticism of the original *Gates Reading Survey* which attempted to cover a range of eight grades (3–10). This range was too great to discriminate among pupils at every level of competency.

Additional information about the tests is available in a *Technical Manual*. Among other topics, there is a discussion of item selection, establishment of norms, reliability, and correlation between subtest scores and reading and IQ-scores. Validity information is not given.

COOPERATIVE ENGLISH TEST: READING COMPREHENSION. These tests are available at two levels of difficulty and in three forms. *Test 2* is designed for pupils in grades nine through twelve. *Test 1* is intended for college freshmen and sophomores. However, *Test 1* is much more discriminating among the good readers in the eleventh and twelfth grades than is *Test 2*.

The authors of these tests have recognized the complexity of reading comprehension and the need to use selections and questions that sample the examinee's ability to think, manipulate verbal concepts, utilize his experience background, and apply various techniques of reading as they relate to purpose. They measure depth of comprehension rather than meaning alone. The following indicate some of the aspects of reading sampled: determining the meanings of words from contextual clues; construing the writer's meaning, tone, intent, point of view, and the reliability of his evidence; and applying conclusions to different situations.

The tests provide four scores: *Vocabulary, Speed of Comprehension, Level of Comprehension,* and a *Total Reading Comprehension* score. There are two parts to the test. *Part I* (vocabulary) is fifteen minutes long and *Part II* (reading) provides twenty-five minutes of working time. The vocabulary test includes sixty multiple-choice items with words chosen to provide a wide range of difficulty. The speed of comprehension score depends on the number of items answered correctly in *Part II*, which also contains sixty multiple-choice items, each based on a reading passage.

An interesting idea, labeled *Level of Comprehension*, is also built into the tests. Experience has shown that most pupils have time to try at least the first thirty items in *Part II*. Hence, the number of items which the pupil answers correctly out of the first thirty in this part is primarily a power score which represents level of comprehension. This score does not contribute to the *Total Reading Comprehension* score, which is computed by averaging the *Vocabulary* and *Speed of Comprehension* scores.

PROBLEMS

10   An elementary school principal has administered a reading survey test designed for grade levels 3–6. In the case of the sixth grade, 80% of the pupils scored above the 75th percentile. Why was the principal displeased with these results? How could this situation be remedied?

11   In the selection of a good general reading test, what kinds of information should the subtests yield? Which of these do you consider most significant?

Test Batteries

In surveying pupil strengths and weaknesses, information is needed concerning relative achievement in the basic skills and the various subject areas. Does the pupil excel in reading but do poorly in arithmetic? Is he a high achiever in the physical and biological sciences but lacking information and skill in dealing with problems in the social studies? Standardized tests can provide information for evaluating a pupil's relative status. However, scores from single tests standardized on different populations are not necessarily comparable. For example, the standardization group for one test may have higher achievement or aptitudes than that for another, resulting in more exacting norms for the first test. Therefore, a pupil would have to show better performance in the former case than in the latter to avoid appearing deficient. This limitation inherent in the use of individual tests is overcome through the use of test batteries standardized on the same population. By comparing subtest scores, it is possible to determine whether a pupil has any real differences in his achievement pattern.

PROFILES.   We have seen that the raw score a pupil earns on a test may be expressed as derived scores that can be classified as test norms (see page 257). Four types of norms are discussed: (1) quartiles, deciles, and percentiles, (2) standard scores, (3) grade equivalents, and (4) age equivalents. If a battery of tests is given and a pupil gets twenty-five vocabulary questions right but only fifteen spelling questions correct, he may not necessarily be better in vocabulary than in spelling. The vocabulary test may be longer or more difficult, so that the two raw scores cannot be compared.

If these raw scores are changed to percentile rank norms based on the same standardization group, units may then be compared. This pupil may, for example, have a percentile rank of 80 in vocabulary and a percentile rank of 90 in spelling. It appears that his achievement in spelling is greater than that in vocabulary. But this is not necessarily so. Neither test has perfect reliability, and the reliability of the difference between two scores is less than the reliability of either test (see page 324). In the better standardized tests, information is included in the manual that will help the test user determine when real differences exist.

When the raw scores of a battery of tests are changed into common derived scores, the result is a pupil's score profile. Profiles may be reported in various ways. A number of batteries have a class record sheet on which all pupils in the class have their profiles presented in tabular form (see Figure 22). Also, they may provide profile sheets for individual pupils (see Figure 23).

Note that Alice White's profile (Figure 23) is recorded in percentile bands. She has earned a *Reading* score of 300. However, because this test, like others, is somewhat unreliable, we cannot be certain that she would earn this same score if she took the test again. On the other hand, we can say that approximately two-thirds of the time a pupil's "true score" will lie within the percentile band. In the case of Alice White's *Reading* score, this band extends from the sixty-first to the eighty-second percentile rank. How then does one compare a pupil's standings in the various areas recorded on the profile? Can we infer that Alice White's score in *Reading* is significantly higher than her score in *Writing* or *Social Studies?* The answer would have to be "no," since these bands overlap. On the other hand, it is reasonable to infer that her scores in *Reading, Writing,* and *Social Studies* are probably greater than her scores in *Listening, Science,* and *Mathematics,* because there is no overlapping of the percentile bands of these two groups.

ELEMENTARY SCHOOL TEST BATTERIES. There are a number of achievement test batteries available for elementary school use. Those batteries listed in Table 14 are widely used. The table presents a rough classification of the emphasis in the different areas or achievement for the intermediate grades. In some cases, this includes grades four, five, and six, and in others, only grades five and six. Time limits allotted to the various subtests are used in determining the percentages listed. Because the total time of test administration varies, caution should be exercised in comparing percentages between tests. They can best be used in noting the degree of emphasis. Another point in interpretation is that, in some batteries, areas are combined. For example, in the *Metropolitan Achievement Tests* some study skills are included in the social studies and science tests.

CLASS RECORD SHEET

Iowa Tests of Basic Skills

Grade **6**   Semester (1st or 2nd) **2nd**   Date **May 1, 1967**   Form **1**

City, or District **Chelsea, New York**   County **Cherry**   School Building **Pleasant View**   State **New York**   Teacher **Susan Allison**

Each cell lists the grade equivalent (upper) and percentile rank (lower).

Names of Pupils	TEST V Vocabulary	TEST R Reading Comprehension	L-1 Spelling	L-2 Capitalization	L-3 Punctuation	L-4 Usage	TEST L Total	W-1 Map Reading	W-2 Reading Graphs and Tables	W-3 Knowledge and Use of Reference Materials	TEST W Total	A-1 Arithmetic Concepts	A-2 Arithmetic Problem Solving	TEST A Total	COMPOSITE V, R, L, W, A
Adams, John	6.3¹ / 40	7.4 / 66	6.5 / 42	5.6 / 18	5.1 / 22	5.9 / 34	5.8 / 27	7.2 / 63	5.9 / 26	6.9 / 54	6.7 / 48	5.3 / 6	5.7 / 12	5.5 / 5	6.3 / 35
Baker, Alvin	8.4 / 80	7.0 / 56	6.5 / 42	7.6 / 64	6.6 / 47	9.7 / 93	7.6 / 67	8.0 / 85	6.6 / 44	7.1 / 60	7.2 / 68	6.5 / 40	6.9 / 55	6.7 / 46	7.4 / 68
Ball, Betty	8.5 / 82	8.6 / 88	8.4 / 86	7.6 / 64	9.5 / 91	10.3 / 97	9.0 / 89	7.8 / 85	10.2 / 99	9.5 / 98	9.2 / 98	8.8 / 98	7.6 / 80	8.2 / 93	8.7 / 93
Carter, Susan	8.2 / 77	7.6 / 70	5.8 / 23	8.8 / 83	6.6 / 47	8.8 / 82	7.5 / 65	6.5 / 40	8.1 / 81	8.0 / 82	7.5 / 76	7.8 / 86	7.4 / 74	7.6 / 81	7.7 / 76
Chenworth, Ellis	9.2 / 91	9.0 / 93	4.9 / 5	5 / 74	4.7 / 54	8.1 / 72	7.0 / 54	7.7 / 78	8.5 / 94	7.4 / 69	7.9 / 85	7.5 / 77	6.1 / 24	6.8 / 50	8.0 / 82
Corson, Margaret	8.8 / 87	7.5 / 68	8.0 / 79	10.8 / 98	10.4 / 97	9.1 / 86	9.6 / 95	6.5 / 40	7.8 / 83	8.5 / 90	7.6 / 78	8.1 / 91	9.4 / 99	8.8 / 98	8.5 / 91
Daig, Herbert	10.0 / 96	8.5 / 87	9.1 / 94	10.8 / 98	10.0 / 94	8.4 / 76	9.6 / 95	7.5 / 72	8.1 / 88	8.7 / 92	8.1 / 89	6.8 / 50	8.0 / 89	7.5 / 75	8.7 / 93
Dall, Amy	10.6 / 98	9.8 / 97	8.5 / 87	9.7 / 92	9.5 / 91	10.3 / 94	9.5 / 94	7.8 / 80	8.7 / 95	9.7 / 98	8.7 / 95	8.0 / 90	8.5 / 95	8.2 / 93	9.4 / 97
Fale, Ann	10.3 / 97	9.8 / 97	8.5 / 87	11.2 / 99	10.5 / 97	10.6 / 98	10.2 / 98	7.7 / 78	8.9 / 97	9.7 / 98	8.8 / 96	8.1 / 91	8.2 / 91	8.2 / 93	9.5 / 98
Green, Carter	5.6 / 25	6.2 / 35	5.9 / 25	6.8 / 50	5.4 / 27	6.5 / 44	6.2 / 36	6.3 / 34	5.9 / 26	6.7 / 48	6.3 / 33	6.9 / 54	6.4 / 45	6.6 / 42	6.2 / 32
Gould, Robert	6.2 / 38	6.5 / 43	7.6 / 71	7.4 / 74	7.3 / 58	10.1 / 96	8.3 / 80	6.3 / 34	7.4 / 71	7.1 / 76	7.1 / 64	8.1 / 91	8.8 / 97	8.4 / 95	7.3 / 65
Hall, William	7.0 / 54	7.0 / 56	6.5 / 42	5.3 / 27	5.1 / 22	6.5 / 44	5.8 / 27	7.7 / 78	7.2 / 64	7.6 / 74	7.5 / 76	7.3 / 70	6.1 / 24	6.7 / 46	6.8 / 51
Heald, Joe	8.4 / 80	8.5 / 87	8.0 / 79	8.2 / 74	8.2 / 73	9.1 / 86	8.4 / 81	8.0 / 85	8.9 / 97	7.2 / 63	8.0 / 80	7.5 / 95	8.5 / 95	8.0 / 88	8.3 / 88
Julson, Patricia	8.5 / 82	7.5 / 68	7.3 / 64	8.2 / 74	6.9 / 52	9.6 / 86	7.9 / 73	8.0 / 85	6.6 / 44	7.1 / 60	7.2 / 60	7.0 / 58	6.7 / 46	6.8 / 50	7.6 / 73
Larson, Alfred	6.9 / 52	6.4 / 41	5.5 / 15	5.9 / 27	6.6 / 47	8.8 / 82	6.7 / 47	6.0 / 26	7.4 / 71	6.9 / 54	6.8 / 52	6.1 / 26	6.7 / 46	6.4 / 34	6.6 / 45
Metz, Connie	7.8 / 70	7.2 / 60	8.2 / 83	8.9 / 89	8.2 / 73	5.6 / 30	7.8 / 71	7.8 / 80	7.4 / 71	8.0 / 82	7.7 / 80	7.3 / 70	7.6 / 80	7.4 / 75	7.6 / 73

Printed in the U.S.A.

From Lindquist and Hieronymous, 1955; reproduced by permission of Houghton Mifflin Company.

FIGURE 22   CLASS RECORD SHEET SHOWING GRADE EQUIVALENTS AND PERCENTILE RANKS

STEP STUDENT PROFILE
SEQUENTIAL TESTS OF EDUCATIONAL PROGRESS

Name _____ White _____ Alice _____ Jane _____
       Last   First   Middle

School _____ Pleasant Grove _____ Grade or Class _____ 11 _____

Age _____ 16 _____ 3 _____ Date of Testing _____ Fall _____ 1967 _____
       Years   Months   Fall or Spring   Year

Norms Used

☒ Publisher's ☒ Fall   Grade or Class _____ 11th Grade _____
☐ Local   ☐ Spring   Other _____

© Copyright 1957, All rights reserved

Cooperative Test Division 🅐 Educational Testing Service · Princeton, N.J. · Los Angeles 27, Calif.

Test	Reading	Listening	Writing	Soc. Studies	Science	Mathematics
Form	2A	2A	2A	2A	2A	2A
Converted Score	300	280	290	280	270	265

PERCENTILE

Here you can profile a student's percentile ranks on as many as six tests in the STEP series. In order for your comparisons between the areas to be valid, all tests included should be administered within a period of 4 or 5 months.

Recording. Directions for recording information and drawing percentile bands on the PROFILE form are included in each STEP MANUAL FOR INTERPRETING SCORES. Consult the manuals for the tests used.

Interpreting. To compare a student's performance on one of the tests in the STEP series with that of students in the norms group used, note the unshaded parts of the column above and below the percentile band. For example, if the Listening percentile band is 24-36, you know that 24 per cent of students in the norms group score lower than this student and 64 per cent score higher. In other words, this student's Listening performance is below average with respect to the norms group.

To compare a student's standings on any two tests in the STEP series, the following rules apply:

1. If the percentile bands for any two tests overlap, there is no important difference between the student's standings on those two tests.

2. If the percentile bands for any two tests do *not* overlap, standing represented by the higher band is really better than standing represented by the lower band.

Examples: According to local norms, a student's percentile bands for three tests are

    Mathematics (2A)   50-62
    Social Studies (2A) 60-71
    Science (2B)   41-52

Bands for Mathematics and Social Studies overlap; there is no important difference between the student's standings in these two areas. The same is true of Mathematics and Science. However, bands for Science and Social Studies do not overlap; the student's standing in Social Studies is higher than his standing in Science. We expect the student to perform better in the social studies area than in the science area.

More detailed discussions of interpretations are contained in each STEP MANUAL FOR INTERPRETING SCORES.

D107RSØV

From *Cooperative Test Division, 1957; reproduced by permission of the Educational Testing Service.*

FIGURE 23   PUPIL PROFILE CHART.

TABLE 14

ELEMENTARY SCHOOL TEST BATTERIES AND PERCENTAGES OF
TOTAL TESTING TIME ALLOTTED TO THE VARIOUS AREAS

	California achievement tests	Iowa tests of basic skills	Metropolitan achievement tests	Stanford achievement test
Reading comprehension	26.6	19.7	10.1	11.2
Vocabulary	5.1	6.1	5.7	4.5
Fundamentals of arithmetic	31.6	10.7	16.2	20.6
Arithmetic reasoning	12.7	10.7	15.0	11.9
Language	16.5	19.7	20.2	17.9
Social studies	0.0	0.0	19.0	9.3
Science	0.0	0.0	6.9	9.3
Spelling	7.6	4.3	6.9	5.6
Study skills	0.0	28.7	0.0	9.3
Total working time (minutes)	158	279	247	267

Note that the *California Achievement Tests* and the *Iowa Tests of Basic Skills* do not include social studies and science. Emphasis is placed on diagnosis in fewer areas. Only two of the batteries listed, the *Metropolitan Achievement Tests* and the *Stanford Achievement Test*, include subtests in social studies and science. The questions in these subtests consist of the "who, what, and when" type, referring to specific facts. This flaw is not so serious because information called for can be learned through numerous references.

IOWA TESTS OF BASIC SKILLS.   This is a multi-level edition test designed for grades three to nine and is representative of most available batteries. Its title is descriptive. By means of eleven separate tests, five areas of basic skills are emphasized: *Vocabulary, Reading Comprehension, Language Skills* (the mechanics of correct writing), *Work-Study Skills,* and *Arithmetic Skills.* It should be noted that pupils of only one grade level take the same test. Although there is overlapping, the tests are designed for specific grade levels. The *Iowa* battery is the longest of the four named above, and provides analytical subtests in *Language, Work-Study,* and *Arithmetic Skills.* There are no tests in the content subjects. These are not course-oriented achievement tests.

The battery is unusual in that all levels are bound in a single booklet. There are actually six batteries, one for each of grades three to eight; grades eight and nine use the same battery. It is possible therefore, for pupils at different grade levels to be tested simultaneously, since the time limits and directions are the same for all levels. Separate answer sheets for each grade level may be either hand-scored with a stencil or machine-scored with IBM equipment.

Instructions for administration are written very clearly, and the mechanics of the test booklet are simple. A test schedule of four sessions is suggested. Some schools administer the battery in four consecutive sessions, one each half-day. Others choose to give the test in the mornings of four consecutive days. The authors rightly recommend that under no circumstances should the entire battery be administered in one day.

The Vocabulary subtest is composed of items requiring the examinee to select from four choices a word having most nearly the same meaning as one designated in a brief context. As in all vocabulary tests of this kind, the examinee needs only to recognize a synonym superficially; there is no measure of the breadth and depth of his concepts.

Reading Comprehension is measured by series of multiple-choice questions on brief selections. The authors are to be commended for including a variety of questions unrelated to fact or detail. For example, there are a number of items on organizational pattern, main ideas, summarizing, and tone and intent. True measures of reading comprehension must determine whether the reader understands more than the sense meanings. Also, he must not be able to select the correct answer by a process of matching words in the test item with those in the selection. In some reading tests, questions can be answered from the reader's general background of information. In either case, a true measure of comprehension is not obtained through answers to the questions. The authors of this test have generally succeeded in eliminating these pitfalls. Another very strong point of this reading test is the variety of the subject matter and style of the chosen selections, which give a better over-all measure of comprehension than simple narrative material alone. Also, the selections appear to be sufficiently difficult to provide for individual differences at each level.

A battery such as this should be considered analytical rather than diagnostic in nature. The difference lies in the thoroughness of sampling rather than in the methodology of the approach. The teacher needs more information than can be obtained from tests of this kind to make a thorough diagnosis.

The Language Skills test actually measures the skills of correct writing-spelling, capitalization, punctuation, and usage. The spelling test uses recognition items. There are five choices, the fifth one in each case being "No mistakes." The pupil's task is to determine if any word is misspelled, and if so, which one. The incorrect spellings are selected from children's frequent errors. Those who favor this approach to measuring spelling achievement should find that, in general, all words have been well chosen for each level.

The tests on *Capitalization, Punctuation,* and *Usage* have four choices in each item, the last choice being always "No mistakes." Pupils are directed to determine whether an error occurs, and if so, to indicate the choice where it is to be found. Various kinds of materials are used, such as letters and conversation. The skills chosen appear in general to be consistent with what is taught at the various levels.

Work-Study Skills are divided into three subtests—*Map Reading, Reading Graphs and Tables* and *Knowledge and Use of Reference Materials.* The subtests represent important aspects of reading skill in addition to development of vocabulary and comprehension of narrative material. The maps, graphs, and tables are clearly printed. No confusion should result from poor reproductions of drawings. Items in the map-reading test determine a pupil's knowledge of direction, distance, symbols, and specific concepts such as latitude, parallels, and elevation. Measurement of ability to read graphs and tables includes pictures, bar, circle, and line graphs, the calendar, and a various assortment of tables. The test is organized so that several items refer to one graph or table. In general, the material is meaningful and should result in greater pupil motivation.

Knowledge and Use of Reference Materials includes such skills as are required in locating words in a dictionary, using an index and table of contents, using an encyclopedia, and locating information through the selection of correct references. There are also items on the interpretation of diacritical markings in the dictionary.

Arithmetic Skills are divided into two subtests, *Arithmetic Concepts* and *Arithmetic Problem Solving.* Among the concepts included are cardinal and ordinal numbers, directional orientation, geometric figures and component parts, telling time, our monetary system, linear measurement, reading a thermometer, size of fractional components, common denominators, Roman numerals and some simple algebra. All of the items in *Arithmetic Problem Solving* are problems requiring the student to set up his own operations. The items have four choices with the last choice being "Not given." The problems require the pupil to use addition, subtraction, multiplication, and division for whole numbers and fractions. Items on percentage are also included. The various skills are introduced at the grade levels where they are generally taught. Problems tend in general to be related to the meaningful activities of children and their families. Readability is geared to the particular grade level for which the problem is designed.

Two manuals are published with these tests. The *Teachers Manual* includes a discussion of the purposes of the test and preparations for testing, directions for test administration and scoring, suggestions for using the test results in the improvement of instruction, and the norm tables. The *Manual for Administrators, Supervisors, and Counselors* (Lindquist and Hieronymous, 1956) is more comprehensive, and explains in detail such technical considerations as data on validity, reliability, sampling, and scaling of scores.

The group on which this battery of tests is standardized represents an attempt to include a sampling of all elementary children in grades three through eight who are in regular attendance in the public schools throughout the United States. A total of 74,174 pupils from 213 school systems in 46 states are included in the normative sample.

Grade and percentile norms are available for each of the eleven tests and for the composite of all tests. There are also percentile norms for interpreting individual pupil achievement and school averages. Norms for school averages are presented for the beginning, middle, and end of the year.

Both the coefficient of reliability and the standard error of measurement for each of the eleven tests and the composite of these are given. The split-half method was used to determine the reliability coefficients, and they range from 0.70 in *Map Reading*, grade three, to 0.96 in *Reading*, grade four, for the subtests. The coefficient for the composite is 0.98 for all grades except grade three, which has a coefficient of 0.97.

A great deal of planning and careful consideration was given to the validity of this battery of tests. Instructional procedures, courses of study, and textbooks were analyzed. The skills tested were identified and studied with considerable care. Attention was given to proper grade placement. Items finally selected were judged on the basis of their cruciality and discriminating power. They were chosen on the basis of the test's objective to emphasize the pupils' ability to use the skills. Tests are longer than usual to provide as adequate a sample in each area as was practically possible.

SECONDARY SCHOOL TEST BATTERIES.   Although achievement test batteries have been constructed for secondary school pupils, meaningful norms for the content subjects are difficult to develop. This is so because the populations are different for each subject area and often pupils included in the norm group have not studied the subject in question. Pupils enrolled in physics have not necessarily completed a course in ancient history. When the same pupils constitute the norm group for all subject areas whether or not they have received instruction in them, the norms are meaningless; the test is invalid for those who have not received instruction.

Two popular test batteries are the *Iowa Tests of Educational Development* and the *Sequential Tests of Educational Progress*. The latter battery is discussed because of its unusual approach in measuring achievement in the content fields. This series of achievement tests, known as *STEP*, was constructed to measure "the critical skills in *application* of learning" in the fields of *Essay Writing, Listening and Reading Comprehension, Writing, Science, Mathematics,* and *Social Studies.* In each area there are tests at four educational levels:

Level 4—Grades 4, 5, and 6
Level 3—Grades 7, 8, and 9
Level 2—Grades 10, 11, and 12 of high school
Level 1—Freshman and sophomore years of college

Two forms of every test are available at each level with the exception of the essay tests, which have four forms. All tests except the Essay tests are allowed seventy minutes of working time. They are broken up into two thirty-five-minute working periods, which may be given separately. The Essay tests have only one thirty-five minute section.

An important objective in the construction of these tests is to measure "the ability of students to use what they have learned in the classroom." It has been pointed out in a previous discussion that tests in the content areas emphasize the content of the subject rather than its outcomes. For example, there is general agreement that one objective of a science course is to promote a scientific attitude, although teachers select different subject-matter content to develop it. Therefore, an attempt to measure specific subject matter results in some items that are too difficult for pupils who have not had an opportunity to learn the information, whereas other items prove too easy. In addition to the difficulty of constructing discriminating items, subject-matter tests of this kind do not measure the pupil's ability to solve new problems through the knowledge he has learned.

When hundreds of teachers and researchers were queried about measurement of student achievement, their answers enabled the authors to set up the following directives for the construction of the *STEP* tests (Cooperative Test Division, 1957, p. 3):

1. Tests must be long enough and broad enough for sound individual interpretation. Short tests are not adequate for measuring an individual student's development.

2. There must be continuity of measurement over nearly all the years of general education. The same skills should be measured over a long range of years on a single continuous score scale. Measurement begins with the early simple learnings and proceeds to the later complex skills. Shifting from one short-range test or battery to another results in loss of continuity.

3. The focus should be on the outcomes of instruction rather than on its content. The items must be centered on critical skills and understandings.

4. Ability to apply learning rather than just to "play it back" must be tested.

In this series, ability to write is measured by the *Essay Tests*. About 5,000 student essays on eight topics of interest at each level were evaluated to provide scoring samples. The teacher uses these products as guides in grading his own pupil's papers. Quality is therefore evaluated on the basis of a national norm.

The following essay topic is for Level 3 (grades seven-nine):

> If you knew that you were going to go blind twenty-four hours from now and that nothing could prevent it, what would you do with the time between now and this moment, this time tomorrow when you could see no more? Where would you go? What and whom would you try to see? Write an account of what you would do from the time you leave this room until your blindness strikes, explaining, if possible, the reasons for your actions.

In the *Listening Comprehension Tests*, the examiner reads the selection aloud once and then continues to read orally the multiple-choice questions and the possible answers. The pupil is given a booklet containing only the possible answers and an answer sheet. He marks his responses on the answer sheet. Each level contains twelve to thirteen selections chosen on the basis of listening requirements common to the pupil's experiences. They sample narration, exposition, directions, argument, poetry, etc. Questions relate to four aspects of the selection: main idea, important details, organizational pattern, and word meaning. Three levels of understanding are measured: plain-sense comprehension, interpretation, and evaluation and application. Interpretation and evaluation represent higher order skills, which go beyond determining the sense of the passage. They involve implied meanings and the validity of the communication. The importance of critical and selective listening is illustrated.

To standardize the examiner's reading of the passage to some degree, suggested time limits are given for each selection. The examiner is cautioned to practice reading the materials to present the author's ideas clearly and effectively. Below is a selection from Level 3 (grades seven-nine). The reading time is one minute and thirty seconds.

The examiner reads:

> Here is the fourth selection. It is a speech by a student running for school office.
>
> "A students, B students, C students, D students, and my friends! As you know, I am running for the office of President of the Student Council. I'd like to tell you what I'll do if I'm elected. In the first place, I think several students ought to sit in on teachers' meetings. They settle too many things for us. I don't think that the teachers always know what's best for us.
>
> "In the second place, I'd like to see our Student Council do something. Take the business of the candy machine, for instance. Just because a couple of doctors and dentists don't like it doesn't mean we shouldn't have one. Candy is good for us. It gives us energy, and I, for one, don't think it hurts either your teeth or your appetite. And if it does, so what? You save the lunch money and can go out on a date.

"Last, you know that my opponents—and you'll hear from them in a minute—are two girls. Now, everybody says girls are smarter than boys. That might be true—but just because they're smarter doesn't mean they'll make better officers. In fact, I think girls are too smart and can't always get along with people because of that. Maybe we need somebody not so smart, but that can get along. That's me, fellow students—vote for me!"

One of the questions asked the examinee about the above selection follows:

20.   It is likely that in the past the speaker has:
       E disagreed with the teachers' decisions
       F disagreed with the opinions he has stated
       G agreed with the doctor about the candy machine
       H agreed with his other opponents about decisions of teachers

Materials in the *Reading Comprehension Tests* were chosen from a wide range of content in order to test breadth as well as depth of comprehension. Questions may be answered from the reading matter. Five reading skills are tested:

1.   Ability to understand direct statements made by the author.
2.   Ability to interpret and summarize the passage.
3.   Ability to see the motives of the author.
4.   Ability to observe the organizational characteristics of the passage.
5.   Ability to criticize the passage with respect to its ideas, purpose, or presentation.

The format of the test commonly used is a short reading selection followed by multiple-choice questions. Other reading tests that do an equally effective job of sampling reading skills are available. The merit of this test, therefore, lies in the fact that it is a part of a battery as well as one of a series of tests with different levels of reading maturity.

The format of the *Writing Tests* consists of a series of unedited selections written by children and followed with multiple-choice questions which suggest possible ways to edit the selections, thereby testing the following writing skills:

1.   Ability to write logically.
2.   Ability to organize materials.
3.   Ability to write for purpose, occasion, and audience.
4.   Ability to write effectively, concerning word choice, emphasis, details, reasons, examples, and so forth.
5.   Ability to use the conventions of writing such as basic form, syntax, and word-form mechanics.

Note the following example for Level 2 (grades ten-twelve).

My Favorite Magazine

1. Many young people of today are taking a great interest in the magazine *Suburbia.* 2. It is of fairly large size with a considerable number of pages. 3. The publishers, Allen and Watts, are well known and reputable; thus providing young homemakers with ideas and practical plans for their present and future homes. 4. Because it also contains articles of family and community relations and hints on home improvement, it is most likely preferable reading to people who are seeking guidance on such matters. 5. The previously mentioned content explains why the advertisements would logically be about products and furnishings for the home. 6. The articles were well written, and all the features of *Suburbia* help to form an interesting and informative magazine. 7. I found one particularly interesting article, it was entitled "Families Are Using Spare Time to Broaden Their Horizons." 8. This article points out that leisure time should be spent in any activity other than usual work, instead of remaining in complete inactivity.

Among the questions asked is the following:

14. Which of these possible additions to the report would be most helpful?
    E. A listing of the advertisers making use of several issues of *Suburbia*
    F. A statement of the rates paid by the publishers for articles purchased
    G. A listing and brief description of the "departments" appearing in every issue, as distinct from the featured articles
    H. A statement, accompanied by authoritative references, of the credit rating of the company which publishes *Suburbia*

The *Mathematics Tests* were organized around the idea of the sequential organization for teaching mathematical concepts. Therefore, content is not confined to any one or a series of mathematics courses. Because there is not complete agreement as to the grade level at which concepts should be taught, there may be a need to shift to higher or lower levels depending on the group's progress. the *STEP* tests assess five skill areas essential to the understanding and application of mathematical concepts:

1. Number and operation: understanding of cardinal and ordinal numbers, the number system, fractions, kinds of numbers, fundamental processes, etc.
2. Symbolism: use and nature of symbols, algebraic symbolism.
3. Measurement and geometry: geometric nomenclature and relations, denominate numbers, significant digits and measurement, etc.
4. Function and relation: graphs, ratio, equations, scale drawing, etc.
5. Proof: deductive and inferential reasoning.
6. Probability and statistics: depicting trends, concepts of mean, median, correlation, sampling, data interpretation, etc.

Note the samples of test material drawn from the four levels of the battery.

Level 4 (grades four-six)

Situation: In Tom's school, some children ride bicycles, some walk to school, and some ride the school bus. The pupils on the safety patrol have to come early.

1. Two children from each class in the school were members of the safety patrol. To find how many patrol members there are altogether, what other fact would you need to know?
    A.   The number of children in the school.
    B.   The number of classes in the school.
    C.   The number of children in each class.
    D.   The number of street crossings.

Level 3 (grades seven-nine)

Situation: Mrs. Cain went to the power and light company to check on her electric bills and obtain information about electrical equipment.

1. Mrs. Cain wanted to buy an electric blanket. The office manager of the electric company told her that the blanket would cost 3 cents a night to use. If she used it 200 nights out of the 365 nights of the year, the yearly cost would be:
    A. $ 4.95
    B. $ 6.00
    C. $10.95
    D. $60.00

Level 2 (grades ten-twelve)

Situation: Mr. Jones has a dairy farm on which he also grows corn.

1. Mr. Jones has two fields of equal size on which he grows corn. If ⅞ of field I and ⅚ of field II are devoted to corn, which one of the following statements is true?
    A.   Field I has more space devoted to corn.
    B.   Field II has more space devoted to corn.
    C.   Equal space is devoted to corn in both fields.
    D.   The amounts of space devoted to corn cannot be compared.

Level 1 (grades thirteen-fourteen)

Situation: The Mill City Statistical Agency conducts opinion polls and surveys and performs related statistical research.

1. A new interviewer for the agency reported at the end of his first day that he had interviewed 100 people. He said that 42 of these were men, of whom 30 were Democrats, and that 49 were Republican women. The agency needed to know how many Democratic women he had interviewed but all that he could remember was that everyone had been either Democratic or Republican. From this information alone, it is possible to determine that:
    A.   The data are contradictory
    B.   There were 9 Democratic women
    C.   There were 19 Democratic women
    D.   There are still insufficient data for an answer

The *Science Tests* emphasize basic scientific concepts and applicational skills. These factors are tested in situational aspects related to economics, culture, social relations, and science in the home. Six skills are sampled:

The ability to:
1. Identify and define a scientific problem.
2. Suggest, screen, and test a hypothesis.
3. Design experiments and collect data.
4. Interpret data and draw conclusions.
5. Evaluate critically the printed and spoken word.
6. Reason quantitatively and symbolically.

The following example shows how items have been based on concepts and skills rather than specific textbook information:

Level 3 (grades seven-nine)
Situation: Tom planned to become a farmer and his father encouraged this interest by giving Tom a part of the garden to use for studying plant life. Tom wanted to find out what effect fertilizer has on garden plants. He put some good soil in two different boxes. To box A he added fertilizer containing a large amount of nitrogen. To box B he added fertilizer containing a large amount of phosphorus. In each box he planted 12 bean seeds. He watered each box with the same amount of water. One thing missing from Tom's experiment was a box of soil with:
A. Both fertilizers added
B. Neither nitrogen nor phosphorus fertilizers added
C. Several kinds of seeds planted
D. No seeds planted

As in the *Science Tests*, the objectives of the *Social Studies Tests* are to measure long-term values rather than specific subject matter. The following basic skills are measured:

Ability to:
1. Read and interpret maps, charts, cartoons, pictures, diagrams, as well as the printed word.
2. Think critically, to distinguish fact from opinion, and to recognize propaganda.
3. Assess and interpret data.
4. Apply appropriate outside information and criteria.
5. Draw valid generalizations and conclusions.

Basic understandings must relate to past, present, and future. The authors list the following as measured by this test:

Basic understandings. Although the following understandings are stated in the present, a thorough appreciation of them will involve a realization of how the past has contributed, what the present situation is, and what the future may bring. With increasing insight and breadth of perception, the student should be able to understand:

1. The nature of social change and its effect on man's ways of living.
2. The profound effects of geographic environment on man's institutions and ways of living.
3. Control over the forces of nature as a major factor in accounting for the ways in which we live today.
4. The nature of a democratic society and the rights, privileges, and responsibilities of free men.
5. The means by which society directs and regulates the behavior of its members.
6. Man's economic wants and the ways of satisfying them.
7. The ways in which man attempts to understand and adjust to his environment and his place in the universe.
8. The interdependence among individuals, communities, societies, regions, and nations.
9. The sources of human nature and personality.

The example on page 363 suggests measurement of an important work-study skill and a long-term value. The pupil is provided with the monthly temperature and rainfall chart and is asked questions about it such as the two following the chart.

In addition to the care exercised in the selection of test content and the construction of items, the norm sample was carefully chosen for meaningful interpretation. Because there is evidence indicating a variance of achievement among the regions of the country, the battery was administered to a standardization group chosen from elementary and secondary schools representing nine regions in the United States. College norm groups were also selected by region as well as for junior or four-year colleges.

Percentile norms have been prepared for each of the six tests for individual pupils in grades four through fourteen. School mean norms for all tests, except *Listening*, in each of these grades are also available.

1. Which of these cities are north of the equator?

    (A)   I and III only
    (B)   II and IV only
    (C)   All of the cities
    (D)   None of the cities

2. In which city would one need the greatest variety of weights of clothing?
    (E) I (F) II (G) III (H) IV[1]

Percentiles on each of the various tests can be compared, since they are based on groups of pupils with the same ability. Individual score norms are listed as percentile bands rather than as percentiles for a given earned score (see Figure 23). You will find the *STEP Teachers' Guide* (Cooperative Test Division, 1959) most helpful for interpreting test scores.

---

[1] These and all other test items from *STEP* included in this chapter are reproduced with the permission of the Educational Testing Service.

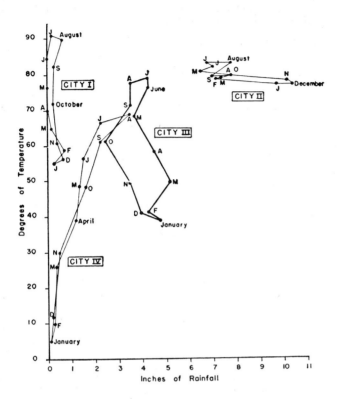

The relationship of the *STEP* tests to the *School and College Ability Tests* should be emphasized. The latter are discussed on page 387. The *SCAT* tests are measures of verbal and quantitative skills. Like *STEP* they are designed for continuity of measurement, having five overlapping levels of instruments extending from the fourth grade through the college sophomore year. Since the *SCAT* and *STEP* tests have been standardized together, they may be used to compare a pupil's achievement with his own ability to achieve. Under- and over-achievement norms are available to determine whether the pupil's *STEP* scores correspond to his verbal and quantitative skills as measured by *SCAT*.

PROBLEMS

12 What, in your opinion, is the outstanding advantage of using the *Sequential Test of Educational Progress* or the *Iowa Tests of Basic Skills* for the purpose of measuring pupil achievement in the elementary school?

13   Table 14 (page 352) compares four achievement test batteries for the elementary school. Which of these four appears most useful to you in your particular subject-matter field? Why?

14   In one study, third-grade norms on the *California Achievement Test* yield grade placements significantly higher than those for four other popular test batteries for the elementary school (Stake, 1961). What are the consequences of a difference such as this?

15   Thelen (1960, p. 19) says that "our tests teach pupils that academic status, not learning, is the goal of education." Do you agree? Why?

Diagnostic Tests

Survey tests, whether individual or battery, help the teacher screen out those pupils who have serious learning disabilities. They provide some diagnostic information. In general, however, the teacher needs much more data on the specific difficulties of a pupil for adequate remediation. Diagnostic tests serve this purpose.

Such tests must, therefore, be considerably longer than the typical survey tests to make the necessary subtests sufficiently reliable. Rather than giving three scores—vocabulary, comprehension, and rate—as is typical of reading survey tests, they may provide numerous scores. A reading diagnostic test may give scores in syllabication, knowledge of consonant sounds, blending, reversals, wrong beginnings, and endings. Whereas an arithmetic survey test may provide two scores, computational and reasoning, a diagnostic arithmetic test may provide information on the difficulties encountered by a pupil in each of the fundamental processes as well as in fractions and decimals. For example, one pupil may have difficulty in long division because he makes mistakes in subtraction. Another makes errors in multiplication which give him an incorrect answer. Still a third has difficulty in his placement of zeros in the quotient. A good diagnostic test will reveal to the teacher the source of the pupil's difficulty.

The more detailed diagnostic tests are individually administered and require greater administrative skill than survey tests. Interpretation is also more complex. Norms are not always provided. Although norms are useful, they are not nearly so important as are the careful tabulation and analysis of the pupil's performance in the varied tasks presented.

Finally, because diagnostic tests often tend to be subdivided into numerous subtests, sampling is frequently limited, thereby casting doubt on the adequacy of their reliability. Such scores should be supported by further data if the test is to realize its potential usefulness.

Diagnostic Tests and Self-Helps in Arithmetic.   A good illustration of this type of test is the *Diagnostic Tests and Self-Helps in Arithmetic* for use in grades four, five, and six. Three kinds of materials are provided.

They are the *Screening Tests*, the *Diagnostic Tests*, and the *Self-Helps* exercises. Three screening tests enable the teacher to survey the pupils' achievement in whole numbers, fractions, and decimals. A fourth screening test, designed for use in grades six and above, is general in nature and contains more difficult examples than the other three. The author suggests that when a pupil makes one or more errors in a screening test, the proper diagnostic tests be administered.

There are twenty-three diagnostic tests in all:

Addition facts	Subtraction of like fractions
Subtraction facts	Addition of unlike fractions
Multiplication facts	Subtraction of unlike fractions
Division facts	Multiplication of fractions
Uneven division facts	Division of fractions
Addition of whole numbers	Addition of decimals
Subtraction of whole numbers	Subtraction of decimals
Multiplication of whole numbers	Multiplication of decimals
Division by one-place numbers	Division of decimals
Division by two-place numbers	Per cent
Regrouping fractions	Operations with measures
Addition of like fractions	

The tests are also cross-referenced among each other. For example, those related to *Multiplication of Whole Numbers*, Test 8, are Tests 1, *Addition Facts*, 3, *Multiplication Facts*, and 6, *Addition of Whole Numbers*. When a pupil makes a mistake in a problem such as 986×357, he may have one of several difficulties. He may place the products of the various steps incorrectly. Possibly he does not know how to carry. Perhaps he does not know his addition facts or understand how to do column addition. Some of these difficulties will be obvious after administering Test 8. By assigning the related tests, the teacher can locate the source of error.

The *Self-Helps* guide the pupil in overcoming his difficulties in a particular skill. Each diagnostic test has its companion self-help material. For example, if a pupil has difficulty in multiplying numbers with zeros in the multiplicand, there are exercises showing all the work required in this type of skill:

760	806	900
$\times$ 59	$\times$ 48	$\times$ 67
6840	6448	6300
38000	32240	54000
44840	38688	60300

The pupils are instructed to study the work to determine how the answers are found. They are then advised to cover the work and answers and solve the exercise on their own.

No coefficients of reliability or validity are reported. However, the author points out that rows of examples testing each step were included to increase reliability. For example, in testing a pupil's ability to deal with one-place multipliers where no carrying is involved, we have the following exercises:

$$\begin{array}{ccc} 34 & 213 & 111 \\ \times\ 2 & \times\ 3 & \times\ 6 \end{array}$$

Content validity is stressed. The tests are based on an analysis of the underlying skills involved in the various operations. These are organized systematically in terms of the development of each skill.

PROBLEMS

16   What particular care must be exercised in the interpretation of the results from the subtests of a diagnostic test such as the *Diagnostic Tests and Self-Helps in Arithmetic?*
17   Would a different type of validity be stressed in a diagnostic test than in a survey test of achievement? Explain.

SUMMARY

Standardized tests differ from teacher-constructed tests in that they have norms and, in general, exhibit greater care in construction of items and more attention to educational objectives. Both the standardized and teacher-constructed tests serve useful purposes. The strength of standardized tests lies in their use as an added criterion of measurement against which the teacher may judge the adequacy of his content selection and the effectiveness of the learning experiences he has organized.

In a testing program, survey tests are generally given first to identify areas of individual and group weakness. Although there are numerous tests of this kind, the trend has been toward the use of test batteries for this purpose. In the past, batteries have been employed almost entirely in the elementary school. However, new batteries designed for the secondary school will probably result in more extensive use of these instruments at this higher level. A distinct advantage of the battery is the availability of a profile providing a more adequate interpretation of a pupil's strengths and weaknesses.

The diagnostic test can be administered to those pupils who do poorly on the survey test. Diagnostic tests include items sampling aspects of learning that have caused difficulty for large numbers of pupils. They therefore aid in analyzing areas of weakness.

The frontier in standardized testing lies in the development of instruments measuring long-term values rather than specific information taught. The teacher-made test can utilize the materials in a specific textbook or reference work as a vehicle for measuring the development of ability to apply scientific method, for example. However, in a standardized test, the authors cannot depend on all pupils having studied the same references and must therefore supply materials, a requirement which presents practical problems, particularly with regard to test length.

Suggested Readings

Anastasi, Anne. *Psychological testing.* (2nd ed.) New York: Macmillan, 1961. Chapters 16 and 17.
An excellent discussion of achievement tests in general and in special areas is presented. Uses and limitations of achievement tests and batteries and problems in construction are emphasized. A number of achievement tests in special areas are described, and some of the items are illustrated.

Bligh, H. F. Trends in the measurement of educational achievement. *Rev. educ. Res.,* 1965, **35,** 34–52.
A review of the literature on educational achievement tests has been made for the three-year period from 1962 to 1965. As is typical of these reviews, a lengthy bibliography is included.

Cronbach, L. J. *Essentials of psychological testing.* (2nd ed.) New York: Harper & Row, 1960. Chapter 13.
Functions of proficiency tests, their validity, norms, and types of items used are discussed. Special attention is given to the relationship between achievement tests and the objectives of the curriculum. Representative achievement test batteries are listed. Discussion of reading tests is included.

Engelhart, M. D. What to look for in a review of an achievement test. *Personnel & Guid. J.,* 1964, **42,** 616–619.
As the title implies, the author discusses the salient factors that make a satisfactory achievement test. Validity and reliability are stressed.

Katz, Martin. *Selecting an achievement test, principles and procedures.* (2nd ed.) Educational Testing Service Evaluation and Advisory Service Series, No. 3. Princeton, N.J.: Educational Testing Service, 1961.
This monograph is designed to help laymen make a more intelligent choice among the many available tests. The basis for test selection consists of certain universal elements; namely, pupil population, school objectives, purposes in testing, methods of accomplishing these purposes through tests, orientation and motivation of school personnel, and available time and money.

Lennon, R. T. *Testing in the secondary school.* Test Service Notebook, No. 20. Tarrytown, N.Y.: Harcourt, Brace and World, 1957.
This pamphlet gives some helpful suggestions on the selection and use of standardized tests.

Rudman, R. C. How good are standardized achievement tests? *Nat'l Elem. Prin.*, 1964, **44**, 32–38.

Standardized tests do measure what a student knows about a subject more reliably than teacher-constructed tests, and can be put to good use because of the degree of uniformity in the school curriculum throughout the nation.

Stake, R. E., and J. T. Hastings. Stanford achievement battery. *Personnel & Guid. J.*, 1964, **43**, 178–184.

This is an excellent critique of a standardized achievement test battery. It provides an insight into many aspects of test construction that determines the quality of the instruments.

Super, D. E., and J. O. Crites. *Appraising vocational fitness by means of the psychological test.* (Rev. ed.) New York: Harper & Row, 1962. Chapter 7.

Both educational achievement tests and vocational proficiency tests are described in this chapter. The latter tests are principally stenographic and typing tests.

Thompson, A. *Test giver's self-inventory.* Tarrytown, N.Y.: Harcourt, Brace and World, 1956.

A well-organized check list is presented for those who have the responsibility for the administration of standardized tests.

Tyler, R. W. Assessing the progress of education. *Phi Delta Kappan,* 1965, **47**, 13–16.

The author emphasizes the need for dependable information about pupil achievement if the national effort for maintaining and improving the quality of education is to be effective. He describes a plan for assessing educational progress on a national scale. Individual pupils who are a part of a national sample are to respond to only a few test items concerning their scholastic achievement. Measurement of achievement of groups rather than individuals is to be made.

References Cited

Cooperative Test Division. *A prospectus, Sequential Tests of Educational Progress.* Princeton, N.J.: Educational Testing Service, 1957.

Cooperative Test Division. *Sequential Tests of Educational Progress.* Princeton, N.J.: Educational Testing Service, 1957.

Cooperative Test Division. *Sequential Tests of Educational Progress teacher's guide.* Princeton, N.J.: Educational Testing Service, 1959.

Educational Testing Service. *ETS builds a test.* Princeton, N.J.: Educational Testing Service, 1959.

French, J. W., and W. B. Michael. *Standards for educational and psychological tests and manuals.* Washington: American Psychological Association, 1966.

Lindquist, E. F. Preliminary considerations in objective test construction. In E. F. Lindquist (Ed.), *Educational measurement.* Washington: American Council on Education, 1951. Pp. 119–158.

Lindquist, E. F., and A. N. Hieronymus. *Iowa Tests of Basic Skills.* Boston: Houghton Mifflin, 1955.

Lindquist, E. F., and A. N. Hieronymous. *Manual for administrators, supervisors, and counselors: Iowa Tests of Basic Skills.* Boston: Houghton Mifflin, 1956.

Stake, R. E. "Overestimation" of achievement with the California Achievement Test. *Educ. psychol. Measmt,* 1961, **21**, 59–62.

Thelen, H. A. The triumph of "achievement" over inquiry in education. *Elem. sch. J.,* 1960, **60**, 190–197.

Measuring Pupil Aptitudes

VISIT ANY CLASSROOM with a democratic social climate and you will observe as many kinds of behavior as there are pupils. Within a fifth-grade class you find some pupils working arithmetic problems while another group turns, fascinated, to the production of a play they have written. One boy is building a model to illustrate the operation of a machine studied in a science unit; one of the girls is writing a poem. Other children are reading and seem to be totally absorbed in a story. You see one pupil staring out of the window; occasionally he will try to work at an assignment, but he seems to give up easily. Another child is buzzing around the room enjoying a series of social calls, and is soon called back to his seat.

You also notice that performance varies considerably. Some children seem adept at manipulating scissors or blocks. Others paint very well, though the art work of their peers seems immature. Certain pupils offer many ideas as they work with others; some tend to follow and do as they are told.

The many individual differences you observe reflect interests, attitudes, experience backgrounds, and innate ability. All of these factors form the basis for the pupil's ability to learn. His ability to learn is his aptitude; his achievement refers to what he has learned. As we shall see, tests that measure aptitude and achievement differ not so much in their content but in the functions they perform.

Certain inherited traits are basic to specific aptitudes. Early studies of individual differences revealed that some people react to stimuli more quickly than others. Take, for example, the case of a certain astronomer engaged in recording the instant at which he saw the images of stars as they crossed the field of his telescope. When a consistent time-lag appeared in his reports, his employers discharged him promptly, thinking him simply careless. This occured before scientists' discovery that individuals react to stimuli with varying rapidity. Those who react quickly have an advantage in some kinds of work. Certain manual skills require long fingers and a deftness of manipulation. In those areas an individual with short stubby fingers which he uses awkwardly will find himself at a definite disadvantage. In most instances, aptitude represents more than innate ability. As in the case of identical twins, two individuals with identical inherited capacities may have quite different aptitudes because their experiences have been different. One may learn or perform a task with ease; he has a high aptitude for that work. The other may find the task difficult; he is inept at improving his skill, and has little aptitude for the work. Theoretically, each could develop this special genetically based aptitude to the same degree, but this may not happen because of the important part achievement plays in aptitude potential.

High general ability is necessary for the development of superior specific aptitudes. The concert pianist has not only high musical aptitude, but high general ability as well. An individual with superior native endowment is also more likely to have a wider range of aptitudes than is his peer who is less intellectually mature. He may be talented in the graphic arts, exhibit physical prowess, and show high scholastic achievement.

Knowledge of a pupil's aptitudes is of value in counseling him on vocational plans and preparation for jobs in which he is likely to succeed. It is also helpful in organizing learning experiences for the individual. For example, low achievement may be the result of lack of effort or ability; we want to know how much a pupil can achieve. Of course, reliability of prediction is dependent on the stability of the aptitude. If an aptitude is unstable, it cannot be measured reliably and will have low correlation to achievement. The findings of research dealing with the problem of the constancy of aptitudes indicate some disagreement among psychologists, but, in general, aptitudes seem to be fairly stable. Super (1962, p. 72) states that ". . . whether largely innate or largely acquired, the aptitudes about which we know something appear to become· crystalized in early childhood and that after that they mature in a predictable way and are generally relatively constant."

In developing instruments for evaluating aptitudes, emphasis has proceeded from general to the "purer" aptitudes. Any list of aptitudes we choose will be arbitrary, depending upon the extent to which we find measurement of discrete aptitudes helpful as opposed to lumping them together for practical purposes. For instance, it is often useful to know a pupil's mechanical aptitude in addition to having a measure of his general mental ability. Yet mechanical aptitude is a composite of spatial visualization, perceptual speed and acuity, and mechanical information. At the present time it is probably more generally useful to take a global approach to aptitude measurement than an "atomistic" one; for example, making a separate analysis of mechanical aptitude. Thus the discussion that follows is centered around special groupings of the purer aptitudes. Those of particular importance to school personnel are classified under the headings scholastic, mechanical, and sensory. There is also a discussion of the basis for differential aptitude testing and of instruments designed for this purpose. A selected list of tests which measure many different aptitudes is shown in Appendix D.

SCHOLASTIC APTITUDE

Someone once quipped that intelligence is what intelligence tests measure. Unfortunately most other definitions do little more to clarify the concept, and though many have been offered, they all fail in some sense. Since intelligence, unlike a muscle, cannot be described, definitions delineate an individual's inherited capacity. Because intelligence can only be inferred from the behavior of the organism, test scores imply a quantity or quality of intelligence rather than measuring it directly.

In measuring achievement, we sample areas of learning, and if our test and testing situation are adequate, we can arrive at some fairly defensible conclusions about the pupil's skills. But in measuring intelligence, we must consider unequal educational opportunities. Since we cannot measure intelligence directly, we establish problem situations which represent important intellectual functions. Though we try to exclude problems whose solutions have been taught in school, the tools the pupil uses are learned. If he is to answer questions on a group intelligence test, he probably will have to know how to read. Some items will demand arithmetic; others the development of specific concepts, such as rod, quarter, capital, civil war, and so forth. Because a pupil's ability to do well on these tests is so closely related to success in school, the commonly used measures of general intelligence are known as scholastic aptitude tests. There is a high correlation between scores on these tests and achievement tests. Test items are often difficult to differentiate. (See page 30.)

Individual Tests

The individual scholastic aptitude test, as the name implies, is designed for face-to-face administration to the individual pupil. Three commonly used instruments in this category are the *Stanford-Binet Scale, Form L-M*, the *Wechsler Intelligence Scale for Children*, (the *WISC*), and the *Wechsler Adult Intelligence Scale*, (the *WAIS*).

STANFORD-BINET INTELLIGENCE SCALE, FORM L-M. The 1960 revision of the *Stanford-Binet Intelligence Scale*, which is designated as *Form L-M*, differs from earlier revisions in both content and structure. Some of the content revisions have relocated or eliminated certain subtests and test items. Many of the non-scholastic items are omitted to put greater emphasis on word knowledge. Others clarify directions for test administration and scoring. By structural changes the authors have attempted to make the intelligence quotients comparable at the various ages, and have tried to correct an inadequacy of the 1937 revision of the scale which yielded intelligence quotients with an arithmetic mean greater than 100. In addition, the intelligence quotient tables in the 1960 revision have been extended to include ages seventeen and eighteen.

Form L-M is grouped into twenty age levels. Beginning at Year II, the levels are placed at six-month intervals up to Year VI; that is, Year II, Year II-6, Year III, Year III-6, and so forth. This grouping allows for the rapid growth of preschool children. Each level has six tests; one month of credit toward the mental-age score is allowed for each test. From Year VI to Year XIV, twelve-month intervals are used. Since there are also six tests in each of these levels, each receives two months of credit. Topping the scale are four increasingly difficult levels, the Average Adult, the Superior Adult Level I, the Superior Adult Level III, and the Superior Adult Level III. The Average Adult level has eight tests counting two months each. Each of the three Superior Adult levels has six tests. In Superior Adult Level I, each test counts four months, in Superior Adult Level II, five months, and in Superior Adult Level III, six months. Form L-M reflects the conclusions of longitudinal studies (Bradway & Robinson, 1961; Bradway & Thompson, 1962), that improvement in performance on the test continues after sixteen years of age. The new form recognized improvement to age eighteen.

The tests demand both verbal and nonverbal performance. In some cases, simple memory is sufficient; in others, reasoning is necessary. The pupil must rely on his past experiences as well as his talent to solve problems in new situations. Test materials consist of toy objects, printed cards, a test booklet for recording responses, and the test manual.

Below are samples of some of the tests (Terman & Merrill, 1960, reproduced by permission of Houghton Mifflin Company) from various age levels:

Year II—*Identifying Objects by Name* (Alternate)
  Material: Card with dog, ball, engine, bed, doll, and scissors attached.
  Procedure: Show the card with the six small objects attached and say, "See all these things? Show me the dog." "Put your finger on the dog." "Where is the dog?"

Year VI—*Mutilated Pictures*
  Material: Card with mutilated pictures.
  Procedure: Show subject the card with mutilated pictures and pointing to each in turn, ask, "What is gone in this picture?" or "What part is gone?"

Year XIV—Orientation: Direction I

Procedure: Read the following directions distinctly, emphasizing the critical
words:

  (a)   "Which direction would you have to face so that your left
        hand would be toward the east?"
  (b)   "Suppose you are going west, then turn to your right;
        what direction are you going now?"
  (c)   "Suppose you are going north, then turn to your left,
        then turn right; what direction are you going now?"
  (d)   "Suppose you are going south, then turn left, then turn
        right, then turn left again; what direction are you going
        now?"
  (e)   "Suppose you are going north, then turn left, then left
        again, then right, and then right again; what direction are
        you going now?"

Superior Adult III—Reasoning

Material: Card on which problem is stated.
Procedure: Let subject look at the card while you read the problem aloud
and while he is solving it. "I planted a tree that was 8 inches
tall. At the end of the first year, it was 12 inches tall; at the end
of the second year it was 18 inches tall; and at the end of the
third year it was 27 inches tall. How tall was it at the end of
the fourth year?"

The authors emphasize three requirements for a valid test:

1.   The standard procedures must be followed.
2.   The pupil's best efforts must be enlisted by the establishment and
     maintenance of adequate rapport.
3.   The responses must be correctly scored. (Terman and Merrill, 1960)

The examiner must have special training in test administration and
scoring before he can meet these criteria. He must also have background
information in testing and a considerable amount of practice with the
instrument to administer it well. Any variation of the standardized procedure somewhat invalidates the test results. Too much attention to details
excludes continuing rapport with the pupil and may result in a less-than-
adequate performance. Test administration is further complicated by the
fact that scoring is simultaneous with administration. Cues for the next
step in the procedure are dependent on the pupil's success or failure.

With younger children, testing is usually begun at an age level about
one year below the anticipated mental age of the child. If all tests at this
level are passed, that is known as the pupil's basal age, and the tests at the
next higher age level are administered. If any tests are failed, the examiner
drops down to the next lower level until a basal age is reached. Tests are
then given through the higher age scales until a level is achieved at which
the child fails all the tests. This is known as his ceiling or maximal age.

At levels of Year VI and above, some examiners may begin with the vocabulary test. This is used for Years VI, VIII, X, and XIV, and all adult levels; the scoring standards change from level to level. The age level for further test administration is determined by comparing the number of words passed by the pupil and the number of correct word definitions necessary for success at a given level. The procedure for determining the basal and maximal ages is identical to that previously described.

It is obvious that no pupil takes all of the tests. He tries only those items that determine the upper and lower limits of his ability. Provision is made for the spoiling of tests by making an alternate test available at each of the age levels. About one hour is usually needed for test administration; the time required may vary from as little as thirty to forty minutes for younger children to an hour and one-half or more for older children.

The test manual specifies the desired performance on each test for credit at a particular level. For example, in *Identifying Objects by Name* for Year II, the child must correctly identify at least five of the six objects to pass. Scoring is on an all-or-none basis. The child who identifies three objects correctly receives no more credit than one who identifies two. Both children fail. Some tests are used at more than one age level and require higher standards of performance for success at the higher age levels. If a test is administered at a lower level, it is not given again at the higher level, but is scored and credited for the proper age level at that time. For example, in the *Opposite Analogies I* test of Year IV, the child needs to have only two of the items correct; however, if three or more are right, he is given credit for the same test in Year IV-6. The items in this test follow (Terman & Merrill, 1960, reproduced by permission of Houghton Mifflin Company):

a. "Brother is a boy; sister is a —————."
b. "In daytime it is light; at night it is —————."
c. "Father is a man; mother is a —————."
d. "The snail is slow; the rabbit is —————."
e. "The sun shines during the day; the moon at —————."

The mental age of a child is determined by adding to his basal age the number of months he earned on those tests passed beyond this age. Traditionally, the intelligence quotient (IQ) had been found by dividing his mental age (MA) by the chronological age (CA) and multiplying by 100. However, this method prevents IQ's having the same meaning at different age levels. At one CA an IQ of 120 may be the highest score of 85% of the age group while, for another age group, an IQ of 115 may be the top figure for the same percentage of that population. To overcome this problem, in *Form L-M* of the *Stanford-Binet*, a deviation or standard score IQ (sometimes known as DIQ) is found by entering a table with the proper M and CA for the pupil in question.

Year level	Number of tests passed	Months of credit per test	Total Credit	
			Years	Months
VI	6 (Basal Age)	—	6	0
VII	3	2	0	6
VIII	1	2	0	2
IX	0 (Ceiling Age)	2	0	0
Mental Age			6	8

This child's basal age is six, and his ceiling age is nine. His mental age is the sum of the various amounts of credit he earned.

In essence, DIQ's are standard scores with an arithmetic mean of 100 and a standard deviation of 16.

Because *From L-M* was constructed from items selected from *Forms L* and *M* of the 1937 revision, data from this earlier revision are still important. For example, *Forms L* and *M* were administered to a group of children with a time period between the two administrations, and a coefficient of reliability was obtained. Appreciable differences among the reliability coefficients for the various age groups were found, as can be noted from Table 15 (McNemar, 1942, pp. 62–63). Reliability of the scores of older children and scores of those having lower IQ's tends to be greater. Most of the coefficients are about 0.90 or only slightly below for the total range, which is excellent considering the greater homogeneity of specific age levels. Reliability of most scholastic aptitude tests has been determined on far more heterogeneous groups.

The validity of *Form L-M* is based on three factors. First, the best items borrowed from the two forms of the 1937 revision assure us that the 1960 revision measures whatever was measured by the previous one. Secondly, items were selected on the basis of an increasing percentage of

TABLE 15

RELIABILITY COEFFICIENTS OF THE STANFORD-BINET SCALE
(1937 REVISION) FOR IQ INTERVALS AND AGE GROUPS

IQ-Interval	Age Group		
	2½ to 5½	6 to 13	14 to 18
140–149	0.83	0.91	0.95
60–69	0.91	0.97	0.98

success as the CA of the children increased. For example, based on both forms of the 1937 revision, a higher percentage of six-year-old children than five-year-olds should pass an item at Year VI. Thirdly, items were chosen on the basis of their relationship with the total score on each form, a criterion of internal consistency.

The criterion-related validity of an intelligence test is of interest to teachers. Scholastic achievement is the criterion generally used in investigations of this kind. Studies show that there is a high relationship between academic achievement and scores on the *Stanford-Binet*, with those courses emphasizing verbal skills tending to show the highest coefficients of correlation; for example, higher than 0.70. Though academic success is influenced by numerous unmeasured factors such as background, persistence, and personal-social adjustment, the *Stanford-Binet* scores are still very helpful to those planning a pupil's education.

Like any other aptitude test, the *Stanford-Binet* does not measure pure native capacity, but innate ability and the effect of learning. Only if we could assume that the test is completely valid and reliable and that influencing environments are identical could we infer that the pupils tested have the same native capacity. At that, it would be sounder to infer only that they had the same ability to learn. But no psychological test has perfect reliability or validity; rapport and effective tapping of a pupil's maximum potential are always problems. He may know the answer to a question and refuse to respond; he may give an incorrect answer for many reasons. Pupils with academic disabilities may have a particularly strong dislike or even a fear of the kinds of items included in the *Stanford-Binet*.

The improbability that children will experience the same environments extends even to siblings. The older children may be asked to assume more responsibility, to supervise younger brothers or sisters. Perhaps more sharing is demanded of them. Because older children serve as models of behavior, younger members of the family are likely to participate in certain activities at an earlier age than their older siblings.

Differences also exist among family environments. One home may provide a great deal of social interaction, another almost none. Reading may be a central interest of all members of one pupil's family; his classmate's family may lack even a daily newspaper. Bilingual homes present a special problem for children. Because the *Stanford-Binet* is highly verbal, a pupil from a bilingual home is likely to be severely affected by lack of verbal stimulation. Although he may have other types of ability, they are not effectively sampled by this test.

It should also be noted that the *Stanford-Binet* is not designed to differentiate among the various aspects of intelligence. There are no separate scores, only a composite.

Despite these limitations, the *Stanford-Binet* has proved over the years to be a valuable instrument. Although superior performance on the test is dependent on success in school, the test may also be the instrument for predicting such success, since verbal ability is an important factor in school success and this highly verbal test enables an examiner to assess the pupil's verbal facility. It also helps spot deficiencies in arithmetic, problem solving, and the fund of information.

During the administration of the *Stanford-Binet*, one can observe a child's reactions. Although the quality of his performance should be interpreted cautiously by an experienced examiner, a pupil's problem-solving ability, his work habits, and his reaction to success and failure can be examined. When he fails, the examiner determines whether he is disturbed, irritable, argumentative, or depressed. When he is successful, his reaction is also observed. Reaction time should be noted; it can be indicative of certain personality problems. Is it delayed, blocked, or irregular? Is there any indication of negativism, or are the responses given quickly and impulsively? On the basis of this and other evidence, the examiner can gain insights into the personality of the pupil.

Problems

1 The *Stanford-Binet test* has proved a valuable, though far from perfect, instrument for measuring individual mental capacity. What are the strengths of this test in terms of its value to the classroom teacher? Can you see any areas of weakness in its construction?
2 Billy and Sally, both 8 years old, received IQ's of 97 on the *Stanford-Binet*. However, the basal age for Billy was 5 and his ceiling age was 12. Sally's basal age was 7; her ceiling was 10. On the basis of this information, what differences might you expect in the pattern of abilities of these two pupils?
3 In the 1960 revision of the *Stanford-Binet*, the authors provide adjusted IQ-scores which are standard scores with a mean of 100 and a standard deviation of 16. What was the reason for this change? How has this improved the test?

WECHSLER INTELLIGENCE SCALE FOR CHILDREN.   Most of the items in the *WISC* have been taken from *Form II* of the earlier *Wechsler-Bellevue Intelligence Scale*. The most important change is the addition of easier items so that young children can be tested. It is planned for children from five to fifteen.

The *WISC* is a series of point scales. That is, each test item is assigned points for a correct response. Points for each test represent raw scores, which are changed to scaled scores by means of a table. The respective tests in the *Verbal Scale* and the *Performance Scale* are added to secure the verbal and performance scores. By the use of tables, the intelligence quotients may be determined.

The pupil's IQ is found, therefore, by comparing the score representing his test performance with those scores earned by the individuals in the standardization sample of a single age group. By holding the standard deviation of IQ's constant and equating the total mean score for each age group, the IQ is made comparable for pupils of different ages. An individual is assigned an IQ on the basis of the amount that he deviates from the average performance of those in his own age group.

The WISC actually has twelve subtests grouped under Verbal and Performance Scales. However, two of these, the Digit Span in the Verbal Scale, and Mazes in the Performance Scale, were omitted in establishing the IQ-tables. Digit Span and Mazes (or Coding) may be used either as alternates or supplementary tests if time permits.

The ten-test scale is therefore as follows:

Verbal tests	Performance tests
General information	Picture completion
General comprehension	Picture arrangement
Arithmetic	Block design
Similarities	Object assembly
Vocabulary	Coding or mazes

Care must be exercised in interpreting differences among subtest scores, and we must anticipate many differences resulting from chance variations. Cohen (1957) concludes that only eighty-six per cent of what a subtest measures is the result of common factors and error.

The WISC Manual emphasizes that the test examiner must be well-trained and have access to a quiet testing room and proper materials. The directions for test administration must be followed specifically. Rather than changing the wording of the questions, the teacher should read the instructions from the manual. The conditions under which the child performs certain tasks have been carefully standardized; norms of performance have been prepared under the conditions of the instructions. As in the administration of the Stanford-Binet, the examiner has an opportunity to note any unusual behavior that bears on the child's personality.

The examiner must always be concerned with securing optimum performance, and very skillful questioning is required. Often the child's response needs clarification which can be accomplished by nonevaluative querying. For example, the examinee may be asked to "Please explain further," or to "Tell more about it." Also, in maintaining rapport it is sometimes necessary to encourage with supporting statements, such as, "This is a little difficult; you will find it easier when you are older." One should not build up an expectancy for approval within the child, because he may come to interpret no comment as disapproval.

The scoring is partly clerical but also highly professional because interpretations must be made. Although the scoring of a certain test, such as Arithmetic and Coding, can be completely objective, the responses children give for Vocabulary, as in the case of the Stanford-Binet, are numerous and demand considerable judgment from the examiner. Test items correctly answered are accorded a certain number of points, and are then added to obtain a raw score which, in turn, is changed to standard scores from tables provided. The IQ's may then be found as previously explained.

Split-half reliability coefficients were determined for Full, Verbal, and Performance Scales for 7½, 10½, and 13½ year age groups. Subtest score reliabilities were also reported. Full Scale reliabilities were 0.92, 0.95, and 0.94 respectively, for these age groups. Verbal Scale reliabilities were 0.88, 0.96, and 0.96. The reliabilities on the Performance Scale were 0.86, 0.89, and 0.90. However, the subtest reliabilities were considerably lower. Digit Span was as low as 0.50 for the 13½ year group. Most of the values lie in the 0.60's, 0.70's, and 0.80's (Wechsler, 1949).

No interpretive data are presented in the manual on the validity of the test. However, many studies have compared performance on the WISC with that of the Stanford-Binet. Coefficients of correlations usually found vary between 0.60 and 0.80. Correlations based on the Performance Scale alone tend to be somewhat lower than those based on the Verbal Scale alone.

The WISC uses a standard deviation of 15 in contrast to the 16 used for Standard-Binet scores. Therefore, if two bright pupils have numerically similar means on the two tests, the DIQ on the Stanford-Binet will be slightly higher than on the WISC. With comparably dull children, the DIQ on the Stanford-Binet will be a little lower.

The WISC is more easily administered than the Stanford-Binet. Moreover, the subject does not undergo the frustrating situation he experiences in the latter during the series of failures as he approaches his ceiling. One of the limitations of the WISC, however, is in testing retarded children because it does not yield an IQ below 45.

WECHSLER ADULT INTELLIGENCE SCALE.   Form I of the original Wechsler Intelligence Scale was published in 1939 and was called the Wechsler-Bellevue Intelligence Scale. Form II was adapted from a scale developed during World War II. Scales of both forms were designed for adults rather than children. The tasks in existing instruments, such as the Stanford-Binet, do not hold enough interest to motivate many adults. In addition, the speed factor is particularly detrimental in assessing adult intelligence when a test is standardized on children.

The items in these scales reflect Wechsler's specific objective, namely, to construct an instrument that would enable him to better understand his adult patients at New York's Bellevue Hospital. Because he had to determine their intelligence and personality aberrations, he needed an instrument with diagnostic properties in addition to those measuring "global" intelligence.

These scales were used for ten to fifteen years, and during that time a considerable amount of research revealed certain limitations that warranted an extensive revision. This was undertaken, and in 1955 the *Wechsler Adult Intelligence Scale*, commonly called the *WAIS*, was published. The significant changes were more adequate norms, based on a broader population sampling, and an increase in the range of difficulty in the items of the subtests and in improved total scale reliability.

Like its two predecessors, the *Wechsler-Bellevue Intelligence Scale* and the *WISC*, the *WAIS* is a point scale designed to yield a deviation IQ. There are eleven tests in the *Full Scale* of the *WAIS*, six of which comprise the *Verbal Scale* and the remaining five are grouped into the *Performance Scale*. The same considerations for interpreting the differences between subtest scores and verbal and performance IQ's mentioned in the previous section should be adhered to.

VERBAL TESTS	PERFORMANCE TESTS
Information	Digit Symbol
Comprehension	Picture Completion
Arithmetic	Block Design
Similarities	Picture Arrangement
Digit Span	Object Assembly
Vocabulary	

PROBLEMS

4 Generally speaking, teachers look only for the actual IQ-score when an individual psychological test has been administered. Few bother to read the detailed report prepared by the examiner. What dangers are inherent in this practice? What information should you as a teacher look for and expect to find in a psychological report? In what respects might a psychological report of a *Stanford-Binet* test differ from one on the *WISC* in terms of the kinds of information given?

5 Which subtests of the *WAIS* or *WISC* do you feel would be most significant as predictors of achievement in your subject-matter area?

6 Prepare a summary of the major differences between the *Stanford-Binet* and the *WAIS* or *WISC*. Compare them in terms of test construction, computation of IQ, statistical data on reliability and validity, and the interpretation of the IQ-score.

Group Tests

In most school situations, there is neither time nor trained personnel for the administration of the individual tests described. Group tests, therefore, are much more extensively used, since they may be administered to a large group by an examiner with minimum training. In general, they are verbal, and if they do not require reading, the examinee must at least be able to understand the verbal instructions of the examiner. Therefore great care must be taken in interpreting test scores, for a low score may indicate a lack of verbal facility rather than intellectual immaturity.

Although many good group intelligence tests are available for school use (see Appendix D), all of them cannot be discussed here. A logical choice is to examine several tests which represent somewhat different approaches to the measurement of mental ability. In addition, a summary of the important college aptitude tests is included.

OTIS QUICK-SCORING ABILITY TESTS.   In the *Otis* group, tests have been designed at three levels, the *Alpha, Beta,* and *Gamma,* for grades 1.5-4, 4-9, and high schools and colleges respectively. The arrangement of the *Otis* tests is of the omnibus type. Instead of using subtests of homogenous items, the designers introduce all easy items first, whatever their nature. For example, in the *Gamma Test, Form EM,* the first item samples information; the second, vocabulary; the twelfth, arithmetic; the fourteenth, vocabulary; the twentieth, alphabetizing; and so on. The difficulty of each item is gradually increased, the last the most difficult of all. This arrangement is more likely to tap the potential of the examinee because he will not spend undue time on very difficult items early in the test.

The *Alpha* test for primary school children is constructed so that the same items are re-used with two sets of instructions to provide verbal and nonverbal scores. If both administrations are used, it is recommended that the nonverbal part be given first. When administering the nonverbal section, instructions require that the pupil draw a horizontal line through the correct picture. In one practice test item (from Otis, 1954; reproduced by permission of Harcourt, Brace and World, Inc.), the directions are given below. It is obvious that the instructions are verbal, thereby introducing an inaccuracy in the test name.

> Now let us look at the pictures in the first row. In the first row there are three things that are alike. What are they? Yes, they are the three girls; so draw a line through the picture of the man because he is *not* like the three girls.

When the verbal part of the test is administered, the pupil is asked to use a differently colored lead or crayon and mark the picture with a vertical line.

> Look at the first row of pictures. Find the girl who is jumping and draw a line through that picture. Remember to draw an up and down line.

There is a different set of oral instructions for each item of the verbal test, some of them quite complex:

Next mark the set of squares in which the smallest square is in the lower right-hand corner of the middle-sized square.

Stencils are provided for ease in scoring. The MA for verbal, non-verbal, and total scores may be ascertained from norm tables. Two procedures determine IQ's. The usual method of dividing a pupil's MA by his CA may be used. In the other method, the deviation of his score from the norm is determined. This value is then translated into an IQ through the use of a table. No data are given on comparability of IQ's with those on other tests; moreover, there is no information on comparability of IQ's at various age levels.

The reliability coefficient of the *Alpha* test is 0.81, based on the scores of a group of second- and third-grade pupils. The same group was used in finding the validity coefficients. Correlation coefficients between the scores of the *Alpha* and the *Primary Examination* and between the *Alpha* and grade placement were 0.65 and 0.86, respectively.

An *Alpha* short form was published in 1953. Unlike the original, it yields only one IQ, which includes both verbal and nonverbal items. This form represents a selection of the forty-five most valid items from the long form chosen under the following criteria stated in the manual:

1. The distribution of item-difficulty values in the shortened form was to parallel the difficulty distribution of the original form.
2. Items having the highest correlation, in both verbal and nonverbal use, with original total score would be given preference.
3. Items yielding the best prediction of school achievement as measured by average reading score would be given preference.

Like the original form, these items are given twice under two sets of instructions. The total time for administering the short form is twenty-two minutes, and a table is provided for converting short form scores into long form scores and vice versa. The correlation of the 1953 short form with the original as reported in the manual is 0.95.

The *Beta* and *Gamma* tests are revisions of the *Otis Self-Administering Tests of Mental Ability*. The tests have six forms, the last two being published in 1953. The items in these tests are largely verbal in nature. Instructions to the examinee are printed in the test booklet, and the problem of administration is further simplified by using a time limit for only the total test.

Scoring is either by hand or machine depending on the forms used. Mental age may be determined from age norms, and the IQ is found by either of the two methods employed in the *Alpha*. Reliability of the *Beta* was determined by correlating odd versus even scores from *Form A* with those from *Form B*. Coefficients varied from 0.79 to 0.95 and from 0.65 to 0.98, respectively. The *Gamma* test manual reports reliability data for odd-even numbered items in grades 10, 11, and 12 with coefficients of 0.90, 0.91, and 0.85, respectively, when corrected with the Spearman-Brown formula.

CALIFORNIA TEST OF MENTAL MATURITY.   The 1963 edition of the CTMM (Long Form) is available for six levels: Level 0 (Kindergarten-Grade 1), Level 1 (Grades 1, 2, 3), Level 2 (Grades 4, 5, 6), Level 3 (Grades 7, 8, 9), Level 4 (Grades 9, 10, 11, 12), Level 5 (Grades 12-College and Adult). There are twelve subtests listed under five factors: *Logical Reasoning, Spatial Relationships, Numerical reasoning, Verbal Concepts,* and *Memory.* Tests results yield a language, nonlanguage, and total IQ. Actually, here again nonlanguage is not accurate terminology since the examinee must understand the verbal instructions of the examiner in the nonlanguage tests.

Probably the total test IQ is the most valid measure to be derived from this instrument. The language and nonlanguage IQ's, however, can aid in educational diagnosis. If the pupil is poor in reading, he is likely to make a lower language IQ score than a nonlanguage IQ on this test, and knowing this can help prevent wrong classification.

The reliability of the total IQ varies from 0.86 to 0.96. The variation for the language factors is from 0.71 to 0.95, and for the nonlanguage factors from 0.79 to 0.93. The deviation IQ has been adopted.

The manual contains an Intellectual Status Index for determining anticipated achievement for a pupil in his actual grade placement. It enables one to predict, for example, whether a pupil can be expected to do average, below average, or above average work in accordance with his score on the CTMM series. When used with scores on the *California Achievement Test* it roughly indicates the status of a pupil's performance in various subjects.

A short form of the test is available for eight levels: Level 0 (Kindergarten-Lower First), Level 1 (Grades High First-Lower Third), Level 1H (Grades 3-4), Level 2 (Grades 4-6), Level 2H (Grades 6-7), Level 3 (Grades 7-8), Level 4 (Grades 9-12), and Level 5(Grades 12-College and Adult). Language, nonlanguage, and total IQ's are also available for this series. Four out of the five factors in the long form are included: *Logical Reasoning, Numerical Reasoning, Verbal Concepts,* and *Memory.* Total score reliabilities vary from 0.78 to 0.95, and the language and nonlanguage score reliabilities vary from 0.59 to 0.94. The short form requires only 34 to 43 minutes of actual testing time for administration while the long form demands 48 minutes to one hour and 23 minutes depending on the particular test level.

KUHLMANN-ANDERSON INTELLIGENCE TESTS.   In the seventh edition of the *Kuhlmann-Anderson Tests* there are eight booklets which are designated by letters: AK, A, B, CD, D, EF, G, and H for use in kindergarten, grades 1; 2; 3 and 4; 4 and 5; 5, 6 and 7; 7, 8, and 9, and 9, 10, 11, and 12, respectively. Although there is overlapping between consecutive booklets, this has been somewhat reduced from the sixth edition. There are now eight tests in the booklets instead of ten, but each test has been lengthened. About forty per cent of the content of this edition has been changed.

Changes also include tables of deviation IQ's with stanine equivalents available. In addition, grade percentile ranks are provided for the beginning, middle, and end of a school year for each test booklet (Kuhlmann and Anderson, 1963).

Although verbal (V) and quantitative (Q) scores may be derived from booklet D upward, the user is warned that these scores for the D and EF booklets are not to be used to predict differential success in these areas because they lack sufficient independence. This limitation has been overcome somewhat at the G and H levels and grade percentile ranks are available for the V, Q, and T scores. The users should interpret the differences between V and Q scores with caution, however.

The tests are easy to administer. They are of the speeded variety and are not corrected for guessing. Test-wise pupils may increase their scores by random marking if they find they do not have time to finish the test.

Test reliability is determined in several ways. First, test-retest coefficients range from 0.83 to 0.92. Secondly, testing pupils on adjacent forms produced coefficients from 0.77 to 0.89. Split-half coefficients of reliability for booklets K to CD range from 0.93 to 0.95.

The validity of the sixth edition of the *Kuhlmann-Anderson Tests* was determined by its ability to discriminate among scores of subjects at successive levels of chronological age, by a comparison of scores of successful and unsuccessful pupils, and by intercorrelations among the subtests. The authors emphasize the test's capacity to discriminate between small increments of mental development. Subsequent studies show a substantial relationship between a pupil's achievement, individual intelligence test scores, and *Kuhlmann-Anderson* scores (Allen, 1944; Dearborn and Rothney, 1963). Acceptable validity for the seventh edition is claimed by virtue of the validity of the sixth edition being built into it. Item analyses were performed using the sixth edition as a criterion.

Problems

7 What kinds of pupils might profit from the spiral omnibus arrangement of the *Otis* tests?

8 Would you expect a higher correlation of *Otis* IQ's with *Stanford-Binet* IQ's or the *WISC* IQ's? Why?

9   What major weakness can you see in the *CTMM?*

10   What advantages can you see in the *Kuhlmann-Anderson* which neither the *Otis* nor the *CTMM* appears to have? What particular advantage does the first have for the intellectually superior child?

11   Compare and evaluate the method of determining validity of the *Kuhlmann-Anderson* with that of the *Otis* or *CTMM.*

12   If you were given the choice among these three group tests of scholastic aptitude, which would you select for a sixth-grade class? Why?

SCHOLASTIC APTITUDE TEST. As more and more high school pupils become interested in going to college, it appears that many admissions offices will rely heavily on test scores as one of the criteria for selecting students. To provide these scores, several independent testing agencies develop tests, arrange for their administration, score the answer sheets, and report information to the pupil and the college to which he wishes to gain admission.

The College Entrance Examination Board *Scholastic Aptitude Test* (SAT) is probably the oldest test for this purpose. Generally, the pupil takes these tests during his senior year in high school. However, because there were demands to have these test scores before the last high-school year, the *Preliminary Scholastic Aptitude Test* was made available to juniors in secondary schools.

The SAT is generally administered five times each year at designated centers throughout the country. Application is made to the College Entrance Examination Board in order to register for the examinations. There are two parts to the *Scholastic Aptitude Test*, the *Verbal* and *Mathematical* sections. Items are of the best-answer multiple-choice type, requiring three hours of working time.

The candidate who has read widely, so that his vocabulary and skill are well developed, has a definite advantage in the verbal section over a peer with the same native ability but inadequately developed verbal skill. Performance on this test depends on developed skills rather than knowledge of specific information. The quantitative part of the test is also a measure of ability for dealing with concepts rather than mathematical achievement. Although a knowledge of elementary mathematics is necessary, emphasis is on the pupil's application of basic knowledge in the solution of problems. The ceiling of this test is high enough to discriminate among able pupils even though their training in formal mathematics may be limited.

AMERICAN COLLEGE TESTING PROGRAM. Another program for testing college-bound pupils has been developed under the auspices of the Measurement Research Center in Iowa. The American College Testing Program (ACT) offers a basic battery of four tests in the fields on English, mathematics, social studies, and the natural sciences. This battery can predict college success, and like other widely used scholastic aptitude tests, includes items sampling the intellectual skills of solving problems which require mathematical reasoning and interpreting passages.

THE COLLEGE QUALIFICATION TESTS. Other tests are available for colleges wishing to do their own testing. The *College Qualification Tests* (*CQT*) requires eighty minutes and provides a total score as well as part scores measuring verbal ability, numerical reasoning, and information with separate scores for science (biology, chemistry, and physics) and social science.

SCHOOL AND COLLEGE ABILITY TESTS. The *SCAT* was developed to replace the *American Council on Education Psychological Examinations*. It is a scholastic aptitude test with a comparatively heavy emphasis on academic achievement.

There are four parts in the test. Part I is a sentence-meaning test. In each item one word is missing, and this word is to be selected from five choices. Part II is arithmetical computation but numerical reasoning is involved. Part III is a vocabulary test. Part IV tests the pupil's skill in numerical problem solving. Parts I and III give verbal scores while Parts II and IV provide quantitative scores. Percentile "bands" for verbal and quantitative aptitude are plotted to obtain a pupil profile.

This test also reflects the trend toward greater emphasis on achievement for the prediction of academic success. The test content is largely material taught in school. In their manual, the authors say the test should determine the capacity of the pupil to continue his schooling successfully. They further state that the tests measure "school-learned abilities" rather than characteristics giving an indirect measurement of capacity to learn.

THE NATIONAL MERIT SCHOLARSHIP EXAMINATION. Still another college aptitude program was initiated in 1955. Under the auspices of the National Merit Scholarship Corporation, it has aroused public interest in scholarship aid for talented youth. At the beginning of each school year, all secondary schools in the United States and its territories are invited to select pupils to take the examination, which is administered through a private testing agency.

On the basis of scores from the selecting test, which measures both the aptitude and achievement of the student, semi-finalists are named. Semi-finalists then are administered the *SAT*. Along with other data, including school records, recommendations, outside activities, work, and so forth, scholarships are awarded in each state roughly proportional to the number of high school graduates in that state. In addition to the National

Merit Scholarships, the Corporation also awards scholarships provided by industry, foundations, and individuals.

PREPARING FOR THE TESTS. Teachers wonder if they can prepare pupils for these tests by tutoring them. The effect of coaching for College Entrance Examination Board *Scholastic Aptitude Test* has been studied extensively (College Entrance Examination Board, 1965 b). Scores obtained by groups coached in private and public schools and by groups given intensive individual tutoring were compared with scores obtained by matched control groups with no special training. Results show that special coaching increased test scores only very slightly. On the average, the increase was ten points or fewer. Remember that the scale extends from 200 to 800; the gains in question are much less than the standard error of measurement of the test.

These findings are not strange. Scholastic aptitude tests require both innate ability and achievement. To demonstrate this fact, solve the problems below:

If 5 post cards cost y cents, how many cents will 15 post cards cost? (A) 3y (B) 15y (C) 5y (D) 75y (E) 16y.

The answer is 3y. However, the purpose of the problem is not to determine whether the pupil can multiply 3 by y, which is one computation that might be used in determining the answer, but to determine if he knows how to attack the solution of the problem—finding the cost of one post card and then 15. Nevertheless, it is obvious that if he cannot divide 15 by 5 correctly and then state the produce of 3 and y, his answer will be wrong. Therefore, achievement in mathematics is basic to success in this test.

The following analogy is similar to those found in the *Verbal* section of the SAT (College Entrance Examination Board, 1965 a):

Trigger: Bullet::   (A) handle: drawer   (B) holster: gun
                      (C) bulb: light   (D) switch: current
                      (E) pulley: rope

The purpose of the item is to determine the examinee's ability to see the relationship among these words rather than to measure his understanding of each. However, the examinee has to know the meanings of trigger, bullet, switch, and current to select response *D* as the correct answer.

Teachers can do nothing to increase the innate intellectual capacity of their pupils, but can do much to improve their effective intelligence. Verbal and mathematical facility are based on good intellectual ability, but poor achievement in language and mathematics precludes the use of this ability. If it were possible to select two pupils of equal capacity, the one who had read widely, had a broad vocabulary, and had developed critical skills in reading and thinking, would be at an advantage in taking the various scholastic aptitude tests. Pupils pay a penalty for a meager educational environment and rightfully so, since pupils with these deficiencies will not do as well in future school work.

Individual vs. Group Tests

The individual intelligence test can be administered to only one person at a time. The only numerical limitation on a group intelligence test are the facilities and proctors available. Administering group tests is not difficult in most instances, although certain problems arise when young children are being tested.

The examiner must cope with their short attention span and their difficulties in following instructions. However, he can be trained rather quickly for group test administration. The same is not true for the individual test; special training is necessary if the examiner is to capitalize on the testing situation to learn something of the individual's work habits and personality. One of the most important factors in any test administration is motivating the examinee to optimum performance. It is much easier to obtain good motivation when the examiner's attention can be concentrated on one person. In group testing, disinterest, lapses of attention and effort are more difficult to determine.

Scoring of responses on individual tests tends to be more subjective than on group tests. Although scoring guides are furnished, the examiner must interpret the correctness of the response. For example, in the *Stanford-Binet Vocabulary* the examinee is asked, "What is an orange?". The response "tree" is listed as a correct answer but "lemon" is not. The *Memory for Designs* test at years nine and eleven requires the examinee to reproduce two designs after looking at them for ten seconds. In scoring, he is allowed full credit for the A designs but only one-half credit for the B design shown in Figure 24. On the other hand, a group test is generally scored in terms of the number of items right and, in most instances, no such fine interpretation need be made. As a matter of fact, a clerk can score as well as a test specialist, and machine scoring can also be employed.

Each type of test has advantages and disadvantages. The group test is used more in the schools because it does not require highly trained personnel for administration and is more economical in time and cost to administer. An individual intelligence test should be administered when one suspects that group-test results are invalid. Because the group test emphasizes reading ability more than the individual test, considerable caution should be exercised lest a low score be interpreted as lack of native ability rather than as low reading achievement.

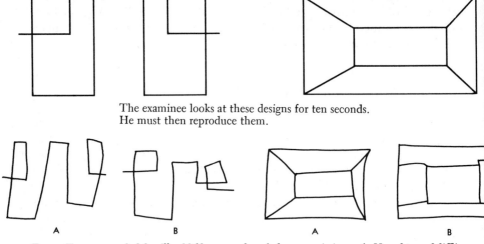

The examinee looks at these designs for ten seconds.
He must then reproduce them.

From Terman and Merrill, 1960; reproduced by permission of Houghton Mifflin Company.

FIGURE 24

MEMORY FOR DESIGNS—STANFORD-BINET SCALE YEARS IX AND XI

PROBLEMS

13   Bill received an IQ of 107 on the *Otis* and 107 on the *Stanford-Binet*. What justification can you see for the additional time and expense involved in the use of the individual test?

14   Tom's score was in the low range of mental ability on all group standardized tests given in elementary school. His achievement was also low. An alert sixth-grade teacher took a special interest in this, because Tom's answers during recitation periods showed evidence of good thinking. He felt that the root of Tom's difficulties might be reading. Describe a convenient way to obtain useful test data concerning his opinion.

Verbal vs. Performance and Nonlanguage Tests

Performance tests generally require the subject to manipulate some object, put parts of a figure or picture together, set up a color design, and so forth. Generally they call for individual administration and are often designed for those individuals with some physical anomaly, such as speech or hearing for illiterates, or for those who cannot speak English. Scoring procedures vary. In some instances, only the time to complete the test is recorded. In other tests, the examiner scores the number of moves in addition to keeping a time record, and sometimes tabulates false movements.

Nonlanguage tests are paper-and-pencil tests designed for group administration. No knowledge of written or spoken language is necessary, and although some test instructions are given orally, they are very simple and can be translated into another language without affecting test validity. Pantomime is often used to clarify instructions. Test items may require a subject to complete paper-and-pencil mazes, determine the number of cubes in a pile, complete a series in which X's and O's have different patterns of arrangement, mark identical pairs of numbers, draw in missing parts of pictures, and solve a spatial relations test.

One test requires the examinee to determine which geometric figure cuts another into parts of a certain shape; find missing parts on reversed geometric figures; determine the resulting design of a pattern synthesis, in which two geometric figures are superimposed; and the examinee must determine the next position of a sequence of geometric figures in a movement sequence; determine spatial relations in a manikin test, in which the position of the manikin is changed and the correct figure in terms of hand placement must be determined; and identify, in paper folding, how the paper would look after it had been folded, cut, and opened again (Pintner, 1945).

It should be understood that both the performance and nonlanguage tests measure different aspects of intelligence from those measured by verbal tests. It is doubtful if they tap higher-order abilities, since the verbal tests demand the manipulation of verbal symbols through thinking. In general, performance and nonlanguage tests rely on spatial and perceptual abilities.

The tests are useful in supplementing data obtained from verbal tests on certain occasions. A child who has failed in school may not be motivated to do items on a verbal test so similar to school work. On the contrary, he may find the tasks in performance and nonverbal tests novel and exciting. Performance tests are also helpful to the clinician in his observation of a child's behavior, but require training beyond that of the average teacher. Despite certain limitations, the verbal test is a better instrument for prediction of academic success.

PROBLEMS

15 What place would you allocate to performance and nonlanguage tests in a public school testing program? Defend your answer.

16   In your opinion, what is the major drawback of the performance or non-language test? Could this be overcome?

Culture-Fair Tests

This type of test is sometimes spoken of as a *culture-free* test, which, of course is not an accurate description. Every individual's development bears the imprint of some culture. The concern is that the typical scholastic aptitude test is unfair to those reared in a deprived environment. We often question whether our commonly used tests give a valid indication of a pupil's intelligence when he comes from an unstimulating environment where verbal communication is not valued.

Various kinds of items have been utilized in an attempt to avoid penalizing this kind of pupil. Mazes, symbol copying, classification of pictures, explaining the essence of a picture, and identification of similar drawings have been employed. Because speed is a cultural factor, it has been de-emphasized. Tests placing a premium on quick recall have not been used.

Despite an attempt to eliminate cultural bias, studies in general show that lower-class children do not perform any better on this type of test than on other tests of mental ability.

Stroud (1957, p. 85) writes that:

> . . . We may find that the problem is really too big for the test author. It may turn out that the kinds of cultural impact associated with social class differences affect the course of *mental development* of children as well as their performance on intelligence tests.
>
> Social class differences are real differences, substantial psychological phenomena with which schools and society must deal. It may be that we cannot build valid intelligence tests which will not at the same time discriminate among the social classes. Or, if we start the other way round by designing tests which will not discriminate among social classes, we may find that the tests are poor predictors of academic achievement.

Educational Loading

Cronbach (1960, p. 235) has constructed a chart for comparing various tests of scholastic aptitude (see Figure 25). Note that he has arranged the tests along a spectrum from those measuring educational achievement (maximal educational loading) to those that are independent of specific instruction (minimum educational loading). He points out the difference in functions of the tests at either end of the spectrum. Those with maximum educational loading are designed to predict future school achievement. Evidence indicates that a pupil receiving low scores on these tests is likely to be a poor achievement risk. If, however, a counselor is

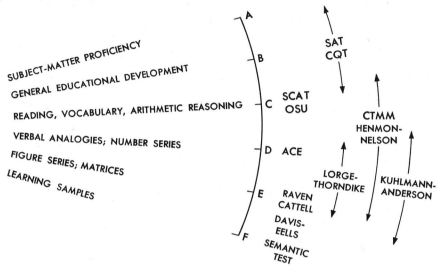

MAXIMUM EDUCATIONAL
LOADING

SUBJECT-MATTER PROFICIENCY

GENERAL EDUCATIONAL DEVELOPMENT

READING, VOCABULARY, ARITHMETIC REASONING

VERBAL ANALOGIES; NUMBER SERIES

FIGURE SERIES; MATRICES

LEARNING SAMPLES

A

B

SAT
CQT

C SCAT
OSU

CTMM
HENMON-
NELSON

D ACE

LORGE-
THORNDIKE

KUHLMANN-
ANDERSON

E RAVEN
CATTELL
DAVIS-
EELLS
SEMANTIC
TEST

F

MINIMUM EDUCATIONAL
LOADING

From Cronbach, 1960; reproduced by permission of Harper & Row.

FIGURE 25

SPECTRUM FOR COMPARING TESTS OF SCHOLASTIC APTITUDE

(Note: Tests with which you are unfamiliar are discussed in Buros' *Mental Measurements Yearbooks*.)

concerned with the potentialities of a pupil, then tests at *E* and *F* on the spectrum would be more helpful. It is further suggested that if the purpose is to compare individuals with diverse educational and cultural backgrounds, the tests from *D* to *F* are most desirable. Those at *F* will best serve when backgrounds are extremely different.

We must carefully consider the criterion behavior that we are predicting. If our concern is with average academic performance in a number of subjects, then a test which samples various abilities such as reasoning, perception, language, mathematics, and memory will be more effective than one that samples skills less widely. On the other hand, if we wish to predict achievement in a particular subject, then a test with high content validity in that subject may well be an excellent aptitude test.

Mental Age

When buying clothing for school-age children, we do not ask for something to fit a ten-year-old; we ask for a definite size because children of the same age vary. Intelligence testing is the same; pupils of the same age do not have the same amount of intelligence. The outstanding feature of the *Stanford-Binet Scale* is that the tests are grouped according to the age at which a majority passed. For example, if a child passes the items at the ten-year level and fails those at the eleven-year level, he has a mental age of ten. If his chronological age is less than ten, he is bright; if his chronological age is greater than ten, he is duller than average. In actual practice, a child may receive a mental age of ten and yet miss some items in the scale below the ten-year level and pass some above this level.

Mental age may be determined in other tests from the raw score, such as the total number of items correct. The mean raw score earned by a particular age group in the standardization sample would represent the mental age for the group. If the group were seven-year-olds, the mental age would be seven. A child who makes a raw score equal to the average of seven-year-olds would, therefore, have a mental age of seven. It should be emphasized that the mental age in itself tells us nothing about the brightness of the child. It refers only to the level of mental development.

Other characteristics inherent in the concept of mental age make interpretation difficult. Unlike the measurement of height or weight, no absolute zero point exists, and it would be difficult to define the point of no intelligence in a human being. Moreover, mental age units are unequal. As the individual grows older, the mental age units represent decreasing development. Since the increase in mental age units compared to the increase in the CA is quite small, the concept of MA becomes meaningless for pupils in their late teens. Actually, the growth pattern is not unlike that for height. Between two and four years of age, there is a much greater increase than between the years of sixteen and eighteen. It is for this reason that percentile ranks and standard scores, rather than IQ's, are used for older pupils.

Another problem is in the interpretation of identical mental ages of two pupils who have different chronological ages. If mental age is assumed to represent a pupil's level of mental capacity, then an MA of eight represents the same degree of intellectual maturity no matter if one child has a CA of six and another a CA of ten. However, these two pupils are quite different intellectually. Further difficulties in the interpretation of the MA must be dealt with when extrapolating to determine an IQ-value for the superior pupil. How does one interpret a mental age of twenty-two obtained from the norm table when the mean adult mental age on the test is fifteen years?

We should not conclude from this discussion or from recent trends indicating use of the DIQ (see page 375) that the MA has no value. When the teacher recognizes the limitations of the concept of mental age, it can be of help in suiting a learning task to the pupil's ability. We know that the understanding of concepts in number, time, and distance requires a certain degree of mental maturity. Much research about teaching children to read has established that general intelligence is the most important factor in reading readiness; mental age is closely related to the pupil's success or failure. Harris (1961, pp. 32–33) summarizes the evidence as follows:

1. There is a substantial relationship between mental age and ease of learning to read; most children who fail in reading in the first grade have mental ages below six years. The more mature children not only learn more easily but also retain what they learn better than the less mature children.

2. Most children who have normal IQ's, and who have MA's above six years, and are free from special handicaps, can be successfully taught to read in the first grade. However, a delayed start does the children no harm.

3. It is not possible to set a definite minimum mental age for learning to read, because too many other factors are involved. Children with mental ages as low as five years can be taught to read first-grade materials. There seems to be no lasting advantage in such an early start, however, and many of these children fail to make any headway when the pace of instruction is geared to the progress of older or brighter children.

Intelligence Quotient

Information concerning a child's rate of mental development is also useful to the teacher. He needs to know whether the child is maturing more or less rapidly than the average child. If his mental age is greater than his chronological age, he is brighter and will eventually be more mentally mature than his duller peers. Other things being equal, he will be a more rapid learner.

Levels of intelligence have been classified in relation to IQ-intervals, as listed in Table 16. These descriptive levels are helpful in communicating about individuals with different degrees of intelligence and in roughly predicting job success. It is well to remember that these classifications are useful guides, not rigid divisions.

CONSTANCY OF THE IQ. How stable is the IQ of an individual? Does it effectively predict an individual's ability over a long period of time? This question is of great importance in educational and vocational planning. You will recall that intelligence is implied from an intelligence test score. Test intelligence demands achievement as a means for sampling innate ability; inherited capacity cannot be measured directly. Heredity and environment are also relatively important, and if heredity is more significant, and if we could measure it accurately, it might yield a more stable

TABLE 16
DISTRIBUTION OF INTELLIGENCE QUOTIENTS FROM
THE 1937 REVISION OF THE STANFORD-BINET SCALE

IQ	Percentage	Classification
160–169	0.03	Very superior
150–159	0.2	
140–149	1.1	
130–139	3.1	Superior
120–129	8.2	
110–119	18.1	High average
100–109	23.5	Normal or average
90–99	23.0	
80–89	14.5	Low average
70–79	5.6	Borderline defective
60–69	2.0	
50–59	0.4	
40–49	0.2	Mentally defective
30–39	0.03	

score. If environment were more important, its influence could vary from time to time and change measurement. We have reason to believe that both heredity and environment influence effective intelligence. Someone has said that "heredity sets the limit, while environment determines how closely an individual approaches this limit." In other words, probably no individual fully develops his innate capacity; nevertheless, heredity is generally considered the more important of the two variables.

Unreliability of measuring instruments may result in the conclusion that the IQ is less stable than is really warranted. Even a test-retest on different forms of the *Stanford-Binet* administered very close together causes a considerable variance in scores for the same individual (Terman & Merrill, 1960). Another limitation of some tests is their lack of an adequately high top score for the brighter pupils in a recommended grade range (Stanley, 1951). The average college freshman has a mental age of around sixteen and one-half years; average college graduates test around eighteen. Graduate students have an average mental age of eighteen and one-half, and those who earn Ph.D.'s in the natural sciences have a mental age of nineteen and one-half, which corresponds to a childhood intelligence quotient of about 130 (Wolfle and Oxtoby, 1952). Suppose John receives an IQ of 160 on the *Stanford-Binet* at nine years of age, which is equivalent to a mental age of about fourteen years and five months; if his IQ does not change, at age fifteen he will have a mental age of about twenty-four. When he is in the tenth grade, tests designed for this grade level are not difficult enough to measure his ceiling, and college tests have no norms for bright youngsters of his age. These tests would have more validity, however, than tests at his grade level.

> Most upper-half tenth-graders in typical schools can be measured adequately by tests designed for Grades IX–XII. A crude but perhaps helpful way to determine the adequacy of a score is to note the number of points it falls short of the maximum possible score; this might well be at least three times the standard error of measurement of the test. If the difference is less than this amount, try administering a higher level of the test or a more advanced test to the student. Testing, like all other phases of teaching, must be individualized. Few instruments are adequate throughout the entire range of abilities found in typical classrooms. At least three different levels are usually needed for optimum assessment of differences among individuals in a single grade. For this reason, the actual range of talent within a class will often be greater than it appears on the basis of only one test. The least able students are crowding the "floor," while the ablest one are bumping their heads on the "ceiling" (Stanley, 1954, p. 33).

The results yielded by tests administered periodically over a number of years have shown that mental growth is uneven (Bayley, 1949; 1955; Freeman and Flory, 1937). Note the fluctuations in the individual mental growth curves of the five boys in Figure 26. Freeman and Flory (1937) point out that growth curves do not indicate which of several explanations cause these fluctuations. Possible causes could be transitory psychological or physical conditions, such as rapport between the examiner and the subject, or illness. On the other hand, the irregularities might reflect real changes in intellectual maturity.

Bayley's studies (1933; 1949) are in agreement with other longitudinal studies that provide correlational results with regard to a pupil's relative standing in a group. A pupil tends to change in his relative position in the group in relation to the amount of time between tests. Less shifting of relative position occurs with increasing age. Reporting the age of the pupil at the time of testing along with the name of the test is therefore important in considering the constancy of the IQ.

Pinneau (1961) emphasizes other considerations. Because standard deviations of conventional IQ's for a given test vary from age to age, he draws certain conclusions. First of all, the same relative standing in a group may result from very different scores at different ages. He explains how, on the 1937 edition of the *Stanford-Binet*, a pupil's IQ might be 125 at age 6 and 140 at age 12. For the same reason another pupil may have an IQ of 75 at 6 years and 60 at 12 years. Both pupils maintained the same relative

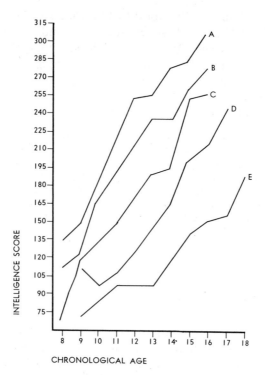

From Freeman and Flory, 1937, p. 56; reproduced by permission of the authors and the Society for Research in Child Development.

FIGURE 26

MENTAL GROWTH OF FIVE BOYS

position in their age groups, and change in their IQ's was a result of changes in the size of the variability. Another conclusion is that the same change in IQ for two different pupils may indicate a different relative standing. Two six-year-olds may drop 15 points in IQ by the age of 12— one from 75 to 60 and the other from 125 to 110. The former does not change in relative position; the second drops from the 87th to the 69th percentile of his age group. Finally, the IQ's of pupils who are tested at an age when the conventional IQ variabilities are large as compared to those of pupils tested at an age when these variabilities are small designate a different amount of change in relative position. Suppose two pupils have conventional IQ's of 90 and they show a 20-point increase on a second test. If the first pupil was tested at the ages of 2 and 12, and the second at ages 5 and 17, the first child changes from the 31st to the 69th percentile and the second from the 24th to the 76th percentile on the second test.

When an individual is tested with different instruments, the measured IQ's are likely to differ. Hence, in reporting an IQ, it should always be identified with the test from which it is derived; e.g., IQ (*Otis, Beta, Form F*) = 93. For a given pupil, test scores from different scholastic aptitude tests may differ greatly (Knezevich, 1946).

CONCLUSIONS. We may conclude that the IQ of an individual is, in general, quite stable throughout his life if we consider it to be a rough classification. Certainly, the child with a high IQ will tend to remain an individual with considerable intellectual prowess. A pupil who has an IQ well below 100 will probably become an adult who functions on a lower intellectual level, unless the score is the result of poor academic efficiency. We are assuming also that the IQ is not based on an infant test since such tests are quite unreliable. Because of the numerous factors that may influence test scores, a teacher should never rely on the results of a single test. In addition to other test scores, data obtained through observation, for example, should be used to evaluate mental maturity.

PROBLEMS

17 An elementary school is grouping pupils in the intermediate grade levels according to MA as measured by a good standardized test. Is this defensible? Explain.
18 When you make the statement, "John has an IQ of 86," what are you *really* saying?
19 There is much current controversy concerning making school records available to parents, including the reporting of actual IQ-scores. Should this be done? Can you justify your answer?
20 Compare the growth curve of mental age with that of chronological age of elementary school pupils.

CREATIVITY

Creativity is difficult to define. Generally, we say that to be creative is to be original. Such originality could be directed toward frivolous activities or highly productive ones. It can be an expression of the inner states of the creator, an effort to meet specific, external needs and goals, or a combination of the two (Carnegie Corporation, 1961).

Despite some criticism of the work of Getzels and Jackson (1962), their research has stimulated a great deal of interest in creativity. In essence, they conclude that pupils making the highest scores on "intelligence" tests are not necessarily the most creative. In their intensive review of the literature, Gaier and White (1965) list four directions that creativity research has taken: (a) the nature and quality of the product created, (b) the actual expression of creative acts and the continuing intellectual process during the creation, (c) the nature of the creator, and (d) environmental factors that fostered creativity. The authors pointed out that unfortunately little empirical research is grounded in theory. Taylor (1964) concludes that biographical items and measures of past achievement appear to be better predictors of creativity than self-ratings, inventories and traditional aptitude and general intelligence measures. At this point, we should not overrate creativity tests at the expense of general intelligence tests. For selection purposes particularly, much more needs to be learned about the stability of standings on creativity tests.

MECHANICAL APTITUDE

Mechanical aptitude is actually made up of a number of quite specific aptitudes. Among those identified through research studies are perceptual, spatial, and mechanical reasoning ability. Manual dexterity should also be included. Moreover, mechanical aptitude is affected by knowledge of mechanical information and experience with mechanics.

Single tests used to measure mechanical aptitude do not sample all these factors. Also, jobs requiring mechanical skill differ in their demands for these specific aptitudes. Although certain tasks require a great deal of manual dexterity, others demand perceptual and spatial abilities. This fact explains in some degree why, in general, the current tests of mechanical aptitude cannot claim high predictive validity. The factors included in the test as well as on the job must both be known. It is important that other means of evaluation, such as observation of performance in shops and a careful study of the record of experience, be used in counseling pupils on mechanical aptitude.

Minnesota Paper Form Board Test

Available tests for measuring mechanical aptitude may be classified either as paper-and-pencil or performance tests. They may also be categorized as measures of perceptual and spatial abilities, as assembly tests, or as tests of mechanical information. Various means are used to measure perceptual and spatial abilities, including construction puzzles, form boards, and paper-and-pencil tests. One of the most popular paper-and-pencil tests is the revision of the *Minnesota Paper Form Board Test*. It consists of items having two-dimensional diagrams cut into separate parts (see Figure 27). The subject chooses one figure out of five that he believes to be made up of the exact parts shown in the original diagram. Numerous validity studies have proved its usefulness in selecting personnel for various mechanical jobs. It possesses some validity for predicting academic success in art, dentistry, drafting, and geometry. It is particularly helpful in

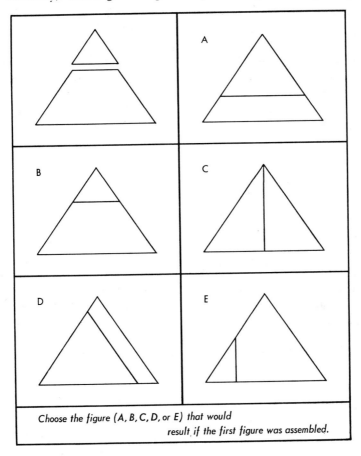

Choose the figure (A, B, C, D, or E) that would result if the first figure was assembled.

Reproduced by permission of The Psychological Corporation.

FIGURE 27
SAMPLE ITEM FROM THE REVISED MINNESOTA PAPER FORM BOARD

measuring an individual's ability to visualize and manipulate objects in space. Reliability coefficients vary between 0.80 and 0.92.

Minnesota Mechanical Assembly Test

In assembly tests the subject works with parts in putting a mechanical object together. One of the better known assembly tests is the *Minnesota Mechanical Assembly Test*, a revision of the *Stenquist Assembly Test*. The test consists of a series of mechanical contrivances, such as a monkey wrench, hose clamp, bicycle bell, spring clothespin, spark plug, flat iron, that can be easily assembled. Most individuals could be successful with the tests if they had enough time. Therefore, time limits are rigidly controlled. Speed is a basic factor for successful completion of the tests.

The instrument is designed for subjects eleven or older. It has not, however, proved particularly valid for women and girls, and mechanically apt men find it too easy. Also, the test is less reliable for men than for junior high school boys. The short form is considerably less reliable than the original test.

Bennett Mechanical Comprehension Test

The *Bennett Mechanical Comprehension Test* is a paper-and-pencil test that can be used with high school pupils and adults and measures an individual's understanding of mechanical and physical relationships. Items consist of pictures illustrating principles of mechanics, fluid pressures, and so forth. Questions related to the pictures have two or three alternatives. Unfortunately, there is little information available on the test's empirical validity. One of the tests in the *Differential Aptitude Test* battery; namely, the *Mechanical Reasoning Test* (see page 407), is similar to the *Bennett*.

Motor Tests

One of the more specific aspects of mechanical aptitude is motor dexterity. A number of tests have been constructed to determine the ability of a subject to manipulate objects. In general, such manual tests require the subject to do any of a number of tasks within specified time limits, such as place pins into holes in a board with the fingers or with a tweezer (*O'Connor Finger Dexterity Test* and *O'Connor Tweezer Dexterity Test*); remove circular blocks from holes, turn them over and replace them

(*Stromberg Dexterity Test*); or use hand tools to loosen and tighten nuts on bolts (*Hand-Tool Dexterity Test*).

Although the reliability of these tests is generally adequate, the same cannot be said of validity. In addition, validity must be judged in terms of the very specific motor tasks of a particular job. Therefore, motor tests are not very useful in the school where the counselor is much more concerned with the broader aspects of pupils' mechanical aptitudes.

PROBLEMS

21 For each of the three tests of mechanical aptitude discussed, describe a situation in a public school in which it might prove to be a useful tool.
22 Can you give any reasons why the degree of validity of motor dexterity tests may be frequently inadequate?

SENSORY APTITUDES

The classification of sensory aptitudes may not at first seem logical, since it includes but a few of the more discrete aptitudes that are the basis for the more global aptitudes already discussed. They are included because of the teacher's concern with certain aspects of vision and hearing.

Vision

Visual examinations are common in our schools, and the most widely used is the *Snellen Test*. The test or modifications of it have become standard for industry, doctors, and schools. Two types of charts are recommended: for those who cannot read, the *E* chart; for other pupils, the letter chart. The symbols on both charts decrease in size with the large letters at the top and the small ones at the bottom. Both charts are to be read from a distance of twenty feet. The subject can show with three fingers the direction in which the *E* of the *E* chart points. He calls out the names of the letters on the letter chart. The adequacy of his vision is determined by the size of the symbols he can read.

The efficiency of the *Snellen Test* and other visual screening tests has been the topic of several investigations. One widely quoted study was conducted in 1948 and 1949 (Crane and others, 1954). The conclusion of this research was that when vision tests are administered under the conditions of the present directions, the *Snellen Test* and the *Massachusetts Vision Test* give better agreement with clinical judgment than other visual tests that can be used in the schools.

A study by Kelley (1951) criticizes the foregoing study. The author states:

> This misconception that the *Snellen* chart will do an effective job of screening out children who need visual care is a major block in the road of those who are trying to establish good school visual screening programs. The fact is that any school which relies on the *Snellen* chart alone as a screening method will fail to detect large numbers of children in urgent need of visual care (Kelley, 1951, p. II–11).

The author concludes from the results of his study that a minimal screening program must include the following tests:

1. A test of the visual acuity of each eye at the far-point.
2. A test of the visual acuity of each eye at reading distance.
3. A test of lateral imbalance (phoria) at far-point.
4. A test of lateral imbalance at near-point.
5. A test of fusion. (Are both eyes seeing an object simultaneously?) (Kelley, 1951, p. V–4).

Hearing

In hearing, the teacher wants to know whether a child has difficulty hearing the ordinary conversation in the classroom. But even if the child can hear ordinary conversation, he may find it impossible to discriminate among letter sounds. If there is a differential loss at the higher frequencies, he may not be able to hear the consonants so important in learning to read. In the sentence "The boy ran around the house," the child may be able to make out the word *ran* even though he does not hear the sound of the *r*. However, he may not be able to differentiate between the sounds of *p* and *r* to find the meaning of a new word *pan*.

Although the "watch tick" and the "whispered speech" tests help detect hearing difficulties, their lack of standardization precludes the use of helpful norms. In these tests the examiner moves farther and farther away from the subject to determine the point at which the watch or the whisper can just be heard.

The pure tone audiometer used for group demonstration gives more reliable and valid results. One company manufactures an instrument that can be used as a pure tone audiometer or with spoken words; the intensity of the sound is controlled in both. When the spoken words are used, the subject has an answer sheet with a series of sets of three pictures each. This makes it necessary for the subject to differentiate among the three consonants in, for example, *rat, cat, hat.*

PROBLEMS

23 In your opinion, what are the major inadequacies in the *Snellen Test?*
24 What kinds of symptoms in the classroom by a pupil would justify a referral for a hearing test?

PROGNOSTIC TESTS

Prognostic tests are designed to predict a pupil's success in a specific subject. At the elementary level, reading readiness tests may be classified in this category. In the secondary school, tests of prognosis in algebra, geometry, foreign languages, and shorthand have been developed. Although these tests are supposedly designed to contain material from the field in question, this has not always proved true. In general, prognostic tests for secondary school pupils have declined in use. Differential test batteries have proved more helpful to the counselor since it is impractical to administer prognostic tests to all pupils for every subject. Only when large groups of pupils are being tested to predict skill in a particular area for which other test results may be unavailable, are they of great importance. This is particularly true in an area such as shorthand.

Probably the prognostic tests most widely used in our schools are those classified as reading readiness tests. Although these tests are very similar to scholastic aptitude tests, their content demands abilities that are specifically related to elementary reading skills. For example, a lesson situation may be presented in which the pupil's ability to learn words is demonstrated. Other items may test his ability to give the names of letters. He may also be instructed to match sounds. Whether a scholastic aptitude test or a reading readiness test best predicts reading achievement is debatable. Some evidence shows that general intelligence tests may better predict ultimate reading achievement, because reading at higher levels requires considerable verbal ability as measured by many general intelligence tests. On the other hand, the reading readiness tests may better predict early reading success because of their high content validity. Another factor to consider in a reading readiness test is its diagnostic value; teachers would do well to select tests with this attribute in mind in addition to the total test score.

PROBLEM

25   In an elementary school faculty meeting, a lively dispute arose over the relative need and importance of various standardized tests. Miss Brown argued strongly for the use of reading readiness tests. Miss Johnson said that the present group mental ability tests could serve the same purpose and warned against the danger of over-testing. Which teacher would you support? Why?

DIFFERENTIAL TESTING

Factor analysis studies show that individuals have different amounts of specific abilities. Knowledge of these abilities is helpful in educational and vocational guidance. General mental ability tests give us only a limited amount of information about an individual. Furthermore, there is reason to question even the supposedly "general" nature of these tests. Certainly, verbal comprehension contributes heavily to their scores.

One of the most interesting theoretical models classifying the factors of the intellect was proposed by Guilford. (1959; 1965). His model shown in Figure 28 provides for 120 cells, each corresponding to a potential factor. His threefold model includes the process of operation performed (cognition, memory, convergent thinking, divergent thinking, and evaluation), products (units, classes, relations, system, transformations, and implications), and contents (figural, symbolic, semantic, and behavioral). Although each cell has as yet not been identified, it proves most helpful in aiding the formulation of hypotheses for further research designed to explore the nature of the intellect.

Theoretically, it may some day be possible to predict any behavior from Guilford's model whether it be performance in algebra or architecture. However, at the present time, validity of available aptitude tests enables us to predict criterion behavior only within certain limits. In some of the widely used instruments, the verbal and quantitative scores are still the best predictors of academic success.

However, useful insights into a pupil's strengths and weaknesses may be found through a battery of tests standardized on the same population. A profile of aptitude scores can be determined and comparisons made among an individual's cognitive, perceptual, and sensory-motor aptitudes. Recently, batteries of tests standardized on the same population have made a comparison of scores more meaningful. Representative of this kind of test battery are the *Academic Promise Tests* (*APT*) designed for grades 6–9,

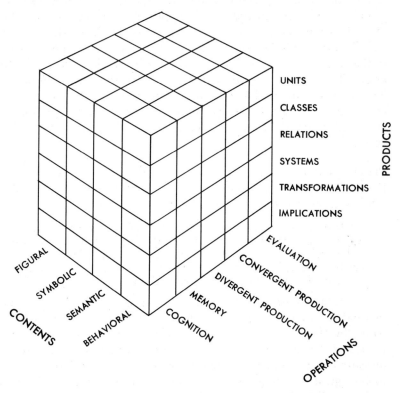

UNITS

CLASSES

RELATIONS

SYSTEMS

TRANSFORMATIONS

IMPLICATIONS

PRODUCTS

EVALUATION

CONVERGENT PRODUCTION

DIVERGENT PRODUCTION

MEMORY

COGNITION

OPERATIONS

FIGURAL

SYMBOLIC

SEMANTIC

BEHAVIORAL

CONTENTS

From Guilford, 1959; reproduced by permission of The American Psychologist.

FIGURE 28

THEORETICAL MODEL FOR THE COMPLETE "STRUCTURE OF INTELLECT"

the Differential Aptitude Test (DAT) for use in the secondary school, and the General Aptitude Test Battery (GATB) for ages sixteen and over. The DAT illustrates such differential testing instruments.

Differential Aptitude Test Battery

The Differential Aptitude Tests is a battery of eight tests: Verbal Reasoning, Numerical Ability, Abstract Reasoning, Space Relations, Mechanical Reasoning, Clerical Speed and Accuracy, Language Usage. The last test has two scores, Spelling and Grammar. Norms are also available for the combined Verbal Reasoning and Numerical Ability scores. The tests are essentially power tests, except the one on *Clerical Speed and Accuracy*, which is actually a speed test. Figure 29 contains two sample test items illustrating the approach. The first represents the *Abstract Reasoning Test*; the second represents the *Space Relations Test*.

By means of statistical procedures, content overlapping is minimized in the various tests, and the level of difficulty is related to the particular age group. These tests are published in groups in the case of *Forms L* and *M*. Two booklets are available, each containing four tests. A separate booklet containing only the *Verbal Reasoning* and the *Numerical Ability Tests* is also used. Since IBM answer sheets are available, the test booklets can be reused.

PROFILE CHART. The authors suggest the use of the profile chart in Figure 30, but they caution against interpreting the bars extending downward as negative and those upward as positive:

> If only the top twenty per cent on a given test are likely to succeed in a given course or job, it is not a "positive" sign to have a bar extending up to the sixty-fifth percentile. Conversely, if all but the lowest ten per cent may be expected to succeed, a bar extending down to the twentieth percentile mark is not "negative." (Bennett and others, 1966, p. III–5).

Through statistical formulas the authors arrived at a convenient method for approximating the significance of the differences between test scores by the use of a ruler on the Individual Report Form shown. The vertical distance between any two scores, as plotted on the form, can be measured. A real difference may be assumed to exist if the distance is one inch or greater. Differences between one-half inch and one inch should be evaluated along with other evidence, as the significance of the difference may be doubtful. Probably no important difference exists if the vertical distance beteen any two scores is less than one-half inch. (The measurements mentioned do not apply to the reduced chart in Figure 30.)

In Figure 30, the difference on the actual profile sheet in the length of bars representing *Verbal Reasoning* and *Clerical* measures over one inch, and we may assume that this is significant. Likewise, the difference between the *Clerical* score and each of the other scores except *Grammar* is also significant. On the other hand, the measured difference between the *Space Relations* and *Mechanical Reasoning* bars is only about one-fourth of an inch and therefore probably insignificant. The measured difference between the *Verbal Reasoning* and *Abstract Reasoning* bars is between one-half and one inch, the value of which is in question.

It is important that the individual tests in a battery have high reliability; it is also essential, however, that tests do not correlate highly with each other if important differences among the abilities of an individual are to be determined. The following tests gave the highest intercorrelations:

Abstract reasoning

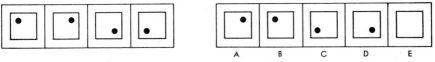

Study the position of the black dot. Note that it keeps moving around the square clockwise: upper left corner, upper right corner, lower right corner, lower left corner. In what position will it be seen next? It will come back to the upper left corner. Therefore, B is the answer, . . .

Space relations

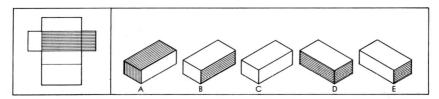

Notice—all the "boxes" made from this pattern are correct in shape, but the sides which you see are different. Some of these figures can be made from this pattern while others cannot. Let us look at them.

—Figure A is correct. If the large gray surface is shown as the top, then the end surface of gray can be shown facing towards you.

—Figure B is wrong. The long narrow side is not gray in the pattern.

—Figure C is correct. The two gray surfaces can both be hidden by placing the large gray surface at the bottom and the gray end to the back.

—Figure D is wrong. The gray end is all right, but there is no long gray side in the pattern.

—Figure E is correct. One can show the box so that the large gray surface is at the bottom (as it was in C), but with the gray end showing at the front. So, you see, there are three figures (A, C, and E) which can be made from the pattern, in example Y and two figures (B and D) which cannot be made from this pattern. Remember that the surface you see in the pattern must always be the OUTSIDE surface of the completed figure.

Reproduced by permission of The Psychological Corporation.

FIGURE 29
SAMPLE ITEMS FROM THE DIFFERENTIAL APTITUDE TESTS

Forms L and M

INDIVIDUAL
REPORT FORM

DIFFERENTIAL APTITUDE TESTS [1963 EDITION]

G. K. Bennett, H. G. Seashore, and A. G. Wesman

Name John Black

	Verbal Reasoning	Numerical Ability	VR + NA	Abstract Reasoning	Clerical Sp. & Acc.	Mechanical Reasoning	Space Relations	Language Spelling	Usage Grammar
Raw Score	36	33	69	43	46	55	46	80	30
Percentile	80	85	85	95	35	80	85	80	60

66F L 10 M

Profiling Your DAT Scores

The numbers that tell how you did on each test are in the row marked "Percentiles." Your percentile tells where you rank on a test in comparison with boys or girls in your grade. These percentiles are based on test scores earned by thousands of students in numerous schools across the country. If your percentile rank is 50, you are just in the middle — that is, one-half of the students in the national group did better than you and one-half did less well. (If your school uses local norms, your counselor will explain the difference.)

In the columns below each percentile you can draw your aptitude profile. For each test make a *heavy short line* across the column at the level which corresponds to your percentile rank on that test.

Your aptitude profile will be more visible if you black in each column *up to* or *down to* the 50-line from the short lines

you have just made. The vertical bars on your profile show the strength of your tested aptitudes, *up* or *down* from the rank of the *middle student* of your grade and sex.

Think of "percentile" as meaning "per cent of people." In your case, the people are boys or girls in your grade in many schools across the country. The percentile shows what per cent of this group scored no higher than you did. If your percentile rank on one test is 80, you are at the top of 80 per cent of the group scores — only 20 per cent made higher scores than yours. If you scored in the 25th percentile, this would mean about 75 per cent of the group did better than you on the test. Thus, a percentile rank always indicates your relative standing among a theoretical 100 persons representing a large "norm" group — in this case, students of your sex and grade. It does not tell how many questions (or what per cent of them) you answered correctly.

How Big a Difference Is Important?

Of course we do not want to over-estimate small differences in ability on tests because a test cannot be perfectly accurate, and your score might not be exactly the same if you could take the same test twice.

To estimate the importance of a difference between your scores on any two tests on this profile, use a ruler to measure how much higher on the chart one mark is than the other. It is the *vertical* distance } that counts, of course, *not* how far *across* the chart / or \

If the distance is *one inch or greater*, it is probable that you have a real difference in your abilities on the two tests.

If a difference between the two percentile ranks is *between a half inch and one inch*, consider whether other things you know about yourself agree with it; the difference may or may not be important.

If the vertical distance between two tests is *less than a half inch*, the difference between the two scores may be disregarded; so small a difference is probably not meaningful.

Reproduced by permission of The Psychological Corporation.

FIGURE 30

SAMPLE PROFILE FROM THE DIFFERENTIAL APTITUDE TESTS

Verbal Reasoning, Numerical Ability, and Grammar; Mechanical Reasoning, Abstract Reasoning, and Space Relations; Spelling and Grammar. Clerical Speed and Accuracy gave the lowest correlations. The average intercorrelation coefficients range from 0.06 to 0.67.

Through a formula utilizing both test reliability and intercorrelations among tests, the differentiating power of the tests was determined. It is believed that tests having a differentiating power of less than 25 per cent should not be used in differential diagnosis. When the formula was applied to all possible pairs among the eight tests for Form L, the 25 per cent value was exceeded for all twenty-eight differences among the girls and for twenty-seven differences among the boys. The results for Form M were the same for boys and slightly less satisfactory for the girls, due primarily to the lower reliability of the Mechanical Reasoning Test when administered to girls.

RELIABILITY. Reliability coefficients are available for each test, each grade, and for both sexes. These data, based on homogeneous and meaningful groups, are of basic importance for interpreting the test scores. The reliability coefficients for Forms L and M, varying from 0.79 to 0.94, were determined by the split-halves techniques except for the Clerical Speed and Accuracy Test. Average reliability coefficients varied from 0.87 to 0.94 for boys, and from 0.79 to 0.93 for girls. Both low coefficients, 0.87 and 0.79 are for the Mechanical Reasoning Test.

Measurements made with the DAT are found to be consistent over an appreciable span of time. The authors point out that this consistency results only in part from test reliability. If the trait measured is not constant, then of course it is impossible to obtain consistency in test scores. In one instance, pupils were tested in the ninth grade and again in the twelfth. The test-retest coefficients for a large group of pupils varied from 0.59 to 0.86. Verbal Reasoning and Spelling were two tests which reflected unusually great constancy of performance. Over this period of time, these data indicate good stability for these tests.

VALIDITY. Numerous validity studies resulting in over 4000 correlation coefficients have been reported on the Differential Aptitude Tests (Bennett and others, 1966). Investigations have included research in the prediction of course grades in secondary school and college, prediction of achievement test results, and prediction of vocational and educational success. An interesting graphic presentation in terms of the number of studies producing validity coefficients with a certain range are reported for final marks in English, mathematics, science, social studies, and history. Although a considerable range in these coefficients is reported for both boys and girls, certain patterns do stand out. The highest relationship with

English final marks exists with the tests of Verbal Reasoning plus Numerical Ability, Verbal Reasoning alone, and Grammar. The test correlating most highly with mathematics is Numerical Ability. Verbal Reasoning plus Numerical Ability, Verbal Reasoning alone, Numerical Ability alone, and Grammar are all highly related to science achievement. Finally, scores from these same tests also seem to be highly related to achievement in the social studies.

A follow-up study reported in the manual produced interesting data showing relationships between scores attained by high school pupils on the DAT and the vocational or educational choice made as college students. Among the groups studied, premedical students were especially high in Verbal Reasoning, Numerical Ability, and Spelling. The science group was outstanding in Numerical Ability. Engineering students were superior in Numerical Ability and much higher in Space Relations and Mechanical Reasoning than other student groups. The various unskilled groups had over-all low performance but average performance in Mechanical Reasoning. The skilled groups were below average in Numerical Ability, Space Relations, and Abstract Reasoning, but about average on the other tests.

In another follow-up study seven years later, the conclusions of the earlier report were reinforced. Profiles of high school pupils entering diverse occupational and educational careers varied widely from one another. For example, the engineers showed marked superiority in Numerical Ability, Mechanical Reasoning, and Spelling; on the other hand, the average of boys who entered the building trades was near the class average in Abstract Reasoning, Space Relations, and Clerical Speed and Accuracy.

The Differential Aptitude Tests represent a model of attention to detail of test construction and interpretation. The care that has been exercised in their development is so well presented in the four editions of the test manual that by studying these discussions, the reader can develop an understanding of the important considerations of test construction in general. However, despite this commendation, one must be aware that many of the reported validation coefficients are low.

PROBLEMS

26 Which test or tests from the DAT would appear to be most significant in terms of predicting (a) rank in class on high school graduation, (b) achievement in mathematics, (c) achievement in industrial arts, and (d) achievement in general science?

27 Figure 30 presents a DAT profile chart for a tenth-grade boy. Is this boy a potential college student? Can you predict areas of subject-matter difficulty for him? What might a vocational counselor point out in discussing this chart with John and his parents?

28 Validity studies on the *DAT* show that the *Verbal Reasoning Test* correlates highly with achievement in English and social studies. Why should this be so?

Use of Aptitude Tests in School

The aptitude test most commonly used by the classroom teacher is the so-called "intelligence" or scholastic aptitude test. Whether a test measures aptitude or achievement depends not so much on its content as on its function. A test at one time may be used to measure present achievement and at other times to predict future achievement. There is a high correlation between the scores on achievement tests and the so-called "intelligence" tests which are most commonly used to determine academic aptitude. If one compares items on the two kinds of tests, he is struck by their similarity.

However, as we have indicated, the commonly used tests of scholastic aptitude differ greatly. Choosing the right test for a given purpose requires careful consideration. Test specialists are not agreed on their utility. Some feel that tests of general mental ability are of limited utility, and argue that most of the uses to which they have been put can be better served by using properly constructed achievement tests of more specialized abilities (Davis, 1964, p. 137). Nevertheless, a pupil's academic potential must be determined and the scholastic aptitude test is helpful for this purpose.

Group, rather than individual tests of verbal mental ability are probably the most useful and can provide helpful information in any school testing program. Because of their economy and practicality, they do not require a trained examiner, and yet they tend to be as reliable as individual tests. For school use their degree of validity is satisfactory.

It must be emphasized, however, that at times a pupil does not give his optimum performance, and this invalidates the score. If the score seems to deviate widely from other data available, a teacher may want a child retested on an individual basis with an instrument such as the *Stanford-Binet* or the *WISC*. In administering the individual test, the examiner can observe the pupil and better evaluate the validity of the test. If personnel trained for administering individual tests are unavailable, another form of the group test already used or a different group test should be administered. The nonlanguage test is a helpful supplementary instrument for discovering pupils whose scores are affected by poor reading or general lack of verbal facility. Some tests give a language and a nonlanguage IQ in addition to a composite IQ, and are popular in some schools. However, in interpreting these scores, one must realize that differences may be due to error. At the secondary school level, differential aptitude testing may provide some information for educational as well as vocational counseling; yet testing alone should not be used as the only criterion for determining the aptitude of boys and girls. The alert teacher is aware of their interests, their performance in and out of the classroom, the kinds of questions they ask, and so forth. Complete evaluation is necessary for valid interpretation.

More and more secondary schools are realizing the importance of obtaining information about other aptitudes of their pupils. With the advent of differential testing, such instruments as the *Differential Aptitude Tests* have provided a means to identify the aptitude patterns in areas other than those most generally measured by the typical scholastic aptitude test. This added information enables the school to help all pupils plan their studies.

To be specific, a few of pupils' special problems more readily identified by differential testing are listed below:

1. The boy who is failing the verbally oriented courses, but who has excellent mechanical ability.
2. The boy from a bilingual home with few cultural opportunities who makes high scores on the *Numerical Ability, Mechanical Reasoning,* and *Space Relations* tests, but is failing in school.
3. The girl whose tested abilities are below average except for *Clerical Speed and Accuracy*.
4. The boy who aspires to be a physicist but whose numerical reasoning score is low.

The school must have adequate information about its superior pupils if it is to help them achieve. The gifted pupil is too often overlooked or unmotivated to continue his education. School authorities should identify such pupils and exercise every effort to appreciate and develop their talents.

It is also important to identify accurately the aptitude patterns of those who are less able. The common practice is to direct them into vocational courses without regard for any other criterion except that they are doing poorly in their academic classes. Yet, the chances of a pupil's succeeding in a commercial course are not good if his score on the *Clerical Speed and Accuracy Test* is low. In addition, the mechanically inept are not served best in a shop course. It is necessary to assign courses that correspond with the interests and abilities of all students.

PROBLEMS

29 What weight would you give to informal teacher observation of pupil scholastic aptitude as opposed to standardized test results?

30 In advising pupils about curriculum choice, what relative weights would you assign to aptitude scores as compared with school marks?

Summary

Schools are committed to help children develop according to their growth potential. It is therefore necessary to measure each child's aptitude to provide the best learning experiences for him. Aptitude testing has progressed from the general to the specific, and performance on general aptitude tests is closely related to school work. Such tests are called scholastic aptitude tests; some can be administered to one pupil at a time, others to groups.

Aptitude tests may be classified as either verbal, performance, or nonlanguage tests. To perform successfully on verbal tests, the subject must understand oral and often written language. Performance tests emphasize the manipulation of objects rather than verbal skill and are individual tests. Although some oral instructions in the administration of a non-language test may be required, in general, no written or spoken language is necessary to give correct responses. Instructions are simple and may even be translated to another language without invalidating the test. Non-language tests are constructed as paper-and-pencil tests and, unlike performance tests, are designed for group administration.

Because aptitude is affected by achievement and innate ability, consideration has been given to the construction of tests that would de-emphasize the role of the examinee's environment and are known as culture-fair tests. They vary in the degree to which they achieve their purpose, but there are substantial relationships between scores of these tests and the common scholastic aptitude tests.

The scores made by younger children on scholastic aptitude tests can be translated into mental ages or IQ's. There is a trend toward the replacement of the ratio IQ by the deviation IQ. A rough classification of an individual's IQ generally holds throughout life; that is, dull, normal, and bright children tend to become dull, normal, and bright adults.

Interest in special aptitudes focused attention on the construction of various tests to measure such specific ones as artistic, musical, and clerical aptitudes. The difficulties in using these instruments are that the standardization population is different for each test, and the units of measurement are not comparable, so that it is impossible to construct a meaningful profile for the examinee. At present an attempt has been made to solve these problems through differential measurement; a series of tests are standardized on the same population so that scoring units are comparable. Low and high scores made on these tests are used to interpret the pupil's strengths and weaknesses.

Suggested Readings

Anastasi, Anne. Psychological tests: uses and abuses. *Tchers. Coll. Rec.*, 1961, 62, 389–393.
> With the themes that no test can eliminate causality, and that a test score, however derived, cannot reveal the origin of the behavior it reflects, Anastasi suggests procedures for using tests more effectively in inner group comparisons describing present differences, investigating their origins in past events, and predicting future outcomes. This article is particularly appropriate in relation to the testing of "culturally-deprived" groups.

Carnegie Corporation. Creativity. *Carnegie Corp. of N.Y. quart.*, 1961, 9, 1–8.
> This issue is a report of research projects supported by the Carnegie Corporation directed at such questions as "What are creative individuals like as people? Do they have patterns of attitudes, values, interest, and personality that distinguish them from less creative persons? How does a creative person think? What effect has the environment on creativity?"

Davis, A. Cultural factors in remediation. *Educ. Horiz.*, 1965, 43, 231–251.
> The important aspect of this article is the discussion of the IQ and its relationship to cultural differences. He emphasizes the great variation in IQ among low socio-economic groups as well as those more fortunate groups of higher status. The author contends that genetic factors are not unequally distributed by socio-economic groups, and that powerful cultural influences affect problem solving of the kind required on scholastic aptitude tests.

Guilford, J. P. Intelligence: 1965 model. *Amer. Psychologist*, 1965, 21, 20–26.
> This is in part an answer to McNemar's article listed below. Guilford discusses the progress he has made in occupying additional cognitive cells in his model of the structure of the intellect that is shown in Figure 28 in this chapter.

Guthrie, F. A. What to look for in a review of an individual intelligence test. *Personnel & Guid. J.*, 1964, 43, 67–70.
> Although the discussion is oriented toward a review of the individual intelligence tests, the principles discussed are pertinent to all measures of scholastic aptitude.

Levine, A. S. Aptitude versus achievement tests as predictors of achievement. *Educ. psychol. Measmt*, 1958, 18, 517–525.
> The author suggests that aptitude and achievement tests are differentiated not so much by the nature of their content as to the use to which they are put. Two different types of achievement tests are discussed.

McCollum, H. W. Relationship of anxiety to intelligence test scores of tenth-grade students. *J. educ. Res.*, 1964, 58, 35–37.
> The hypothesis that high anxiety is related to low IQ-scores was not proven. However, a tendency of this nature was noted. The predicted relationship was stronger for girls than for boys.

NcNemar, Q. Lost: our intelligence? Why? *Amer. Psychologist*, 1964, 19, 871–882.
> The author makes a strong case for general intelligence as opposed to special abilities determined by factor analysis for predictive purposes. In addition,

he severely criticizes some of the research done in creativity. Note Guilford's article listed above for another point of view.

Millman, J., and M. D. Glock. Trends in the measurement of general mental ability. *Rev. educ. Res.*, 1965, **35**, 17–24.

The authors indicate that the environment of the young child, especially his educational experience, plays a key role in the development of intelligence. Therefore, intelligence tests are important in controlling the environment as well as in predicting future intellectual development.

Pinneau, S. R. *Changes in intelligence quotient, infancy to maturity.* Boston: Houghton Mifflin, 1961.

Four major topics are emphasized in this book. First, the constancy of the IQ from the early years to late adolescence is analyzed. Secondly, accurate mental age scores and revised IQ-tables for the *Stanford-Binet Intelligence Scales* have been developed. Thirdly, a table of IQ-changes with age has been prepared and explanations provided. Fourthly, consideration is given to the rate of mental maturation by individuals of different levels of ability.

Sigel, I. E. How intelligence tests limit understanding of intelligence. *Merrill-Palmer quart.*, 1963, **9**, 39–56.

The author relates evidence suggesting that general intelligence test scores are influenced by the cognitive style of the individual. This has implications not only for the construction of tests, but also for scoring them. He concludes that much more information could be obtained from tests.

Stalnaker, J. M. Psychological tests and public responsibility. *Amer. Psychologist*, 1965, **20**, 131–135.

The author discusses the National Merit Scholarship Program and alludes to some very interesting prediction problems. He is also concerned with the great social responsibility that those associated with the administration of this program accept.

Super, D. E., and J. O. Crites, *Appraising vocational fitness by means of psychological tests.* (Rev. ed.) New York: Harper & Row, 1962. Chapters 5, 6, 8, 9, and 10.

Separate chapters are devoted to intelligence tests, clerical tests, manual dexterity tests, and mechanical aptitude tests. Considerable detail is included.

References Cited

Allen, Mildred M. The relation between Kuhlmann-Anderson tests and achievement in grade IV. *J. educ. Psychol.*, 1944, **35**, 229–239.

Bayley, Nancy. Mental growth during the first three years. A developmental study of 61 children by repeated tests. *Genet. psychol. Monogr.*, 1933, **14**, 1–92.

Bayley, Nancy. Consistency and variability in the growth of intelligence from birth to 18 years. *J. genet. Psychol.*, 1949, **75**, 165–196.

Bayley, Nancy. On the growth of intelligence. *Amer. Psychologist*, 1955, **10**, 805–818.

Bennett, G. K., H. G. Seashore, and A. G. Wesman. *Differential Aptitude Tests, Forms L and M, manual.* (4th ed.) New York: Psychological Corporation, 1966.

Bradway, Katherine P., and Nancy M. Robinson. Significant I.Q. changes in twenty-five years: a follow-up. *J. educ. Psychol.*, 1961, **52**, 74–79.

Bradway, Katherine P., and Clare W. Thompson. Intelligence at adulthood: a twenty-five year follow-up. *J. educ. Psychol.*, 1962, **53**, 1–14.

Carnegie Corporation. Creativity. *Carnegie Corp of N.Y. quart.*, 1961, **9**, 1–8.

Cohen, J. The factorial structure of the WAIS between early adulthood and old age. *J. consult. Psychol.*, 1957, **21**, 283–290.

College Entrance Examination Board. *A description of the College Board Scholastic Aptitude Test.* New York: Author, 1965 (a).

College Entrance Examination Board. *Effects of coaching on Scholastic Aptitude Test scores.* New York: Author, 1965 (b).

Crane, Marian M., and others. *Screening school children for visual defects.* Washington: U.S. Department of Health, Education and Welfare, 1954.

Cronbach, L. J. *Essentials of psychological testing.* (Rev. ed.) New York: Harper and Row, 1960.

Davis, F. B. *Educational measurements and their interpretation.* Belmont, Calif.: Wadsworth, 1964.

Dearborn, W. F., and J. W. M. Rothney. *Predicting the child's development.* (2nd ed.) Cambridge: Sci-Art Publishers, 1963.

Freeman, F. N., and C. D. Flory. Growth in intellectual ability as measured by repeated tests. *Monographs of the society for research in child development*, 1937, **2**, No. 2.

Gaier, E. L., and W. F. White. Trends in the measurement of personality. *Rev. educ. Res.*, 1965, **35**, 63–81.

Getzels, J. W., and P. W. Jackson. *Creativity and intelligence.* New York: John Wiley and Sons, 1962.

Guilford, J. P. Three faces of intellect. *Amer. Psychologist*, 1959, **14**, 469–479.

Guilford, J. P. Intelligence: 1965 model. *Amer. Psychologist*, 1965, **21**, 20–26.

Harris, A. J. *How to increase reading ability.* (4th ed.) New York: David McKay, 1961.

Kelley, C. R. *Visual screening and child development.* Raleigh: North Carolina State University, 1951.

Knezevich, S. J. The constancy of the IQ of the secondary school pupil. *J. educ. Res.*, 1946, **39**, 506–516.

Kuhlmann, F., and Rose G. Anderson. *Kuhlmann-Anderson Intelligence Tests, handbook.* (7th ed.) Princeton, N.J.: Personnel Press, 1963.

McNemar, Q. *The revision of the Stanford-Binet scale.* Boston: Houghton Mifflin, 1942.

Otis, A. S. *Otis Quick-Scoring Mental Ability Tests.* Tarrytown, N.Y.: Harcourt, Brace and World, 1954.

Pinneau, S. R. *Changes in intelligence quotient, infancy to maturity.* Boston: Houghton Mifflin, 1961.

Pintner, R. *Pintner General Ability Tests: non-language series.* Tarrytown, N.Y.: Harcourt, Brace and World, 1945.

Stanley, J. C. On the adequacy of standardized tests administered to extreme norm groups. *Peabody J. Educ.*, 1951, **29**, 145–153.

Stanley, J. C. Identification of superior learners in grades ten through fourteen. *Educ. Monographs*, 1954, 81.

Stroud, J. B. The intelligence test in school use: some persistent issues. *J. educ. Psychol.*, 1957, **48**, 77–85.

Super, D. E., and J. O. Crites. *Appraising vocational fitness by means of psychological tests*. (Rev. ed.) New York: Harper & Row, 1962.

Taylor, C. W. (Ed.) *Creativity: progress and potential*. New York: McGraw-Hill, 1964.

Terman, L.M., and Maude A. Merrill. *The Stanford-Binet Intelligence Scale: manual for the third revision*. Boston: Houghton Mifflin, 1960.

Wechsler, D. *Wechsler Intelligence Scale for Children*. New York: Psychological Corporation, 1949.

Wolfle, D., and T. Oxtoby. Distributions of ability of students specializing in different fields. *Science*, 1952, **116**, 311–314.

13 ✐

Evaluating Personal-Social Adjustment

THE GREEK MYTH OF DAEDALUS AND HIS SON ICARUS tells how Icarus met his death because he could not adjust to a new situation. When Daedalus, who had been held captive, made his escape from prison, he found no other way to flee the heavily guarded island but by air. Rarest of craftsmen, he set to work making great feathered wings for himself and for his son, binding the large feathers with thread, the small with wax. When all was ready for flight he gravely cautioned the boy Icarus always to fly close to him in a moderate course between sky and sea, warning that if they flew too low the weight of sea spray in their feathers would drag them down, and if too high, the heat of the sun would melt the wax that bound them.

All went well until Icarus, lacking his father's realistic caution and giddy with the joy of flight, soared away into the heavens. The blazing sun melted the wax and as the feathers fell away, nothing was left to hold the boy in the air but his flailing arms. Suddenly missing his beloved son, Daedalus cried out to him but was answered only by the terrible sight of scattering feathers swirling in the sea beneath.

Icarus' behavior seems to defy explanation. What foolhardiness caused him to behave so? Men have always concerned themselves with human behavior. It was once believed that patterns of adjustment were entirely inherited, and personality traits passed on to children in the same way as blue eyes and red hair. Even today we hear people say of nonconforming children: "Well, he comes by it honestly; he's a chip off the old block," assuming, however unconsciously, a hereditary basis for atypical behavior.

Modern psychology has shown that personal-social development depends on the interplay of many factors, not only on learned patterns of adjustment, but on such elements as the chemical function and physical structure of the body, and the general level of intelligence. The small boy may become aggressive to compensate for his size, or withdraw from physical contact and compensate through intellectual prowess or fantasy. The dull girl with high standards may resort to atypical actions in an attempt to adjust to an impossible situation, but her reaction is learned, not inherited.

The maladjusted individual is no longer assumed to be immoral or suffering over his sins. Neither is he accused of deliberate nonconformist behavior. The clinician accepts the individual and approaches his problem with sympathy, but objectifies the situation and tries to determine its antecedents. Instead of focusing on symptoms, he seeks causes.

Yet some parents and teachers still subject "different" children to sarcasm, and believe that if these children would only "try," they would improve. The shy child is urged to show more spunk; daydreamers are asked to wake up. Too often this approach convinces the child that he is right in his estimation of himself, that he is indeed inadequate, and, too often, he accepts the situation as hopeless. Thus, his behavior may actually be reinforced by exhortations to reform. Admonishing or ridiculing are not effective ways to initiate a positive change in behavior.

The process of adjustment is the individual's attempt to create a more congruous relationship between himself and his environment. The process may consist of an attempt to change the environment, his behavior, or to modify both. The teacher should play a very important role in helping the child manage the adjustment. Certainly, he cannot assume that the burden to adjust rests entirely on the individual alone. Yet, if he is careless of his responsibility, he may establish a social climate in which it is impossible for his pupils to meet even their basic personality needs. A teacher who stipulates equal requirements for all is frustrating many pupils by denying them any opportunity for success. Equally, when able children are forced to repeat much that they have already experienced and learned, the teacher is denying them the challenge that comes through new experience and that stimulates new learning and growth. The authoritarian taskmaster who expects everyone in his classroom to conform is stifling creativity and the satisfaction that comes through self-expression.

TEACHERS' CONCEPTS OF ADJUSTMENT

One of the most difficult problems in evaluating the personal-social adjustment of pupils lies in the teacher's understanding of adjustment. Just because certain kinds of behavior disrupt the well-oiled machinery of a carefully controlled classroom is no defensible reason to label them maladjustment. Yet a number of studies indicate that teachers fail to differentiate between behavior that disturbs the activities of the classroom and behavior which may lead to serious emotional difficulty (Wickman, 1928; Dale, 1941).

In one study (Sparks, 1952), teachers were asked to rank fifty-five problems, those most serious for the pupil and those most troublesome to the teacher. Table 17 shows clearly that the participating teachers did not have an accurate concept of what constitutes evidence of serious adjustment problems. Apparently they considered traits that violate society's social and moral code as most likely to produce adjustment problems in the individual. They list as most "serious," traits which prove troublesome to them as teachers, not symptoms related to the emotional conflicts of children. They tend to make no differentiation between academic success and emotional health. In general they consider pupils who do satisfactory academic work to be well-adjusted individuals, while if a pupil's achievement is low, they are inclined to think of him as a behavior deviant or just stupid.

One of the classic studies (Wickman, 1928) trenchantly exhibits the differences between teachers' and mental hygienists' concepts of problem behavior. In 1928, when members of each group were asked to rank behavior problems according to their importance, they sharply disagreed. Stouffer (1952) repeated this study after a period of twenty-five years. Although some change is noticeable, there are still numerous points of wide disagreement. A comparison of these rankings is shown in Table 18. Note the high teacher-ranking given in 1942 to problems which might tend to disturb class routine or defy society's code of right and wrong, such as stealing, truancy, untruthfulness, unreliability, cheating, and impertinence.

TABLE 17
TRAITS RANKED MOST TROUBLESOME TO THE TEACHER
AND MOST SERIOUS TO THE PUPIL

	Traits	
Rank	Most troublesome to teacher	Most serious to pupil
1	Interrupting	Stealing
2	Carelessness to work	Untruthfulness
3	Inattention	Unreliableness
4	Restlessness	Cruelty and bullying
5	Silliness, smartness	Cheating
6	Whispering and note writing	Heterosexual activity
7	Tattling	Impertinence
8	Thoughtlessness	Imprudence
9	Disorderliness	Selfishness
10	Inquisitiveness	Laziness

TABLE 18

COMPARISON OF BEHAVIOR PROBLEM RANKINGS BY
MENTAL HYGIENISTS AND TEACHERS IN 1928 AND 1952

Behavior problem	Ranking by mental hygienists	Ranking by teachers	
		1928	1952
Unsocial, withdrawing	1	40	6
Unhappy, depressed	2	22	3
Fearfulness	3	36	23
Suspiciousness	4	37	35
Cruelty, bullying	5	8	4
Shyness	6	50	34
Enuresis	7	19	30
Resentfulness	8	29	11
Stealing	9	2	2
Sensitiveness	10	48	24
Dreaminess	11	41	40
Nervousness	12	20	18
Suggestible	13	28	13
Over critical of others	14	45	27
Easily discouraged	15	23	10
Temper tantrums	16	13	16
Domineering	17	33	15
Truancy	18	6	7
Physical coward	19	31	33
Untruthfulness	20	5	5
Unreliableness	21	12	1
Destroying school material	22	10	12
Sullenness	23	35	32
Lack of interest in work	24	14	22
Cheating	25	9	9
Selfishness	26	24	17
Quarrelsomeness	27	27	28
Heterosexual activity	28	1	14
Restlessness	29	49	45
Inattention	30	26	36
Slovenly in personal appearance	31	34	31
Tattling	32	46	47
Impertinence, defiance	33	7	8
Obscene notes, talk	34	4	29
Laziness	35	17	20
Stubbornness	36	32	37
Attracting attention	37	39	43
Thoughtlessness	38	38	41

TABLE 18 (*Continued*)

Behavior problem	Ranking by mental hygienists	Ranking by teachers	
		1928	1952
Imaginative lying	39	42	46
Disobedience	40	11	19
Carelessness in work	41	25	25
Masturbation	42	3	26
Imprudence, rudeness	43	16	21
Inquisitiveness	44	44	44
Disorderliness in class	45	21	39
Tardiness	46	30	38
Interrupting	47	43	48
Profanity	48	15	42
Smoking	49	18	49
Whispering	50	47	50

From Wickman, 1928; Stouffer, 1952; adapted by permission of the Commonwealth Fund.

Failure to understand children's emotional conflicts is evident in the low ranking given such problems as suspiciousness, shyness, enuresis, and dreaminess.

PROBLEMS

1   What important problems of pupil adjustment seem to have been omitted in Table 18? Suggest a procedure for composing a complete list.
2   Can you see any important trends emerging as you analyze the data presented in Table 18? What might account for this?
3   Choose five behavior problems from the list in Table 18 and illustrate concretely how you would attempt to deal with each in class.
4   On the basis of your own classroom experience, list those teacher characteristics which seem to promote a high degree of personal-social adjustment among pupils.

METHODS OF EVALUATING PERSONAL-SOCIAL ADJUSTMENT

The discussion in this chapter is confined to personal-social adjustment rather than personality. The latter is much broader in meaning, as is emphasized by Shaffer and Shoben (1956, p. 310):

Personality does not depend on one or a few characteristics only, but upon the interplay of practically all of an individual's qualities. Physical structure, chemical functioning, learned motives, and habits of adjustment all contribute to personality, and not as separate entities but as interacting aspects of an organized system.

Of course, the individual must adjust to his physiological needs; he eats when he is hungry, he seeks warmth if he is cold. But much broader dimensions of adjustment are assumed than this simple adaptive behavior. We must consider the pupil's relationship to his social environment as well as his behavior in relation to his own psychological needs.

In the lives of most civilized people, social adjustments are more significant than responses to physiological wants. Human beings are social persons as well as biological organisms. Social interactions among people and between groups of people are required to fulfill even some of our most elementary needs. On the other hand, people often work in competition or at cross purposes so as to thwart one another's satisfactions. When a child feels insecure and unwanted by his family, when a student feels isolated from his fellows, or when a man is unsuccessful in his work, adjustments are required to mediate between the socially defined needs and the socially determined frustrations (Shaffer and Shoben, 1956, p. 4).

Behavior patterns such as these are partial reflections of the degree to which some important educational objectives have been achieved in the pupil, and it is necessary, therefore, to attempt to evaluate them.

A variety of instruments for evaluating personal-social adjustment is available to the teacher. Some of these are based upon formal observations, some are paper-and-pencil inventories to be administered to a group of pupils, others are individual instruments designed primarily for use by clinicians. The following outline is indicative of the variety of useful instruments and techniques in this area of evaluation.

Evaluation methods based on observation
　　Anecdotal records
　　Rating scales
　　Check lists
　　Interviewing
Projective techniques
Sociometric and related techniques
　　Sociograms
　　Social distance scales
　　"Guess who" questionnaires
Self-report inventories
　　Biographical data blank
　　Personal inventories
　　Interest inventories
　　Attitude scales and questionnaires

As long as this list is, it does not include all the variations in use today, such as analyzing writings by pupils, in the form of autobiography or the completion of an unfinished story or sentence, as a means of sampling feelings and attitudes. For the teacher's use, however, the list is sufficiently comprehensive.

A selected group of standardized instruments for measuring aspects of personal-social adjustment is given in Appendix E. In general, neither these methods nor less formal ones are as reliable or valid as the better standardized achievement and scholastic aptitude tests. As there are extremists who harbor an indefensible degree of enthusiasm for the measurement possibilities of these tests, there are at the other extreme many prophets of gloom who mistrust them altogether and advocate a "hands off" policy. It seems reasonable to adopt a middle-of-the-road position. The following discussion emphasizes the limitations of various methods and techniques included in the outline above, but goes on to suggest some practical approaches to this area of evaluation.

Evaluation Methods Based on Observation

What a teacher can learn from observation of students in natural situations is generally useful to him and is, for many reasons, a valuable addition to the study of personal-social development.

First, the results of such observation supplement information gathered elsewhere. A pupil may do well on a mechanical aptitude test, but be awkward and uninterested in the shop. Another may give the desired answers on an adjustment inventory, but be unable to work cooperatively with any of his peers.

Second, they provide the teacher with information unobtainable in other ways. He has an opportunity to notice numerous significant incidents and attitudes in the daily activities of the pupil, an opportunity which may be lacking in artificial situations. When a pupil answers "yes" to the question "Is it fun to do nice things for other boys and girls?", his behavior may not be indicative of his adjustment to a peer group; the teacher may observe that the child is really self-centered.

Third, they afford an opportunity to sample the student's actual behavior. Under informal observation, a pupil is not asked to conform to what he might feel in an artificial situation, as in answering a questionnaire, and is not requested to report on his own behavior. Direct observation will, therefore, be more valid in certain instances.

Finally, the results of such observation benefit the observer. It is important that the teacher develop proper relationships with the pupils. Too often teachers judge their pupils in terms of their own feelings and prejudices and therefore find it impossible to help them. It should be said, however, that the teacher may need help in developing the skill of accurate reporting. A serious limitation of observation may lie within the observer himself, for what a person sees or hears depends in part on what he is predisposed to see or hear (Froehlich and Darley, 1952, pp. 84–87).

WHAT THE TEACHER OBSERVES. What should the teacher observe in the behavior of children in a natural situation? An important place to observe is in class. Does the pupil volunteer or offer to share experiences, or does he withdraw and fail to participate? What kind of questions does he ask? Does the nature of his questioning indicate that he has a genuine interest in learning, or is he more interested in his marks? What does he like to talk about? Does he ever mention his interests, problems or family? How does the group react to contributions by individual members? The teacher will find that the group will support certain individuals, contradict some, and ignore others.

The teacher should also observe the group and its interactions. Which pupils are aggressive, withdrawn, or hostile? Which lead and which follow? Does group behavior in the freedom of the playground differ from that in the classroom? The pupil who appears listless and uninterested in the classroom may come alive in a ball game. Are some more aggressive when freed from the teacher's control?

Finally, a great deal is revealed about a pupil's personal-social development through observation of his creative activity, which enables him to translate his feeling into action. Does he prefer working with abstract symbols or concrete objects, enjoy participating in dramatics and role playing? Is he anxious when he appears before others? What emotions does he tend to express in his drawings and paintings?

PROBLEMS

5   Describe the major personality traits of those teachers who might experience the most difficulty with the observational method. Might training in this technique serve as a therapeutic aid in improving a teacher's own personal-social adjustment?

6   Make a check list of factors which you feel are of importance in recording observed behavior.

7   How can "creative" activity be observed through your particular subject-matter field?"

DANGER OF BIAS. Bias in observation is common. Take, for example, the commonly accepted fallacy that "only" children are spoiled. Teachers often interpret negative behavior in pupils without siblings as being a direct result of having their own way at home. This may or may not be the cause underlying the behavior. Mere knowledge that a pupil is an only child, without further examination of his actual relationship with his parents, is not grounds for assuming that his "onliness" will result in a handicap. Although recent research disproves the assumption that only children are universally spoiled, and disliked by peers and adults alike, "onliness" is still labeled the cause for many classroom problems.

Bias may also result when an observer does not admit his own feelings and weaknesses to himself. Failing to do so, he may attribute his inadequacies to others, and a pupil's behavior will be interpreted as similar to his own inhibited desires.

> In everyday life we often see illustrations of judgments passed on others that reflect as much of the personality of the one who judges as the one who is judged. For example, a person with pronounced authoritarian tendencies, who has a strong urge to show respect for his superiors, and to demand respect from his subordinates may see a student's frankness as a form of being "fresh"; he may regard a student who has opinions of his own as impudent, or one who voices disagreement as disobedient. The teacher who is insecure may interpret calculated flattery as genuine appreciation and regard those who make a policy of agreeing with him as true scholars. A person who is unsure of himself may take offense, and assume that an offense was intended, when someone offers a bit of well-meant criticism. A person who is defensive about his opinions may interpret an innocent question as a form of attack. A teacher who suffers from intense feelings of guilt because of his sexual impulses may interpret a little exchange of whispers or notes between two people as evidence that they have "filthy minds"; and if a student actually is guilty of behavior that is indiscreet or in poor taste, the teacher may magnify the indiscretion into a heinous crime (Jersild, and others, 1953, pp. 6–7).

This same projective type of weakness in reporting may also be reflected in a "Pollyanna" attitude toward all pupils. While it is commendable to look for strengths in children, their total behavior must be evaluated objectively, and that is not easy. Many people well versed in factual knowledge of human behavior, have never learned to apply this information to themselves or to others. An astute observer is able to analyze his feelings toward others as they relate to his own behavior, and attempts to discover their causes through an objective approach. Why does he dislike certain pupils and champion others? What makes him unhappy with the behavior of some students? Observation alone cannot yield valid answers. Lack of objectivity makes it impossible to report behavior truthfully.

Objectivity in reporting may be improved by separating description from judgment. "Johnny is undependable," and "Mary will assume no responsibility" are judgments which do not specify what happened and how, nor do they specify the responsibilities Mary failed to assume. As they stand, there is no way to check their validity; possibly they express only the teacher's dislike for a child. The following illustrates a more useful description of behavior.

> I said, "Eddie, you haven't done the work assigned you this period. Don't you understand it?" Eddie answered by saying, "I don't know." When I checked to see if he understood, he knew the answers to all of my questions relating to the assignment. Eddie seldom completes more than one assignment per week during the allotted time.
> On the playground I overheard Susie say, "Don't choose Eddie, because he won't try hard if he doesn't like the game." Janie said, "But someone has to choose him."

Note that the above is a report; it injects no judgment. This is what the teacher said, how Eddie answered, and what was done as a result. In the same manner, the playground incident consists simply of the children's conversation.

SAMPLING. Adequate sampling is also important for valid observation. The teacher who concerns himself only with classroom behavior may have a very biased picture of pupils' total personal-social adjustment. The same boy who is hostile and aggressive in English class may be a cooperative and respected leader in the chemistry club, or have a helpful attitude toward his mathematics classmates.

To improve sampling, it is necessary to make observations in varied situations. However, care should also be given to timing. A pupil under observation may have a toothache on the day you have chosen to make mental notes about his actions, or perhaps difficulties have arisen in his home, and what you see or hear may not be at all typical of his behavior. Naturally, the more you observe him in a variety of situations, the more likely you are to synthesize an accurate picture of his problems of adjustment, and the more reliable your observation will become.

The teacher must plan for reliability and economy of effort. It is not practicable for him to use the technique, valuable in certain researches, of planning a schedule of short observations in advance where, by randomizing the schedule, numerous pupils are seen in more or less comparable situations. Nevertheless, the teacher can schedule, and, through a conscious effort, somewhat avoid the bias resulting from observation of a nonrepresentative or improperly timed situation.

PROBLEM

8 Elementary school teachers who remain with the same children all day have ample opportunity to obtain a wide variety of behavior samples. In what specific ways might junior and senior high school teachers meet the problem of less opportunity to sample behavior?

PURPOSE IN OBSERVATION.   Although the point has not been stressed, it is obvious that effective observation is useful. Of course, the teacher is seeking information that will help him promote learning, but this is a very general objective. It is more helpful to look for something specific. Why does one pupil seem to have difficulty in getting along with other boys? Why does another refuse to make reports or enter class discussion? An intelligent search for the answers will be guided by what we already know. It may be necessary to arrange some special occasions in which there is an opportunity to test guesses and hypotheses about the source of difficulty. These are artificial situations. Some simple structuring can elicit reactions to social stimuli that are encountered in the normal course of events— perhaps by assigning certain pupils specific responsibilities, by formulating key questions, or organizing games that present some individual and social problems.

ANECDOTAL RECORDS.   Observation techniques function most effectively when the information is written. One way of recording this information is in anecdotal records, systematic and significant records of the pupil's behavior, which generally form part of the permanent record passed on with him from grade to grade. In studying a behavior problem, it is important to look for signs of its development, because change can be evaluated only through knowledge of previous happenings.

A sample anecdotal record is shown in Figure 31. Notice that the

---

ANECDOTAL RECORD FORM

Date 1/24/66   Pupil's Name Sue Collings
Observer Dorothy Larson

Description of incident:

Sue had won our first essay contest. When she was offered a prize for her second success, she gave it to Marlene, who was runner-up. Marlene accepted it without any expression of appreciation.

Comment:

Sue seems to be a very well-adjusted child and quite sensitive to the needs of the other children. It was a particularly noble gesture for her to give Marlene the prize since Marlene is very selfish and uncooperative with her peers.

FIGURE 31
SAMPLE ANECDOTAL RECORD

description of the incident is separated from the teacher's comments about it. In both instances, more details can be added if necessary. Incidentally, a copy of this anecdote could be placed in the files of both girls mentioned.

The following running report on an eighth-grade boy was made over a period of several weeks. It is a condensation of a series of anecdotal records.

> September 30. Bill was late to class and was sent to the principal's office for a pass. He did not return.
> Upon checking up, I found that Bill had gone to the school nurse with a complaint of illness.
> Interpretation: This may have been a deliberate attempt to avoid class.
> October 7. Bill responded to my question on the assignment with "I didn't read it. It doesn't seem very important to me."
> Interpretation: Bill seems to be hunting for ways of justifying his behavior.
> October 10. Bill continued to whisper, make various remarks about the class discussion, shuffle papers, and drop pencils or books. When I reprimanded him, he got up and left the room.
> Interpretation: Bill seemed to be intent on disrupting the class.
> October 13. In looking at the data in Bill's cumulative file, I found a history of reading difficulty. His *Stanford-Binet* IQ was 120.
> Interpretation: Bill's inability to read might be the source of his behavior problems.
> October 14. I asked Bill if he would help me build a cage for some snakes that I wanted to exhibit in the science room. He said that he would be happy to come in after school. It was 5 o'clock before we had finished.
> Then he leafed through some books and materials on snakes that I had on the shelf. He chose a booklet with low reading difficulty and asked if he could take it home with him.
> Interpretation: I believe that I am establishing a good relationship with Bill and have found a way to help him.
> October 15. The interest of the class was centered around Bill. He had some information to share on the booklet he had read. He stopped after class to return the booklet and ask for another.
> Interpretation: Bill expressed satisfaction with this new role. He seemed genuinely pleased with his ability to make a contribution to the group.
> October 17. Bill stopped in after school and asked if there was any way in which he could improve his reading.

Because Bill was a particular problem to him, the teacher concentrated his attention on him; it is best to select one or two pupils to observe at a time. That way teachers find they compile better records of each pupil and can separate the child's behavior from their own feelings and biases. It is an almost hopeless task to write daily or weekly records for all pupils, but when significant incidents occur involving others, they should be recorded.

The teacher has made an objective report of the incidents above, separating interpretation from report. He is, therefore, able to make an accurate description of Bill's behavior and to hypothesize the source of his difficulties. Notice in this case that it is extended observation that points up the reading difficulty and its relationship to Bill's behavior problems. In effect, he has been trying to escape from responsibilities that involve reading, yet his need is not evident from any single anecdote; the pattern emerges as a number of situations are reported.

Deviant behavior may appear periodically among some pupils. Possibly certain taxing school events, like issuing report cards, coincides with this behavior. The amount of security that home life affords a child varies as it does in school. Therefore, it is necessary to have adequate sampling to make a valid interpretation of behavior. Extended observation also provides an opportunity to detect improvement or lack of it in an individual's behavior.

Problems

9   As you look at the anecdotal records of Bill can you see other plausible interpretations of his behavior?
10   An important use of the anecdotal record is to serve, along with other data, in making inferences and formulating hypotheses about behavior. What other major uses can you see in this technique?

RATING SCALES.   Rating scales are also useful in making and recording observation. These instruments are popular in many schools because they emphasize important aspects of adjustment and provide data that can be treated statistically. They also make it possible for several judges to rate the same pupil, a procedure that usually increases the reliability of the rating.

Most of the rating instruments used in the elementary and secondary schools are graphic scales, constructed so that the rater can mark any point along a continuum.[1] For example:

Is he moody?		✓						
	never		seldom		usually		always	

How does he accept authority?					✓	
	poorly		well		very well	

The rater may check any one of the defined points or rate the pupil between the points. In these examples, the rater has classified the pupil's degree of moodiness between the defined points of "never" and "seldom," but his acceptance of authority as "very well."

[1] See Guilford, 1954, pp. 267–268, for a list of issues concerning graphic rating scales.

The foregoing scales (from Haggerty and others, 1930; adapted by permission of Harcourt, Brace and World, Inc.) can be greatly improved by substituting behavioral statements for the more general terms of "poorly," "well," and "very well." For example:

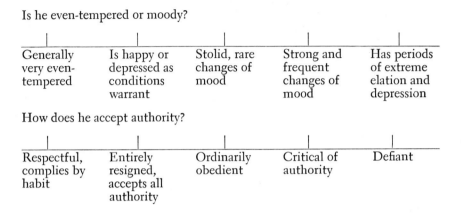

Is he even-tempered or moody?

| Generally very even-tempered | Is happy or depressed as conditions warrant | Stolid, rare changes of mood | Strong and frequent changes of mood | Has periods of extreme elation and depression |

How does he accept authority?

| Respectful, complies by habit | Entirely resigned, accepts all authority | Ordinarily obedient | Critical of authority | Defiant |

If some of these items, such as "even-tempered" and "defiant" were defined more specifically, they would provide a more common basis on which to evaluate the pupil. Specific examples of behavior, such as "refuses to hand in papers" and "talks back in a belligerent tone," will do much to offset disparity of judgment which arises because different raters employ different criteria in judging pupils according to general descriptive terms.

Another method of defining the points on a scale more clearly is by determining the approximate number of pupils which should be placed at each point. If one assumes that a trait is normally distributed for the population, and that the group of pupils in question is unselected, then the trait will approximate a normal distribution for the group.

Table 19, which is derived from tables of the area under the normal curve, can be used as a guide to determine the percentage of the group that should be placed at each point on the scale. The ratings of observers will tend to be more comparable if the number of pupils at each point is established in this manner.

There are several types of error affecting the reliability and validity of ratings; namely: (1) rating all pupils either too high or too low ("personal bias" or "personal equation"); (2) rating everyone near the central point of the scale (error of central tendency); (3) inaccurate rating because of ambiguity in the scale or misunderstanding on the part of the raters; and (4) allowing one's general impression of the pupil to affect the rating ("halo effect"). The fourth type of error results if the rater is favorably impressed by a pupil and so tends to give him a higher evaluation than he

TABLE 19

PERCENTAGE DISTRIBUTIONS FOR A CLASS OF FORTY PUPILS FOR SCALES
HAVING DIFFERENT NUMBERS OF POINTS

Three points	Four points	Five points	Six points	Seven points
20	11	7	5	4
60	39	24	15	10
20	39	38	30	22
	11	24	30	28
		7	15	22
			5	10
				4

From Symonds, 1931, p. 81; reproduced by permission of Appleton-Century-Crofts, Inc.

deserves on many items. Lower ratings may result for a pupil of whom the rater is not particularly fond (Wrightstone, 1960, p. 931).

The reliability of ratings can be improved by increasing the number of judges. This poses a practical problem in the elementary school where a child generally has only one teacher. In secondary school, the large pupil-teacher ratio prevents teachers from knowing all their pupils well, but because each pupil has contact with a number of teachers, there is a better opportunity to get reactions from several observers. It should be emphasized that rating pupils without sufficient evidence to make a highly reliable and valid opinion is a waste of time.

One might well be skeptical of the relative validity of ratings because of the many human errors attributable to the rater. However, some recent studies of the validity of rating scales definitely support their use. For instance, ratings of aptitude for military service proved to be more highly related to ratings of performance in the field than was any other information (Technical Research Report, 1953).

An interesting variation of the common rating scale is that involving the forced-choice technique. This, in its simplest form, requires the rater to choose between two descriptive statements, deciding which is more characteristic of the person rated. In one instance, both paired choices may represent desirable behavior, in another instance, undesirable behavior. In either case, the members of the pair appear to be equally acceptable in terms of desirability, but actually they represent different kinds of behavior. Instruments have been developed using groups of three, four, and even five statements.

Below is a pair of statements concerning one aspect of a pupil's social relationship:

A.   Shares his interests with the group
B.   Listens attentively while others relate their experiences

Since the rater must choose between what appeears to him to be equally complimentary statements, the "halo effect" is counteracted, and the judge is prevented from giving only cursory attention to the items. Actually, as determined by validity studies, the choices do not represent equal degrees of personal-social development. Choice A might reflect more maturity than choice B.

Although there is still much research to be done and many problems to be resolved, the forced-choice technique may prove to be helpful in developing more adequate instruments for evaluating personal-social adjustment in our schools. This technique is also being used successfully in self-report inventories, such as the *Gordon Personal Profile* (see Appendix E). In this case the pupil himself determines which statements best describe his behavior.

PROBLEMS

11   Some research specialists who make frequent use of behavior rating scales ask teachers to rate each child on a continuum using as a base all children they have known. Why is this done?

12   The United States armed forces have made use of the "man-to-man" type of rating scale in evaluating officers. The individual doing the rating is first asked to think of the best, the poorest, the average, etc., officer in his experience. Each man to be rated is then compared with these models. Could this procedure be successfully adapted to the classroom situation?

13   Merit ratings of teachers by either the administrators or fellow teachers is a highly controversial issue in the public schools. What do you think of the practice? What problems must be met if it is to be used successfully?

CHECK LISTS.   Check lists make it possible to record aspects of behavior rapidly. They are simply lists of personality descriptions or traits which the recorder notes as present or absent in individual pupils. Some schools construct their own, which results in a particularly valuable device if done with the cooperation of the whole staff under a leader who is well informed about child growth and development. The experience of constructing a check list may then prove to be effective in service training.

One of the best known standardized check lists is the *Vineland Social Maturity Scale.* The items are arranged in the order of their increasing average difficulty and represent progressive maturation in self-help, self-direction, locomotion, occupation, communication, and social relations.

Below are some excerpts from the scale, ranging from those designed for very young children to those for an adult:

> "Crows"; laughs
> Follows simple instructions
> Relates experiences
> Goes to school unattended
> Makes telephone calls
> Performs responsible routine chores
> Buys own clothing
> Looks after own bath
> Assumes responsibilities beyond own needs
> Shares community responsibility

This scale has many possible uses. It can serve as: (1) a standard schedule of normal development that can be used repeatedly for the measurement of growth or change; (2) a measure of individual differences and, consequently, of extreme deviation that may be significant in such problems as mental deficiency, juvenile delinquency, and child placement or adoption; (3) a qualitative index of development variation in abnormal subjects such as the maladjusted, the unstable, the psychopathic, the epileptic; (4) a measure of improvement following special treatment, therapy, and training; and (5) a schedule for reviewing developmental histories in the clinical study of retardation, deterioration, and rates of growth and decline.

INTERVIEWING.   An interview with a pupil often supplements and verifies other information about his adjustment. Since the teacher is able to observe a child in a limited variety of situations, a face-to-face encounter with no peers present provides an opportunity to observe his reactions closely and with greater attention than is possible in the classroom.

There are several schools of thought about the approach to a pupil in an interview. Part of the disagreement concerns the degree to which the pupil is allowed to dominate the interview; in other words, the permissiveness the teacher exercises. Despite differences of opinion on this point, a number of suggestions will serve as guides for effective interviewing.

1. Be certain that you have a desirable purpose for the interview. If this is done, you can prepare for it by checking other available data and formulating, at least in your mind, what you hope to accomplish.
2. Rapport must be established. Certainly a teacher cannot propose to get helpful information if he calls in a pupil after a misdemeanor and uses this as the basis for a conference. Good relationships between the pupil and the teacher can hardly be expected if the discussion revolves around an interpersonal difficulty. It should be remembered that what the teacher says in establishing rapport is not nearly so important as how he says it and whether he is encouraging good feeling between the pupil and

himself. Try to help the pupil to see that you are sincerely interested in him and his problems.

3. Guide the discussion so the pupil has an opportunity to express his feelings. If you ask questions that can be answered with a "yes" or "no" he may respond with the expected answer.

4. Avoid communicating a note of finality at the end of the interview. Suggest that there will be opportunities for other conferences if they seem desirable. It is important for the pupil to feel that the interview has been helpful and satisfying to him. If it appears that this is not the case, it is perhaps well to set a time for another interview.

5. After the pupil has left, make a short written summary of the salient points of the interview that can be placed in his cumulative record. Do not trust your memory.

Interviews with parents can also yield useful information for evaluating a pupil's personal-social adjustment. As in interviewing the pupil, it is important to have a purpose in mind. Know what gaps of information you need to fill; parents can be an excellent source of missing information about behavior problems.

There are advantages in having the parents come to the school for interviewing as well as in visiting them at home. As a home visit gives the teacher a picture of a pupil's home life, a school visit lets the parent see how his child spends the day. Some parents may feel more secure in their homes because many of them recall painful childhood experiences that are, unfortunately associated with school. Among the disadvantages to visiting the home are the shame some parents may feel about their home's physical appearance and the possibility of other family members interrupting the interview.

In learning to know the father and mother, a teacher may come away with a better understanding of the pupil in the light of parental reactions. One teacher wrote of a home visit:

> The time could have been spent to no better advantage. I developed an insight into Ann's problems that I've never had before. It will be much easier for me to be sympathetic with her at school now. I'm certain that I shall conserve considerable emotional energy. Frankly, I wonder how Ann has been able to adjust so well to our classroom environment. Coming from a middle-class home, I'm afraid I didn't realize how some people live.

PROBLEMS

14 What are some highly useful ways of establishing good rapport in a pupil interview? How might you proceed with a hostile, withdrawn child?

15 What symptoms by the pupil might indicate the need for a home visit? What factors should the teacher keep uppermost in his mind when interviewing parents?

Projective Techniques

The general idea of projective techniques is to present the pupil with some unstructured and ambiguous situation and then to note his reaction to it. Since the individual has no clues from the examiner, he will tend to react to the situation in terms of his own personality. Whatever he does or says in such a situation will be influenced by his experiences and his state of mind at the moment.

Two very common projective tests used by highly trained specialists in clinical diagnosis are the *Rorschach Inkblot Test* and the *Thematic Apperception Test,* commonly called the *TAT.* (The *Children's Apperception Test (CAT)* is similar in type to the *TAT* and is designed for children of ages 3–10). The *Rorschach* is composed of ten inkblots which serve as unstructured and ambiguous stimuli, exciting the individual to a performance giving expression to the pattern of his personality. They are presented to the subject in a given order and he tells what he sees in each. The *TAT* consists of a series of pictures that may be interpreted in many ways. The subject is asked to tell a story about each picture, emphasizing how the scene was initiated, what is happening, how the characters feel, and what will probably result. The test is based upon the well recognized fact that when a person interprets an ambiguous social situation, he is likely to expose his own personality as much as the phenomenon under scrutiny. Absorbed in his attempt to explain the objective occurrence, he becomes naively unconscious of himself and of the scrutiny of others and, therefore, less vigilantly defensive. To a trained ear, he is disclosing certain inner tendencies and cathexes,[1] wishes, fears, and traces of past experience (Murray and others, 1938).

Cronbach (1960, p. 569) emphasized the difference between the two kinds of test. He classifies the *Rorschach* as a stylistic type test and the *TAT* as a thematic type. In other words, the stylistic type indicates the style with which a pupil handles a problem, while the thematic type emphasizes the content of his thoughts and fantasies. He indicates, however, that the specific strengths are not mutually exclusive and that of the two, the thematic test more nearly examines "the whole person" yielding possible information on emotions, attitudes, and cognitive processes.

The classroom teacher is not generally trained to use either of these instruments. Their administration and interpretation require the knowledge and experience of the trained clinician. Schools fortunate enough to have psychologists on their staffs may find that they will employ projective

[1] Webster's Third International Dictionary defines a cathexis as an "investment of libidinal energy in a person, object, idea, or activity."

testing for certain difficult behavioral problems. These tests may provide helpful information with a comparatively small outlay of time and effort.

PROBLEM

16 Projective techniques such as the *Rorschach* and the *TAT* are administered only by highly trained clinicians. List the types of information which the classroom teacher should know about these tests. In what kinds of situations might you refer a child for testing of this type?

Sociometric and Related Techniques

One of the most valuable sources of information about the personal-social adjustment of pupils is their peers. Instruments that cause pupils to rate their classmates in various ways are known as sociometric techniques. Teachers will find it helpful to use these means to verify their judgment of pupils for a number of reasons. First, the teacher has an opportunity to observe boys and girls only in a limited number of situations. Second, the relationship between teachers and pupils is different from that between pupils and their peers; teachers represent authority and children respond to authority in different ways. Third, it is possible that a teacher may lack objectivity in his observation, a problem that has been discussed already.

It is possible that teachers may look on sociometric techniques as a lot of unnecessary bother, feeling that very little additional information can be obtained through their use, since, on the whole, good teachers have been quite successful in determining the degree of a pupil's adjustment to the group. There continue to be some very bad misjudgments, however. One study (Bonney, 1947) showed that the adolescent who is "smooth" and successful with his teachers is generally overrated, while those who get along well in the small group but antagonize the teacher, or respond poorly to him, are often underrated. In another report (Cunningham and others, 1951) a fourth-grade girl who was judged as most accepted by her teacher was ranked by her peers only twenty-first in a class of thirty-two on a social distance scale. The teacher had based his judgment on the observation that "some boys remarked that Pearl is pretty. Children take up for her when she is in trouble. When they hurt her feelings in a group and make her cry, they voluntarily go to apologize to her."

Teachers who use sociometric techniques are quick to admit that they have at times misjudged the relationship among pupils. Social interaction is so complex a process that many feelings are expressed in such a way even the keenest observer cannot detect them. Pupils may admire certain traits in each other that completely overshadow behavior the teacher considers undesirable. It is also possible that the observer may, because of his own background, emphasize undesirable characteristics disproportionately.

SOCIOGRAMS.	The sociometric test is a device for getting preferences among associates to determine the social structure of a group. One method of administering the test is to ask pupils to list in order of preference the three persons in the class with whom they would most like to work on a project. A sociogram is constructed by drawing a map showing, by means of names and lines, the choices of each pupil. This depicts the social structure of the group for a particular moment in a particular situation that prompted the members' choices. To obtain a complete picture of the social interaction in the group, it is necessary to give several tests involving varied situations. Pupils do not always choose the same persons for work on different assignments. The choices expressed by a pupil represent what he would like. They do not necessarily indicate what it is. For example, several students may indicate by their choices that they would like to be a part of the group populated by two or three leaders. If one were to observe them in the classroom, however, he would find no interaction between them and the pupils of their choice. This explains why the sociometric test can provide information that may not be available to an observer.

A natural circumstance should be selected to initiate the test, such as reseating a group, forming committees, or a similar activity. The teacher should emphasize that he will keep the pupil's preferences confidential. They must understand they may choose anyone; in some schools, where separation of boys and girls is encouraged, children may think that they must choose only from their own sex. Finally, sufficient time should be given for all pupils to make their choices.

The following is an effective way of wording the sociometric question:

> "Our next unit is on the western movement in the United States. You have decided that you would like to take certain projects and work on them in committees. Each of you knows with whom you would like to work. Now I am going to pass out some cards. Print your name in the upper right-hand corner and then number from '1' to '3' on the left hand side of the card like this. (Illustrate on the blackboard.) Beside the '1' write the complete name of the person with whom you would like most to work in a committee. After '2' indicate your second choice and after '3' your third choice. You may choose either a boy or a girl, but of course the person must be in this class. I will arrange the committee members so that you will be with at least one of those whom you have chosen" (adapted from Jennings, 1959).

It is also possible to ask the children to list at the bottom of the card the name of anyone with whom they would prefer not to work. This procedure has serious limitations, however, since it is in contradiction to the social philosophy that the teacher should wish to develop in his class.

When a group of eleventh graders was asked to list classmates whom they preferred not to have on their committees, a number of parents said that the pupils were disturbed by the request. Even though there were a number of cliques, students were unhappy about having to "blackball" someone.

The primary-grades teacher may have to have the children give their choices orally if they cannot write. One second-grade boy reported that he had chosen Tom because he couldn't write Marjorie, the name of his best friend. A problem also arises when children do not know each other's names. Pupils must be well acquainted before the sociometric test can be used effectively.

Figure 32 is an illustration of a sociogram of a fourth-grade class of twenty-five pupils. Only first and second choices are shown; the solid lines

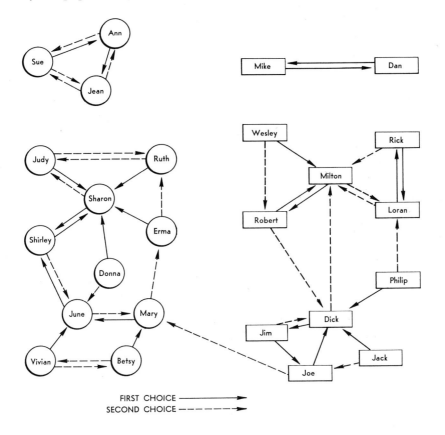

FIGURE 32
SOCIOGRAM OF A FOURTH-GRADE CLASS

indicate first choices and the broken lines, second choices. The boys' names are enclosed by boxes, the girls' by circles.

Notice the sex cleavage in this class. Only one pupil, Joe, has chosen another of the opposite sex. Sue, Ann, and Jean form a clique. There are a number of mutual choices. Prominent among these are Mike and Dan, Rick and Loran, Sharon and Shirley, and Milton and Robert. There are also several isolates—pupils whom no one has chosen: Donna, Wesley, Philip, and Jack. Complete directions for constructing a sociogram such as this are given by Jennings (1959).

After the sociogram is constructed, it should be evaluated. The individual pupil should be considered first: Who are his preferences? Who has chosen him? The pupils should then be considered as a group: Who was chosen most often, very seldom, or not at all? Are there any small groups who have chosen each other and seem to stand apart from the class as a whole? Does the group tend toward cleavages, boys choosing boys and girls choosing girls? Do urban children fail to choose rural children and vice versa? The answers to these questions may prove surprising when the teacher compares them with his own reactions.

The sociometric interview, a by-product of the sociometric test, is used to obtain information and explanations from children. For example, John, a high-school junior, said that he chose Bill because he wasn't as cocky as Tom. Actually, the sociogram indicated that Tom was well liked and had shown his effectiveness as a leader many times. John and Tom were rivals for high marks as well as for social position in the school, and this struggle had had its effect on John's feelings toward his rival. Tom, on the other hand, had given John his first choice for committee work. When queried about his reasons for this choice, he said simply, "John has good ideas."

Care must be taken in the interview not to place the pupil on the defensive because of his choices. The teacher should not say, "Why did you choose Bill?", but "How did you decide to choose Bill?" If the teacher finds that his duties do not leave him time to interview the whole class, he may select those few about whom he is most concerned. He might also get from all pupils written statements of the reasons for their choices. Of course, he must assure them of his intent to keep the information confidential. Written statements of this kind are seldom effective unless the teacher has excellent rapport with his class.

PROBLEM

17   In a junior high school, sociograms of each seventh- and eighth-grade section were constructed by the guidance counselor on the basis of choices made in group guidance sessions during the fall semester. These data were then released to the teachers. Evaluate this procedure.

SOCIAL DISTANCE SCALES. The sociogram is limited in the degree to which it can show the complete social structure of the group. Since each pupil typically has only three choices, we have no information on why he failed to choose other classmates. As one fourth grader said, "I didn't have enough choices to choose Sally." However, she did not choose Billy because "He is such a tattletale."

The social distance scale overcomes this particular weakness. It is possible to use this instrument to determine the degree to which the individual accepts or rejects the group as well as the degree to which the group accepts or rejects him. Table 20 shows how thirty-two elementary school pupils reacted to two classmates in terms of certain social situations. The number of checks for each item on the scale received by the most accepted child and the least accepted child are listed. Interestingly enough, this researcher found in studying many children that everyone was accepted by at least one person and even the most popular were not approved by everyone. In the above study, only four of the thirty-two children did not have their names checked on the entire range of the scale.

Nevertheless, the questions used in this technique are definitely limited. If our objective is to promote peer acceptance, we may wonder about the effect of an item like "Wish he were not in our room." Some teachers prefer not to use social distance scales because items of this kind are in opposition to their goals.

"GUESS WHO" QUESTIONNAIRES. Another method of obtaining reports from pupils is to have them match their peers with a list of behavioral characteristics. The teacher makes a list of characteristics ranging from complimentary to unfavorable. The pupils then indicate those classmates who, in their opinion, fit each description (Hartshorne and May, 1929). Since pupils often know each other better than the teacher does, it is possible to get a great deal of information about many aspects of their adjustment. The following examples illustrate the kind of item that has proved helpful (Cunningham and others, 1951, pp. 419–422).

> Here is someone who likes to talk a lot, always has something to say ————.
>
> Here is someone who waits for somebody else to think of something to do and always likes to follow the suggestions which others make ————.
>
> Here is someone who is very friendly, who has lots of friends, who is nice to everybody ————.

Children may list themselves or as many pupils as fit the description. It is also possible that some pupils will feel that certain items apply to no one in the class. When the teacher tabulates the number of times each pupil is mentioned for each description and finds some individuals referred

TABLE 20

SOCIAL ACCEPTANCE OF TWO PUPILS

Item on scale	Checks for pupil 1 (Most accepted)	Checks for pupil 2 (Least accepted)
1. Would like to have him as one of my best friends.	20	2
2. Would like to have him in my group but not as a close friend.	7	15
3. Would like to be with him once in a while but not too often or for a long time.	3	4
4. Do not mind his being in our room but do not want to have anything to do with him.	1	3
5. Wish he were not in our room.	1	8

From Cunningham and others, 1951, p. 172; reproduced by permission of the Bureau of Publications, Teachers College, Columbia University.

to by a large number of the class, it is significant information. No doubt he should disregard mention by only one or two, although possibly some children are not well known and are mentioned infrequently for this reason.

Self-Report Inventories

Since no one has an opportunity to observe an individual under as many or as varied situations as he himself, a biographical data blank elicits important factual information. The self-report test attempts to tap the wealth of information that a person has about his feelings, interests, and attitudes. If a number of standardized questions are chosen that can be relied upon to show differences among individuals, one has the basis for the so-called paper-and-pencil "personality," interest, and attitude inventories. It is obvious that the reliability and validity of these instruments depend to a great degree on how adequately the individual can or will report the facts. It is possible that some pupils with severe emotional problems cannot satisfactorily interpret their feelings and behavior to make a valid report.

BIOGRAPHICAL DATA BLANK. Factual information about an individual's past history has been found helpful in predicting a pupil's future success on the job or in higher learning. Hobbies, special activities in and out of school, skills, success with past education, etc., can be used by an evaluator to make a clinical judgment about an individual. In some cases, items have been analyzed to determine the relationship of responses to future behavior of the individual. For example, it may be that in a question such:

How many things have you built out of wood?
  (a) none
  (b) several
  (c) many

the pupil answering *many* probably is more successful in shop class than one answering *none* or *several*. On the other hand, the question may have no predictive value for success in general mathematics. A *Pilot Biographical Data Blank* was useful during World War II to predict success of applicants. More recently, *Project* Talent employed numerous questions of the biographical-data-blank type in the nationwide inventory of human talent. Typical of the questions used are the following:

How many times have you been president of a class,
a club, or other organization (other than athletic)
in the last 3 years?
  (a) none
  (b) once
  (c) twice
  (d) three times
  (e) four times
  (f) five or more times

How many books are in your home?
  (a) none, or very few (0–10)
  (b) a few books (11–25)
  (c) one bookcase full (26–100)
  (d) two bookcases full (101–250)
  (e) three or four bookcases full (251–500)
  (f) a room full—a library (501 or more)

Instruments of this type probably have predictive value because they reflect interests, personality traits, and certain abilities related to performance.

PERSONAL INVENTORIES. One of the typical personality inventories designed for school use is the *California Test of Personality*. This instrument was developed in five series so that it can be administered to pupils from kindergarten to adulthood. According to the authors, the major purpose of the inventory is to reveal the extent to which the pupil is adjusting to the conditions facing him and is developing a normal, happy, and socially effective personality. Each series is divided into two sections. The first part indicates the pupil's feelings about himself (personal adjustment), and the second reflects social adjustment. Each division is further subdivided into six headings having an equal number of questions: eight in the primary series, twelve in the elementary series, and fifteen in the intermediate, secondary, and adult series. Such questions are asked of primary children as: "Do the children think you can do things well?" "Are you asked to play in other people's yards?" Older pupils are queried as follows: "Do you visit with several young men and women in your neighborhood?" A "yes" or "no" response is made to each question. The authors suggest that a profile be made for each pupil so that serious deviations may be determined and dealt with.

The foregoing inventory is designed to be a measure of traits or components of adjustment. Another approach to the evaluation of personal-social adjustment is through the determination of problem areas. The *Mooney Problem Check List*, which can be used with junior and senior high school pupils, is a self-report instrument whose purpose is to help individuals express their personal problems. The pupil reads through the check list and underlines the problems that concern him. After completing the first step, he is asked to go back over the items he has underlined and circle the numbers of those of greater concern to him. In the high school form there are 330 items representing common problems of adolescents which were collected from reports of pupils. Some of the items in this form are:

Getting sick too often
Awkward in meeting people
Not being attractive to the opposite sex
Being different
Too little freedom in class
Worrying about grades
Afraid of the future

The items are set up in problem areas to facilitate counseling. For the high school form there are eleven areas: health and physical development; finances; living conditions and employment; social and recreational activities; social-psychological relations; courtship, sex, and marriage; home and family; morals and religion; adjustment to school work; the future: vocational and educational; and curriculum and teaching procedures.

It would appear offhand that the pupil who has checked the most problems would be in serious need of counseling. However, an individual may check an item even though it bothers him very little. Since the number of problems checked depends on the willingness of the pupil to express himself, some individuals may not check their most serious problems. It is also possible that one problem may be more difficult for one pupil than a series of problems for another. It should be noted that what may not seem to be a problem to an adult, or at least one of little importance, may be a very real source of concern to the pupil. The first step in helping pupils to better adjustment is finding out what seem to them to be their problems. In some instances, pupils have checked problems which arise out of school or community peculiarities. Thus it is often helpful to get a group summary of the marked items. In one school a large number of pupils checked "teachers lacking interest in students." This was quite revealing information to the faculty, but happily a problem that they could rectify.

Extensive investigations of the reliability and validity of the adjustment inventories, particularly of the type represented by the *California Test of Personality*, have been made. One reviewer states:

> There is at best one chance in two that these tests will validly discriminate between groups of adjusted and maladjusted individuals, and there is very little indication that they can be safely used to diagnose *individual cases*, or give valid estimations of personality traits of specific respondents (Ellis, 1946, p. 425).

In a later survey of personality inventories, the same reviewer states:

> . . . it was found that in most instances the inventories are not measuring the independent traits they are supposed to be measuring; they do not agree too well with each other nor with the results of *Rorschach* and projective tests; they are easily faked; and they usually do not give significant group discriminations when used with vocational, academic, sociometric, and disabled and ill groups. It was especially found that in none of the areas in which they are commonly employed, do personality inventories consistently show significant group discriminations (Ellis, 1953, p. 48).

According to Ellis, these inventories are valid if they adequately discriminate neurotics from nonneurotics, introverts from extroverts, dominants from submissives, and so forth. But the teacher administers the inventory for other purposes as well. The instruments provide an opportunity for pupils to inform school personnel of their problems. Test scores may also be used to inform pupils how they compare with their own age group. In view of this, the conclusion by Ellis must be evaluated in relation to the school's purpose.

It is suggested that pupil profiles based on subtests of the *California Test of Personality* containing as few as eight or twelve items be used to determine specific peculiarities of an individual's personality traits. Referring to the table of norms for one of these subtests, we find the pupil's score is at the twentieth percentile if he answers five questions correctly; however, if he circles the "yes" for one additional item, his score jumps to the thirty-fifth percentile. A total of seven correct answers places it at the fifty-fifth percentile. This certainly does not inspire confidence in the utility of the norms of this particular inventory. Furthermore, no systematic attempt has been made, in many instances, to validate the items in terms of the descriptive headings under which they are subsumed.

The lack of precision found in the typical personal inventory precludes their satisfactory use in the construction of diagnostic adjustment profiles. If any score is used, the total score would seem to be the wisest choice. Its reliability and validity are superior to those of the subtests.

Despite the limitations mentioned in the foregoing discussion, adjustment inventories can be helpful if they are used in conjunction with other evaluation data. The teacher must understand their weaknesses and under no circumstances, use the scores from these instruments as his sole source of information about the pupil. It is possible that the pupil with a low total score may have adjustment problems; on the other hand, the teacher should not assume that a high score necessarily means good adjustment. Faking is common with this type of instrument.[1] Since the test results are much more likely to be valid if the subject wants to be truthful, rapport in the administration of this kind is very important.

One defensible use of these instruments is to screen populations for adjustment problems. Some pupils, especially those who do not interfere with the class routine, may have serious difficulties that an administration of a personal inventory may bring to the teacher's attention. On the other hand, a screening may identify pupils as maladjusted when, in effect, they have no serious problem. These cases are labeled as "false positives." In industry or in the military, large numbers of adequately adjusted individuals referred to as maladjusted may prove troublesome. However, in the classroom where teachers are concerned with children as individuals at all stages of development, there is less harm unless the teacher fails to study the child further and to compare test results with additional data. On the other hand, the test scores may well direct the teacher's attention toward some child who was not identified as needing help. Remember, however, that screening should be done on the basis of the total score rather than through the use of subscores.

Despite this admonition, checking on the answers to individual questions of personal inventories may provide leads for further investigation of a pupil's problems. The boy or girl who never enters class discussions and who answers "yes" to the question, "Do your classmates seem to think that your ideas are usually poor?" has given the teacher a basis for helping him. Likewise, the pupil who seems willing enough, but who gets discouraged easily, indicates that he needs help in developing independence when he

[1] An attempt has been made in the *Minnesota Multiphasic Personality Inventory* to detect faking, evasion of questions, and habitually giving oneself the benefit of the doubt or vice versa. The subject is rated on these problems through another set of scores. This helps the evaluator to determine how much confidence can be placed in the answers given by the respondent.

answers affirmatively the question, "Do you need someone to give you a great deal of encouragement in order to do your work well?"

Personal inventories are only one source of information about pupils. If these data are used critically along with other knowledge, they can be of considerable help in evaluating pupil growth in terms of the educational objectives in this area. To suggest that they should not be employed in the classroom because of their limitations is to deny teachers a source of information in an area seriously lacking in effective evaluation tools and techniques.

PROBLEM

18 Of what specific value are personal-social adjustment inventories in the classroom? Who among the school personnel would be best fitted to interpret and utilize results gained from these inventories?

ETHICAL CONSIDERATIONS. Questions have been raised about the ethics of requiring individuals to answer very personal questions included in some personal-social adjustment inventories. These have caused some to inquire as to whether such questions constitute an invasion of privacy. Particular attention has been focused on requiring individuals who are not thought to be emotionally ill or "mentally disturbed" to answer questions about private feelings in such areas as religion, family relationships, patriotism, and so forth. Comments in the press and testimony before Congressional committees delineate some of these concerns.

In general, psychologists defending the use of personal-social adjustment inventories stress their present basic limitations, but emphasize their usefulness when the results yielded by them are considered along with other data. Self-regulation by the psychological profession is helpful, but a basic conflict exists. At the same time the psychologist believes firmly in the dignity and worth of the individual, he is committed to increasing man's understanding of himself and others. Hence, is the use of personal-social adjustment inventories in a given instance an invasion of privacy or a legitimate investigation of man's behavior (Messick, 1965)?

INTEREST INVENTORIES. The experienced teacher knows that interest plays an important part in the personal-social adjustment of children. The boy who likes sciences and has books available to him in this area will be motivated to read, thereby developing his basic reading skill and his sense of adequacy at the same time. The teacher who involves his pupils in a project that interests them will find that facility in social situations will develop much more readily than if they are made to do uninteresting or irrelevant work.

A particularly important interest for secondary school pupils is the vocation for which they wish to prepare. Two standardized inventories, Strong's *Vocational Interest Blank* (sometimes called the *VIB*) and the *Kuder Preference Record-Form C-Vocational,* have been used extensively for vocational guidance in the secondary schools. The *Kuder-Form E-General Interest Survey* is a recent revision and downward extension of *Form C.* It is designed for grades 6–12. Two other *Kuder* inventories, *Form D-Occupational* and *Form DD* are similar to the *VIB* in that they compare a pupil's response with those of a number of occupational groups. With *Form DD* there are direct item-by-item comparisons between an individual's responses and those in numerous occupational and college-major groups.

The *Kuder Preference Record-Form A-Personal* taps an individual's personal and social preferences rather than those related to vocations. It is therefore more like an adjustment inventory than the other *Kuder* forms. Its five scales reflect the following personal and social preferences: (1) preference for being in active groups; (2) preference for familiar and stable situations; (3) preference for working with ideas; (4) preference for avoiding conflict, and (5) preference for directing or influencing others. Only the Strong *Vocational Interest Blank* and the *Kuder Preference Record-Form C-Vocational* will be discussed at length in this chapter.

In developing the Strong *Vocational Interest Blank,* a large number of items relating to an individual's everyday living was selected. These items were submitted to persons engaged in various occupations. It was found, for example, that engineers tended to express similar likes and dislikes. Persons in other fields showed the same tendency toward common interests within the occupational group differing from those of other occupational groups. This means that an individual could be questioned about his interests to determine how closely they compared to those of individuals who were successful in their chosen fields.

Separate forms of the *VIB* are available for men and women. The 1966 edition for men contains 399 items. To most of these the examinee responds with *like, indifferent,* or *dislike.* For example, he selects one of these three words to represent his feelings toward various occupations, school subjects, amusements, activities, and types of people. He responds, for example, to words such as actor, history, poker, skiing, picnics, arguments, optimists, and foreigners. The inventory is scored for more than fifty different occupations. These are listed in eleven groups on the profile sheet. The occupations in each group have roughly similar interests; for example, the biological sciences.

Keys for specialization level, occupational level, masculinity-femininity, and academic achievement have also been developed. The specialization level key was first designed for differentiating between the interests of the medical specialist and the general practitioner. It has since been used as a possible means of predicting whether the examinee would like specialized graduate study. Occupational level represents a measure of differences in interests between those in the professions or business or labor. Masculinity-femininity refers to the degree to which a person's interests compare with those of men or women. Scores from the academic achievement scale correlate significantly with final marks in college.

Strong found that interests change very little from age 25 to 55, that there is a little change from 20 to 25 years of age, but that the shifts are considerable between the ages of 15 and 20. He therefore suggests that it would be wise not to use the test with boys under the age of 17 unless they are unusually mature; in any event, an allowance should be made for their youth (Strong, 1943).

The Kuder Preference Record—Vocational illustrates another method of construction. As in Strong's Vocational Interest Blank, a large number of items were collected describing everyday life. However, instead of emphasizing the interests of those in the various occupations and then attempting to determine if a person's interests were like theirs, Kuder sought to describe the interests of a subject through a logical grouping of items. If a pupil showed an interest in a certain group of items, it could be said that he had an interest in activities related to that group. Altogether there are ten areas of interest and a verification scale to identify those who answer the items carelessly or without understanding.

The Kuder Preference Record—Vocational has 168 items organized in groups of three. The pupil decides which of the three he likes most and which he likes least. He is forced to choose even though he likes or dislikes them equally. In the first example shown in Figure 33, the examinee has punched a hole in the left-hand circle in front of the letter R. In this way, he has indicated that the three activities, P, Q, and R, he would most like to visit a museum. By punching the hole in the right-hand circle beside letter Q, he indicates that of the three activities he would like least to browse in a library. Similarly, in the second example, he would like most to collect autographs and would least like to collect butterflies.

A sample Kuder profile is shown in Figure 34. This profile of Jim Spencer, a high school junior, shows that he has very little interest in the computational and scientific areas. Jim's father is an engineer and holds an important executive position in his firm. Both parents are anxious for their son to choose engineering as a vocation. Jim's record throughout elementary school has been satisfactory. His IQ on the Henmon-Nelson Tests of Mental Ability administered at the end of the eighth grade was 136. His scores on the Iowa Tests of Basic Skills showed no difficulty in the basic

DIRECTIONS:

A number of activities are listed in groups of three. Read over the activities in each group. Decide which of the three activities you like *most*. There are two circles on the same line as this activity. Punch a hole with the pin through the left-hand circle following this activity. Then decide which you like *least* and punch a hole through the right-hand circle.

P	Visit an art gallery	O	P	O
Q	Browse in a library	O	Q	O
R	Visit a museum	O	R	O
S	Collect autographs	O	S	O
T	Collect coins	O	T	O
U	Collect butterflies	O	U	O

From Kuder, 1951; reproduced by permission of Science Research Associates.

FIGURE 33

ITEMS FROM INSTRUCTIONAL EXAMPLE OF THE KUDER PREFERENCE
RECORD—VOCATIONAL, FORM CH

subjects. However, in high school his final marks in algebra, plane geometry, and general science were below average. He had to repeat biology during the summer session. During his junior year he was in serious difficulty with his mathematics and science courses, though he had completed one of the best projects in social studies. He had also become a behavior problem and was absent from school quite often. Because he refused to cooperate at band practice, he was suspended from that organization.

Although the preceding data do not represent a complete case history, it seems apparent that Jim's interests are most closely related to other vocational fields than to engineering. His superior academic ability will probably be wasted if he is forced to continue his present course of study. Quite possibly a career in a social science would be appropriate for him.

The descriptive nature of the *Kuder* provides a suitable basis for counseling. Through statistical analysis, it has become possible to translate *VIB* scores into descriptions of traits as well. The form for the *Kuder* is also the same for both sexes, while the *VIB* for women is less complete than the men's form. The scoring of the *VIB* is complex and time consuming, although it can be scored commercially for a nominal fee. On the other hand, the pupil can score his own *Kuder* record in a few minutes and the results are available immediately. It is not surprising, therefore, to find the *Kuder* used much more extensively in the secondary school than the *VIB*.

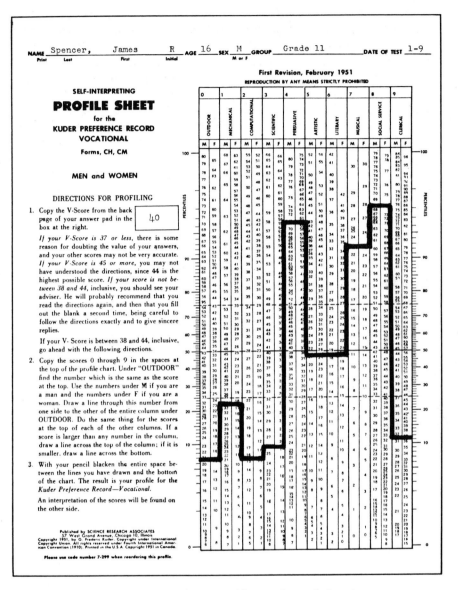

From Kuder, 1951; reproduced by permission of Science Research Associates.

FIGURE 34

KUDER PREFERENCE RECORD PROFILE SHEET

Studies indicate that the *VIB* odd-even reliability coefficient is about 0.80. The *Kuder Preference Record—Vocational* reliability coefficient is about 0.90. No adequate consideration has been given to the stability of the *Kuder*, however. One study shows a considerable shift of high school pupils' low and high interest areas when there is a difference of several years between initial and second testing (Millinson and Crumrine, 1952). Retest scores reported in the manual on the *VIB* over long periods of time, when compared with initial scores, show a relationship as high as 0.80.

A number of studies by Strong (1951; 1952 a; 1952 b) have shown that scores on the *VIB* have considerable criterion-related validity. In several follow-up investigations, he found a very definite relationship between the occupations in which the subjects were employed and their interest test scores. The *Kuder*, on the other hand, has not had this thorough an investigation of its criterion-related validity.

The problem of faking is an important consideration in the test validity of interest inventories, just as it is in the personal-adjustment inventories. An examinee suitably motivated can successfully fake the *Kuder Preference Record*. Because the intent of the items is not so obvious in the *VIB*, it is less easily faked. When tests are given for employment purposes, apparent motives could promote untruthful answers, but when used with secondary school pupils, it would seem that little is gained from faking.

Despite its shortcomings, the *Kuder* has earned a place in the secondary school testing program. It is of some help to the counselor and teacher, since it focuses attention on general fields of interest rather than on the interests of successful people in various occupations, as in the case with the *Vocational Interest Blank*. However, the teacher or counselor needs to exercise caution in over-interpretation. Effective evaluation must include the use of other data gathered from varied sources as an adjunct to the interest inventory scores.

Problems

19 The *Kuder Preference Record* is frequently administered during the ninth grade as an aid in the selection of high school courses and for pre-vocational planning for the pupil. Although counselors know that interests may shift, they find the inventory useful. Why?

20 Interest inventory results must be reported to parents with the greatest of care. Describe the most troublesome misconceptions that frequently occur.

Attitude Scales and Questionnaires. The concept of attitude refers to the way individuals act and think toward and about people, objects, and situations they encounter, as a result of their previous experiences. The school is committed to the development of certain basic social attitudes in its pupils. Among the attitudes that can be learned are those toward race prejudice, bigotry, consideration, religion, democracy, and quality of man. The evaluation of attitude formation and change becomes just as important, then, as achievement in the basic skills.

The formal instruments for attitude measurement fall into two categories: opinion polling and attitude scales. Neither is very useful to the classroom teacher. Their value lies chiefly in their utility as research tools. The Gallup poll is a typical opinion survey. A person is generally approached with a single question which he is usually asked to answer with "Yes," or "No," or "Undecided." The results are typically reported in terms of the percentages of answers given in each of those categories.

Attitude scales are generally of the Thurstone (Thurstone and Chave, 1929) or Likert (1932) types. Thurstone sets up his scales so that an attitude can be measured on a continuum from unfavorable to highly favorable. A number of statements representing various degrees of favorableness give the subject an opportunity to express his feelings. For example, in measuring attitude toward the law, the excerpt in Figure 35 shows that a favorable attitude is given a higher value. Those with low numerical values suggest an unfavorable attitude. The subject identifies those statements with which he agrees and those with which he disagrees. His score is the average of the scale values of the statements toward which he is favorable.

A subject's position on the scale of attitude toward the law is then determined by finding the average of all the scale values of statements with which he agrees. Suppose that out of the twenty items on this scale he checked statements having the following values: 10.1, 10.5, 9.1, and 6.1. He would then have an average of $\frac{35.8}{4} = 8.95$ or 9. The items on Thurstone scales are generally on a continuum from one to eleven. Therefore, this individual appears to have a favorable attitude toward law.

In the Likert method, statements are never neutral toward the object in question but are favorable or unfavorable in varying degrees. The subject reacts to each statement on a five-point scale, indicating that he either strongly agrees, agrees, is uncertain, disagrees, or strongly disagrees. His score is computed simply by weighting the responses from five to one for a favorable statement beginning with strong agreement. Values are assigned in reverse order for unfavorable statements.

The Likert method is illustrated by the following two items (from Likert, 1932; reproduced by permission of the Science Press) taken from a scale designed to measure one's attitude toward the Negro. It will be noted that both items have the A circled, which means that the subject agreed

DIRECTIONS:
Put a check mark (√) if you agree with the statement.
Put a cross (×) if you disagree with the statement.

			Value
( )	6.	I believe in the use of force to overthrow the law.	0.2
( )	15.	The law is made in response to the pressure of lobbies in Washington.	2.9
( )	16.	Some laws command our respect while others are mere regulations.	6.1
( )	9.	The law is more than the enactments of Congress; it is a sacred institution.	10.5

From Thurstone and Katz, 1931 reproduced by permission of the University of Chicago Press.

FIGURE 35

EXCERPT FROM THURSTONE'S SCALE FOR MEASURING ATTITUDE
TOWARD THE LAW

with both statements. However, since the first item is favorable to Negroes, the "Agree" has a value of four. The second item is essentially unfavorable, and so the reverse order of scoring gives it a value of two. The total score on the scale is the sum of the values of all items. The maximum possible score is five times the total number of items.

Encircle one of the symbols preceding each of the following statements A stands for "Agree," SA for "Strongly Agree," D for "Disagree," SD for "Strongly Disagree," and "?" for "Uncertain."

SA (A) ? D SD If the same preparation is required, the Negro teacher should receive the same salary as the white.

SA (A) ? D SD Negro homes should be segregated from those of white people.

Reliability of the Thurstone-type scales by the split-half method yields an average coefficient of about 0.80, which is good for an instrument with so few items. The coefficients of reliability for the stability method are much lower. Likert scales have been found to have roughly equivalent reliability coefficients.

Determining the relative validity of attitude scales has been a difficult problem, chiefly because of a lack of adequate criteria by which to judge test scores. The question arises as to whether verbalized opinions actually represent attitudes. Although behavior can be checked, of course, individuals behave in different ways for different reasons. A pupil may say that he likes school and show outward signs of full cooperation. He may nonetheless dislike teachers and his classwork intensely, but find it expedient to foster good will so that he can stay on the basketball team. As is true of other self-report techniques, attitude evaluation is likely to be most valid when the pupil has no reason for falsification.

Unfortunately, standardized instruments for attitude measurements have not developed to the point where they can be practically useful to the classroom teacher, who must in large part depend on other evidences of attitude formation and change. Through observation and sociomatric data, he will be able to evaluate these changes if he directs his attention toward them and systematizes his approach.

To obtain objective data, a teacher must look for attitudes in pupil behavior. Pupils may say that honesty is the best policy, but do they cheat, lie, or steal? Do they accept other pupils despite their social status? Are they responsive to the needs of others? Do they have a scientific attitude? Do they get all the facts? Do they draw logical conclusions? The teacher who has stated his educational objectives in terms of changes in pupil behavior will be able to infer attitude development and change from the modified actions of his pupils. If he then records this development in anecdotal records, if he files some of the answers to open questions, and if he summarizes these data for the group, he will make progress toward effective evaluation of attitudes.

PROBLEM

21 There is common agreement that the degree of validity of attitude scales is generally low at best. Nevertheless, describe possible uses of these instruments in a classroom or in a group guidance session.

SUMMARY

The importance of adequate personal-social adjustment in school children is emphasized by the needs of our society. Fostering achievement in this area of development is as much the responsibility of our schools as is the teaching of basic skills. To provide effective learning situations leading to maturity, teachers must understand emotional problems. They must be able to differentiate between adequate adjustment and atypical behavior. It is apparent that they need to develop skill in diagnosing many less serious behavioral problems. They must determine causes and effect solutions.

Evaluation of personal-social adjustment, therefore, plays an important role in the school's instructional program. There are many approaches to this evaluation. Observing children is one of the best ways of determining how well they get along with their peers and the degree of their emotional maturity. Often this can be done in the natural situation, although care must be exercised to prevent the biases of the observer from interfering with objective reporting. To this end, it is helpful to separate reports from interpretations in anecdotal records.

Rating scales and check lists, which direct and objectify observation, can also provide quantitative data, making it possible to pool the evaluations of several observers. A number of schools have constructed instruments to meet their own needs. Unfortunately, not many helpful standardized scales or check lists are available to the teacher. Still another source of information about a pupil's personal-social growth is the teacher-parent interview.

Standardized projective instruments, designed chiefly for use by clinical psychologists, are available. The present standardized instruments provide situations in which ambiguous stimuli allow an individual's personality to influence his reactions. The teacher should be informed about the utility of these instruments so he can refer pupils for testing if the need arises.

Children can report much information about each other that is not always available to teachers and parents. Such devices as the sociogram, social distance scale, and "guess-who" questionnaire can indicate how well a pupil is accepted by his peers and can reveal specific strengths and weaknesses of his personality. Follow-up interviews, in which an attempt is made to find reasons for specific choices or descriptions of children, may reveal certain adjustment problems.

Pupils should also be able to tell much about themselves since no one has so good an opportunity to observe an individual in so many different situations as he has himself. Self-report tests, such as personal inventories, interest inventories, attitude scales, questionnaires, and biographical data blanks, are based on self-reporting. One of the most severe drawbacks of these instruments is the faking of answers by pupils who are motivated by a desire to make themselves appear different than they really are.

In the final analysis, a teacher should collect as much information about a pupil from as many different sources as possible. No one test score or single observation should be relied upon for complete evaluation. Because personal-social adjustment is such a complex process, it demands extensive and varied approaches in evaluation.

Suggested Readings

Amos, R. T., and R. M. Washington. A comparison of pupil and teacher perceptions of pupil problems. *J. educ. Psychol.*, 1960, **51**, 255–258.

Twenty-one teachers were asked to identify pupils with problem behavior and to rate them on the *Mooney Problem Check List*. Their ratings were compared with the pupils' self-ratings. Differences between the two show that teachers are more aware of problems which disrupt classroom order, and are relatively insensitive to problems in the areas of money, work, the future, and health and physical development.

Amrine, Michael (Ed.) Testing and public policy. *Amer. Psychologist*, 1965, **20**, 857–993; 1966, **21**, 401–478.

These two issues of the *American Psychologist* contain testimony presented to committees of the Congress which were investigating the criticism of the use of psychological tests, particularly paper-and-pencil personality inventories. Invited comments from government officials and other individuals are also included.

Bauernfeind, R. H. What to look for in a review of an interest inventory. *Personnel & Guid. J.*, 1964, **42**, 925–927.

The author raises important questions in determining whether an interest inventory is appropriate for a specific group and purpose.

Berdie, R. F. Strong Vocational Interest Blank scores of high school seniors and their later occupational entry. *J. appl. Psychol.*, 1965, **49**, 188–193.

Significant relationships were found between VIB scores and later occupations.

Cunningham, Ruth, and others. *Understanding group behavior of boys and girls*. New York: Bureau of Publications, Teachers College, Columbia University, 1951. Chapter 11.

Chapter 11 represents the techniques used in this particular study and gives many illustrations and helpful suggestions for the use of anecdotes, time sampling, log of activities, autobiographies, children's reactions, and projective techniques.

Gaier, E. L., and W. F. White. Trends in the measurement of personality. *Rev. educ. Res.*, 1965, 63–81.

Research reports concerning means of measuring personality are reviewed. A lengthy bibliography is included.

Gronlund, N. E. *Sociometry in the classroom*. New York: Harper & Row, 1959.

The three parts into which this book is divided constitute a detailed description of how to construct and administer the sociometric test in the classroom, and how to interpret its results.

Hutson, P. W. Recent studies in character-trait rating. *Personnel & Guid. J.* 1960, **38**, 364–368.

This is a report of the findings of recent research on the use of rating scales by high school teachers. By using the recommended procedure of Gardner and Ritenour, teachers' ratings of pupil proved to be better predictors of college marks than either mental ability tests or high school marks. The rating procedure used is described.

Kuder, G. F. A rationale for evaluating interests. *Educ. psychol. Measmt*, 1963, **23**, 3–10.

This article is useful for those who wish to further explore the rationale and history of development of the vocational interest inventories. The article emphasizes several points such as the development of vocation keys and the importance of overlapping of the keys.

Layton, W. L. *The Strong Vocational Interest Blank*, research and uses. Minneapolis: University of Minnesota Press, 1960.

 This volume includes a series of papers read at an institute concerning the *Vocational Interest Blank*. Such topics as longitudinal studies of interests, validity, correlates of interest, and maturity are presented.

Masia, B. B. What to look for in a review of a personality inventory. *Personnel & Guid. J.*, 1964, **42**, 1030–1034.

 Three major functions traditionally assigned to personality measurement in the schools are discussed. Limitations of achieving these purposes are indicated. The author cites information that the user of personality inventories should know to interpret a review intelligently.

Messick, S. Personality measurement and the ethics of assessment. *Amer. Psychologist*, 1965, **20**, 136–142.

 The author points out that self-regulation of psychological assessment is very complex because the normative standards and values that should govern such regulation are in conflict. On the one hand, a psychologist believes in the dignity and worth of the individual. On the other hand, he is dedicated to the search for a better understanding of man's behavior. These two goals could be in conflict when personal-social adjustment inventories are used in certain instances.

Super, D. E., and J. O. Crites. *Appraising vocational fitness by means of psychological tests*. (Rev. ed.) New York: Harper & Row, 1962. Chapters 16, 17, 18, and 19.

 The first three chapters are devoted to interest tests whereas the fourth concerns the measurement of attitudes and temperament. Paper-and-pencil techniques are emphasized.

Taba, Hilda, and others. *Diagnosing human relations needs: studies in intergroup relations*. Washington: American Council on Education, 1951.

 This booklet presents very practical discussions on the use of diaries, parent interviews, participation schedules, sociometric procedures, open questions, and teacher logs. Its clear instructions to the teacher provide an adequate guide for classroom use.

Taylor, R. G. Personality traits and discrepant achievement. *J. consult. Psychol.*, 1964, **11**, 76–82.

 This article deals with the relationship of academic anxiety, self values, authority relations, and several other personality variables and their relation to academic achievement.

References Cited

Bonney, M. E. Sociometric study of agreement between teacher judgments and student choices. *Sociometry*, 1947, **10**, 133–146.

Cronbach, L. J. *Essentials of psychological testing*. (2nd ed.) New York: Harper & Row, 1960.

Cunningham, Ruth, and others. *Understanding group behavior of boys and girls*. New York: Bureau of Publications, Teachers College, Columbia University, 1951.

Dale, G. A. A comparison of two groups of elementary school children classified for school adjustment on a basis of teacher rating. *J. educ. Res.*, 1941, **35**, 241–250.

Ellis, A. Recent research with personality inventories. *J. consult. Psychol.*, 1953, **17**, 45–49.

Ellis, A. The validity of personality questions. *Psychol. Bull.*, 1946, **43**, 385–440.

Froehlick, C. P., and J. G. Darley, *Studying students.* Chicago: Science Research Associates, 1952.

Guilford, J. P. *Psychometric Methods.* New York: McGraw-Hill Book Company, Inc., 1954.

Haggerty, M. E., W. C. Olson, and E. K. Wickman. *Haggerty-Olson-Wickman Behavior Rating Schedules.* Tarrytown, N. Y.: Harcourt, Brace and World, 1930.

Hartshorne, H., and M. A. May. *Studies in service and self-control.* New York: Macmillan, 1929.

Jennings, Helen H. *Sociometry in group relations.* (Rev. ed.) Washington: American Council on Education, 1959.

Jersild, A. T., and others. *Education for understanding.* New York: Bureau of Publications, Teachers College, Columbia University, 1953.

Kuder, G. F. *Kuder Preference Record-Vocational, Form C.* Chicago: Science Research Associates, 1951.

Likert, R. A technique for the measurement of attitudes. *Arch. Psychol.*, 1932, No. 140.

Messick, Samuel. Personality measurement and the ethics of assessment. *Amer. Psychologist,* **20**, 136–142.

Millinson, G. G., and W. M. Crumrine. An investigation of the stability of interests of high school students. *J. educ. Res.* 1952, **45**, 369–383.

Murray, H. A., and others. *Explorations in personality.* London: Oxford University Press, 1938.

Shaffer, L. F., and E. J. Shoben, Jr. *The psychology of adjustment.* (2nd ed.) Boston: Houghton Mifflin, 1956.

Sparks, J. N. Teachers' attitudes toward the behavior problems of children. *J. educ. Psychol.*, 1952, **43**, 283–291.

Stouffer, G. A. W., Jr. Behavior problems of children as viewed by teachers and mental hygienists. *Ment. Hyg.*, 1952, **36**, 271–285.

Strong, E. K., Jr. *Vocational interests of men and women.* Stanford University: Stanford University, 1943.

Strong, E. K., Jr. Interest scores while in college of occupations engaged in 20 years later. *Educ. psychol. Measmt,* 1951, **11**, 333–348.

Strong, E. K., Jr. Nineteen-year follow-up of engineer interests. *J. appl. Psychol.*, 1952, **36**, 65–74. (a)

Strong, E. K., Jr. Twenty-year follow-up of medical interests. In L. L. Thurstone (Ed.), *Applied psychology.* New York: Harper & Row, 1952. Pp. 111–130. (b)

Symonds, P. M. *Diagnosing personality and conduct.* New York: Appleton-Century-Crofts, 1931.

Technical Research Report, PRB 1077. Personnel research for the United States Military Academy, Washington: The Adjutant General's Office, 1953.

Thurstone, L. L., and E. J. Chave. *The measurement of attitude.* Chicago: The University of Chicago Press, 1929.

Thurstone, L. L., and D. Katz. *The measurement of social attitude toward the law.* Chicago: The University of Chicago Press, 1931.

Wickman, E. K. *Children's behavior and teachers' attitude.* New York: The Commonwealth Fund, 1928.

Wrightstone, J. W. Observational techniques. In Chester W. Harris (Ed.), *Encyclopedia of educational research.* (3rd ed.) New York: Macmillan, 1960. Pp. 927–933.

14 ✐

A School-Wide Program of Evaluation

SOONER OR LATER MOST OF US GO ON DIETS. One day a man whose habits are satisfying takes an honest look in the morror and finds the familiar terrain has developed unfamiliar bulges, and that once-trim clothes are now straining. The concerned self-observer establishes a weight to be reached, and the campaign is on.

A feature accompanying such programs is the organized, continuous, and comprehensive evaluative effort. The serious dieter establishes a pattern of daily checks on progress: numerous type measurements and trips to the bathroom scales, honest scrutiny in the mirror, an informal check on physiological reactions following the rapid ascent of a flight of stairs, and perhaps an occasional secretive attempt to button the tuxedo of a more streamlined era. These evaluations continue for the duration of the program, and perhaps beyond.

With versatility and persistence, a school should determine the degree to which its pupils are achieving its educational objectives. Too often, however, a school's evaluative efforts stop with administering a few classroom paper-and-pencil tests or a standardized achievement or scholastic aptitude test at infrequent intervals, efforts neither coordinated nor adequate. With such spotty and incomplete findings, the school cannot effectively evaluate the real state of things.

PURPOSE OF AN EVALUATION PROGRAM

An evaluation program informs the school how to enable each pupil to develop his potential within an educational framework. To accomplish this, the school must know the pupils' capacities, interests, and achievements, and have objectives that can be evaluated. It does little good to state high-minded objectives like "To develop good citizenship," if good citizenship is not defined and its aspects stated so that the degree of the pupil's development can not be determined. How much less bewildering it is to assess progress toward the well-stated objective, "The pupil develops an awareness of property rights and of truth and falsehood."

Educational objectives should reflect the needs of pupils in a particular school. Although the objectives of various schools are more similar than different, important differences inevitably exist. Some schools have a large percentage of college-bound pupils, while most students in a neighboring school will remain in the community. Out-of-school activities and their impact on the educational program will differ among communities. Many children of higher socio-economic families have access to a variety of books and magazines and may attend concerts, plays, and art exhibits at least on occasion, but pupils in certain rural areas may do little reading, and have no access to cultural opportunities. Community resources and the vocational goals of children must influence a school's objectives.

A school-wide program of evaluation is based on the set of educational objectives held by that school. The task is exceedingly complex. Too often testing is confused with evaluation, and the school initiates a testing program per se. Though an important part of the evaluation program, testing is still only one part. Many kinds of evidence are needed, and from various sources. Because we do not have effective tests to measure all aspects of behavior, many other approaches including observation, rating scales, questionnaires, and interviews must be used. Data collected can then be used as a basis for evaluating individuals in terms of their abilities and needs.

Problems

1 The board of education of a small community hired a team of educational specialists from a nearby university to evaluate the testing program of the school system and to make specific recommendations for improvement. The team prepared a comprehensive report which was then presented to the faculty. Although this report was complimentary for the most part, there was a general feeling of dissatisfaction among both faculty and administration. Criticize the procedure followed by the board of education. Suggest a better approach.
2 Prepare a list of educational objectives for a secondary school program in a slum area in a large city, and another list for a secondary school program in a small rural community. In what respects are your lists similar? Are the differences sufficiently large to cause the school-wide evaluation program at one school to be greatly different from that of the other school?

Initiating the Program

Since a program of evaluation cannot be separated from the total educational program, school personnel in administration, guidance, and instruction must participate in its inception, organization, and promotion. It should be a truly cooperative venture. The authoritarian principal who dictates a program may compel his staff to comply mechanically. They may administer, score, and record the results of tests, but it is doubtful that they will be motivated to understand pupil behavior, and motivation which only comes through in-service education and democratic participation of a staff, is the basis of a good evaluative program.

In a small school, the general staff meeting involves all teachers. For everyone has a chance to ask questions and discuss. The administrator should probably assume leadership to stimulate interest, perhaps by posing such a problem of "Why do our pupils always do better on the mathematical parts of standardized achievement test batteries than on the verbal parts?" Perhaps community criticism of achievement may prompt the staff to evaluate its educational program. It is also possible to interest the staff by showing them the results of the administration of a standardized achievement test, such as a reading survey test from which they can determine the strengths and weaknesses of the pupils. When properly directed, this approach will stimulate thinking about the total evaluative problem in the school.

In the large city system it is impractical, if not impossible, to involve the entire staff in the initial evaluation discussions, so a representative committee should work out preliminary details. Before any final action is taken, the entire staff should discuss and evaluate the proposals, a necessity if the evaluation is to be integrated with the total educational program.

In the initial discussions, teachers should understand that evaluation is a comprehensive process requiring continuous administrative and guidance functions in addition to the more obvious instructional ones. Suggestions of the kinds of evidence needed for evaluating in terms of a group of related objectives, and where that evidence can be sought, can be made meaningful if presented in chart form, as illustrated in Table 21. This will help prevent the limited approach of paper-and-pencil testing alone.

The objectives concerning communication shown in Table 21 are adapted from Kearney (1953). Although it is desirable to refine the wording of some of the objectives in this table in terms of the discussion in Chapter 2 concerning the guidelines for stating specific objectives (Mager, 1962), note that these are not vaguely phrased. Rather than statements such as "to develop comprehension," the objective listed is "he reads third-grade material with a comprehension of 80 per cent." Rather than "to read rapidly," the objective is stated "he can read from 95 to 120 words silently each minute." The last objective could be improved by adding "and is able to answer correctly 80 per cent of the comprehension questions sampling the passage." The criterion of acceptable performance is now definite. A few other objectives could be more crisply stated in behavioral terms such as "he can read orally in a meaningful way." The term "meaningful" should be clarified.

In Table 21, the statement of objectives is followed by a suggested means for gathering information to be used as a basis for evaluation. Although teacher-constructed and standardized tests are often very helpful, there are some areas of achievement where they are inapplicable. For example, no test can determine whether a pupil does his assigned reading independently. Certainly improved skill will be reflected in test results, but the teacher can only observe him in the classroom for effective evaluation of this achievement. Incidentally, not all pupils will be limited to the specific objectives stated in Table 21, which are only general guides for

TABLE 21
EDUCATIONAL OBJECTIVES IN COMMUNICATION FOR
THE PRIMARY PERIOD AND MEANS OF EVALUATION

Educational objective	*Means of evaluation*
Knowledge and Understanding	
He can recognize basic reading sight-vocabulary.	Standardized oral reading tests Informal word recognition tests Standardized word lists
He can define common words that he uses orally.	Standardized word meaning tests Observation: teacher listens to his use of words Informal tests: Pupil writes definitions of words
He can read orally in a meaningful way.	Standardized oral reading tests Informal tests Check lists: smooth reading, good phrasing, correct interpretation of punctuation marks.
He has developed an acquaintance with children's literature.	Check lists: books checked out of library, brought to school. Observation: talks about books
He understands that many words "pair off" as opposites, e.g., yes-no, little-big.	Informal and standardized tests Workbook exercises Informal questioning during group instruction
He can distinguish between the names of persons and things and action words.	Informal tests Observation: ability to act out directions, to make up directions for others to follow Classification lists

TABLE 21 (*Continued*)

Educational objective	Means of evaluation

Skill and Competence

He does assigned reading independently.	Informal questioning during group instruction Observation: independent reading Written work
He can recall the sequence of a story or the facts read in a story.	Standardized reading tests Informal reading tests: recalls and writes facts Observation: answers well-phrased questions during group discussion, illustrates sequence in pictures, acts out sequence
He reads simple informational material with comprehension.	Informal reading tests Written work: brief written reports Observation: discusses material read
He reads third-grade material with a comprehension of 80 per cent.	Standardized reading tests Informal tests
He can read seven out of ten paragraphs of third-grade material and recognize many of the main ideas.	Standardized reading tests Informal tests Working with him independently and questioning him
He can read from 95 to 120 words silently each minute.	Standardized reading tests Informal tests (timed)

Attitude and Interest

He enjoys reading for recreation or information.	Observation: talks or writes about his reading, anxious to read new books, brings in objects about what he has read
He likes to recite poems and retell favorite stories.	Observation: reflects interests by what he says and does
He is interested in the sounds of words in word-families, in rhymes, and in secret languages and codes.	Observation: ability to act out direc- indicate this interest, knows how to determine word-families

Educational objectives adapted from Kearney, 1953, pp. 102–110; by permission of the Russell Sage Foundation.

primary teachers. A number of pupils should be able to read more difficult material than those at third grade level, just as some will read faster than 120 words per minute.

Problems

3   Table 21 presents in chart form a suggested manner of listing educational objectives in reading and a means of evaluation for each objective. Prepare a similar table for your subject-matter area but improve your statements of objectives by following the suggestions in Chapter 2.

4   Choose one or more of the educational objectives that you have stated for your subject matter and devise reasonably reliable and valid methods by means of which you might systematically and objectively evaluate each pupil in a class.

The Cumulative Record

The cumulative record is a device for recording and filing all pertinent data which will lead to a better understanding of the pupil for educational and vocational guidance purposes. Various kinds of data from many sources are more helpful than data obtained from a single source. A systematic, long-range accumulation of data clearly produces more intelligent interpretation than data collected at one time.

Cumulative records take various forms, the most common of which are the card, the folder, or a combination of them. The folder is printed for recording data, and any pertinent materials such as anecdotal records may be placed inside. A typical cumulative record of the folder type for the elementary grades is shown in Chapter 15 (pages 514–515). Notice the information required, the recording method, and the insert for recording additional health data. A surprisingly large amount of information can be permanently recorded on such a form.

Traxler (1953, pp. 74–75) suggests that the school staff should plan the record form cooperatively, and lists the following guiding principles for its construction:

1. It should agree with the educational objectives of the local school.
2. It should be the result of the group thinking of the faculty member.
3. It should either provide for a continuous record of the development of the pupil from the first grade to the end of the junior college or be one of a series of forms which make provision for such a record.
4. It should be organized by time sequence; that is, it should be set up by yearly divisions which run throughout the form.
5. It should contain ample and carefully planned space for a record of the results of all types of tests and for an explanation of the norms in terms of which the results were interpreted.

6. It should provide for the annual recording of personality ratings of behavior descriptions, which represent the consensus of the pupils' counselors and teachers.
7. While it should be as comprehensive as possible it should be simple enough to avoid overwhelming the clerical resources of the school.
8. It should be accessible to the teachers as well as to the counselors and principal. Highly confidential information which the counselor may possess should be filed elsewhere.
9. The record form should be re-evaluated periodically and revised as needed to take account of educational change and progress.

A number of Traxler's suggestions are followed in many cumulative record forms on the market.

Information Needed

One of the best ways to select data to include in the cumulative record is to determine the usefulness of each in understanding the pupil. In general, the following information is thought helpful.

1. *Identifying data.* These include items such as name, address, age, and date of birth.
2. *Scholastic achievement and mental development.* This would include not only information about the pupil's achievement in various areas but data concerning his general and special aptitudes. Some of this information can be recorded in anecdotal form. Other data can be tabulated as the results of informal and standardized tests and as school marks.
3. *School Attendance record.* Many factors, such as the suitability of the curriculum, home conditions, and the pupil's health, are related to a poor attendance record. These should be reported as well as the source of this information.
4. *Home and family background.* The educational and cultural backgrounds of the parents should be noted. It is also important to know the father's occupation, whether parents are living together, and any other information about home conditions that may be reflected in the pupil's behavior.
5. *Personal-social development.* Such factors as a pupil's degree of self-confidence, emotional stability, predominant moods, relationship to peers and authority figures, and his general mental health should be recorded.
6. *Health.* Under this category, items such as a history of medical and dental care, disabilities, and special information on vision and hearing are included. If a pupil has a disability, it is also wise to record his attitude toward it.
7. *Special activities and interests.* Discovering how a pupil uses his free time in and outside school often provides answers to important questions about his behavior. Any skills in athletics, music, or art, and any other special talents, as well as any work experience that he had, should be reported.

8. *Educational and vocational plans.* For the pupil in secondary school, this item becomes a prime factor in his selection of subjects and in his decision for the future. As his plans develop they should be noted, even though the pupil may be somewhat vague about them.

Sources of Information

Observation is an important source of data about the pupil's personal-social adjustment, special activities, and interests. If critical incidents are recorded over the years, the pupil's teachers and counselors at every level will be able to see his problems. The anecdotal record is an excellent means of recording these observations. Also useful are self-report devices, such as personal-social-adjustment inventories, interest inventories, and attitude scales; the pupil's responses to open questions; and diaries.

Such sociometric techniques as the sociogram and the "guess-who" questionnaire indicate the pupil's relationship to the group. Rating scales and check lists also record certain aspects of personal-social development. Conferences with pupils and parents often enable the teacher or counselor to complete needed information. Informational methods of evaluating achievement are very important sources of information as are the standardized achievement and aptitude tests which form part of the school's continuous testing program, and provide objective data for evaluating scholastic achievement and mental development.

Interpretation and Use of the Cumulative Record

The cumulative record will be useful to all school personnel concerned with educational and vocational guidance. The three key persons involved are the teacher, the counselor, and the school administrator.

THE TEACHER.   The teacher facilitates learning through improved instruction. Though he must consider the individual differences in his class, the practical demand is that he instruct the group. The discussion of the class record and class analysis chart in Chapter 15 shows how an orderly presentation of data enables the teacher to analyze the needs of his class and know the strengths and weaknesses of the group as a whole. For example, a large percentage of the class may be having trouble with decimals, finding the main idea in a paragraph, or problem-solving in science. Knowing this, the teacher can use group instruction effectively. Those pupils who do not need help can explore new material.

But the teacher must go further than releasing pupils from areas they have already mastered. He must help them select projects and materials.

The direction the students need should be readily available in the cumulative record from achievement and aptitude scores, samples of the pupil's work, and indications of his interests.

The cumulative record can also find a pupil's weaknesses. For example, a pupil often appears to succeed, but only in comparison with his lackluster classmates. A mediocre performance often looks good if the competition is weak. Because the pupil seems to be doing all right, the teacher attends to those whose difficulties are more obvious and who are generally the less able. But when the teacher matches achievement with ability, and notices from the record of the able pupil that he does poorly in areas hitherto unnoticed, instructional problems are seen that would otherwise have gone overlooked.

After the teacher has located learning difficulties, he must prescribe remediation and try to prevent such difficulties in the future. Chapter 15 includes a discussion of the process of identifying group and individual difficulties, and suggests remedial help. Again in attacking remedial problems, the importance of data from the cumulative record is emphasized.

The cumulative record also plays an important role in marking and reporting a pupil's progress. Obviously a teacher cannot prepare a progress report without adequate information. To make marking and reporting meaningful to parents, he must have such data as objective test scores, illustrative work samples, and reports of critical behavioral incidents.

THE COUNSELOR. Darley and Anderson (1951, pp. 74–75) list seven significant measurements needed in the counseling process:

1. General scholastic ability
2. Differential measures of achievement
3. Evidence of special aptitudes or disabilities
4. Interests
5. Personality structure and dynamics, including attitudes and beliefs
6. Socio-economic and cultural derivation and relations
7. Health and physical attributes

They also give four types of questions with regard to counseling pupils that may be answered by data obtained from the above measurements.

1. Questions regarding vocational planning
2. Questions regarding underachievement
3. Questions regarding personal development and adjustment
4. Questions regarding motivation and interest

The choice of a vocation should depend on the pupil's ability, often with emphasis on scholastic aptitude. In certain cases, vocational choice must be made on the basis of past achievement, health, physical attributes, or the ability to adjust to people. Jobs are classified into families; if the pupil is interested in a particular area, he may select a vocation appropriate to his talents. The low IQ pupil who is interested in medicine can, after all, be a hospital orderly.

Although the pupil may have excellent academic potential, and be a well adjusted individual, his lack of interest can result in underachievement. To determine the causes, it is helpful to turn to interest inventory scores, notations of hobbies, leisure time activities, and anecdotal records. Possibly a pupil's parents may be insisting on a particular course of study because they think it is prestigious or, thwarted in their own lives, are trying to live through their children. Parents may exhort their children so violently to greater effort that the child refuses to try at all.

To be most effective, counselors and teachers must cooperate. Evaluation is improved as additional data are added to the record available to both. Teachers, through observation of pupil behavior, can give important information to the counselor, just as the counselor can share interpretations of test scores and other information found in the pupil's cumulative record.

An important objective for the counselor is to develop in the pupil a capacity for self-evaluation. The pupil should see test scores and other discreetly selected portions of information in the cumulative record to help him understand his strengths and weaknesses, so that his decisions can be based on sound judgment.

THE SCHOOL ADMINISTRATOR.   Data from cumulative records prove helpful to the school administrator in organizing class groups, and in providing information to colleges, prospective employers and schools to which pupils may transfer. Some of the data can be used in a public relations program, particularly such elements as recorded results of standardized achievement and aptitude tests.

As our population increases, even small schools must have more than one class at each grade level. Combination grades, such as a fifth and sixth, may be formed. At other times, particularly at the secondary level, pupils may be grouped into more or less homogeneous groups on the basis of their educational and vocational aims, or of scores from standardized scholastic aptitude tests. Achievement is related to these variables, though not perfectly correlated. In other cases some pupils may be grouped because of such things as their lack of basic skills in English.

As applications for higher education increase, college officials must have data on which to base selection, and one source is systematic records of standardized tests. Because final marks given in small schools are often not comparable to those assigned in larger ones, and because the quality of instruction varies from school to school, standardized test data provide a basis for comparison of candidates across the country. Though many colleges use college entrance examinations, the data from a school testing program present a child far more completely than the single test administration.

Many pupils work after high school. As recently as fifty years ago, graduation from secondary school was a measure of achievement, but when most children receive high school diplomas and variability of achievement becomes the rule, the wise employer must contact the high school administration about a prospective employee. As requests of this kind increase, the administrator must have a well-kept cumulative record.

But this is not the whole of the administrator's informational obligation. He must also interpret the school program for the general public, a task which may involve brochures, speechmaking, and public discussion. Since most standardized achievement tests measure those fundamentals which the public considers important, criticism can be very effectively dealt with if students are achieving in terms of their ability. It is particularly important to have this information available when some curriculum innovation is introduced. The cry, "Let's teach the basic skills," may well be raised. Adequate achievement scores are a satisfactory answer to this demand. If test scores show achievement comparable to ability in arithmetic and the language arts, the school will not be on the defensive.

The school administrator should not evaluate the effectiveness of the school's program only by standardized achievement tests. He should also consider the pupils, keeping in mind that achievement tests are not designed to measure attainment of all the school's educational objectives. For example, none of the instruments in common use measures critical thinking.

Nevertheless, test results help keep him alert to development. In teaching the basic skills of reading and arithmetic, continuous and systematic attention must be focused on their development. Some skills are prerequisite to learning others. A pupil cannot do long division unless he can subtract and multiply. The pupil who does not know his basic word attack skills will be at sea reading difficult materials. Standardized test results help keep the busy administrator abreast of the effectiveness of various educational programs.

Problems

5   Traxler (1953 pp. 74–75) recommends that the cumulative record should provide for the annual recording of personality ratings of behavior descriptions. Do you agree? Explain your answer.

6   Information about home and family background is considered most helpful but is often lacking in many school records. What are some ways in which this information could be obtained effectively and systematically?

7   The cumulative record folder accompanies the pupil as he moves from elementary to junior high school and also when he enters senior high school. At the transfer points, many counselors go through the folders and discard materials which, in their opinion, are no longer useful or which might jeopardize the child in a new setting. What kinds of material might they prefer to discard? Is this a wise practice?

8   An eighth-grade English teacher noticed that one of his pupils seemed to have a reading difficulty even with material on a fourth-grade level. He noted, however, that the boy had a high interest in electronics, and, much to his amazement, could read related material with comparatively little difficulty. What kinds of helpful information might he find in the boy's cumulative record? What defensible hypothesis would he test?

9   Pupils frequently ask teachers or counselors if they may see their cumulative records. Would you grant these requests? Why?

10   Darley and Anderson (1951, pp. 74–75) present a rather comprehensive list of measurements to be used by counselors. Other schools of counseling theory, such as the Rogerian school, reject this viewpoint; they point to serious dangers, which, in their opinion, are inherent in counseling based on measurement results. With which counseling theory are you more in agreement? Why?

11   Imagine that you are the principal of a high school in a small city. You have been asked to speak before a joint meeting of the local service clubs. Your topic is "Curriculum Evaluation." Prepare an outline for your speech.

Use of Standardized Tests

Although standardized tests represent only one means of obtaining data in an evaluative program, they are very important tools in measurement. Therefore their selection, administration, scoring, and interpretation are significant aspects of educational evaluation. A great deal of research has gone into test construction. Selection of the wrong test, its improper administration or scoring, or inadequate interpretation of the results can waste time and money, and harm pupils.

Scope of the Program

Elementary and Junior High School. A minimum testing program for the elementary and junior high school consists of a periodic measurement of scholastic aptitude and a yearly achievement testing. Although authorities differ about the best grade level for administering scholastic aptitude tests, they generally agree that four or five administrations should occur between the time the child enters school and his completion of high school. A suggested sequence is at the beginning of the first, fourth, seventh, and tenth grades. Some schools add two more administrations in the second and eighth or ninth years. These are transitional points in the pupil's educational life, representing the beginning of formal study and of the intermediate, junior high, and senior high periods. In addition to the administrations suggested above, the pupil should be tested again whenever results are at variance with the teacher's judgment.

Another argument for frequent administrations of scholastic aptitude tests is the variation in the test results which typically occurs. It is common for IQ's to vary as much as ten or more points when two or more tests are given. A pupil may, therefore, be penalized unless previous test results are continually checked.

Achievement batteries should be administered yearly. The minimal program should emphasize tests of basic skills. The basic responsibilities of the school at this level are proficiency of work-study skills, language arts, and arithmetic—of greater importance than content areas.

An optimum program for the elementary and junior high school would include access to all available tests that would help the pupil. In addition to survey tests of achievement, diagnostic tests would be administered whenever necessary. Special reading tests, such as readiness tests, could be added to the first grade battery. An optimum program would also include personal-social adjustment and interest inventories. Although these instruments are inadequate in several important respects, they can be used as screening devices to identify problem children.

SENIOR HIGH SCHOOL. The minimum program in the senior high school should include a test of scholastic aptitude or a differential aptitude test and measures of achievement in various subjects. It is particularly important that college-bound pupils know their adequacy in such areas as mathematics, social, biological, and physical sciences, and the language arts. Every program should also include a recheck of the basic skills. The optimum program for the secondary school would employ personal-social adjustment inventories, problem check lists, and interest inventories. These can be used for screening purposes or educational and vocational guidance.

PROBLEMS

12 At what levels would you administer reading tests in the elementary and junior high school program? When might an aptitude battery such as the DAT be most useful?

13 Many colleges and universities are now asking that college-bound high-school pupils provide scholastic aptitude test scores obtained either during the junior or senior year of high school. Some school personnel feel this is unnecessary. Do you agree?

Selecting the Test

Tests should be selected on the basis of their contribution to evaluation in terms of the school's educational objectives. Therefore, a test must be studied carefully to determine both its content and its relationship to other tests and information available. The best way to do this is to take the test oneself. This points up the processes required for correct responses, makes clear the obvious content, and enables the teacher to anticipate difficulties in administration.

In selecting tests, the teacher should consult Buros' *Mental Measurement Yearbooks*. These references are revised continually and provide quantities of information about all types of tests. At least one specialist discusses the strengths and weaknesses of most of the popular tests. Often individual items are criticized, and sometimes problems in administration and scoring are discussed. As well as being helpful in selection, these volumes provide a great deal of general learning about tests.

After tests have been selected, administered, and proved functional for a school, they should not be replaced unless it appears that other instruments will be more effective, since it is necessary to compare results from year to year if the cumulative record is to be meaningful. A more recent copyright date on another test doesn't necessarily guarantee a better test. At times, because of the development of new instruments, it is wise to make a change. Then study of the results of groups of pupils will be helpful in making comparisons with previous test data.

VALIDITY. Validity is defined as the extent to which a measuring instrument serves the purpose for which it is intended. There are three kinds of validity: content, criterion-related, and construct. Each test in the evaluation program must possess a satisfactory degree of one or more of these types to justify its use. Hence, thoughtful attention must be given to certain questions concerning the validity of a test before it is selected. Among those of importance are the following:

Questions of general interest:
1. Are the kinds of validity reported those required by the role to be played by the test in the testing program?
2. Is evidence available that supports the validity of each of the interpretations of each of the test scores as suggested by the authors?

3. Is the basis on which the particular scope of the test was determined a sound one?

4. Do the test items seem to be well constructed and suitable in all important respects for the pupils to be tested?

5. Does the validity of this test compare favorably with that of similar tests?

6. What opinions do reviewers, critics, and research workers have about the validity of the test?

Questions concerning standardized achievement tests:

1. Are the sources from which the test items are drawn satisfactory ones?

2. Is the method of sampling the content a defensible one?

3. Is a table of specifications or the equivalent provided for each test or sub-test, and are the relationships between the test items and these tables identified?

4. Are these tables very similar to those based upon the educational objectives of the class that is to be given the test?

5. If a degree of criterion-related validity is claimed, is the validation sample representative and are the independent criteria adequate and meaningful?

Questions concerning standardized aptitude tests:

1. Are the correlation coefficients resulting from validity determinations so high that the likelihood of misclassifying a pupil on the basis of the test scores is slight?

2. Are variability measures of the test scores reported with each correlation coefficient and, as far as can be determined, are they similar to those for the pupils to be tested ?

3. Are suitable expectancy tables available?

4. Is the author's definition of the aptitude to be measured clearly stated and is it appropriate in terms of needs of the testing program?

5. Is there adequate evidence to show how the individual test items represent a part of this definition?

6. Are the independent criterion measure described accurately and with sufficient detail?

7. Were criterion scores determined independently from the scores of the testing being validated?

8. Is the validation sample representative of the pupils with whom the test is to be used?

Questions concerning standardized instruments for evaluating personal-social development are much like those for standardized aptitude tests in that construct and criterion-related validity are particularly important.

RELIABILITY. If a test does not give consistent results, it has low reliability. Caution should be exercised in interpreting scores from tests of questionable reliability. This is especially true when test results are used in the diagnosis of an individual pupil's difficulties. If test results are used with groups of individuals, reliability coefficients can be lower and the data still be helpful in pointing up trends, weaknesses and strengths. In studying the reliability of a standardized instrument, questions such as the following should be posed:

1. What types of reliability determinations have been made, and have they been described in sufficient detail?
2. Is evidence presented that enables one to determine whether the test and all of its subparts, if any, are sufficiently reliable for their recommended uses?
3. Is the standard error of measurement small enough to justify the uses of test scores which are planned?
4. Is the reliability of the difference between test scores reported when the construction of a profile is suggested and is it relatively low?
5. Is the sample used in the reliability determination comparable to the pupils with whom the test is to be used?
6. Are measures of variability reported with each reliability coefficient and, as far as it can be determined, are they similar to those for the pupils to be tested?
7. Do the reliability coefficients of this test compare favorably with those of similar tests?
8. What opinions do reviewers, critics, and research workers have about the reliability of the test?

NORMS.   An important feature of the standardized test is the availability of norms, which reflect relative performance. In determining their adequacy, questions such as the following should prove helpful:

1. Are various types of norms reported or easily obtained from test data presented?
2. Is there an adequate description of the distribution of the raw scores on which the norms are based?
3. Is the standardization group described clearly?
   (a)   Is the method of sampling a defensible one?
   (b)   Is the group described in detail with respect to talent, training, age, sex?
   (c)   Is the size of the standardization group sufficiently large?
4. Are separate sets of norms available for all important subgroups of the standardization group that are known to differ in terms of the test?
5. Do the norms for this test compare favorably with those of similar tests?
6. What opinions do reviewers, critics, and research workers have about the norms of the test?
7. Are norms available for groups with which you want to compare your class members?

EASE OF ADMINISTRATION. The information concerning validity, reliability, and norms is meaningful only if the test is administered in the same way that it was administered to the standardization group. Because untrained personnel often administer tests, the simplicity and readability of test instructions are of prime importance. Tests with complicated timing procedures often give invalid results. Tests with inadequate instructions to the examinees, inadequate sample exercises, or poor typographic makeup stimulate excessive questions.

The time required for test administration is also important. Because some tests can be administered in parts, they can be scheduled during the regular school periods; others require a reorganization of the daily schedule. Before a test is selected, its length must not hamper local conditions. The arrangement of the test booklet is an important factor in the administration of a test. In some tests pupils must turn the booklet around or fold under pages. The examinee who often finds it difficult to follow instructions may lose his place and invalidate results.

EASE OF SCORING. A test may be well administered, but the results are of little value if scoring is inaccurate. When scoring is completely objective, fewer problems arise, and, of course, instructions for scoring should be clearly worded. However, when some subjectivity is involved, the scoring becomes more complex, and machine scoring is no longer possible.

The mechanics of scoring the test should be checked, and a simple scoring key provided for efficient checking. Some arrangements are awkward, time consuming, and inaccurate. The calculations for scoring should be simple and brief.

ECONOMY. The old adage "penny wise and pound foolish" is certainly applicable to the selection of tests. The price of a test book is a very minor part of the total cost of an evaluation program. Administration, scoring, and interpretation represent teacher and pupil man-hours of considerable magnitude. Scoring alone is very expensive for certain tests. Primarily, of course, tests should be selected for their ability to measure the achievement of school objectives. Basing choice on any other reason is false economy.

MISCELLANEOUS. Equivalent forms should be available to allow the testing of different classes at different times, or multiple testing of one class. Also, aids should be provided for interpretation of test results. Class charts and profile blanks ease and clarify recording and interpreting test results. Even a survey test will serve some diagnostic purposes if results can be adequately interpreted, and some manuals give suggestions for such remediation. Suggestions are correlated with the various subtests.

PROBLEMS

14 Some schools recommend that teachers study the content of a standardized achievement test very carefully. Others, fearing that teachers will begin to teach for the test, discourage this practice. What would you advise?

15 A junior high school is using a new battery of achievement tests this year. A faculty committee has been appointed to evaluate the usefulness of the new tests and to recommend either retaining or discontinuing them. Outline a procedure for the committee to follow.

16 Give an example in which the kinds of validity reported in a test manual might not correspond to the role to be played by the test in the testing program.

17 Teachers tend to be confused by statistical reports of validation studies in test manuals and therefore skip over them. List four basic questions which can serve as guides in reviewing this material.

18 A senior high school is concerned about the reliability of the scholastic aptitude tests which they are now using. In contrast to the information reported in the manual, the guidance department has pointed out several instances in which there has been a discrepancy in scores from one test administration to another. Design a plan whereby the guidance personnel can resolve this apparent inconsistency.

Administering the Test

If test results are to be successfully interpreted, they must be carefully administered according to the specific instructions. Results from various classes cannot be compared unless administration is standardized, nor can norms be of any value. This applies not only to reading printed instructions carefully, but to motivating the pupils to do their best on a test. Time limits must be followed rigidly.

THE TEST ADMINISTRATOR. Who should administer the tests? Some individual tests will be given by the school psychologist. Possibly in large school systems, a testing specialist is employed to administer group tests. In most instances, however, the teacher gives tests, and to some advantage. Not only does it identify the teacher with the testing program, since he must familiarize himself with the tests, but because he knows his pupils, he can motivate them more effectively, interpret their reactions, and establish the necessary rapport.

Those who criticize teacher administration usually focus their arguments on inaccurate timing or improper instructions. Teachers should be given instruction in the administration of the tests. The first step is to familiarize them with standardized test construction, for they must understand the importance of standardized procedure. Group instruction is advised when provision can be made for a question period. Instruction had best be given by a specialist in testing, whether from the local school or from a college or university.

If the instructions are particularly complex, teachers should be encouraged to give the test to each other. Many a test has been spoiled because instructions were not completely understood.

Special emphasis should be given to proper timing. Instructions generally appear quite simple, but when an ordinary watch is used as the timing instrument, it is easy for the examiner to err in finding the termination point. When possible, the teacher should use a stop watch which he has operated with checks on his readings before he administers the test. When a regular watch is used, the starting time should be recorded in minutes and seconds. Then the testing time should be added to record the exact moment to stop the test. Memory should never be trusted in timing any more than in memorizing instructions. Record the time and read the instructions.

GIVING THE TEST. Scheduling is one of the biggest problems in a testing program. On the surface it may appear simple, but when test booklets are being re-used for economy, when IBM answer sheets are used on which all the answers for several sittings are recorded, or when test length does not coincide with the length of the class periods, some complicated situations can arise. For example, since the test booklets must be checked for marks after each administration, the same booklets cannot be used in consecutive periods. Getting pupils started at the right place when their answer sheets are collected at the close of one sitting is another problem. When testing time is longer than class periods or a combination of them, it is probably wise to set up a testing timetable.

Proper physical conditions for testing will allow pupils to work with freedom without crowding, poor lighting, or interruptions. A sign should be placed on the door indicating a test in progress. All testing equipment must be in the room and readily available, along with extra pencils and erasers, and carefully-spaced functional chairs. Cheating should not be tolerated, but dealt with firmly without emotional outbursts to disturb the other pupils.

Even though details are carefully provided for, directions carefully followed, timing accurately completed, and interruptions eliminated, test results may not be highly valid if the pupil is not motivated to do his best. The pupil must be confident that testing is for his own welfare and not for determining promotion or for assigning final marks. He must understand the purpose of the test and the demands it will make on him. Unless testing is of value to him, he may not do his best work.

On the other hand, overstimulation produces anxiety which interferes with good performance. It is particularly aggravated among those pupils who have the greatest need to earn high marks (Sarason, 1960). The test administrator provides the best testing atmosphere for dealing with anxiety when he establishes a relaxed, business-like atmosphere with a touch of humor. He encourages the pupil to do his best, but does not threaten.[1]

Furthermore, pupils need to have a certain amount of sophistication or testwiseness to give evidence of their best performance. Teachers should exhort pupils to listen carefully to instructions, mark their papers neatly and accurately, plan wise use of their time, leave enough time to recheck their answers, and understand when to omit or answer a question.

TIME OF YEAR FOR TEST ADMINISTRATION.   An important decision in any evaluation program is the time for test administration. Should standardized tests be administered in the spring or fall? Fall administration has a number of advantages:

1. With today's itinerant population, fall administration assures the teacher a record for each pupil. Transfer pupils may not bring adequate records with them from other schools. If tests are administered in the spring the teacher is more likely to have inadequate data for some pupils throughout the year, a deficit which prevents him from focusing his attention on pupil needs rather than on what is supposed to be taught in a certain class. If pupils have specific weaknesses and he knows about them, he can plan remedial work. If they rank high in achievement, he won't make the serious mistake of having them repeat what they already know just because it appears in the syllabus. The information enables him to meet the needs of individuals through grouping or through any other practical approach.

2. Fall testing provides a more realistic measure of pupils' achievement. During the summer vacation, certain skills may improve; others may deteriorate. If the child does know arithmetic, he may not be as proficient in September as he was in June. On the other hand, he may have done considerable reading during the summer, thereby improving his skill in this area.

3. Testing can be helpful to pupils in self-evaluation. If the results are used wisely, they can provide aid in formulating goals. The objective data from standardized tests can give the pupil direction and purpose for the new school year.

[1] A self-inventory for those who administer tests has been prepared by Thompson in which many of the important details of test administration are listed. See Thompson, Anton, *Test-Giver's Self-Inventory*. Test Service Bulletin No. 85. Tarrytown, New York: Harcourt, Brace and World, Inc. Thompson, Anton, "Test-Giver's Self-Inventory," *California Journal of Educational Research* (1956, pp. 67–71).

4. Too often it appears that tests are administered to determine the effectiveness of the teacher rather than the status of the pupils. This may result in coaching the pupils for tests or in invalid administration such as lengthening time limits. Fall testing lessens this possibility.

5. Testing in the spring is generally done under pressure of time. As the school year draws to a close, teachers are busy filling out reports and completing final details. Testing may tend to be more of a chore than an aid to good teaching.

Although fall testing is generally recommended, certain conditions may require spring testing. This is particularly true when ability grouping requires that data be available for determining programs of the pupils for the following year.

Problems

19 Imagine that you are in charge of a school-wide achievement testing program in which classroom teachers will administer the tests. What steps would you take to insure standard testing procedures? What difficulties would have to be anticipated?

20 Many school systems do not tell pupils in advance when standardized tests are to be administered, in the hope that undue anxiety and absenteeism will thereby be avoided. Evaluate this practice.

Scoring the Test

Although essay and objective tests of the supply type are generally scored by hand, many standardized and informal objective tests can be machine scored. Central agencies providing this scoring service at a nominal fee offer some definite advantages:

1. Accuracy is greater; machine-scoring results in fewer errors.
2. It saves time for the busy teacher, who can spend his time more profitably than doing clerical work.
3. Item-analysis data can be quickly prepared when needed.

Hand-scoring by the teacher also results in certain benefits:

1. Results are generally more quickly available.
2. It is possible that by scoring some tests the teacher will gain better insight into a pupil's strengths and weaknesses. However, this is not as likely to occur in the case of the objective test as it is in the case of the essay test.

The advantages and disadvantages of hand-scoring notwithstanding, the fact remains that many test papers are scored in this manner, so the scorer must avoid injustice with inaccuracy. This is so important a matter that school officials must exert considerable effort and care in training teachers and checking scoring accuracy.

Two types of errors are frequently made: compensating and biased. In the first category are those errors made by carelessness in checking, adding, or using formulas; they score too high in one instance and too low in another. The other type of error is a misinterpretation of a scoring formula, which slants scores all in one direction, high or low. There is no opportunity for them to be cancelled out.

How should these errors be prevented? Teachers must be taught how to score, and carry out the scoring instructions to show they have understood them. A discussion of procedures is not enough. The papers first scored should be rescored. When maintaining high accuracy, only a sampling of papers need be checked. One out of five or ten papers may be selected for this purpose. Because biased errors prove to be so serious, the second scoring should be done by a different person. In some schools all papers are scored twice with different colored pencils. One helpful idea is to have one or more teachers responsible for each subtest. They can then become thoroughly proficient in their task; scoring becomes much more efficient and accurate.

Another check is to see if any extreme scores show up in a pupil's profile. It is possible that they are valid, but if such scores occur, these subtests should be scored again. Also, if scores seem unrealistic in terms of a pupil's past achievement, the corresponding parts or the entire test should be rescored.

Problem

21   Some argue that, if each teacher scores the tests of those pupils whom he meets every day, test results become meaningful to the teacher; in the process of scoring the teacher will become conscious of specific areas of subject-matter difficulty. Evaluate this position.

Interpreting and Using the Testing Results

Regardless of the care with which the tests have been selected, administered, and scored, little value will accrue from them unless the results are used in the evaluation program. This means that they must be available to teachers, counselors, and school administrators. In Chapter 15, summarization and interpretation of group and individual test scores provide information for improving diagnostic and remedial programs. In

Chapter 16, suggestions are given for the use of test scores in reporting to pupils and their parents.

It is sometimes advantageous to use test scores in interpreting the school program for the public or special community groups. It is often useful to have information comparing pupil achievement with national norms of those having comparable ability. It may focus attention on a school's educational objectives to portray achievement in various subjects, and at different grade levels. Such a summary may, on the other hand, point up specific weaknesses that should be remedied through increased financial support by the community.

Test data should be presented in the most meaningful ways. The use of numerical or graphic charts is clearer than a narrative. Figure 36 shows the distribution of ability scores of a senior high school class compared with national norms. It would also have been possible to graph the achievement of the group to provide a comparison with their ability. Note that stanines are employed (see page 269).

The group of pupils from School X tends to be above the national

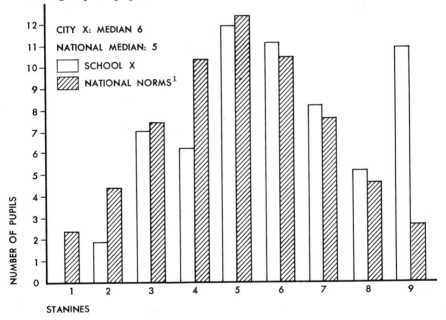

[1] Expected frequencies of a representative sample; the same number of pupils were selected from the standardization group.

FIGURE 36

DISTRIBUTION OF THE SCHOOL AND COLLEGE ABILITY TEST, TOTAL SCORE, FOR A TWELFTH-GRADE CLASS.

norms. No pupils have a stanine score of 1, and fewer have stanine scores of 2, 3, 4, and 5 than is true of those from the national norm group. However, in the case of stanine scores of 6, 7, 8, and 9, there is a larger proportion of pupils from School X.

Summary

A sound evaluation program is based on the measurable educational objectives of a particular school. A testing program is only one of the techniques for collecting data which are used as the basis for evaluating the progress of a school's pupils in terms of its educational objectives for them.

For an evaluation program to be successful, it is mandatory that all school personnel, teachers, counselors, and school administrators, be involved from its initiation throughout its integration with the other educational activities of the school. In many schools this means providing in-service education programs to prepare staff members for their parts in the evaluation.

Methods of recording evaluation data and their availability to school personnel largely determine their contribution to the program. There can be no substitute for a cumulative record in which many kinds of data are filed. Both counselors and teachers use cumulative records in helping pupils attack their problems in vocational planning, underachievement, personal development and adjustment, and motivation and interest. Both have their own means, unavailable to the other, of securing data about pupils, so it is in sharing and working cooperatively that they can be most helpful to pupils.

The school administrator is vitally concerned with the evaluation program. He needs information for organizing class groups and to provide to colleges, prospective employers, and schools to which his pupils transfer. Evaluation data are the basis for keeping him and the public informed about the educational progress of the school.

Tests, whether teacher-constructed or standardized, are an integral part of any evaluation program. A minimal testing program includes tests of scholastic aptitude and achievement. The optimum program adds interest and personality inventories. While standardized achievement tests are most helpful when administered yearly, scholastic aptitude tests can be scheduled at the beginning of the first, fourth, seventh, and tenth grades.

In selecting a test, the first consideration should be its usefulness to the evaluation program as a whole. Attention should be given to its validity, reliability, and norms, and to the complexity of its administration and scoring. One of the most helpful reference works, including much data on tests, is Buros' *Mental Measurement Yearbooks*, which will provide effective guidance in test selection.

Valid test results depend on effective administration and scoring. Teachers must be carefully instructed in both. It is not only necessary to review all instructions, but advisable to give a mock test, as well as to practice scoring and then re-check the papers initially scored. Time and place are also important considerations in test administration. In general, the fall of the year is preferred to the spring. In many cases, tests are administered in the pupil's own classrooms, but there must be ample lighting, space to work, and freedom from interruptions. Of course, adequate physical facilities must always be supplemented by a good testing atmosphere for the pupil to be motivated to do his best work.

Test scores can be used to help interpret the school's program to the public. Charts are helpful aids here.

Suggested Readings

Belanger, L. L. Policy statement on the use of standardized tests in California schools. *Calif. Educ.*, 1964, 2, 8–10.
> Official representatives of various educational organizations in California have developed a statement on test usage that classroom teachers will find useful.

Brim, O. G. American attitudes toward intelligence tests. *Amer. Psychologist*, 1965, 20, 125–130.
> According to this study, the general public is critical of the use of intelligence tests. Laymen criticized them on five counts: Inaccessibility of test data; invasion of privacy; rigidity in the use of test scores; types of talent selected by tests; and fairness of test to minority groups.

Buros, O. K. (Ed.) *Tests in print.* Highland Park, N.J.: Gryphon Press, 1962.
> As a companion to the *Mental Measurements Yearbooks*, this volume provides (a) useful information concerning more than 2,000 currently available tests, (b) cross references to additional information about these tests, (c) short descriptions of more than 800 tests now out of print, and (d) index-directories of test publishers. The editor suggests that, for the most efficient use of the first six *Mental Measurements Yearbooks*, *Tests in Print* should be used.

Crook, F. E. Elementary school testing programs: problems and practices. *Tchers Coll. Rec.*, 1959, 61, 76–85.
> Three testing programs are described. They point to the need for involving the teacher to a greater extent in a testing program.

Ebel, R. L. External testing: response to challenge. *Tchers Coll. Rec.*, 1962, 64, 190–198.
> The author replies to six concerns which the school administrators have expressed about external testing. These are included in the report from the National Association of Secondary-School Principals which is listed below.

Educational Testing Service. *Essential characteristics of a testing program.* Educational Testing Service Evaluation and Advisory Service Series, No. 2. Princeton, N.J.: Educational Testing Service, 1956.

> This bulletin summarizes the principal characteristics of a continuous evaluation program. Of importance are a careful identification of the purposes of such a program and a full understanding of these by teachers, pupils, administrators, and parents.

Findley, Warren G. (Ed.) *The impact and improvement of school testing programs.* Sixty-Second Yearb. nat. Soc. Stud. Educ., 1963. Chicago: University of Chicago Press.

> Highly useful information is contained in this volume. Individual chapters have been prepared by a number of well-known testing specialists. Particularly pertinent are Chapter 10, which deals with the selection and use of tests, and Chapter 12, which contains recommendations concerning the interpretation of test scores.

Foose, R. L., and C. Vroman. How much and what kind of testing program for today's secondary school? *Nat'l Assn. Sec. School Prin. Bull.,* 1960, **44,** 205–210.

> A secondary-school principal and a college director of admissions discuss the problem of providing an adequate testing program in secondary schools without overloading the pupil with superfluous tests.

National Association of Secondary-School Principals. *Testing, testing, testing.* Washington: National Education Association, 1962.

> This report is a protest with regard to the increase in testing in the schools. In particular, concern is expressed about the large "external" testing programs and their usefulness.

Morrison, Wilma. *The school record, its use and abuse in college admissions.* Princeton, N. J.: College Entrance Examination Board, 1961.

> The author presents a very frank and insightful discussion of the problems faced by college admissions officers and secondary school personnel in evaluating pupils' cumulative records. Such topics as the validity of rank in class, the need for better personality appraisal, and the problem of faulty communication point up the difficulties inherent in the selection process. The *Secondary-School Record* form is shown.

State Committee on Cumulative Records. *Handbook on California cumulative records.* Sacramento: California State Department of Education, 1956.

> The purpose of this handbook is to serve as a guide to school personnel who wish to develop adequate cumulative records. Not only does it give thorough instructions on how to initiate and keep these records up to date, but it has illustrations of completed records.

Traxler, A. E. Ten essential steps in a testing program. *Educ.,* 1959, **79,** 357–361.

> The various steps to be followed when developing a testing program are listed and discussed. Faculty involvement in this process is stressed.

References Cited

Buros, O. K. (Ed.) *The sixth mental measurements yearbook.* Highland Park, N.J.: Gryphon Press, 1965.

Darley, J. G., and G. V. Anderson. The functions of measurement in counseling. In E. F. Lindquist (Ed.), *Educational measurement*. Washington: American Council on Education, 1951.

Kearney, N. C. *Elementary school objectives*. New York: Russel Sage Foundation, 1953.

Mager, Robert F. *Preparing instructional objectives*. Palo Alto, Calif.: Fearon Publishers, 1962.

Sarason, I. G. Empirical findings and theoretical problems in the use of anxiety scales. *Psychol. Bull.*, 1960, 403–415.

Traxler, A. E., and others. *Introduction to testing and the use of test results in public schools*. New York: Harper & Row, 1953.

15 ✐

Diagnosis and Remediation of Problems

THERE IS MORE TO GARDENING than having a "green thumb." When the expert gardener's plants do not grow well, he knows there is a reason, and he tries to determine the source of the trouble. Is an insect, a fungus, or an improper soil condition causing the damage? He searches for evidence that will help solve his problem. When he has identified the parasite or disease, he determines the treatment, which may consist of spraying fungicides or insecticides on the affected plants. The gardener knows, however, that all insecticides are not lethal to all insects, that a certain fungicide will not destroy all fungi, and that plants differ in their tolerance of various kinds of chemicals.

The gardener's approach is like that of the teacher who realizes that all members of the group of pupils he is teaching do not have the same abilities. Some of them are not growing well scholastically, and the causes must be found and remedies applied. He knows that the textbook for the class will be too difficult for some pupils, too easy for others. Some children are not able to do long division exercises because they lack skill in multiplication, addition, and subtraction. Others are proficient in long division and can be challenged only by more advanced work in mathematics. The teacher tries to avoid the mistake of frustrating the slower pupils or boring the more able. With a range of ability and achievement from three to nine grade levels in most classes, he knows that good teaching must begin with information about the ability and achievement of each pupil.

THE MEANING OF DIAGNOSIS AND REMEDIATION

If a school is to reach its educational objectives, each teacher must recognize and understand the complex aspects of behavioral changes. Since a pupil's development tends to be sequential, schools must provide the most effective sequence of experiences; that is, those that will bring about behavior consonant with the abilities of the individual (Cook, 1951). Because growth patterns differ among individuals, causing various degrees of maturity at the same age, and because a developmental sequence in behavior is necessary, the teacher must determine where the individual pupil stands in this sequence, and what marks the limits of his potential.

The teacher sees each individual within the group as having different problems. In practice, of course, pupils in a class have many common difficulties and can be grouped for instruction. For example, in a class where a few advanced pupils know how to multiply common fractions, those who do not can be taught as a group. And certainly, as a gardener waters the whole garden, there are many opportunities to bring the entire class together for instruction, like listening to a poem or story, watching a demonstration, or discussing initiation of a project.

In helping the individual, the teacher must determine the stage of his development and his peculiar learning difficulties. This is educational diagnosis. Some years ago, educational diagnosis was confined for the most part to academic knowledge and skills, but its scope has kept pace with the modern concept of education which emphasizes all aspects of development. Thus the development of the nonintellectual aspects of the pupil's personality is as much the legitimate concern of his teacher as his academic knowledge and skills. Indeed, research has shown that personal-social adjustment and personality development cannot be divorced from learning knowledge and skills.

Remediation, which is nothing more than good teaching, is possible only when the teacher understands the basis of a pupil's difficulty, and seeing his needs, teaches to meet them. Good teaching implies several things: first, that we meet the child at his own level of achievement and start from there; second, that we know something of the experiences and problems he has met in reaching that level; third, that we are aware of how present learning relates to the future sequences. The child who has suffered agonies of frustration and humiliation in arithmetic classes will present a more complex problem of remediation than his friend who simply doesn't understand long division.

Diagnosis

Educational diagnosis centers on three questions. Which pupils have learning difficulties? What are the strengths and weaknesses in their achievement? What factors have caused their unsatisfactory achievement?

Identifying Pupils Having Difficulty

There are a number of ways to locate pupils with learning difficulties. One of the most effective is the survey approach. Survey achievement tests of the kind included in a school testing program are specifically designed to find pupils who need remediation. When a serious lack of achievement shows up, the teacher will need information about the pupil's scholastic aptitude to make the achievement score more meaningful. Perhaps the child is achieving as well as can be expected in terms of his potential; a pupil is not retarded simply because his score is lower than the class average. Perhaps some pupils, particularly at the secondary level, need to change their educational and vocational goals. Others may have average or above average achievement but are still below their potential. It is these brighter pupils who generally benefit most from remediation because there is a wider disparity between their achievement and their ability.

A teacher will often discover from test data that his entire class has a specific weakness. One fifth-grade teacher found that all of his pupils were below the grade norm in rate of reading, although they were above average in scholastic ability. Another uncovered a weakness in study skills; a third, difficulties with fractions; a fourth, spelling.

Many sources of information are helpful in locating the pupil who needs help. One may contact a child's former teacher, because past achievement must be evaluated. Attendance records and data on personal-social adjustment may provide clues. Information in a pupil's cumulative record, such as an anecdotal record, perhaps, may prove helpful. For example, some of the highest academic achievers are in serious need of guidance in their social relations. Case histories show that some pupils, having no friends, strive for high scholastic achievement as a means of compensating for lack of personal-social development.

PROBLEMS

1   Define retardation with regard to academic achievement. Illustrate with specific examples. The general public customarily links the term "remedial instruction" with the below-average pupil or slow learner. What subtle influence has this exerted on educational programs?
2   A high school biology teacher who meets with 150 pupils per day along with being responsible for a tenth-grade homeroom, maintains that, under these circumstances, individual pupil diagnosis is an impossible task. What arguments would you use to refute the position he is taking?

Determining Strengths and Weaknesses

The pupil's improvement is the goal of all diagnosis and remediation, and to achieve it, a good teacher helps the pupil correct his weaknesses by building on his strengths. For example, if he has a reading disability, it is just as important to know that he is good in his word attack skills as it is to know that he is poor in his use of context clues. One of the basic principles in effective remediation is that the pupil must experience success, and building on his strengths makes this possible.

COMPETENCIES IN DIAGNOSIS. Determining a pupil's strengths and weaknesses requires essential diagnostic skills which a teacher must develop even though he is not a trained clinician. He should first understand the principles of learning and their application. Second, he should be able to recognize behavioral symptoms that suggest the causes of specific difficulties. Third, he should be able to apply diagnostic and remedial techniques.

Before a teacher can be a successful diagnostician, he must be familiar with the psychology of learning in general, and with regard to specific subject areas. He can formulate useful hypotheses about the nature of a child's difficulties far more readily if he has a grasp of the way learning normally develops in a subject area and is aware of the difficulties most frequently encountered in it.

Take, for example, the problem of transfer of learning. If we learn how to shift gears in a Chevrolet, most of us can then shift gears in a Ford. Learning from the original task has transferred to the new. But if we are then asked to drive a Volkswagon with a four-forward-speed shift, our previous learning tends to interfere with the new task, and this psychological process is known as the negative transfer effect.

Research in transfer of learning indicates that though considerable transfer occurs from some learning tasks to others, there are cases in which there is little transfer unless we teach for it. In one such case, a teacher discussed word endings and rhyming with his class. He followed the prescribed procedures carefully; *Jane* rhymes with *rain, cane, train*. A little girl went home and announced, "We learned about rhyming today. Try me. You say *Jane*." When the parent dutifully obeyed, the child responded with a triumphant "*rain, cane, train*." Asked whether other words rhymed with *Jane*, the child said no, only the three she had just given them. Clearly her concept of rhyming was the relationship among four specific words and no useful learning transfer was gained.

We can further illustrate the importance of understanding in learning as it applies to concept formation. A teacher cannot *give* a pupil a concept; they can only be formed by the individual out of his own experiences. Research shows, for instance, that difficulties in all arithmetic processes can be traced to a failure to understand basic number concepts. Too often understanding is evaluated on the basis of the products of learning without considering learning processes. When a pupil's answers are correct, does he understand the problem? He may not. It is possible that he got the correct answer by coincidence or, having dutifully learned a method, followed it blindly down a corridor of computation to the proper reply. Can you explain why you invert and then multiply when you divide by a fraction? If you cannot, you were probably taught how to perform the operation without understanding the process. Understanding number concepts comes through many experiences in which the pupil is required to think through the reasons for performing an operation. Therefore, diagnosis in mathematics should begin with a study of the pupil's concept of a number as it relates to his particular difficulty.

A second competency in diagnosis is the ability to recognize symptoms related to the physical and psychological aspects of growth. Sometimes the underlying causes of a pupil's difficulty are so complex that the teacher will need to rely on the services of a specialist for diagnosis, but he should be familiar with symptoms of poor vision, inadequate hearing, and lack of energy. Further, the informed teacher understands the common mental mechanisms used by poorly adjusted children to reduce their tension. Pupils with severe anxieties are not ready for learning. Remediation is, after all, exceedingly demanding of the pupil, requiring both concentration and a high degree of motivation.

The psychological bases of a problem may be hard to reach. One pupil of above average intelligence was having great difficulty with arithmetic. His achievement in subjects demanding verbal facility was high, relationships with his peers appeared satisfactory, and his rapport with his teacher was excellent. The teacher tried every approach he could think of to help the pupil but made little progress. Finally, in a case history, he discovered the child's mother had always done poorly in arithmetic and persisted in talking about it. The youngster had identified with his mother, building up a self-concept of his inability that completely negated his efforts.

The third competence is the ability to use the various diagnostic and remedial techniques, devices, and materials with understanding. Among these devices are standardized and informal tests and practice exercises. Detailed discussions of specific difficulties, particularly in arithmetic and reading, are to be found in the literature, and suggested remedial procedures are outlined in detail. The teacher can do much diagnosis and remediation without a clinical specialist. Available printed materials help him in the classroom, and this experience expands his knowledge.

Factors Causing Unsatisfactory Achievement

The teacher who knows the more common causes of unsatisfactory achievement has some basis for making intelligent hypotheses about the difficulties of his pupils. Lack of achievement may be attributed to personal and/or environmental factors, reflected in scholastic aptitude, physical development, and health, with special emphasis on visual and auditory abilities, and personal-social adjustment.

SCHOLASTIC APTITUDE. If a child has low scholastic aptitude, lack of achievement cannot necessarily be interpreted as the result of faulty teaching or lack of application. He may be doing as well as he can. Many pupils who are poor in reading and mathematics have low scholastic aptitude scores, but a low score does not necessarily mean that a pupil has low innate mental ability. His score on most group tests of scholastic aptitude can be seriously affected by poor reading ability, lack of motivation, or distractions from poor test administration. Therefore, a principal diagnostic problem is to get as accurate an estimate of the pupil's ability as possible. The teacher should not conclude that a pupil has a low scholastic aptitude unless he has considered various data. If at all possible, an individual intelligence test should be administered to those pupils who have low achievement and low group scholastic aptitude scores. It is often surprising to learn that some of these pupils have higher mental ability than some of the high achievers. Too often teachers equate ability to pass tests, conformity, good grooming, and verbosity with high intelligence. Many shy, withdrawn, poorly groomed or nonconformist pupils excel intellectually.

HEALTH. A pupil's health influences his ability to achieve, because learning is hard work. Many things cause inadequate stamina: malnutrition, glandular difficulty, or improper rest. In one fourth-grade class a teacher discovered that forty per cent of the pupils were consistently watching television until after ten o'clock on school nights. It is understandable that this group was difficult to teach. Poor health may also cause excessive absences which are especially detrimental to achievement in such subjects as arithmetic and reading, which require cumulative sequences of skills.

There is no unequivocal evidence that visual anomalies are a major cause of educational disability. While some pupils with good vision are poor readers, others who fail to pass vision tests read well, but these may perform with considerable discomfort. Many cannot attend to print and can only read for short periods of time. If a pupil is nearsighted, and if his teacher uses a visual approach, the pupil may miss basic instruction.

Poor hearing is a distinct disadvantage. Pupils may successfully camouflage hearing anomalies with apparent attention and go unnoticed by the teacher. Even pupils who pass common hearing tests may have serious auditory deficiencies. If there is a high tonal frequency loss, it is difficult to differentiate among consonant sounds so that an oral approach to beginning reading distinctly handicaps such a pupil.

An alert teacher can often detect symptoms of poor hearing. Pupils so handicapped may speak without expression and with the voice pitched unnaturally. Because they cannot differentiate among sounds, they are often poor spellers, and their speech and pronunciation lack clarity and precision. When they cannot understand what is being said, their attention often wanes; they may stare out the window or disturb other students. Others may frequently request that statements or questions be repeated. Whether speech defects result from loss of hearing or some other cause, they seriously impair a pupil's achievement.

There are also organic symptoms of poor hearing, such as earache, sinus condition, and ear discharge. Because such disorder can be corrected, teachers can prevent permanent disabilities by referring these pupils for medical attention.

Motor coordination is another physical factor to which the elementary teacher in particular should be attentive, since it can have a detrimental effect on handwriting. Because handwriting is important in developing other skills, a disability may have far-reaching effects. If a student writes slowly, he may understand test items but find it impossible to complete them within the time limit. His score implies low achievement but the real deficiency lies in the handwriting.

PERSONAL-SOCIAL ADJUSTMENT. The emotionally disturbed pupil dissipates his energy before he can apply it. It is difficult to determine whether emotional difficulties are causing learning difficulties or vice versa. Learning difficulties can at times be cause or effect. Indeed, a pupil may become an outstanding achiever to compensate for some emotional problem. But too often the child with an emotional disturbance finds himself caught in a vicious circle, anxious over lack of achievement, and performing poorly because of the emotional disturbance.

Harris (1961, pp. 265–269) lists ten kinds of emotional problems that contribute to reading disabilities, but which can also be applied to other subjects.

1. Conscious refusal to learn
2. Overt hostility—Because some children have built up intense feelings of resentment, they find it difficult to exercise control of their emotions. Pupil-teacher relationships are not conducive to learning.
3. Negative conditioning to reading—Reading has been associated with something the child dislikes intensely like a teacher or punishment. Therefore, he learns to dislike reading.
4. Displacement of hostility—Suppose a child dislikes or fears a parent or a teacher. The child realizes that this person enjoys reading. Since it may arouse feelings of anxiety and guilt to direct his hostility toward this individual, he expresses these hostile feelings toward reading.

5. Resistance to pressure—When an over-ambitious parent pressures his child to achieve, the reaction of the child may be a disinterest in reading.

6. Clinging to dependency—To avoid growing up a child may cling to a symbol of early childhood—inability to read.

7. Quick discouragement—Because some children lack a feeling of security, they become quickly discouraged. They have little confidence and respect.

8. Success is dangerous—Success may symbolize entering adult society and competing as a rival with a parent. There is an implication for the child that this competition will result in extreme retaliation.

9. Extreme distractability or restlessness—When a child has a high degree of tension, he finds it difficult to control his physical activity. This results in inattention and inability to learn.

10. Absorption in a private world—Day dreams through which some children fulfill their wishes result in lack of concentration and inability to learn.

The teacher should be continually aware of symptoms. If a pupil cannot solve his problems in the classroom, he may need to be referred for clinical treatment. Symptoms of aggression, withdrawal, and general problem behavior are often indicative of personal-social adjustment problems. Sometimes anti-social behavior results from a particular incident and passes quickly. Serious and deep-seated problems, however, can be identified by persistence of symptoms.

ENVIRONMENTAL FACTORS. Although it is difficult to identify outside causes of a pupil's learning difficulties, the difficulties quickly show up in the pupil. A poor home environment where the parents are separated or the child is rejected may cause personal adjustment difficulties in the child in short order.

Some pupils are handicapped by a lack of intellectual interests in the home. Their parents provide few, if any, books or magazines for them. Lack of travel and other cultural opportunities make it difficult, if not impossible, for them to develop the concepts so readily attainable by those with broader experiences.

Poor teaching may be the cause of learning problems. The pupil may have learning disabilities that become cumulative. He may be underequipped to learn and emotionally disturbed. Suffice it to say that in diagnosing learning difficulties, one must investigate a pupil's environment to find if the principal cause lies there.

SPECIFIC SUBJECT DIFFICULTIES. Learning difficulties often stem from the subject itself. The complex skills demanded by mathematics, language, spelling, and reading present learning problems. Considerable research on learning disabilities has indicated typical and specific errors and has resulted in the design of many diagnostic instruments to help locate them. But the teacher need not always administer a standardized instrument in diagnosis, because informal techniques are effective when used competently.

Buswell and John (1926) studied the common errors made by pupils in arithmetic. Table 22 shows some of their findings. Note the errors made by pupils in the third, fourth, fifth, and sixth grades when they add and subtract; similar data are also available for multiplication and division.

TABLE 22
FREQUENCY OF TEN COMMON ERRORS IN ADDITION, SUBTRACTION, MULTIPLICATION, AND DIVISION OF WHOLE NUMBERS

	Grade level				
Type of error	3	4	5	6	Total
Addition					
Errors in combinations	81	103	78	58	320
Counting	61	83	54	17	215
Added carried number last	39	45	45	26	155
Forgot to add carried number	37	38	34	17	126
Retraced work after partly done	26	34	39	22	121
Added carried number irregularly	26	30	28	18	102
Wrote number to be carried	34	25	18	12	89
Carried wrong number	28	19	26	14	87
Irregular procedure in column	16	29	23	18	86
Grouped two or more numbers	25	22	21	16	84
Total number of pupils	96	124	116	78	414
Subtraction					
Errors in combinations	62	75	69	40	246
Did not allow for having borrowed	19	50	57	36	162
Counting	43	44	39	10	136
Errors due to zero in minuend	25	39	26	15	105
Said example backward	21	38	29	12	100
Subtracted minuend from subtrahend	47	33	12	4	96
Failed to borrow, gave zero as answer	21	20	14	4	59
Added instead of subtracting	18	9	19	1	47
Error in reading	14	5	13	10	42
Used same digit in two columns	18	15	3	4	40
Total number of pupils	84	109	109	70	372

From Buswell and John, 1926, pp. 136–139; adapted by permission of The University of Chicago Press.

The inter-relationships among the fundamental processes must be taken into account in any diagnosis concerning them. For example, if a child is struggling with long division because he cannot subtract or multiply, giving him more division problems to work without analyzing his difficulty is an inefficient way of helping him. Learning to subtract will make him competent in long division.

Among the common errors in language are those related to oral speech. Abney (1944, pp. 181–186) lists the following:

1. Incorrect vowel quality: Frequently heard in such words as *get, was, pretty, catch, because, creek, just.*
2. Incorrect consonant quality: Frequently heard in *length, what, luxury, immediately, walking, talking.*
3. Misplaced accent: *positively, research, museum, umbrella, discharge.*
4. Omission of requisite sounds: As in *recognize, family, really, mirror, nearer, February.*
5. Sounding silent letters: In such words as *often, toward, evening, parliament, salmon, corps.*
6. The addition of superfluous sounds: As in *athlete, mischievous, once, prairie, film, portentous, elm.*
7. The utterance of sounds in their improper order: Frequently heard in *children* (not *childern*), *hundred, larynx.*

Willing (1926) analyzed grammar errors in compositions written by secondary school pupils and developed a series of proofreading exercises

TABLE 23
FREQUENCY OF GRAMMATICAL ERRORS—
AGREEMENT OF VERBS AND SUBJECTS

	Number Errors per 1200 Words		
Error classification	8th grade	9th grade	Both grades
Compound subject with single parts	4	1	5
Intervening expressions	5	5	10
Expletive *there* constructions	3	3	6
Don't usages	0	0	0
Subjects such as *each, everyone*	1	0	1
Attraction of predicate nouns	0	1	1
Other cases, verbs following subject	9	4	13
Miscellaneous	3	1	4

From Willing, 1926, pp. 55–63; reproduced by permission of the Bureau of Publications, Teachers College, Columbia University.

that teachers may find helpful in diagnosis. Table 23 gives a number of error classifications concerning the agreement of verbs and subjects. As expected, ninth-grade pupils had fewer errors than eighth-grade. Other categories reported by Willing are spelling, capitalization, punctuation, sentence structure, and word usage.

Failure to write legibly often requires attention. It is possibly the result of inadequate motor development, but considerable evidence shows that careless formation of a very few letters contributes greatly to this problem. Table 24 presents Newland's (1932, p. 256) data on illegible writing. The table lists the percentage contributions of twelve of the twenty-four common types of error to the total illegibilities recorded. Newland notes that a, e, r, and t contribute about fifty per cent of the illegibilities recorded for all age groups. If legibility is to be improved, the teacher must check these letters and correct errors. It is a waste of valuable time to have intermediate grade pupils drilling on every letter of the alphabet.

Spelling errors may be related to mispronunciation, speech disability,

TABLE 24
ANALYSIS OF LETTER MALFORMATIONS

| Common types of error | Percentages Contributed | | | |
	Elementary	Secondary	Adult	Total
Failure to close letters (a, b, f, g, j, k, o, p, q, s, y, z)	24	20	16	18
Top loops closed (l like t, e like i)	13	14	20	18
Looping nonlooped strokes (i like e)	12	27	12	16
Using straight up-strokes rather than rounded strokes (n like u, c like i, h like li)	11	10	15	13
End stroke difficulty (not brought up, not brought down, not left horizontal)	11	6	9	9
Difficulty crossing t	5	5	9	7
Difficulty dotting i	3	5	5	5
Too short (b, d, f, h, k, l, t)	6	7	3	5
Letters too small	4	5	4	4
Closing c, h, r, u, v, w, y	4	3	3	3
Part of letter omitted	4	4	3	3
Up-stroke too long	2	3	1	2

From Newland, 1932, p. 256; adapted by permission of Dembar Publications, Inc.

or inability to use phonic skills. A classification of typical spelling errors can reveal this relationship and give the teacher a basis for helping the pupil. Spache (1940) analyzed the errors made by poor and average spellers in the third, fourth, and fifth grades (Table 25) and showed that the average spellers make more phonetic substitutions than poor spellers who, in turn, are inclined to make more nonphonetic substitutions. Also, average spellers add fewer letters than poor spellers, which may be accounted for by greater use of phonics by the average spellers. Mistakes occur because English words are not always spelled as they are pronounced.

Pupils having difficulty with spelling often have difficulty with reading and vice versa; the skills are closely related. Another, and subtler, cause of reading disability is lack of background, a difficulty in all grades and areas. A first-grade pupil may not have had the visual and auditory experiences to acquire a sight vocabulary. A pupil in secondary school may lack the vocabulary to comprehend his assignments in social studies and physical science. One gifted pupil thought that a cow was about the size of a large dog. He had never seen a cow, though he could very well talk about one. Field trips provide experiences that help make classroom learning meaningful. A lesson in conservation will be much more effective if pupils have actually seen the results of erosion. A discussion of city government will be aided by a visit to the municipal buildings. Words have no intrinsic meaning; they trigger associations from the experiences of the individual. When he has no experiences to associate with the symbol, he can only memorize.

Another cause of poor reading is lack of the systematic development of the basic skills in reading, such as a sight vocabulary, techniques of word recognition, comprehension, and the work study skills. For example, if a child has not developed an adequate sight vocabulary, he may become overanalytical in his reading and break words apart without learning how to blend the syllables or use meaningful phrases and the context to help him understand. In other cases, structural, analysis, syllabication, phonics, etc., have been too little emphasized, and the pupil finds himself handicapped in attacking new words. Independent reading demands a system of word attack skills.

Failure to transfer reading skills to other assignments is another difficulty. Teaching reading without applying it to assignments in, for example, biology, too often results in the pupil's inability to do everyday reading tasks. The science teacher needs to discuss main ideas of paragraphs with his students. He should show how skimming, thorough reading, and rapid reading can be applied to his assignments. He should help his pupils initiate vocabulary development programs for themselves, because skills must be applied, not allowed to remain in isolation.

TABLE 25
MEAN PER CENT OF ERRORS OF POOR AND AVERAGE SPELLERS
IN THIRD, FOURTH, AND FIFTH GRADES

Spelling error	Poor spellers	Average spellers
Omissions		
Single letter		
Silent	12.0	13.5
Sounded	12.7	9.5
Doubled	5.7	7.4
Syllable	3.4	1.7
Total	30.7	29.9
Additions		
Single letter		
Doubling	3.0	3.3
Nondoubling: phonetic	2.1	5.5
Nondoubling: nonphonetic	9.5	9.2
Syllable	0.8	1.1
Total	14.0	18.0
Transpositions		
Phonetic	1.5	1.5
Nonphonetic	3.2	3.7
Total	4.4	4.8
Phonetic substitutions		
Vowel	17.0	19.8
Consonant	9.3	10.0
Diphthong	2.6	2.6
Syllable	3.5	6.0
Entire word	2.8	1.7
Total	33.5	37.9
Nonphonetic substitutions		
Vowel	3.2	1.6
Consonant	4.3	3.0
Diphthong	0.7	0.7
Syllable	2.0	1.4
Entire word	1.1	0.9
Total	9.5	6.2
Homonyms	1.4	1.7
Incomplete	4.5	2.1
Unrecognizable	3.8	1.8

From Spache, 1940, p. 185; adapted by permission of Dembar Publications, Inc.

PROBLEMS

3 Explain the following statement: "The emotionally disturbed pupil dissipates his energy before he can apply it to learning." Illustrate your answer.
4 A sixth-grade teacher reports that his pupils can do arithmetic computations fairly well but that they are experiencing frustration and defeat in the areas of arithmetic reasoning and problem solving. Apply the principles of diagnosis to this situation by outlining specific steps for this teacher to follow to gain a thorough understanding of the learning problem he faces.
5 Common learning difficulties in the basic skill subjects have been presented. How might teachers in the following curriculum areas approach similar analyses?
   a. Junior high school physical education
   b. Elementary art
   c. Eleventh-grade American history
   d. French I
6 Before classifying a pupil as mentally retarded, what factors must be thoroughly investigated?

REMEDIATION

Remediation would be much simpler if we could apply a trusted formula to each learning disability—a notion as sadly impossible as every other cure-all. Pupils differ, and learning disabilities are rooted in different soils. The source of one pupil's difficulty may be emotional while another suffers from faulty teaching. One pupil's handwriting is illegible because of inadequate motor development while his neighbor is simply careless.

Despite the different techniques and methods for remediation, certain guiding principles apply to all subjects and provide an operational framework.

1. Remediation should be accompanied by a strong motivational program.
2. Remediation should be individualized in terms of the psychology of learning.
3. A continuous evaluation which informs a pupil of results is vital.

Providing Motivation

No remedial technique will be successful unless the pupil can see the relationship between the purposes of the technique and his own needs. Many failing pupils have acute feelings of inadequacy and feel they are unable to succeed, that they are different. Some of them withdraw, and refuse to try; others rationalize by thinking success is unimportant; that which they might learn will never be useful.

The teacher is the catalyst for changing these attitudes. Such pupils long to be understood. Many of them have been lectured, threatened, and rejected until often the first task is to help them rebuild self-confidence. Good remedial teaching has all the hallmarks of good teaching anywhere. The teacher lets the pupil know that he is liked and appreciated; above all he is optimistic and stays optimistic during the pupil's "downs" as well as his "ups." By accepting the pupil, the teacher helps him build a self-security which is vital for effective learning.

Since a pupil develops confidence when he experiences success, it is important that the teacher know his strengths as well as his weaknesses, for the teacher must build on those strengths, starting at the child's level of achievement. It helps if the pupil's first success is dramatized. Presenting progress concretely is effective, particularly for younger children. Charts, graphs, and pictures can all be used successfully, though the device must be attuned to the maturity of the pupil. A device that lets him see his improvement works well. When he competes with himself, he can better his past record and this proves highly motivating.

To sustain motivation, the teacher should stimulate interest in the remedial program and monotony should be avoided like smallpox. Different approaches prevent mental fatigue, as do materials with high motivational value. If the pupil can help plan his program by selecting materials and procedures, his involvement will often generate a permanent interest basic to the development of his independence.

A pupil's interest may droop if he is forced into remedial activity because some pupils honestly feel that their skills are adequate in spite of painful indications to the contrary. Sometimes allowing them to take a standardized test and helping them analyze the results produces the desired effect. Ingenious teachers use many methods to help a student want to improve, and social recognition is not the least of them. Most pupils find it rewarding to demonstrate progress to their peers and parents. Above all, remedial activities should not be scheduled when they conflict with other things the pupil would like to do. To be required to work a sheaf of arithmetic exercises while a "big game" is going on is hardly motivating.

Evaluating the Program

No remedial program can be based on initial diagnosis without consistent follow-through. In the first place, the pupil's needs will change as he overcomes his learning difficulties. Just as his problems have been cumulative in nature, remedial instruction will be cumulative in its impact. The new is learned in terms of the old.

Secondly, the teacher will want to judge the success of his program. He may have to shift methods and materials to help the pupil learn; all pupils do not respond equally to the same treatment. Only a continual evaluation can determine progress and future procedure.

In the third place, evaluation is important because it lets a pupil know how he is progressing. Motivation to learn goes up when the pupil knows the results of his effort. The less mature the child, the more it is necessary to depict results graphically.

Using Clinical Personnel

Although most teachers are responsible for remedial work, special teachers are occasionally employed to help regular teachers with their problems and often to work with pupils who show severe retardation. Because reading problems are the source of much educational retardation, a number of schools employ reading specialists. Although they are most often found in the elementary schools, some secondary schools are also providing their services. In other schools a subject specialist handles problems in all basic skill or curriculum areas rather than with reading alone.

Another specialist who can substantially contribute to a child's improvement is a school psychologist. Although a great share of his work will be corrective in nature, much of it will also be preventive. His task is to sensitize school personnel to the needs of pupils, and to diagnose individual problems and make the proper referrals when necessary. In this role, he serves as a coordinator for all the special services in the school as well as the community. Through him, the varying contributions of remedial teachers, mental health clinics, social agencies, and the home can be effectively utilized.

PROBLEMS

7 Imagine that you are a foreign language teacher. Three of your pupils are having difficulties. Robert works hard but stumbles desperately in dictations and oral work. Al has a natural ear for the language but seemingly cannot understand the grammar. Donna is a rote learner who memorizes long vocabulary lists with ease, but cannot grasp the essential meaning when translating. Describe how you would provide individualized remediation for these pupils.

8 Some teachers do not report standardized test scores to their pupils as they fear that poor results may be discouraging. Do you agree?

9 Many regard the school psychologist as a sort of second-class psychiatrist who should solve each pupil's problem in a few brief interviews. What is your conception of the role of this specialist? What kinds of pupils would profit by referral to him?

SURVEYING CLASS ACHIEVEMENT

It is effective to identify pupils with learning difficulties by administering a survey achievement test and a scholastic aptitude test. Pupils who appear to be underachieving may then undergo thorough diagnosis and remediation. The discussion that follows is based on the results of the *Stanford Achievement Test* (Partial Battery) and the *Lorge-Thorndike Intelligence Test* (Verbal) administered in October to twenty-three pupils of a fifth-grade class who attended an elementary school in a small city. Their families were of varied socio-economic status. In analyzing the data, description is given of the use of the class record and the class analysis chart in identifying group as well as individual strengths and weaknesses. Suggestions for individual diagnosis and remediation are presented through a discussion of one pupil's difficulties.

Class Record

A class record was prepared on the basis of the test scores from both tests and is shown in Table 26. The pupil's names are listed in the order of their overall achievement as presented by their battery median grade equivalents. To find the battery median grade equivalent, the grade equivalents for the seven subtests are ranked in order of magnitude; the fourth score from the top or bottom is the battery median grade equivalent. The sex of the pupil is recorded in the first column following the name. His age is listed in the next two columns, his *Lorge-Thorndike IQ* in the fourth column, and the grade equivalent and stanines for the seven subtests of the battery in the following columns.

Class Analysis Chart

The numbers preceding the pupils' names serve as identification numbers when preparing a class analysis chart, such as that shown in Table 27. A column is available for each subtest score. Note that these scores are in terms of stanines. The distribution of stanines for each column is found

TABLE 26

CLASS RECORD OF STANFORD ACHIEVEMENT TEST SCORES FOR A FIFTH-GRADE CLASS

Pupil's name	Sex	Age Yr-Mo	Lorge-Thorndike	Word mean.	Par. mean.	Spelling	Language	Arith. comp.	Arith. concepts	Arith. applic.	Batt. median
1. Mary Jones	G	10-2	132	8.8-9	9.2-9*	7.0-7	8.6-8	7.9-9	8.2-9	9.6-9	8.6
2. William Seeber	B	10-1	128	8.8-9	9.2-9	8.0-9	9.0-9	6.5-8	8.2-9	8.0-9	8.2
3. Mary Hillhouse	G	9-8	125	8.8-9	7.8-8	8.0-9	10.5-9	5.2-5	5.2-5	5.4-6	7.8
4. Ann Chitwood	G	9-10	130	8.3-9	9.2-9	6.0-6	8.6-8	5.9-7	7.6-9	7.7-8	7.7
5. Celia Graham	G	10-4	120	7.5-8	6.7-7	7.1-8	10.5-9	5.6-6	5.2-5	5.6-6	6.7
6. Carol Smith	G	10-5	125	6.7-7	6.1-6	6.3-7	6.4-6	6.8-8	6.6-8	7.1-8	6.6
7. Gloria Behrens	G	10-7	122	6.2-7	6.4-7	8.0-9	7.3-7	5.6-6	5.9-6	7.1-8	6.4
8. Sandra Black	G	10-4	123	6.7-7	7.3-8	6.3-7	10.0-9	4.6-4	5.2-5	5.6-6	6.3
9. June Nelson	G	9-10	128	6.7-7	5.1-5	6.3-7	6.4-6	4.1-3	6.1-7	7.1-8	6.3
10. Trudy Lincoln	G	10-4	115	7.1-8	6.1-6	6.3-7	7.5-7	5.1-5	5.6-5	5.4-5	6.1
11. Joe Sills	B	10-3	110	6.4-7	5.9-6	6.4-7	7.3-7	4.6-4	5.2-5	5.6-6	5.9
12. Albert Uken	B	9-11	115	5.7-6	6.1-6	6.3-7	7.7-8	4.6-4	5.6-6	5.1-5	5.7
13. John Sevaar	B	10-2	110	6.2-7	5.3-5	5.3-5	6.2-6	2.9-1	4.9-5	5.1-5	5.3
14. Cindy Bockwitz	G	10-5	104	4.4-4	2.6-1	7.1-8	4.8-5	5.1-5	4.6-4	5.4-5	4.8
15. Florence Weber	G	10-6	.98	5.7-6	4.6-4	4.8-5	4.5-4	3.8-3	3.6-3	4.0-3	4.5
16. Meg Adams	G	10-8	102	4.4-4	5.1-5	4.3-4	2.7-2	4.1-3	4.0-3	4.4-4	4.3
17. Stanley Seward	B	10-4	98	4.2-4	4.4-4	3.3-2	4.9-5	3.6-2	3.6-3	4.4-4	4.2
18. Beverly Hill	G	10-8	122	3.8-3	3.6-3	3.6-2	3.4-3	4.6-4	6.3-7	6.1-7	3.8
19. Carol Jones	G	10-6	94	3.9-3	3.2-2	4.5-4	3.6-3	2.9-1	3.1-2	4.0-3	3.6
20. Peter White	B	9-10	98	3.9-3	3.6-3	3.1-2	3.6-3	2.9-1	3.1-2	4.0-3	3.6
21. Floyd Echart	B	9-9	90	3.8-3	2.6-1	3.1-2	2.4-1	2.9-1	3.6-3	3.4-2	3.1
22. Oscar Biggs	B	10-1	88	2.7-1	2.5-1	2.8-1	2.4-1	2.9-1	2.2-1	2.9-1	2.7
23. Helen Brown	G	10-7	85	2.5-1	2.5-1	2.8-1	2.5-1	2.6-1	2.2-1	2.9-1	2.5

* The first score is the grade equivalent; the second score is the stanine based on the standardization group.

TABLE 27
CLASS ANALYSIS CHART FOR A FIFTH-GRADE CLASS

Stanine	Word mean.	Par. mean.	Spelling	Language	Arith. comp.	Arith. concepts	Arith. applic.
9	1, 2, 3, 4	1, 2, 4	2, 3, 7	2, 3, 5, 8	1	1, 2, 4	1, 2
8	5, 10	3, 8	5, 14	1, 4, 12	2, 6	6	4, 6, 7, 9
7	6, 7, 8, 9, 11, 13	5, 7	1, 6, 8, 9, 10, 11, 12	7, 10, 11	4	9, 18	18
6	12, 15	6, 10, 11, 12	4	6, 9, 13	5, 7	7, 12	3, 5, 8, 11
5		9, 13, 16	13, 15	14, 17	3, 10, 14	3, 5, 8, 10, 11, 13	10, 12, 13, 14
4	14, 16, 17	15, 17	16, 19	15	8, 11, 12, 18	14	16, 17
3	18, 19, 20, 21	18, 20		18, 19, 20	9, 15, 16	15, 16, 17, 21	15, 19, 20
2		19	17, 18, 20, 21	16	17	19, 20	21
1	22, 23	14, 21, 22, 23	22, 23	21, 22, 23	13, 19, 20, 21, 22, 23	22, 23	22, 23

by writing the identification number of each pupil in the box on the same line as his stanine score. For example, Margaret Adams (#16) has a stanine score of 5 for the *Paragraph Meaning* test. Therefore, a "16" is written in the paragraph meaning column in the box opposite the stanine score of five. The remaining twenty-two numbers are similarly recorded in this column.

For each column, the median stanine score was determined by locating the twelfth score from the top or bottom, and plotted by placing a large dot at the appropriate point in each column. The class profile is found by joining these dots with straight lines.

As you can see, the class analysis chart is a summary of the test results for the entire class. At a glance, the teacher can identify the areas in which the best and poorest work is being done. There is considerable variability in all areas of achievement. Few pupils have scores at the very top or bottom of the class in all subtests. Notice that the low point of this class is arithmetic computation. In Table 28, an item analysis indicates that pupils tended to miss items demanding certain computational skills. If these skills are not taught, it is unlikely pupils will develop them. The class does somewhat better in arithmetic application, because needed skill in computation is on an easy level. Typical of test items in arithmetic application are:

1. Ninety children are assigned to three classrooms. What is the average number of pupils in a class?
2. Three pencils cost 10 cents. How many could you buy for $1.00?

The highest points of achievement are in word meaning and spelling. Word meaning is related to good scholastic ability. In this connection, note that the median IQ of the group is 115, which is above average. Spelling ability can be attributed to the school staff's special emphasis on this subject.

As the teacher studies the class analysis chart, he becomes aware of other problems. For instance, Cindy Bockwitz (#14) has a much higher score in spelling than in other parts of the achievement test. Is this an indication that Cindy could improve in other areas? Does it mean that her parents have been drilling her in spelling and find that she excels in this skill? Spelling is not as high level a verbal skill as is reading for comprehension. Cindy's IQ supports the idea that she may be giving spelling special attention.

The teacher cannot assume that two pupils with the same battery median are alike in achievement. Margaret Adams (#16) and Stanley Seward (#17) have battery medians almost alike, yet Margaret is in the second stanine in language usage, while Stanley is in the fifth. There is also considerable difference between them in spelling.

Item Analysis

Another useful aid is an item analysis chart constructed from the right and wrong answers to each item in a subtest. Table 28 lists the responses of the fifth-grade class on the arithmetic computation subtest of the *Stanford Achievement Test*. This diagnostic device gives the teacher a more detailed picture of his pupil's achievement. For example, the content represented by items like 1, 4, and 6 is fairly well learned by the class as a whole, while several items missed by a large percentage of the group represented areas of low achievement.

Items 16, 23, 24, 26, 29, and 35 all require skill with fractions, but there was little instruction in fractions when these pupils were in the

TABLE 28

ITEM ANALYSIS OF THE ARITHMETIC COMPUTATION SUBTEST
OF THE STANFORD ACHIEVEMENT TEST

Test item	Right No.	Right %	Wrong No.	Wrong %	Test item	Right No.	Right %	Wrong No.	Wrong %
1	19	83	4	17	24	3	13	20	87
2	17	74	6	26	25	9	39	14	61
3	16	70	7	30	26	8	35	15	65
4	19	83	4	17	27	16	70	7	30
5	16	70	7	30	28	8	35	15	65
6	18	78	5	22	29	5	22	18	78
7	16	70	7	30	30	8	35	15	65
8	16	70	7	30	31	17	74	6	26
9	8	35	15	65	32	6	26	17	74
10	14	61	9	39	33	7	30	16	70
11	11	48	12	52	34	4	17	19	83
12	7	30	16	70	35	4	17	19	83
13	14	61	9	39	36	9	39	14	61
14	12	52	11	48	37	5	22	18	78
15	5	22	18	78	38	3	13	20	87
16	3	13	20	87	39	9	39	14	61
17	11	48	12	52	40	13	56	10	44
18	10	44	13	56	41	11	48	12	52
19	12	52	11	48	42	6	26	17	74
20	11	48	12	52	43	3	13	20	87
21	7	30	16	70	44	5	22	18	78
22	10	44	13	56	45	4	17	19	83
23	4	17	19	83					

fourth grade. They had only been introduced to these skills since all pupils were taught according to a syllabus which made little allowance for individual differences. This was also true for decimals, and resulted in incorrect answers or omissions for items 25, 33, and 36. The pupils had been instructed in division, yet a large percentage missed items 15, 19, and 37. In item 19, a short division exercise ($4860 \div 8$), the problem of placing a zero in the quotient seemed to confuse many pupils, indicating lack of understanding of that particular skill. Many of them selected "67½" as their answer. By a simple check of their work, they should have discarded this possibility.

In a multiple-choice test, it is possible to determine the number of pupils choosing each of the distractors as well as the number answering correctly. When items are machine-scored, the IBM test scoring machine can easily run the analysis. Because a good test item included plausible distractors, a study of pupils' choices will often give the teacher insight into their difficulties. He will be in a better position to diagnose and, as a result, to prescribe effective remediation.

PROBLEMS

10   Table 26 contains both achievement and mental ability test scores. What general statement can be made about the correlation of each of these sets of achievement test scores with the mental ability scores?

11   Can you find specific instances of retardation in achievement in the fifth-grade class in question? Are any of the pupils overachievers? In your opinion, what is the major problem confronting the teacher of this class? What additional information about the pupils would be highly useful to him?

12   Which pupils in the fifth-grade class under discussion might profit by referral to a reading specialist?

INDIVIDUAL DIAGNOSIS AND REMEDIATION

At this point it is clear that group strengths, weaknesses, and range of ability can be determined from the class record and the class analysis chart. Some individual problems also become apparent. Consider the case of Beverly Hill (#18) who is significantly below the average achievement in language skills of a normal fifth-grade child in the second month of the school year. Beverly has ability that surpasses the average child. Her mental age is 13 years. Therefore her "mental grade" is 8 years (Bond, 1948).

Fifth-grade pupils with normal mental ability have a "mental grade" of 5 years 2 months at this stage of the school year. Despite her superior scholastic aptitude, she is definitely below the point a pupil with average mentality should be, except in arithmetic. Even her arithmetic scores represent retardation considering her scholastic aptitude.

Inability to Read

Because there was evidence that inability to read might be the cause of Beverly's difficulties, the teacher wanted to explore several related elements, but needed more information about her specific reading difficulties. Many teachers like to use an informal oral reading test for this purpose. Beverly's teacher selected several interesting narrative passages, each about 200 words long, from material that Beverly had not read. The reading level of the first passage was of first- or second-grade difficulty, the others of increasing difficulty.

This procedure threw considerable light on Beverly's reading problems. Typical questions asked in an informal reading test are: Does she know the sounds of the vowels and consonants? Can she break a new word into syllables? Can she blend individual sounds together so that she can recognize the word? Does she read with expression, indicating that she is using the context to help identify new words? Does she rely too much on context and fail to recognize certain words, substituting those that make sense but distorting the meaning?

In addition to the informal reading test, the teacher administered the *Gates-McKillop Reading Diagnostic Tests* which is a standardized instrument to analyze reading difficulties. Table 29 contains some of Beverly's grade scores on these tests. Her oral score is 3.8, approximately the same as

TABLE 29
SCORES ON THE GATES-MCKILLOP READING DIAGNOSTIC TESTS
FIRST ADMINISTRATION

Subtests	Beverly's grade score	Highest possible grade score
Oral Reading	3.8	7.5
Reversals	Poor Score	
Recognizing and Blending Common Word Parts	Very Low Score	
Syllabication	Low Score	

her silent reading score. The other scores indicate her serious weakness in reading fundamentals.

Beverly had developed no systematic method for attacking words. She tended to concentrate on words themselves, rather than on the relationship among them, and thereby lost the train of thought. Even her word-by-word reading was marked at times with considerable confusion. Not only did she make a considerable number of reversal errors, but she had difficulty in blending word parts. A number of letter sounds were confused, particularly a and e. Recognition of syllables and phonograms was weak and because of her undue attention to word parts and units, she made very little use of context to aid her in pronunciation or comprehension.

Determining the Cause

The teacher found from Beverly's cumulative record, Figures 37 and 38, that she had a long history of retardation. She had complained of headaches during her first year of school and, in the second grade, was required to wear glasses for close work. Also, during that year her father had been killed in an accident and her mother had to work. Beverly was anxious and insecure, and her early school experience probably accounts for the reading difficulty. She was severely handicapped because learning basic skills is cumulative and she lacked a foundation on which to build. Beverly's mother remarried, and both parents expressed concern about the child's achievement. They asked for a conference, so the teacher had an opportunity to enlist their help.

The teacher realized the importance of involving the parents in learning and giving them a positive role in the process. He understands that parental nagging, forcing children to forego normal social activities, or a lack· of genuine parental interest in the child can prevent a remedial program from being a success. He also knows that he must give parents specific instructions before they can help. If possible, he must avoid telling them that there is nothing they can do, that everything will work out all right.

Of course it is sometimes difficult if not impossible to elicit parental cooperation. Some parents own lack of personal-social adjustment prevents them from being close to their children. Some are so absorbed in their own interests and professional lives that they find it impossible to become involved in their children's problems.

During the conference with Beverly's parents, the teacher explained that their child was bright and that her difficulty stemmed from immature word recognition skills and lack of concentration on the meaning and the relationship among the words. It was decided that Beverly should have

CALIFORNIA CUMULATIVE RECORD
ELEMENTARY FORM
Confidential Information for use by Professional Personnel

FILE No. (Pencil)

1. IDENTIFICATION DATA

PHOTOGRAPHS

LAST NAME	FIRST NAME	MIDDLE NAME	NICKNAME: (Pencil)	CHECK SEX M / F
Hill	Beverly	Jane		X (F)

BIRTH DATE	BIRTH DATE VERIFICATION	CITY (OR COUNTY)	STATE (OR NATION)
2/20/56	Birth by Certificate	Suburban	New York

HOME			DATES PHOTOGRAPHED (Pencil)	SCHOOL DISTRICT

NAME	ADDRESS	TELEPHONE	IN CASE OF EMERGENCY NOTIFY				
Mary L. Hill	101 Olds Ave.	3218					

IN CASE OF EMERGENCY NOTIFY

NAME	ADDRESS	TELEPHONE (Pencil)		NAME	ADDRESS	TELEPHONE
Joe S. Brown	1805 Lotus St.	8-4532	Dr. Ralph Ogden	16 Main St.	8072
COMMENTS Uncle			COMMENTS		

2. GROUP SCHOLASTIC CAPACITY TESTS (LABEL OTHER SUB SCORES USED, e.g., PERFORMANCE, PERCEPTION, ETC. DOUBLE SPACES PROVIDED.)

DATE TEST GIVEN	GRADE	NAME OF TEST	FORM	LEVEL	C.A.	M.A.	Total	Verbal	Non-Verb.	7	8	9	10	11	12	13	COMMENTS	EXAMINER
10/62	1	Otis Alpha (Verbal)	A	Alpha	6-8	9-0	124											
10/66	5	Lorge-Thorndike			10-8	13	122											

3. INDIVIDUAL TESTS

DATE TEST GIVEN	GRADE	NAME OF TEST	C.A.		RESULTS AND REMARKS	EXAMINER
11/66	5	Revised S-B, L-M		130 I.Q. Had trouble with tests demanding reading skill.	A.J.Smith

4. GROUP ACHIEVEMENT TESTS (including Reading Readiness) (LABEL VARIOUS SUB SCORES, e.g., VOCABULARY)

DATE TEST GIVEN	GRADE	NAME OF TEST	FORM	LEVEL	2 READING	3	4	5 ARITHMETIC	6	7	8 LANGUAGE	9	10	11	12	13	14	15	COMMENTS	EXAMINER
11/63	2	Stanford	J	Prim	Par Wd M 1.1	1.5		Reas Comp 3.1 1.8			Spell 1.5									
10/64	3	Stanford	W	Prim	Par Wd M 1.8	2.3		CompConc 2.9 2.9			Spell 2.5									
10/65	4	Stanford	W	Int I	Par Wd M 2.3	2.7		Appl CompConc 5.1 3.8 5.0			Spell Lang 3.6 3.6									
10/66	5	Stanford	W	Int II	Par Wd M 3.6	3.8		Appl CompConc 6.1 4.6 6.3			Spell Lang 3.6 3.4									

5. PERSONALITY AND INTEREST INVENTORIES, APTITUDE TESTS, AND OTHER TESTS (LABEL VARIOUS SUB SCORES, e.g., EMOTIONAL, SOCIAL)

DATE TEST GIVEN	GRADE	NAME OF TEST	FORM	LEVEL	2	3	4	5	6	7	8	9	10	11	12	13	14	15	COMMENTS	EXAMINER
11/66	5	Calif. Test of Personality	AA	Elem	Per'l Soc Adj. Adj. %ile%ile 50 60															

Reproduced by permission of A. Carlisle and Company.

FIGURE 37   INSIDE HALF OF AN ELEMENTARY SCHOOL CUMULATIVE RECORD

6. INFORMATION CONCERNING INDIVIDUAL ADJUSTMENT

YEAR AND GRADE	INTERESTS, ACTIVITIES, LEADERSHIP	FAMILY AND HOME RELATIONSHIPS OUT OF SCHOOL RESPONSIBILITIES	ATTITUDES AND FEELINGS ABOUT: SELF; PEERS; SCHOOL	REFERRALS TO SCHOOL SERVICES AND/OR COMMUNITY AGENCIES
YEAR 19 61-62 KINDERGARTEN	Quiet child. Very cooperative.	Shares family experiences. Close family ties.	Has adjusted well to school and to her peers.	
YEAR 19 62-63 GRADE 1	Likes to do activities with hands. Doesn't choose books in free time.	Family watches television a great deal.	Sometimes appears to be day-dreaming.	
YEAR 19 63-64 GRADE 2	Seems withdrawn since death of father.	Mother is now working. Does not spend as much time with Beverly.	Retarded in reading. Seems un-interested.	
YEAR 19 64-65 GRADE 3	Evidences of some leadership. Has several close friends.	Seems to be a close relationship with the Mother.	Has shown considerable interest in arithmetic.	
YEAR 19 65-66 GRADE 4	Continues to be liked and accepted by her peers.	Has done some baby sitting with neighbor children during the day hours.	Has applied herself to her school work.	
YEAR 19 66-67 GRADE 5				
YEAR 19 -19 GRADE				
YEAR 19 -19 GRADE				
YEAR 19 -19 GRADE				
YEAR 19 -19 GRADE				

Reproduced by permission of A. Carlisle and Company.

FIGURE 37   INSIDE HALF OF AN ELEMENTARY SCHOOL ACCUMULATED RECORD

7. GROWTH AND DEVELOPMENT THROUGH SCHOOL EXPERIENCES

INDICATE MAJOR CURRICULUM UNIT, DESCRIPTION OF EXPERIENCE, AND DURATION. INITIAL EACH ENTRY. THIS SPACE MAY ALSO BE USED FOR INDICATING DEGREE OF SUCCESS IN SCHOOL EXPERIENCES AND READERS USED.

FORM L.M.—A. Carlisle & Co., S.F., 1955

YEAR 19 61-19 62 KINDERGARTEN	YEAR 19 62-19 63 GRADE 1	YEAR 19 63-19 64 GRADE 2	YEAR 19 64-19 65 GRADE 3	YEAR 19 65-19 66 GRADE 4	YEAR 19 -19	YEAR 19 -19
Works well with group and plays independently. Neat; follows directions. Sings in tune; knows many nursery rhymes.	Reading: S-F series. Readiness bks., 3 pre-primers, Jr. pre-primer and primer completed. Also 3 pre-primers of supp (H-M) rdrs.	Readers: S-F series. $1\frac{1}{2}$ reader ..11/20 $1\frac{2}{2}$ " (H-M)..2/2 1^2 " 4/15 L-C phonics bks, A & B Cowboy Sam, 1 & 2	Readers: S-F series. 2^1 of S-F and of H-M; workbooks. Eye & Ear Fun, 1, 2, 3 L-C Phonics, bk C	Readers; In lowest group. S-F 3^1 & 3^2 Workbooks: S-F & Readers Digest Skill Builders, 2, 3, 4 Merrill Skilltexts: Nibs, Nicky, Uncle Funny Bunny		
Knows the letters of the alphabet, names of the colors. Can write her name.	Did not start first reader, but should be ready for it in Sept. Did all bks.	(started 2^1 reader in May, but finds it difficult. Cannot concentrate. Wears glasses, but forgets them.)	Completed S-F 2^2 and began 3^1, but finds it difficult. Dislikes reading.	Math: S-B bk 4. Neat, accurate. Understands problems but has trouble reading them.		
Cooperative	Math: Knows combinations and understands meaning of concepts	Math: Understands add. & sub., knows basic facts. S-B bk.	Social Studies: Local history, Indians	Social Studies — Foll. Regional studies. Can't read text. Does not participate in disc.		
Seems ready for first grade work			Math: Average in class S-B bk 3; knows all combinations and 4 processes; accurate and neat.	Science: enjoys experiments, can't read text.		

YEAR 19 66-19 67 GRADE 5					YEAR 19 -19	YEAR 19 -19 GRADE

Requirements of U. S. Constitution, American History, State and Local Government satisfactorily completed.

Date Certified _____ INITIAL _____

Reproduced by permission of A. Carlisle and Company.

FIGURE 38 OUTSIDE HALF OF AN ELEMENTARY SCHOOL ACCUMULATED RECORD

8. SCHOOL HISTORY

DATE ENTERED	HOME ADDRESS & TELEPHONE	CITY OR COUNTY	SCHOOL & SCHOOL DISTRICT	GRADE	TEACHER	ATTENDANCE	TRANSFERRED TO:	DATE LEFT
9-61	101 Olds 3218	Suburban	Suburban Central	K	Shapiro	Perfect		
9-62	"	"	"	1	Wilson	1st week -- trip		
9-63	"	"	"	2	Eddy	1 week -- death of F.		
9-64	"	"	"	3	Wood	Periodic absence		
9-65	"	"	"	4	Banner	No absences		
9-66	"	"	"	5	Green			

COMPLETED GRADE 6 OR 8 (CIRCLE) OR ON | Month | Day | Year

9. PARENTS' EDUCATIONAL AND/OR VOCATIONAL PLANS FOR PUPIL: (Pencil)

	HOME ADDRESS (Pencil)	SPECIFIC OCCUPATION (Pencil)	BUSINESS ADDRESS AND TELEPHONE (Pencil)	CIRCLE (Pencil)	CIRCLE
10. FATHER'S NAME Deceased				Pupil Living Wth Yes (No)	Lives? Yes (No)
11. MOTHER'S NAME Mary L. Hill	101 Olds Ave.	Teacher	Elmwood School	Pupil Living Wth (Yes) No	Lives? (Yes) No
12. OR GUARDIAN'S NAME				Pupil Living Wth Yes No	Lives? Yes No

13. CHILDREN OF FAMILY

NAMES	Year of Birth	RELATIONSHIP TO PUPIL	Living at Home (Circle)
Beverly Hill	1956		

15. SIGNIFICANT HEALTH FACTORS

DATE	RECOMMENDATIONS OF HEALTH ADVISER	ADVISER'S NAME
9/63	Glasses prescribed	Jones
	Audiometer reading normal	Jones

DATE	TEACHER'S COMMENTS ON PUPIL'S HEALTH CONDITIONS	TEACHER
11/63	Symptoms of extreme anxiety.	Eddy

14. ADULTS OTHER THAN PARENTS LIVING CONTINUOUSLY IN PUPIL'S HOME (Pencil)

DATE	NAME	RELATIONSHIP TO PUPIL

Reproduced by permission of A. Carlisle and Company.

FIGURE 38   OUTSIDE HALF OF AN ELEMENTARY SCHOOL CUMULATIVE RECORD

individual remedial reading instruction each day. Her parents were helped to realize the need for supporting the child emotionally and were asked to praise her liberally for any improvement. They were advised against exerting pressure either overtly or through expression of concern about her progress.

The teacher was also able to discuss television and its relation to Beverly's reading problem. He helped her parents to see that if their own chief interest was television, not reading, it would be impossible to convince the child of the importance of improving her reading, that their habits would have a marked effect on Beverly's. They were advised to discuss both television programs and their reading, drawing Beverly into the conversation, thereby pointing up the importance of both in acquiring and formulating ideas.

Providing Remedial Instruction

Removing the cause of a learning difficulty is only the first step. Now Beverly had to be taught to read. In her case, stress was placed on recognition of sounds, syllables, and blending. She was given opportunity for practicing a systematic attack on unfamiliar words and helped to use context for determining meanings. Her left to right orientation was developed.

Attention was also given to improving her reading rate. Beverly was encouraged to time herself on short easy exercises and to keep a record of her progress. To keep her abreast of class work, the teacher made available easy materials on topics under study.

A pupil who has had difficulty in such a basic skill as reading is probably short on confidence. Beverly was given an opportunity to read an

TABLE 30

SCORES ON THE GATES-MCKILLOP READING DIAGNOSTIC TESTS,
SECOND ADMINISTRATION

Subtests	Beverly's grade score
Oral Reading	7.2
Reversals	Normal progress
Recognizing and Blending	
Common Word Parts	Normal progress
Syllabication	Normal progress

easy passage to the class occasionally, but first her teacher made sure that she was well prepared. Recognition of this kind provided a high degree of motivation.

At the end of the year, several tests from the second form of the *Gates-McKillop Reading Diagnostic Tests* were administered to Beverly. The scores are listed in Table 30. Notice the vast improvement. The total score in oral reading increased from 3.8 to 7.2. All other scores are now satisfactory. Moreover, her scores on the *Gates-MacGintie Reading Tests* are as follows:

Test	Grade level
Vocabulary	6.8
Speed and Accuracy	6.3
Comprehension	6.5

Beverly kept a record of the books she read during the year, and at the last count, she had over forty to her credit. Although some were very short and easy, she also had read a number of considerable substance.

All remedial teaching does not have to be done on an individual basis, as has already been pointed out. Elementary school teachers can group pupils in various ways so that special help can be given for special difficulties. More secondary school teachers need to utilize these grouping procedures. The teacher might begin with two groups. Four or five pupils who excel in the course may be grouped for special projects while the teacher works with the majority of the class. Gradually, as the teacher's skill and confidence increase, he can increase the number of groups.

PROBLEMS

13 An analysis of Beverly's reading scores has been presented. Does the interpretation given indicate a need for a certain degree of sophistication on the part of the teacher to make maximum use of these tests? How would you explain the meaning of the *Gates* subtest scores to a parent?

14 Parental conferences can be highly important in helping a child. Conversely, if not handled correctly, such meetings may aggravate the situation. Formulate a simplified set of rules or guideposts for the inexperienced teacher.

15 Figures 37 and 38 duplicate Beverly's cumulative record. What additional information do you wish had been included?

SUMMARY

Good teaching implies that each pupil should achieve in terms of his interests, needs, and potential. There are several reasons why pupils may not be learning. Among these is the promotion of "lock-step" teaching, where every pupil is required to read the same materials, spell the same words, and work the same problems. This is bound to result in some pupils repeating what they already know while others are confronted with tasks too difficult for them because they have basic disabilities.

In diagnosing learning difficulties, the first step is to identify the pupil with a learning problem and then pinpoint his strengths and weaknesses. If possible, the underlying cause of the difficulty should be eliminated before remedial instruction begins. Although the teacher cannot be expected to develop the proficiency of a clinician, he must have several competencies in diagnosing and providing for remediation: (1) an understanding of the psychology of learning as it applies to specific subject areas; (2) an ability to recognize those physical and psychological aspects of human development related to learning; and (3) an understanding of the important diagnostic techniques and the remedial methods and materials in various subject areas.

Research has uncovered a number of factors affecting pupil achievement. Scholastic aptitude, health, vision, hearing, motor co-ordination, personal-social development, and environment either contribute toward achievement or prohibit successful school work. Difficulties peculiar to a specific subject may be responsible for learning problems, and such elements have been identified in arithmetic, language, handwriting, spelling, and reading.

As in diagnosis, certain guiding principles should be applied in remediation: motivation, individualizing learning, and keeping pupils aware of the effects of remediation through continual evaluation. Individualizing learning does not mean the abolition of group instruction; both elementary and secondary school teachers can group pupils with common problems to help them.

A school testing program is an excellent way to initiate a sound program of diagnosis and remediation. By administering a general survey test, it is possible to screen out pupils who may be in need of special help. Devices such as the class record, class analysis chart, and results of a test item analysis prove helpful in getting a clear picture both of the group and its individual members. Analyses supported by diagnostic tests and data from cumulative records are the basis on which to build a remedial program.

Suggested Readings

Blair, G. M. *Diagnostic and remedial teaching.* (Rev. ed.) New York: Macmillan, 1956.

This book is designed for both elementary and secondary teachers. In addition to discussing the problems of diagnosis and remediation in reading, arithmetic, handwriting, spelling, and English fundamentals, the author outlines remedial programs for elementary, junior high, and high schools.

Brueckner, L. J., and G. L. Bond. *The diagnosis and treatment of learning difficulties.* New York: Appleton-Century-Crofts, 1955.

The authors direct their discussion to the typical classroom teacher. Special emphasis is given to learning problems in arithmetic, language, spelling, and handwriting.

Daly, W. C. *Test scores: fragment of a picture.* Test Service Notebook, No. 24. Tarrytown, N,Y.: Harcourt, Brace and World, 1959.

The "pattern" technique in child study is recommended. The goal of this technique is to make a diagnostic formulation for prediction. A large quantity of various kinds of information about the pupil is needed.

Goldman, L. *Using tests in counseling.* New York: Appleton-Century-Crofts, 1961. Chapters 7, 11, and 13.

These chapters present a discussion of test interpretation, including illustrative cases.

Harris, A. J. *How to increase reading ability.* (4th ed.) New York: Longmans, Green, 1961.

This is one of the best and most widely used references in the field of diagnosis and remediation in reading. The author bases his discussion on research and practical experience. The book is a thorough and practical source of information.

Henry, N. B. (Ed.) *Individualized instruction.* Sixty-First Yearb. nat. Soc. Stud. Educ., 1962, 177–282. Chicago: University of Chicago Press.

Section III of the yearbook discusses school practices for individualizing instruction. It presents some of the current thinking on the problems of individual differences within the schools.

Horst, P. How much information on test results should be given to students: views of a research psychologist. *J. counsel. Psychol.*, 1959, 6, 218–222.

Problems of communicating test results to pupils are considered. Teachers are urged to improve this type of communication by learning more about tests and the meaning of the scores they produce.

Kough, J., and R. F. De Haan. *Teacher's guidance handbook.* Chicago: Science Research Associates, 1955–1957.

This work in four volumes gives practical and concrete suggestions to aid the classroom teacher in identifying and helping the following groups of special children: the gifted and talented, the emotionally, socially, and educationally maladjusted, and the physically handicapped.

Strang, Ruth, C. M. McCullough, and A. E. Traxler. *The improvement of reading.* (3rd ed.) New York: McGraw-Hill, 1961.

This book deals with problems of reading in the secondary school and college. Such topics as special reading groups, appraisal of reading proficiency, overcoming difficulties in word recognition and vocabulary, special problems of slow and able learners, personality, and individual treatment make this an exceptional resource.

Thorndike, R. L. *The concepts of over- and under-achievement.* New York: Bureau of Publications, Teachers College, Columbia University, 1963.
The author reviews the research studies on over- and under-achievement. He points out incidents of faulty design and suggests precautionary measures for future research.

References Cited

Abney, Louise. Speech, voice, and pronunciation. *Teaching language in the elementary school.* Forty-Third Yearb. nat. Soc. Stud. Educ., 1944. Chicago: University of Chicago Press.

Bond, G. L. Identifying the reading attainments and needs of students. *Reading in the high school and college.* Forty-Seventh Yearb. nat. Soc. Stud. Educ., 1948. Chicago: University of Chicago Press.

Buswell, G. T., and L. John. *Diagnostic studies in arithmetic.* Suppl. Educ. Monogr., 1926, No. 30.

Cook, W. W. The functions of measurement in the facilitation of learning. In E. F. Lindquist (Ed.), *Educational measurement.* Washington: American Council on Education, 1951. Pp. 3–46.

Harris, A. J. *How to increase reading ability.* (4th ed.) New York: David McKay, 1961.

Newland, T. E. An analytical study of the development of illegibilities in handwriting from the lower grades to adulthood. *J. educ. Res.*, 1932, 26, 249–258.

Spache, G. Characteristic errors of good and poor spellers. *J. educ. Res.*, 1940, 34, 182–189.

Willing, M. H. *Valid diagnosis in high school composition.* Contributions to Education, No. 230. New York: Bureau of Publications, Teachers College, Columbia University, 1926.

16 ✒

Determining and Reporting Growth

SUPPOSE YOU HAVE ASKED YOUR PHYSICIAN to give you a thorough physical examination. He runs through a complex series of clinical and laboratory examinations, evaluates them, and says "Well, I guess you're worth about a B+." You leave cheerfully enough—a B+ always sounds good when you are told achievement test results—but a bit puzzled. Perhaps it means that there are not many people as physically able as you. Perhaps there are more things right than wrong with your health. But these seem to be the only conclusive judgments you can come to. You do not know how to improve your health, because you do not know what deficiencies kept you from getting an A.

Clearly a letter grading system is inadequate for summarizing the results of a physical examination. If your physician discovers circulatory difficulties, he discusses the ailment with you. Often he must interpret extensively before you understand the meaning of the evaluation. Many bits of information are related and balanced. Furthermore, a physician relates his diagnosis to remediation, and is likely to modify your activities or diet.

Similarly, evaluating a pupil's competence requires careful reflection on many aspects of his personality and abilities. Much more is examined than his knowledge of subject matter; his teachers are concerned with his personal-social adjustment, the way he represents his school, and the quality of his response to the learning situations he experiences.

Composite evaluation of something as nebulous as human behavior must be highly complex. Not all evidence can be completely objective. Every source of data available for assessing both psychological and physical characteristics must be tapped. It is almost impossible to summarize the evaluation with a single symbol.

Teachers agree that giving and reporting marks is one of their most uncomfortable responsibilities. Some lack confidence in the marks they assign; others believe their marks are fair, but find them difficult to defend. Behind these negative attitudes lies the fact that the basis for assigning marks is often unclear. Should the intelligent pupil who loafs be given a low mark? Should the pupil who works very hard but whose mental capacities are inadequate be upgraded in spite of his below-average performance on tests and assignments? Should the pupil who adjusts well to his peers but receives failing marks be promoted? What would be the effect on this child's future development if he were held back? With so many factors to consider responsibly, it is small wonder that teachers regard giving final marks as a chore.

Marking and reporting have come a long way since the earliest report cards in American education. Generally these were colorful, artistic, and vague. They contained simple little messages like "To a very industrious little girl from her affectionate teacher," or "Studiousness and good deportment in a young man are a credit to his parents and a satisfaction to his teacher." Comments about achievement in important subjects like penmanship, spelling, and reading developed later. These evaluations, together with a report on attendance and deportment, persisted in our schools for many years. Though less common today, this type of report is still in use. It informs parents of their child's attendance and tardiness, deportment, achievement in subject matter according to grade standards, and his chances of promotion or failure (Goodykoontz, 1955).

In many modern schools, there is a definite trend toward revising methods of marking and reporting. Child psychology and a redefinition of the objectives of the school have had their influence. Attention has been centered on the whole child, emphasizing his achievement in relation to his own potential for development. The complexity of this kind of evaluation is reflected in changed methods of reporting, leading to such devices as check lists, personal letters, and teacher-parent conferences.

Purposes of Reporting

The purposes of marking and reporting can best be defined in terms of those who use them—pupils, parents, teachers, school administrators, and employers. In the final analysis, reports should serve the paramount purpose of facilitating the educational development of each pupil in relation to his ability, and their effectiveness should be judged by this criterion. Reports succeed insofar as they help each pupil realize his potential.

Informing the Pupil

MOTIVATION. Originally, one of the purposes of reports was to exhort pupils to greater effort in school. Fear of failure, it was argued, would produce greater achievement, while if the pupil knew he would be passed on automatically from grade to grade, he would work less. Research does not support this conclusion. One study compared seventh grade groups in nine elementary school systems employing almost universal "social-promotion" and nine school systems maintaining rigid standards of promotion. No significant differences were found either in achievement or intelligence between groups. In the school where failure was common, the range of abilities aggravated the instructional problem. In fact, grade standards tended to be lowered (Cook, 1941).

It has been found that certain pupils will be challenged to work for higher marks. Although they may have little interest in the subject matter at first, it may develop through feelings of accomplishment and success. Yet there are dangers in working for marks. A pupil who conforms rigidly to a teacher's set standards for an A may sacrifice his creativity and imagination in the process. Another, lacking the mental ability to meet the standards set by his teacher, is not motivated to learn when he knows he cannot succeed despite his efforts. Yet if marks represent his improvement rather than status alone, he may have incentive to strive for them.

GUIDANCE. One of the conditions for effective learning is that a pupil know the results of his study. For example, a diagnostic evaluation that shows the reader his mistakes in word attack skills and commends him for effective use of context clues is important for continued growth in reading. The pupil who is constructively criticized after his talk in speech class learns from suggestions. Research emphasizes that the best time to correct an error is immediately after it is made. Learning is facilitated by the help a pupil receives from the comments of his teachers and peers in day to day contacts. Therefore, the teacher should inform the pupil continually of his strengths and weaknesses. These daily evaluations also make possible more effective summaries at the end of a report period. The secondary school pupil has much to gain from an over-all appraisal of his abilities in specific academic fields. He needs to know his possibilities for success in further education to help him decide what course of studies he should follow. Secondary school marks are useful in predicting college marks; a number of studies show relationships represented by correlation coefficients well above 0.50 (Smith & Dobbin, 1960, pp. 783–791).

On the other hand, standardized achievement test scores have been shown to have about as high a relationship with college marks as secondary school marks (Lindquist, 1951). They also provide the individual with an opportunity to compare his performance with a regional or national norm, a comparison more likely to give him a valid estimate of his achievement.

Final marks must be interpreted in terms of the quality of instruction and the general ability of the pupils in the class. In some schools where there may be a lack of talent among the pupils, it is possible for high marks to give a distorted picture of a pupil's achievement. The lower marks of some pupils in our better schools may represent more achievement than A's in schools inadequately staffed and equipped. A final mark of C in an honor's class may represent greater achievement than an A in an average class.

The interpretation of marks, then, is very important. The value of the report increases as the pupil is helped to understand what it means. This implies that the teacher is prepared to defend its accuracy and show its significance. There are teachers who make it a practice to explain the meaning of marks and other data to pupils before the reports go home. This procedure also provides an opportunity to review the school's objectives with the pupils.

Informing the Parent

Parents must understand the school's objectives to advance cooperation between home and school; otherwise there is likely to be conflict. Some parents feel that academic achievement should be the only concern of the school. Many think certain kinds of academic achievement are more important than others. Learning dates, names, and places may be more desirable in their eyes than understanding the social issues. A large vocabulary may seem more important than understanding what is read. Therefore, field trips to provide background experience for reading are frowned on as a waste of time.

Such parents are perplexed when the school is concerned with group living and personal-social adjustment, despite the fact that our greatest national health problem is mental health. They fail to understand that we cannot divorce the pupil's intellectual growth from other aspects of his development. Not until a parent can accept the educational objectives of the school is he in a position to support and supplement the educational program for his child, but he can neither accept nor support without understanding. A truly informative system of reporting is formulated in terms of these objectives and of his child's growth and progress toward them, and provides a basis for understanding and the intelligent cooperation of the parent with both teacher and child.

Informing Teachers, School Administrators, and Employers

A composite evaluation of a pupil's achievement and growth should be available for his future teachers and the administration. The cumulative record is most helpful. Periodic reports should be filed here, since they represent evaluations of much of the data. Whether or not the pupil remains in the same school system, his teachers will have information about his progress in previous grades.

The school administrator or guidance officer often must evaluate the competence and potentiality of the school's graduates. As more pupils continue their formal education, colleges and universities must exercise increasingly stringent selection, and well-organized evaluations of college-bound pupils should be available for them. Many aspects of achievement—oral expression, laboratory skills and creativity among them—cannot be evaluated by paper-and-pencil tests. Colleges are also interested in such facets of a pupil's school life as his personal-social adjustment, his participation in extra-class activities, and the nature of his interests and goals.

Pupils who do not go to college generally seek employment. Because the tendency to practice social-promotion has changed the meaning of a high-school diploma, their prospective employers often request information about them. While competence in secretarial or machine-shop skills are important for certain types of jobs, employers also want people who can get along with others, assume responsibility, have leadership potential and an attitude of cooperation. Periodic reports over the years provide an indication of the future pattern of behavior that an employer might expect of an individual.

PROBLEMS

1 If we accept the premise that report cards and final marks exist to help each pupil develop according to his ability, how then can we justify the use of rigid standards of passing and failing?
2 If standardized test scores yield information comparable to secondary school marks, could we then abolish report cards and concentrate on thorough interpretation of the achievement test results in individual conferences with the parents and child? Explain your answer.
3 Many guidance counselors schedule routine conferences with individual pupils for the purpose of discussing achievement as recorded on the report card. What additional kinds of information must the counselor have available as preparation for these conferences?

BASES FOR REPORTING

Objectives of the School

Effective intruction and evaluation are based on the educational objectives of the school. These should be stated in terms of desired pupil behavior, which should enable a pupil to satisfy both his immediate and adult needs. It is not possible to identify the most important educational objectives for all schools and all times, or to determine when they are to be emphasized. This must be decided in terms of the individual differences of pupils, teachers, and communities.

If evaluation is to be made in terms of all of the school's objectives, general and specific, marking and reporting become very complex. In the first place, evaluation of some parts of a pupil's behavior cannot be as adequate as we would like, yet even so may be more valuable than a paper-and-pencil test indicating only what the pupil says he will do. If one of our objectives is to develop effective citizenship, statements such as "He votes in all elections for which he is eligible," and "He assumes responsibility in group work," give some direction and basis for evaluation. Secondly, it is impractical to sample enough behavior of every pupil to obtain an adequate evaluation. This is especially true for the secondary school where a teacher meets many pupils every day. Third, to report on each one of a great number of behavioral patterns would give the false impression that valid judgments can be made in every instance. A fourth problem would arise in presenting such a report to parents, since it would be too long and complex to be interpreted easily.

So the teacher faces something of a dilemma. On one hand, he wants to base his marking and reporting on all pertinent educational objectives, general and specific. On the other, the list of these objectives is so long, and sometimes the evidence concerning them so difficult to obtain, that he faces an almost impossible task. To make his reporting task more manageable, he compromises, however reluctantly. Rather than trying to report pupil progress in terms of all educational objectives each time a report is to be made, he may select a group of objectives, perhaps reporting on a different group on the next occasion. Or he may report on each pupil on each reporting occasion in terms of a group of basic objectives of special importance to the pupil and the school. Each of these may really be a combination of related specific objectives.

Growth and Achievement

Reports may depict growth, achievement, or both. These are distinct concepts. Growth means change or gain. To interpret it adequately, we must consider the individual, his ability, background experience, present environmental stimulation, and so on. Achievement means the pupil's present status—what he knows or can do now. Achievement is generally judged against norms or teacher's standards, and all too often is evaluated without respect to ability and prior experiences.

Differences between the two concepts can be described by use of diagrams. Figure 39 is a record of John's and Bill's growth and achievement in reading comprehension. The top line is a description of John's progress, the bottom line describes Bill's. Clearly there was a point in the life of each boy when his achievement in this basic skill was zero; this is represented on the far left of the two lines by the position labeled absolute zero. Proceeding to the right represents an increase in achievement. Let us assume that John and Bill have just entered the fifth grade. Each boy's achievement in reading comprehension at this particular time is represented by a point called prior achievement. Bill's prior achievement in reading comprehension exceeds John's considerably.

If we examine the boys' achievement at the end of the academic year (final achievement) we find that Bill still surpasses John. Their growth in reading comprehension is represented by the difference between prior and final achievement. Both boys have grown in this skill, but John has made a tremendous spurt. Several interpretations are possible, depending on the other information we have about these pupils. Suppose that they have equal potential in reading. We might then conclude that Bill is an over-achiever who could not be expected to make tremendous growth strides, whereas John may be achieving according to his ability. It is more likely

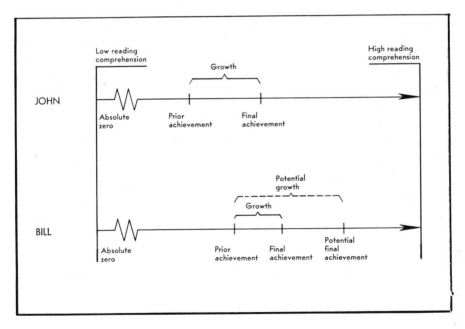

FIGURE 39

DIAGRAM OF GROWTH AND ACHIEVEMENT IN READING
COMPREHENSION OF TWO FIFTH-GRADE PUPILS

that John was retarded in the earlier grades and, through good teaching, was able to make great strides in the fifth grade. Bill, on the other hand, may or may not have shown adequate growth during the year. But suppose that Bill is a brighter boy than John. His actual growth is then inadequate; his potential growth may then be as great as that shown in Figure 39. Although his final achievement may be the highest in the class, it is still unsatisfactory in terms of what he could do.

We see from the above illustration that both growth and final achievement guide the teacher in evaluating pupil progress. However, it is questionable whether to assign marks on the basis of achievement gains rather than present status. First, gains are very unreliable because they include the errors of both the initial and final measurements. Second, if initial scores are obtained from instruments that are too easy, able pupils will have little opportunity to improve on the final assessment. Third, it is much more difficult to raise a high score even higher than to raise a low score. A gain of one-half standard deviation from a score below the mean may not be of the same substance as a gain of one-half standard deviation above the mean.

The problem confronting teachers is psychological. How does one prevent a pupil who receives only low marks from getting discouraged. One way, of course, is to have him compete against himself; that is, to evaluate him on the basis of his gains. However, if this is not defensible, then we can give all pupils opportunities within the school and the class an opportunity to excel in some way even though it is not through over-all achievement status in the subject matter. The hard facts of life dictate that all pupils must learn eventually that present status rather than growth is what counts for the most part.

IN THE ELEMENTARY SCHOOL. During the elementary school years, the teacher is concerned with helping each individual achieve as much and as rapidly as possible. Studies in child development inform us that children mature at different rates; every child is different and has environmental problems peculiar to him which affect his learning. Thus, it is not always possible to predict which pupils will eventually lead the group in specific areas of achievement. The elementary school teacher is in a position to manipulate the school environment so that pupils are not thwarted and stunted in their growth before they reach a degree of maturity at which they can evaluate their own strengths and weaknesses realistically. Therefore, the teacher often emphasizes self-improvement—growth, in other words. Emphasis on growth stresses the child rather than the subject matter. It can apply to all kinds of learning situations, academic and non-academic.

Bloom (1964, p. 127) has shown how important growth in achievement is in the first three grades of elementary school. Research findings indicate that approximately 50% of general achievement at grade 12 (age 18) has been reached by the end of grade 3 (age 9). This means that the first few years of school as well as the preschool period contribute greatly to the development of learning patterns and general achievement.

Furthermore, Bloom's study shows the importance of the early years for the development of intelligence. He states that "in terms of intelligence measured at age 17, about 50% of the development takes place between conception and age 4, about 30% between ages 4 and 8, and about 20% between the ages 8 and 17."

IN THE SECONDARY SCHOOL. Even in the secondary school, evaluation based on final achievement alone does not tell the whole story of the pupil's development. Achievement scores, for example, do not indicate whether he is at a particular level from lack of effort or talent. Neither does a single achievement score give an indication of whether there has been improvement or not. A teacher should consider pupil growth in evaluating her teaching. But in the secondary school, the pupil is looking forward to higher education and professional life, and it is imperative that his grades reflect achievement status. The standards that students must meet for the professions of medicine, law, and teaching, for example, exist as much to protect society as to select qualified students.

Standards and Ability to Learn

Whether to evaluate pupils in terms of standards or achievement in relation to ability to learn is in some ways similar to the growth-versus-achievement question. Standards of achievement are often thought of as the teacher's estimate of the level of achievement that a pupil must reach before he has done acceptable work. The use of such standards is sometimes defended in the following manner:

> When I pass a student in this course I am certifying to his next instructor that he has covered the material of the course, and that if he works reasonably hard he is capable of continuing with the next course in this field at least approximately at the level indicated by his letter grade. In the first place, I will not give a fraudulent certification. In the second place, it would be no kindness to your child to let him get into college or into a job only to find out that he is not prepared to do good work. Morever, if I lower the standards, the result is a disservice to your children and your community, handicapping all future students by making colleges and universities reluctant to accept them or give them scholarships, and prospective employers mistrustful of them (Green, 1956, p. 72).

Yet when a pupil is evaluated in terms of his ability to learn, his efforts must be considered. Then all pupils, whether talented or not, will receive praiseworthy reports if they achieve as much as they possibly can under existing circumstances. This focuses on the pupil, as did the method by which he was taught.

These two points of departure for evaluating pupils are not so different as one might suppose. Evaluating in terms of standards does not mean ignoring individual differences, nor does evaluating in terms of ability to learn mean abandoning standards. When standards are the criterion for evaluation, it does not follow that the talented pupils will be discouraged from progressing above the passing level nor that less able pupils will never experience success. When evaluation is based on a pupil's ability to learn, greater achievement is expected of the able pupil than his less talented classmate.

In other words, whether instructing or evaluating, the teacher cannot disregard either standards or individual differences in the ability to learn. Standards are multiple; those for the superior pupil differ from those for the less able. Moreover, the level of the standards changes from one grade level to the next, form one curriculum area to another, and from teacher to teacher. Nevertheless, there is a minimum level of achievement that a pupil must reach before he receives credit for a course or can be promoted to a higher grade level. If a pupil fails to achieve at this level or one higher because of inadequate ability, he should be moved to a classroom situation which presents educational experiences better suited to his ability. Hence the selection of appropriate classroom experiences is an important factor in providing for individual differences. Special provisions may be necessary for the elementary pupil. Guidance in the selection of appropriate courses is basic for secondary school pupils.

Problems

4 Can numerical marks reflect differences in growth as described in the example of John and Bill? How?

5 If a school emphasizes self-improvement in elementary school and then suddenly shifts to group standards of achievement at the secondary level, is it creating confusion and uncertainty within adolescent children by doing so?

6 Ability grouping has been suggested as a means of accommodating to some degree individual differences on the secondary school level. Is this a satisfactory procedure? Why?

7 If there are to be multiple standards of achievement in the interests of healthy psychological development on the part of the pupil, is there a need to revise the high school diploma system as it now exists in many schools? Why?

Specific Evidence of Pupil Progress

The specific evidence needed for accurate assessment and reporting of a pupil's progress must come from the many measuring instruments and techniques discussed in detail in other chapters. Certainly data from both teacher-constructed and standardized paper-and-pencil tests, ranking and rating scales, and check lists, must be used. Data from observation of class participation and pupil success in projects and reports are helpful as well.

Test Performance

TEACHER-CONSTRUCTED TESTS. The teacher-constructed achievement test is used extensively in common practice as a partial basis for determining final marks and making reports. As well as measuring the level of a pupil's knowledge and understanding, it can provide helpful diagnostic information. When well constructed, it is invaluable in direct learning, and can focus on topics under discussion in class. In reading, comprehension tests can give an indication of the ability to select main ideas, to summarize, to determine meanings of unfamiliar words from context. Classroom arithmetic tests check skill in number combinations and processes, and accuracy and speed in working them out. Varied test items will analyze difficulties encountered by pupils at all levels in working word problems. Daily or weekly spelling tests reflect a pupil's progress in spelling and the legibility of his writing. Knowledge of facts can be checked in the content areas. Understanding of various skills and uses of equipment in science can be determined. Such skills as map reading and knowledge and use of various kinds of reference materials can be evaluated in social studies classes.

Classroom tests can also deal with learning difficulties that are of particular concern to the group. Of course, teachers should take care that their tests do not place a premium on verbalization and rote memorization of facts. It should also be remembered that if tests are not used correctly, they can set the learner for short-term retention. The pupil may be able to pass the quiz, but fail to see the broader relationships in a unit of work.

STANDARDIZED TESTS. The workmanship in the better standardized tests is generally far superior to that of the typical classroom test. Great care and extensive trial administrations result in test items that are more likely to test the pupil in the desired terms, and there are norms by which a pupil's progress can be compared with national averages. In most instances, however, it would be unwise to base reports entirely on these test scores.

Standardized tests are based on objectives generally agreed upon by educational authorities. There is no consensus as to the emphasis these objectives should have or, in many instances, at what grade level they form the base for instruction and evaluation. These decisions must be made by the local school and community. To depend entirely on the use of standardized tests in marking and reporting would presuppose that the teacher has established the same objectives and emphases as the test makers. Only if this were true would the standardized test give a valid evaluation of the extent to which the class objectives have been reached.

Standardized tests can make a genuine contribution to the instructional program and effective reporting. They provide a more accurate total picture of a pupil's strengths and weaknesses in subject-matter achievement than teacher-constructed tests. Available norms also make it possible to compare the pupil's achievement with that of pupils in other schools. The diagnostic tests in particular can be helpful in determining the basis of a learning difficulty. The aptitude test scores, of course, indicate a pupil's ability to achieve, and provide criteria for judging the adequacy of achievement. In addition to the achievement and aptitude tests, personal-social adjustment inventories can provide helpful data if used with caution.

Procedure and Product Evaluation

Achievement of certain educational objectives cannot be evaluated effectively by paper-and-pencil instruments. Operating a microscope, writing a theme, delivering a speech, or preparing food products are kinds of behavior related to some of these and are classified as procedures and products. Ranking and rating methods, checklists, and anecdotal records are generally used in evaluating procedures. Product scales as well as ranking and rating methods are used in product evaluation. Sample products prepared by the pupil serve well as a means of explaining to him and his parents the degree of his achievement. Data yielded by procedure and product evaluation often require less explanation than some test scores.

Class Participation

Class participation here means the broad aspects of the pupil's participation in group activities rather than simple recitation. Evaluation should not be based on the number of times a pupil answers questions in class. While some students crave attention, others may be far better problem solvers and think more creatively than their more vocal peers. We can learn about pupils through the comments they make. Do they show that they have an understanding of the subject? What attitudes are reflected in their discussion? How does the class react to comments of individual pupils? Are they accepted or rejected because of the personality of the contributor rather than the essence of the remark?

Participation in class also involves getting along with others and playing one's roles as a leader and follower. Class observation is the only way in which certain personal-social aspects of the pupil's behavior can be evaluated, but reporting this behavior objectively, presents a problem. Some of the subjectivity can be eliminated by evaluating in terms of educational objectives stated as observable behavior.

Projects and Reports

Some pupils prove adept at learning facts and following prescribed directions and outlined procedures. Achievement here is simple to check, but certain important educational objectives representing higher intellectual abilities are harder to evaluate with the conventional instruments. Such objectives include problem solving, creative and independent thinking, and the ability to locate and select pertinent information. Achievement here can be evaluated through the use of projects and reports which provide occasion for the pupils to muster their inner resources apart from the artificial atmosphere of the paper-and-pencil test and attack a problem on their own. Projects and reports often help determine pupil interest; perhaps effort lacking in teacher-dominated activities will come out with opportunities allowing greater freedom of action. Remember that achievement in terms of these objectives is not easy to assess. Reliability may be low. If we feel that such activities should be included in the determination of final marks, then we will have to cope with the problems of inadequate degrees of validity and reliability.

PROBLEMS

8 Parents and pupils are seldom as aware of standardized achievement test scores as they are of final marks. Does this indicate a failure in communication on the part of the teachers? Would you advocate the systematic reporting of standardized achievement test results?

9   In addition to numerical marks, a junior high school requires ratings of class participation ranging from unsatisfactory to excellent. A seventh-grade science teacher objects strongly to this procedure. He states that it is impossible for him to keep a daily record of 180 students in terms of their class participation. How would you help this teacher?

Methods of Marking and Reporting

Typical procedures for marking and reporting are letter-number systems, check lists, correspondence with parents, and teacher-parent conferences. It is important that these methods be critically evaluated in terms of purposes, bases, and the sources of information available for reporting. Whatever system is used must be established as the best possible under existing circumstances.

Letter-Number Systems

The letter-number system has been and remains a popular method of reporting pupil progress. In essence it is an effort to summarize a variety of information about such characteristics of a pupil as his growth, final achievement, effort, ability, and general deportment. The summary is given in the form of a letter, usually A through E or F, or a number, usually 100 through 0, reported for each subject-matter area each report period.

There are two reasons why these marks are difficult to assign. First, the teacher cannot be certain whether appropriate credit is being given to growth and to final achievement for each educational objective considered. Second, since the mark represents pupil progress in terms of a combination of objectives, the teacher is uncertain whether each objective within the combination is being appropriately weighted.

DUAL MARKING SYSTEMS. An interesting variation of the traditional letter-number system is the use of two marks for each subject-matter area. The first represents the pupil's final achievement in relation to the teacher's standards. The second is often an evaluation of effort put forth by the pupil; in other school systems it represents pupil growth in the area of achievement listed. A three-point letter system is sometimes used for recording the pupil's effort: H if the pupil exceeds what is expected of him, S if his level of work corresponds approximately to his level of ability, and U if he is capable of better work. Pupils evaluated according to this system might receive marks such as A/S or 91/S, each indicating high final achievement and normal effort. Marks such as *C/H* or *83/H* mean that the pupil is average in terms of final achievement, and that his effort is superior.

Clearly the success of dual marking systems depends on a teacher's ability to evaluate final achievement and effort by a letter or number. Some teachers find evaluation of effort particularly troublesome since satisfactory judgment requires more accurate evaluation techniques than are available. If the second mark represents growth rather than effort, an extensive pre-testing program must be set up to establish achievement levels before instruction begins and then careful consideration must be given to the problems of interpreting gains.

In actual practice, Halliwell and Robitaille (1963) found a halo effect on assigning good marks to bright students on their relative achievement as well as on subjective factors such as effort. Teachers tended to equate effort with achievement disregarding individual differences of intelligence. To correct this type of problem, no doubt teachers should have better in-service training and orientation with respect to dual reporting, and more accurate measuring techniques of pupil effort are needed.

These are central issues. If they can be resolved, dual marking systems can be expected to give a clearer picture of a pupil's progress than a single mark. However, dual reporting could still present an oversimplified picture of the teacher's evaluation. Each subject-matter area encompasses many educational objectives. Theoretically, with suitable instruments, adequate teacher preparation and time, a pupil's final achievement and effort or growth could be determined and reported in terms of each one of them. Practical considerations, however, would impose some limitations.

RELATIVE VERSUS ABSOLUTE STANDARDS FOR MARKING. Because there is no absolute zero for achievement test scores, it is impossible to assign marks on an absolute scale or standard. If a pupil responds correctly to all items on a test, it does not necessarily mean that he knows 100% of what is to be learned in the subject, as a mark of 50% does not mean that he has learned half of the subject matter. Test items are a sampling of what is learned. Furthermore, whether a pupil receives credit for knowing a particular concept depends on how his understanding of it is measured by a particular test item. Even a question about a difficult concept may be answered correctly by almost all pupils if the question requires only super-ficial understanding. In other words, the difficulty of an item often depends as much on how a concept is measured as what is measured.

Actually teachers who convert raw scores or percentages directly into final marks usually adjust them near the end of the year by giving bonus points, by constructing an easy or difficult test as the situation may warrant, or some such procedure, until the raw scores or percentages will convert to a distribution of final marks which was largely predetermined. This distribution involves an arbitrary decision. It may be determined by school policy, the ability and vocational plans of the pupils, gaps in the distribution of composite scores, and so forth. In a high ability class, for example, a teacher might give 30 per cent A's, 40 per cent B's, 20 per cent C's and 10 per cent D's. Rarely are there as many F's as there are A's; the median final mark in many classes is often B rather than C.

Regardless of the marking system adopted, it is important that the marks present a clear message to pupils, parents, employers, and college admission officers. The meaning of marks is much clearer when school personnel agree on the criteria for choosing the percentage of pupils in a given class who will be assigned a particular mark.

To illustrate how final marks may be assigned unfairly, imagine three English classes taught by different teachers. Classes 1 and 2 are made up of college-bound pupils of comparable ability, class three of pupils of lesser ability. The teacher of Class 1 assigns 60 per cent A's and B's. The teacher of Class 2, who is less liberal, gives only 40 per cent A's and B's. Consequently a pupil whose English achievement is typical of college-bound pupils would probably receive a B if he were in Class 1, a C if in Class 2, and an A if he were a member of Class 3, in which he would probably be one of the best students.

One way of rectifying this situation is to obtain some common and relevant measure by which the three English classes could be compared. Scores from a scholastic aptitude test or from standardized or teacher-constructed English achievement tests with acceptable degrees of content validity might be used. Suppose it is decided that 15 per cent of the pupils will recieve A's. Then the cut-off score, above which only 15 per cent of the pupils score on the common measure, would be determined. The number of pupils in a particular class who surpass this cut-off score provides the approximate number of A's to be given in that class. The same is true of the percentages of B's, C's and so on. Note that the final mark which a particular student receives depends on his total performance in his class, not on his scholastic aptitude score. The scholastic aptitude tests serve here to determine percentages of letter-grades assigned, not the pupils to whom they will be assigned. Some pupils will receive higher final achievement marks than their fellows who scored higher on the scholastic aptitude test.

Michael (1960) reports another system to prevent able pupils from being penalized in terms of final marks because of ability grouping. He suggests that in a subject such as English, pupils are usually grouped into three to five categories. There may be a top section designed to prepare pupils for advanced placement. A number of classes either homogeneously or heterogeneously grouped are the designated standard college preparatory sections. Then there may be several low ability classes of pupils who in general do not intend to go to college.

When a school reports letter marks, it is common to assign a certain number of points to a letter: A-5 pts; B-4 pts; C-3 pts; D-2 pts. A multiplying factor which varies according to the ability category is applied to each pupil's mark. Suppose there are three categories. The pupil in the highest group will have his A multiplied by 6; an A received in the middle group will be multiplied by 5; A's in the low section are multiplied by 4. The plan has the effect of raising marks in the top section by one letter while lowering those in the bottom section by one letter.

Michael emphasizes that the point system affects only class rank. It does not appear on the report card. However, because rank is one important criterion determining college admission, pupils in the higher groups are compensated for possible lower marks than pupils receive in lower ability groups.

WEIGHTING DATA.   One of the problems the teacher encounters in giving final marks is weighting the data gathered from such various sources as informal quizzes, final examinations, and reports to obtain a valid composite score for ranking his pupils. There is no consensus on the emphasis each of these types of data should receive in the total evaluation. Some teachers maintain that a final examination should count far more than the quizzes and other tests given during the course. They point out that since the final examination measures long term retention, and the ability to organize and deal with large units of subject matter, this score should logically be weighted more heavily than others. Other teachers are quick to retort that it is unfair to the pupil to determine such a large proportion of his final evaluation from his performance at a specified time within an interval of several hours at most. They also object to the limitations of most final examinations that preclude measurement in terms of many important educational objectives. This is a very important consideration. The weighting of various data must be determined in terms of the educational objectives of the specific grade level or class. Those data that reflect pupil progress in terms of the most important objectives must be given greater weight when computing a composite mark than those relating to less important objectives. This is equally true whether the data come from a final examination or any other measuring instrument.

There is a precaution that must be taken in determining a composite mark no matter what weightings are chosen. Suppose we wish to base one-fifth of the final mark for a course on class reports, one-fifth on daily assignments, one-fifth on quizzes and unit tests, and two-fifths on the final examination. Inspection of the ranges and standard deviations of these measures in the following table reveals a definite lack of uniformity. If we hope to maintain the weighting scheme originally chosen, we must take into consideration these differences in variability. A failure to do this will result in inequities. To illustrate this point, let us suppose that Mary made a total of 55 points for class reports, the highest number of points for this category. However, on quizzes and unit tests her score was the lowest, 30 points. For daily assignments and the final examination she earned 61 and 91, respectively. Frank, on the other hand, did the poorest of anyone in the group on class reports; his score was 29. On the quizzes and unit tests he had a high score of 140. It happens that he also made the same scores as Mary on daily assignments and the final exam, namely 61 and 91.

Source of points	Nominal weight	Range	Standard deviation
Class reports	1	26	5.1
Daily assignments	1	46	8.6
Quizzes and units tests	1	110	20.8
Final examination	2	90	16.4

If we weight Mary's and Frank's scores for each source and add them to obtain a composite, we have the following:

Mary	Frank
$55 \times 1 = 55$	$29 \times 1 = 29$
$61 \times 1 = 61$	$61 \times 1 = 61$
$30 \times 1 = 30$	$140 \times 1 = 140$
$91 \times 2 = 182$	$91 \times 2 = 182$
Total $= 328$	Total $= 412$

Note that although class reports and quizzes and unit tests are to have the same weight, Mary is penalized because of the lesser variability of scores of class reports when compared with that of quizzes and unit tests. In other words, class-report scores with a relatively low standard deviation ($\sigma = 5.1$) have less influence than scores of quizzes and unit tests ($\sigma = 20.8$) in determining the class rankings on the composite score.

A procedure for avoiding errors like the one above would be to convert the raw scores into standard scores so that the variability of the scores for each category would be the same. When the scores for each category are converted into stanines the following formula to compute the composite is appropriate:

$$C = \frac{\Sigma \, WS}{\Sigma \, W}$$

where

C = composite average
Σ = the sum
W = weight for a particular category
S = standard score for that category for each pupil

To illustrate the use of the formula let us assume that Mary received stanine scores of 9, 5, 1, and 7 for class reports, daily assignments, quizzes and unit tests, and the final examination respectively. Frank's stanine scores were 1, 5, 9, and 7. The composite averages would be:

Mary

$$C = \frac{(1 \times 9) + (1 \times 5) + (1 \times 1) + (2 \times 7)}{1 + 1 + 1 + 2} = \frac{29}{5} = 5.8$$

Frank

$$C = \frac{(1 \times 1) + (1 \times 5) + (1 \times 9) + (2 \times 7)}{1 + 1 + 1 + 2} = \frac{29}{5} = 5.8$$

Although these composite averages are not stanines, they do provide means for the ranking of pupils which reflects the desired weightings of the scores for the several categories. On the basis of this distribution, the teacher may assign final marks.

RELIABILITY AND VALIDITY. The reliability of scores from paper-and-pencil tests is sometimes not as great as we wish it to be. Reliability of data from a teacher's observations of a pupil's procedures and his personal-social adjustment is usually even lower. Yet both are used to determine final marks. Consequently, the reliability of final marks is often less than is to be desired.

Such evidence as is available suggests that the usual reliability coefficients of semester marks may be as high as 0.70 to 0.90. This means that in many if not all cases it is difficult to defend the practice of interpreting such differences as those between an 83 and an 84 or a 91 and a 92. For that matter, the difference between a C+ and a B− may be due purely to chance.

Evidence of the validity of final marks is also limited. They seem to be quite valid as a measure of mastery of subject matter by the pupil, the correlation coefficient estimated to be 0.70 or possibly higher. This estimate was arrived at by summarizing the results of a number of studies concerning the correlation between the final marks in question and (1) other marks in the same subject matter area, (2) test scores from appropriate standardized tests, and (3) the pupils' estimates of the marks they deserved.

The validity of final marks has been investigated with respect to a number of different criteria, such as college entrance examination scores, college marks, economic success, and success on the job. The correlation coefficients vary a great deal. The most widely investigated use of secondary-school final marks is that of predicting academic success in college. The correlation coefficients are often as high as 0.50 and seldom higher than 0.70. It has been repeatedly shown that final marks in secondary school are one of the best means of predicting college success, whether used alone or as part of a prediction battery.

INTERPRETATION.   The typical letter or number system of marking is based primarily on final achievement. Confusion results when a teacher also attempts to include an evaluation of effort and other personality traits in this single mark. Interpretation becomes almost impossible. There is no way to determine whether a low mark is the result of lack of achievement or effort. Even when a single letter mark is used to report final achievement alone, it is very difficult to make a valid interpretation. What does a B in general science mean? Does it show that the pupil did A-work in quizzes, C-work in laboratory, B-work in class participation? Or more important still, does it mean that the pupil achieved at an A-level with respect to one educational objective, a B-level with respect to another and a C-level with a third? We have no way of knowing. Therefore when letter or numerical marks are used, there must be additional data in the report that provide diagnostic information. The mark is also influenced by other factors, one of which is the nature of the pupil population. Too often pupils who have been graduated magna cum laude from their high schools find to their dismay when they face competition in a university that they do not have exceptional ability. Another factor is the peculiarity of the individual teacher who does the marking. Some teachers give consistently high marks, while others pride themselves in never being so easy as to give an A or a 95. A pupil may find it very difficult to identify a criterion by which he can judge the value of his marks.

Marks as they are now generally assigned are far from being as meaningful as people think. They are being overinterpreted; they reveal far less about the pupil than is commonly supposed, and their meaning is often ambiguous. Hence it is imperative that standardized test scores be used to supplement final marks whenever possible. It is particularly important for secondary school pupils to have this objective basis for comparing their own capacity and achievement with a broader sample of pupils, giving them a better opportunity to interpret their potentialities for future academic work.

PROBLEMS

10 What effect might dual reporting have on each of these pupil groups: below average, average, and gifted?

11 On the basis of your educational experiences, can you demonstrate in a simple, clear-cut fashion the necessity of considering score variability when weighting data to obtain a composite score?

TYPES OF REPORT CARDS. The report cards used to record the assigned marks can take many different forms. Commonly they provide for the recording of marks for all marking periods during the school year. Parents or guardians are requested to sign the card before it is returned at the end of each marking period.

Reports of academic achievement are often accompanied by a check list of personality traits and attitudes. The teacher may generally place a check in any one of several categories, such as "unsatisfactory," "satisfactory," or "improving." If these check lists are carefully worded, the instrument can save the teacher time and effort.

Reporting must not become a stereotyped procedure. In the past, many pupils have been checked "satisfactory" in every characteristic from kindergarten through the sixth grade. The "halo effect" seems to keep some teachers from making a realistic evaluation of the pupil. This can be eliminated if the teacher bases his report on adequate data, carefully compiled and critically interpreted. Space left on the check list form for comments on pupils' problems will help individualize the method.

At the secondary level, check lists are usually used to supplement numerical or letter marks, both providing information not discernible from the mark alone, and helping to clarify the mark itself. In elementary school, check lists are often the only report given. The example shown in Figure 40 represents the type that can be used for this purpose. Observe that all major aspects of the academic program are included, as are health, music, art, and personal development. The common three-point letter system is used to represent the teacher's judgment of the pupil's success. In this case, the letters are O for outstanding, S for satisfactory, and N for not satisfactory. Such a check list as this can give a great deal of information about the pupil's school ife.

A number of schools, wishing to conserve time, are employing computers for reporting marks and organizing and analyzing data about them.

REPORT CARD FORM

What the letters mean:

O—Outstanding for your child; commendation for special effort and achievement.

S—Satisfactory for your child; achievement consistent with ability.

N—Not Satisfactory for your child; improvement needed.

Note: Any further information in regard to the standing of your child may be secured in personal conference.

Growth in Skills	1st Report	2nd Report	3rd Report
Reading			
Understands what he reads			
Works to develop independent reading habits			
Writing			
Expresses himself well			
Uses basic writing skills			
Writes legibly			
Spells correctly			
Uses good sentence structure			
Learns to use new words			
Arithmetic			
Knows arithmetic facts			
Understands arithmetic processes (addition, subtraction, multiplication, division)			
Applies skill in solving problems			
Social studies			
History, geography, civics, government, development of American ideals			
Works to develop a knowledge and understanding of home, community, state, country, world			
Works to develop skill in the use of materials (newspapers, maps, encyclopedias, etc.)			
Science			
Works to develop keen observation			
Is growing in scientific knowledge			
Listening			
Understands what he hears and responds wisely			
Health			
Works to develop good health habits			
Helps to maintain safety			
Plays and enjoys games			
Works to develop skill in physical education			
Music			
Takes part in group singing			
Responds to rhythm			
Works to develop basic music skills			
Art			
Expresses ideas creatively			
Works to develop a variety of skills			

Personal development				
Is developing a variety of interests _____	_____	_____	_____
Is courteous and considerate _____	_____	_____	_____
Respects the rights and property of others _____	_____	_____
Shares outside experience, skills and materials with others _____	_____	_____	_____
Accepts responsibility _____	_____	_____	_____
Works to the best of his ability _____	_____	_____	_____

From Heffernan and Marshall, 1955, pp. 75–76; reproduced by permission of the California State Department of Education.

FIGURE 40

MODIFIED FORM OF CHECK LIST

In one school system (Crisler and Wogaman, 1963) each school's master class schedule and individual pupil programs are converted into punched cards. There is a deck of cards for each class with one mark-sense card for each pupil (See Figure 41). All the decks are arranged alphabetically by teacher name and each teacher's decks by period sequence.

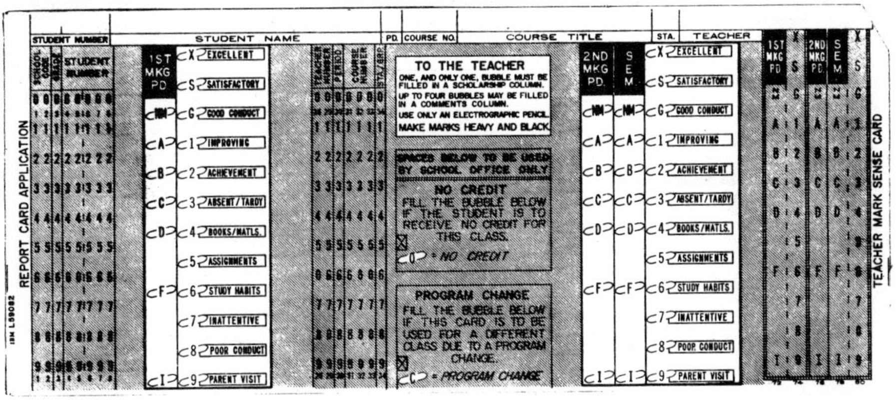

Reproduced by permission of the Richmond (California) Schools.

FIGURE 41

PUPILS MARK-SENSE CARD

At the time of reporting, a teacher receives a deck of mark-sense cards for each of his classes. He marks these in the space representing the final mark earned by each pupil. One to four comments, such as "excellent," "satisfactory," etc., from a list of nine on each card are also marked.

The cards are then returned to the processing center where the teacher marks are printed on the report card (See Figure 42). Four copies of this report are available. The original is given to the pupil to take home and the other three copies are for office use. The report cards are cumulative during a semester; that is, the pupil's previous marks also appear on successive reports. Parents do not sign these cards and pupils do not return them.

This system of reporting provides readily available data about marks to the school staff. The number of times each pupil received each letter mark and each comment is totaled along with his average mark. Data on

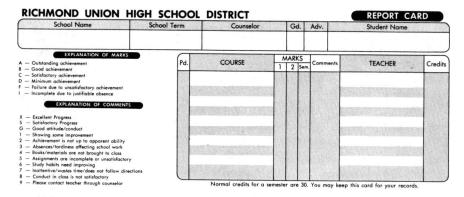

Reproduced by permission of the Richmond (California) Schools.

FIGURE 42
REPORT CARD

teachers include the number of times they made a comment, such as "excellent," or "inattentive." The average mark of each teacher's class and the average for all his classes are tabulated. Marks are also available for each class grouped by subject-matter area, as are the comments marked, the percentage of each mark given, and the average mark for the class.

With information showing how teachers mark, this school has the basis to set up guide lines for assigning marks and give the teacher feedback on his own marks as well as those of his colleagues. There is an excellent opportunity to make marks more meaningful to pupils and their parents.

PROBLEMS

12 What difficulties might parents face in interpreting information from a check list? How can these be minimized?

13 What are goal cards? Study the illustrations of their use in elementary school (Bauernfeind, 1966) and evaluate their usefulness as a means of solving some of the problems related to marking and reporting.

Correspondence With Parents

Communications sent to parents may range from a little notation on a report card to a long letter discussing many aspects of their child's school experiences and growth. Here it is possible to emphasize both pupil development and subject-matter achievement. With an adequate cumulative record, the teacher has evidence to interpret patterns of development. He may discuss problems and emphasize factors pertinent to the individual pupil. If some phases of his work would profit from help at home, this can be explained to the parents. As parental comments are requested, there is provision for two-way communication. The interchange of information may lead to some fruitful conferences between teachers and parents.

One of the serious weaknesses of letters to parents is that they tend to be generalized and sterotyped, all too often appearing to have been run off an assembly line, with little variation in wording to relate to a particular pupil. For instance, the following letter is far less helpful to the parent than it might have been:

Mary is an exceptionally likeable child. In general her progress has been quite satisfactory in all phases of her school work. She seems to be interested in all activities and is purposeful in the tasks she undertakes. Her personal-social adjustment is proceeding at a very normal rate.

What has the parent learned? Do Mary's peers accept her, or is she just liked by the teacher? Perhaps the teacher likes her because she is retiring and does not bother anyone. Certainly there must be some strength or weakness in her academic progress that could be emphasized. Does she question what she reads or is she inclined to accept it without critical evaluation? Do her reports show imagination or does she tend to string together some of the words she has read in the encyclopedia? What does the teacher mean by "purposeful?" What is "normal" personal-social adjustment?

Often the reason for inadequate reporting can be traced to vaguely-stated objectives. Objectives like the following do not assure that the teacher understands the criterion behavior. There is no suggestion of how she is to determine whether an objective has been achieved (See Chapter 2).

> To develop good citizenship.
> To improve health habits.
> To understand the scientific method.

Even with sharpened objectives, communicating with parents by letter is not easy. In one community a parent received among other comments the statement "Your child is nervous." He reacted at once with concern about the youngster's mental health, a notion the startled teacher had not meant to convey at all. Letters may annoy the parent or fail to express what the teacher means. The following note concerning a fifth grade pupil is not helpful in cementing effective relations between home and school:

Dr. Mr. and Mrs. Knowles:

John has been a real problem in our class this year. Unlike most of the children in the group, he doesn't enjoy working with others. He is really a lone wolf. Instead of cooperating, he seems to find satisfaction in disturbing others, and he . . .

This could be changed to a much more effective report for securing parental cooperation.

Dear Mr. and Mrs. Knowles:

We find that it is difficult to summarize in a single mark the things we would like to share with you about John's development this year. In addition to achievement in academic skills, there are many other aspects of growth that we feel are important.

John can be depended upon to see a task through to completion. In preparation for a recent play, he volunteered to get a number of props and he had them for us on time. When he offered to interview several city officials about our town's history, he brought back information that was exceptionally well organized and interesting. Even in activities that require considerable effort, John will finish the task. I recall a particularly long assignment in fractions with which he had some difficulty. He worked longer than he usually has to, but the paper he handed in was well done.

John seems to have no serious trouble in mastering the basic skills. He reads with understanding and he has learned how to make effective use of source materials for research reports. He is a good speller and has missed no words on our weekly spelling tests. In class discussions, he expresses himself well and reflects a background of reading and travel.

We have been trying to help John this year in associations with his classmates. He tends to prefer working by himself rather than with others. At times he is quite aggressive in a group and finds it difficult to cooperate with his classmates on a project. We feel, however, that he has made considerable progress in this respect. Of late he has commented favorably on the good ideas of his group members. He was also chosen as chairman of the entertainment committee for the last day of school.

John tells us that most of the children in his neighborhood are younger than he. It might be helpful if John had some opportunities this summer to play with children of his own age. This would enable him to enter into the "give and take" that is so important for his continued development.

I have enjoyed working with John this year. We anticipate that he will have a good relationship with his sixth-grade teacher and class group.

Sincerely,

Because poorly written letters may cause serious trouble, many principals supervise this type of reporting closely. Some schools have provided such suggestions as the following:

SUGGESTIONS FOR WRITING LETTERS TO PARENTS

I. Begin the letter with encouraging news.
II. Close with an attitude of optimism.
III. Solicit the parents' cooperation in solving the problems, if any exist.
IV. Speak of the child's growth—social, physical, and academic.
    A. Social (Citizenship traits)
        1. Desirable traits attention, attitude toward school, care of property, cooperation, honesty, effort, fair play, neatness, truthfulness, obedience, promptness, reliability, self-control, self-reliance, concentration, courtesy and consideration, thrift, patience, appreciation, kindness, sympathy, orderliness, interest in associates, discrimination, politeness, respect for the rights of others.
        2. Undesirable traits: selfishness, wastefulness, untruthfulness, dishonesty, spitefulness, slow to respond, impudence, carelessness, untidiness, rudeness, noisiness, insolence, cheating, inattention, lack of self-reliance, discourtesy, tattling, snobbishness, conceit, impatience, stealing.
    B. Physical (Health conditions): posture, weight, vitality, physical handicaps, cleanliness (personal), muscular co-ordination, nervousness, emotional traits.
    C. Academic
        1. Interests: (a) in school activities; (b) in extra-school activities.
        2. Methods of work: (a) methods of attack; (b) purposing; (c) planning; (d) executing; (e) judging; (f) consistency in finishing work.

　　3.　Achievements: (a) growth in knowledge, appreciation, techniques; (b) list subjects in which the child is making progress and those in which he is not making progress; (c) relationship of his accepted standards to his capacities.

V.　Compare the child's efforts with his own previous efforts and not with those of others.

VI.　Speak of his achievements in terms of his ability to do school work.

VII.　Remember it is our professional duty to know the reason why if the child is not making what, for him, is normal progress. (Some suggestive reasons for lack of progress—late entry; absence; lack of application; health defects, such as hearing, sight, undernourishment.)

VIII.　Teacher's advice to parents in matters pertaining to health in which the home is a vital factor; such as diet, rest, clothing, exercise, etc.

IX.　Please remember that every letter is a professional diagnosis, and as such is as sacred as any diagnosis ever made by any physician.

Reproduced by permission of the Santa Monica City (California) Schools.

Obviously it requires a great deal of time to compose a thoughtful and helpful letter and the teacher is faced with an enormous task if he must report on thirty or forty pupils. Some elementary schools have abandoned reporting by letter for just this reason. It is impractical in most secondary school situations.

The problem can be eased if reports are sent out in staggered lots rather than on all pupils at once. The number of letters for each pupil can be limited. It is better to have one good letter than three poor ones, and to use other methods for other reporting periods. Perhaps some pupils will benefit more by frequent letter reports than others, thereby reducing the load.

Time spent on reporting is never lost and often produces rich dividends in parental cooperation. If the report concerns a problem child, the energy saving from better relations may be very rewarding. Too often teachers become so involved in unimportant details that they overlook more fruitful approaches.

Problems

14　An elementary school supervisor has decreed that all written reports and letters to parents must bear his signature along with that of the classroom teacher, a requirement that some teachers resent for a variety of reasons. Suggest reasons why the supervisor adopted this practice. Should he continue to do so?

15　What is the most serious limitation in reporting both positive and negative pupil behavior by means of a letter? If a school system requires this type of evaluative procedure, what steps can be taken to avoid poor public relations?

Teacher-Parent Conferences

The conference method of reporting is most generally used in the elementary school, although for special situations it should be more widely employed at the secondary level. It has potential for providing more information and better understanding between home and school, for misunderstanding can be eliminated far more readily when either conferee is able to raise questions than when communication is by letter. Certainly there are optimum conditions for conferences. They should not be called only when a special problem arises—rapport can hardly be at its best if this is the only basis for meeting. They should be planned periodically to serve as a regular report on the child's progress.

Sufficient time must be allowed—a minimum of thirty minutes. Attempting to rush through one interview to be prompt for the next is unfair to parent and teacher. Conferences are just as much a part of a good instructional program as teaching the multiplication table, and the teacher should be given time to prepare and hold them during his working schedule. Some schools dismiss classes for half day periods; others provide substitutes to relieve the teacher of classroom responsibilities. Because conferences involve a great deal of time, some schools arrange only one per pupil during the school year, using other methods for the remaining report periods.

CONFERENCE PREPARATION. Preparation is basic to an effective conference. Some school systems orient their teachers in the conference technique by distributing bulletins describing the conference purpose, policy, records to be kept, time and preparation. These typically contain numerous illustrations suggesting ideas for preparation. The following are examples:

> Bobby Bates, in second grade, an only child, is 7 years, 6 months. He is sturdy and well-developed physically, energetic and active. He seems to have superior mental ability, reads very well and possesses distinct creative language ability. He loves music and the arts, expressing himself creatively and freely. He is doing very satisfactory number work. Bobby has never been able to get along in a group—he exhibits a quarrelsome and domineering attitude and a tendency to be very aggressive with his peers. He also evidences a negative and often openly resistant attitude toward adults. His parents need to give him more experience in childrens' groups, gradually add responsibility for certain home tasks. They have a "perfectionist" attitude, want him to excel.

Show Mrs. Bates puppet stage (point out Bobby's ideas)
Refer to room-mothers' meeting
Growth in skills
    Reading (books, reading records)
    Language arts (sample stories—dictionary—broad writing vocabulary)
    Doing two-column addition, gaining mastery of facts

Attendance records
Help in broadening interests
Group adjustments
Home interests and attitudes
Seems resistant to suggestion (examples)
Sometimes domineering—aggressive (examples), makes group accept-
ance difficult—good ideas
Plans for helping Bobby—home—school (boys' groups? hobbies? help to
share his ability)
Individual work habits
Perfectionist
Sharing and helping others is difficult (examples—games, books, Mon-
day play)
How can we help him accept and profit by occasional failures?
Parents' support and encouragement (suggestions)

James, age 12–8, entering junior high school, has reached sixth grade
with normal physical and social growth and development. His academic
achievement ranges from a year to a year and one-half beyond normal sixth
grade as per the fall testing scores.
Safety Patrol work—fine job
Review academic progress Kgn through 6
Indicate seventh-grade adjustment problems
Emphasize adequate social growth for age
Successful six years of growth
Meeting of sixth-grade parents and junior high school guidance teachers
on May 20.

Reproduced by permission of the Schenectady, New York, Public Schools.

Some schools have organized workshops and various kinds of training
sessions for their teachers. Role playing, in which teachers assume the roles
of both parent and teacher, is helpful. Writing a script of a hypothetical
conference and inviting criticism from colleagues develops insight into
conference skill. Often bulletins are issued outlining suggestions including
"do's and don'ts." They include such helpful materials as the following:

1. A teacher's guide sheet for each child, with appropriate headings, to be
filled in prior to the conference.

2. Lists of characteristics of boys and girls at different age levels. Such lists
are most helpful if these characteristics are described in terms of specific
behaviors. They help teachers to identify possible problems in their early
stages and to find strengths in pupils that might otherwise be overlooked.

3. An outline of the school program to help parents understand the goals
of the school and the ways in which the school works to attain these
goals.

4. A reminder sheet of effective and ineffective conference techniques.

5. A form to report what actually took place at the conference. Ample
space is provided for the contributions made by parents. One copy of
this report is often given to the parents, the other is retained in the
cumulative folder (Weckler, 1955, pp. 120–121).

It is helpful to anticipate some of the questions parents may ask in a conference. A list of such inquiries and suggested answers is usually included in the conference bulletins for teachers. The following are typical:

Why can't my youngster sound a strange word? He's in the third grade now.

Answer: This is what he can do. He can recognize beginning consonant sounds. He is beginning to be able to sound consonant combinations. I am working with him toward . . . (an opportunity here to present a phonetic program grades one through six). It takes some children longer to reach various stages.

My older boy's first year in junior high school leads me to believe that he wasn't ready for the seventh grade. Do you send children to junior high school who aren't ready for seventh grade?

Answer: It is the policy of this school system to accept a pupil at his level of achievement in each succeeding grade level and bring him along from there. Perhaps your boy was doing arithmetic, shall we say, below seventh-grade achievement level. His seventh-grade teacher will recognize this from information sent along in the boy's folder and record and will begin his instruction where he is . . . (opportunity for interpretation of variances in the promotion policy).

I like marks. I want to know whether my youngster is an A or B student.

Answer: We have discussed the work of your child and find that he works hard and with understanding at easy material for his grade. We're satisfied with what he is doing and the effort he is putting forth. At present, he is working at a lower level of achievement than the average student in the class. If you want to think of his work in terms of marks with which you are familiar, you can apply a letter or a grade to the usual three divisions of a group such as A, B, C, and thereby indicate to your satisfaction the mark that you are giving your child.

Reproduced by permission of the Schenectady, New York, Public Schools.

One reason why teachers do not get as much needed information from parents is that they don't ask good questions. Typical questions like the following lack the sharpness so necessary to get at specific behaviors that would be helpful for teachers to know about.

Is Jimmy generally good natured?
Does Mary like mathematics?
Does Jack seem to be in good health?

Parents can and will provide, under adequate stimulation, information that will help the teacher determine how effective his teaching has been in transferring to pupils' behavior outside of school. Note the questions below:

Is Mary interested in graphs printed in the local newspaper?
Does she ask questions when the stock and bond quotations are broadcast?
Does Jack accept food that he has disliked or ask for a substitute to maintain a healthful diet?

Parents can also provide information to aid in remediation. Too often in answer to queries about their child's difficulties they have been told that everything is all right. They are advised not to concern themselves with instructional problems. Nothing is more frustrating to the interested and intelligent parent than this approach.

In addition to his skill, the teacher's attitude about the conference determines its success to a large degree. He has to accept the parent and look objectively at his problems and their relationship to the child's welfare. Resenting the parent for his treatment of the child is more likely to reinforce the parental attitude than to change it.

USING SPECIFIC INFORMATION. The mother of one kindergarten child must have been perplexed to hear the teacher sum up a conference during the eighth month of school by saying, "You know, I just haven't learned to know Ann very well." This teacher violated an important rule of a good conference, namely, always have specific information available for each pupil. Anecdotes and dated illustrative examples of daily work and quizzes can mean the difference between a generally unproductive visit, however friendly, and a purposeful, helpful conference. Rather than saying "Bill is a very cooperative child," how much more informative to report "Bill is always willing to help out with class activities. He's dependable. The other day he mentioned that he could bring a book on trucks from home, and he didn't forget." Or instead of "Mary is a well-adjusted child," it is far more meaningful to the parent to hear "Children are always choosing Mary for their games and activities. She is very thoughtful of other pupils. Yesterday she helped Jim and Sally clean up their paints so they could go out to recess with the rest of the group."

Rather than comparing elementary school pupils with each other, discuss the child's progress in terms of his past achievement, and his own strengths and weaknesses. Instead of "Jack is the best reader in the room," the comment would be better phrased, "Jack reads a great many books during his free-reading period. He's always willing to discuss what he's read, and really enjoys recommending books to other children. You may be interested in this list of books that he's read since the beginning of school. Notice how varied his interests are. You may remember he wasn't nearly so interested in books last year." Try to be constructive and positive in discussing pupils. For example, rather than stating, "Sally lacks the ability to do independent reading," say "Sally is slowly becoming interested in reading books on her own. She told me you had given her a very exciting book for her birthday. It was clear that your family discussion of the hero of the story impressed her. I'm pleased to learn of your interest in this aspect of Sally's work."

A teacher can report a great deal more on children's reading if he has data to draw on. Evaluation of the child's reading rate, the adequacy of his oral reading and the grade level of the reader he comprehends present objective data for reporting. Many of the basal reading series provide tests that can give a still clearer picture of his progress. Numerous standardized tests provide information on achievement which can be meaningfully interpreted to the parent. Test norms give additional information. Areas like music and art can also be reported specifically. Can the pupil match tones, keep rhythm, and follow a tune? Does he read syllables? How effective is he in handling specific media such as crayons and watercolors? Does he show indications of creativity and originality? Can he show perspective? Does he have a grasp of the vocabulary?

Along with information about his academic work, there should be reports on a pupil's health, attendance, tardiness, and personal-social adjustment. It is important to relate these data to his scholastic achievement, for they are part of the total picture of his progress.

LIMITATIONS. Conferences have several important limitations, one of which is the time factor. Yet as in the case of letters to parents, this time can be very important in developing learning readiness. Educating the parent may be as important as working with his child in the classroom. Teachers also find that the information gathered and the thinking they must do in preparing for the conference may be very useful in class instruction. Often they are forced by a conference to collect information they should already have.

Another limitation sometimes mentioned is that parents will not come to conferences. A great deal of the blame for this can be attributed to the school administrators, and to teachers ill trained in the technique. The effective administrator will involve the community leaders as well as his staff in affairs of the school, and is concerned about the community's understanding of the purpose of conferences. Of course he and his staff need to exercise the greatest care that the conferences prove worthwhile and do not degenerate into sheer generalizing and passing of pleasantries. The inadequately trained teacher can do more harm than good, for the parent is often antagonized and refuses to cooperate readily in the future. In such a case, the usefulness of conference-type reporting is greatly reduced.

A third limitation is that the conference technique is difficult to use in the secondary school. It is true that most experimentation with conferences has been in the elementary school. Moreover, the consensus of many writers is that secondary school pupils do not want their parents to participate in formal teacher-parent conferences. A study of 248 junior high school pupils does not support these conclusions, however (Richardson, 1955). One hundred ten students, or 44 per cent, favored teacher parent conferences; seventy-five, or 30 per cent, favored teacher-parent-pupil conferences, and only forty-five pupils, or 18 per cent, wanted to exclude the parent.

No one would maintain that the child ceases to grow after he leaves the sixth grade or that parents have no place in his educational program. As the educational level of parents increases over the years, there is likely to be as great parental concern about pupil growth in the secondary school as there now is in the elementary grades. Indeed, there are some indications that such a trend is developing. Nonetheless, there is a very practical problem that must be solved before there can be extensive conferences at the secondary school level. The large pupil-teacher ratio will prevent conferences with the parents of all pupils during the year. The teacher's need for better home understanding and parental cooperation to help some pupils must form a basis for selection. The guidance staff will be able to alleviate the teacher's load by conferring with some of the parents. At any rate, secondary schools need to plan closer contact with the home.

PROBLEMS

16   The teacher-parent conference is often more helpful to the teacher than to the parents in terms of understanding that child. If you were allowed only one conference each year, during what month would you prefer to schedule these meetings? Support your answer.

17   Kenneth is in the low group of his eighth-grade class; mental ability test scores show him to be in the borderline defective classification. His teachers and guidance counselor feel that he probably cannot complete the ninth-grade academic requirement. His mother, resenting her own lack of education, is demanding that her son take a college-preparatory course in high school. In previous conferences she has steadfastly refused to accept the true situation. The guidance counselor is now meeting with all eighth-grade parents for the purpose of assisting in the selection of ninth-grade subjects and of making tentative plans for high school. How should the conference with the pupil's mother be structured?

Self-Evaluation

One aspect of the total evaluation program that is being emphasized more and more is the need for pupils to evaluate themselves. It has been pointed out that self-evaluation might well be used as a means of reporting pupil progress. After reviewing the literature, Russell (1953, p. 566) concludes:

Children's self-evaluation of their development of habits and attitudes contained in some of the usual concepts of personality or "good citizenship" in school bears a positive but slight relationship to the other criteria of adjustment, teacher and peer ratings.

Relative to self-ratings in academic achievement he says:

Elementary school children who have received no special instruction do not appraise their academic progress much like their teachers or peers do, although they may be fairly consistent in overestimating or underestimating their achievement (1953, p. 568).

He also finds that socio-economic class and a pupil's level of aspiration affect achievement as well as the opinions of his teachers and peers concerning his achievement. It has been known for some time that teachers tend to approve middle-class standards of behavior because of their own backgrounds.

Though there is insufficient evidence to support self-evaluation as a valid part of any marking and reporting system, teachers should guide pupils in learning to evaluate themselves. This is an important educational objective, and one helpful way of achieving it is to discuss a pupil's progress with him. He should be able to interpret his own achievement as it relates to his strengths and weaknesses and the teacher should help him to understand the various reports sent to his parents.

PROBLEM

18 Outline a specific program in your subject-matter area for implementing self-evaluation procedures. What are your underlying objectives for following this program?

BY-PRODUCTS OF MARKING AND REPORTING

Emotional Problems

Invariably a cartoonist playing on some aspect of reporting will emphasize the defensive behavior of the pupil or his fear of adult disapproval. The judgment always seems to be punitive, and the implication that life would be wonderful if report cards could somehow vanish. Certainly in many instances parents do withhold privileges or administer corporal punishment when their child brings home a bad report. Some offer prizes and rewards for A's; then the child's problems may be overlooked and the mark becomes all important. Other parents identify with their children and may blame the school for bad reports, and the necessary cooperation between the home and school is hard to come by.

In other cases, the pressures for getting high marks result in cheating, or at best, in conforming to a teacher's wishes as a ploy in working for marks. Some pupils develop feelings of inferiority and the resulting self-concept keeps them from trying to solve their difficulties. It is not uncommon for gifted children with specific difficulties in arithmetic or reading to be convinced of their general lack of intellectual prowess.

Anxieties are further aroused by threats of failure. Excessive fear does not promote effective learning; it creates tensions and disorganization. Energy is dissipated through the emotions fear creates and pupils find it difficult to learn. One seventh grade boy wrote this when asked what he worried about:

> I worry about what my folks will say about my low marks. I hate to take home my report card. My folks get mad and scold me. I try hard, but it doesn't seem to do any good. I wish I could do better.

This is what happens with loss of perspective on the defensible use of marks. Marking and reporting need not cause these reactions. In many school systems children are eager for reporting time. The spirit is one of helpful cooperation, with the child standing to gain. Prevailing attitudes promote helpfulness rather than criticism.

Effect of Marking on Teaching

Some teachers present marks in the light of rewards or prizes, but even with this approach there will be pupils who face failure. For those able to earn high marks, it would be better for the teacher to foster interest in learning. Trying to motivate through marks seems an easy way out for the teacher, eliminating the need to provide interesting and worthwhile learning experiences. The typical textbook assignment with equal requirements for all can be followed regardless of individual differences in learning ability. Academic achievement can be emphasized while ignoring other aspects of pupil growth. It is a simple process to evaluate only in terms of test and examination averages, marks on papers, and participation in recitation, much simpler than trying to understand each pupil and evaluate his growth in terms of his own inherent characteristics and environmental problems. When marks are used for motivation, they too often degenerate into an end in themselves. They should be a tool for improvement of learning, not a crutch for ineffective teaching.

Problem

19   A high-school teacher felt that Johnny was lazy, and was concerned about
his sloppy work in algebra. He reasoned that this boy needed a good jolt.
Knowing that Johnny's father held rigid, high standards for his son, the
teacher assigned his pupil a particularly low mark. Evaluate this decision
by the teacher.

Improving Marking and Reporting

The following seven steps include various suggestions advanced by
schools that have studied their marking and reporting systems seriously and
initiated programs of effective improvement (Strang, 1955, pp. 15–17).

Have teachers, parents, and pupils study the problem cooperatively.
Involving representatives of all groups who will be concerned with marks
and reports is the best way to insure understanding and cooperative effort
for continued critical analysis and improvement of the system. This means
calling on teachers from a range of grade levels and subjects as well as a
variety of specialists among school personnel, such as administrators and
guidance staff. There should be representatives from the parent-teacher
association and other interested organizations. It is important to provide a
hearing for a cross section of the pupils, and for parents from several socio-
economic backgrounds, as their goals for their children will differ.

Begin by studying the present reporting system.   The experience of
all representatives with the existing marking practices of the school will
generate interest, should produce profitable discussion, and do much to
involve all members of the group. They should determine the effectiveness
of communication under the current reporting system and the usefulness
of the information which reports give to pupils and parents. Teachers can
comment on how easy and effective they feel their communication to be.
Certainly the group will be concerned with how well the marking and
reporting evaluate in terms of the educational objectives of the school.
This provides an excellent opportunity to interpret the school program to
parents and pupils. Teachers will need to rethink their teaching in relation
to the objectives.

Determine what marking and reporting should accomplish.   The
answer to this problem will evolve from the previous discussion. The group

must decide what it believes important to know about the pupil, and whether it is feasible to report it. There must be exploration of such issues as the use of universal standards in marking and marking achievement in terms of the pupil's ability. The breadth of achievement and growth must be determined. If only final achievement is to be assessed, the group's problem is comparatively simple; if there is a desire for some of the reporting to be based on pupil growth, then serious consideration must be given to the problems involved.

Explore the marking and reporting systems of other schools. The group can often glean helpful ideas from the experiences and reports of other schools. Though no two school systems have identical problems, there is enough similarity to make it helpful to examine effective methods, difficulties that have been met, and suggestions made for improvement elsewhere.

Prepare a tentative form. The starting point for a reporting system is always the objectives of the school. The group must select those objectives on which they wish reports made, examine the feasibility of various methods of reporting in terms of those objectives. It is important to consider such factors as time available to the teacher. Possibly there should be time released from teaching to prepare and make the reports. If a printed form of some kind is to be used, specific suggestions should be made for its construction.

Present the tentative form to pupils, teachers, and the general public. A considerable amount of study may be necessary if a basic change in reporting is involved. Questions which may not have been considered in the representatives' group will surely be raised upon general presentation. Another meeting of the group may be necessary to resolve some of them. Possibly teachers will find it helpful to meet in special session to study means of administering the system effectively. Understanding and agreement should be reached. If there is a change to teacher-parent conferences or the writing of letters, in-service training conferences will undoubtedly be needed. Possibly some basic curriculum changes will be recommended if educational objectives are reformulated. A new look at school and community relationships may be in order, and some aspects of the school program may have to be revised, such as promotional policies, guidance services, and curriculum offerings.

Give the tentative form a trial. When the basic groundwork has been completed, the new system is ready for its trial run. Plan on several semesters to appraise its strengths and weaknesses. Set up machinery to collect all possible suggestions and criticisms from pupils, parents, teachers, and the general public. Emphasize the growth of the pupil as the criterion for judgment. Has his attitude toward learning been improved? Has his personal-social adjustment matured? Is there a better relationship among pupils, teachers, parents?

We should not stop here. The new system must always be subject to revision. Parents and pupils should be involved continuously in a study of the educational program of the schools. This includes evaluation of the extent to which the program achieves the educational objectives. It also means that evaluation must keep pace when objectives are changed.

Schools and communities which follow the seven steps above to the best of their ability will not necessarily arrive at the same system of marking and reporting, for there is no single system that is the best for schools of all types or for all grade levels within these schools. Because of differences, however slight, in educational objectives, pupil talent, and points of view about the function of reports, the reporting systems selected vary from place to place and time to time. Furthermore, it is common to find variations within a school system. Different combinations of several of the reporting techniques may be used.

Regardless of which reporting system or combination of systems is chosen, it is most important that the result receive widespread approval and that its purposes be clearly understood by all concerned. If understanding and approval exist, cooperation among teachers, pupils, parents, and school administrators will come more easily, and the likelihood of misinterpretation (usually in the form of overinterpretations) of the reports themselves will be greatly lessened.

PROBLEMS

20 A suggested program of improving marks and reporting has been outlined. Choose one of the seven steps, and assume that you are to head a committee which is to carry out this phase of the program. Describe in detail the procedures you and your committee would follow.

21 The role of the parents and community in the development of the marking and reporting system is very often overlooked. What advantages are to be gained from enlisting this cooperation? What disadvantages may exist?

PROMOTION AND FINAL MARKS

Problems and Principles

If the philosophy of the school is concerned with the most effective development of the whole pupil, policies for promotion must be consistent with the criterion of "what is best for the pupil." Widely different practices are currently in effect in an effort to meet this criterion. Pupils in some schools must meet or exceed a "passing level" of achievement before they are promoted. Other schools have the policy of "social promotion," or one hundred per cent promotion. Both of these approaches have serious limitations.

Requiring all pupils, without respect to their talents and goals, to reach a "passing level" before promotion creates a threat of failure, that can in some cases, do great harm to the pupil. To a pupil of modest ability, it becomes a perpetual threat of failure that can undermine his confidence in himself, creating feelings of inadequacy and insecurity which can do irreparable damage to his personality. Moreover, failing him not only leaves the cause of his difficulty unchanged, but aggravates the situation by his feelings of inadequacy. Some pupils are doomed to repeat failure because they do not have the intellectual capacity to meet certain standards necessary for promotion. The bad effect on their mental health is obvious.

The very nature of today's school population greatly complicates the mental health problem of the schools. They are committed to accept all children with few exceptions and to give them twelve or thirteen years of free education. State laws force the children to stay in school for most of these years. Great heterogeneity results. Unfortunately the curriculum of many schools has not been expanded to meet the different needs of their pupils. Consequently those placed in classes in which they may have no interest and for which they are ill prepared, are faced with failure. The result may be boredom, apathy, anxiety, belligerence, or hostility. The teacher is confronted with a complex teaching situation.

Thus the use of a "passing level" is not the source of the problem. A much more basic cause is the limited nature of the curriculum in many schools. Until they are placed in classes better suited to their needs and talents, some pupils will experience a series of failures. To assume that every pupil should receive the same dosage of subject matter in a particular grade level is to ignore the fact that, at any grade level, there are pupils at all levels of achievement with a wide range of learning capacities. There must be appropriate levels of instruction with appropriate standards.

Yet "social-promotion" is not the answer. In the first place, there are some pupils who profit by repeating a course or grade level. A pupil who is generally immature might find considerable satisfaction in being with a younger group of children and a teacher who instructs accordingly. A second and more important factor is that pupils do not become a homogeneous group by some magic after they are promoted. The fact that they are all now fourth graders or sophomores in high school does not suddenly emulsify heterogeneity. Pupils must still be taught on the basis of their experience backgrounds and learning capacities. Data show that there are from three to nine grades of achievement levels in any one grade level.

Indeed, effective teaching tends to make a group more heterogeneous relative to achievement. Therefore, if we are to promote pupils regardless of achievement, considerable attention must be given to the individual pupil and the problems peculiar to him.

Trying to establish the best promotion policy is about as difficult as trying to find the best marking and reporting system. In fact, there are many problems common to the two issues. In both cases, differences among schools in terms of educational objectives, pupil populations, and the opinions of all parties concerned can be reasons for differences in policies.

Six basic principles that can be used as the basis for a policy for promotion are the following (National Education Association, 1931, pp. 18–22):

1. Promotion should be decided on the basis of the individual pupil.
2. Promotion should be on the basis of many factors. The final decision as to whether a particular pupil should be promoted should rest not merely on academic accomplishment, but on what will result in the greatest good to the all-around development of the individual.
3. In order that promotion procedures may be more or less uniform throughout a particular school system, a definite set of factors should be agreed upon, which each teacher will take into consideration in forming his judgment as to whether or not a particular pupil should be promoted.
4. Criteria for promotion must take into consideration the curriculum offerings of the next higher grade or unit and the flexibility of its organization, its courses of study, and its methods.
5. It is the duty of the next higher grade or unit to accept pupils who are properly promoted to it from the lower grade or unit and to adapt its work to fit the needs of these pupils.
6. Promotion procedures demand continuous analysis and study of cumulative case history records in order that refinement of procedure may result, and guesswork and conjecture be reduced to a minimum.

The principles above were stated a number of years ago, and then only as a basis for discussion. However they are sound and applicable in today's classrooms. Notice that they stress the individual child as the central factor. In many instances, uniform promotion is the answer, yet to make this a blanket policy would work against the needs and interests of some pupils. There can be no substitute for the careful study of the individual. Decisions must be made on the basis of what is best for him.

Problem

22 Nancy has failed four seventh-grade subjects. She is of average mental ability and has a stable home background. She is physically immature, has

low vitality, and has grown very little in the past few years. This year she has been absent a great deal due to illness. The seventh-grade teachers have made the decision that she should repeat the seventh grade. What other information would you like to have before you could evaluate their action?

The Ungraded School

Goodlad and Anderson (1963) criticize present patterns of school organization which foster common expectations for all pupils, both in content of what is to be learned and in the time given to learn it. They label non-promotion as an adjustment mechanism to counteract problems resulting from specified graded content, graded materials, and limited provision for individual differences. They propose nongrading; that is, the removal of grade levels, as a device for breaking this lockstep. Nongrading is in tune with the realities of individual differences; it provides both for the slow moving pupil and the high achiever. It facilitates pupil progress, in terms of his readiness, by using sequentially organized subject matter with closely related instructional materials and evaluation based on individual progress rather than comparison with others. Pupils can be placed, not simply because they pass or fail, but on the basis of whether they "fit" into the group.

In one ungraded high school (Brown, 1963) pupils are placed in temporary learning situations which they can leave at any time depending on their ability to move into the next higher "phase." These "phases" are designed to group students in terms of their skill level; namely, low, minimal, medium, high, superior.

The challenge of the ungraded system is for the teacher to take advantage of a school organization that focuses on meeting individual needs. An opportunity is provided for him to break the lockstep that too often persists in the graded school.

SUMMARY

Determining and reporting pupil growth is one of the greatest concerns of teachers, parents, and pupils. Although teachers dislike it, probably no other activity has greater potential for interpreting the school program, for securing cooperation between home and school, and for promoting pupil development.

Reporting exists to inform pupils, parents and the administration on the degree to which teachers judge the pupil to be achieving certain educational objectives. The most important aspect of this judgment deals with the growth of the pupil in terms of his own capacity. The chief sources of information used for evaluating the pupil are informal and standardized tests, procedures and product evaluation, class participation, and projects and reports.

Common methods of marking and reporting are the letter and number system, check lists, correspondence to parents, and teacher-parent conferences. The letter and number system has the very definite weakness of telling only part of the story. Correspondence with the parent and teacher-parent conferences are as broad in their evaluation of all aspects of the pupil's growth as the teacher cares to make them. Their limitations lie in the difficulty of effective communication and in the time required.

Probably the best plan of reporting is a combination of the different methods. There should be a regular program of teacher-pupil conferences and, insofar as possible, teacher-parent conferences. Parents can be active participants in the evaluation process. They have opportunity to observe many phases of their children's development which the teacher does not see. Cooperative participation is the key concept in any program for improving marking and reporting. Parents, teachers and pupils must first study the school's educational objectives and then determine the most effective way to communicate the results of pupil progress in those terms. Only after thorough study, trials of tentative suggestions, critical reactions, and revisions can a school hope to effect a defensible system of marking and reporting.

Promotion policies should be based on what is best for the pupil. Since learning at school takes place in a group situation, the pupil should be placed in circumstances which result in the greatest interaction between himself and the other pupils. In general, interaction increases in homogeneous age groups. Therefore a definite trend has developed toward adapting "social-promotion." But promoting all pupils does not solve all the problems of organizing effective learning experiences. Since typical promotional policies cannot eliminate differences among pupils, individual differences must be considered in every grade level.

A suggested solution to the problems of failure and promotion is nongrading. A pupil progresses in terms of a curriculum arranged sequentially based on important principles and concepts rather than on expectations for a particular grade.

Suggested Readings

Alexander, W. M., and others. Special feature on reporting. *Nat'l educ. Assn. J.*, 1959, **45**, 15–28.
This issue contains articles by seven authors expressing differences of opinion

as to the most effective way of reporting pupil progress. Discussion centers around "what" should be reported—that is, pupil standing in class or individual progress—and "how" it should be reported—that is, by various forms of report cards or parent-teacher conferences.

Bailard, Virginia, and Ruth Strang. *Parent-teacher conferences.* New York: McGraw-Hill, 1964.

The setting and conditions necessary for successful parent-teacher conferences from kindergarten through high school are considered. Illustrative interviews from elementary, junior, and senior high schools are reproduced and evaluated.

Brown, B. F. *The non-graded high school.* Englewood Cliffs, N.J.: Prentice-Hall, 1963.

The non-graded high school at Melbourne, Florida, is described. Some of the topics discussed are breaking the grade lockstep, a concept-centered curriculum, and marking and reporting in the non-graded school.

Chansky, N. M. Report cards and teacher personality. *J. educ. Res.,* 1964, **57,** 492–494.

A relation between certain teacher personality characteristics and preference for type of report card was found. For example, personality characteristics like empathy, aggression, confidence, anxiety, were correlated with a preference for one of seven types of report cards.

Goodlad, J. I., and R. H. Anderson. *The non-graded elementary school.* (Rev. ed.) New York: Harcourt, Brace and World, 1963.

Problems of promotion are considered in Chapter 2. In Chapter 6 the reporting of pupil progress in the non-graded school is explained.

Halliwell, J. W., and J. P. Robitaille. The relationship between theory and practice in a dual reporting program. *J. educ. Res.,* 1963, **57,** 137–141.

The history of marking and reporting is reviewed. A bibliography on various related studies is provided, and a research study pointing up some of the problems in a dual reporting program is presented.

Hawes, G. R. *Educational testing for the millions: what tests really mean for your child.* New York: McGraw-Hill, 1964.

This book is written primarily for parents and is also useful to teachers in improving communications with parents. The author classifies tests under several headings, thereby separating achievement tests and aptitude tests.

Jarrett, C. D. Marking and reporting practices in the American secondary school. *Peabody J. Educ.,* 1963, **41,** 36–48.

The author contends that marking systems are often anti-democratic. He argues for final marks which show individual growth and against competitive marks.

Johnson, M., Jr. Solving the mess in marks. *N. Y. S. Educ.,* 1961, **30,** 12–13.

A differentiation is made between a motivational and a descriptive marking system. The need for understanding the meaning of marks is emphasized.

Johnson, R. R. Better ways of measuring and reporting student achievement. *Nat'l Assn. Sec. School Prin. Bull.,* 1961, **46,** 94–97.

A procedure for sending home individual report cards and progress reports is described. Reporting by this system is staggered so that the burden of marking is distributed over a period of time.

Long, F. How improved grade reporting can help your district. *Sch. Mgmt,* 1963, 104–108.

Eight standards that a superior report card should meet are listed.

Smith, Ann Z., and J. E. Dobbin. Marks and marking systems. In Chester W. Harris (Ed.), Encyclopedia of educational research. (3rd ed.) New York: Macmillan, 1960. Pp. 783–791.

Research reports concerning marking and reporting are summarized for the periods 1910–20, 1920–30, 1930–40, and 1940–57. Over one hundred references are cited.

References Cited

Bauernfeind, R. H. "Goal cards" and future developments in achievement testing. In Proceedings of the 1965 Invitational Conference on Testing Problems. Princeton, N. J.: Educational Testing Service, 1966. Pp. 73–84.

Bloom, B. S. Stability and change in human characteristics. New York: John Wiley & Sons, 1964.

Brown, B. F. The non-graded high school. Englewood Cliffs, N. J.: Prentice-Hall, 1963.

Cook, W. W. Grouping and promotion in the elementary school. Series on Individualization of Instruction, No. 2. Minneapolis: University of Minnesota Press, 1941.

Crisler, R. D., and T. D. Wogaman. Educational data processing at Richmond. J. sec. Educ., 1963, 38, 71–76.

Goodlad, J. I., and R. H. Anderson. The non-graded elementary school. New York: Harcourt, Brace and World, 1963.

Goodykoontz, Bess. Helping children get along in school. Chicago: Science Research Associates, 1955.

Green, C. D. What shall we do with the dullards? Atl. Mon., 1956, 197, 72–74.

Halliwell, J. W., and J. P. Robitaille. The relationship between theory and practice in a dual reporting program. J. educ. Res., 1963, 57, 137–141.

Heffernan, Helen, and L. E. Marshall. Reporting pupil progress in California cities. Calif. J. elem. Educ., 1955, 24, 67–77.

Lindquist, E. F. Manual, Iowa Tests of Educational Development. Chicago: Science Research Associates, 1951.

Michael, K. E. What are some of the new trends in reporting student growth and achievement to parents? Nat'l. Assn. Sec. School Prin. Bull., 1960, 44, 146–149.

National Education Association. Pupil promotion problems. Five Unifying Factors on American Education, Ninth Yearb. Washington: Author, 1931.

Richardson, Sybil. How do children feel about reports to parents? Calif. J. elem. Educ., 1955, 24, 98–111.

Russell, D. H. What does research say about self-evaluation? J. educ. Res., 1953, 1953, 46, 561–573.

Smith, Ann Z., and J. E. Dobbin. Marks and marking systems. In Chester W. Harris (Ed.), Encyclopedia of educational research (3rd ed.) New York: Macmillan, 1960, 783–791.

Strang, Ruth. *How to report pupil progress.* Chicago: Science Research Associates, 1955.

Weckler, Nora. Problems in organizing parent-teacher conferences. *Calif. J. elem. Educ.,* 1955, **24**, 117–126.

Appendices

Appendix A: Statistical Methods[1]

Part One

Measure of central tendency: the arithmetic mean. The arithmetic mean is a measure of central tendency. In other words, it is a value that attempts to represent the clustering that is so commonly found in test-score distributions. In the cases in which the test scores are for all practical purposes normally distributed, the arithmetic mean corresponds closely to two other measures of central tendency, the mode (the most common score) and the median (the point below which 50 per cent of the test scores fall).

The arithmetic mean is the sum of all test scores in a distribution divided by the number of test scores. Many people call it "the average." This definition can be translated into the following equation:

$$M = \frac{\Sigma X}{N}$$

where:

M = arithmetic mean
Σ = the sum
X = any test score
N = number of test scores

This formula can be applied to any set of ungrouped data to determine the arithmetic mean.

The following table contains intelligence test scores of twenty fifth-grade pupils.

107	123	112	97	100
93	88	83	109	91
101	96	98	114	106
115	105	85	118	111

The sum of the twenty values (ΣX) is 2,052. The arithmetic mean is 2,052 divided by 20, or 102.6. The substitution in the formula is as follows:

[1] For those who wish to engage in independent study of statistical concepts useful in tests and measurements, a programmed textbook is available entitled *An Introduction to Statistics and Measurement: A Programmed Book*, by L. A. Shoer, Allyn and Bacon, Inc., 1966.

$$M = \frac{2,052}{20} = 102.6$$

Test scores are not always available in the ungrouped fashion illustrated in the foregoing table. Occasionally they are grouped in a frequency distribution, as in the case of the 360 vocabulary test scores shown in Table 4 (Chapter 8). In a frequency distribution the exact test score for any particular pupil is unknown, and the formula for the arithmetic mean as presented above cannot be applied.

One method of computing the arithmetic mean of test scores included in a frequency distribution is to guess the arithmetic mean and then correct the guess. The only requirement for a guessed mean is that it be the midpoint of one of the intervals of the frequency distribution. The guessed mean is corrected by a simple coding operation.

The first steps of the computation of the arithmetic mean of the 360 vocabulary test scores included in the frequency distribution cited are shown in the following table.

Raw-score interval	Frequency (f)	Deviation (d)	fd
90–94	4	7	28
85–89	6	6	36
80–84	12	5	60
75–79	20	4	80
70–74	28	3	84
65–69	36	2	72
60–64	40	1	40
55–59	46	0	0
50–54	43	−1	−43
45–49	39	−2	−78
40–44	32	−3	−96
35–39	24	−4	−96
30–34	13	−5	−65
25–29	9	−6	−54
20–24	5	−7	−35
15–19	3	−8	−24
Total	360		−91

The guessed mean is 57, the midpoint of the 55–59 interval. The values in the deviation column are found by counting, in terms of the number of intervals, how far each interval deviates from the interval containing the guessed mean. Thus, the d-value of the 60–64 interval is +

1 because it is one interval above the 55–59 interval; the d-value of the 50–54 interval is − 1 because it is one interval below the 55–59 interval. The fd-values are determined by multiplying each frequency by the corresponding d-value.

The complete formula for finding the arithmetic mean of a frequency distribution is as follows:

$$M = G.M. + (h)\left[\frac{\Sigma fd}{N}\right]$$

where

$$M = \text{arithmetic mean}$$
$$G.M. = \text{guessed mean}$$
$$h = \text{size of the intervals of the frequency distribution}$$
$$\Sigma fd = \text{alegbraic sum of the entries in the } fd\text{-column}$$
$$N = \text{number of test scores}$$

The expression following the plus sign corrects the guessed mean by increasing it if it is too small or reducing it if it is too large.

The appropriate values can be readily taken from the table and substituted in the equation as follows:

$$M = 57 + (5)\left[\frac{-91}{360}\right] = 55.7$$

The fact that the guessed mean is slightly higher than the actual arithmetic mean causes the sign of the Σfd to be negative.

The formula for computing the arithmetic mean of test scores arranged in a frequency distribution is nothing more than a convenient substitute for the definition formula for the arithmetic mean that is applied to ungrouped data. The frequency distribution formula is none too satisfactory at times. It often yields inaccurate answers when the number of cases in the frequency distribution is small.

The formula for computing the median of test scores included in a frequency distribution is shown in Part Four of Appendix A. For the frequency distribution of 360 vocabulary test scores the median is 55.8. Since the distribution of test scores is approximately normal, it is very close to the arithmetic mean.

Part Two

Measures of variability: the standard deviation. The standard deviation, like the range, is a measure of variability, or dispersion, as it is sometimes called. It is a distance expressed in test-score units rather than a point such as the arithmetic mean. If the test scores of a distribution are widely scattered above and below the arithmetic mean of the scores, the standard deviation is large; the distribution has considerable variability. If the test scores of a distribution cluster closely around the arithmetic mean, the standard deviation is small; the distribution has little variability.

Like the arithmetic mean, the standard deviation can be computed for ungrouped data or test scores arranged in a frequency distribution. The formula for computing the standard deviation of ungrouped data can serve as a definition of the standard deviation. The formula for computing the standard deviation of test scores arranged in a frequency distribution is a somewhat imperfect substitute for the first formula.

To compute the standard deviation of ungrouped test scores, the following formula is used:

$$\sigma = \sqrt{\dfrac{\Sigma X^2 - \dfrac{(\Sigma X^2)-}{N}}{N}}$$

where:

$\sigma =$ standard deviation
$\Sigma =$ the sum
$X =$ any test score
$N =$ number of test scores

This formula was used to determine the standard deviation of the 200 American history achievement test scores cited in Chapter 10.

In the following chart are a few of the 200 test scores, and opposite each is its square.

Pupil	Test score (X)	X²
1	80	6,400
2	21	441
3	62	3,844
4	76	5,776
5	32	1,024
6	47	2,209
•	•	•
•	•	•
•	•	•
200	75	5,625
Total	10,620	585,979

Summing the two columns yields the two values needed for the numerator of the standard deviation equation. Substitution of all values gives the following equation:

$$\sigma = \sqrt{\dfrac{585{,}979 - \dfrac{(10{,}620)^2}{200}}{200}} = 10.5$$

Finding the standard deviation of test scores arranged in a frequency distribution is a simple extension of the process used to compute the arithmetic mean of those test scores. A convenient interval is selected, the deviations of the remaining intervals from the selected interval are identified, and a systematic series of multiplications follow.

The frequency distribution of vocabulary test scores shown in Table 4 (Chapter 8) is reproduced in the following table.

Raw-score interval	Frequency (f)	Deviation (d)	fd	fd^2
90–94	4	7	28	196
85–89	6	6	36	216
80–84	12	5	60	300
75–79	20	4	80	320
70–74	28	3	84	252
65–69	36	2	72	144
60–64	40	1	40	40
55–59	46	0	0	0
50–54	43	−1	−43	43
45–49	39	−2	−78	156
40–44	32	−3	−96	288
35–39	24	−4	−96	384
30–34	13	−5	−65	325
25–29	9	−6	−54	324
20–24	5	−7	−35	245
15–19	3	−8	−24	192
Total	360		−91	3,425

The 55–59 interval is chosen as the starting point and all other intervals are identified in the deviation column according to the number of intervals they happen to be above or below the selected interval. The entries in the fd-column are found by multiplying each frequency by the corresponding d-value. The entries in the fd^2-column are determined by multiplying each fd-value by the corresponding d-value.

The sums of the fd-column and fd²-columns are needed if the standard deviation is to be found. The complete formula for the standard deviation is as follows:

$$\sigma = (h) \sqrt{\frac{\Sigma fd^2}{N} - \left[\frac{\Sigma fd}{N}\right]^2}$$

where:

σ = standard deviation
h = size of the intervals of the frequency distribution
Σfd^2 = sum of the entries in the fd²-column
Σfd = algebraic sum of the entries in the fd-column
N = number of test scores.

Substitution of the values computed in the table yields the following:

$$\sigma = (5) \sqrt{\frac{3,425}{360} - \left[\frac{-91}{360}\right]^2} = 15.3$$

A simpler method of determining the size of a standard deviation is available provided that the distribution of the test scores is approximately normal. All that is necessary is to (a) sum the scores for the top sixth of the group of pupils, (b) sum the scores for the bottom sixth, (c) find the difference between these two values, and (d) divide the difference by half of the number of pupils in the total group. The formula is as follows:

$$\sigma = \frac{\Sigma X_t - \Sigma X_b}{\dfrac{N}{2}}$$

where:

σ = standard deviation
ΣX_t = sum of scores for top sixth
ΣX_b = sum of scores for bottom sixth
$\dfrac{N}{2}$ = half of the number of pupils in the total group

Values yielded by this formula are often quite satisfactory for the needs of a classroom teacher.

Part Three

Measure of relationships: the product-moment coefficient of correlation. The Pearson product-moment coefficient of correlation represents the degree of straight-line relationship between two sets of measurements, such as those of two characteristics of each of a group of pupils. The correlation coefficient reflects the tendency of these pupils to have, in some systematic manner, similar relative positions or dissimilar relative positions in the two distributions. If pupils who are high in one distribution tend to be high in the second, and if pupils who are low in one distribution tend to be low in the other, the correlation coefficient is positive; a direct relationship exists between the two characteristics. If pupils who are high in one distribution tend to be low in the other, and if pupils who are low in one distribution tend to be high in the other, the correlation coefficient is negative; an inverse relationship exists between the two characteristics.

The amount of straight-line relationship between two characteristics is indicated by the size of the correlation coefficient. If the correlation coefficient is + 1.00 or − 1.00, the straight-line relationship is perfect, that is, plotting one measurement against the other will yield a series of points that can be joined by a single straight line. If the correlation coefficient were 0.00, there would be absolutely no straight-line relationship between the two characteristics. Thus, correlation coefficients can vary in size from + 1.00 to − 1.00, the sign reflecting the direction of the relationship and the size reflecting the amount of the relationship. The fact that two characteristics are correlated does not necessarily mean that one is the immediate cause of the other.

A correlation coefficient is useful in situations such as that described in Chapter 9 in connection with the discussion of criterion-related validity. Table 8 (Chapter 9) shows the test scores of the scholastic aptitude and social studies achievement of each of twenty pupils.

The following formula is used to compute the coefficient of correlation:

$$r = \frac{\Sigma XY - \dfrac{(\Sigma X)(\Sigma Y)}{N}}{\sqrt{\left[\Sigma X^2 - \dfrac{(\Sigma X)^2}{N}\right]\left[\Sigma Y^2 - \dfrac{(\Sigma Y)^2}{N}\right]}}$$

r = product-moment coefficient of correlation

Σ = the sum

X = any test score of one characteristic (i.e., any scholastic aptitude test score)

Y = any test score of the other characteristic (i.e., any social studies test score)

N = number of pupils

Solution of the formula can be simplified by preparing a worksheet. The following table, based upon Table 8, is such a worksheet.

Pupil	Scholastic Aptitude Test (X)	Social Studies Test (Y)	XY	X²	Y²
Jim	135	66	8,910	18,225	4,356
Sam	130	90	11,700	16,900	8,100
Ruth	120	68	8,160	14,400	4,624
Mary	117	85	9,945	13,689	7,225
John	116	81	9,396	13,456	6,561
Louise	114	47	5,358	12,996	2,209
Ralph	113	69	7,797	12,769	4,761
Mae	112	77	8,624	12,544	5,929
Quinton	111	65	7,215	12,321	4,225
Sandra	109	56	6,104	11,881	3,136
Larry	107	89	9,523	11,449	7,921
Norma	106	49	5,194	11,236	2,401
Frank	101	57	5,757	10,201	3,249
Milton	100	58	5,800	10,000	3,364
Dave	97	71	6,887	9,409	5,041
Joe	95	60	5,700	9,025	3,600
Bill	94	38	3,572	8,836	1,444
Sally	90	31	2,790	8,100	961
Margaret	88	40	3,520	7,744	1,600
Sue	87	59	5,133	7,569	3,481
Total	2,142	1,256	137,085	232,750	84,188

The new entries in the worksheet are products, either the square of a test score or the crossproduct of two test scores for a pupil. The sums of these products as they are listed in the last row of the table are the values necessary to solve the r-formula. The following needed values can be taken from the table:

$$\Sigma X = 2,142 \qquad \Sigma Y = 1,256$$
$$\Sigma X^2 = 232,750 \qquad \Sigma Y^2 = 84,188$$
$$\Sigma XY = 137,085 \qquad N = 20$$

Substitution of these values into the formula for the correlation coefficient yields the following:

$$r = \frac{137,085 - \dfrac{(2,142)\,(1,256)}{20}}{\sqrt{\left[232,750 - \dfrac{(2,142)^2}{20}\right]\left[84,188 - \dfrac{(1,256)^2}{20}\right]}} = 0.61$$

As in the case of arithmetic means and standard deviations, co-efficients of correlations can be computed using measurements arranged in frequency distributions as well as ungrouped data. The formula must be altered somewhat to do this. A complete description of the computation of a correlation coefficient from a two-way frequency distribution can be found in most introductory textbooks of statistical methodology.

A simple means of obtaining a somewhat accurate estimate of the size of the product-moment coefficient of correlation is to compute a tetra-choric correlation coefficient. Such coefficients can be determined by finding the percentage of pupils who are in the top half of the class in terms of *both* sets of test scores being correlated, and then looking up the correlation coefficient corresponding to this percentage in a table published by the Educational Testing Service. The table is as follows:

%	r	%	r	%	r	%	r	%	r
45	.95	37	.69	29	.25	21	−.25	13	−.69
44	.93	36	.65	28	.19	20	−.31	12	−.73
43	.91	35	.60	27	.13	19	−.37	11	−.77
42	.88	34	.55	26	.07	18	−.43	10	−.81
41	.85	33	.49	25	.00	17	−.49	9	−.85
40	.81	32	.43	24	−.07	16	−.55	8	−.88
39	.77	31	.37	23	−.13	15	−.60	7	−.91
38	.73	30	.31	22	−.19	14	−.65	6	−.93

Unfortunately, the tetrachoric correlations yielded by this table are not precise. At best they can be thought of as a rough approximation of the size of the product-moment coefficient of correlation for the data in question.

Part Four

Measure of relative performance: the quartile, decile, and percentile. Quartiles, deciles, and percentiles are points in a distribution of test scores. The first quartile, often identified as Q_1, is the point in the distribution below which 25 per cent of the test scores fall; the first decile (D_1) is the point below which 10 per cent of the test scores fall; the first percentile (P_1) is the point below which 1 per cent of the test scores fall. Other quartiles, deciles, and percentiles are similarly defined and symboli-cally identified.

Quartiles divide the test-score distribution into four equal parts in terms of the number of test scores. Deciles divide such a distribution into ten equal parts, and percentiles divide it into one hundred equal parts.

A computation of any quartile, decile, or percentile can be based upon a frequency distribution of test scores such as that shown in Table 4 (Chapter 8). This frequency distribution contains English vocabulary test raw scores obtained by testing 360 pupils. It is reproduced in the following table.

Raw-score intervals	Frequency (f_w)	Cumulative frequency (f_c)
90–94	4	360
85–89	6	356
80–84	12	350
75–79	20	338
70–74	28	318
65–69	36	290
60–64	40	254
55–59	46	214
50–54	43	168
45–49	39	125
40–44	32	86
35–39	24	54
30–34	13	30
25–29	9	17
20–24	5	8
15–19	3	3
Total	360	

The formula for determining any quartile, decile, or percentile is as follows:

$$Q, D, \text{ or } P = 1 + (h)\left[\frac{(F)\ (N) - f_c}{f_w}\right]$$

where:

$1 =$ theoretical lower limit of the interval containing the quartile, decile, or percentile desired

$h =$ size of the intervals in the frequency distribution

$F =$ a fraction that varies according to which quartile, decile, or percentile is desired

$N =$ number of test scores

f_c = cumulative frequency below the interval containing the quartile, decile, or percentile desired

f_w = number of test scores within the interval containing the quartile, decile, or percentile desired

Two of the values used in the formula, l and F, deserve further explanation. That l is a theoretical lower limit of an interval and not a reported lower limit simply recognizes the fact that all measurements are limited in accuracy. Although test scores are reported to the nearest whole number, theoretically each score represents the interval that extends from 0.5 below the test score in question to 0.5 above it. A reported score of 50 represents an interval from 49.5 to 50.5 in a test-score distribution. Whenever test scores are reported to the nearest whole number, the value of l is 0.5 less than the reported value of the lower limit of the frequency distribution interval containing the quartile, decile, or percentile to be computed.

The value of F is defined as the size of a fraction associated with the quartile, decile, or percentile. For the median, the point below which 50 per cent of the scores fall, the fraction is 50/100, or 1/2. For the third decile (D_3), the point below which 30 per cent of the scores fall, the fraction is 30/100 or 3/10. For the sixty-third percentile (P_{63}), the fraction is 63/100. All other fractions can be found in a similar manner.

Suppose that P_{32} is to be computed. The first step is to find the interval containing P_{32}. The most rapid way of doing this is to determine F, which is 32/100, and multiply it by N, which is 360. The answer, 115.2, is entered in the cumulative frequency column of the table. Observe that 86 pupils have test scores of 44 or less, whereas 125 pupils have test scores of 49 or less. Therefore, P_{32}, which corresponds to 115.2, falls somewhere within the 45–49 interval.

Now that the interval is identified, three of the required values can be quickly identified. The number of test scores within the interval (f_w) is 39; the cumulative frequency below the interval (f_c) is 86; the theoretical lower limit of the interval (l) is 44.5. Substitution of these and other needed values yields the following equation:

$$P_{32} = 44.5 + (5)\left[\frac{\dfrac{32}{100}(360) - 86}{39}\right] = 48.2$$

The determination of a decile or quartile is equally simple. The steps needed to compute D_6 are as follows:

1. $F = \dfrac{60}{100}$, or $\dfrac{6}{10}$

2. $(F) (N) = \dfrac{6}{10} (360) = 216$

3. Therefore, the interval containing D_6 is the 60–64 interval.
4. $f_w = 40$
5. $f_c = 214$
6. $1 = 59.5$

Therefore:

$$D_6 = 59.5 + (5) \left[\dfrac{\dfrac{6}{10}(360) - 214}{40} \right] = 59.8$$

A quartile, such as Q_3, is computed as follows:

1. $F = \dfrac{75}{100}$, or $\dfrac{3}{4}$

2. $(F) (N) = \dfrac{3}{4} (360) = 270$

3. Therefore, the interval containing Q_3 is the 65-69 interval.
4. $f_w = 36$
5. $f_c = 254$
6. $1 = 64.5$

Therefore:

$$Q_3 = 64.5 + (5) \left[\dfrac{\dfrac{3}{4}(360) - 254}{36} \right] = 66.7$$

Quartile, decile, and percentile ranks can be determined by inspecting the appropriate quartiles, deciles, and percentiles; inspecting an appropriate ogive curve; or computing from ungrouped test scores arranged according to size from low to high. These techniques are described in many introductory testbooks of statistical methodology.

Appendix B: Publishers and Distributors of Standardized Evaluation Instruments[1]

Name	Address
1. American Chemical Society	Examinations Committee, University of South Florida Tampa, Florida 33620
2. American Guidance Service, Inc.	720 Washington Avenue, S.E., Minneapolis, Minnesota 55414
3. Association Press	291 Broadway, New York, New York 10007
4. Bobbs-Merril Co., Inc.	4300 East 62nd Street, Indianapolis, Indiana 46206
5. Bureau of Educational Research and Service	Extension Division, State University of Iowa, Iowa City, Iowa 52240
6. Bureau of Publications	Teachers College, Columbia University, 525 W. 120th Street, New York, New York 10027
7. California Test Bureau	Del Monte Research Park, Monterey, California 93940
8. Center for Psychological Service	Suite 419 Columbia Medical Building, 1835 Eye Street, N.W., Washington, D.C. 20006
9. Committee on Diagnostic Reading Tests, Inc.	Mountain Home, North Carolina 28758
10. Consulting Psychologists Press	577 College Avenue, Palo Alto, California 94306
11. Cooperative Test Division, Educational Testing Service	20 Nassau Street, Princeton, New Jersey 08540
12. Educational Test Bureau American Guidance Service, Inc.	720 Washington Avenue, S.E., Minneapolis, Minnesota 55414
13. Educational Testing Service	20 Nassau Street, Princeton, New Jersey 08540

[1] Other publishers are listed in Buros' *Sixth Mental Measurements Yearbook*.

14.	Harcourt, Brace & World, Inc.	757 Third Avenue, New York, New York 10017
15.	Houghton Mifflin Company	2 Park Street, Boston, Massachusetts 02107
16.	Institute for Personality and Ability Testing	1602 Coronado Drive, Champaign, Illinois 61822
17.	Iowa State University Press	Press Building, Ames, Iowa 50010
18.	Personnel Press, Inc.	20 Nassau Street, Princeton, New Jersey 08540
19.	The Psychological Corporation	304 East 45th Street, New York, New York 10017
20.	Science Research Associates, Inc.	259 E. Erie Street, Chicago, Illinois 60611
21.	Sheridan Supply Company	P.O. Box 837, Beverly Hills, California 90213
22.	Stanford University Press	Stanford University, Stanford, California 94305
23.	C. H. Stoelting Company	424 N. Homan Avenue, Chicago, Illinois 60624

APPENDIX C: SELECTED LIST OF STANDARDIZED ACHIEVEMENT TESTS

Name of test	Publisher[a]	Year of publication	Age or grade level[b]	Time	Recent review in Buros' M.M.Y.[c]
Anderson-Fisk Chemistry Test	14	1966	X–XIII	40	TIP–1604
Barrett-Ryan-Shrammel English Test, New Edition	14	1954	IX–XIII	60	TIP–403
Blyth Second Year Algebra Test, Revised Edition	14	1966	X–XII	40	TIP–986
Brown-Carlsen Listening Comprehension Test	14	1953	IX–XIII	45–50	6–739
California Achievement Tests	7	1957	I–XIV	110–190	6–3
California Arithmetic Test	7	1957	I–IX	39–78	6–616
California Basic Skills Tests	7	1954	IV–IX	119–152	6–4
California Surveys of Achievement	7	1957	VII–XII	30–40	TIP–1344
Contemporary Mathematics Test	7	1965	III–XII	35–45	None
Cooperative English Tests	11	1960			6–256
Reading Comprehension			IX–XII, College	40	
English Expression			IX–XII, College	40	
Dictionary Test			VII–XII	30	
Literary Comprehension and Appreciation Test			X–XII, College	40	
Usage, Spelling, Vocabulary Test			VII–XII, College	70	
Cooperative Foreign Language Tests	11	1964	H.S., College		
Skills tested are: Listening				25	
Reading				35	
Speaking				10	
Writing				35	
French Tests					None
German Tests					
Italian Tests					
Russian Tests					
Spanish Tests					

APPENDIX C (Continued)

Name of test	Publisher[a]	Year of publication	Age or grade level[b]	Time	Recent review in Buros' M.M.Y.[c]
Cooperative French Listening Comprehension Test	11	1955	H.S., College	30	TIP-635
Cooperative General Achievement Test	11	1956	IX–XII	40 each	6–7
Cooperative Latin Test	11	1941	H.S., College	40	TIP-668
Cooperative Mathematics Tests	11				
Arithmetic		1962	VII, VIII, IX	40	6–607
Structure of the Number System		1964	VII, VIII	40	6–655
Algebra I		1962	VIII, IX	40	6–594
Algebra II		1962	H.S.	40	6–594
Algebra III		1964	H.S., College	40	6–594
Geometry		1962	H.S.	40 each	6–645
Analytic Geometry		1964	H.S., College	40	6–643
Trigonometry		1964	H.S., College	40	6–657
Calculus		1964	H.S., College	40 each	6–654
Cooperative Science Tests	11				
General Science		1964	VII–IX	40	6–872a
Advanced General Science		1964	VIII–IX	80	6–876a
Biology		1964	H.S.	80	6–887a
Chemistry		1964	H.S.	80	6–909a
Physics		1964	H.S.	80	6–931a
Cooperative Sequential Tests of Educational Progress (Step)	11	1963	IV–XIV	70 each 35 essay 40–80	6–25
Cooperative Social Studies Tests	11	1965			
American History			VII–IX		None
Civics			VII–IX		None

Test					
American History			X-XII		TIP-1763
Modern European History			X-XII		TIP-1765
World History			X-XII		TIP-1766
American Government			X-XII		TIP-1801
Problems of Democracy			X-XII		None
Cooperative Test on Foreign Affairs	11	1953	XII-College	60	6-980
Crary American History Test, Revised Edition	14	1965	IX-XIII	40	TIP-1768
Cummings World History Test, Revised Edition	14	1966	IX-XIII	40	TIP-1769
Davis Reading Test	19	1962	VIII-XI	40	6-786
Diagnostic Reading Tests	9	1963	II-XIII	40-60	6-823
Diagnostic Tests and Self-Helps in Arithmetic	7	1955	III-XII	Unspecified	TIP-1054
Dunning Physics Test	14	1950	XI-XIII	45	TIP-1634
Durost-Center Word Mastery Test	14	1950	IX-XIII	60	6-330
Durrell-Sullivan Reading Capacity and Achievement Tests	14	1944	II-VI	40	TIP-1468
Engle Psychology Test, Revised Edition	14	1966	XI-XIII	7-55	TIP-1295
Gates-MacGintie Reading Tests	6	1965	K-XII	30-60	None
Gates-McKillop Reading Diagnostic Test	6	1962	II-VI	120	6-824
Greene-Stapp Language Abilities Test	14	1952	IX-XIII	279	TIP-440
Iowa Tests of Basic Skills	15	1956	III-IX	329-459	6-13
Iowa Tests of Educational Development	20	1963	IX-XII	30-65	6-14
Kelley-Greene Reading Comprehension Test	14	1952	IX-XIII	75	TIP-1415
Lankton First-Year Algebra, Revised Edition	14	1965	IX-XII	40	TIP-1005
Madden-Peak Arithmetic Computation Test	14	1955	VII-XII	49	6-624
Metropolitan Achievement Tests	14	1962	I-IX	105-240	6-15
Metropolitan Achievement Tests: High School Battery	14	1962	IX-XII	315	6-15
Michigan Vocabulary Profile Test	14	1949	IX.,-XVI, Adult	50	TIP-572

Appendix C (Continued)

Name of test	Publisher[a]	Year of publication	Age or grade level[b]	Time	Recent review in Buros' M.M.Y.[c]
Nelson Biology Test	14	1965	IX–XIII	40	TIP–1592
Nelson-Denny Reading Test	15	1960	IX–Adult	30	6–800
Nelson Silent Reading Test	15	1962	III–IX	30	6–802
New Purdue Placement Test in English	15	1962	IX–College	65	6–276
Peltier-Durost Civics and Citizenship Test	14	1958	IX–XII	55	6–1019
Read General Science Test, Revised Edition	14	1965	IX–XIII	40	TIP–1570
Seattle Algebra Test	14	1951	IX–XII	40	6–601
Seattle Plane Geometry Test	14	1951	X–XII	45	TIP–1122
Shaycoft Plane Geometry Test	14	1950	X–XII	40	TIP–1124
Snader General Mathematics Test	14	1950	IX–XIII	40	TIP–975
SRA Achievement Series	19	1964	I–IX	360–480	6–21
Stanford Achievement Test	14	1964	I–IX	180–330	6–26
Stanford Achievement Test:					
High School Battery	14	1966	IX–XII	320	None
Stanford Diagnostic Arithmetic Test	14	1966	III–VIII	205–250	None
Stanford Diagnostic Reading Test	14	1966	III–VIII	110–160	None
Understanding the Meanings in Arithmetic	19	1959	VII–XII	75	6–641

[a] The number designating the publisher refers to Appendix B.
[b] Age levels are given in Arabic numbers, grade levels in Roman numbers.
[c] The number before the dash indicates the Yearbook; TIP refers to Buros' Tests in Print; the number after the dash indicates the instrument entry.

Name of test	Publisher[a]	Year of publication	Age or grade level[b]	Time	Recent review in Buros' M.M.Y.[c]
SCHOLASTIC APTITUDE TESTS					
Academic Promise Tests	19	1962	VI–IX	90	6–766
California Short-Form Test of Mental Maturity	7	1963	Kgn–Adult	34–42	6–443
California Test of Mental Maturity	7	1963	Kgn–Adult	48–90	6–444
College Entrance Examination Board Scholastic Aptitude Test (SAT)	13	1957	Cand. for College	180	6–449
College Qualification Tests	19	1961	XI–XIII	80	6–450
Cooperative School and College Ability Tests (SCAT)	11	1963	IV–Adult	70	6–452
General Ability Test Battery	USES	1963	XII–Adult	120–150	6–771
Henmon-Nelson Tests of Mental Ability, Revised Edition	15	1961	III–XII, College	30–40	6–462
IPAT Culture-Fair Intelligence Tests	16	1963	4–Adult	30	6–453a
Kuhlmann-Anderson Tests, Measure of Academic Potential, Seventh Edition	18	1963	Kgn–XII	40–60	6–466
Kuhlmann-Finch Intelligence Tests	2	1960	I–XII	45–60	TIP–785
Lorge-Thorndike Intelligence Tests	15	1964			6–467
Multi-level			3–13	62	
Separate Level Edition			Kgn–XII	20–61	
Ohio State University Psychological Test, Form 23	20	1959	IX–XIII, Adult	120	TIP–808
Otis Quick-Scoring Mental Ability Test	14	1954	I–XII	25–40	6–481

Appendix D (Continued)

Name of test	Publisher[a]	Year of publication	Age or grade level[b]	Time	Recent review in Buros' M.M.Y.[e]
Pintner General Ability Tests:					
Non-Language Series	14	1945	IV–IX	50	TIP–826
Pintner General Ability Tests,					
Revised Edition	14	1965	Kgn–IX	25–45	TIP–827
SRA Primary Mental Abilities Test	20	1962	Kgn–XII	35–60	6–780
Terman-McNemar Test of Mental Ability	14	1941	VII–XIII	40	TIP–860
TESTS FOR OTHER APTITUDES					
Differential Aptitude Tests (DAT)	19	1963	VIII–XII, Adult	181	6–767
Engineering and Physical Science					
Aptitude Test	19	1951	Cand. for Tech. School	80–90	TIP–2001
Finger Dexterity Test: Work-sample No. 16	23	1926	14 & over	10–20	6–1078
Flanagan Aptitude Classification Tests					
(FACT)	20	1960	IX–Adult	258	6–770
Graves Design Judgment Test	19	1948	VII–XVI, Adult	20–30	TIP–588
Horn Art Aptitude Inventory	23	1953	XII–XVI, Adult	50	TIP–589
Iowa Silent Reading Test: New Edition	14	1942	IV–XIII	45–49	6–794
Lee-Clark Reading Readiness Test	7	1962	Kgn–I	20	6–846
Lee-Clark Reading Test	7	1958	I–II	20–30	6–795
MacQuarrie Test for Mechanical Ability	7	1943	VII & over	20	TIP–1922
Meier Art Tests: I, Art Judgment	5	1940	VII–Adult	45–60	6–346
Metropolitan Readiness Tests	14	1965	Kgn–I	60	TIP–1500
Minnesota Clerical Test	19	1959	VIII–XII, Adult	15	6–1040

	[a]		[b]		[c]
Minnesota Mechanical Assembly Test	23	1930	11 & over	17–21	TIP–1928
Modern Language Aptitude Test	19	1959	IX–Adult	30–60	6–357
Multiple Aptitude Tests	19	1959	VII–XIII	177	6–766
Revised Minnesota Paper Form Board Test	19	1948	IX–Adult	20	6–1092
Seashore Measures of Musical Talents, Revised Edition	19	1939	IV–Adult	60	6–353
SRA Tests of Educational Ability	20	1962	IV–XII	49–67	6–495
Test of Mechanical Comprehension	23				TIP–1946
Form AA: Men		1940	IX & over	25–45	
Form W-I: Women		1942	IX & over	25–45	
Tests in Fundamental Abilities of Visual Art	7	1927	III–Adult	85	TIP–594
Tweezer Dexterity Test: Worksample No. 17	23	1928	14 & over	10–20	6–1078

[a] The number designating the publisher refers to Appendix B.

[b] Age levels are given in Arabic numbers, grade levels in Roman numbers.

[c] The number before the dash indicates the Yearbook; TIP refers to Buros' Tests in Print; the number after the dash indicates the instrument entry.

APPENDIX E: SELECTED LIST OF STANDARDIZED INSTRUMENTS FOR EVALUATING PERSONAL-SOCIAL ADJUSTMENT

Name of test	Publisher[a]	Year of publication	Age or grade level[b]	Time	Recent review in Buros' M.M.Y.[c]
Bell Adjustment Inventory, Revised Student Form	10	1963	VIII–XVI	20–30	6–59
Billett-Starr Youth Problems Inventory	14	1961	VII–XII	70–80	6–66
Bonney-Fessenden Sociograph	7	1955	Kgn–Adult	Indefinite	TIP-119
Brainard Occupational Preference Inventory	19	1956	VII–Adult	30	TIP-1856
California Psychological Inventory	10	1960	13 & over	45–60	6–71
California Test of Personality	7	1953	Kgn–Adult	40–50	6–73
Edwards Personal Preference Schedule	19	1959	College–Adult	40–55	6–87
Gordon Personal Inventory	14	1963	IX–XVI, Adult	15–20	6–102
Gordon Personal Profile	14	1963	IX–XVI, Adult	15–20	6–103
Guilford-Zimmerman Temperament Survey	21	1955	IX–XVI, Adult	50	6–110
Institute of Child Study Security Test	2	1957	IV–VIII	20–30	TIP-196
IPAT Children's Personality Questionnaire	16	1963	8–12	10–50	6–122
IPAT High School Personality Questionnaire	16	1963	11–18	6–120	6–131a
Johnson Home Economics Interest Inventory	17	1955	College	60	TIP-1271
Kuder Preference Record–Personal (Form A)	20	1960	IX–Adult	40–45	6–132
Kuder Preference Record–Vocational (Form C)	20	1962	IX–Adult	40–50	6–1063b
Kuder Preference Record–Occupational (Form D)	20	1963	IX–XVI, Adult	25–35	6–1062
Kuder Preference Record–General Interest (Form E)	20	1964	6–12	45–60	6–1061a

Instrument	[a]	Year	Grade/Age Level [b]	Time (min.)	Reference [c]
Kuder Preference Record—Occupational (Form DD)	20	1966	XI–XII	30	None
Minnesota Counseling Inventory	19	1957	IX–XII	50	6–142
Minnesota Multiphasic Personality Inventory, Form R	19	1966	16–Adult	Indefinite	6–143
Minnesota Vocational Interest Inventory	19	1965	9–Adult	40–50	None
Mooney Problem Check Lists	19	1950	VII–Adult	20–50	6–145
Occupational Interest Inventory (Lee-Thorpe)	7	1956	VII–Adult	30–40	6–1064
The Personality Inventory (Bernreuter)	10	1938	IX–Adult	25	6–157
Sixteen Personality Factor Questionnaire	16	1963	15 and over	30–70	6–174
SRA Junior Inventory	20	1956	IV–VIII	45	TIP–274
SRA Youth Inventory	20	1956	VII–XII	30–45	6–170
Study of Values, Third Edition	15	1960	XIII & over	20	6–182
Thorndike Dimensions of Temperament	19	1965	XI–Adult	35–45	None
Thurstone Interest Schedule	19	1947	IX–Adult	10	TIP–1889
Thurstone Temperament Schedule	20	1953	IX–XVI	20	6–192
Vineland Social Maturity Scale	12	1953	Birth–Maturity	20–30	6–194
Vocational Interest Blank–Men (Strong)	19	1966	17 & over	30–60	6–1070
Vocational Interest Blank–Women (Strong)	19	1962	17 & over	30–60	6–1071

[a] The number designating the publisher refers to Appendix B.

[b] Age levels are given in Arabic numbers, grade levels in Roman numbers.

[c] The number before the dash indicates the Yearbook; TIP refers to Buros' *Tests in Print*; the number after the dash indicates the instrument entry.

Appendix F

FREE AND INEXPENSIVE MATERIALS
CONCERNING MEASUREMENT AND EVALUATION

I. Test Bulletins Published at Irregular Intervals
   Test Data Reports, Harcourt, Brace and World, Inc.
   Test Service Bulletins, Harcourt, Brace and World, Inc.
   Test Service Bulletins, The Psychological Corporation
   Test Service Notebook, Harcourt, Brace and World, Inc.
   Testing Today, Houghton Mifflin Company

II. Annual Reports and Proceedings
   Annual Reports, College Entrance Examination Board
   Annual Reports, Educational Testing Service
   Proceedings, Annual Invitational Conference on Testing Problems, Educational Testing Service
   Proceedings, Annual Western Regional Conference on Testing Problems, Educational Testing Service

III. Newsletters Concerning Measurement
   The ACT Newsletter, American College Testing Program
   ETS Developments, Educational Testing Service
   Items, Cooperative Test Division, Educational Testing Service

IV. Educational and Psychological Journals
   American Educational Research Journal
   Educational and Psychological Measurement
   Journal of Educational Measurement
   Journal of Educational Psychology
   Psychological Abstracts: "Methodology and Research Technology: Testing" and "Educational Psychology: Testing"
   Review of Educational Research: "Educational and Psychological Testing"

V. Paperback Books and Bulletins
   Brim, O. G., and others. *Experiences and Attitudes of American Adults Concerning Standardized Intelligence Tests*. New York: Russell Sage Foundation, 1965.

   Brim, O. G., and others. *The Use of Standardized Ability Tests in American Secondary Schools and Their Impact on Students, Teachers, and Administrators*. New York: Russell Sage Foundation, 1965.

   Educational Testing Service
   ETS Builds a Test, 1959.
   Locating Information on Educational Measurement: Sources and References, 1965.
   Making the Classroom Test: A Guide for Teachers, Second Edition, 1961.
   Multiple-Choice Questions: A Close Look, 1963.
   Selecting an Achievement Test: Principles and Procedures, Second Edition, 1961.

Short-Cut Statistics for Teacher-Made Tests, Second Edition, 1964. *Testing in Perspective and Context*, 1961.

Engelhart, Max D. *Improving Classroom Testing*. Washington: National Education Association, 1964.

French, J. W., and W. B. Michael. *Standards for Educational and Psychological Tests and Manuals*. Washington: American Psychological Association, 1966.

Goslin, D. A., and others. *The Use of Standardized Tests in the Elementary School*. New York: Russell Sage Foundation, 1965.

Mager, Robert F. *Preparing Instructional Objectives*. Palo Alto, Calif.: Fearon Publishers, 1962.

McLaughlin, K. F. *Interpretation of Test Results*. Washington: U.S. Government Printing Office, 1964.

Rothney, J. W. M. *Evaluating and Reporting Pupil Progress*. Washington: National Education Association, 1955.

Tyler, Leona E. *Tests and Measurements*. Englewood Cliffs, N.J.: Prentice-Hall, 1963.

Index of Names

Index of Subjects